Making the Grand Figure

# Making the Grand Figure

*Lives and Possessions in Ireland, 1641–1770*

Toby Barnard

Yale University Press
New Haven and London

For information about this and other Yale University Press publications, please contact:
U.S. Office: sales.press@yale.edu        yalebooks.com
Europe Office: sales@yaleup.co.uk        www.yalebooks.co.uk

Set in Minion by Northern Phototypesetting Co. Ltd
Printed in China through Worldprint

Library of Congress Cataloging-in-Publication Data

Barnard, T. C. (Toby Christopher)
Making the grand figure: lives and possessions in Ireland, 1641–1770 / Toby Barnard.
p. cm.
Includes bibliographical references and index
ISBN 0–300–10309–3 (alk. paper)
1. Ireland—Social life and customs—18th century. 2. Ireland—Social life and customs—17th century. 3. Material culture—Ireland—History—18th century. 4. Material culture—Ireland—History—17th century. 5. Collectors and collecting—Ireland—History—18th century. 6. Collectors and collecting—Ireland—History—17th century. I. Title.
DA947.3.B37 2004    941.507—dc22        2004001542

A catalogue record for this book is available from the British Library.

10  9  8  7  6  5  4  3  2  1

Published with assistance from the Annie Burr Lewis Fund.

# Contents

# Preface

A beginning and an end to the writing of this book can be identified. In the late 1970s, Peter Thornton, then at the Victoria and Albert Museum, was excited by the graining painted on the wooden doors in the house in West Cork where I was staying. He ignored the porcine physiognomies of the ancestors hanging in the dining room. The skill with which a costlier wood had been simulated on imported pine by a local artificer alerted me to a hitherto unsuspected fact of life not just in Jack Lynch's Ireland but in its seventeenth- and eighteenth-century predecessors. A terminus, after this book was completed, is when a gold coin went on display in the Ashmolean Museum in Oxford. It is a gold *aureus* of the Emperor Vespasian, minted in the eastern empire shortly after the sack of Jerusalem in AD 70. A unique find in Britain, it was unearthed by a ploughman more than a century and half ago in fields across which I often walk. The treasure was quickly acquired by a female collector. The Romans never reached Ireland, so Vespasian is irrelevant to its history. However, the ways in which objects as well as people migrated, how they were valued and collected, are topics raised in the following pages.

Peter Thornton and others at the Victoria and Albert Museum pioneered an approach into the ways in which houses were furnished, used and regarded. Their work influences what follows. So, too, more directly, do the heroic researches into hitherto neglected aspects of the material cultures of Ireland. Many of these enquiries were afoot at the same time as mine. I have benefited greatly from the information and insights which the pioneers have shared so willingly with me, and often before they were published. Building on the foundations laid by Ada Leask, Rosemary ffolliott and Maurice Craig, recent workers have revealed the richness and inventiveness of architects, artists, craftworkers and retailers. I have shamelessly pillaged the work of Anne Crookshank, Jane Fenlon and Nicola Figgis on painting; Mairead Dunlevy on clothing, textiles, ceramics and glass; Peter Francis, also on ceramics and glass; Alison Fitzgerald and Helen Clifford on silver (the first in Ireland, the second in England); Sarah Foster on shopping; Desmond Fitzgerald, the Knight of Glin, on architecture, painting and indeed virtually every aspect of eighteenth-century Ireland; Claudia Kinmonth on furniture;

of Marie-Lou Legg into the worlds of the Limerick agent Nicholas Peacock and the diocese of Elphin in the 1740s; Edward McParland on public architecture (and much else); Charles Nelson on Irish horticulture; Finola O'Kane about gardens; Vivien Pollock on humbler lives in Ulster; Nessa Roche into glass and furniture; William Roulston on building, especially in the north-west. I have learnt, too, from the investigations of Daniel Beaumont and Rosemary Richey into the cultures of the landed gentry, respectively in the midlands and the north-east. David Fleming's exciting findings about provincial life in eighteenth-century Ireland have constantly stimulated and helped me.

This book tackles subjects usually relegated to the margins, if not ignored, in histories of Ireland. In attempting to recreate and understand the contexts of lives in Stuart and Hanoverian Ireland, I have also benefited from the writings that have delineated the contours and detail of the economy (notably those of Louis Cullen, David Dickson and Leslie Clarkson) and of high politics (David Hayton, Paddy McNally, Ivar McGrath, Eoin Magennis, Anthony Malcomson, Jimmy Kelly and Sean Connolly).

Many friends have ferried me to libraries, houses and sites, and shown me documents and objects from which this account has been fashioned: Claire Asquith, Valerie and John Bunn, Peter Busch, Bernadette Cunningham, Jason Dorsett, Derry Falvey, Desmond and Olda Fitzgerald, Christopher and Hanne Gray, Biddy Gwynne-Howell, Michael and Anne Harnett, David and Deirdre Hayton, Joanna Macintyre, Eoin Magennis, Anthony Malcomson, the late William O'Sullivan, and Brendan and Alison Rosse. Others have generously shared their knowledge: Andrew Carpenter, David Dickson, Roy Foster, John Ghazvinian, Ultan Gillen, Raymond Gillespie, Patrick Guinness, Amy Harris, Alan Harrison, David Hayton, Jimmy Kelly, Rolf Loeber, John Logan, John Loughman, Tadgh O'Sullivan, Tom Power, Marieke Riethof, the late Jeanne Sheehy, and James Woolley.

Numerous owners of manuscripts, archivists and librarians have also assisted. For allowing me to read documents which they own, some of which have subsequently passed into public collections, I am grateful to Mrs Eileen Barber, Mrs Valerie Bunn, Viscount de Vesci, the Duke of Devonshire and the trustees of the Chatsworth settled estates, the Knight of Glin, Mr Michael Harnett, the Marquess of Lansdowne, Dr Marie-Louise Legg, the Duke of Leinster, the Earl of Rosse, Canon George Salter, the Earl of Shelburne, Mr Allen Synge, Major-General Marston Tickell and Captain Richard Turner. Other custodians in public repositories throughout Ireland and Britain have helped me to the materials on which this volume relies: at PRONI, David Lammey, Ian Montgomery, Jean Agnew, Andrew Sneddon and Anthony Malcomson; at the Presbyterian Historical Society, Bob Balfour; in the RCB library, Ray Refaussé, Heather Smith and Susan Hood; in NLI, Catherine Fahy, Colette O'Flaherty, Elizabeth Kirwan and Tom Desmond; at Marsh's, Muriel McCarthy and Ann Simmons; at RIA, Siobhan O'Rafferty and Bernadette Cunningham; at NA, Aideen Ireland; in IAA, David Griffin; at Pearse Street, Maire Kennedy; at RDS, Mary Kelleher; in the Dublin

City Archives, Mary Clark; at the Friends' Historical Library, Mary Shackleton; at the King's Hospital, Leslie Whiteside; in the Cork Archives Institute, Patricia MacCarthy; at the Boole Library, Helen Davies and Julian Walton (as earlier in Waterford); and at Chatsworth, Peter Day. Financial assistance from the Leverhulme Foundation, the British Academy (including a research readership from 1997 to 1999), the Modern History Faculty in Oxford, the Harding Fund of Hertford College and the governors of Archbishop Narcissus Marsh's library in Dublin (who benevolently made me a visiting fellow) have eased the research and writing. The Irish Georgian Society has generously assisted towards the costs of the illustrations. The support and expertise of Robert Baldock and Diana Yeh at Yale have again made the final stages of this labour easy and agreeable.

Younger colleagues are ground between the upper millstone of faculty obligations and the nether of college duties, and so disabled from adopting the ambling gait of this excursion. My colleagues, notably Geoffrey Ellis and Christopher Tyerman, have spared me by shouldering many chores. Some parts of the enterprise have engaged me for thirty years: a luxury unlikely to be enjoyed in the foreseeable future by those in academic institutions in Britain, where first the cycle and now the contents and tone of publications are determined by strange planetary conjunctions.

Many who have helped were met first at Eddie McParland's convivial table or over informal Saturday lunches in Dublin *trattorie*: research 'clusters' *avant la lettre* as well as sociable groups of the kind (if not so riotous) described in chapter 11. Funding bodies keen to stimulate historians into greater productivity might do better to underwrite such ventures, or the Drumcondra Centre maintained by Bernadette Cunningham and Raymond Gillespie, to which I owe more than I can properly express, than yet more research institutes with sesquipedalian names. David Fleming and Mary-Lou Legg, understanding my quirky interests, have fed me with numerous references. If in the end the leopard skins imported through Skibbereen by Major Arabin and the transmogrified pug have not seemed apposite to advancing or illustrating my arguments, many more of their discoveries have been. My interest in objects, their owners, sellers, genealogies and meanings owes much to early mornings at Bermondsey (and elsewhere). Anthony O'Connor fostered this curiosity. He has added to my indebtedness by being a patient and perceptive companion on numerous rambles (along with the pugs), and also indexer of this book.

In 2002, hitherto unknown drawings by Hugh Douglas Hamilton, an Irish painter at the very start of his career, came to light in Australia. They had been mounted in an album entitled, 'The Cries of Dublin, 1760'. On first examining them at Christie's in London, I was astonished by the visual confirmation of much that I had surmised from written fragments. Immediately a misty world was clarified. Subsequently, I was introduced to William Laffan and the purchaser of the volume, through whose generosity the drawings have been put into the public domain with a facsimile edition. A further happy chance – and a remarkable series of coincidences – caused Valerie Bunn to contact me. As a result I was able to read a remnant of a collection, the bulk of it originally at Barbavilla in Westmeath but now in the National Library of Ireland, which has proved one of the most helpful for the reconstruction of eighteenth-century Ireland. In addition, I was shown the portrait of Barbara Smythe, *née* Ingoldsby, for whom the Smythes' seat in Westmeath was named. Again a wraith took on substance. The iridescence from the past is as difficult to capture as the flash of a kingfisher's wing. Something of the solidity of seventeenth- and eighteenth-century Ireland, and perhaps a glint of its delights, follow.

# Abbreviations

| | |
|---|---|
| Barnard, 'Cork settlers' | T. C. Barnard, 'The political, material and mental culture of the Cork settlers, 1649–1700', in P. O'Flanagan and N.G. Buttimer (eds), *Cork: history and society* (Dublin, 1993), pp. 309–65, reprinted in T. Barnard, *Irish Protestant ascents and descents* (Dublin, 2003), pp. 35–83 |
| Barnard, 'French of Monivea' | T. C. Barnard, 'The worlds of a Galway squire: Robert French of Monivea, 1716–1779', in G. Moran and R. Gillespie (eds), *Galway: history and society* (Dublin, 1996), pp. 271–96 |
| Barnard, 'What became of Waring?' | T. C. Barnard, ' "What became of Waring?" The making of an Ulster squire', in V. Carey and U. Lötz-Heumann (eds), *Taking sides? Colonial and confessional mentalities in early modern Ireland. Essays in honour of Karl S. Bottigheimer* (Dublin, 2003), pp. 185–212, reprinted in T. Barnard, *Irish Protestant ascents and descents* (Dublin, 2003), pp. 235–65 |
| Barnard, *New anatomy* | T. C. Barnard, *A new anatomy of Ireland: the Irish Protestants, 1649–1770* (New Haven and London, 2003) |
| Barnard and Fenlon (eds), *Dukes of Ormonde* | T. C. Barnard and Jane Fenlon (eds), *The Dukes of Ormonde, 1610–1745* (Woodbridge, 2000) |
| BH | Bowood House, Wiltshire |
| BL | British Library |
| *CARD* | *Calendar of the Ancient Records of Dublin*, ed. J. T. Gilbert and R. M. Gilbert, 19 vols (Dublin, 1898–1944) |
| Chatsworth | Chatsworth House, Derbyshire |
| Christ Church | Christ Church, Oxford |

| | |
|---|---|
| *CJI* | *Journals of the House of Commons of Ireland*, 20 vols (Dublin, 1796–1804) |
| CRO | County Record Office |
| Crookshank and Glin, *Painters of Ireland* | A. Crookshank and D. Fitzgerald, Knight of Glin, *The painters of Ireland*, c.1660–1920 (London, 1978) |
| Crookshank and Glin, *Ireland's painters* | A. Crookshank and D. Fitzgerald, Knight of Glin, *Ireland's painters, 1600–1940* (New Haven and London, 2002) |
| *CSP, Dom, Ireland*, etc. | *Calendar of State Papers, Domestic, Ireland* |
| Delany, *Autobiography* | Lady Llanover (ed.), *The autobiography and correspondence of Mary Granville, Mrs Delany*, 2 series, 6 vols (London, 1861–2) |
| *EHR* | *English Historical Review* |
| GEC, *Complete peerage* | GEC, *The complete peerage of England, Scotland, Ireland, Great Britain and the United Kingdom*, ed. V. Gibbs and H.A. Doubleday, 13 vols (London, 1913–40) |
| GO | Genealogical Office, Dublin |
| *HJ* | *Historical Journal* |
| HMC, *Buccleuch Mss* | Historical Manuscripts Commission. *The manuscripts . . . of the duke of Buccleuch and Queensberry . . . at Montagu House*, 4 vols (London, 1899–1926) |
| HMC, *Dartmouth Mss* | Historical Manuscripts Commission. *The manuscripts of the earl of Dartmouth*, 3 vols (London, 1887–96) |
| HMC, *Egmont Diary* | Historical Manuscripts Commission. *Report on the manuscripts of the earl of Egmont. Diary of Viscount Percival, afterwards first earl of Egmont*, 3 vols (London, 1920–3) |
| HMC, *Egmont Mss* | Historical Manuscripts Commission. *Report on the manuscripts of the earl of Egmont*, 2 vols (London and Dublin, 1905–9) |
| HMC, *Ormonde Mss*, n.s. | Historical Manuscripts Commission. *Calendar of the manuscripts of the marquess of Ormonde, K.P., preserved at Kilkenny Castle*, new series, 8 vols (London, 1902–20) |
| HMC, *Stopford-Sackville Mss* | Historical Manuscripts Commission. *Report on the manuscripts of Mrs. Stopford-Sackville, of Drayton House, Northamptonshire*, 2 vols (London, 1904–10) |
| HMC, *Various Collections* | Historical Manuscripts Commission. *Report on Manuscripts in various collections. Vol. VIII* (London, 1913) |

| | |
|---|---|
| IAA | Irish Architectural Archive, Dublin |
| *IESH* | *Irish Economic and Social History* |
| *IHS* | *Irish Historical Studies* |
| Ingamells, *Travellers* | J. Ingamells, *A dictionary of British and Irish travellers in Italy 1701–1800* (New Haven and London, 1997) |
| *JCHAS* | *Journal of the Cork Historical and Archaeological Society* |
| Johnston-Liik, *HIP* | E. M. Johnston-Liik, *History of the Irish Parliament, 1692–1800*, 6 vols (Belfast, 2002) |
| JRL | John Rylands Library, Manchester |
| *JRSAI* | *Journal of the Royal Society of Antiquaries of Ireland* |
| Legg (ed.), *Synge letters* | M. L. Legg (ed.), *The Synge letters: Bishop Edward Synge to his daughter Alicia, Roscommon to Dublin 1746–1752* (Dublin, 1996) |
| Loeber, *Architects* | R. Loeber, *A biographical dictionary of architects in Ireland* (London, 1981) |
| McParland, *Public architecture* | E. P. McParland, *Public architecture in Ireland, 1680–1760* (New Haven and London, 2001) |
| Marsh's Library | Archbishop Narcissus Marsh's Library, Dublin |
| NA | National Archives, Dublin |
| NAM | National Army Museum, London |
| NAS | National Archives of Scotland, Edinburgh |
| NLI | National Library of Ireland, Dublin |
| NLS | National Library of Scotland, Edinburgh |
| NLW | National Library of Wales, Aberystwyth |
| NUI | National University of Ireland |
| *P & P* | *Past and Present* |
| Petworth | Petworth House, West Sussex |
| *PRIA* | *Proceedings of the Royal Irish Academy* |
| PRO | Public Record Office, Kew, now the National Archives |
| PRONI | Public Record Office of Northern Ireland, Belfast |
| RCB | Representative Church Body Library, Dublin |
| RD | Registry of Deeds, Dublin |
| RDS | Royal Dublin Society |
| RIA | Royal Irish Academy, Dublin |
| RO | Record Office |
| RSAI | Royal Society of Antiquaries of Ireland, Dublin |
| *Statutes* | *The Statutes at large, passed in the parliaments of Ireland*, 13 vols (Dublin, 1786) |

| | |
|---|---|
| Strickland, *Dictionary of Irish Artisits* | W. G. Strickland, *A dictionary of Irish artists*, 2 vols (Dublin and London, 1913) |
| TCD | Trinity College, Dublin |
| *TRHS* | *Transactions of the Royal Historical Society* |
| UCNW | Department of Palaeography and Manuscripts, University College of North Wales, Bangor |
| *UJA* | *Ulster Journal of Archaeology* |
| UL | University Library |
| V & A | Victoria and Albert Museum, London |
| Williams (ed.), *Correspondence of Swift* | H. A. Williams (ed.), *The correspondence of Jonathan Swift*, 5 vols (Oxford, 1963–5) |

Dates before 1752 are given in Old Style, with the year adjusted to begin on 1 January. Prices are in £ s. d., sterling. In quoting sources, I have silently modernized spelling and punctuation, except for a few occasions, where phonetic renderings may convey an accent or brogue. I have referred to the earls, marquess and duke of Ormond, and their wives, before 1688 as Ormond and Ormonds; after 1688, and the dynasty in its entity, as Ormondes. Derry refers to the city; Londonderry to the county. William King, while bishop of Derry between 1690 and 1703 is Bishop King. After 1703, when archbishop of Dublin, he becomes Archbishop King. Similarly, the second earl of Cork is Cork until 1665 when he received the additional (English) earldom of Burlington. Thereafter he is referred to as Cork and Burlington.

# Illustrations

## Plates

For help with the illustrations I am particularly indebted to Daniel Beaumont, Charles Benson, Tom Desmond, Mairead Dunlevy, Derry Falvey, Jane Fenlon, Alison Fitzgerald, David Fleming, Peter Francis, Elizabeth Kirwan, William Laffan, Simon Lincoln, John Logan, Eddie McParland, Anthony O'Connor, Dermot O'Hara, Valerie Pakenham and, above all, to Desmond Fitzgerald, the Knight of Glin. For permission to reproduce objects in their possession, I am grateful to Valerie Bunn (plates 11, 48, 75); Desmond Fitzgerald, the Knight of Glin (plates 21, 22, 24, 25, 29, 30, 41, 47, 64–6, 81–3); Peter Francis (plates 31, 32); Captain Christopher Gaisford St Lawrence (plates 29, 47); Michael Harnett (plates 6–8); Norman Ievers (plate 46); Thomas and Valerie Pakenham (plate 63); The Bodleian Library, Oxford (plates 28, 38, 43, 49, 52, 55, 67, 68, 72, 77, 82, 87–9); Christ Church Picture Gallery, Oxford (plates 44, 45); an anonymous owner and The Churchill House Press, Tralee (plates 33, 34, 60–2, 69–71, 73, 74, 76, 78); Messrs. House, auction-eers, Bournemouth (plate 42); The Irish Architectural Archive, Dublin (plates 21, 22, 24, 25, 29, 30, 41, 47, 64–6, 81–3); The Museum of Art, Rhode Island School of Design (plate 79); The National Archives, Dublin (plate 53); The National Library of Ireland (plates 27, 80); The Representative Church Body Library, Dublin (plate 40); The Board of Trinity College, Dublin (plate 59); The Ulster Museum, Belfast (plates 36, 85); Victoria and Albert Museum, London (plate 35). Plate 86 is reproduced from *Memoir of the Lady Freemason* (Cork, 1914).

## Tables

## Map

Introduction

# The Grand Figure

This volume fleshes out the skeleton exhibited in *A New Anatomy of Ireland*. It has several aims. First, it attempts to reveal a profusion and variety of goods hitherto unsuspected even by specialists. Second, it considers how buildings, lodgings, furnishings and objects were made, used and regarded. These issues lead naturally into a series of problems, many of them common to other societies, the material worlds of which have been investigated. Among them are the extent to which factors other than money determined who possessed what. Then, too, there are suggestions that places peculiar to élites and the populace were more precisely demarcated, along with those for public and private activities, and for men and women. Other questions arise from what are seen as the distinctive characteristics of Ireland. Its uncertain and evolving relationship with England meant that it was viewed as a colony, a distant province (or collection of provinces) and as a kingdom in the composite monarchy of the Stuarts and Hanoverians. Dublin in particular, populous and – in some quarters – prosperous, thanks to its public buildings, luxurious interiors, varied and specialist retailers, dexterous craftworkers, and charitable and associational endeavour met (and sometimes surpassed) expectations of what the second city of the Hanoverians' empire should be. It came to be regarded as a metropolis in its own right and a worthy capital for a proud kingdom.

At first glance, the economy goes far to explain the chronology, pace and limits of Irish enjoyment of the diversifying array of goods. From the 1750s, the rents of the landed increased; so, too, did those charged by Dublin landlords and landladies. Numbers in the middling orders were also growing. By the 1790s, it has been estimated that 30 per cent of Ireland's inhabitants had annual incomes between £5 and £20.[1] This moderate prosperity, modestly diffused, allowed more to purchase from an enlarged selection of wares, wear and diversions.[2] However, improved finances do not help greatly in explaining what is described in succeeding chapters, since so much of the activity happened before the more favourable conditions of the 1750s. Average incomes and outgoings earlier than the mid-eighteenth century remain shrewd guesses or isolated instances.[3] Only in the later eighteenth century are imports recorded continuously, so allowing what arrived to be quantified.[4] Few kept full accounts. At different social levels, the squire Richard Edgeworth and the land agent Nicholas

Peacock watched minutely over receipts and spending. The careful not the careless are those whose habits can be reconstructed with a semblance of precision. Edgeworth and Peacock warn against assuming that all purchases were governed by rational calculation. Prescript, as to what a family required either to subsist or to live creditably, even genteelly, diverged from what was bought – sometimes strikingly so. Consumers, faced with an abundance of commodities, exercised choice. The results have been interpreted variously: on the one hand, as evidence of the ingenuity and unscrupulousness of makers and sellers in stimulating demand; on the other, the cravings of consumers goading traders into strenuous efforts to satisfy them. Those outside the conventional cantonments of privilege – the middling and lower ranks and women – participated. Buyers did not always choose the cheapest or what the lofty presumed would be most useful.[5] Goods, assorted in price and quality, circulated more widely what had recently been the monopoly of the rich and fashionable. In addition, sales, bequests and even pilfering passed the second-hand to new and often humbler owners.

Housing, possessions, dress and deportment, intended to deepen economic and social striations, blurred and even erased them. Unfortunately, the patterns of purchasing among all but a few from the landed élites have left only the faintest traces. The spending habits of the anonymous bulk of the population, including the respectable town-dwellers and professionals, have to be inferred from aggregated estimates of income and consumption. Want of evidence also impedes any sustained attempt to decide how other factors influenced lives in Stuart and Hanoverian Ireland. Gender mattered there, as elsewhere. In general, women lacked independent control over finances. Yet, notwithstanding the constraint, many fashions – and not only in dress – are more readily explained if the preferences of women are acknowledged. In Ireland, further forces – confession and ethnic background – came into play. Little of the show described in the following chapters could be achieved without money, or at least credit. In Ireland, from the mid-seventeenth century, money was linked intimately with confession and – more hazily – with ethnicity. Put crudely: repeated confiscations and prohibitions left a large majority of the Catholics – at least 75 per cent of Ireland's population – poor. Most, although far from all, Catholics in Ireland were of Irish rather than Old or New English lineage. Protestants contended that Catholics possessed distinctive traits including a fondness for show.[6] Even if this were true, after the 1650s, Catholics had scant opportunity to indulge it. The Catholics' enthusiasm for distinctive fashions, often taken directly from continental Europe rather than mediated through Britain, was stunted.[7] One paradox to result from the good fortune of many Protestants in Ireland was the chance to engage in ostentation and extravagance. Catholics, owing to their prevalent penury, were manoeuvred into frugality and restraint. Prisoners of meagre incomes, Catholics could nevertheless escape as the lower-priced commodities were put on sale by hawkers, hucksters and higglers and at markets, fairs and patterns.

The brilliance of the few coexisted with, and maybe thrived on, endemic underdevelopment, poverty and recurring famines. The splendour was precarious, depending on incomes lower and prices often higher than in England.[8] Much of the glitter was dismissed as that of pinchbeck rather than of the real alloy. The grand figure, when achieved in Ireland, relied on legerdemain, illusionism or brazen deceit. Frequently it bequeathed debts. As a consequence, unabashed enjoyment was tempered by disquiet about the excesses and neglects of the rulers and owners of Protestant Ireland. Criticism made the thoughtful reflect, but seldom stopped the headstrong in their traces. The full-blooded satisfaction of appetites was censured everywhere. In Ireland, critiques were capable of wounding deeply since they impugned those who had only lately gained mastery. So, the appurtenances of living aroused feelings sharper and more complex in Ireland than in Britain.

The objects that excited, variously, condemnation and commendation are worth lingering over. They existed in an unexpected quantity and variety. This account differs from the more specialized ones in not seeking to measure quality. Simply the intention is to establish the ubiquity of objects, next to return them to the contexts in which they were made and used, and then to ponder the values that led to their being constructed, traded, treasured and discarded. First and foremost, this is an investigation of Ireland – at a specific time, as the Protestants' ascendancy was being created and enjoyed. However, the study addresses questions that have preoccupied historians of other societies. The issues range from a quest for privacy, through the reservation of particular spaces either for women or men, to the semiotics of both everyday and outlandish objects. The findings detailed here may allow Ireland to be incorporated more plausibly into the larger picture of a consumer revolution (or not) across western Europe and colonial America. Those whose concern is to decide conclusively how Ireland in the seventeenth and eighteenth centuries is best conceived – colony, province or kingdom – may seek ammunition from this report. They will do so in vain. Although alert to the matter, this study leaves the conundrums unsolved. Artificers and customers in Ireland can be found plodding in the tracks of others in Britain, conforming in habits to those of like circumstances in Wales, western England and colonial America, or, independent of any mediation through Britain, going directly to the sources of fashion in continental Europe and so acting as cultural innovators. Neither Protestant nor Catholic Ireland constituted a homogenous unit. Characteristics of the colonial, the provincial and the metropolitan were to be found in the same places and at the same times.

More promising is a second recent concern of historians of Ireland: the comparison of Irish developments with those in Wales, Scotland and the remoter areas of England. Throughout this examination, such an approach has been attempted, but it is hampered by the lack of comparative analyses. Wales has been subjected to more intensive study than either Scotland or the remoter western and northern regions of England.[9] The potential remains. As the yields from mining the political histories of the three kingdoms of England, Wales and Ireland near exhaustion, the cultures of the three, and specifically their material culture, could still prove a rewarding seam.[10] Artefacts common to all three kingdoms possibly brought a greater degree of integration than laws and institutions.

Most surviving evidence documents the exceptional within the Protestant minority. This dangerous imbalance has been worsened by later studies which, in the main, focus either on the nineteenth century (and later) or on one of the two ducal families in Ireland: the Butlers, earls, marquesses and dukes of Ormonde, and the Fitzgeralds, earls and marquesses of Kildare and dukes of Leinster. Nineteenth-century Ireland, with its striking economic and cultural divergences, is no sure guide to life there in earlier centuries. The grandeur, in succession, of the Ormondes and the Leinsters, although a standard at which the competitive aimed, affected few, and is untypical of how even most peers lived. Treatments of Ireland, with honourable exceptions, follow the charts of English explorations and have searched for (and found) the inventive and arresting in country houses.[11] Given that the majority of the well-to-do, mostly Protestants, lived in Dublin and other towns, it is there that many sociable and cultural initiatives began. A predominantly rural perspective brings further risks. Any inclination towards magnificence among landowners is easily connected with the rawness and insecurities of the recently settled. Everywhere, parvenus are derided for their crass advertisement of wealth. If proprietors were guilty of vulgarity, they were not alone. Newcomers who behaved like the well-established were universally ridiculed as vulgarians or were condemned as pushy *arrivistes*. Yet, both inherited and recently gained money was spent on the same things. Among them were many of the requisites for projecting the grand figure. In 1749, Lord Chesterfield (a recent and supposedly successful governor of Ireland) lectured his son on how 'to make a figure in your country'.[12] Chesterfield's exhortation provided Sir Lewis Namier with a key to unlock the motivations of public men in England.[13]

A preoccupation with making the right impression helps to explain the scheming and spending set out in later chapters. It united Protestants (and Catholics) in Ireland with many contemporaries throughout Europe and America.[14] A few examples introduce the notion. Early in the 1730s, a squire in the Irish midlands, hoping to be an MP, congratulated himself on winning the support of 'all the gentlemen of figure and fortune' in his locality. The aspirant laboured to cut a dash with his own and his horse's equipage, in his house and through his mien. A second, also anxious to be in the Dublin parliament, campaigned on several fronts. All his strategies – house, entertainments, local offices and personal manner – contributed to 'the grand figure'.[15] Being on a public stage made actors jittery about 'interest', 'credit' and 'figure'. The important, self-important and would-be important fretted and fussed about 'genteel fancy', 'a perfectly genteel fancy' or 'the most fashionable way'. Clothes and accessories were to be 'as handsome and genteel as possible', 'the best and newest', 'to make me very fine and sparkish', and to fend off any 'slur or discredit'.[16] Varied devices were used to impress: house, furniture, collections of books and *objets de vertu*, clothes and hospitality. In this way, a haunch of venison, a creel of eels, the choice of music or the tulips and carnations in borders became elements in assessing credit and esteem.[17]

Things loom large in what follows. However, they cannot be detached from people who made, sold and bought them. Nor were they divorced from ideas.[18] So, this account reads rather differently from most recent histories of Ireland. Commodities, so far from being ornamental and incidental, are integrated into daily lives. Inevitably, the approach sheds most light on a prospering minority of Protestants. Wherever possible, it tries to consider the impact of the material on humbler producers and consumers. The study starts with the viceroyalty, the agency through which the impressionable in Ireland might have been brought closer to English ways. In redirecting Irish tastes, its effect, although not altogether negative, was negligible. Accordingly the focus quickly swivels from Dublin Castle to the houses of those usually – if not habitually – resident in Ireland. How they were arranged and furnished, and the grounds in which they were set, reveal more about Irish participation in the feverish consumerism gripping western Europe. Unfamiliar goods and ideas arrived in Ireland. Yet, a greater diversity at home did not stem the stampede from the countryside into the town, forsaking the provinces for the capital, and even Ireland for Britain and the rest of Europe. A footloose minority left behind the sedentary. Lucky Protestants, free to travel over-seas, can be compared with Catholics condemned to dolorous exile. Activity, whether at home or away, was gregarious not solitary.

Occasions of sociability and conviviality multiplied. Some remained essentially domestic; others were assertively public. Many, it will be argued, belonged typically both to the town and to men. However, as an examination of recreations suggests, towns were not yet rigidly sepa-rated from the countryside. More important in segregating participants in society, societies and sociability from the excluded were gender, money (often evident in dress and conduct) and confession. The final factor alone distinguished Ireland sharply from its nearest neigh-bours. However, the prevalence of poverty debarred a larger proportion of its people than in neighbouring lands from the more highly variegated worlds of goods. This affected Protes-tants and Catholics alike, but the latter predominated among the impecunious. Lives stripped of material possessions were readily equated with backwardness, even with barbarism. The more friendly made a virtue of what was usually a financial necessity and ascribed frugality to Catholics. The corollary was that the Protestants' zest for buying and consuming novelties, once seen as the goal of the English mission in Ireland, began to be criticized.[19]

Despite the compass of this study, several relevant subjects are omitted. They include diet, hospitality and intoxicating print. The omission of the last underscores the danger that, transfixed by the scintillating husk, the vital kernel is ignored. More in the minds of those who inhabited seventeenth- and eighteenth-century Ireland needs to be rediscovered. Yet, this account is unrepentant in lingering over what some may dismiss as trivia. This is not from any intention to trivialize the often grim experiences of so many in Ireland throughout the period. The underlying contention is that the often humdrum settings and materials of daily life were inescapable. Most struggled simply to survive, and many failed. Yet the strug-gle was not without pleasures, snatched, evanescent and (to grandees) derisory. A few are still visible; most have vanished. Both appear in what follows.

# Chapter 1

# The Viceroyalty

## 1

In 1737 the incoming lord-lieutenant, the duke of Devonshire, was congratulated by the Irish lord chancellor on being advanced to 'the greatest and most honourable government under the crown of Great Britain'. The young Edmund Burke echoed the opinion in 1747. 'The grandest place His Majesty can bestow on a subject is to represent himself in Ireland'.[1] Occupants of the post did not always value it so highly. Devonshire himself dressed casually, and so offended the always critical Dubliners. He struggled thereafter to correct the unfavourable impression created by his appearance. One of Devonshire's entourage noted, 'the generality of the people of this country . . . are known to esteem the patrons and the patronised according to the figure they make'.[2] In particular, 'the little town of Dublin, so censorious', judged its rulers severely.[3] More than deportment and dress weakened the lord-lieutenant. Stripped systematically of powers of patronage and of initiating policies, the viceroy by the 1750s seemed to have declined into 'a mere figure of state pageantry'.[4] Even so, Lord Chancellor Wyndham was technically correct. Scotland, united with England since 1707, had no equivalent of the viceroyalty. The Hanoverians' more distant territories in America or India did not, or had yet to, develop the office. The need for such an officer testified to the standing of Ireland as a kingdom in its own right, entitled still to be ruled through its own institutions. Its absent monarch, king of Great Britain and elector of Hanover, had to be represented by an impressive substitute.

The identities of each lord-lieutenant, the 'silver substitute of day', throughout most of the seventeenth and eighteenth centuries, together with the diminished powers and cramped accommodations, sat awkwardly with the pomp of the office.[5] Furthermore, in comparison with the arrangements through which, for example, the Spanish and Austrian monarchs governed their satellite kingdoms, such as Flanders, Bohemia and Hungary, the English did little to flatter the self-esteem of their Irish dependants. No prince of the royal blood was ever dispatched. Late in the 1670s it was rumoured that the popular bastard of

Charles II, Monmouth, would be sent to govern Ireland.[6] This scheme recalled one of the 1520s when the duke of Richmond was designed as deputy to his father, Henry VIII.[7] Neither project was adopted. Except when the monarch himself briefly descended on the island – in 1689, first James II, then William of Orange – it was fobbed off with motley noblemen. From 1713, they were not even of Irish lineage.

The likelihood of these visiting grandees ingratiating themselves – and the monarchy which they represented – with the inhabitants of Ireland was lessened by the short spells for which most alighted on Irish soil. The reputations of these mainly overwintering migrants were burnished or spotted according to the figure that they cut. This was variously judged: sometimes by their political system with its resulting alliances and triumphs in the Dublin parliament. Increasingly, these successes resulted from the right choice of intermediaries and undertakers rather than from the exertions of the kingling himself.[8] Political acumen and affability could influence the outcome of such manoeuvres. However, most governors were constrained by the programme of their masters back in England, so that it was through style and steering that the successful relaxed tensions. The glitter from public fêtes delighted but seldom disarmed critics. In 1692, the court of Lord Sydney, the first lord-lieutenant since the Glorious Revolution, was cried up by a sycophantic office-holder. Sydney, it was reported, 'lives magnificently to the honour of his country [England], and the relief of the Protestants and Irish nobility who crowd his table'. In addition, 'he is affable, easy of access, and popular enough, without descending too low, at the same time tender of the king's prerogative, and careful to preserve the dependence of this kingdom on England in parliamentary proceedings according to the ancient constitution, for which some turbulent factious men only are displeased with him'.[9] What pleased some angered others. The latter, even when written off as 'turbulent factious men' (and women), would not be silenced. Achievements could melt away as fast as the fun and fare offered in the Castle.

Contrary observers adjudged expansiveness extravagance, even debauchery; decorum, as standoffishness or niggardliness. Of Clarendon, lord-lieutenant in 1685, it was said, 'my lord and his train go to mend and not mar fortunes'.[10] In 1700, the imminent disembarkation of Rochester, the new viceroy, brought the prospect of 'a full court' and 'a great change in our figure'.[11] Three years later, the return of the second duke of Ormonde to Ireland as lord-lieutenant attracted 'a mighty court in Dublin'. Two hundred coaches – thirty of them drawn by six horses – were said to have greeted the duke: a measure of the Ormondes' popularity.[12] Carteret, lord-lieutenant between 1725 and 1730, was approved more than most from England. Spirits lifted with his prospective landing. Katherine Conolly, the wife of the leading politician with whom he would have to deal, cheered. 'We are like to have a fine gay court here'.[13] Other Dubliners agreed. 'He hath rattle, wit and humour to a great degree, and the later, the sprightlier'.[14] Carteret was eased into his local popularity by his brief from his masters in London: to reverse unpopular measures.[15] He and his family played their roles to perfection. The sensitive suspected that it was acting, with Carteret affecting a bluff manner foreign to his sophisticated nature. His clowning at the Castle, playing 'merry Andrew', was generally liked.[16] Carteret's successor, Dorset, was scrutinized minutely from the moment when he disembarked. He was immediately reckoned, 'grave, civil, yet retired'. A stickler for forms and dignity, his was likened to a sombre Spanish court after the vivacity of the Carterets' regime.[17] A similar contrast had been drawn between the *bonhomie* of the duke of Ormonde and the reserve of his replacement, Pembroke, back in 1707.[18] In the intimate spaces of Dublin Castle, differences between governors tended to be magnified. Each had favourites. But, on their side, those hunting for favours adjusted to changed viceroys. The incumbent in the Castle was an obvious focus of hopes. In this spirit, the many who did not know the current viceroy snatched at any who could claim kinship or acquaintanceship with and access to the important. The shrewd concurrently explored other avenues to the influential, especially any which led directly to courtiers and ministers in England.[19] The disappointed – the majority – subsequently questioned where real power was to be found.

The frostiness of and towards Dorset thawed as he spent prodigally to delight his guests in the Castle, first in 1731 and again in 1733. An exacting visitor from England attended the festivities for the king's birthday. The ballroom, tricked out especially for the event with gilt leather, 'was the prettiest thing I ever saw'. Similarly, the supper, served at midnight, 'was finer than anything I ever saw'. The Dorsets were 'excessive civil to everybody', so much so that Lady Anne Conolly cooed, 'I like Queen Dorset much better than Queen Caroline'.[20] Political systems were inseparable from the physical impact of the changing regimes. In 1710, it was noted that the departing governor 'by courting nobody gained . . . [his] point and pleased everybody that is what we call the ascendant'.[21] Just as Carteret had welcomed different politicians into the viceregal presence, so it was remarked how Dorset caressed his own favourites.[22] Before that, the younger Sir John Temple, a confidant of Essex and Ormond, noted plaintively in 1687 that he was seldom invited to the Castle and had dined only once with the new (and Catholic) viceroy, Tyrconnell.[23] Much later, an egregious Ulster clergyman congratulated himself that Lord-Lieutenant Halifax 'has at every time I appeared at his levée condescended to distinguish me by particular notice and conversation'.[24] The small viceregal entourage which always accompanied the lord-lieutenant was enlarged with local recruits. Yet, for the most part, the court at which the hopeful and bored congregated palely reflected its original in London, and seldom eclipsed the other diversions on offer elsewhere in Dublin. Lady Anne Conolly dismissed the junkets under Dorset as 'our sham court'.[25] Among hosts, frank impatience was expressed sometimes about 'the trail of grandees' that tagged along behind the viceroy.[26] Others despised the alacrity with which their neighbours fawned on the visitors. In the autumn of 1733, at the prospect of Dorset's return, 'tho the people here are generally poor, they are preparing for gaiety and folly to make a figure for him'.[27]

On their side, companions of the visiting dignitary questioned the posting to Dublin. In the 1680s, one reluctant attendant was urged to consider 'whether you can stoop to the duty and uncertainty of a little court and how far Ireland is agreeable to you'.[28] For this courtier, as for the majority who danced on the viceroy, his stay did not outlast that of his master, so that the remainder of his career was passed outside Ireland. One brought in the train of Devonshire mused on his lot. His dignity, 'a place of no profit, only procures a man the liberty to appear often at court and of improving himself'.[29] Another young officer, chosen by Devonshire to be one of his gentlemen at large at the Castle, was equally disenchanted. These attendants paid heavily to maintain a fitting style and to entertain comrades. The second officer was left with debts of £60 after his short tour of duty.[30] 'A way of life where a person has neither his time nor his actions at his own disposal' rapidly palled.[31] The tedium was alleviated by the chance to plunge into Dublin society away from the cantonment of the Castle.[32] A secretary at the Castle in the 1720s, the poet Thomas Tickell, was satirized in an invented list of his smart acquaintances in Dublin. The catalogue may have been a cod, but it revealed how personable viceregal attendants insinuated themselves into local society.[33] Through charm even temporary sojourners acquired permanent connections with Protestant Ireland.

To the hopeful it seemed that the lord-lieutenant had an inexhaustible cornucopia. The viceroy thought differently. The stock that he distributed was limited, and shrinking.[34] Even positions formally in the lord-lieutenant's gift were seldom bestowed with complete freedom. He had patrons, allies and rivals back in England to please. Competitors sought to control appointments to positions nominally within his purview. Failure of an incumbent in Dublin to place his nominees depressed his standing, usually irreparably. The man in Dublin Castle needed to command a good share of patronage, 'as a mark of power'.[35] Lord Capel, newly invested with the Irish government in 1695, begged that his first recommendation for ecclesiastical preferment should succeed. Otherwise, he would be weakened from the start.[36] Sometimes, in failing to prefer hopefuls, a lord-lieutenant sheltered behind procedures in which he was imprisoned. Sales and exchanges of offices were blocked in the 1720s as contrary to George I's stated wishes.[37] In 1755, Hartington explained his refusal to grant Lord Mountcharles the aulnager's office because he had already agreed with the king not to make appointments for life with rights of reversion.[38] Five years later, Bedford candidly admitted to Nathanael Clements that he could not prefer the latter's candidate to a living in County Meath, because 'I have had so many prior applications'.[39] In many cases, the Irish governor was powerless; in others, he feigned impotence. Either way his credit in Ireland dropped.

The feebleness of the lord-lieutenant was aptly shown in the failure, despite repeated pleading, to improve his housing. Dublin Castle, the main viceregal residence, served as fort, arsenal and government offices. Its importance, both as emblem and headquarters of the English administration in Ireland, had made it the target for attacks. In October 1641, conspirators aimed to end the oppressive rule associated with Lord Deputy Wentworth and his

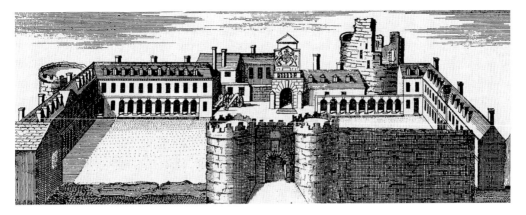

1. Dublin Castle, *c.* 1728, from C. Brooking's map of Dublin, showing the ramshackle fabric with as yet few ranges in a regular, classical style.

successors by seizing the Castle. Again in 1659 and 1663, its capture was central to intended coups. Once, early in 1660, its seizure did initiate political changes.[40] Nervy lords-lieutenant continued to fear fresh attempts on the Castle. Cramped in the ancient centre of the city, it was open to surprise. Yet the threats receded as British rule apparently entrenched itself more deeply. By the 1740s, the uninvited within its precincts were women pilfering silver and pewter.[41] Other worries increasingly preoccupied the Castle's residents. Chief among these was the danger from fire, magnified by the storage of gunpowder in the towers. Twice in Charles II's reign, in 1671 and 1684, flames destroyed parts of the fabric. Had it not been for timely action, in the second case directed by the lord deputy, Arran (imitating the king's role in the Fire of London), worse damage might have been suffered.[42] The destruction intensi-fied the complaints of those who had long argued that the Castle needed radical overhaul. Some proposed that its multiple functions end. The arsenal and citadel should be removed, so that they no longer risked detonating the governor, government and many of the gov-erned in the surrounding streets.[43] The other bodies which met within the precincts – including, for a time, parliament – could be accommodated elsewhere. If the lord-lieutenant was left as sole occupant, the premises might then be upgraded to make them more appro-priate to his status as surrogate sovereign. Yet, not all were happy to leave the viceroy in pos-session, including some of the viceroys themselves. They ached for adequate gardens, paddocks and pleasure grounds. They wilted in the foetid air of the stinking city. Like the smart among their Dublin neighbours, they looked longingly to the more spacious suburbs springing up away from the crowded centre of the capital.

Lord-Lieutenant Essex commented bleakly in 1673, 'this castle is of itself one of the most incommodious dwellings that ever I came in and there is no place of pleasure belonging to it, nor any house to retire to for a little air upon reason of sickness'.[44] Such complaints, voiced earlier by Wentworth and often repeated, failed to mend the defects. Necessary repairs were allowed; rooms were redecorated; fresh sequences were created to allow ceremonial more in keeping with changing notions of court etiquette; occasionally, additions announced greater architectural pretensions. As so often was the case, in London and continental capitals as well, the prospect of building a splendid palace mesmerized projectors and architectural amateurs.[45] Lord Orrery, Sir William Petty and Sir William Robinson all turned their minds to the possibilities. Robinson, as surveyor-general, had formal responsibility for the upkeep of the state's buildings. He probably designed what was built in the 1680s.[46] Remembering that the ambitious schemes for remodelling the warren at Whitehall between the 1620s and the 1690s were never executed, it is not surprising that Dublin did not acquire a startling classical viceregal residence. The money was lacking. So, as importantly, was the will. With a driving force, funds could be found and ambitious structures were erected. Notable in this regard were the military hospital of Kilmainham, the library for Trinity College, the Royal Barracks and the Parliament House on College Green.[47] Each could be seen, both in terms of spending and ideologically, as an alternative to expensive works on the Castle. Indeed, the new parliament building was hailed variously as 'one of the finest pieces of architecture in the world' and 'the finest building that was ever beheld in this kingdom'.[48] Similarly, a bishop commented on the recently completed complex, 'it is indeed too fine for us, but it hath employed our own hands'.[49] The Castle never attracted equivalent plaudits.

Ormond, conscious of his dignity as Ireland's sole duke and as – in his mind – its natural viceroy (a judgement with which Charles II more often than not concurred), certainly interested himself in the look of Dublin Castle. So, too, did the duchess of Ormond. Shortly after Ormond re-entered the viceroyalty in 1678 he wrote plaintively that his wife and Robinson 'have been conspiring to put me to more charge than my purse but not the place require'.[50] Without any adequate Dublin billet of their own, the Butlers (dukes of Ormonde) were inconvenienced not to have continuous occupancy of the Castle. While there, between 1662 and 1669 and again from 1678 to 1685, they remade it in the Butlers' image. In the main, this was achieved economically, by tricking out rooms with tapestries, gilded leather wall-coverings, table carpets or upholstered seat furniture, gilded, silver and brass sconces and mirrors, not through major structural alterations.[51] Ormond, although wealthy – a rental of perhaps £25,000 – was enmired in debt and sinking fast. He was not going to spend his own money on a state residence. Instead, he switched furnishings and staff between his private houses, notably Kilkenny Castle, and Dublin Castle.[52] Thereby, the glory of the state was enhanced, but so too was that of the Ormonds. Ormond, owning extensive property in Ireland, had an advantage denied to all his English successors.[53] When the stench of the city proved insupportable, he retired to his own estates. There he could refresh his entourage with hunting and diversions. At Kilkenny, as much as in Dublin

2. Michael Dahl, *James Butler, 2nd duke of Ormond (1665–1745)*, lord-lieutenant of Ireland, 1703–7 and 1710–13, engraved by S. Gribelin, 1713.

Castle, he held court.[54] In the Ormonds' world, private and public functions merged. Ormond, uniquely among Irish subjects, enjoyed regalian rights thanks to the palatinate of Tipperary. He also presided over an estate where he enjoyed formal and informal legal powers. Simultaneously, as the king's deputy, he dispatched business, heard petitions, adjudicated disputes and dispensed favours. His castle, site of this mixture of activities, was transformed. Robinson advised.[55] Alongside the concentration on Kilkenny, Dublin Castle tended to be neglected. Neither Ormond nor his grandson, the second duke, who followed him as viceroy between 1703 and 1707 and 1710 to 1713, had the same pressing urge felt by the visiting English governors to find a rural and recreational refuge. Simply they could remove with their followers to Kilkenny.

Throughout most of the period only the minimum was spent to keep the Castle habitable. By the eighteenth century, if successive lords-lieutenant (and their ladies) lamented the discomforts, they stayed too short a time to inaugurate dramatic changes. They mitigated the inconveniences of the buildings by camping among their own furnishings either carried backwards or forwards with them or sold to them by their predecessors.[56] Viceroys were disinclined to spend heavily from their own purses; nor did they enjoy the leverage with the British Treasury to secure grants for grandiose rebuilding. The Irish Parliament viewed the viceroyalty askance, as the embodiment of an irksome and sometimes controverted constitutional dependency on England. If parliament was to spend on architectural extravaganzas it was on a library for the educational institution (Trinity College) which – at least after 1717 – upheld 'revolution principles', a barracks that helped to guarantee the security of the Protestant interest, and the assembly place of the representatives of that interest. Expert at the petty insult, patriotic Irish Protestants kept the king's deputy in cramped discomfort while professing service and loyalty. England had sent this functionary; England, therefore, could pay to house him. But the paymasters in Whitehall ordered Ireland low among their priorities, with any idea of funding a splendid viceregal pad far down the list.

Uncomfortable and discomfited, ingenious viceroys schemed over what to do. Some, as has been mentioned, imported impressive props with which they could surround themselves and radiate grandeur. Others took refuge in elaborating ceremony. In this they were abetted by local impresarios. The official with the greatest interest in inventing appropriate rituals was Ulster King of Arms. William Hawkins, holder of this heraldic office between 1698 and 1736, dedicated himself to the matter. Continuity in aspiration if not of accomplishment was ensured when Hawkins was succeeded by first his son and then his grandson.[57] From the moment when the new deputy disembarked, either at Ringsend or Dun Laoghaire, next as he was conducted into and through the city to the Castle, until finally he surrendered the sword of state and sailed away, the processions were carefully choreographed. Similarly, the regular occasions when the viceroy ventured abroad – to open or prorogue parliament, publicly to worship, to receive worthies or to view the provinces – were to be stage-managed.[58] Some occupants of the high office proved more apt than others as pupils of the heraldic masters of ceremonies. In the 1690s, Archbishop Marsh of Dublin fretted because neither lord justice, Drogheda and Mountrath (both Irish peers), had taken communion during the Christmas festival at the Church of Ireland cathedral. As the Primate warned, since 'the common people judge by outward appearance', any imagined or real slight to the state church might damage it.[59] The dignity of the viceroy was further compromised when members of the commonalty repeatedly invaded the gallery reserved for his use in the cathedral.[60] Any damage could be offset by magnificence. Rochester, riding in state as lord-lieutenant to Christ Church cathedral for the commemoration of 5 November in 1701, elicited admiring gasps. The eight greys which hauled his carriage and the livery of the footmen impressed.[61]

## II

Public mishaps depressed viceregal reputations. The duke of Devonshire's dishevelled appearance offended some. Similarly, the informal civilian garb sported by a successor, Devonshire's own son, Hartington, on a visit to Limerick in 1755 drew more criticism.[62] Devonshire upset the punctilious. Each year, the viceroy publicly received the lord mayor of Dublin. The latter mimed the municipality's loyalty to the English crown and reminded that Dublin's privileges derived from the same source by presenting the sheathed sword of the city. Devonshire, in drawing it from the scabbard, used such force that the aged and portly lord mayor was pulled over and tumbled down the steps. Onlookers took this as an unlucky omen.[63] As the viceroy's work became more civilian and sedentary, rather than peripatetic and martial as so often it had been during the sixteenth and first half of the seventeenth centuries, the calendar was crowded with days when locals were entertained. Already in the 1680s two days were dedicated to the lord mayor and lady mayoress of Dublin. The year 1690 was the first time the sovereign's birthday was celebrated. A lord justice wrote ruefully of his sore head after two days of feasting in early November.[64] In this decade, both the special Irish Protestant festival of 23 October and St George's Day were marked exuberantly.[65] The ceremonial calendar was swollen as local, topical and British festivals were added to the red-letter days.[66] All had to be managed in seemly manner. By 1703, Rochester, the lord-lieutenant, although absent in London, decreed that the queen's birthday should be celebrated appropriately. However, he believed it unnecessary to serve supper at the Castle: fireworks, music, dancing and a play sufficed.[67]

In the first decade of the eighteenth century, each of the national saints of the Stuarts' realms was celebrated. How far these observances arose spontaneously in Dublin, with its confessionally and ethnically mixed population, how far they were devised by the authorities, and how far exploited by avaricious functionaries to add to their perquisites is not easily ascertained. When Scottish union was being promoted before 1707, and some hoped for similar treatment for Ireland, St Andrew's crosses were distributed near the end of November. The Welsh exiles in and around the Castle sustained the market for leeks on St David's Day.[68] St Patrick's crosses were sported in mid-March. Habitués of the Castle wore these favours. Archbishop King received his from servants of the viceregal establishment. Prices rose steeply, hinting that profit mattered more than patriotism. By 1714, King ceased to buy these offerings.[69] Maybe the blatant commercialization had turned him against this particular manifestation of national feeling. Despite the archbishop's abstention, St Patrick's tide continued to be marked, with favours worn or treats given. In 1734, the bishop of Down and Connor had to give the viceroy's servants a not inconsiderable 5s. 5d. for his 'Patrick's Cross'. (The same money would buy a seat at a concert of Handel's music.) In 1756, Squire Edgeworth, a member of parliament, obtained his shamrock from the servants at the Castle.[70]

St Andrew's Day also retained a following.[71] Festivities for St George seem to have declined. A conspicuous failure, and consequently a lost opportunity, on the part of the English rulers of Ireland was to use the cult of St Patrick to bind those in Ireland tighter to the monarchy. During the 1630s, it was mooted that an order of chivalry peculiar to Ireland and dedicated to St Patrick might be invented. Not until 1783 was this scheme adopted. By then, it could be argued, it was too late to reverse an offensively anti-English particularism.[72]

The lord-lieutenant when resident – usually for part of every second year – presided over a busy court. In 1742 a bemused visitor described the offerings. Every Tuesday, the duke held a levee for the men. This was followed by the vicereine's, for both ladies and gentlemen. In the evening, beginning at nine and not ending until 1 or 2 a.m., a ball was held. It usually attracted at least 200 ladies. Friday also saw a levee. In the evening there would be a drawing-room, at which cards were played. This attracted fewer and lasted a shorter time. The *haut ton* otherwise amused itself with plays on Mondays and Thursdays and concerts on Wednesdays. The musical evenings, at which Handel's compositions were performed, could attract 600, mostly subscribers. On Saturdays there would be a ball, attended by between 600 and 800. These routines were later varied.[73] Fashionable Dubliners did not depend solely – or even primarily – on the viceroy for their diversions.[74] Yet, socialites, thirsting for novelty, appreciated what astute lords-lieutenant offered. Many were invited to the Castle, but fewer were accorded personal recognition. By 1761 it was noted that the viceroy customarily acknowledged none under the rank of member of parliament.[75] More select were the dinners to which one or two dozen were bidden. Most guests were office-holders or members of parliament, although women were also entertained, especially in the 1760s. Often these occasions had an overt political purpose.[76] Less blatantly, the sociable lords-lieutenant, such as Carteret, wooed the important of Protestant Ireland. Some suspected that the charmer played to the gallery. A tune, 'Lustrum pony', came into vogue, to which Carteret persuaded 'my poor silly country men' to perform 'a most ungraceful set of steps that would become any one above the degree of those who carry a cake at a maypole or a hat at a codling match'.[77] This theme of provincial uncouthness was reprised by a satirist in 1757. 'The grand menagerie' in the Presence Chamber was dominated by army officers and clergy. The formal squires 'bow in the press/ Their hinder parts recoil as far as/ Guns fired on a level terrace'. Instructed by the foremost dancing master of the age, Delamain, they 'aped, but aped in vain', his courtly steps.[78]

Other governors kept their distance, and scarcely concealed their disdain for the bucolic company. In 1761, Lord Halifax whined that his gathering on 6 November was not as full as usual owing to meetings of parliamentary committees. He confided, 'assembly night was as dull as usual, and I had as many disagreeable assemblages to salute'. Yet, Halifax also knew that the concourse could be read as an index of his own standing in Ireland. Other instincts came into play. Of a ball, he was delighted to record that it attracted handsome women, 'which I had not seen before at the Castle'. An autonomous society functioned in Dublin, into which the astute lord-lieutenant was content to slide. Halifax donated ten guineas to a charity for clergymen's widows. However, as he himself appreciated, by attending a concert in aid of this cause, he did more: 'the great advantage the charity got by my company was that it filled the room'.[79] Sycophants took up causes that the lord-lieutenant and his lady were trying to popularize. But, as Lady Carteret remembered, 'it used to be easy enough to get subscriptions but not quite so easy to get the money paid'.[80] By the 1760s, some of those invited to the Castle declined the invitations. On 23 October 1769, twenty-five diners appeared, but twenty-one had refused. The absentees probably registered political estrangement from Lord Townshend's system.[81] Earlier, Dorset's imperiousness, matching his zeal to curb Irish Protestant querulousness, angered many. These feelings sometimes mutated into personal animosity. In 1752, it was gleefully reported how at a regatta on choppy seas in Dublin Bay, Dorset proved as poor a sailor as parliamentary manager. The lord-lieutenant was 'like to have puked' in his neighbour's pocket.[82]

Towards the end of the 1750s, the measures and methods adopted by Lord Bedford were scrutinized. Charles O'Hara, a cosmopolitan squire from County Sligo, invited to the Castle, played guinea whist there until after eleven. Any good effects of Bedford's management were soon nullified – at least in O'Hara's eyes – by the conduct of the viceregal entourage. 'The Duke and all his people drunk, even his first chaplain', it was noted after a February party. In contrast, O'Hara insisted, he had not seen an Irishman inebriated throughout the winter. Again, though, he was shocked by the entertainment at Nathaniel Clements' spanking new house in Phoenix Park. At this 'private undress party' for a dozen, the duchess of Bedford wore a hat, the viceroy his regimentals. Again drunkenness reigned, with 'dancing, blindman's buff, and such riot [as] never was'.[83] Most worrying perhaps was an encounter with the chief governor at supper during a ball given by Clements. This, O'Hara admitted, beat anything he had ever seen before. Bedford turned up, 'drunk from Annesley's, where they had been settling the plan for future power'.[84] As with Dorset, Bedford's political ambitions spilled over into the physical settings of his viceroyalty. He forwarded schemes of rebuilding, addition and redecoration at the Castle. These had been on the carpet since the later 1740s. The surveyor general, Thomas Eyre, provided designs of dignified functionalism. He aimed to enlarge and improve the existing apartments, and add to their number, so giving the castle 'the appearance of a palace'.[85] Conscious of the dignity of the lord-lieutenancy, Eyre aimed to stop Dubliners peering down on the incumbent as he rode in the garden. Nor did he feel that a wooden 'shed' in the garden was a fitting place in which Bedford should work.[86] A few years earlier, a campaign of rebuilding under Eyre's predecessor as surveyor-general, Arthur Jones Nevill, had created a sequence of state apartments for the then viceroy, Harrington. A staircase led into a guard room (the Battle Axes' Hall) and on into the Presence Chamber and Drawing Room. Something of the martial atmosphere lingered still in the Castle, partly through the continuing presence of guards and also in the plainness and severity of the architecture. Nevill's Presence Chamber used the austere Doric order, rather than the more festive Corinthian or Composite.[87]

This greater architectural assertiveness of the lord-lieutenant, and the willingness of the British Treasury to finance it, coincided with a period in which successive viceroys tried more aggressively to curb the unruliness of local politicians. But, if these modern edifices were resented as symbols of the greater British intrusions into Irish affairs, they were partly annexed by the locals. The ancillary ranges in the Castle accommodated the state and semi-state panels, such as the Linen Board.[88] The grandeur did not always strengthen Dubliners' respect for their immediate and distant rulers. A visitor from Ulster in 1757 considered the public places of Dublin inferior to those in London.[89] Only in 1770 did this same observer, now familiar with the West Indies and St James's Palace in London, allow that 'the brilliancy' of official entertainment at the Castle 'far exceeded my expectations or anything of that nature I had ever seen before'. He judged Dublin Castle, 'the most elegantly furnished place I ever had the opportunity of seeing', whether in Havana, London or Caribbean outposts. The Irish festivities, continuing through the night until six in the morning surpassed what had been provided the previous year in London.[90] An Irish pride may have inspired this praise. However, changes had occurred since 1757, with a more regularly resident lord-lieutenant and fresh spending (£4,817 is recorded) on the buildings.[91]

Lords-lieutenant had difficulty in avoiding the extremes of parsimony and profligacy. In 1755, the newly installed Hartington reassured his father, Devonshire, a predecessor in the lieutenancy, 'we were very sober, there having been but one bad bout'. The father himself had been reckoned a prodigious drinker. This capability, coupled with a readiness to patronize the spectacles of the town rather than moping in the Castle, recommended him.[92] From another quarter in 1755, 'a very great Castle ball, and the night before a very prodigious great Castle drinking bout from dinner till past eleven' were reported. Over these rites, Hartington concluded fresh political deals with the Speaker, Boyle, and the restless Lord Kildare.[93] Kildare himself admitted to his wife after the Castle thrash, 'I don't think I ever drank so hard and fast in my life: every one of the company complain today'.[94] As Hartington settled into the sociable politics of the town, enjoyment occasionally degenerated into excess.[95] Hartington congratulated himself on doing rather well in taxing circumstances. He regained some of the popularity forfeited by Dorset's high-handedness. Hartington had interests of his own in Ireland as well as a father who had himself served as viceroy. His bride, the heiress to the great Cork and Burlington (Boyle) estate, brought him a stake in the kingdom such as no lord-lieutenant since the Ormondes had possessed. Although affable and with a large Irish rental, Hartington did not please all. Lord Kildare, on discovering that Hartington could not be moulded like soft wax, complained: 'I fear he is a very young man, and has already got into bad hands without his knowing it'.[96] Hartington, despite his qualities, represented a governmental system which, if amended since the time of Dorset, affronted patriots through its subservience to Britain.[97] At least he avoided the opprobrium that enveloped his successor, Bedford. By the time the latter departed in 1760, local opinion had swung violently against him. His going, one Dubliner reported, was 'to the great joy of almost all the whole kingdom, for we began to fear he was doing us at least no good. Indeed, some people think that a great deal of our present calamities is owing to his administration'.[98]

## III

The freedom of lords-lieutenant to initiate policy was severely curtailed by the mid-eighteenth century. Accordingly, their impact was felt chiefly in the social and cultural spheres. The subtle used amusements to steer their guests into better courses, and to wile away the *longueurs* of their tours of duty. Repeatedly, the well-meaning sought to make de rigueur the wearing of Irish textiles: prickly frieze (or tweed), poplin and linen.[99] Immediately after Charles II's restoration, a parliamentary bill to compel the use of clothes made in Ireland was promoted, but was never enacted.[100] The duke of Dorset took this patronage of Irish wares further. He commissioned a service of pottery, painted with his own armorials, from the manufacturer who had lately set up in Dublin. Dorset, on his return from his first tour of duty in 1737, in his second capacity of lord steward of George II's household, removed the contract for supplying the royal household with table linen from the Low Countries to Ireland.[101]

Once in Dublin, no lord-lieutenant could be ignored. Such was the magnetism of power that all, even the inept, attracted some followers. However, he was not the only planet in the Dublin constellation. The Ormondes while out of Irish office tended to locate themselves outside Ireland. Thereby they did not obviously challenge the incumbent viceroy. But, by the eighteenth century, English lords-lieutenant struggled not to be eclipsed by local notables: first the Conollys and then the Kildares. Their wealth enabled both dynasties to set up as formidable hosts and hostesses, in Dublin and the Kildare countryside. Their establishments at Kildare (later Leinster) House, Carton and Castletown rivalled what was on offer in the Castle and certainly outshone dull Chapelizod, the modest viceregal refuge outside Dublin. The Conollys co-operated cosily with the Carterets, but during the 1730s, the widowed Katherine Conolly developed Castletown as a rival court to Dorset's alien regimen. The chatelaine of Castletown happily invited Devonshire and 'the government' to holiday there. In 1755, Hartington, a widower keen to avoid summer in Dublin, was given the use of the mansion.[102] Meanwhile, the Kildares re-established themselves as the social leaders in the Protestant Pale and Dublin. By the 1750s, splendidly housed in Dublin, they staged a series of balls.[103] Bedford responded by hiring a town house for himself: Lord Powerscourt's.[104] Looking to the future, Bedford set in train improvements to the Castle which would permit his successors to live there more creditably.

Transient fashions in dress, diet and décor were reflected in the viceregal arrangements. In 1758, it was alleged that a Dublin alderman died of a surfeit of ices after a reception in the Castle. In earlier times, custards would have killed the greedy. Moreover, breakfasts of beef-steaks were supplanted by less robust fare.[105] Dorset and his haughty adjutant Archbishop George Stone felt that a low-grade yellow-label champagne would suffice for Castle balls. But 'a better kind' was needed 'for select meetings'.[106] It is doubtful, nevertheless, how many novelties were first introduced by the viceroy and vicereine, and how far their influence reached within, let alone beyond, Dublin. Furthermore, differing in temperament, viceroys relaxed variously: with the chase, the bowling green, card tables, theatricals, music or venery. Also, the tone at the Castle depended on whether or not the governor was accompanied by his wife. In 1707, Lord Pembroke did not intend to bring his spouse or family because of the want of appropriate accommodation.[107] Their absence explained the austerity of his regime. Nevertheless, under his patronage a group of virtuosi briefly resurrected the Dublin Philosophical Society. Pembroke and his cultivated aides, such as Andrew Fountaine, encouraged collectors and savants, with whom they maintained contact long after returning to England.[108] The group may have been a rarefied taste among the rumbustuous habituated to the ways of the camp associated with Ormonde or of the whorehouse, the resort of his immediate successor, Wharton. Again, Carteret's popularity owed much to the ease with which he combined vivacity with cultivation. In 1728, his wife revealed that he 'walks miles every day, and reads folios every night'.[109] Lasting influences tended to be subterranean and personal. The nostalgic harked back to a particular viceroyalty, whether of an Ormonde, Pembroke or Carteret, because then they had been in favour and bright morning promised. One elegist of the first Ormond contrasted his 'skilful hand' with the 'ignorance' and 'errors' of the English viceroys.[110] The second duke of Ormonde was credited with similar dexterity in tuning 'the Irish harp'. In addition, he was approved because he 'lives very great'.[111] The brilliance was long remembered and overshadowed his English successors. Among the latter, a few – like the Carterets – kept up with some acquaintances in Ireland after they had left the kingdom.[112] Any affection which survived in Ireland was for individuals rather than the institution of the viceroyalty itself.

In comparison with continental courts, including those of viceroys in Milan and Brussels, the Irish viceroyalty achieved little.[113] Even such an adjunct as the chapel royal, because inadequately housed and manned mainly by imported clerics, was little noticed. Early in the seventeenth century, the parish church closest to the Castle, St Werburgh's, where sometimes the viceroy worshipped, did promote the approved brand of Protestantism. By the eighteenth century, lords-lieutenant went through the motions in their devotions. Their larger contribution in the ecclesiastical sphere, frequently decried, was to move their chaplains into Irish bishoprics. Lords-lieutenant, from the time of Wentworth and Ormond (and before) liked music and plays.[114] At the Castle, diversions of this kind were arranged. Other performances under viceregal auspices took place in the town. Subsequently, as Halifax so complacently remarked, a lord-lieutenant's support could decide the success or failure of a play, actor or actress, concert, composer or singer. Successive governors sat dutifully through the concerts in St Andrew's church which raised funds for Mercer's Hospital. The programme, mainly Handel, had become set in stone, and owed nothing to the promptings of the viceroy.[115] Indeed, no musical or dramatic innovations can be traced definitively to the prodding of a particular viceroy or vicereine.

Some lords-lieutenant aspired to lead through another pastime. The bored at the Castle refreshed themselves at the races or with the chase. The expanding metropolis devoured easily accessible hunting grounds. Governors from the time of Ormond and Essex pleaded to preserve Phoenix Park as a handy recreational retreat.[116] Stags were hunted by the favoured few; deer parks were the playgrounds of the grand.[117] Ormond and his sons removed parties to enjoy the sport on their own lands around Kilkenny. One son, Arran, hired Maddenstown in County Kildare essentially as a hunting box.[118] English lords-lieutenant lacked any such escape of their own, and begged for a viceregal country estate. Wentworth, in the later 1630s, started to build such a retreat at Jigginstown outside Naas. Ingeniously he justified the massive project as a place to which the king or his progeny could repair when in Ireland. The shell was abandoned by 1640 and then cannibalized – among others by the Ormondes for fittings at Kilkenny. In this detail, the ambitions of Wentworth, on behalf both of his monarch and the Irish viceroyalty, were not repeated.[119] The reasonable argument that the lord-lieutenant needed an alternative setting to Dublin never overcame the penny-pinching of the Irish and English state. Instead, the locally popular, such as Devonshire and Hartington, were invited into the mansions of the Irish Protestants.

Horse-racing was actively promoted.[120] In the short term, sport, and in the longer, bloodstock, may have benefited. Viceregal enthusiasm for this activity paralleled the support offered by some lords-lieutenant to the Philosophical Society, Incorporated Society and Dublin Society. However, their patronage seldom translated into regular and continuing attendance, and could not preserve ailing institutions. There remain two possible contributions of the viceroys. One is negative. The viceroyalty failed to fasten Ireland more firmly to Britain. Individuals, notwithstanding their foibles, were hardly to blame. Rather it was the way in which the post was used. Even the fact that, as a matter of policy, it was conferred only on English noblemen after 1713 need not have enfeebled it. The swapping of high functionaries between different parts of an empire, practised by the Habsburgs and in seventeenth-century France, could achieve greater administrative uniformity and smooth away awkward regionalism. During the later seventeenth century, there were some signs that Ireland might be better integrated into the Stuarts' composite monarchy. The Irish-born could still rule their own kingdom. At the same time, the lucky could make profitable careers elsewhere. Ormond, sometimes in plurality with the lord-lieutenancy, but also in isolation, held the lord high stewardship and a variety of other English offices. His contemporaries Anglesey, Conway and Ranelagh also occupied prestigious jobs: lord privy seal, secretary of state and gentleman of the bedchamber.[121] This promising interchange of the personnel of government between the two kingdoms did not last. Whereas Englishmen grabbed many of the best bishoprics and judgeships in Ireland, it was rare for any of Irish origins to rise so high in eighteenth-century England.

## IV

The secret springs through which the lord-lieutenant gave life to Irish politics remained hidden from the generality of the population. Instead appearances counted for much. The seeming ephemera of décor, design and decorum quickly decided the standing of a viceroy. Stinted in what could be spent on permanent buildings, the greatest ingenuity went into temporary stages. The magnificence to which Wentworth aspired in the 1630s was affected by Ormond in the 1660s, in this respect the heir of Wentworth. He installed chairs of state under canopies to denote the majesty which Ormond represented.[122] Yet, as at Charles II's court, so in Ormond's, loftiness alternated with accessibility and informality. The Ormondes, idolized – at least retrospectively – as the last Protestants among the English of Ireland to be trusted to govern the kingdom, set a standard by which successors were measured and generally found wanting. In 1677, it was noted, by an unsympathetic commentator, that a 'magnificent banquet and ball' had been staged at the Castle.[123] Clarendon in 1685 and Sydney in 1692 used Ormond's establishment at the Castle as the model. Their agents hunted for furnishings now missing or mislaid. Feverishly, canopies and hangings were sought. Those on the spot advised the strangers where they should buy their candles, milk and sausages.[124] The knowing carried over many necessities. They also imported accoutrements calculated to dazzle. Essex accordingly shipped into Dublin massive silver dishes and trenchers made in London. They copied a French pattern introduced into England by Lady Northumberland.[125] Styles first observed at the Castle might be copied by artificers and customers, but had at best only a limited impact on tastes in Ireland. Lords-lieutenant who carried over too much risked angering Dublin tradespeople. Once installed in the Castle, the shrewd did not reallocate contracts too dramatically. Dorset was one of several who encouraged innovative locals. Hartington offended some with his restrained garb, but he spent lavishly. In one month in 1755, he ran up bills of £1,105. They included £274 spent with a Dublin silversmith, Calderwood, and another £257 paid to 'Mr. Kelly' for linen.[126]

The custom of the Castle consolidated rather than created the pre-eminence of a few Dublin suppliers. To this trade was then added that generated by the fashionable summoned to the viceregal presence. Notwithstanding ambivalence about the system that the lords-lieutenant personified, an invitation necessitated the right rig. This impulse was less to honour the host than to stand out in the crush. In 1751, when the splendours of Dorset's court were admired, so too were the three most striking ladies in the company: Miss Gardiner, Miss Foster and the daughter of Mark White.[127] Finery was displayed: as much by men as by women. Lord St George from County Galway had tailored 'a fine suit of clothes . . . trimmed with gold', so that he could dance the night away with Lady Carteret.[128] Richard Edgeworth, a County Longford squire, allowed his new wife £20 for an outfit to sport at the Castle on the next 'birthday' in 1733.[129] One wit imagined that, for the costume of one heir, 'whole woods must fall'.[130]

Dublin Castle was a place to be seen. Whether, with seemingly promiscuous resort to the thronged assemblies, viceregal summonses were as prized as those to Carton and Castletown is harder to ascertain.[131] Invitations to the Castle were sought and usually accepted. Outward deference to governors, and ultimately the monarch for whom they deputized, combined with invective and contempt. Sometimes it was puzzling to decide which stance most accurately represented attitudes. What is clear is that the Castle was not the sole setting which extorted costly displays. To outsiders, 'us poor Irish chimney corner folk', it was inseparable from the magic of the capital. A woman marooned in the Wexford countryside, 'this stupid part of the world', dreamt of Dublin 'as prodigious gay and polite this winter, for there is a vast many fine people come and coming with the Duke of Grafton', the lord-lieutenant.[132] The better informed, habituated to the life of the city, knew that it functioned fully only for about six months in every two years.

More constant, and therefore, more characteristic of Dublin's allure were its many private and communal diversions.[133] Much detracted from the local authority of the viceroy. Rivals exploited and magnified the weaknesses. Even so, open warfare seldom existed between the interloping English administration and the locals. More commonly the separate groups jogged along amicably. The Carterets and the Devonshires happily enough holidayed at the Conollys' palace of Castletown in County Kildare. Yet, it can hardly have been lost on these visitors, and was certainly remarked by contemporary observers, how Mrs Conolly queened it over the gathering. The state in which she lived, especially once widowed, surpassed that of the vicereine. Furthermore, her invitations emphasized what the unfortunate English governors lacked: a country seat to which they could retreat or where they could entertain less formally. By the 1730s, Mrs Conolly was enlivening her widowhood by running a casino at Castletown. This gambling den, reviled by the prudish, offered, whether deliberately or not, an alternative to the amusements of the Castle. Indeed, it directly contravened the recent orders from the lord-lieutenant which had banned gambling.[134] It was Mrs Conolly who also pressed her numerous acquaintances into taking tickets for the charity at which *Messiah* was first performed. She had a cold and kept away. Her reach was long and strong enough to oblige the ladies of Dublin to while away their leisure in knotting or sit through the oratorio.

Katherine Conolly had the resources, personality and (perhaps) reasons to outshine the transients at the Castle.

Protestant notables were not completely estranged from the viceroyalty. During the lengthy absences of the lord-lieutenant, substitutes – lords justices – were appointed. In the 1690s, while a workable system of rule was being hammered out, even these deputies were English. Some were written off as distinctly sub-standard. William Duncomb, in the triumvirate with Capel and Sir Cyril Wyche in 1694, was described as 'very snappish in humour', and better fitted for a 'frozen embassy in Gothland . . . or to be a punning, cavilling justice of the peace and squire at his dirty seat in Bedfordshire'.[135] Duncomb did not last long in Dublin. Nor indeed did the habit of dispatching English functionaries. It made better political sense to use those on the spot. Most commissioned as lords justices in the eighteenth century were chosen by virtue of the high offices which they held in Ireland: Primate; lord chancellor; speaker of the house of commons. They were interspersed with Irish Protestant peers. Blessington, Mountrath, Drogheda, Mountalexander and Kildare were gratified by being given their turns between 1696 and 1715. The practice, especially after 1715, ensured that the principal local politicians – Conolly, Henry Boyle and John Ponsonby – and the notoriously awkward customer, Archbishop King, were involved in the honorific as well as functional duties of government. Yet most of the regal attributes allowed a lord-lieutenant were denied the lords justices. The distinctions between the two kinds of authority – lieutenancy and justiceship – only reminded of the lowlier regard in which the British held the Irish. Furthermore, this regular share in the ceremonial side of government ended in the 1760s when it was decided to try a more active and continuously resident viceroy, but still an imported Briton. Through continuous residence rather than brief stays, the incumbent might endear Britain to Ireland. It has yet to be shown that the first of the residents, Lord Townshend, solved Irish conundrums or turned the Castle into more of a focus for the anglicized, loyal and ambitious. Some viceregal guests, as has been suggested, detected a new magnificence; others stayed away.

After 1713, the British government withheld the viceroyalty from Irish magnates. Recent occupants, Tyrconnell and the Ormondes, had pushed their own and their clients' interests alongside rather than in advance of the crown's. A British nobleman, although less encumbered with local obligations than the Ormondes or Tyrconnell, was not free from them. Moreover, as has been suggested, he suffered from other disadvantages. Whether the repute of the office would have been raised and the difficulties of governing Ireland eased had Britain abandoned its restrictive approach and reverted to the tradition of appointing, for example, the Kildares, is debatable. Some of the splendour that was concentrated in Kildare House and the country residence at Carton might have been directed into the viceregal appurtenances. But, as in the seventeenth century, when the Butlers and Talbots basked in sunshine, the Geraldine affinity once warmed by official favour might have grown to dan-

3. Anon, *A lady in court dress*, early eighteenth century. Robust enjoyment of festivities at the Castle led to caricatures like 'Miss Hoyden'.

gerous proportions. As it was, the lords-lieutenant from England, because strangers, craved assistance. Those who proffered it profited.

In the absence of consistent and effective leadership from successive viceroys, locals looked to others for political and cultural direction. In Queen Anne's reign, it was acknowledged that 'for the grand figure', a visiting noblewoman proved 'the topping spark'.[136] The local society into which the viceroy's secretary, Tickell, slipped was well populated. The long catalogue – Lady Drogheda, Lady Rosse, Lady Blessington, Lady Prendergast, Molly Westenra, Mrs Hamilton, Mrs Brookes, Mrs Spencer, Miss Eustace, Lady Mary Moore, Mrs Nugent, Molly Warburton, Miss Bury, Miss Bell Ludlow, Mrs Rogerson, Mrs Mary Bligh and Mrs Cramer – hinted at the memorable personalities who ruled smart Dublin. Their foibles and follies were well known within an intimate world. A Mr O'Hara could be characterized as 'the lying lover or fluting fop'. The unlucky Mrs Cramer became 'Miss Hoyden country dancing in perfection', while Lady Levinge was linked with 'the art of getting a good jointure and losing an old husband'.[137] Tickell's acquaintances formed a privileged legion in touch with the rituals of the Castle but also securely entrenched in the society of Protestant Ireland. They and their kind thread through the following chapters, as they acquire and don the staples and novelties of the material world. Sadly, they eclipse the majority outside the encampments of political and economic privilege. Nevertheless, it will be suggested that the middling and lower ranks, thanks to wigs, fresh linen, brightly dyed cloth, striking engravings, boldly patterned pottery, the electricity of the race meeting and the society of the tavern, were not strangers to the delights. What is also clear is that neither the notables in their Palladian mansions with walnut tallboys, silver salvers and champion stallions, nor the worthies priding themselves on the respectability which possessions conferred took their lead from their English rulers in the Castle.

Chapter 2

# House

*I*

Early in 1715, a landowner near Athlone received a letter of advice from Dublin. It related to a projected new house. Some questions – about tree-planting and the exact situation of the building – could be 'resolved on among yourselves and by some sensible gentlemen of the country and neighbourhood, who may be very competent judges thereof'. In addition, 'men of good sense, not artists', could settle details of orchards, kitchen gardens, *cour d'honneur* and offices. The Dublin expert limited himself to spelling out essentials: shelter from the prevailing winds; an 'agreeable prospect fronting the east and not surpassing the south sun'; a site on rising ground; and a dependable water supply. Architectural style, safely decided by 'a good fancy guided by a solid judgement', could also be left to those on the spot. It was acknowledged that there 'may be variety of opinions on that subject'; indeed, 'in regard [to] so many men, so many minds'.[1]

The surprising confidence in the judgement of provincials contradicts the widespread assumption of rustic ignorance of correct design. This unexpected thread needs to be followed. Some inhabitants of later-Stuart and Georgian Ireland showed ingenuity and expertise in housing themselves fittingly. Other evidence from architectural projects in Ireland at the start of George I's reign also assumed a degree of expertise in the provinces. Kean O'Hara, about to build at Annaghmore in County Sligo, was advised by his brother-in-law, George Mathew. The latter, a wealthy proprietor in Tipperary and briefly knight of the shire for that county (1713–15), had recently enlarged his own mansion at Thomastown, rendering it 'the completest seat in this kingdom'.[2] O'Hara was told to procure 'a good model'; in other words, detailed plans. Further, he was cautioned, 'let your model be well approved of by men of skill or else you and your posterity will be ever blaming without being able perhaps to amend it'.[3] Another whose opinion O'Hara sought was Sir Edward Crofton, a Roscommon notable. Crofton, having been shown the designs by the mason in charge of O'Hara's works, commented: 'which I like very well, only the roof you have fixed upon, will make it look very mean, so that you must alter your design in that, which wont cost much, and resolve to put on the other which he showed me'. Crofton – so far as is known – had no particular architectural facility. Indeed, he entreated O'Hara's mason to tell him whether a scheme for his own house at Moate 'be good or bad'.[4] The correspondence, nevertheless, supported the belief that there now existed in Ireland a pool of the interested and adept. O'Hara's circle enfolded other informed amateurs of architecture. William Flower was building on almost as grand a scale as Mathew, at Castle Durrow. Dean William Perceval, a distant kinsman and erstwhile neighbour, channelled architectural information from Oxford into Ireland. In addition, craftsmen built up expertise; so, too, did Kean O'Hara's wife, herself a Mathew. When O'Hara was absent from Sligo and as his health deteriorated, she oversaw operations. She continued as director when house and gardens were embellished throughout the 1720s. Like other wives, she was unlikely to have been indifferent to the Annaghmore project, and may well have influenced its look from the start.[5]

These discussions in early-eighteenth-century Ireland recalled the attitudes and advice offered more than fifty years earlier in England by Sir Roger Pratt and Roger North. The number of patrons and craftsmen versed in the correct classical principles rapidly increased thanks to foreign travel and treatises. Knowledge of the approved architectural idioms differentiated the cultivated few from the uncouth many. Buildings everywhere contained a powerful moral charge. This had long been true in Ireland. There, the capacity to build with stone and mortar, and to insert glazed windows and brick chimneys, was thought to separate newcomers from the indigenes. Indeed, even to have a fixed abode improved on the nomadic habits of the locals content to dwell in cabins and creaghts. In 1665, a despairing observer likened the Irish tenantry to snails, which 'carry their houses on their heads, and will easily abscond themselves as never more to be seen by us . . . '[6] The importance of building with the proper materials and in the right fashion was frequently reiterated by the champions of the English and Protestant interests in Ireland. In 1738, the zealous improver Samuel Madden derided the impermanent dwellings in the Irish countryside as 'bird's nests of dirt wrought together and a few sticks and some straw'. The typical shelters of 'the common people' connoted a barbarism that the ardent wished to end.[7] In 1747, Burke in *The Reformer* compared the peasants' huts to dunghills.[8] Private reactions also registered shock. Another bishop, lately arrived in the diocese of Meath, was aghast at the single-storey house in which his predecessor had lived. The floorboards were easily punctured with a stick to reveal the earth below.[9] Anne Langford, a Welsh woman installed at Castlereagh (County Roscommon) in 1738, confessed that she had visited one other house in the town. Only a couple more could be entered 'without stooping very low to get in'. The inhabitants crept in on hands and knees. The Roscommon cabins, built of mud and thatched with straw, made the houses of the humble in Wales appear as palaces.[10]

4. Interior of Ballyhaise, Co. Cavan, the seat of the Newburghs, held up as a model of improved architecture.

The deficient housing of most Irish Catholics was repeatedly mentioned. Its improvement continued to feature in the agenda of reformers, such as Madden and his colleagues in the Dublin Society. Proprietors were repeatedly urged to popularize better practices. Either through example and subsidy or by incentives and penalties, the homes of the poor might be made 'snug, warm and decent'. Improvers schemed to implant 'a taste and desire for the reasonable satisfactions of life'.[11] In order to satisfy these impulses, it was argued that the cottiers would be obliged to work. Thus, the discipline of regular labour would be introduced. Landlords who gave a lead were commended. One such was Colonel Brockhill Newburgh of Ballyhaise in County Cavan. Newburgh was praised for substituting stucco for panelling in his own mansion, so reducing the risk of fire. Furthermore, he had arched all his rooms as a protection against damp. The proprietor of Ballyhaise was elevated into the epitome of the public-spirited squire. Architecture was an essential among attributes which encompassed service in parliament, county office and an 'old English hospitality . . . without the foppery of French refinements'. Newburgh had inherited an estate on which both landlords and tenants lived in 'thatched mud-walled houses'. In the first half of the eighteenth century, it was noted how Irish gentlemen 'began to quit their cottages and build mansion houses suitable to their estates and fortunes'.[12] Newburgh set an example in his own mansion, designed by Richard Castle.[13] He also built the nearby town of Ballyhaise in the form of a circus. The houses were again all supported on arches and arranged around a central market house, 'a building, in the opinion of some good judges, not unworthy the plan of a Vitruvius or a Palladio'. It was even likened to the Pantheon in Rome.[14] Unlike the Pantheon, however, as Dean Swift reported sardonically in 1736, the 'fine arched market-house, quite finished with a grand cupola on the top, fell flat to earth'. Unabashed, Newburgh had it rebuilt.[15] Newburgh's civic worth had manifested itself – at least for his panegyrist – as much in this concern with a proper architecture as in sponsoring the linen industry, having roads built, establishing a town and occupying a variety of public offices. In sum, it could be concluded that no man in 'a private station of life' was more respected.[16]

This theme, that physical and moral advances in Ireland were displayed and furthered through appropriate building, was frequently reprised. A poet linked the urge of gentlemen to improve 'their splendid seats' with 'social bonds of amity and love'.[17] The Reverend William Henry, keen to broadcast what had been achieved in the north-west, trumpeted Samuel Madden's accomplishments at Manor Waterhouse. However, the latter's collections of paintings, performances of music and replanting of the demesne, although all had ethical purposes, were too rarefied for the generality of squires to imitate. Instead, Henry held up as a model another work by Castle: Hazelwood, the Wynnes' mansion outside Sligo. Henry believed that the house 'far excels all the rest' in the vicinity. Accordingly, he described it in detail, 'to drop some useful hints in the way of gentlemen who have a spirit for building'.[18] Whereas Malone and O'Hara turned to knowledgeable neighbours and kinsfolk to guide them towards an acceptable architecture, by the 1730s Ireland afforded more solid examples from which the interested could learn. As yet, the increase was modest and hardly constituted the boom in country-house building which has been detected in England after 1714.[19] Exiguous incomes and political uncertainties hampered architectural exhibitionism in Ireland. So, also, did the greater distance from the sources of inspiration, whether the treatises, printed generally on the continent of Europe, or ancient and modern buildings in a rational classicism. Nevertheless, housing was increasingly conceived as something more than mere shelter. In Ireland, as elsewhere, it could be a stratagem – albeit costly and cumbersome – to contrive the grand figure.

In general, a rough congruence was maintained between income, rank and scale of residence. Through style as much as size, not just financial superiority but also cultural discernment was conveyed. Propagandists of the Protestant order in Ireland were keen that its leaders

5. Castle Salem, Co. Cork. An example of a modest gentleman, Fortunatus Morris, attaching a late-seventeenth-century dwelling to an earlier tower house.

adopt the appropriate architecture. To build at all had once sufficed, at least in the imaginations of the English, to differentiate civil immigrants from rude aboriginals. However, to that basic had been added more sophisticated expectations. The superiority of Ireland's new rulers and owners was best communicated through buildings based on harmonious mathematical ratios. The symmetries of classicism, mediated through Vitruvius and his more recent disciples such as Alberti, Serlio, Palladio and Scamozzi, expressed a simplicity and rationalism which was the physical counterpart of Protestantism. This ideal, insisted on with increasing stridency by the late seventeenth century, took time to enslave the Protestants of Ireland, among whom penny-pinching and utility often prevailed. Economy frequently dictated the adaptation of older fabrics. So, too, did the unsettled state of the island. The fashionable who, during the reign of Charles II, forsook a precautionary defensiveness rued their optimism when – as with Orrery's Charleville or Perceval's Burton – these residences were wrecked during the Williamite War of 1689 to 1691.[20]

Thereafter lingering anxieties about Irish Catholic intentions combined with small rentals to recommend the re-use of existing structures. Incongruous amalgams might result, but also ingenious juxtapositions. Cutting their cloth according to their means, the cautious patched up antiquated structures or tacked modern additions onto them. Goresgrove in County Kilkenny and Castle Salem in County Cork attest to this habit.[21] Some thought this niggardliness unwise. In 1686, it was remarked how 'several builders in Ireland have incommoded their new houses by striving to preserve some incurable or smoky castle'.[22] Catherine O'Brien, chatelaine of Dromoland in County Clare, noted the same tendency in 1718. The old castle, being 'half pulled down', stood 'all open at the top and so ill joined to the new wing, that we are always swimming in some part or other of the house'.[23] She had to call in the top man, the surveyor-general, Burgh, to staunch the leaks.[24] Notwithstanding the obvious problems, the practice continued. An ancient tower house was retained as the centre of a symmetrical block by Robert French at Monivea in the 1740s.[25]

Pragmatism rather than any dawning taste for antiquity explained these choices: at least until the mid-eighteenth century. At Castle Durrow – or Ashbrook – in 1715, William Flower had the stump of an ancient castle ruthlessly removed as he reordered the estate.[26] In contrast, the absent Lord Abercorn was keen to retain the old castle at Magavelin in County Fermanagh, perhaps because of a new alert over the Young Pretender in 1745.[27] Hints of a relaxed appreciation of relics from the Irish past were offered by the Hills in County Down. By 1758, although the ancient fortress at Hillsborough had fallen into decay, Lord Hillsborough vowed 'to keep it up . . . as it is a testimony of the antiquity of his family'.[28] The Hills had arrived in the district about 200 years earlier; the fort was scarcely older. However, the ramparts evidently impressed wayfarers with the age and standing of the dynasty to which they belonged.[29] The head of a more unequivocally venerable house, Lord Kildare, like Janus faced both past and future. Shortly before he had Castle reconstruct his Kildare seat at Carton, he was presented with a stone that had been discovered near the top of Ardglass Castle in County Down. This relic, inscribed with words about the earlier history of Kildare's house, was saved and cleaned.[30]

The Protestants installed as proprietors during the seventeenth-century disappointed the most fervent reformers by the tardy embrace of classicism. In Britain, too, the craze for the new was moderated by an affection for the familiar and by financial constraints.[31] Equally disappointing to the zealots for an English and Protestant Ireland was the unwillingness of all to accept the obligations which went with property. Houses were conceived and functioned as the centre of communities which radiated outwards from the immediate family and household into the neighbourhood, and beyond.[32] Properties from which the owner and his family were missing failed to fulfil all their functions. Both as emblem and generators of industry and wealth, these dynamos faltered and slowed without the presence of the master or mistress. Absences, when intermittent and temporary, could be extenuated. Indeed, stays in Dublin, London, Bath or continental Europe introduced provincials from Ireland to ideas, styles and articles which they might then adopt on their estates. From the first earl of Orrery and the first duke of Ormond to the first Viscount Molesworth, Samuel Waring and Robert

French of Monivea the impact of travel outside Ireland eventually showed in their houses and grounds. Other travellers, such as the Southwells or Temples, loosened their links with Ireland. Yet their enthusiasm for innovative architecture, inseparable from the more general well-being of their remittances from Ireland, affected their Irish holdings.

Since both property-owning and architecture were suffused with ideologies of ethical improvement, it was inevitable that the styles in which the Protestants of Ireland built should be scrutinized closely by admirers and adversaries alike. On occasion, excess could be justified as an affirmation of the English and Protestant missions to Ireland. But ostentation whether in the exterior or interior of a dwelling might be censured as mercilessly as squalor and primitivism. In 1682, the recently built sessions house at Naas was roundly criticized. It stood on 'pillars, which yet are so disproportioned and dwarfish that a mean artist might judge them set up in darkest time of barbarism and before proportion or symmetry was thought on'.[33] The grounds for this attack suggested a gradual permeation of the rudiments of classical theory among the country gentlemen who, as grand jurors, had to commission public buildings.[34] These remarks modify the portrait of the typical provincial squire, if not sunk in sottish torpor, as excited only by the design of stables, coaches, fences and paddocks.[35] During sociable gatherings, at the assizes or in private homes, evidently the talk might turn to architecture. Collective responsibilities as grand jurors, magistrates and members of parliament meant that this was a matter to which attention increasingly had to be paid. Even those who were not prepared to uphold the Protestant interest in Ireland by a costly display of harmony, 'natural' proportions assembled in bricks, stone and lime, expressed personal preferences or succumbed to the wishes of spouses by undertaking new works. How pervasive these interests had become is shown by the statements with which the chapter began. In the group around O'Hara in Sligo, some of the tributaries down which floated the baggage of classicism can be charted. More difficult, and therefore more interesting, is the other example.

The prospective patron outside Athlone was Edmund Malone. His guide in Dublin was Thomas Hewlett. Malone lived at Cartron on the Westmeath side of Athlone.[36] He came of a family some of whose members were embracing Protestantism, but others remained in the Catholic fold. The more settled conditions inaugurated by George I's accession and the repulse of the Jacobites may have made 1715 a propitious moment to build. However, in Malone's case – as in that of many more – personal rather than national events probably determined the timing of his architectural plans. Malone proceeded cautiously. 'As for the model of the house, I would have it but small in regard [my] estate and family is but small and the expense in building and furnishing it will be very great'. What he did specify was that ground should be reserved for pleasure gardens with gravelled walks.[37] This priority reflected a common concern with utility and recreation among patrons. The setting of a house mattered. Malone was touched by the ideology with which classical architecture had been invested. The order and harmony of the proposed structure would match his own values, for he boasted that 'no man in Ireland lives with more regularity and temperance than I do'.[38] Through his house, no less than his conduct, he would confound raffish neighbours with their ramshackle seats.

Malone suggests the surprisingly long reach of architectural understanding into the Irish countryside. His adviser, Hewlett, discloses a little more of the unexpected aptitude available in George I's Dublin. Hewlett, not otherwise known as a designer, was linked with speculative builders in the capital.[39] Furthermore, his membership of the Smiths' Guild in the city may have signified membership of the building fraternity.[40] Hewlett made clear that architecture 'is not my profession nor whereon I do depend'.[41] Although reticent about dictating specifics, he gave Malone sound advice. How he had come to the situation in which Malone sought his help is unknown. Equally mysterious are the processes by which Hewlett had acquired his architectural interests. He may have been a craftsman who underpinned his technical mastery with a grasp of theory. Alternatively, he could have belonged to the growing band of gentlemanly amateurs who, thanks to reading or travel, familiarized themselves with the rudiments of classicism. In the same year that Hewlett advised Malone, another Dublin resident, George Boyd, guided a provincial correspondent. Boyd promised Caesar Colclough, like Malone of a family of strong Catholic antecedents, to 'send you a plan of the house I intend to build'.[42] The planned residence was probably more modest than Malone's. Nevertheless, the remark again suggests a reservoir of interest and expertise in the capital.

The Smythes' new mansion at Barbavilla, also in Westmeath, was another venture helped by the architectural competence within the extended family. The owner, William Smythe, consulted a brother-in-law, Thomas Burgh, as well as acquaintances with an amateur interest in architecture. Barbavilla, when built, was taken as the 'model' for the houses of others, such as a brother and a son-in-law in County Meath. Furthermore, some involved in its construction then moved on to fresh projects. The mason, for example, was subsequently employed at Castle Forbes in County Longford.[43] In addition, visits to and by neighbours allowed the spread of new notions. One who came to view the recently completed Barbavilla was Richard Edgeworth from County Longford, who would soon remodel his own seat at Edgeworthstown.[44]

Manuals and treatises which dispelled ignorance among would-be builders appeared more slowly among the prosperous in Ireland than in England.[45] By 1747, Samuel Chearnley, from a family of minor landowners, was persuaded by the proprietor of Birr, Sir Laurence Parsons, to design a column to commemorate the triumph of Cumberland at Culloden. Chearnley, confessing that 'I have been always a lover of architecture, but this is my first essay', filched the design from Perrault, the seventeenth-century French designer and theorist.[46] The exercise might be novel, but neither Chearnley nor his patron Parsons lacked cultural preparation. Chearnley's brother, Anthony, made topographical drawings which were subsequently engraved to illustrate histories of Irish counties. Samuel Chearnley entertained himself by sketching a series of grotesque but learned garden buildings. In addition, his backer, Parsons, had ambled around Europe.[47]

## II

Books, talk and travel spread the principles of Vitruvian classicism. Another instructor was freemasonry. This movement gained popularity in Dublin and the provinces during the 1720s. Its mythology promoted a history of building. The Temple of Solomon represented the ideal of the mason's craft. Initiates in masonic lodges were taught the geometry underlying creation. They were reminded, too, of the need for correct proportions when erecting edifices. The era of Augustus in Rome was venerated as the apogee of 'wisdom, strength and beauty'. The recent revival of this style was hailed, with St Peter's in Rome lauded as 'the largest and most accurate temple now in all the earth'.[48] Any Irish freemason who studied his handbook would be offered a quick resumé of the highlights of revived classicism. Michelangelo, Bramante, Scamozzi and Palladio were all praised.[49] Next, the renaissance of the craft in England under Inigo Jones and Christopher Wren, and its subsequent reception into Ireland, were traced. According to the masonic version, disciples of Jones had initiated an improved Irish masonry with the construction of Kilmainham Hospital in the 1680s. This had then continued with the Custom House, Burgh's Royal Barracks and Library for Trinity College, and had culminated late in the 1720s with the Parliament Building. A significant omission from the catalogue was Dublin Castle. The surveyor-general, Burgh, 'the great Vitruvius of our Isle', was also proudly claimed as 'a true and faithful brother'.[50] Others high in the masonic hierarchy, like John Putland, developed an acute architectural understanding.[51] The gatherings of the masonic lodges added to the occasions when the consciously polite and cultivated, in the midst of other diversions, might swap views on architecture.[52] At best, these conversations consolidated an interest already apparent among the élites of Protestant Ireland.

Clues about the routes by which a better understanding of classical theory and practice reached Ireland in the later seventeenth century shift the focus away from the leadership of viceroys, first to the self-appointed virtuosi like the first earl of Orrery and Sir William Petty, then to less familiar adepts and amateurs and, finally, to practising craftworkers. Among grandees, a maxim took hold, picked up from England and ultimately from Italy and France, that a gentleman was properly furnished only when he knew the essentials of classical architecture.[53] This was part of the process that elevated architecture – and the often allied disciplines of siegecraft and fortification – from craft to liberal art. Thanks to this transformation, the sons of the smart, including the youthful Orrery, were dragged around the sights and through the theory of correct building. One instructor was Dr Jeremy Hall.

Hall's lengthy career spanned the viceroyalty of Wentworth, who had first brought him to Ireland, to that of Tyrconnell. Hall ingratiated himself with a succession of Irish peers: Orrery, Roscommon, Donegall and Strafford. He knew the sights and perils of continental Europe. In consequence, he was in great demand to escort of the heirs of noble Irish families through western Europe. Confidant, trusted man of business, troubleshooter, banker, tutor: Hall was equal to all demands. He amassed enough to endow charities in his native Halifax and adopted Limerick. In preparation for his benefaction to the city of Limerick, he had Simon Cowell draw a plan. Cowell had worked in County Cork with his father-in-law Captain William Kenn on schemes for Orrery and the Percevals.[54] However, we can hardly suppose that Hall left Cowell free to follow his fancy. Hall was a well-travelled man used to overawing the insubordinate.[55] He had seen at first hand the master-works of western Europe and kept them in mind through his library. In short, Hall was part of a stock of architectural expertise in Ireland which the baffled and uncertain could raid. Moreover, he was a channel through which the untravelled, like (presumably) Cowell could be introduced to the detail of approved styles.

Hall, for all his versatility, did not (so far as is known) himself sketch designs. Therefore, he can scarcely be ranked as an amateur architect. In this he differed from another who again attests to the growing familiarity with classical styles in late-seventeenth-century Ireland gained through travel. In 1703, Samuel Waring inherited an estate in County Down, worth about £600 p.a. Before coming into this inheritance, he had been prepared for his duties: first, at Trinity College, Dublin, and then through a foreign tour. The personable Waring was selected as companion for Charles Butler, the grandson of the aged duke of Ormond, on a protracted European tour. Waring equipped himself carefully. He listed the addresses of helpful contacts, both Irish and English, in the towns through which the party would pass. He stocked up on guides: the 'beauties of Italy', 'the courts of Rome', 'the delights of Holland', a 'description' of Venice and a 'guide to Naples'. Burnet's account of Italy, which he also acquired, was a favourite for the intending English visitor.[56] Less predictable among his book purchases were Evelyn's translation of the Frenchman Fréart's treatise on architecture, and the same author's 'perfection of painting'.[57] Waring and Butler were expertly shepherded by Maximilian Misson, a Huguenot refugee.[58] Waring, obedient to the injunction of the most influential English printed guide to Italian journeys – 'I would have him then to be not only a virtuous man but a virtuoso too' – recorded and systematized his impressions.[59]

Later, back in Ireland, Samuel Waring remembered fondly the journey which had opened eyes and mind. He told Misson that the crowded trip constituted 'one of the chiefest and most satisfactory occurrences of my life'.[60] Various devices – his own notes, worked up after his return, engravings he had collected, drawings he had made, the guidebooks that he still studied and Misson's published version of the travels – aided his happy recollections. Tastes aroused by the expedition were retained. On the road, he noted agricultural and manufacturing novelties. Some were dismissed as inefficient or odd; others – especially those observed in the Low Countries – might possibly be applied in Ireland. Relevant to what he attempted at Waringstown were the questions of how bogs could be drained, waterways improved and the nascent linen industry fostered. These were all matters with which Waring was concerned even before he inherited the estate from his father.[61] He also prided himself on arboreal and horticultural experiments, in much the same way as his vicarious mentor, Evelyn.[62]

Buildings fascinated Samuel Waring. On his travels, rather than react randomly, he classified what he had seen. On his return to County Down, he ordered these impressions. He listed what he took to be the chief differences in the treatment of windows and interior circulation within houses. One innovation which he appreciated was the introduction of two separate staircases – 'a large public pair and a private one' – into houses of any pretension. 'The public ones', he noted, were intended 'as much almost for ornament and state as use'. In contrast, 'the lesser or private stairs' were designed 'only for back lodgings and the servants [or] children to make use of'.[63] This convenience appeared in Waring's own house in County Down. It eased the division of the building into two units: the one for his mother once widowed and the other for himself and growing family. Soon it would feature in the modest Sligo residence of the O'Haras – Annaghmore, later Nymphsfield – taxed on only eight hearths.[64] Waring reflected succinctly on building. In the manner of Pratt and North in their notes, he advised on materials, measurements and costs more than he theorized. In doing so, he prefigured Hewlett, Malone's instructor, and – considerably later – John Aheron, an enterprising architect from County Clare. By the time Aheron compiled his conspectus, in 1751, the craze for building had created an urgent need for 'small plans of houses suitable to gentlemen of small fortunes and farmers'. Modest means, often related to Catholicism, arrested ambitious projects. Aheron, in common with Waring, offered 'to guard gentlemen of small as large fortunes from being hurt by either the imposition or ignorance of unskilful pretenders to architecture'.[65] Waring and Aheron concerned themselves with the practicalities of building, so that proprietors would not be cheated. For the same reasons, Kean O'Hara was told to engage a supervisory mason and carpenter, who would expertly execute the Annaghmore plans.[66]

The accomplished Waring moved easily among the main patrons and practitioners of architecture. As early as 1699 he had come across 'Captain' Thomas Burgh, the leading architect of his generation. Whether this was a friendship which blossomed thanks to shared architectural interests or through a common social network is unknown.[67] Waring applied his knowledge to rejigging his father's house. Waringstown, enlarged already in the 1670s, expanded with the family's prosperity and social importance. By the 1690s, extra domestic servants were engaged in order to free Mrs Waring to entertain her guests. At the same time, the names of the rooms – 'purple', 'blue', 'green', 'old' and 'new' parlours – told of spaces more fashionably decorated and differentiated. The interior also reflected the availability of new

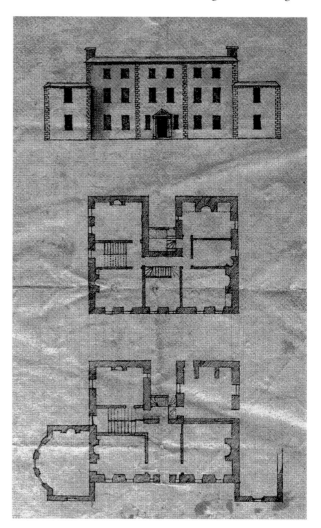

6. Samuel Waring, elevation of
Waringstown House, Co. Down, *c.* 1720.

commodities. Where these had first been encountered – in the houses of local notables like
the Brownlows of Lurgan and the Hills of Hillsborough, in Dublin and London, or by Samuel
Waring on his continental rambles – is unclear. On inheriting, he imprinted his residence
with his own firm stamp. A symmetrical façade of greater grandeur with curving blind walls,
gate piers and a reordered court and garden brought this modest mansion closer to what was
widely esteemed by people of figure.

Waring's architectural fancy, tickled as he journeyed, was disciplined by studying continental publications and the volumes of *Vitruvius Britannicus*. He had not subscribed for any
of the handsome set. Nevertheless, he had access to the first two volumes (published between

 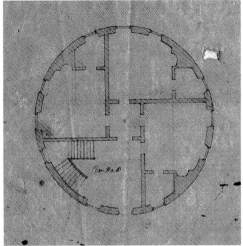

7. Samuel Waring, elevation and plan of a circular house, *c*. 1715. An invention of a talented amateur.

1715 and 1725). With careful, even elegant draughtsmanship, he copied plates. These included the depictions of the house which Vanbrugh had built for the Southwells at King's Weston in Gloucestershire. Waring knew Edward Southwell, secretary to the lord lieutenant Ormonde, who had commissioned Vanbrugh to remodel King's Weston. Southwell, indeed, had married a grand acquaintance of the Warings, Lady Betty Cromwell, and as a result entered the inner circle of County Down. These connections may have prompted Waring to take a special interest in the King's Weston plates in *Vitruvius Britannicus*. It is possible that he talked to Southwell, when in Dublin or the Ulster countryside, about building and buildings. In addition, he experimented with schemes of his own: some for Waringstown itself. One *jeu d'ésprit* was a ground plan and elevation for a circular house. Sketched ground plans of 'a house for Mr. Walker in Dundalk' and 'Captain Chichester's house in Belfast' may have represented designs of his own that were executed. The harassed widow of Hillsborough, Anne Hill, consulted Waring about works there.[68] Later, he hinted that he advised on the erection of the new Parliament House in Dublin, although he had ceased to be a member of parliament in 1727.[69]

Samuel Waring was never other than an amateur in architecture. He, like Jeremy Hall, was assisted by foreign travel and publications to develop and refine this interest. The importance of these experiences in habituating the grandees of Stuart England to the norms of classicism is well known; less so, the similar if later development in Ireland.[70] Apparently, Waring applied these skills only to his own and a few friends' properties. Virtuosity in this particular accorded well with the formation of Waring as 'gentleman', as it did with Squire Newburgh at Ballyhaise. Examples such as those of Waring and Newburgh confirm the other hints that

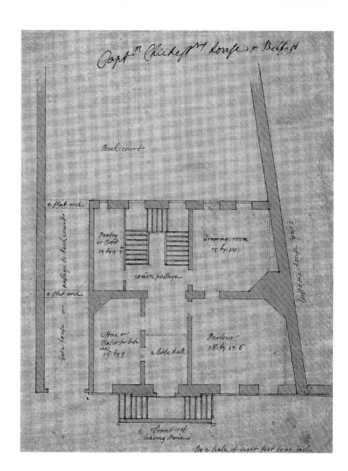

Captn Chichesrt house in Belfast

Back court

a flat arch

Pantry
or Closet
14 by 5 7

Drawing room
15 by 14

comon passage

a flat arch

Office or
Closet for beds
only
16 by 9

a litle hall

Parlour
15 by 11 6

Gate house or passage to back court

Coach house house yard

Front of
coach house

On a scale of eight foot to an inch

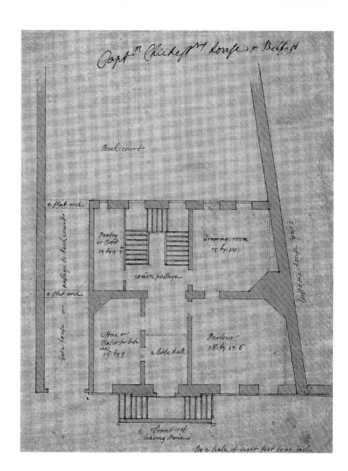

8. Samuel Waring, 'Captain Chichester's House in Belfast', *c.* 1715. It is not clear whether this was a new house designed for Chichester by Waring or simply a survey of an existing house.

later Stuart Ireland was not impervious to the architectural novelties engulfing England. It further reminds that an informed and practical interest in such matters, so far from depressing, enhanced local standing. In the case of Waring, his repute within and beyond the county community was strengthened by his aesthetic expertise. Facility in art and architecture did not reduce him in contemporaries' estimation to a fop or dandy; it sat well with acumen over linen, leases and trees. By training himself in these recondite arts, Waring made himself more useful to family, tenants, his neighbourhood and the nation at large, and exemplified the axiom that the virtuoso could indeed be a virtuous man.[71]

Few in later Stuart Ireland as cultivated as Samuel Waring can be exhumed. Clearer is the record of construction.[72] By the standards of England, activity, both in scale and style, looked modest. A survey during the 1690s of the seats in County Cork inventoried about a score. A second survey in the 1740s recorded almost 200. In the interval, the criteria for inclusion were probably relaxed. Nevertheless, the growth attested both to an increase in the number of gentry and in building more conspicuously.[73] In Queen's County, a map of the 1760s showed only ten inhabited castles (itself a sign of architectural conservatism) and thirty-five mansions.[74] By the 1790s, County Down contained forty-eight noteworthy seats at a time when the commission of the peace numbered eighty-seven.[75] In the decades before 1740, Dublin most visibly responded to the need for more and better accommodation. In the countryside, a common architectural taste only slowly permeated the prosperous squirearchy. Individual circumstances and purses usually dictated what was built. Often necessity ruled. Crazy fabrics battered in recurrent warfare or by tempests had to be shored up or replaced. Fancy could play a part, especially when inheritance of a property or marriage brought an infusion of funds with which the reconstruction could be financed. Yet, well into the eighteenth century, some who took their turns in the magistracy, grand jury or subsidy commissions dwelt still in houses too decrepit or small to interest cartographers and chorographers.

Mrs Catherine O'Brien, married to the heir of one of the leading families in County Clare, dwelt in 'a little box' at Corofin. The description was not altogether fanciful. Having (as yet) only a 'little fortune . . . makes me contented with such a habitation as I can make warm and decent . . . being 'tis independent of any thing but ourselves which is a great satisfaction to me'.[76] In time her circumstances would alter, and for a spell she would move into Dromoland nearby, only, once widowed, to abandon it to the heir. At Dromoland, she interested herself in improvements and consulted Burgh. By then, new buildings were under way across the kingdom. Typical were those for Lord Tyrone. About 1700, he returned to his Curraghmore estate in County Waterford. There he intended to lodge in the red house 'and see our building well done'.[77] When a scheme was proposed in 1716 for a house on the Annesley estate at Clough in County Down, a seven-bay residence in the Pratt–May idiom was sketched. In England, it would have seemed old-fashioned, but not absurdly so; in Ireland, such was the time lag, it looked unusually smart.[78]

## III

To build in the correct style was turned into a sign of cultivation, even gentility, in Augustan England. In Stuart and Hanoverian Ireland, to build at all had cultural and ethical resonances. Houses aptly embodied the antiquity, eminence and superiority (not just in wealth but in judgement) of owners. Accounts of counties, in Ireland no less than England, flattered would-be subscribers and purchasers by itemizing local notables and their residences. Showy buildings furnished a ready measure of who mattered most in the shire. Surveyors followed convention in setting sketches of their employers' residences alongside stylized cabins of a single storey and with thatched roofs. Maps continued to concentrate on the residences of the important into the late eighteenth century.[79] The same was true of England where a rough correlation continued between social standing and size of house. In remoter areas, where esquires and gentlemen enjoyed smaller revenues, dwellings tended to be smaller, and more frequently in a local idiom.[80] Similar variations distinguished the remoter westerly regions from the generally more prosperous east of Ireland.[81] It was not self-effacement alone that made Francis McNamara of Moriesk in County Clare describe 'two small offices' which he had built lately. 'I live in one of 'em', he reported, 'and my horses in the other'.[82]

Landlords in Ireland generally subscribed to the prevalent doctrine which equated English-style houses with peace and prosperity. Accordingly, through leases and gifts of materials, they encouraged construction. What they understood by suitable habitations for themselves and their tenants varied considerably. Lord Arran, son of the lord-lieutenant Ormond, happily recommended a place in County Kilkenny to a courtier in England as suitable for 'a private gentleman'. More modest, but still with an aura of respectability, was 'a middling farm house with a double chimney', sitting in hedged enclosures and sheltered by a band of 'forest trees'.[83] Those with a residual memory of comparable accommodation in Britain were faced with a bewildering variety of types.[84] The materials available in Ireland further complicated and inevitably modified the imitation of imported regional genres.[85] Nevertheless, where durable materials – stone, lime, mortar, slate and shingles – had been used and a dwelling of some pretension erected, observers were favourably impressed. Advances were customarily attributed to relative newcomers. In comparison, the accommodation of the indigenes, when not dismissed brusquely as barbaric, was seldom analysed in detail. The perambulating Charles Smith was delighted by the abundance of farmhouses in Tipperary. They presided over 'a well-improved country producing plenty of all kinds of grain and stocked with vast flocks of sheep and horned cattle'.[86] A similar sight cheered Adolphus Oughton when riding south into Munster from the bleaker north-west. 'The warm houses of the farmers and the elegant ones of the country gentlemen diversified and enriched the scene'.[87] Elsewhere, the owners' agents praised physical changes which could only enhance the value of their employers' portions. In this vein, they catalogued 'a good new built farm house slated, one storey and a half high', 'a good mansion house, slated two storeys high, with stable and barn thatched a good orchard and ornamental ash trees about the house', 'a good mansion house . . . large orchard, walled gardens and summer house, with handsome new built pigeon house' or 'one good stone-walled house'.[88] Such buildings revealed the velocity of anglicization and the rising worth of lands. For these reasons, newcomers to Ireland were not content with what in late-seventeenth-century Chesapeake has been termed an 'architecture of transience'.[89]

Efforts were made to fashion town and country houses in what western Europeans would deem correct styles earlier and more widely in Ireland than in Maryland. Yet, as in colonial America, a vast gulf opened between what the few and the many could command. At Westover in Virginia, William Byrd, schooled earlier in Europe alongside the Percevals and Southwells, aimed to make 'a good figure'. He, like some counterparts in Ireland (William Flower at Castle Durrow) consoled himself for absence from the metropolis with 'the more solid pleasures of innocence and retirement'. Byrd felt his economic, cultural and ethnic difference from others on his estate and in the neighbourhood. However, and again paralleling contemporaries in Ireland, he regarded the care and improvement of his estate as 'an amusement in this silent country'.[90] Elsewhere in early-eighteenth-century Virginia, Ralph Wormeley of Rosegill hankered after a civility, in architecture as much as in behaviour, which he associated with England rather than with his neighbourhood.[91] Building carried some of the same resonances for settlers in north America and Ireland.[92] But aspirations, attitudes and achievements in Ireland more often resembled those among the prospering and consciously respectable of Britain and continental Europe.[93] Lower revenues and the geographical remoteness of most in Ireland keen to build or rebuild ensured that their dwellings had more in common with the country houses of Scotland, west Wales and provincial France than with lowland England. The opinionated Mary Delany thought the polite society of Protestant Ireland akin to that of her native Cornwall.[94] The insight could be extended to the manners and housing of provincial Ireland if more were known about the landed gentry and the material worlds of Georgian Cornwall.

What some commended as comfortable and hygienic, even decent or genteel, others attacked as wasteful pretension. Tenants, in particular, were expected to obey the terms of their leases but to avoid excess. Those who engaged in ambitious building, such as the lessees on the Wentworth holdings in south Wicklow and north Wexford, threatened to blur the distinction between landlord and tenant, just as their behaviour confused the boundaries between social orders. Critics supposed that the ostentatious mistook improvement for self-aggrandisement. Envy sometimes coloured these unfriendly assessments. Enquiries in the 1730s revealed how resident tenants had interpreted the generous terms in leases made immediately after the dislocations of 1685–91. Stipulations to raise 'substantial' structures of stone, brick, lime, sand and mortar, and to plant orchards, empark designated acreages and wall, hedge or ditch fields had been obeyed. At Coolekenny, for example, the occupier, Squire Lorenzo Hodson, tenant to 656 acres at an annual rent of £117 2s., presided over 'a stone and lime slated house and outhouses in good order, with handsome garden, orchards and plantations of fir trees, &c., fine old hedges and ornamental trees'.[95]

Habitation remained one of the readiest reckoners of worth, both monetary and ethical. A quick inspection told the knowing if the programme of the English and Protestant interest in Ireland was being executed. On the Wentworths' estate, it had been. However, by the 1730s, this was no longer praised unreservedly. Tempted to essay the grand figure, ambitious tenants had built unnecessarily large houses and surrounded them with ornamental rather than useful plantations. Thereby future generations were encumbered with expenses which their farms might not meet.[96] One prominent inhabitant typified the trend. John Nickson, heir of a former Wentworth agent in the district, rented Nunny for a yearly £113. On the property stood a 'handsome, well-contrived and well-built lime and slated, stone-walled and slated new house', embowered in a walled garden, orchard, groves and hedgerows, all 'very good and handsome'. More ominously, perhaps, Nickson leased a second Wentworth farm in the vicinity, for another £113 16s. 6d. This had not been renovated, but nevertheless retained 'a pretty good old house, with orchard and garden, some ornamental trees about the house and park'. Captain Abraham Nickson's son continued what his father had begun, with the 'same elegancy and beauty'. The younger Nickson was celebrated for taking 'a particular pleasure in planting and improving', and reputed 'to have a genius for it'.[97]

In many respects, these improving tenants performed their allotted role, and provided a model of what had to be done, not least in the matter of accommodation. The absence of nominal overlords, such as the Wentworths, threw into higher relief some of the practices of the prosperous tenants. It was understandable, and indeed desirable, that the latter should undertake the responsibilities on which the lords of the soil had defaulted. Unfortunately the underlings' unabashed enjoyment of their happy situation once the Wentworths had scuttled back to Yorkshire drew criticism. Vanity over housing was merely one charge on a lengthy indictment. But in a sense it embodied what was awry in this society, at least in the eyes of the censorious. The sons of these 'half-gentlemen' were addicted to sport. They kept horses, setters and greyhounds, and passed the winter shooting woodcock. Meanwhile, the daughters disdained useful handicrafts such as spinning and instead haunted the dancing schools. Whereas good mounts and smart dress had once been objectives of the English mission for Ireland, by the 1730s the same traits disquieted. Politeness and gentility in overbearing tenants, so far from being applauded, were mocked. On the Wentworth property, 'no tenant would drink a drop of ale at any public meeting except good claret, sack or punch . . . The wives and daughters had coffee, tea or chocolate'.[98]

Material plenty, instead of announcing industry, too often went with parasitism, even luxury, which would enervate and eventually overthrow the Protestant interest in Ireland. It was widely – and deservedly – suspected that these pleasures had been bought at the expense of the distant Wentworths and the numerous under-tenants who tilled the soil. On other estates, similar evidence, usually manifest in housing and other appurtenances, alarmed rather than pleased. In the south-west, the absence of another owner, Lord Orrery, allowed privileged tenants to flourish. Reasonably enough they usurped much of the cultural and political leadership of the absentee. In 1754, Orrery's agent warned his employer that about a dozen of his tenants kept coaches. These expensive vehicles – normally costing £80 or £100 – proclaimed the prosperity of tenants such as Sir Maurice Crosbie and the Knight of Kerry under Orrery's loose rein. Ostentation extended beyond carriages to their residences, and (worse still) to their demeanour. The notables, although nominally dependents of Orrery, were 'not as manageable as tenants of inferior degree'.[99]

## IV

In the main, the signs of physical excess were the penalties of success. By the mid-eighteenth century, some of the English programme for Ireland was achieved. The exteriors and interiors of houses, both of owners and substantial tenants, conformed better to the desired norms of civility. Scattered suggestions as to how this could happen have been collected. Even so, much in the process eludes us. Other, more familiar examples help to explain how an often bucolic classicism and rough civility were diffused throughout late-seventeenth- and eighteenth-century Ireland. In south Munster, cultural as well as political direction was offered by some of the largest proprietors. Ambitious remodellings or new building could back the claims of a particular house to local primacy. They remained awkward, slow and costly means to assert such pretensions. Among the Boyles, the greatest profiteers from the recent plantation in Munster, neither the first nor second earl of Cork, heads of the tribe, bothered much about architectural exhibitionism. Both preferred to direct resources into furnishings and surroundings. In addition, the second earl, having married an English heiress, acquired lands and ambitions in England. As a result, he spent most on metropolitan, suburban and country residences there.[100] Similarly, the Butlers, the chief rival of the Boyles and from 1660 dukes of Ormonde, limited what they did at their principal seat: Kilkenny Castle. They, too, lavished more on buying and embellishing English houses.[101] This tendency of some among the wealthiest in Protestant Ireland to transfer their personal and architectural ambitions to England ceded artistic as well as political leadership to others. Absentees did not all forget Ireland. Most, such as the Cork and Burlingtons, Orrerys, Egmonts and Palmerstons still depended on Irish remittances for the bulk of their revenues. Accordingly, the well-being of estates and tenants remained matters of moment. Improvement, in both its physical and metaphysical forms, swelled their rentals. From afar, and sometimes on visits, through exhortation and example, they showed how to build, dress and behave.

In south Munster after 1660, the initiative in these matters was seized by a cadet of the Boyles, the first earl of Orrery. As lord president of the province between 1660 and 1672, he had formal precedence. He took his duties seriously. An immediate need was a worthy presidential seat. With shameless but effective toadying, he named his settlement Charleville, and dated the start of building there to 29 May 1661: the first anniversary of the restored Charles II's re-entry into London. A prodigy house soon rose in the north Cork plain. It grew alarmingly. In 1664, it was taxed on twelve hearths; by 1667, fifty-six and by 1680, sixty-five. Orrery with characteristic hyperbole alleged that he had doubled his intended spending to £20,000 in order that the house accommodate his public functions. As Orrery's heir complained, 'the only fault' was ''tis too big by one half'. Too big it certainly proved when, in 1672, Orrery was summarily stripped of his lord presidency. The *raison d'être* for a setting which had served as court and private house vanished. In dudgeon, Orrery removed himself to a second house closer to the Cork coast. This, Castlemartyr, had been intended for his second son. Modest in comparison with Charleville, it more closely resembled the manor houses of the region built earlier in the century (such as Coppinger's Court). Economy rather than sentiment persuaded Orrery to preserve the older castle – erected by the original owners, the Fitzgeralds – alongside the modern ranges.[102]

Orrery, a deft courtier, knew that an understanding of architecture was as necessary an attribute in the circle of Charles II as wit, playwriting, intrigue and military skills. His boast that he would turn his property in Limerick into 'the Covent Garden of that city' hinted that he had learnt the right idiom. He knew the principles as well as the vocabulary of modern architecture. During his travels in Europe during the 1630s, he studied the modish curriculum of mathematics, fortifications and architecture. In the next decade, fighting in Ireland afforded him ample opportunities to apply some of what he had learnt. Thereafter, doubtful that Ireland was permanently pacified, he balanced in his buildings the demands of defence and elegance. In the event, he allowed the latter to triumph over the former. Massive Charleville was sacked and more modest Castlemartyr badly damaged during the Williamite War. In the 1680s, a neighbour of Orrery warned that any new house must be capable 'of making some short defence if occasion arise'.[103] Orrery, it seemed, had disregarded this warning. Only in the star-fort which guarded entry to the harbour at Kinsale did he apply his understanding of the science and practice of fortification.[104]

All notables needed appropriate housing. But what they deemed appropriate varied. Temperament as well as inherited and acquired rank determined how deeply they plunged into building. The interest of the first Lord Orrery skipped several generations. When, eventually, it reappeared in the fifth earl, it was focused not on south Munster, where Charleville mouldered as a neglected wreck, but on Caledon, the estate acquired by Orrery with his wife. Castlemartyr, Orrery's secondary residence had, as intended, passed to his second son, and so, through him, to a junior line. Throughout the first half of the eighteenth century, this branch was headed by Henry Boyle, speaker of the Irish House of Commons and eventually earl of Shannon. By virtue of his offices, Boyle had regularly to be in Dublin. Yet those offices had come to him thanks to a political campaign in which he had insisted on – and exaggerated – his provincialism. Necessarily, in order to secure his political base, he kept close to his origins. In Dublin, he affected the squire; at Castlemartyr, he lorded it. True to this strategy, he invested the minimum in metropolitan life. In Dublin, he rented, and escaped to Castlemartyr as soon as he could.[105] As with his forbear, the first Lord Orrery, Speaker Boyle directed his spending towards his first love, his Munster home. William Kent supplied advice and some furnishings; later, a leading stuccodore, Robert West wrought the ceilings for Boyle's son. Canals were dug, vistas opened and plantations of saplings cherished.[106] Henry Boyle skilfully elevated these preferences into a political statement, which numerous neighbours applauded. This showed his inventiveness as a politician. The truth was that the

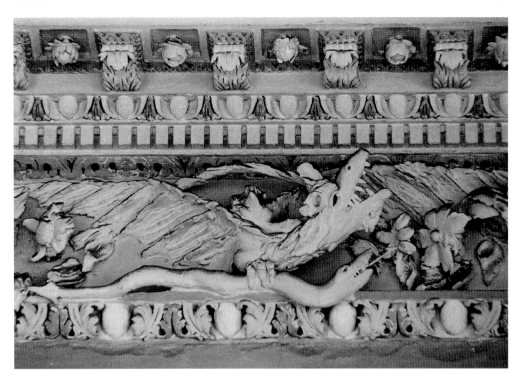

9. Stucco ceiling, former ballroom, Castlemartyr, Co. Cork. The virtuosic and naturalistic style, found particularly in Dublin houses and associated with the *stuccodore* Robert West, spread into the provincial residences of the grand, like Speaker Boyle, owner of Castlemartyr.

Speaker, like his shrewd ancestor, wanted the wherewithal simultaneously to run sumptuous establishments in Dublin and in the country.[107] Money certainly disabled this branch of the Boyles from architectural profligacy on multiple sites. Where and how they lived shaped their politics, and their political following, and – in turn – as they prospered as politicians, the location, look and nature of their houses mattered even more.

The lumbering attempt of the first earl of Orrery to claim an artistic supremacy over his region, while never openly challenged, was quietly subverted. Others in the neighbourhood, such as the Southwells and Percevals, with fewer public responsibilities and a less inflated sense of their importance, arguably set more influential examples. The Southwells of Kinsale, on visiting terms with the Medici, tramped around western Europe. By the 1680s, they had shifted their main interests from County Cork to London and Gloucestershire. Opportunists, they let their town house in Kinsale to naval victuallers. The ancestral home, although noteworthy in the small port, lacked any strong architectural character. The Southwells, customarily absent from Kinsale, nevertheless guarded its interests. On these, a substantial segment of their wealth and influence rested. Keen to see a better harbour, they believed it should impress. In 1696, Sir Robert Southwell commanded his agent, when letting ground in front of the Southwells' house, to press tenants to build so as 'to look well and uniform'. To achieve this aim, Southwell requested that the design 'will be a sort of rule or model for others on the other side [of the street]'.[108] This planned development may have owed something to what Southwell had seen recently in Dublin, where, at Smithfield and other new quarters, regularity was achieved. It would, of course, be familiar from working for so long in post-Fire London. The Kinsale scheme echoed the regulated development which another owner of a port was imposing on his tenants: Lowther at Whitehaven in Cumberland.[109] Southwell, through his many maritime and official contacts, is likely to have known Lowther and what he was doing with his town, the prosperity of which rested on its coal exports to Dublin. But, the Southwells, although they owned much of, sat in parliament for, and occasionally stayed in Kinsale, possessed less power than their equivalents in northern England and Scotland to dictate to their tenants how they should build. The Southwells, having set up in England, concentrated on enterprises there, notably King's Weston redesigned by Vanbrugh. But, directly and indirectly, they still had an impact on fabrics in Ireland. Sir Robert Southwell bespoke a mural monument for the church in Kinsale from Grinling Gibbons. It commemorated Southwell's parents. Prominent in its setting, it was neither so aggressively baroque nor so large as to convert all who saw it to the style.[110]

From the 1650s, the Southwells were sent abroad to gain polish. Well drilled, they recorded and analysed what they saw. The sights included many buildings. This training meant that on their rides around Ireland they also noted the remarkable. In company, whether in Dublin or the provinces, what they talked of with the likes of Samuel Waring can only be guessed. In England, the Southwells, by virtue of Sir Robert's presidency of the Royal Society and his descendants' access to the important, offered a variety of services to their dependants and tenants in Ireland. Visitors streamed through King's Weston. The Southwells' guests, such as Archbishop King, fascinated by and eager to reform architecture, have not, so far as can be discovered, recorded their reactions to Vanbrugh's façades and spaces.[111] For these frequent travellers between Ireland and England, the Southwells' mansion was merely one handy stop among many, effaced in the memory perhaps by the larger collections of the new in London or Oxford. King's Weston contained a 'Kinsale room'.[112] Its highly idiosyncratic style was unlikely to find many imitators around Kinsale. At best, its impact on Irish designs was indirect, even subterranean. The Southwells also acquired Downpatrick through marriage. There, in the 1720s, Edward Southwell endowed almshouses. Again, they were decently symmetrical but unremarkable. His son, the younger Edward Southwell, advised on the projected new sessions house, urging 'that the longest front of their building may be to the street to make a better show'.[113]

The cosmopolitan Southwells, so often out of the country, exercised an uncertain influence over the small-town societies of Downpatrick and Kinsale. When away, they corresponded with numerous acquaintances and subordinates. Sometimes they journeyed through Ireland. They gossiped over politics and intrigued over the next appointment. In Dublin, the first two Edward Southwells served cultivated lords-lieutenant – Ormonde, Pembroke and Shrewsbury – as secretaries. In some cases, the Southwells equalled and may indeed have surpassed their nominal masters in aesthetic discrimination. On the south Munster trail, they saw what other landowners – Sir Emmanuel Moore and Sir Richard Cox – were contriving on their estates.[114] In County Cork, the Southwells had intermarried with another family of powerful office- and land-holders, the Percevals. In the later seventeenth century, the heads of the Percevals resided intermittently on their estates. Thereafter, they directed operations from England. The Percevals' main Irish residence at Burton was rebuilt in the 1670s. In style, it followed the double-pile configuration associated in England with Pratt and May. Burton in its unadorned simplicity and domestic rather than martial air introduced different standards into the district. The contrasts were accentuated both by the lavishness and quality of the furnishings, and – probably – by the manner in which the interiors were organized. There were novelties in the uses of the spaces and in the disposition of the furniture.[115]

Sir John Perceval, planning an Irish life, also had a house built on Merchants' Quay by the river in Dublin. For this commission of 1682 he went to the obvious man in the city, Sir William Robinson, the surveyor-general. Robinson owed his office to qualities other than architectural virtuosity, but he did not lack the last attribute. Working for Ormond at Kilkenny and at Kilmainham for the state (and Ormond again), he supplied striking public architecture. More modest ventures such as Perceval's riverside house were undemanding and details could be deputed to competent craftsmen. With twenty transom windows, the Merchant's Quay property resembled other brick buildings with Dutch echoes going up in the Dublin of the time. Only a pair of columns with capitals under the balcony gave the Percevals' town house a flourish.[116]

Burton, like Charleville, a casualty of the Williamite War, stood for too short a time to inspire many aspiring builders. It was, nevertheless, remembered how Sir John Perceval shook his locality. Neighbours were encouraged to visit him; he seldom ventured into the houses of others. 'This way of life', it was admitted, 'might have seemed to savour too much of pride and grandeur in any country, and especially as men were then modelled in that kingdom' of Ireland. Seemingly, the haughtiness was tolerated. Yet, Perceval's was an exemplary tale, not only because 'his manner of life . . . was magnificent to a very high degree'. He neglected elementary economy and ran up debts of £11,000 through his building.[117] Despite occasional extravagances like Perceval's, the belief persisted that new Protestant owners should promote better modes of building and furnishing alongside innovative crops and techniques on their holdings. Those, such as the Percevals, Southwells and Boyles, with property on both sides of the Irish Sea, were ideally placed to ferry personnel, artefacts and ideas between the two.

## V

The value of travel between Ireland and England (and beyond) in enlightening the benighted was frequently reiterated. One who illustrated the theme was Samuel Molyneux. He inherited wanderlust from his father, William Molyneux, whose curiosity encompassed visible and invisible worlds, and his uncle, the medical doctor Thomas Molyneux. Frank curiosity was wedded to a zest for improving himself, his fortune and Ireland. A spell in England refined Samuel Molyneux's tastes in painting, architecture and gardening. Comments on what he encountered in 1712–13 showed that he was not untutored in these subjects when he arrived. A forbear had acted as surveyor-general in Ireland: facility with fortifications could naturally lead into an understanding of the principles and practice of classical design. In addition, Samuel Molyneux inherited an excellent library which he enlarged. Exposed to both the latest and ancient buildings, he expressed the contemporary preference for 'the antique Roman manner of architecture' over the Gothic. The latter was appositely likened to the futile exercises of the scholastic philosophers: 'a great and noble genius ill managed'. In this light, his enthusiasm for classicism was the counterpart of his interest in experiment and observation in the natural sciences. He admired unreservedly the works of Inigo Jones. The Banqueting House at Whitehall alone of the royal palaces lived up to his expectations of 'grandeur and the sublime'.[118] Yet, Molyneux allowed that association and atmosphere played a part in the impact of a building. Accordingly, Windsor, 'tho of the old Gothic architecture and built castlewise', was praised for possessing 'something so grand and uncommon as to set off the court very well'. He praised 'that happy sublime naïveté and greatness in its walls . . . which has never been seen in modern buildings'.[119] This willingness to find merit in the unexpected and even unfashionable had further scope as Molyneux journeyed into continental Europe. Yet, moderns who tried to recreate something of the castle air, notably Vanbrugh at Blenheim, were reproved. Molyneux criticized the entrance façade as 'clumsy and crowded'. The 'eminencies' on the skyline were disliked as 'extremely Gothick and superfluous'. The ensemble was characterized – perceptively – as 'surprisingly odd'.[120] At Cambridge, Wren's library at Trinity College was singled out as the best building in the town.[121]

The importance of the likes of Jeremy Hall and Samuel Waring can be retrieved only with difficulty; that of Molyneux, merely guessed. As Molyneux's knowledge of architecture deepened, so his links with Ireland loosened. His career – as secretary to the Prince of Wales – transplanted him to England. Yet, he remained a substantial landowner in Ireland and in touch with numerous kinsmen and acquaintances in official and professional Dublin. How they were advised and assisted in their architectural projects cannot now be ascertained. Even deeper obscurity hides those on the frontier between craftsman and architect. The works at Burton for the Percevals were overseen, and may have been designed, by Captain William Kenn. The captain, already used by Orrery at Charleville, belonged to a masonic dynasty. His military title suggested that he had not always been a builder. Like others (including the first

Samuel Molyneux), he had probably picked up his building skills in the army. His principal patron, Orrery, also demonstrated how architecture assisted the arts of war. It was a short step from designing star-forts and citadels to domestic dwellings. Others involved in design in later Stuart Ireland – Captain Rice[122] and Captain Baxter[123] – had military titles. Thomas Burgh, surveyor-general, first demonstrated his architectural proficiency while an army officer, and his subsequent commissions betrayed something of that martial training.[124]

The army, so important as a source of employment for Irish Protestants and such a constant presence throughout Ireland, continued to educate in architecture. However, the expert, in demand as more proprietors contemplated renovations and rebuilding, blended with others – such as Jeremy Hall – who had learnt the Vitruvian tripos in a different school. Architects tended to be distinguished from craftsmen socially as well as intellectually. In some cases, these distinctions were seconded by perceived superiorities in skill among those who had studied the theory of architecture rather than simply learning on the job. Viscount Weymouth, financing an ambitious school at Carrickmacross, questioned the wisdom of employing a local, John Curle. From England, Weymouth protested to his agent, 'I could have wished you had given more some account of him, as what building he has made, where he lives . . . and whether he undertakes to build by the great'. The absentee, sceptical about what talents lurked in provincial Ireland, had expected his subordinate to 'procure some good architect from Dublin to make a draught'.[125] In actuality, Curle had a number of valuable projects – Beaulieu (Louth), Castle Coole (Fermanagh) and Conyngham Hall (Meath) – to his credit.[126]

In Ireland, a Curle might be likened to the master masons in England who revealed talents as designers, such as Grumbold, Kempster, the Strongs and Townsends.[127] The presence and busy practices of Wren, Talman, Vanbrugh and Hawksmoor enabled subordinates to pick up the latest styles, but the professional architect emerged only slowly. In late-seventeenth-century Ireland, the institutional base for architectural activity was much narrower. In essence, it consisted of the one established office: that of the surveyor-general. Between 1670 and 1730 it was held by two of the most talented designers in Ireland: Sir William Robinson and Thomas Burgh.[128] Yet the office itself hardly acted as a repository of knowledge and designs and therefore as an unofficial architectural academy, in the manner of its English counterpart.[129] However, Robinson and Burgh (and their successors), thanks to the volume of their official and private commissions, needed assistants, who then received a firmer grounding. Furthermore, the quickening of work in town and country meant more jobs for the proficient (and not so proficient). Among those who profited were Richard Woodley and Benjamin Crawley. Woodley was engaged to oversee work for the O'Haras at Annaghmore in County Sligo. His services commanded a salary of almost £100 p.a.[130] At the close of the century, Crawley was described as 'an eminent builder'. On the strength of this reputation he was employed to build an ambitious new mansion in County Carlow for the newly rich Dublin trader and banker, Alderman Benjamin Burton.[131]

Crawley moved from Burton Hall to superintend buildings for William Flower at Castle Durrow. As overseer and in effect clerk of the works from 1715, he was paid £40 p.a.[132] The sum compared unfavourably with that given to Woodley. Crawley contracted to supervise the erection of the shell of the mansion for £673, according to detailed plans and agreed dimensions. He was obliged to be on site for four hours daily throughout the winter, and for six during the summer. Also, he supplied and paid the workmen for the main pile, making him akin to a master mason.[133] Flower signed separate contracts with a variety of specialist craftsmen: stone-carvers, bricklayers, plumbers, slaters, glaziers, carpenters and paviers.[134] Some, recommended to Flower by Crawley, were in demand for other prestigious ventures. At Durrow, the dimensions – 96 feet long and 53 feet deep – and such specifications as a 'handsome frontispiece' or pediment, six chimney pieces of black marble 'of the newest fashion' and 'architraves and frieze, eight figures on the corners of the battlements, rustick quoins, pilasters and pediments', proclaimed Flower's ambitions. Sanguinely, Crawley had calculated that the shell could be completed for about £1,100. Already by 1718 this budget had been overshot, perhaps by a factor of three.[135]

It is unlikely that Crawley designed Flower's mansion, not least because Flower belonged to a group of amateurs well informed about the latest in Oxford and continental Europe. What might be required of a supervisory master mason was revealed by one of Crawley's own underlings. In 1699, Joseph Gill, earlier employed as a mason and then as clerk of the works at Burton Hall, was given complete oversight. As well as keeping the accounts and paying the workers, Gill was entrusted with 'laying out the building and carrying it on conformable to a draft or ground plat of the same'. Gill, in contrast to Crawley, functioned primarily as a building contractor and supplier, not as a putative architect.[136] Building, thanks to its potential profits and prestige, advanced a few into the urban gentry. Michael Wills, member of a Dublin dynasty of carpenters, leapt the gap.[137] The possibilities and the rare successes attracted a few not born into the craft. Jack Crofton, a younger son of a respected and respectable family, opted for the trade of building. Initially he was apprenticed to the leading ironmongers in the city of Dublin. Thus equipped, he set up as an interior decorator, happy to furnish the unsuspecting with the conveniences of modern life. These he picked up when the contents of big houses were auctioned and from the same importers as his former master, the ironmonger. Crofton's venture did not prosper. Instead, in what looked a natural progression, Crofton tried to design buildings. Disarmingly, he admitted in 1732, 'if I improve myself in drawing, I could find sufficient business concerning building'.[138] By 1742 the hoped-for improvement had not occurred. To overcome Crofton's inadequacies, a kindly squire, Godfrey Wills, provided Crofton with a design for the court house and gaol at Roscommon. Wills suggested that Crofton copy it and submit it as his own to the committee of the county grand jury which was going to award the contract. It is unlikely that Crofton wrested the Roscommon commission away from the competent Ensors.[139] Subterfuge failed to rescue Crofton from want, and involved him in a more dangerous deceit. He had the signature on a

10. Castle Durrow, Co. Laois. The seat of the Flowers, largely constructed between 1712 and 1750.

kinsman's will forged, and, as a result, only narrowly escaped hanging.[140] Crofton clung on in Roscommon town as a 'builder': a designation which hardly comported with the gentility into which he had been born.[141] He had failed, notwithstanding kinship with numerous squires and gentlemen, to elevate himself into an architect, which would have entitled him at least to a quasi-gentility. Even greater tribulations awaited another builder, John Hickey, with aspirations to a higher standing. He agreed to undertake the renovation of Lohort Castle in County Cork, a property of the absent Percevals, now earls of Egmont. Hickey named a price – £450 – for the whole job, only to discover that he had miscalculated the costs of materials and labour. Bad weather and unsuspected defects in the building added to Hickey's difficulties. His debts led to his being imprisoned in 1741.[142]

In the early seventeenth century, settlers, like Lord Cork, contemplating ambitious works, sent to England for artefacts and artificers. By the middle of the century one local defended Irish workmen as 'more handy and ready in building and ordering houses' than the English.[143]

The opinion was not widely held. Instead proprietors bemoaned the lack of proficiency among builders and 'the clumsy work of the country'.[144] In addition, the intellectual and social gap between craftsmen, master builders capable of sketching and reading designs, and the well-travelled and well-read connoisseurs widened. In 1755, Lord Abercorn's agent in Fermanagh excused the plans of a local, Ramsay, 'as no great drawer of plans or estimates; his skill consists in practice'.[145] In the area, not all could boast even this competence. The same agent lamented the inability of artificers to master the technicalities of constructing a staircase.[146]

In 1715, John Stearne, recently consecrated bishop and removed to Dromore, summoned the carpenter who had worked for him at the deanery of St Patrick's in Dublin. Only a Dubliner could be trusted to execute Stearne's Ulster scheme.[147] As late as 1745, Lord Grandison, master of Dromana on the west Waterford bank of the River Blackwater, enquired after lead-workers in the city of Cork. None was to be found nearer. The specialists in Cork were inundated with work.[148] Reputable craftsmen were in demand. As in England with Wren and Talman, so in Ireland, designers took their favourites with them from site to site. John Coltsman, who had worked under Crawley at Castle Durrow, moved on to the Bernards' house outside Bandon, and may also have been used by Richard Edgeworth.[149] In the midlands, the stone-carvers, the Mulvihills, worked for both Edgeworth in County Longford and the Brabazons of County Mayo.[150] For highly wrought plaster-work 'after the Italian manner', whether 'superficial flowers' or festoons of fruit and flowers, increasingly in demand by George II's reign, the virtuosi were concentrated in Dublin. Hugh Kelly, working for 'the top gentlemen of the kingdom', offered to travel into the provinces on payment of his usual wage of a crown (five shillings) per day.[151] Altogether more modest, but probably more typical of Protestants' houses, was that of Nicholas Peacock, near the River Shannon. Peacock employed Cyprian Purcell for assorted services. These ranged from preparing a plan of a house and orchard, through the making of a kitchen dresser and 'a case' for glasses, mending a bed and failing to repair a clock.[152] Especially in remote districts, with few opportunities to work on a large scale or with other than local materials, craftsmen needed versatility as much as familiarity with the prevailing fashion.

Occasional builders, prospering from the abundant work of the early eighteenth century, in time were transformed into urban gentlemen. More belonged to the middling sort. Specialist stonemasons, plasterers, carpenters, bricklayers, plumbers, glaziers and painters, although in demand and repute, laboured with their hands. As such they continued to rank below the few who learnt and practised architecture as a liberal art. Even the rarities, such as Robinson or Burgh, who might be regarded as professionals followed several callings. The place and perquisites of surveyor-general gave them status which a soldier-turned-builder, like Kenn, lacked. The official position brought Robinson and Burgh private as well as public commissions. Robinson, a self-made man, advanced through industry, talent and ruthlessness.

Burgh – the son of an Irish bishop – came from a background in which an amateur appreciation of and competence in architecture were increasingly to be found. He was educated at Dublin University and then inclined to architecture after serving in William III's army in the Low Countries. Good connections in Protestant Ireland secured his appointment as surveyor-general in 1700. The stated salary, of £300 yearly, together with the unofficial fees and gratuities, added usefully to the modest rents that he had inherited. In 1713, Burgh's income was estimated at an unsensational £500 p.a.[153] Burgh practised pluralism. He retained his military commission, acting from 1706 to 1714 as lieutenant of the ordnance in Ireland with the rank of a lieutenant-colonel. These earnings enabled him to set up in earnest as a landowner, purchasing the Oldtown estate in Kildare.[154] He discharged the customary responsibilities of a squire, being pricked as high sheriff of Kildare in 1712 and sitting for the neighbouring borough of Naas in Parliament.[155]

As with his predecessor Robinson and his successors, Edward Lovett Pearce and Arthur Jones Nevill, it was as office-holder and landowner that Burgh commanded a high station in Irish Protestant society. He would hardly have achieved the same prominence through architecture alone. Rather his expertise as a designer enhanced a reputation, in much the same way as it did among the amateurs within the squirearchy, notably Waring. Work came Burgh's way, not least because he mixed easily with other members of the Protestant élite.[156] He was consulted by neighbours and kindred. Burgh's brother-in-law, William Smythe at Barbavilla, was one beneficiary. Burgh diffused the accomplishments of mathematics, geometry and drawing throughout his immediate family.[157] Sons busied themselves about the design of additions to their houses and exchanged information and instruments with their kinsmen, the Smythes, who were also building.[158] Aptitude in measuring and mapping fields, devising schemes to drain bogs and reroute rivers or outlining how a new house should be framed enhanced standing as a gentleman. Less clear is what other rewards followed. Burgh is unlikely to have been paid for much of his casual advice. Rather he obliged friends and acquaintances, and might hope eventually to exploit those obligations. A need for paid commissions was one reason why he involved himself in designing canals. Of one project Burgh wrote in 1726, 'if I thought I could do my family a service by engaging in a work of that sort I would cheerfully undertake it'.[159]

With so little in the way of even an incipient architectural profession, patrons had either to consult the informed amateurs of their acquaintance or turn to craftsmen. The paucity of architects was obvious. More subjective was the complaint about the ignorance of correct architecture throughout much of Ireland. It was voiced by those who set themselves up as arbiters. Usually they had travelled abroad, as with first Lord Molesworth, or were snooty visitors from Britain. In 1757, patrons in Ireland were laughed at for their 'vein of extravagancy' in attempting ambitious works, but without knowing the correct use of the 'chaste Ionian' and 'gay order of the Corinth'.[160] Another self-appointed arbiter, while finding fault, conceded that a particular house (Caledon) 'makes a good, showish figure'.[161] Lady Anne Conolly arrived in Ireland as the bride of the younger William Conolly, ultimate inheritor of what was commonly seen as the grandest house in Ireland, Castletown. She refused to be impressed. After a perfunctory tour, she concluded that the kingdom boasted 'few places that are any way like a seat'. For one familiar with Wentworth Woodhouse (her ancestral home) and a smart country house circuit in England, even Castletown barely passed muster.[162] More pertinent, but equally damning, was her observation that grandees lavished money on their buildings, but to poor effect. The disappointing results could be blamed on want of skill among designers and operatives alike.[163] In part, her strictures told of a metropolitan disdain for the provincial. Furthermore, assessments of buildings were subject to the vagaries of fashion. The young tended to despise what their seniors treasured.[164] Subjectivity continued to colour assessments, notwithstanding the efforts of theorists to propound universal laws. Lady Anne Conolly enthused over the presence of venerable trees at Rathfarnham: an asset that had nothing to do with its architecture. Unpleasant as these sneers might be, it has to be conceded that until the brief career of Pearce in the 1720s, even the most accomplished in Ireland derived their designs from elsewhere, and frequently from older patterns.[165]

Would-be builders risked not only offending exacting judges but being tricked. Just as in England, where the concerned like Pratt and North guided the innocent who strayed into building, so in Ireland Waring advised. Friends, on the basis of their own experiences, warned of crafty artificers, defective materials and soaring costs. Cautionary tales shaded into suggestions about the design itself. This was natural, since planning and execution could not be divorced. Kean O'Hara was lectured loudly by his brother-in-law, Mathew: 'remember the ornaments of hewn stone are your own extravagance and not my advice'. Mathew allowed that 'the building will be much the handsomer for it, but much the greater cost'.[166] The question of money was paramount. The candid warned that works customarily exceeded estimates. Dean Perceval reminded William Flower, 'I have talked with several who have laid out money in building, who have all found themselves dipped in an expense at least to that sum half as much more than what they originally intended'.[167] Advisers suggested how best to remain within estimates. Too often, as Hewlett had implied in his guidance to Malone, opinions differed and even contradicted each other – 'so many men, so many minds'.[168] Confusing as these discussions might prove, they were an element in any ambitious project. Its planning was shared among intimates and acquaintances. In this way, the conception and evolution of the design, as much as the executed work, had social dimensions. Speaker Conolly, contemplating Castletown, consulted widely; so much so that the authorship of the finished house has always been unclear. The resulting confusion led one learned amateur, George Berkeley, to refrain from tendering advice. 'As I do not approve of a work conceived by many heads, so I have made no draught of my own'.[169]

## VI

Lines of architectural and artistic communication criss-crossed Ireland, and indeed reached into Britain, continental Europe and – by the middle of the eighteenth century – North America. At one nodal point stood William Smythe, soon to erect a new seat on his Westmeath estate. Smythe pestered his brother-in-law, Surveyor-General Burgh, who may have drawn or amended the designs for the resulting mansion, Barbavilla. The name honoured Squire Smythe's wife, Barbara. An Ingoldsby by birth, she had been reared in the grand purlieus of a north Dublin mansion and Carton in County Kildare.[170] Barbara Smythe, like numerous wives (including Kean O'Hara's at Annaghmore), supervised the building when her husband was away.[171] While the plan was on the drawing board, she brought to it her preferences and prejudices, having already lived in sizeable houses. Another with much to contribute was Smythe's brother, the Reverend James Smythe. Squire Smythe himself knew London; Archdeacon Smythe had toured Europe. The latter had trenchant opinions, which he voiced. In one direction, the brothers could draw on Burgh. In a second, James Smythe could exploit the connections of his own wife, a daughter of Sir Thomas Vesey, the bishop of Ossory. Vesey had been educated at Oxford, then at its zenith as an architectural academy under John Fell, Henry Aldrich and George Clarke.[172] Assorted Boyles, Butlers, Southwells and Percevals were also sent there. This network of old boys was capable of helping prospective builders in Ireland. The worldly Vesey bettered his temporal condition. At Abbey Leix in County Laois, he built. He knew what he was doing. Memories of Oxford and his mentor Aldrich faded, but he had stocked his library with the best treatises on classical architecture. In 1707, for example, he bought a copy of Palladio's *Architectura* from a Dublin bookseller.[173] After 1714, as a notorious Tory, Bishop Vesey was unable to commission major public works. In so far as he could translate paper schemes into stone, bricks and mortar, it was on his own and his extensive kindred's properties.

Within Vesey's ambit were not only his son-in-law, James Smythe, but a close ally in high church politics, William Perceval, dean of Emly.[174] Perceval, an alumnus of Christ Church, was distantly related to the Percevals of County Cork and Somerset, and so through them to the Southwells.[175] Perceval, a quondam don, preserved his Oxford links. Through them arrived news and illustrations of what was lately erected. Thus he learnt of the latest productions of Hawksmoor, Aldrich and Clarke.[176] Several were precocious exercises in neo-Palladianism.[177] Independently, Perceval dealt with continental booksellers: another potential source of architectural instruction.[178] The Rochforts took Perceval under their wing, and their estate at Gaulston in Westmeath may have offered one outlet for Perceval's frustrated architectural interests. Others were the projects of Flower and O'Hara. Perceval, like Vesey, languished as a Tory after 1714.[179] However, he did not die in the backwoods. Presented to the Dublin living of St Michan's in the 1720s, Perceval was well placed to exert at least covert influence over fresh projects. His continuing importance in the intellectual and associational life of the capital was indicated by active membership of the Dublin Society after 1731.[180] The Society would in time stimulate reforms in building: a matter taken very much to heart by its chief animator in the late 1730s, another cleric, Samuel Madden. Much of William Perceval's contribution in spreading a better understanding of architectural theories and practicalities in Ireland has to be inferred from his contacts and correspondence. Particularly tantalizing are those occasions in 1733 when he and Edward Lovett Pearce attended the same meeting of the Dublin Society.[181] The capillaries of friendship and consanguinity slowly suffused eighteenth-century Ireland with classicism. Burgh, Pearce, Bindon and Castle all received substantial commissions through their networks.

## VII

Not the least of Perceval's services was to warn about costs. He urged O'Hara to set aside £3,000 for his undertaking. For others, expense deterred ambitious building. Modest incomes meant modest houses. Also, the very factor which obliged many to build, the damage and destruction wrought by two wars (from 1641 to 1653 and 1689 to 1691), reduced revenues, multiplied debts, and so disabled. Cassandras descanted on the dangers of addiction to architecture. However, since credit was limited and local materials and labour could be used, few were ruined by building. Works were staggered to match receipts; grandiose schemes were scaled down or abandoned as the money ran out; fitting up interiors could be postponed. Until the 1740s, spare, even spartan houses contrasted with the giant scale of public – and publicly funded – ventures such as Kilmainham Hospital, the library at Trinity College, the Royal Barracks in Dublin and the new Parliament House. Only Speaker Conolly commanded resources equal to his grandiloquent architectural ambitions. Castletown resulted.

Precise costs for building houses are hard to establish. Orrery, cavalier with figures, plucked a total of £20,000 to cover his spending on Charleville. If true, the sum equalled his declared income for about five or six years. Orrery's subsidiary seat, Castlemartyr, was said – more plausibly – to have cost £2,900.[182] The greatest English mansion of the same era, Clarendon House in Piccadilly, was reputed to have needed £50,000. In the 1670s, Orrery's kinsman, Michael Boyle, concurrently archbishop of Dublin and lord chancellor, spent at least £2,300 on a stylish country seat at Blessington in County Wicklow. At that date Archbishop Boyle may have had yearly revenues of nearly £3,000.[183] Mathew of Thomastown predicted that O'Hara's project for Annaghmore should require no more than £1,500.[184] Others were less sanguine; Dean Perceval told O'Hara to set aside double that sum.[185] Between 1715 and 1718, William Flower's rebuilding at Castle Durrow had consumed at least £1,584.[186] By 1718, Flower himself confided to Perceval, that the house had taken treble what he had predicted.

11. Anon, *Barbara Smythe*, née Ingoldsby, *c.* 1720. The sitter, painted before her marriage in an imaginary and ideal landscape, may have exerted considerable influence over the design of the house and grounds at Barbavilla.

However, it is impossible to know whether Flower had pitched his original estimate at £1,500, £3,000, or lower.[187]

The new bishop of Kilmore, Thomas Godwin, intended to spend £2,000 on a house in his northern diocese. By 1720, he reckoned he had disbursed £3,000 on gardens and house. This outlay bought him a residence esteemed the best in Ulster. It had a frontage of 100 feet, was three storeys high, and with subsidiary offices of two storeys. The ground floor contained seven rooms; the first, six; and the second, seven.[188] During the 1730s, Archbishop Theophilus Bolton erected a palace in Cashel. The shell cost £1,484. Final costs have been reckoned at £3,611.[189] Smythe at Barbavilla prudently set aside £2,000 for rebuilding there.[190] Between 1737 and 1740, the Taylors of Headfort paid Richard Castle more than £2,100.[191] At these prices, Castle was presumably acting as contractor as well as designer of some parts of the enterprise. In the 1740s, the Dublin designer Michael Wills submitted house plans for a competition organized by the Dublin Society. Wills adjusted them to different purses. The most modest, with two principal rooms on two floors, was costed at £508. A similar scheme, with three rooms on each of the two storeys, was estimated at £585 7s. 8d. The addition of four or five rooms raised expenditure to £1,307 or £1,312. Only in a house priced at £1,377 did two stair-cases appear. Wills's grandest houses would take between £1,530 and £7,541 to build. Some support for these costings came from a description of a 'noble' house erected before 1731. It had six rooms on each of its three floors. To acquire it would take £800.[192] Designs and prices for town houses varied in whether they had three or four storeys. The former might be built for £949 15s. 4d.; the larger, for £1,387 10s.[193] In 1763, the municipality of Dublin granted land to Lord Mornington on condition that he expend at least £3,000 on building a house at Hoggen Green.[194]

What a modest squire might do is suggested by William Waring. Bills for work on his County Down residence in 1673 totalled £586 15s. 4d.: probably not the total disbursed on Waringstown. It related only to a second campaign of building and enlarged an existing, modest dwelling. It also included outbuildings, such as walls to enclose the bawn, stables (at £50) and cow house with more walls (£70).[195] Waring's calculation at least reminds that most mansions doubled as farms or centres of farming enterprises, and had yet to become simple family homes. Waring's spending amounted to slightly more than his annual income. Stretched over several seasons and devoid of any great stylistic quirkiness, his was a building tailored closely to function and to the family's local position and means. In 1672, three Kilkenny carpenters contracted to build (or perhaps merely remodel) a house for the bishop. It incorporated the stylish appurtenances of a 'drawing room' and back stairs. The quoted price was £134 14s.[196] Utilitarian housing came considerably cheaper. By 1769, it was thought that a 'very good farmhouse' could be built in County Fermanagh for £150.[197] In the 1780s, two builders – one from Dublin and the other from Bray in County Wicklow – tendered to build houses of the 'best materials', mainly brick. Two-storied houses with outbuildings would cost

£408; those with a single storey, £194.[198] Fourteen 'good dwelling houses' in Tandragee (County Armagh), destroyed by fire early in the eighteenth century, were valued in all at £1,000. Considerably lower was the valuation a house in Aghavilly (County Down). Belonging to Agnes Weir, it was computed at only £8. As with the Tandragee properties, the total may have included contents.[199]

The clergy of the established Church, obedient to their role as exemplars of more civilized ways, were enjoined to build. In the early eighteenth century, the incumbent of Termona-mungan in the diocese of Derry had erected a parsonage. Described as no more than 'a thatched cabin', it was valued at £55 10s.[200] The Reverend James Smythe, while stranded in the cold country of north Antrim during the 1720s, diverted himself with building. He erected a dwelling for a curate of three rooms, kitchen and cellars. Smythe's wife counselled him to be content with a glebe house and the necessary offices, which could be erected for £200.[201] Another cleric, in the western diocese of Elphin, proposed spending £150 on the construction of a glebe house in 1734.[202] Other incumbents in Ulster, such as the Reverend John Leathes and Archdeacon Andrew Hamilton, took seriously the business of how they lived, knowing it could reflect both on their sacerdotal standing and the English Protestant interest which they personified.[203] The Reverend George Bracegirdle, an English cleric preferred to the living of Donogheady, worth £500 or £600 annually, was agreeably surprised by the residence. It was thought to surpass 'common farm houses', with a parlour twenty foot square out of which opened two 'tolerable' rooms with beds. The kitchen was open to the roof, and the servants were accommodated in two rooms. All was arranged on a single floor, since the locals were unable to construct a staircase.[204]

By way of comparison, a yeoman farmer in Restoration Lancashire could have 'a house, parlour, kitchen and buttery, an inside staircase, one good hearth and chimney', with rooms upstairs and an adjoining barn for £100.[205] This represented greater elaboration than occurred in most dwellings in rural Ireland. The same was true the higher the social and economic scales were ascended. Few in Ireland, even if they aspired to the grandeur of the residences of English peers, knights and baronets, enjoyed comparable incomes.[206] The modesty of their incomes constricted what they erected, for grandiose piles might be started but could not be completed on credit. In what they could spend on building, the Protestant proprietors of Ireland were closer to their counterparts in the uplands and remoter quarters of Britain or (indeed) France.[207] Accordingly, the domestic architecture of the later seventeenth and eighteenth centuries is more usefully compared with that of Scotland, Wales, Cornwall, Cumberland, Northumberland and provincial France.[208]

Utility required that houses satisfy several needs: of family; of the owner's public duties; and as the headquarters of an estate, often with the farm and stables adjacent. Again this conformed closely to the practice in the Veneto of Italy and in rural France. Thoughtful ecclesiastics like Archbishop Bolton, Bishop Vesey, Dean Perceval and Archdeacon Smythe and laymen, such as Smythe of Barbavilla, his kinsman, John Digby of Landenstown in Kildare, Robert French of Monivea, Richard Edgeworth and Samuel Waring in County Down, saw architecture as part of the duties and delights of everyday life. Many took it for granted as the unnoticed backdrop to daily doings, as they did the furnishings and decoration, but a minority obeyed the injunctions that the civil and truly genteel should attend closely to these matters. Intending builders and patrons talked about architecture when they met at the assizes, the hunt, parliamentary committee or Dublin drum, and at their own supper tables. Few made their living as architects. Rather it was an attribute, one of the liberal arts, which any aspirant to true civility should burnish. As with all varieties of book learning, the zest for or permanence of what had been picked up on continental sightseeing tours and in the academies varied with the pupil. Some on their return to their inheritances had not been cured of visual illiteracy. They remained indifferent to the look of their surroundings or at the mercy of strong-minded spouses and advisers. Except in the rarest circumstances, domestic buildings could not afford to be ideological gestures. Yet, through the simple act of building in durable materials and with such refinements as chimneys, some insisted that the English and Protestant interests in Ireland were upheld and even advanced. By the same token, members of those communities who failed in these responsibilities were criticized. When they dwelt in accommodation indistinguishable from that of the indigenous Catholics, they risked assimilation to the other supposedly offensive habits of the majority.

Newcomers to the Irish hinterlands swiftly realized that the modes of the locals suited available materials and the idiosyncracies of terrain and climate. These extenuations did not stop zealots for English ways from castigating anything that smacked of the impermanence and supposed backwardness of Gaelic society. Such shelters tended to be dismissed as 'cabins'. In 1720, William Nicolson, a bishop recently translated from Carlisle to Derry, was shocked that Church of Ireland clergy – in his view – preferred 'to live in a cabin on a lay farm sooner than upon any inheritance of his Church'. The term need not be pejorative. Another Englishman deposited in an Irish bishopric, Henry Downes, wrote ironically of 'our little cabin at Elphin'. Already he had spent £100 on it, so raising it above the common run of Irish housing.[209] The term was also applied neutrally to houses of some pretension but, through the single storey and thatch, reproducing the indigenous idiom. Mrs Delany called Archdeacon Golding's house not just a cabin, but 'a lowly one'. Yet, it was 'elegantly neat, and decorated in a pretty taste with some very fine pieces of china'. Moreover, guests were refreshed with 'very good tea, very good supper and above all very good conversation'. In this astringent account, humble settings concealed genteel lives. So it was that the same visitor, entertained by another clerical household in the north of Ireland, conceded that her hosts, although they 'have not much address or elegance in their manner . . . are clean and more tidy in their house' than any others recently visited.[210] Less enthusiastic were the disoriented clerics and distressed gentlefolk who, marooned in remote locations, crouched in primitive 'cabins'.

Condemned to earth floors and no chimneys, these unfortunates were reduced to the depressed level of the Catholic Irish. In 1756, a Westmeath gentleman, Thomas Smythe of Drumcree, was aghast when his sons had had to sleep for some nights in 'a mud-walled cabin, with clay walls and no plastering within'. The father was 'frighted and vexed by this dreadful usage' of his treasured progeny.[211] In the same mood, Bishop Synge described some in County Roscommon who had come down in the world by first expatiating on the character of their habitations.[212] Such comments showed that the settings of everyday life mattered. They offered evidence of material success, industry (or indolence), and orderly (or disorderly) habits. The discerning, especially numerous among the clergy of the established Church, looked into houses as into mirrors to spot inner qualities.[213]

## VIII

The extent, nature and importance of architectural activity are easily overlooked. Little from the late seventeenth and early eighteenth centuries stands. Moreover, as in the example of Hewlett's dealings with Malone, it involved obscure, even unknown figures, with no recorded place in the annals of Irish art and architecture. In general, accounts of architecture, as of painting and gardening considered below in chapters 5 and 6, have been preoccupied with the innovative and 'important', especially if they survive and (even better) if they can be traded. Morphologies of houses and gardens which confine themselves to those which can still be seen or can be ascribed to a particular author, while including some undoubted high points, such as Carton, Castletown, Powerscourt, Castletown Cox and Castle Durrow, hardly tell how buildings and parks fitted into Irish lives throughout the later seventeenth and eighteenth centuries. The teleology that views architecture, or painting and design, as moving steadily forward to better forms informed judgements in the eighteenth century no less than in the twentieth and twenty-first.

Phrases from the language of classical architecture were heard in later seventeenth-century Ireland. The sophisticated opposed 'Gothic barbarism' to the simplicity and harmony of symmetrical classicism. The vocabulary entered Ireland by a variety of routes and at varied paces. Sharing of ideas about buildings, landscapes and paintings, whether through visiting the most modern houses and parks, sitting over designs, engravings and books in closets, lending and being lent treatises and manuals, even sightseeing together, were not rarefied pursuits. They were pursued alongside what is conventionally treated as important: the government of country and county or the stables, paddocks and chase. Indeed, the subjects were incorporated into sociability. In addition, building, furnishings, dress, deportment and diet all had exemplary functions as aspects of improvement. Dangerous and backward habits were to be banished from Ireland. Successes were publicized. Perhaps inevitably the publicity flattered the grand rather than the obscure. Only exceptionally were the latter celebrated. Cummin, the seat of the Sligo squire Thomas Ormsby, was described by a neighbour as the 'Hibernian Versailles'. The neighbour, having travelled at a leisurely pace in France, may not have been entirely fanciful.[214] In west Waterford, Lord Burlington's agent, Andrew Crotty, was satirized for his pretension in building a mansion at Modeligo which surpassed in size (if not in taste) the residences of his betters, Henry Boyle at Castlemartyr and Lord Grandison at Dromana. Yet Crotty, thanks to his intimacy with Burlington and forays to continental Europe, had opportunities to pick up the latest idioms.[215] Travel enabled the likes of Jeremy Hall and Samuel Waring, and later Robert French and Richard Edgeworth, to return home, their minds excited by what they had seen and their portmanteaux bulging with engravings, artefacts and sketches made by themselves and others. The travellers, to the chagrin of sticklers such as the first Lord Molesworth, were emboldened themselves to design and oversee the improvements on their estates rather than to hire specialists.

Modest projects abounded which typified how the generality of houses responded to new notions of comfort, convenience and style. But because so few can be reconstructed in useful detail, it is difficult to avoid the grandiose, such as Castle Durrow, Carton and Castletown. Viewed from fresh perspectives, even these familiar places can yield clues about the extent to which they were conceived and functioned as elements in an impressive figure. Moreover, it is possible to retrieve something of what was being attempted by squires with smaller incomes. In particular, Robert French at Monivea in County Galway and Richard Edgeworth of Edgeworthstown in County Longford, both members of the Irish House of Commons, extended and modernized their homes.

French descended from one of the 'tribes' established in Galway during the middle ages, which had converted from Catholicism only in his father's generation. The parent, a lawyer, had undertaken improvements at Monivea. However, Robert French, inheriting in 1744, was dissatisfied with what the earlier generation had achieved. The core of Monivea was a stone tower-house dating back to the sixteenth century, or earlier. First, French repaired the fabric, spending £210. However, in the following year – 1747 – he commissioned 'a new front building and house at Monivea', at a cost of £276 1s. 6¼d. In 1750–1, a 'new parlour', costing £197 9s. 10d., was added.[216] Thereafter, French's recorded spending on the house related only to repairs and additional furnishings. The demands of his own residence were balanced against those of the larger estate. Over two decades, he spent liberally on a model settlement with dwellings for linen-weavers and labourers, bleachyards and a charter school, and rebuilt both the Protestant church and market house.[217]

One incentive for Robert French to improve his accommodation was the simple excitement of coming into his inheritance. Impatient or contemptuous of what had pleased his parents, he wanted quickly to remake Monivea in his own image. He possessed neither the wealth of a Conolly nor the expertise of a Waring. However, he was not innocent of artistic and architectural interests. He could appeal to a brother-in-law, Francis Bindon, skilled as a

The front of Monivae House to y.e Wood as it now Stand

Part of Kill

Road to Guam

127 feet

The front of Monivae House to y.e Wood as intended to be alterd.

127 feet

12. Monivea, Co. Galway, as it looked in 1755 and with planned changes. The sketches show Robert French's embrace of architectural classicism while retaining the core of the earlier house behind the pedimented centre.

painter and house designer.[218] Two factors may have made French attend urgently to how he lived. The first was marriage in 1746. At first, his wife wished for the hectic Dublin round, so a house there was hired. Twelve years later, it was given up.[219] A second reason for embellishing Monivea was political ambition. French, eager to break into Galway politics, fought a by-election in 1745. He had to wait until 1753 to be returned to the Commons. Needing to cultivate patrons and allies and to impress electors, French may have conceived his house as useful to this foray into public life. Alone, political aspirations did not explain the improvement of Monivea. Indeed, the bid to enter parliament cost French so much that there would be little left to house himself and his family better.

Travel opened fresh vistas to French, as earlier to Waring. French went first to England as a law student, then with his wife in 1751. Alert to what he encountered, he – like Waring before

13. Monivea, Co. Galway, *c.* 1880. The essentials of French's classical reconstruction and the earlier tower can still be seen.

him – sometimes recorded features that might profitably be copied on his own lands.[220] The decision to add a new parlour at Monivea, in effect the drawing room, may have arisen from what he and his wife had seen and liked in England. French, although he spent heavily in the 1740s, was regarded as a paragon of prudence. After the initial investment, only occasional additions and running repairs varied the annual totals spent on buildings and furnishings. Just as work on the fabric could often be staggered, so too could campaigns of redecoration and refurnishing. French, with annual revenues moving steadily upwards from an average of £1,300 in the 1740s to £2,300 by the 1770s, was not embarrassed financially as he and his wife adopted the style of their kind. Reasoned choices were made about extensions, landscaping, décor and artefacts which were of a piece with French's rising reputation as a civic activist. Rationalism but not asceticism marked his activities.

Shortly before French busied himself, Richard Edgeworth took in hand his patrimony at Edgeworthstown. There he found disorder, to which he applied his skills as a barrister. So far as the fabric of Edgeworthstown was concerned, he started modestly: in 1734, a joiner made a new cornice for its front.[221] Not until 1739 did Edgeworth begin a major remodelling. By then he was married, had children and had been elected to parliament for the borough of Longford two years previously. While the work was done, Edgeworth moved from the old mansion and lodged nearby with his sons. The scale of the building was shown by a rise in the tax liability on the property: from eight to eighteen hearths between 1737 and 1742. The house was dressed modestly but with classical rectitude. Pediments surmounted each door. Gate piers were erected at the entrance to the avenue, so that the setting and approach of the mansion were enhanced. The interior was similarly smartened. Much – wooden and turned banisters, marble chimney-pieces, and the carved capitals for the pilasters on the staircase – were procured in and dispatched from Dublin. Other specialists, Rudd the joiner, Mulvihill a stone-cutter, and Masterson, the stuccoist, used to moving between provincial jobs, worked on site. Edgeworth, like French, in improving his house was governed more by family circumstances and personal whims than public ambitions. A drawing room – the acme of elegance – was created only in 1748. By the mid-1750s, Edgeworth had the essentials for living as befitted his station. Thereafter, he indulged personal fancies. He had heraldic tombstones carved for ancestors in Edgeworthstown graveyard.[222] The same carver, Michael Fitzpatrick, embellished the entrance to the mansion by fixing a pelican on a ducal coronet and two stone urns on the doorcase.[223] Concurrently, Edgeworth was assembling a gallery of family portraits, most specially commissioned copies.[224] As late as 1764, marble chimney-pieces were again being bought in Dublin and dispatched to Edgeworthstown. At this time, probably to meet the wishes of maturing children, rooms were redecorated and replastered.[225] Also, Squire Edgeworth continued to concern himself with the ancestral monuments, having them repaired in 1767.[226]

Richard Edgeworth's house at Edgeworthstown was scorned by his son when he inherited the property in 1770. The mansion, although tolerable, had been 'built according to the taste of the foregoing half century, when architecture had not been much studied in Ireland'.[227] That same arrogance which spurred the son to alter Edgeworthstown had earlier inspired his father. The itch to change, justified by the doctrine that architectural techniques and taste were constantly advancing, explained much of the building in Stuart and Hanoverian Ireland. Waringstown and Monivea had resounded to hammers and saws as Samuel Waring and Robert French substituted their own visions for their fathers'. As with the residences of other members of the parliamentary squirearchy, so at Edgeworthstown a growing family had to be accommodated, the estate invigorated and public duties discharged. Training and practice as a barrister, then marriage and membership of parliament obliged Edgeworth to be in Dublin regularly. As his circumstances altered, so – like French – he graduated from lodging with relations to renting a town house. The incentive to incur this extra expense was marriage, not entry into parliamentary politics. Family circumstances also explained why Edgeworth uprooted his family from Ireland and removed to Bath during the 1740s. Whereas the illness of Nicola French took her and her husband to Mallow, Mrs Edgeworth went with her family to Bath. Long stays there influenced what the family expected of Edge-worthstown when at length they returned to live there in the 1750s. After his wife died in 1764, Edgeworth – like French – again adjusted his habits. He indulged his children; new decorations and furnishings pleased daughters still living at home.

Squire Edgeworth resembled Robert French in his awareness of responsibilities to family, ten-ants and neighbours. A meticulous accountant, he acknowledged that his position obliged him to live in a certain way. Convention explained why he cared about outward appearances.[228] As a member of parliament and during the year of his tenure of the county shrievalty, he acted the public part. His country house assisted. Yet, it would be far-fetched to argue that Edgeworth undertook his expensive improvements primarily to further his political career. The timing of the main building campaign, after he had been elected to parliament and before he served as sheriff, hardly supports such an interpretation. Again, a growing family, improving rentals and even personal preferences were more powerful forces prompting him to rebuild.

The factor that seriously hampered any wide embrace of imported styles in Ireland was money. In general, squires who sat in the Dublin House of Commons such as Waring, French and Edgeworth commanded lower incomes than their equivalents in England. They were closer, both in means and ways of life, to the gentry of the uplands and westerly and northern peripheries of England and Wales. It is with the manors and manners of Devon and Cornwall, mid- and west Wales, Northumberland, Cumberland and Westmorland that the resident squires of Protestant Ireland are best compared.[229] Rank, inherited or acquired, carried expec-tations that they house themselves in an appropriate fashion. The propertied wished through their houses to show that they belonged to the same elevated and respectable orders as were found across Europe and North America. Locally, they needed to differentiate themselves from those – usually Catholic and 'Irish' – whom they had supplanted, and from the middling and lower sorts. As is argued in later chapters, it was often easier and cheaper to alter contents, decoration and uses of houses than to build afresh.

Few in Ireland overtopped the annual revenues of £1,500 to £2,300 which the likes of French and Edgeworth drew from their properties. Longer rentals allowed larger houses to be built. Yet, size alone no longer sufficed to differentiate the residence of a magnate from that of the humble. The grandee must build in a style which displayed cultural elevation. Under the later Stuarts, Orrery had striven, not altogether successfully, for this effect; the Percevals and Warings, with rather better results. The mansion erected by William Flower at Castle Durrow after 1712 proclaimed his virtuosity and virtue as well as an income rising to £3,000 p.a. The house and park, briefly renamed Ashbrook, gave the name for the viscountcy con-ferred on Flower's son in 1751. At first glance, then, the ambitious works could be interpreted

14. Edgeworthstown, Co. Longford, follows much the same formula as Monivea, as can be discerned in this mid-nineteenth-century photograph.

as a stratagem in his quest for ennoblement. Indeed, Flower confessed disarmingly how much of his spending was calculated to 'cut a figure'.[230] In addition, he was reminded, 'money is always best spent where one makes the best figure'.[231] Fashionable dress, hospitality, patronage of sports, the tenure of local offices: all served this end.[232] Flower's problem was that he was not entirely sure where to bloom. With property in Wales as well as Ireland, educated at Oxford and frequently in England, his choice was a problem common among the functionally Anglo-Irish.

Flower, although elected to parliament in 1715 for County Kilkenny, practised the cult of rural retirement at Castle Durrow. He was ribbed for contracting in the countryside 'a strange, old-fashioned rust'.[233] Rather than rust away completely, he bestirred himself over house, park and estate. In 1727, he contested a new election. During this campaign, Flower was reminded, 'you can't buy a county without money, and if your Irish savings are gone, touch your English ones'. Half jocularly, Flower was told that 'your marble palaces, your woods and streams, parterres, orchards and plantations set you in a more elevated view' than skulking in London.[234] In 1731 after Dorset, a friend from Flower's youth, arrived as lord- lieutenant he basked in favour.[235] In 1733, he received a peerage and became Lord Castle Durrow. Even then, he wavered between country life, Dublin and London.[236]

Among ventures in early-eighteenth-century Ireland, Flower's is unusually well documented. Inevitably, the size of the building has excited speculation about his intentions. Its timing, begun in 1712, does not fit neatly with his public career, or even with public events. Protestants in Ireland relaxed after 1715, but could still be discouraged from lavish building by continuing apprehensions about Jacobite invasions.[237] Any interpretation which explains the new house primarily as a strategy to forward Flower's political career seems crude and simplistic. Much of the activity throughout the 1720s consoled him for his political eclipse as a one-time Tory. Nevertheless, in a more general sense, Castle Durrow belonged to a campaign of display – making the 'grand figure' – unavoidable if Flower was to retain his place among the leaders of the district. Neighbours and rivals, Sir Thomas Vesey, the worldly and high-living bishop of Ossory, ensconced at Abbey Leix, or Ephraim Dawson, his rival in the 1727 election, set standards to which Flower would conform. Flower, like Bishop Vesey, had been bred in the architectural seminary of Oxford. Aware of what *cognoscenti* decreed, Flower obeyed.[238] So, in the precocious use of the applied giant order, the elaboration of detail and the monumentality of scale and cost, he set a furious pace which few in the area could match. Flower, fresh to his Irish inheritance, newly married and beginning to breed, elected to build. As his annual rental crept towards £3,000, he was already eminent. Modern quarters would confirm and enhance his importance. Flower's revenues bought a magnificence unthinkable for a Waring, French and Edgeworth, with less than half that sum. Inheritance or marriage seemed most often to trigger rebuilding or major additions to seats. In Flower's case, the wish to imprint his newly acquired inheritance with the stamp approved by his smart mentors and friends and favoured by himself and his bride best explains the inauguration of a scheme which continued into the 1740s.

Exactly how its creator used Castle Durrow can only be conjectured. It offered Flower one setting among several: Dublin and London billets, Dublin Castle, the houses of his relations. The park with its decoys, canals and houses for waterfowl offered recreations through which acquaintances and neighbours were gratified. Exteriors, whether of the mansion itself or of ancillary buildings on the demesne, impressed. Interiors ranged from the dazzling with gilded capitals and marble chimney-pieces, exuberantly grained and the floors geometrically flagged in contrasted colours, to the intimate. Inside, although ambitious architectural features of stone, wood and marble were expensive, the look depended in part on illusionism. Cheap materials counterfeited the costly. Sometimes, *trompe l'oeil* tricked the eye. These effects were not always easily achieved. Typical of the simulation of the more costly were the kitchen dressers at the Percevals' Lohort Castle which were 'painted in red oak colour'.[239] Devices like marbling, graining, refitting and refurnishing, not necessarily cheap or easy, allowed a quicker response when fickle taste veered in a new direction than a rebuilding of the house itself.

Flower paced his spending to match his receipts. As late as 1726, 'eight pilasters made according to the Corinthian order' were commissioned for the dining room.[240] In a venture of this complexity, setbacks occurred. One of Crawley's jobs was to solve them. But, in 1726, the surveyor-general, Burgh, was called in to adjudicate on the right price for other carved Corinthian pillars, nine feet high, ten inches broad and with pedestals. These he rated at a lower price than that which the carpenter demanded.[241] There is no sign that Flower was seriously incommoded by the unforeseen costs. Some of the principal interiors were being fitted up fully a decade after the shell was complete. Embellishment of the park, which consisted more of remodelling in a modern fashion than hacking it from a wilderness, waited until the 1720s and 1730s. As late as 1743, the stone-carver Barnaby Demave, employed at the house in 1715, provided 'marble ornaments for the obelisk opposite Castle Durrow' and cut-stone gate piers.[242] In 1746, John Jellycumb was paid for stuccoing the ceiling of 'his lordship's dining-room'. However, this was not a belated effort to complete what had begun decades before.[243] It told rather of the recent passage of the estate to the second baron, William Flower's son, and his impatience with his parents' taste, now deemed old-fashioned. It also showed the initiative of Jellycumb, since the owner protested that he had not authorized all the lavish redecoration and thought the price for 'a plain slotted stucco ceiling . . . very dear'.[244]

The documentation for Flower's spending to improve his habitation, although abundant, is jumbled and incomplete. It hardly allows total costs to be established convincingly. Flower, like other large landowners, benefited from materials available on his own holdings and from tenants who could be set to labour on the projects. Accordingly, it is impossible to gauge what proportion of materials and artificers had to be imported from outside the estate. In the accounts, payments for labour do not distinguish between agricultural routines and reordering the mansion and park.[245] In beautifying the landscape, purely decorative enterprises such as the pleasure garden and wilderness merged imperceptibly into utilitarian ventures of potential profit to all in the locality. Recorded spending by the Flowers fluctuated. The tendency was upwards, but so too was that of their receipts, aided by the capital investment in the estate and adjacent township of Durrow. Spread over more than thirty years, there is little suggestion that the Flowers overstrained their resources by raising a grand house and surrounding it with increasingly intricate planting.

Castle Durrow made an apt setting for a cultivated and public-spirited squire en route for an Irish peerage. Its architect, like those of many similarly ambitious projects, is unknown. Slightly earlier in date than Flower's mansion was that of General Henry Conyngham at Slane in County Meath. The Flowers had appeared in Ireland in the middle of the seventeenth century, and had flourished thanks to military service and the backing of Ormond. The Conynghams had achieved prominence even more recently. Again they owed much to the army. Henry Conyngham's father, Sir Albert Conyngham, had been killed in the Williamite War.[246] In 1706, the general himself died in the Iberian peninsula while fighting in the War of Spanish Succession. Henry Conyngham belonged to a group of interconnected families from the north-west which flourished as a result of the opportunities created by the Williamite reconquest. Indeed, the Slane lands were part of the spoils of war. In his will, General Conyngham left money to 'set up' the unfinished Slane residence – Conyngham Hall – for his widow and children.[247] Before this, Conyngham may have overreached himself. As much was hinted when he mortgaged the estate to Alan Brodrick, currently speaker of the Irish Commons. Brodrick in turn assigned the mortgage to William Conolly, Conyngham's brother-in-law and a future Speaker.[248] Building was supervised by John Curle, designer of Beaulieu, Castle Coole and the Weymouth school at Carrickmacross.[249] The general may have hoped to import into his seat the high style which he had learnt and adopted while campaigning in the Iberian peninsula, but death robbed him of the chance to do so.[250] By 1712, Conyngham Hall was taxed on twenty-one hearths. It boasted a gallery, the convenience of back stairs and the old-fashioned feature of a 'great parlour', not yet called a drawing room.[251]

The vagaries of death, marriage and career often determined the fate of a house: when and in what mode it was built; how and how continuously it was used. These vicissitudes certainly hit Conyngham Hall. The general's widow, Lady Shelburne, soon remarried and left.[252] Care of the children, and of their properties, was vested in William Conolly, their uncle. Conyngham Hall was destined for the heir, Williams Conyngham. His shortcomings would soon be revealed in the life that he adopted, both inside and outside the family mansion. The Conollys, having engaged a strict master for their nephew, were soon dismayed at Conyngham's vices.[253] His Aunt Conolly alleged that the boy had been 'clapped' thrice before he was fourteen and delivered into the clutches of quacks. As Williams Conyngham wasted his inheritance and ruined his health in dissipation, rumours of the latest exploits reached the Conollys, who, aghast, vowed to sunder all links. Nothing better showed the follies of this rake than how he comported himself in Ireland. In 1721, when he travelled down to Conyngham Hall, it was noted that his cavalcade included two running footmen. Mrs Conolly, a close observer of social niceties, had never before seen *two*.[254] Worse still, it was whispered that he preferred the company of menials to that of his social equals. The Nick Shadow to Conyngham's Rakewell was identified as a former footman to two Irish peers, since an ensign in the army and currently a half-pay cornet. It was muttered darkly that this pander had ruined other young Irish gentlemen.[255]

In 1724, when the squire and his wife returned to reside at Conyngham Hall, title-tattle soon reached Katherine Conolly that they were living 'in an odd sort of way, without care or thought'. Williams Conyngham appealed for a sub on the ingenious grounds that he was going to improve the estate village. The vision of him endowing Slane with new houses, a mill and church did not convince his aunt. His bride was next deputed to write to the long-suffering Conollys. The hapless Conynghams, to their consternation, had found themselves

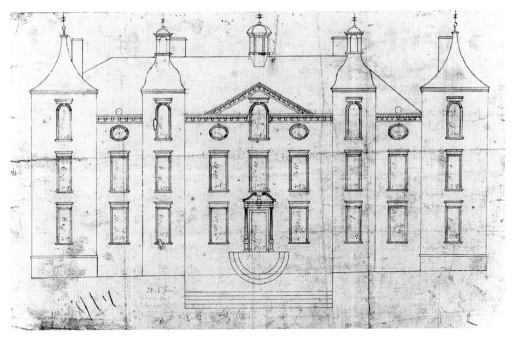

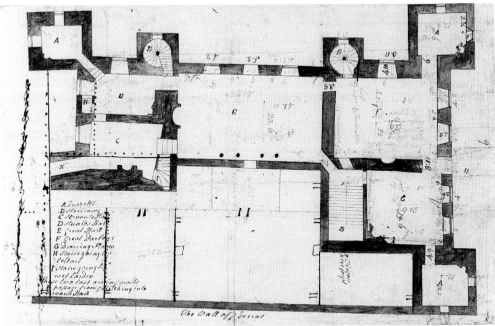

15 and 16. Conyngham Hall, Slane, Co. Meath, elevation (*top*) and ground plan, *c.* 1710. John Curle's drawings show the ambition of the new Conyngham seat. The names of the rooms – great hall, great parlour and drawing room – reveal a tension between modernity and tradition in the internal arrangements.

obliged to spend heavily on repairing their own and tenants' houses at Slane. Constance Conyngham grizzled, 'tho we thought this house was thorough furnished, we did not find one chair in the whole house nor indeed any other furniture, except for old stuff beds and a few pictures'.[256] Conyngham, unequal to his part as Squire of Slane, made the place over to creditors and returned to racket about in London.[257] The consortium to which the property passed included an Irish lawyer working at the Middle Temple in London, and a tailor, coachmaker and mercer, all from central London.[258] Meanwhile, Williams Conyngham's oppressed wife left him, and strove to bring up their son in England with the help of her English relations. Conyngham Hall decayed.

The final scenes in the rake of Slane's progress were played out in Ireland. Again the settings and manner of living showed how far he had deviated from the accepted. He roistered all night and slept during the day. His Aunt Conolly had heard that 'hardly a gentleman' would keep him company. Instead, he passed his time with the 'lowest, scandalous wretches he can pick up'.[259] His estranged wife returned to witness his end. But she too failed to live in a fitting way – forced to lodge in Dublin in a mean room, up 'two pair of stairs'.[260] Early in 1737, Conyngham returned to Slane to meet his maker. Even as he departed from Dublin, he parodied the expected behaviour of a man of his standing. Mrs Conolly ridiculed his quitting the capital with his equivalent of a company of horse, 'I mean a troop of ragamuffins'. 'He took but one hussy in the coach to Slane with him and used always to take two or three, but they had such quarrels he grew tired of so many'. Forty or fifty 'blackguards' from Slane accompanied him from the capital. 'The noise they made alarmed all the streets they went through'.[261]

The house and estate, neglected, even wasted, was saved by Williams Conyngham's death.[262] The property passed to a younger brother, Henry Conyngham. A mortgage of £15,000 and debts of at least £15,000 had to be cleared. Bit by bit, Henry Conyngham, through an advantageous marriage and his pay as an officer in the British army, salvaged the inheritance.[263] He, like his elder brother, was undecided whether to concentrate on Ireland or England. The locals around Slane hoped that their landlords would resume residence there. After an unpromising overture, Henry Conyngham slipped into the required character. He was loaded with Irish dignities: governor of two counties, a privy councillor and vice-admiral of Ireland, and moved from membership of the lower into the upper house as a baron in 1753, viscount in 1756 and, in the year of his death (at Bath in 1781), earl of Mount Charles.[264] Before this rehabilitation, physical settings reminded how *roués* failed to discharge their inherited responsibilities. Private vices first distracted and then disabled them. Williams Conyngham used house and estate as the springboard to excess, not civility and benevolence.

Parallel to Conyngham's career as wastrel, but varying it, was that of the heir to another ample estate. Henry Ingoldsby inherited Carton in County Kildare in 1712. Until the Conollys' Castletown overtopped it, Carton was one of the largest mansions in the Pale.

Ingoldsby was a member of parliament and son-in-law of the combative Tory lord chancellor, Sir Constantine Phipps. His predecessors as owners had been public men: first Richard Talbot, earl of Tyrconnell and Catholic lord deputy of James II; then, when forfeited by the Talbots, the Ingoldsbys. Of Cromwellian provenance, the Ingoldsbys soldiered under King William and Queen Anne, and thereby gained high public positions. General Sir Richard Ingoldsby shared in the government as a lord justice between 1709 and 1712. When he died, he was accorded a state funeral through the streets of Dublin. Carton was used by Tyrconnell and Ingoldsby as both a retreat from and an alternative venue for the affairs of state.[265] Remodelled in dress reminiscent of the Dutch classicism popularized in England by May and Pratt and surrounded by extensive gardens, rides and plantations, it satisfied both the owners' and visitors' expectations of the imposing.[266]

By 1714, Henry Ingoldsby, closely associated with the now discredited Tory administration, lost his political prospects. His eclipse affected how Carton was used. Its frustrated owner quit Ireland and plunged headlong into the sensations of London. During the subsequent riot, he did not altogether forget Carton. In England, he bought articles with which he intended to ornament the Irish house and gardens. But Irish obligations were met intermittently. Ingoldsby's death in 1731 led immediately to the sale of his Dublin house. Soon Ingoldsby's executors concluded that Carton with its gardens cost too much to keep up. In 1738, it was sold to the earl of Kildare.[267] By then, the Kildares, having been depressed in circumstances for much of the second half of the seventeenth century, were reviving. By the 1730s, Lord Kildare, although not universally admired, had money to spend. Much went on a thorough overhaul of Carton. Castle, the Kildares' architect, did not entirely rebuild it: he wrapped the older fabric in a new surcoat. Castle's Carton was not so startlingly innovative as the Conollys' prodigy house at Castletown. Yet Castle's reticently conventional mansion sounded a fanfare for the Kildares' re-entry into politics and high society. Architecture played a role in their public careers.

More strident than the remodelling of Carton was the construction of a massive town house on the edge of the south-eastern sector of Dublin.[268] The twin residences allowed the Kildares, as earlier Speaker Conolly and then his widow, to preside over salons which rivalled the court of the lord-lieutenant. Particularly in the 1750s, as Kildare adopted an aggressive and opportunistic patriotism, his residences housed entertainments designed to further his cause. As has been seen, the viceroys eventually persuaded a penny-pinching treasury to improve their quarters in the Castle. Yet, they lacked a retreat comparable to Castletown or Carton. On his side, Kildare was disappointed that his own high estimate of his merits did not bring the sort of appointment for which he craved. If the lavishness of his houses and the extravagance of his entertaining had aimed to increase his political power, they failed. In practice, the pursuit of power by these means were only one reason – and not the most important – for the feverish activity at Carton and Leinster House. Inheritance, the tastes of

17.  William van der Hagen, *View of Carton, Co. Kildare, c.* 1720.

a bride and a sharper awareness of status as the senior among resident Irish peers, all impelled Kildare into building and decorating.

The renaissance of Carton after its decline under the Ingoldsbys, clear in its essentials, remains elusive in many details. Its vibrancy under its young proprietors was remarked in the later 1740s. By then it was assuming the role as a setting for high politics and society previously performed by its neighbour, Castletown. The latter, despite the gusto with which it was run by its ageing chatelaine, Katherine Conolly, no longer enjoyed the same cachet as when, early in the 1730s, it had first come fully into use. Yet, if the accidents of age and descent threatened Castletown with the gloom which had earlier enveloped Carton, the Conollys' mansion remained without rivals in scale and style. It, like Carton and more modest houses – Conyngham Hall, Castle Durrow, Waringstown – accommodated both the public and domestic. Castletown also reflected the facts that its builders, William and Katherine Conolly, were the wealthiest commoners in the Ireland of the 1720s, and among the richest in the island. Also, Conolly, thanks to his dual positions as Speaker of the House of Commons and chief among the revenue commissioners in Dublin, towered over all in the kingdom. Accordingly, Castletown would be his monument: the nonpareil of Irish houses in the early eighteenth century.

Much about Castletown baffles. The technical arguments over how the plan evolved and who its authors were are important, but it is the swagger of the house in conception and execution, and so its success in making the grand figure, which matter here. As a recent survey states, 'Castletown is Ireland's most important house . . . it represented the highest aspirations and first triumph of Ireland's post-medieval culture.'[269] Yet, with so little by way of precursors to prepare for its style, the willing embrace of strict Italianate classicism puzzles. Part of the explanation has to be in the social, economic and political worlds of its owner, Conolly, and his cronies. Cultural avatars in Ireland no less than in England turned to connoisseurs and virtuosi for guidance. Already, it has been suggested that more expertise than has sometimes been imagined was available in early eighteenth-century Ireland. Malone in Westmeath had his local and Dublin advisers. Later, William Smythe in the same county turned to kinsfolk and acquaintances, some of them well travelled and versed in continental theory and practice. Similarly, Flower had amateur and expert advisers. Conolly consulted a cultivated coterie. Thanks to his own eminence and wealth, his was a project with which the ambitious and opinionated would gladly associate.

William Conolly, in common with Conyngham (his brother-in-law), profited from the Williamite War, the last great upheaval which allowed Protestants already in Ireland to add to their property. Conolly belonged to the buccaneers from north-west Ulster, who rapidly colonized the official, legal and financial worlds of Protestant Dublin in the 1690s. He was further helped by marriage to Katherine Conyngham, a daughter of Sir Albert Conyngham, 'a sober gentleman'.[270] She came (in 1694) with a portion of £2,300. Conolly quickly invested

18. Carton, Co. Kildare, designed by Richard Castle, after 1739. The scale of the building announced the revived importance and wealth of its owners, the earls of Kildare, soon to be advanced to be dukes of Leinster.

this, supplemented by some shadier earnings, in lately confiscated lands. He followed the Conynghams into the northern marches of the Pale. Counties Kildare and Meath were handy alike for Dublin, where Conolly's official duties multiplied, and the north-west, where as member of parliament for County Londonderry, landowner and favourite son, he kept his links in good repair.

By the early 1720s, Conolly was reckoned to have at least £16,000 or £17,000 p.a. In 1724, when Castletown was being planned, he was negotiating the purchase of the Rathfarnham Castle estate on the western outskirts of Dublin. For this he was prepared to give £62,000. He planned to pay £32,000 of the price within four months and without borrowing. Another £10,000 would be raised at 5 per cent interest.[271] Fortune continued to favour him, for, in 1728, he received a handsome bequest.[272] At Castletown, traditionally his wishes are thought to have determined the conception, if not all the detail. He did not want for advice. Some was solicited; some not. Bishop Berkeley of Cloyne reported that the design was said to be 'chiefly of Mr. Conolly's invention'.[273] Yet, none of Conolly's contemporaries supposed that he had the virtuosity of an Orrery or Petty to act entirely as his own architect. Nor was he an architectural autodidact like Waring. Following paymasters such as the Ormondes or Flower, he might spell out or even sketch what he envisaged. However, one characteristic of the house could be traced to Conolly: its size. A main block of thirteen bays was linked by curved colonnades to pavilions of one and half storeys. In scale and look it parallels the splendours commanded by Conolly's equivalents in Scotland and England, such as Braco at Duff House and (more conspicuously) Walpole at Houghton.[274]

Little considered as an influence over either conception or completion is Conolly's wife. Yet, Katherine Conolly had been born into a world of country houses – albeit in remote Donegal – at the reticent but unequivocally symmetrical Conyngham seat of Mount Charles.[275] In 1722, shortly after Castletown had been started, Mrs Conolly, as forthright as her husband, boasted to her Dublin friends that her own bedchamber would be twenty feet high and the hall forty.[276] There is no way of knowing whether she had specified these dimensions. She liked the country place, not least because she thought it better for her husband's health.[277] Only in the last year of the Speaker's life, 1728–9, was the still unfinished mansion used much. Even then, the press of affairs in Dublin limited the time that either could spend in the country. The Conollys' Dublin house in Capel Street, just north of the River Liffey, was ideal for Parliament, Castle and the Custom House. Nevertheless, the wish to set up William Conolly as country squire, if only posthumously, led to his being interred at Cellbridge, the parish church closest to Castletown. It was also at Cellbridge that his widow tried to erect an effigy, ordered from London. It proved too big for the modest chapel and ended incongruously in a barn.[278] During her long widowhood, from 1729 to 1752, Katherine Conolly moved restlessly between her Dublin and country house. She had the time and money – £5,000 p.a. under her husband's will – to give Castletown her own distinctive look. Her comments on the extent to which the disorder of Conyngham Hall matched the dissipation of her nephew, Williams Conyngham, showed how she, like many contemporaries, thought that physical arrangements affected and – ideally – should reflect the qualities of a life. So, at Castletown, she mixed an amplitude both in its size and economy worthy of a duchess with a prosy domesticity. The house embodied her personal regime just as did Flower's at Castle Durrow or Conyngham's in County Meath.

Grief, genuine despite its theatricality, at first dulled Widow Conolly's appetite for fun. In time, her relish for life reasserted itself and banished melancholy. By the spring of 1730, it was reported how she had retained all her dead husband's servants and equipage, kept 'a very handsome table', entertained lavishly and 'is toasted by the young gentlemen in town by the name of Miss Kitty Conolly'.[279] With no surviving child of her own (there were rumours of at least one bastard fathered by her husband), she devoted herself to favourite relations. In particular, a great-niece was taken up, originally because her mother, Molly Burton, was disabled by illness from caring for her. Other relations resented the extent to which the household and spending at Castletown centred on the girl. Mrs Conolly's widowed sister, Mary Jones, always caustic, chronicled the endless indulgences: £200 spent furnishing a suite of bedroom, dressing-room and closet; a further £200 to create a garden adorned with statues, a grotto and walks cut through the woodland.[280] Molly Burton, aged fourteen, spent too long in the company of the servants and played with her doll's house, 'as if she were a seven year old'. When a pair of earrings for her arrived from London, at a price of £100, Mary Jones expostulated, 'no young lady in Ireland is kept so fine, nor at so great expense'.[281] Indeed, the envious Mrs Jones calculated that the girl's expenses must cost Mrs Conolly £400 p.a.[282]

Care of the young favourite caused Mrs Conolly to modify arrangements at Castletown. Rooms were reordered and redecorated, gardens created and furniture commissioned, but these alterations barely touched the shell of the house. The addition for which the widow is best remembered, the folly or 'obelisk', was built 'to answer a vista from the back of Castletown house'.[283] A whimsy, it also employed the poor in the severe winter of 1740–1.[284] Wealth and widowhood allowed Katherine Conolly openly to show her preferences in a manner not vouchsafed to most wives. The public functions of Castletown were abbreviated by the Speaker's death. At first, his widow shunned the public ceremonies in which so recently she had been a principal performer. Deliberately she absented herself when new governors were installed.[285] However, the life of an anchorite was not for her. During the winter of 1731–2, Mrs Conolly was seen at a ball, sitting up until three or four in the morning.[286] She put aside any thoughts of a secluded widowhood from a sense of duty towards the nephew, William Conolly, who inherited the bulk of the Speaker's estate and (it was vainly hoped) his political role. His frequent absences from Ireland and his unwillingness to don his uncle's Irish

19. Charles Jervas,
*Katherine Conolly and
Molly Burton*. The
widow of Castletown
with her favourite niece.
The doting aunt planned
some features in the
house and grounds to
please the girl.

mantle, disappointed many, including Widow Conolly. Yet, the younger William Conolly's passivity allowed his aunt to exert herself the more. Her hospitality, whether in Dublin or at Castletown, had public purposes. The *palazzo* regularly resounded to politically inspired gatherings. It was rumoured that Mrs Conolly heightened the state in which she lived from an undeclared but well-understood competition with the viceroy. So numerous were her guests that three tables were needed for dinner. At one, the hostess and the first rank dined. 'This many ridicules her for, and friends grieves for her doing anything that is not very proper'.[287] This was not the first time that she had thrown propriety to the winds. The extravagant mourning in which she had attired herself and her large household on Conolly's death was much censured. Her nephew agreed it was 'a matter of great observation to the town, being usual only to persons of the first quality'.[288] Katherine Conolly was not indifferent to convention, but – as in the grandeur of Castletown – she was free to follow her own rules.

Katherine Conolly had long watched interestedly the quirks of the migrants roosting in the Castle. She, no bird of passage, made the local habitat her own. She seldom mobbed or mocked the transients. Outwardly the courtesies were maintained. Cosy evenings at the Castle with the duchess of Grafton in the early 1720s, presumably while their husbands were closeted, told of an intimacy which was repeated under the popular Carterets, but did not survive the arrival of the stiff Dorset in 1731.[289] Castletown, whether intentionally or not, during the 1730s offered an alternative focus to Dublin Castle. Mrs Conolly, abetted by another favourite, Frank Burton, a member of parliament and a nephew by marriage, unfolded gaming tables and lured crowds to Castletown. Basset was played. Of all card games, it was deemed 'the most courtly'. 'Only fit for kings and queens, great princes, noblemen, &c.', it suited Mrs Conolly's mood.[290] Burton and Mrs Conolly, acting as bankers, were said to have lost £100 on the first night, and £131 on another.[291] This raffishness contrasted strikingly with the restraint which the viceroy imposed at the Castle. In other ways, Castletown offered a finer setting for pomp than the makeshifts and stage scenery of the Castle,

20. Castletown, Co. Kildare.

especially under Dorset with whom the widow established no rapport.[292] Katherine Conolly evidently shared and continued the stance of her husband: Whiggish and patriotic. With Dorset's successor, Devonshire, she was friendlier. In 1739, Lord-Lieutenant Devonshire happily accepted Katherine Conolly's invitation and fled the city over Christmas. Proudly, Mrs Conolly reported that at Castletown, she had had 'the government and 100 more with me at the holydays'.[293] Mrs Conolly's death, not the Speaker's, provoked the lament of 1754, 'a huge house, now empty and forlorn, that used to be crowded with guests of all sorts'.[294] Its accustomed liveliness revived in 1755, when the viceroy, Hartington, passed the high summer there.[295] He found it 'a large good house and much pleasanter than staying in Dublin'. Thither he invited politicians in order to hammer out a workable system of government.[296]

Katherine Conolly's revenues, even as a widow, surpassed those of all but a few peers in Ireland. In addition, as legatee of her husband's formidable political interests, she remained a focus of incumbent and aspiring public figures. In degree, if not always in character, what she did in the County Kildare and Dublin residences differed from the regimes of most contemporaries. These differences are immediately apparent from a perfunctory comparison with her two sisters. By the 1730s, all were widows; each had been married to a public figure. Jane Conyngham's husband, James Bonnell, had acted as accountant-general and then secretary to the commissioners who disposed the forfeited lands of the defeated Jacobites in the 1690s. Bonnell reckoned that his positions earned him £300 p.a. He lived in modest comfort in Dublin. Bonnell was unusual in his extreme piety, which eventually led him to retire from office and contemplate ordination.[297] Jane Bonnell, widowed in 1699, for a time kept on the Dublin house, but then removed to England. She remained in touch with a lively and devout circle in Ireland. It was clear that she lived in a genteel but sometimes straitened fashion, which was eased by gifts in kind or of money from Katherine Conolly. The situation of the third sister made a yet more poignant contrast with that of the widow of Castletown. Mary Conyngham married Richard Jones, a member of the Dublin parliament. The Joneses' establishment at Dollanstown in County Meath was admired. In 1704, the couple were said to live 'finely'. Richard Jones was accounted 'a very pretty gentleman'.[298] But as politics and wealth of the Conollys and Joneses diverged, relations between them were strained.[299]

Widowhood reduced Mrs Jones's resources. She had been bequeathed an annuity of £200. She trimmed her expenses accordingly, taking lodgings in Dublin by the year and dismissing most of her servants. Meanwhile, her son, Roger Jones, struggled to make a success of the estate that he had inherited. Of its estimated annual value of £330, £200 was earmarked for his mother. Essentially he became a farmer, experimenting with assorted crops in the hope of improving yields. Mary Jones, conscious of the penury which constantly threatened to topple her son from his flimsy gentility, resented the state so insouciantly kept by Katherine Conolly.

In particular, the sums expended – apparently with little thought – on the reigning favourites grated.[300] Mrs Jones was torn between jealousy and grudging admiration of her rich sister. On occasion, she consoled herself, not always convincingly, that at Dollanstown, her son's place, she had more satisfaction from her children and grandchildren, together with 'a homely dinner than with crowds at her table and great variety'.[301] She found fault with the arrangements at Castletown. Staying there, she had to climb eighty stairs.[302] Her *amour propre*, ruffled because Katherine Conolly's invitations 'are very general', was soothed when she was treated as important in her own right rather than as a poorer relation. She was delighted to be given the bedchamber intended originally for Lady Santry, or to have the fashionably late hour of dining moved earlier to suit her convenience.[303]

The mother felt acutely slights offered to young Roger Jones. The shabby gentleman farmer refused an invitation to Castletown because he owned no smart carriage. 'My son's equipage was too bad to appear where there was so much company with a great deal of finery'. For a season, the Gores, connections by marriage and groomed by the Speaker to manage his political interests, reigned in Katherine Conolly's favour, being her 'whole heart's delight'.[304] When Sir St George Gore's wife had to cry off, because she 'makes water every three or four minutes', Katherine Conolly was left with 'no women with her, but a parcel of young men'. Indeed, the merry widow of Castletown blossomed in male company. In her seventies, Katherine Conolly bowled along in a one-horse chaise with Loftus Hume, 'the giddiest young man I ever saw'. Mrs Conolly, it was reported by her disapproving sister, 'thinks [this] a fine exploit. But most folks thinks it was not very well done to venture herself to be drove at that rate'.[305]

The confidence, even arrogance, with which Mrs Conolly dominated her family and its extensive affinity could be resented. She knew this. She recognized and punctiliously met familial obligations. Her houses were the settings for domestic and grand occasions. She was sensitive enough to realize the ambivalent responses to her ostentation among poorer relations. Katherine Conolly knew that her cross-grained sister, when she declined summonses to Castletown, wanted to be cajoled into coming. And Mary Jones, despite her complaints, did come. In 1736, she lodged at Castletown for six weeks. The Joneses were embarrassed that they could not keep up with the Conollys. Yet Katherine Conolly enticed Roger Jones and his family over to Castletown.[306] But the rich widow did not bail out the impecunious Jones as his mother had hoped. Instead, Mrs Conolly followed affectionately the efforts of the household. The younger Mrs Jones was approved as 'a very sober discreet woman, and I believe he [Roger Jones] is happier than if he had got money with a wife'. In 1738, Katherine Conolly was pleased to hear that 'they begin to thrive; he is mighty careful and a great manager'. But without the mother's rosy spectacles, the aunt added, 'had he been so some years ago, he would not have been reduced to the many straits he has gone through'.[307] Roger

Jones's death in 1746 led his aunt to lament that he had left 'a poor miserable family and, I fear, in very bad circumstances'.[308] There was a note of complacency when Katherine Conolly reflected, 'I have a great fortune, it's true, more than I ever expected, but the more one has, the more is expected from them'.[309] Similarly, she reassured herself when she wrote of Mary Jones, 'I have done her and hers great kindnesses but never hurt'.[310] From Mary Jones's angle, matters looked different. Hackneyed it might be, but it was heartfelt when she exclaimed, 'it's the rich that gets most'.[311] Long observation of Castletown and Katherine Conolly's establishment there led Mrs Jones to conclude, 'I find folks are now esteemed according to the figure they make'.[312]

Chapter 3

# Interiors

*I*

Two articles were particularly dear to Katherine Conolly. When she died, it was recalled how she was wont to sit in her great chair of grey cloth.[1] At Castletown, she had demonstrated her devotion to her Burton great-niece by commissioning (and herself ornamenting) a painted and lacquered cabinet, which survives today. It is simply inscribed 'Mrs Conlly to Miss Burten', in the manner of a particularly cumbersome keepsake.[2] These convey a more homely impression than the cavernous spaces of Castletown itself. Association, utility and look endeared objects to owners, or made others wish to own them. A façade could awe – and overawe – by its scale or ingenuity. But what was encountered inside houses often made a stronger impact. Interiors, although not lightly to be redesigned, were more easily altered than the entire fabric. Décor and possessions most quickly reflected new fashions. Moreover, discerning choices demonstrated as vividly as architecture the excellent judgement – or 'fancy' – of the owner and impressed visitors. Yet, even those who craved for the latest could hardly discard the complete backdrop to their lives every year. Possessions, like coral, built up by accretion. Bequests and auctions, typically of silver and pictures, but also of furniture and clothing, passed objects down the generations. The smart seldom disdained the second-hand if of good quality, useful and with a respectable provenance. As a result, houses throughout Ireland, but especially in Dublin and larger towns, contained an unexpected variety of con-tents, some of which succeeding chapters will inventory.

Affection attached to apparently humdrum pieces. Objects embodied associations with people or places. Sometimes they beguiled through look or feel. Legacies carried artefacts to unexpected destinations, thereby treating the humble to an incongruous splendour. In 1665, Bishop George Wilde of Derry, left to his kinswoman, Elizabeth Saxey of Faugher, not just silver, but also the wrought bed of her own making.[3] In 1708, the widow of a Donegal rector excepted from her effects a chest of drawers, which was given to her eldest daughter.[4] Joseph Gill, a prosperous Dublin merchant, in 1741 willed to one daughter 'my fine old-fashioned

21. Katherine Conolly's
cabinet, Castletown, *c.* 1738.

chest of drawers', which had been her mother's. To a second child, he left 'one pair of the
walnut-tree chest of drawers which her mother had made for her'.[5] A prosperous farmer from
County Kildare bequeathed to his wife, along with many other goods, the 'best armed chair'.[6]
In a similar manner, a widow in the north-west of Ireland in 1750 passed to her son six large
silver spoons, her wedding ring and 'a writing desk in my lodging room', all of which were to
be kept 'until he is fit to use them'.[7] At Clonmel in 1746, Ellen Comerford took great care with
her legacies of silver, jewellery, clothing, linen and furniture.[8] Other than in the grandest
establishments, possessions were sparse. Because few, they were easily identified and could be
cherished. Often their individual histories, the moment of arrival and subsequent usage, were
vividly recollected. Household objects became so familiar that they were imbued with a per-

sonality and even a gender, especially if handled and cleaned regularly. Some were ornamented with startlingly anthropomorphic features that added to their individuality.

New possessions were shown off. A proud housewife struggling to make ends meet in the north of County Cork about 1740 gratefully acknowledged a gift of Liverpool pottery. It was reported that the earthenwares 'are very much liked by every body that sees them'.[9] This lust for goods was exploited when auctioneers laid out tempting arrays of wares. One potential bidder, having viewed what was to be sold in a grand Dublin house in 1758, exclaimed, 'there was a great deal of curiosities and a table thirty foot long covered with old china and everything you can think of, down to a pair of Chinese shoes'.[10] Sentiment periodically conquered pragmatism in deciding how possessions should be rated. From Derry in 1739, John Lenox, inheriting furniture from a relation, wrote – somewhat apologetically – that he would keep 'an old family bed my wife has a mind to fix with ourselves'.[11] In 1741, a gentleman of Killeshandra in County Cavan attended carefully to the disposition of 'one large oval table I brought out of the county of Longford'.[12] Family feeling perhaps induced James Ware in Dublin and Richard Edgeworth in County Longford to secure chairs sold at country auctions because they had belonged to kinsfolk.[13] Similarly, the Reverend Dudley Cuffe admitted his love of an old set of 'straw chairs', which had been sent to him from a family home. 'You'll say

22. Detail of an Irish mahogany table, *c.* 1740. The naturalistic carving was regarded as a distinctively Irish trait.

I am whimsical but certain it is I would send much further for such remembrances of Agher'. It may have been further evidence of Cuffe's eccentricity, but, once he had placed the chairs in 'my brick room, *al[ia]s* flagged hall' at Kilmacow, they were copied by neighbours' 'operators'.[14] An unaffected delight in domestic surroundings, and how to suit them to needs and temperament, was expressed by a Waterford resident in the 1730s. A day had been passed busily with 'Aunt Molly', 'putting up pictures, glasses and beds', until it could be said of the house, 'a most comfortable look it begins to have'.[15] Here, comfort as much as the grand figure was the aim.

A Church of Ireland clergyman in County Londonderry also appreciated the pleasures in fiddling about with domestic fixtures and fittings. The Reverend John Leathes, something of a recluse, disarmingly told a brother, 'I am in a manner a stranger to the arts and niceties of polite conversation'. Among the people of 'fine genius and accomplished behaviour' with whom his more assured relations consorted, 'you may imagine I should make but an odd figure'.[16] Nevertheless, Leathes was well attuned to cultural and physical shifts. In 1717, he reported that 'the way of living amongst the better sort of people is much altered' over the last decade.[17] Philosophically, he concluded that change was inevitable because 'human nature is fond of variety'. The restless quest for novelty, whether or not innate, was stimulated and satisfied by manufacturers, wholesalers and retailers. Leathes ran with the flock. His habitation, a rented farm, at first projected 'but an indifferent figure'. He aimed to 'make it a little more fashionable and convenient'.[18] By doing so this provincial surrendered to the same impulses to amass and display objects as his two brothers, enriched by military service in the Low Countries.

Men fussed about the details of fitting up their houses. In part, this was because it continued the business of erecting or modifying a place in order to add credit to its owner. Also, men, as controllers of finances, sanctioned heavy spending.[19] Usually they had travelled further than their wives and daughters, and were enamoured by what they had glimpsed abroad. In addition, men were more likely, especially in the seventeenth and early eighteenth centuries, to be able to read, write and cast accounts. Often, then, they dealt with the craftsmen and suppliers, although in doing so they might communicate the wishes of their womenfolk. Masculinity had not yet been constructed to exclude minute attention to these niceties. Touring or soldiering in Europe – male preserves – refined tastes. General Henry Conyngham, General Frederick Hamilton and Major Henry Crofton, having campaigned overseas, adopted habits not yet known to squires (or indeed to their wives) in provincial Ireland.[20] Such matters preoccupied an official high in the Irish treasury. In 1745, he worried over how he should furnish a room. Having confided his difficulties over portraits, fire grate, pier glasses and lighting, he joked to a male colleague, 'I believe by this time you think I have very little care in my head when I trouble myself and you about these trifles'.[21] Alongside the fate of a kingdom and the plight of its inhabitants, these matters certainly paled. But it did not mean they were of no moment to public persons. Indeed, notables, precisely because they were active in public life, worried about achieving the right look: in their own houses as much as in their attire and demeanour. Nor was it felt that these matters were more properly delegated to women. In London and Dublin, Samuel Waring executed numerous messages for women whom he knew at home in County Down; the Reverend Toby Caulfield performed the same tasks for his Sligo neighbours while in Dublin in the first decade of the eighteenth century.[22] John Digby, member of parliament and squire of Landenstown, shopped for family and friends while in London.[23] Bishop Francis Hutchinson, having returned to County Down, left to a cousin the execution of various commissions in Dublin.[24]

In households, decisions about decoration and purchases, like questions relating to the upbringing of children, may be presumed but cannot be proved to have been joint concerns. Occasional clashes, notoriously at Castle Ward over the style of the architecture – classical or Gothick – left tangible evidence: in the case of Castle Ward, two façades in strikingly opposed idioms.[25] A clash of wills and culture was revealed by the prohibition reported by Mrs Catherine O'Brien. Her father-in-law, Sir Donough O'Brien, had insisted that she should not erect a field bed in the 'parlour'.[26] Mrs O'Brien as a kinswoman of Queen Anne might be supposed to know what was correct. Yet, at first glance, it seemed that the baronet from remote County Clare wished to banish beds from rooms which, according to the latest notions, were to be reserved for daytime uses. The strong-willed Catherine O'Brien was happy to have a bed in the parlour of her little box at Corofin.[27] In these skirmishes, objects, although important in themselves, served as proxies for personal antagonisms. More harmonious relationships were also revealed in decisions about furnishing. Sir John Temple, eager for the rich and rare, was dismayed when a suite of hangings arrived for his new Dublin house while his wife was away. He confessed, '[I] know not what to do', but was relieved a few days later when the tapestries had been hung and looked 'well'.[28] At the other extreme, Sir Thomas Newcomen cited the extravagance of his wife as the reason for his separation from her. Not only had she procured clothes from merchants under specious pretences, but she had removed two silk beds and gold and silver plate worth £300. Newcomen expostulated, 'such insolencies would provoke any man living to throw her out of the windows, for no woman brought out of the stews could do worse things'.[29]

In England, ample evidence has allowed the spread of a greater variety of articles to be traced, and sometimes quantified. As the houses of the genteel grew in size, so rooms acquired more specialized functions. Changes in the ways in which rooms were furnished and used have been reconstructed chiefly from plans and inventories. Although the documents are not always interpreted easily, they reveal the increasing popularity of such articles as looking-glasses or clocks, the elaboration of upholstered furniture and the craze for exotic woods and textiles. In turn, the qualitative consequences have been pondered.[30] The quizzical, occasionally more ingenious than plausible, postulate a new specialization in the uses of rooms, a stronger wish for privacy, and sharper demarcation of public from domestic spaces.[31] Interiors may have been reordered according to gender, with certain rooms – dining room, study and library – turned into male domains, while kitchen, nursery, drawing room and tea room were annexed by women.[32]

The types of documentation available for parts of Britain, continental Europe and north America survive only erratically for seventeenth- and eighteenth-century Ireland. Without substantial series of inventories, wills and plans, trends are at best gauged impressionistically. Any attempt to demonstrate statistically the chronology and extent of the arrival, adoption and spread of consumer novelties is foredoomed to fail. In addition, such information as can be retrieved relates mainly to the important and rich, who were most likely to participate early and eagerly in fashionable consumption. Moreover, the exiguous evidence can mislead. On plans and in inventories, the names of rooms suggest single purposes. In reality, many interiors had still to be used flexibly. Pressure on space meant that beds stood in reception rooms. One – a 'Savoy' bed – graced the little parlour at Conyngham Hall in 1711. During the 1730s, a bed stood in the parlour of Bishop Francis Hutchinson's Dublin lodgings.[33] In the middle of the eighteenth century, a 'turn-up bed' cluttered Colonel Bourke's 'little parlour'.[34] A chaff bed was placed in the hall – not the servants' hall – of Peter Dalton's house near Nenagh in County Tipperary.[35] This flexibility resembled that of the larger houses in west Wales during the eighteenth century. So too did the scant concern for and practical impossibility of privacy.[36] What the plan drawn by the designer separated – sleeping from eating, cooking from converse, family from guests, servants from owner, the domestic from the public – inventories and the chance remarks in letters confuse.

In even the grandest houses in eighteenth-century Ireland (as in France at the same time), public and private rooms were seldom precisely demarcated. At Carton in the 1760s, rules closed some spaces to servants. But this was a ducal regime, unique in Ireland, with a retinue of more than fifty servants. The scale of the establishment brought a need to regulate the staff. Stratified already by status, wages and refinement, they were further differentiated by the spaces into which they were admitted. Niggling exclusions were neither feasible nor wanted in more modest houses.[37] Virtually all houses in Ireland were smaller than Carton. Inmates, although fewer than those in the Leinsters' houses, were numerous, and bedchambers few. Indoor servants, because of their duties and the configuration of rooms, were rarely banished. Even the respectable lived cheek by jowl, so that cramped conditions brought enforced intimacies. When, for example, the atrabilious bishop of Meath died in 1724, his servant was in the next room.[38] Privacy was occasionally craved. Lady Arbella Denny, as a widow of title and ample means, could afford both town house in Dublin and seaside *dacha* on Dublin Bay.[39] Taking pity on younger (female) relations, she was concerned that each should have a modicum of privacy. For this reason she would not make two girls share one room, but gave each 'a little cell to herself'.[40] Another young woman, Jane Hamilton, exchanging confidences by letter, complained how few opportunities she had to write in private. It seemed that she could do so only by locking the door to her bedroom.[41] The more important rooms might have locks, but since door furniture was pricey it was not a universal practice. Furthermore, wooden partitions, panelling and doors frequently fitted so poorly that few were ever truly alone.[42]

A hazy picture emerges. It suggests – not unexpectedly – that the propertied in Ireland adopted commodities popular elsewhere, but were rarely in the vanguard. Even the modest could join the movement, thanks either to imports or cheaper versions made locally. At the same time, it has to be allowed that the majority of homes, whether of Catholics or Protestants, were sparsely furnished. Swift in 1728 imagined the contents of the house of a principal farmer in the provinces. 'His whole furniture consisted of two blocks for stools, a bench on each side the fireplace made of turf, six trenchers, one bowl, a pot, horn spoons, three noggins, three blankets'.[43] The tally was completed with a small churn, wooden candlestick and broken stick that served as a pair of tongs. Drudging curates were depicted in indigent surroundings with rudimentary furnishings. One of their number, Richard Barton warned,

> *his study, kitchen, parlour and saloon,*
> *Contained in twelve feet square, do make but one*
> *Nor wonder much to see spits, pots and hooks*
> *With Homer, Plutarch mixed and Latin books.*

Another curate reprised the theme.[44] Meagre means limited the spread of novelties. Yet, change occurred: pewter and ceramics supplemented and sometimes displaced tin, wood and horn. There were methods – the second-hand, presents and cheaper versions – through which goods conventionally associated with the important and prosperous could enter humbler homes. Thereby, an unexpected, even incongruous figure was achieved.

## II

The most flamboyant interiors of seventeenth-century Ireland – as elsewhere – made their effect chiefly through the quantities and qualities of textiles. In this they followed the fashion throughout much of Europe. Tapestries hung on the walls; Turkey carpets were draped over tables; chair seats and backs were either upholstered or covered with embroidered and figured cloths; sumptuous fabrics, gathered in abundant folds, screened beds and windows.[45] All added to warmth and comfort. They told onlookers of the wealth of the owners. Cork House in Dublin, abandoned by its owners during the 1640s, abounded in just such articles. There in 'my Lord Cork's chamber' were to be found four pieces of hangings, two window curtains, two carpets, one embroidered chair, one great green chair, two small green silk stools, two small green silk chairs, two great silk stools and one little embroidered stool. The effect continued in the chambers of two of his daughters. Otherwise, the principal contents were jointed and turned wooden furniture: tables, chairs and cupboards.[46] A similar impression is conveyed by an inventory of the Dublin house of the earl of Cork's son-in-law, Kildare, a few years later in 1656. In the earl's and countess's own chambers, in Lady Eleanor Fitzgerald's room and in the dining room were sets of hangings. The last room also contained two carpets, probably for covering tables.

Goods of this kind were not monopolized by the peerage. In other Dublin houses shortly before 1641 there are signs that colours of upholstery and hangings were being co-ordinated. In one room of the brasier Thomas Ottowell, green was the predominant colour. Francis Barker, a gentleman, had a set of six 'high' stools covered with 'yellow spotted silk stuff', and a high-backed armchair to match. Another half dozen stools were richly upholstered in 'red philip and chiney', and had a small chair en suite. Window curtains added to the richness.[47]

The Kildares' Dublin place contained a few prizes as well as the ubiquitous and valuable linen and standard carpentered furniture. Lady Frances Fitzgerald's chamber, for example, had a cabinet, valued at £2, perhaps to stand on a table or maybe free-standing, of rare woods, precious metals, stones or lacquer. There were also looking-glasses, screens, and 'a standard for books'. In the 'parlour' survived some dishes needed for meals.[48] Both Cork House and the Kildare residence betrayed signs of the disruption of the war and the absences of the owners. Much that was portable and valuable, notably silver, had been removed. By 1663, peace brought new requirements of hospitality and display to Restoration Dublin, the resort of the important, as parliament and a court of claims deliberated. Now, the Kildares were furnished with an array of napery, metalwares, glass and crockery.[49]

The magnificence unleashed on Dublin by peers like Cork and Kildare differed little from the state kept by their colleagues and themselves in the countryside. Duplicates were not kept in town and country, but instead prestigious items were moved as needed. The will of Francis Aungier, Lord Longford, in 1628 already hinted at the opulence of his household in the midlands. Particularly noteworthy were six pairs of 'forest work' hangings and three 'turkey-work carpets' used in the dining room. Again, the textiles that covered the seat furniture and beds caught attention. The Longfords possessed fourteen 'new, high needlework stools', two 'great needlework chairs', two new needlework stools, a red velvet chair with two [matching] stools and beds hung with taffeta and damask. Two features distinguished this family from the generality of the Irish peerage of the time. The baron had a varied library to bequeath, which was split, according to subjects, between three sons. Also, there was a collection of substantial silver articles.[50]

At the same moment, Lord Digby's effects at Portlester in County Meath attested to similar priorities in spending and show. He concentrated the greatest effect in the Great Chamber in which hung 'five pieces of fine Arras hanging of forest work'. Some variations on the customary themes were rung by a 'green carpet and cupboard cloth', presumably for the court cupboard, 'both bordered about with needlework'. There were, too, three long cushions; two of 'caffa' (a rich silk) and one of figured satin, and a foot carpet of Turkey work. The 'withdrawing chamber' at Portlester may have been dominated by a high bedstead, with green silk top and 'old green silk coverlet'. This room was hung with green and yellow say, a lightweight serge associated with Amiens and East Anglia. Lady Digby's chamber also contained a bed and was decorated with four pieces of 'coarse hanging of imagery' and window curtains. If there were novelties at this establishment, they lay in the 'Banqueting House', where a bed with dornix hangings stood (coarse tapestry originally from Tournai), and a pair of virginals in the 'outward chamber', also hung with green and yellow fabric.[51] This style of furnishing is repeated in the effects of another midlands grandee, Malby Brabazon, who died in 1638.[52] Apparently more sparing was the establishment of a more recent settler in the midlands, Sir Matthew De Renzy. He preferred to stockpile specie rather than goods. Differences in the willingness to participate fully in the consumption of fashion and luxury arose more from income and temperament than from particular ethnic or confessional affiliations.[53] A settler in County Limerick, Captain Hardress Waller had imported one or two novelties. These included a clock from England, valued at £6, and a barrel and box of Venetian glass, also brought from England, though whether also manufactured there in imitation of *façon de Venise* or originating in Italy is uncertain. Otherwise, the bed-hangings and other textiles, the cloth carpets, cupboard clothes and wooden furniture covered in Turkey-work upholstery, together with pewter, impressed.[54]

During the 1630s, Irish notables decorated their homes more lavishly. Some may have been influenced by, and been keen to surpass, Lord Deputy Wentworth's projects at Dublin Castle and Jigginstown. Especially those in contact with the English or continental courts had the incentives and (sometimes) the wherewithal to introduce fresh décor. None was more inclined to engage in this kind of show than Randall Macdonnell, the earl of Antrim. He was abetted, or maybe prompted, by his wife, the widow of the duke of Buckingham. The last had set exacting standards in extravagant settings for himself and his intimates.[55] These persisted with his widow, who transferred them into Dunluce, remote on the north coast of County Antrim. The Catholicism of the Antrims' household explained the costliest fittings. Sixteen pieces of rich embroidered green satin vestments, with matching cloths for pulpit and altar, were valued at £40: more than any other item. In all, the furnishings of Dunluce were appraised at £989 15s. 3d. Diversions in this 'whimsical' eyrie had been provided with an Irish harp and books. The castle had also been adorned with framed paintings: at least fourteen were noted, but not their subjects.[56] In worth and profusion the Antrims' possessions could have had few, if any, equals in the Ireland of their day.[57] Soon, the goods were shipped to England and dispersed.

This fate reminds of the hazards to which material effects, even more than the buildings which housed them, were subject in seventeenth-century Ireland. It also adds to the difficulties

23. Brussels tapestries of
Decius Mus, after
designs by P. P. Rubens,
at Kilkenny Castle.

both of reconstructing the settings of life before the 1650s and determining how much survived from earlier campaigns of building, decorating and furnishing. It would be easy to conclude that outside the wealthiest and smartest aristocratic residences, the comforts expected by the sophisticated had yet to appear. This easy assumption is corrected by two other documents. The household effects of a Waterford merchant, John Skiddy, were valued in 1640 at £189 8s. 6d. Clearly not in the same league as the Antrims, the Skiddys nevertheless revealed the affluence of successful traders. Their metalware was entirely of brass, iron or pewter, not silver. Other than playing tables, perhaps for backgammon or chess, liveliness was given to the interiors by the dyes and patterns of the fabrics. Three pieces of taffeta bed curtains were in red and green; curtains were of blue and yellow; tables were covered with 'Scottish' and 'Irish' cloths; six Turkey-work cushions were strewn about. Notable, too, were no fewer than ten pictures in the house.[58] What these were – ancestors, family, religious, allegorical or landscapes – there is no clue; nor how they might compare in size and subject with those at Dunluce.

The Skiddys belonged to a group with well-developed contacts in British and continental ports, whose prosperity would be threatened and usually reduced by the physical and legal upheavals of the rest of the century. As a result of government engineering, they would generally be supplanted by more recently established Protestants. Yet the ability of merchants, handling consignments of the exotic and fashionable, themselves to adopt some of the commodities in their own homes, even in advance of the rural gentry, cannot be discounted. Further evidence from Dublin in the late 1630s reveals a patchy spread of comforts and novelties. Oliver Weston, a maltster, owned a variety of upholstered seat furniture, and a pair of 'playing tables', to amuse himself and guests at chess, backgammon or dice.[59] Mrs Sarah Darworthy had a splendid bedstead of 'Indian work', varnished blue, presumably lacquer. Its valence and

24. Jan van der Beaver, *George II*. A propagandist piece advertising local textile works and the loyalty of Protestant operatives to the Hanoverian dynasty.

curtains were of 'coloured printed stuff'.[60] Notable, too, in Dublin at this time is the elaboration of the décor of inns, already apparently beguiling topers with displays of pictures and
abundant chairs and tables.[61] In Dublin as well as Waterford, the appearance of 'pictures'
reminds of a taste not confined to the aristocracy and which, thanks to the availability of
numerous types of images – some painted, others drawn or engraved – could be indulged
cheaply. In 1627, Francis Lovell, a settler at Newcestown in County Cork, owned a picture of
Adam and Eve.[62] As the century progressed, although only a minority of those whose material world is known in any detail owned pictures, they occurred at assorted social levels, as
chapter 5 will suggest. Evidence of material possessions should also caution about supposing
that all purchases were dictated either by simple utility or by unthinking imitation of trend-
setters.

More could be learnt of the surroundings of some from settler communities by analysing
the claims for losses suffered during the uprising in and after 1641. Claimants may well have
inflated the value of what they had lost to the insurgents, but were unlikely to have invented
items that they had never possessed. The depositions in which these claims were set out have
of late attracted attention as a means by which more of the nature of everyday life immediately before 1641 can be ascertained. As yet, unfortunately, there has been little enthusiasm for
using them to reconstruct the elaboration – or lack of it – of the physical settings. In the
absence of an analysis, isolated examples continue to be the main basis on which to trace
changing tastes and perhaps rising standards of life.

In houses of pretension, in Ireland no less than in England, tapestries stayed in vogue.[63]
As wall-hangings, they covered large areas, conserved heat and dazzled with their colours
and imagery. Alternatives were appearing: gilded leather, wooden panelling, and displays
of paintings or engravings. But they did not kill the demand for tapestries or other woven
wall-coverings. A standard was set by the Ormonds at Kilkenny. Their set of Brussels tapestries, designed by Rubens, which showed the history of Decius Mus, decorated the dining
room of their subsidiary residence at Dunmore in 1684. The family also owned other sets,
some from Antwerp. Four pieces depicting Polyphemus decorated the duchess's bedchamber.[64] In one of the recurrent bids to curb imports, tapestries were to be woven in Ireland
itself. The textile factory, set up under viceregal patronage at Chapelizod outside Dublin in
the late 1660s, intended to offer such lines as hangings, seat-backs and chaircovers.[65] This
intention continued into the 1720s. Then, as the new parliament house announced the perfection to which architecture and building had been raised in Ireland, so its contents were
to proclaim local skills. It would be adorned with tapestries made in Dublin. The victories
of William III and Marlborough in Ireland were selected as subjects: these heroes, it was
widely argued by members of the Protestant parliament, inaugurated the system over
which the parliament presided and which had stimulated the economic and technological
advances of which tapestry-making would be a fine example. Political points were reiter-

ated when the nascent Irish industry produced a woven portrait of the king, George II.[66] By this time, lighter and more fanciful schemes which displayed the virtuosity of other crafts-men – painters, stuccodores and joiners – were pushing tapestries from the walls of the wealthy.

Most houses of pretension were furnished with a mixture of the locally made and the for-eign, and of different vintages. A sale of goods from Sir Arthur Gore's residence in County Donegal in 1676 included leather carpets and leather coverings for chairs. Gore's 'green room' took its name apparently from the green cloth bed which it housed. Conspicuous in the ensemble were hangings which depicted hunting and shooting: apt for the lives of the country-dwellers.[67] In 1676, the bishop of Down's country residence had hangings that needed to be brushed.[68] Lady Shelburne, the widow of Sir William Petty, bequeathed tapestries and damask hangings to a son in 1706.[69] Archbishop King on first occupying his palace in Dublin had a dressing-room hung with two pieces of 'Arras'. In 1715, King paid £27 for 'tapestry hang-ings'.[70] In his palace at St Sepulchre's, he had a 'tapestry room', which took its name from four large pieces of tapestry. The chamber served as a bedroom. The bed and its furniture, in yellow tabby, with matching window curtains and chair covers, may have overpowered the tapestries.[71]

A contemporary of Archbishop King, William Whitshed, a judge and Dublin resident, had a bedchamber decked with 'arras'. He thought it fitting to leave both bed and hangings to his mother, perhaps because they represented an older taste.[72] In 1720, the County Down notable, the landed lawyer Michael Ward, ordered two tapestries from London. One depicted a fish-market, the other a corn harvest.[73] In 1737, Sir Henry Tuite of Sonnagh in Westmeath was bequeathed 'six pieces of tapestry hangings of the story of Joseph' by George Clarke, the Oxford connoisseur. Clarke apparently took pity on Tuite, 'having heard that his house was left him quite unfurnished'. The legacy, which also included silver, *objets d'art* and a green damask field bed, recalled a friendship that may have started when Clarke was in Ireland as part of William III's commissariat. Those stirring days were also evoked through the paint-ings of the Battle of the Boyne and of Lord Athlone, 'who finished the war in Ireland', willed to the Westmeath baronet.[74] Other grandees in Dublin – General Frederick Hamilton and Lord Kildare – looked to the Low Countries for their tapestries. Their orders were executed by William Leathes from Ulster, first a soldier and then an ambassador in the Low Countries. In Brussels in the early 1720s, Leathes, ever helpful to his compatriots, was ideally placed to order hangings. The trade had received a fillip from the war: victors desired sets of tapestries which depicted the recent victories. The Brussels factory met this demand.[75] Leathes steered would-be purchasers in Ireland away from what was no longer in vogue: floral borders were decidedly *passé*.

The taste for these heavy textiles, redolent of pre-1641 Ireland, long survived. Sir John Temple, the legal functionary under Charles II, had at least two expensive suites of hangings in his new seat at Palmerston, down river from Dublin. One set had been bought for £40 from Lady Lanesborough in 1684.[76] Hints of taste changing come from the country house that Lady Lanesborough was vacating. During the 1680s, the Lanesboroughs' mansion at the eponymous Lanesborough, formerly Rathcline, in County Longford, passed from the father to his heir. The elder Lane, born into a family of modest midland squires, had dedicated himself to the service of Ormond and Charles I. As Ormond's secretary he had spent much of the 1650s in foreign exile. As a result he, like other refugees, saw how differently life was ordered on the continent. Memories from that period, coupled with his longing to rise in the courtly and official worlds of Dublin and London, perhaps influenced what he created in the Irish provinces. Ideas for decking out Rathcline may have been filched from Dublin Castle or the Ormonds' private houses. By 1688, Rathcline blended the traditional and the novel. 'The castle room' (its designation presumably meant that it was located in the older fabric) was decorated with five pieces of tapestry. Lord Lanesborough's dressing-room was hung with grey cloth; similarly, the room over the 'damask room' was hung with 'grey serge striped'. Combined with caned furniture, brass sconces, looking-glasses and walnut stands, the seat furniture covered also with grey cloth, the interiors were considerably lightened. Yet, the contrast was not just with neighbouring houses of an earlier epoch but with other rooms in Rathcline. Some were still embellished with Turkey-work carpets. The dining room achieved a more orthodox impression of richness through twelve Turkey-work chairs with red-caps.[77] That same mixture was in evidence at Temple's Palmerston. There he had had some of the main apartments – such as the dining room – panelled. The contract extended to a carved wooden chimney-piece and entablature, all of which invested the room with an architectural magnificence.[78] Elsewhere in the house, however, the Temples had elected a simpler look, using, for example, painted calico for the walls of one room.[79]

Another who brought back into the Irish provinces what he had seen and admired in Dublin, England and continental Europe was Samuel Waring, encountered already as a proficient amateur architect. Gradually, he released his inheritance from the old husk in which his father had had it encased. Simpler and quicker than any rebuilding were brightening and re-arranging the interior. The principal apartments, 'purple', 'blue', 'brown', 'yellow' and 'red' rooms, presumably took their names from the dominant colour of the textiles. Some had 'hangings', but these may be presumed to be more in the mode of Rathcline than heavy tapestries.[80] By the turn of the seventeenth and eighteenth centuries, when Waring came into his patrimony, the walls of the well-to-do were ceasing to be muffled in verdure tapestries. Others had chambers whose names revealed the dominant colour or shape. Near Nenagh, Peter Dalton, a squire, had 'new blue' and 'old blue' rooms, as well as the 'bow room' and more neutral parlour and little parlour.[81] The rooms in Squire Peter Marsh's house included 'striped', 'wrought' and 'blue' rooms, together with a parlour and 'common parlour'.[82]

Other interiors were enlivened with paintings and prints: often a cheaper alternative to tapestry. This lighter look was endorsed by the viceregal couple at Dublin Castle in 1705. The Ormondes filled the drawing room with engravings, bought in Dublin. They included engraved versions of paintings by Poussin, Simon Vouet, Albani, Le Brun, Vandermulen, Hannibale Caracci and Oudry.[83] The second duke of Ormonde, first travelling and then campaigning in continental Europe during the 1680s and 1690s, was exposed to a multiplicity of cultural currents. His wife, too, had strong preferences which she followed most obviously in her Richmond hideaway.[84] At the Castle, the introduction of prints into the drawing room was of a piece with the changed furnishing of this important apartment. It was crammed with a dozen walnut armed chairs upholstered in blue velvet trimmed with silver, and another dozen smaller chairs to match. All had been made in Ireland. The theme was continued in the three sets of window curtains, also of blue satin and trimmed with silver lace. Two large panel glasses and three pairs of glass sconces with silver branches and sockets further brightened the chamber. Even the fire implements and a japanned chest were trimmed with silver. The rooms embodied and announced a changed style of viceregal entertainment, in which the drawing room to which the select were bidden varied the promiscuous resort to levees and assemblies and the solemnity of the council chamber.[85] Much in the fittings of the Castle proved as transient as the lords-lieutenant themselves. It is hard to gauge how many took a lead in their own homes from what they saw in the public rooms of Dublin Castle. Little there was obviously relevant to the way in which most in Ireland lived. Moreover, those keen to be in the forefront of fashion could go independently to the same sources used by the Ormondes, or later by Pembroke, Carteret and Dorset.

Older and newer types of decoration continued to be combined. As late as 1750, General Richard St George hung tapestries in at least three of the principal apartments in his County Kilkenny seat.[86] The house at Drumcondra on the outskirts of Dublin of the cultivated functionary Marmaduke Coghill (a bachelor) boasted a gilt leather parlour. By 1773, this had been displaced by the 'new parlour'. Similarly, wavering taste was perhaps indicated by the alternative names of another room at Drumcondra: the drawing room or 'tapestry room'. By 1773, furnished in crimson Genoa velvet, it betrayed no traces of old hangings.[87] At another suburban retreat, Delville, the owners, the Delanys, always vain about their artistic discernment, favoured tapestries for the drawing room and Mary Delany's own apartment. The Delanys conceded that nothing matched the richness of tapestry.[88] By this date alternatives were multiplying. A fresher feeling seems to have been intended by the Ingoldsbys in their Dublin residence. The 'back room', important for entertaining, had 'two panels of worked hangings, with pearl coloured bugle ground'. In the best bedchamber, three pieces of tapestry hangings had been framed, achieving a different effect from using them simply to muffle the walls.[89] Dexterous artificers achieved a new – and sprightlier – impact through plaster.[90] At Killeen Castle in County Meath, the earl of Fingall had apparently adopted the medium by 1736.

Again rooms were named after their predominant colour: green, yellow, grey and scarlet. Fabrics were less oppressive: calico, paragon or striped Kidderminster. Already, Fingall favoured a new solution to the problems of covering walls. Green paper hangings decorated one room, aptly the 'green room'.[91]

This economical option increasingly won favour. It supplanted tapestry and fabric hangings, wooden panelling and elaborate plaster frescoes or bas-reliefs.[92] Soon the novelty spread from the capital. In 1747, stamped paper appeared at the Flowers' Castle Durrow. It was also hung in a bedchamber and the drawing room at Edgeworthstown.[93] As early as 1742, blue and white paper had been bought to decorate Mrs Edgeworth's closet. 'Stamped paper' was used for several rooms in 1749. In 1755, blue paper hangings were put up in her room; green, in her

25. Needlework panel associated with Yielding family, Tralee, Co. Kerry, 1738.

26. Stucco ceiling decoration, Castle Durrow, Co. Laois. A surviving detail from one of the best documented projects of interior decoration in the first half of the eighteenth century.

husband's study.[94] Meanwhile, this new decorative material had appeared in the Dublin house of Bishop Synge of Elphin. There the doting father left to his adolescent daughter the choice of pattern and colour. 'Please your own fancy', he told her.[95] Nevertheless, Synge counselled economy by not papering behind large pieces of furniture. At the same time, paper was hung in Cork houses and bought for Castlecoole in County Fermanagh.[96] By 1759, the material graced Dublin Castle. The Bedfords were asked whether they would prefer their new apartments to be hung with paper or silk. If the former, they could choose between flock or a chintz pattern. In either case it must match the curtains. For attic rooms, a cheaper paper sufficed.[97] The popularity of wallpapers led to local production. By the 1760s, Limerick and Waterford had their paper stainers.[98] Once more, viceregal patronage merely endorsed what had been in use among the smart for a couple of decades. An enterprising Dublin furnisher, Thomas Fuller of Temple Bar, offered to hang 'India and Chinese paper in a newer and better taste than was ever done before'. Moreover, he announced that he 'will wait on gentlemen, &c. in the country if desired'.[99] Through such means, Dublin vogues spread quickly into the provinces.[100]

## III

Catalogues of auctions warn how the lines of descent for showy goods could quickly become confused. Sales, in the same way as bequests, allowed prestigious articles to descend the social scale. Records of auctions, like inventories, reveal the rich assortment of goods in eighteenth-century Ireland: sometimes, indeed, remote in the countryside.[101] They can also – again in common with inventories – indicate how rooms were used. Name alone – 'parlour', 'dining room' and 'tea room' – sometimes speaks of function. In other cases, contents disclose how rooms were used, often for multiple purposes. The evidence of inventories contains as many pitfalls, although different ones, as the prescriptions of designers with their schematic room plans. After an owner had died, especially when possessions were about to be dispersed, effects may have been shifted from their original locations and piled in convenient spaces. Articles were also omitted from probate inventories, either because they were reserved for particular members of the testator's family, because they had already been removed, or because they were considered too paltry.[102] Valuers, called in to assess effects, were far from infallible. One aggrieved widow remonstrated against the common practice of jumbling together 'the whole furniture of rooms', instead of setting down 'the true worth of every single thing'. Such imprecision, if it sometimes betrayed ignorance, could also help frauds. Laetitia Ford expostulated to her daughter, 'some fine pieces of tapestry there is and several other hangings, and window curtains without mentioning of what they are, but by the rates one would guess them to be some old Kidderminster and scarce worth anything, as almost all the rest . . . It seems to consist only of some very worthless lumber'. The inventory failed to record eight tapestries of the Labours of Hercules, 'I had so long in my keeping; nor china, nor jewels of any kind . . . all which I told you must be appraised to the full value and so I desire they may be'.[103] To allay such suspicions, specialists might be summoned, especially to deal with items like gold, silver and paintings.[104]

The printing of a catalogue of the contents of the Ingoldsbys' town house in 1731 marked an innovation in marketing.[105] It suggested that the old or merely second-hand was in demand. This supposition is confirmed by earlier instances. In the 1670s, the lordly Archbishop Boyle had his son-in-law enquire after upholstered furniture 'at second hand' for his imposing new seat at Blessington.[106] In the same decade, Sir John Temple bought tapestries and a costly black-framed mirror from the departing vicereine, Lady Essex – a reputable enough provenance.[107] During 1711, more than £30 was spent on Archbishop King's behalf for bed curtains, hangings and furniture at an auction.[108] Economy frequently recommended this method of equipping establishments. In 1742, the new bishop of Kilmore, Joseph Story, setting up in episcopal splendour, bought much at auction. At one, he spent £28 10s. 5d.[109] Snobbery or sentiment sometimes commended what had previously been owned by kinsfolk or the grand. The no-longer-new was valued for its rarity or quality. In 1711, the sale of some of

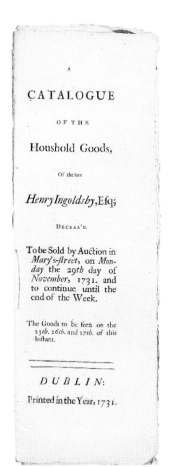

A

CATALOGUE

OF THE

Houshold Goods,

Of the late

*Henry Ingoldsby*, Efq;

DECEAS'D.

To be Sold by Auction in *Mary's-ftreet*, on *Monday* the 29th day of *November*, 1731. and to continue until the end of the Week.

The Goods to be feen on the 25th. 26th. and 27th. of this Inftant.

*D U B L I N*:

Printed in the Year, 1731.

27. Sale catalogue for the Ingoldsbys' Dublin house. The earliest surviving printed catalogue of an auction of house contents in Ireland.

the Conynghams' effects startled one observer. 'A great part of their goods were sold yesterday at great rates; some old things for more than new could be bought for'.[110] Others, with more modest furnishings, expected them, once used, to depreciate.[111] Moreover, the squire of Stradbally, when he furnished a house 'very handsomely', for a poorer relation, stressed that they were 'good *new* things of all sorts and kinds'.[112]

Auctioneers skilfully turned auctions into social events, at which the modish would compete. Refreshments were provided and, in time, printed catalogues. In 1715, when Lord Perceval's showy effects were to be sold in Dublin, an upholsterer arranged the auction. Two thousand tickets were printed.[113] The sly misrepresented what they were selling and ran up prices. In 1724, the agent of an absent vendor assured his master whose furnishings were to be sold in Dublin, 'I would be here to bid for them if they were going off at a low rate'.[114] Despite these tricks, public sales greatly expanded the opportunities to buy.

The catalogue of the moveables in the Ingoldsbys' Dublin residence uncovers something of how the house, on the north side of the city, was organized as well as furnished. The

28. Advertisement of Bart. West, upholder and auctioneer, Dublin. During the eighteenth century, auctions became an increasingly common feature of the city.

family, settled in Ireland since the 1650s, had had ample opportunities to amass goods. In Queen Anne's reign, the head of the house had served as one of the lords justice. This public role recognized substance, and in turn required a fitting setting. The Ingoldsbys divided their lives and their possessions between Dublin and the Kildare countryside. In 1732, the contents of the country seat at Carton were also sold.[115] With no catalogue of what had been there, it is impossible to know how different the two interiors looked. The town house in Mary Street was crowded with relics of the Ingoldsbys' military careers and recent purchases in London.[116] The furnishings may also have reflected the presence and preferences of two young girls.

The first room of consequence was the street parlour. It was well appointed with a dozen cane-seated chairs and a large mahogany table. The appearance of mahogany, imported from Central America, itself exuded an extravagance which the patriots of Ireland rebuked. Another novelty was the dumbwaiter. Glasses and cups were placed on it for easier service. Over the marble chimney-piece was set a 'chimney glass' to reflect the contents of the room and probably daylight from the window. Illumination also came from a glass sconce with gilt frame and brass arms. A passage led from this room to the back parlour. Here, to judge from the mahogany quadrille table covered with green baize, cards were played. Striking was a suite of seat furniture comprising a settee, eight matching chairs and two stools. These were upholstered in 'red silk Indian damask' and supplied with 'case covers of red serge' to protect them when not in use. Here, as elsewhere in the house, the arrival of lighter and more exotic designs either from the orient or in imitation of the eastern signalled a shift of taste away from the heaviness, evident for example in the tapestries from western Europe so popular in the previous century and still to be seen in some Irish houses. Otherwise, front and back parlours were similarly furnished.

The tone set by the rooms on the ground floor echoed throughout the house. The oak staircase, another space calculated to impress any caller, was dominated by its light fittings. Illumination came from 'two lamp glasses with bell covers, brass sockets and arms'. In the centre, suspended from a gilded rose in the ceiling, hanging from a red silken cord with a tassel, was a large glass lantern with four branches for candles in a gilt frame. On the wall was hung a weather glass or barometer, in a 'brazil frame'. The dining room was another chamber designed to stun. Eating was one of the first activities to be given its own specific space in grander houses. In the Ingoldsbys' residence, diners sat on twelve large chairs, two of them with arms, 'with worked covers and red paragon loose cases'. Important to the look of the dining room was a large pier glass, measuring 43 inches by 23 inches, in a glass frame. The manufacture and decoration of these massive mirrors challenged the techniques of local artificers and depleted the purses of the purchaser.[117] Once more, the purpose was to introduce more scintillating effects of light: by day, maximizing what was caught and refracted; and at night magnifying the play of the flames from candles and coal on silver, jewels, polished wood and glass.

A passage led from the dining room into a 'back room', where guests retired once they had eaten. Here, too, cards could be played at the black lacquer table. Over the 'black, gold-veined marble chimney piece' hung a chimney glass in three sections. Adding further to the brilliance of this interior was another pier glass, again framed in glass. The middle plate measured 41½ inches by 24 inches. As in other contemporary houses of any consequence, the bedchambers were dominated by splendid beds. Often their ornate hangings matched the window curtains and the covers of the seat furniture. The lavishness of these apartments was confirmed by the extensive use of walnut, a costly imported wood: for example, in an escritoire in the closet adjoining the 'best bed-chamber'. Distinctive touches were added by a walnut cabinet for medals and a 'couch bed' with red and white stuff curtains. The pewter kept in the kitchen, humbler earthenware located on the back stairs and the glass stored in a closet off the servants' hall were all to be sold. So was the flotsam and jetsam left from earlier campaigns of redecoration: curtains, fire-screens, sections of marble (probably for or from chimney-pieces or table tops), and two panels of 'Indian paper', i.e. painted Chinese wallpaper. The last was a particularly precocious embrace of a stylish novelty.

In an establishment of this importance, the upper servants were well accommodated. The butler, with his separate room, had green Kidderminster hangings for the window and bed curtains. Kidderminster, a woollen fabric, was used in rooms of importance in other houses, such as Fingall's Killeen. In the Ingoldsbys' residence, a distinction between family and even upper servants was maintained through the woods used. The butler's bedstead and chair were fashioned from oak; his table, not from expensive and foreign walnut and mahogany, but from workaday deal or pine.

Many of the Ingoldsbys' possessions had been imported. In particular, the east had been plundered for the painted paper and the large collection of porcelain which – with its own separate printed catalogue – was auctioned a few days later.[118] The services, either gilded *famille rose* and *famille verte* or blue and white, showed the success of the East India Company in introducing its wares to notables in Dublin. Over the course of the eighteenth century, it has been calculated that as many as a hundred Irish families ordered armorial porcelain, mainly through the East India Company in London.[119] These commissions told of the taste for tea, chocolate and coffee. Some of the Ingoldsbys' Chinese porcelain was intended for more robust uses: punch bowls, sets of soup plates, large platters. The largest pieces, covered jars, were entirely ornamental. So, too, were the blue-and-white flowerpots. One pair, of 'delft', probably came from Holland rather than from the orient, and may have been the free-standing tulip vases for which Dutch potters were renowned. The Ingoldsbys had campaigned in the Low Countries during William III's and Anne's reigns, and may first have seen these massive ornaments there. Patriots urged the duty to buy Irish wares. But, whether it was wine, cloth or ceramics, the allure of the foreign proved irresistible. Henry Ingoldsby, although impatient with the cost and inconvenience of London, ransacked it for the choice which he could send to Ireland.

## IV

The configurations and contents found in the Ingoldsbys' north-side property were repeated in the Dublin residences of the comparably circumstanced. Houses of notables, whether in the countryside or capital, met several needs. In them, business shaded into pleasure; the domestic and familial imperceptibly into the social, public and emulative. The expense of furnishing different rooms indicates one hierarchy within the house. Usually, priority was given to the areas where visitors were received. In 1742, two valuations of what was in the rooms of the Balfours' house on St Stephen's Green – one of the best addresses in Dublin – showed how rooms ranked.[120] There are dangers in deducing too much from valuations. In advance of the auction, a leading Dublin furnisher appraised the contents.[121] His totals differed from the sums raised by the auction itself. As in other houses of similar size, linen, silver, china, glass and firearms were listed and sold separately. In the case of the Balfours, their linen fetched £116 8s. 7d., and their silver £561 13s. 3d.[122]

Table 1. Valuations of the contents of the Balfours' Dublin House, 1742

| Room | 15 March 1741[2] | | | | Coleman's valuation | | | |
|---|---|---|---|---|---|---|---|---|
| | £ | s. | d. | Percentage | £ | s. | d. | Percentage |
| Back parlour | 42 | 14 | 4 | (13.3) | 37 | 2 | 8 | (14.4) |
| Street parlour | 66 | 2 | 6 | (20.7) | 63 | 0 | 0 | (24.5) |
| Dining room | 40 | 0 | 4 | (12.6) | 40 | 16 | 5 | (15.9) |
| Bedchamber over the stairs | 26 | 7 | 5 | (8.2) | 20 | 18 | 11 | (8.1) |
| Street room (first floor) | 20 | 18 | 0 | (6.5) | 21 | 0 | 3 | (8.2) |
| Back room (first floor) | 11 | 18 | 5 | (3.6) | 6 | 9 | 10 | (2.5) |
| Street garret | 4 | 17 | 11 | (1.5) | 3 | 14 | 11 | (1.4) |
| Back garret | 1 | 4 | 8 | (0.4) | 5 | 0 | 6 | (1.9) |
| Kitchen | 33 | 19 | 0 | (10.6) | 26 | 15 | 10 | (10.3) |
| Yard | 1 | 5 | 1 | (0.4) | | | | |
| Coal | 10 | 15 | 1 | (3.3) | | | | |
| China | 26 | 18 | 1 | (8.3) | 16 | 15 | 6 | (6.5) |
| Armour, guns, weapons | 18 | 13 | 9 | (5.8) | 4 | 3 | 11 | (1.6) |
| Drinking glasses | 12 | 14 | 2 | (4.0) | 3 | 8 | 8 | (1.3) |
| Total | 318 | 8 | 9 | | 258 | 2 | 7 | |

The street parlour, the ground-floor room into which most visitors were ushered first, was evidently a sumptuous apartment. It was rated above the dining room in the value of its appurtenances. The need for these richly decorated spaces told also of an elaboration in patterns of sociability. Visiting, with its increasingly intricate etiquette, flourished.[123] This was confirmed by an incident involving Dean Swift in 1734. An enraged caller, bent on insulting – if not assaulting – Swift, was shown into the street parlour. Eventually the dean was summoned from the back parlour where he had been playing cards with his host.[124]

The evidence from the Balfours gives some clue as to the richness with which different rooms were furnished. Similar information from country houses shows how priorities varied over time and between city and provinces. In 1682, the County Armagh seat of Sir Hans Hamilton was inventoried. Hamilton's Bawn was well stocked with cattle, horses, and a few sheep and pigs. Names for rooms, other than 'dining room', 'nursery' and 'withdrawing room', give no definitive indication of how they were used. By value of contents, the parlour was surprisingly bare, whereas the mysterious rooms over the parlour and kitchen had the most valuable furnishings.[125]

Table 2. Valuation of the contents of Hamilton's Bawn, Co. Armagh, 1682

| Name of room | Valuation | | |
|---|---|---|---|
| | £ | s. | d. |
| Room above kitchen | 39 | 5 | 6 |
| Room above kitchen room | 9 | 11 | 0 |
| Little room | 2 | 10 | 0 |
| Women servants' room and Mr Smiley's chamber | 2 | 5 | 0 |
| Withdrawing room | 1 | 16 | 0 |
| Dining room | 10 | 7 | 0 |
| Room over parlour | 22 | 0 | 0 |
| Room over hall | 10 | 18 | 0 |
| 3rd room over parlour | 7 | 1 | 0 |
| Room over dining room | 7 | 11 | 0 |
| Nursery | 7 | 1 | 0 |
| Parlour | 1 | 18 | 0 |
| Room over stable | 3 | 9 | 10 |
| Pewter | 12 | 8 | 0 |
| Silver plate | 64 | 0 | 0 |
| Total | 888 | 16[126] | 0 |

By 1741 when the goods in a country house of a squire, Marsh, were valued, names of the rooms hinted at changing habits; so, too, did the relative values of what each chamber held. Most lavishly appointed, if measured by the appraisal, was the 'large parlour'. There almost a quarter of the worth was concentrated. The parlour was followed by the 'wrought' and 'blue' rooms, the designations of which suggested recent campaigns of redecoration.[127] Unfortunately the names of the chambers did not reveal which was the principal bedroom, either in Marsh's or Hamilton's house. In many residences, it was the most expensively furnished space.

Table 3. Valuation of the contents of Squire Marsh's house, 1741

| Name of room | Valuation | | | |
|---|---|---|---|---|
| | £ | s. | d. | Percentage |
| Wrought room | 14 | 8 | 9 | (16.9) |
| Cellar room | 4 | 4 | 0 | (5.0) |
| Striped room | 9 | 11 | 0 | (11.2) |
| Blue room | 10 | 4 | 11 | (12.0) |
| Dark room | 1 | 13 | 0 | (2.0) |
| Maids' room | 3 | 17 | 6 | (4.5) |
| Men's room | 1 | 15 | 0 | (2.1) |
| New room | | 8 | 0 | (0.5) |
| Hall | 1 | 10 | 0 | (1.8) |
| Large parlour | 18 | 2 | 3 | (21.3) |
| Common parlour | 5 | 16 | 6 | (6.9) |

(*cont.*)

| | £ | s. | d. | % |
|---|---|---|---|---|
| Kitchen | 11 | 0 | 3 | (12.9) |
| Cellar | 2 | 17 | 0 | (3.6) |
| Servants' hall | | 12 | 6 | (0.7) |
| Total | 85 | 4 | 10 | |

The physical characteristics of country-house life are also evoked in the arrangements of General Richard St George's house at Kilrush in County Kilkenny. In 1750, some rooms were designated by the colour of their main furnishings: 'yellow' and 'crimson'. Others took their names from the fabrics, 'mohair' and 'chintz', which embellished them. A chief chamber was still called 'the great parlour', not in the modern parlance a drawing room. In the recorded valuations, 'the colonel's room', occupied by the general's nephew, in which his bed stood, was reckoned to house the most valuable possessions. Again this suggested continuities with long-established priorities, in which bedrooms of the important ranked high. The colonel was the nephew and heir of General St George. Because certain categories of goods were excluded from the inventory – silver and other metalwares, paintings, linen – the proportions may be distorted. A distinct oddity was the concentration in the brewhouse.[128]

Table 4. Valuation of the contents of General Richard St George's house, Co. Kilkenny, 1750

| Name of room | Valuation | | | |
|---|---|---|---|---|
| | £ | s. | d. | Percentage |
| Great parlour | 16 | 19 | 9 | (9.2) |
| The Colonel's room | 27 | 12 | 3 | (15.0) |
| Hall | 9 | 18 | 9 | (5.4) |
| Little parlour | 2 | 13 | 7½ | (1.4) |
| ?Mohair room | 12 | 6 | 3 | (6.7) |
| Yellow room | 22 | 3 | 3 | (12.0) |
| Closet to yellow room | 2 | 0 | 0 | (1.1) |
| Dressing room | 14 | 15 | 0 | (8.0) |
| Chintz room | 12 | 14 | 7 | (6.9) |
| Crimson room | 10 | 7 | 9 | (5.6) |
| General's room | 4 | 12 | 1 | (2.5) |
| Closet to General's room | 2 | 1 | 4½ | (1.1) |
| Brewhouse | 34 | 18 | 0 | (18.9) |
| Nurse's room | 4 | 2 | 7 | (2.2) |
| Maid's room | 1 | 2 | 9 | (0.6) |
| Room 16 unspecified | 1 | 8 | 1½ | (0.8) |
| Still room | 4 | 11 | 0 | (2.6) |
| Total | 184 | 17 | 7½ | |

Returning to the dispersal of the Balfours' effects, the deaths in rapid sequence of Captain Harry Balfour and his widow precipitated sales at their residences in County Fermanagh and Dublin. The yields respectively of town and country auctions offer clues about how possessions were distributed between the separate houses. Assessed by value, 34 per cent of goods came from Castle Balfour, the seat in Fermanagh, and 52 per cent from the city house. The remaining 14 per cent resulted from miscellaneous payments. Since the sales at Castle Balfour included much of the livestock, it seems that the greater show was reserved for Dublin.[129] These priorities were not necessarily consistent even in the same family: successive generations reversed them, as they built up local interests or absented themselves entirely from Ireland. Alternative choices were made by a second family situated in County Fermanagh. Between 1747 and 1751, Margetson Armar, having recently inherited Castlecoole, spent £1,533 on its furnishings. Glass, marble, damask, cutlery, carving and paintings arrived from leading Dublin craftsmen and retailers. One of the major items was £109 for damask from the Dublin shop of Grogan.[130] Textiles for hangings and upholstery remained a quick, if not cheap, way to transform interiors.

Too much should not be rested on stray examples. However, the possessions favoured by the Balfours on St Stephen's Green in the 1730s were to be found in the town houses of those of similar rank. The St Lawrences, Barons Howth, owned both a castle overlooking Dublin Bay and a house in St Mary's parish, near the northern bank of the River Liffey. By 1751, two trends had affected the arrangements in the Howths' town house. Spaces were more sharply differentiated on the basis of function. Thus, to the familiar street and back parlours on the ground floor were added breakfast and dining rooms, apparently on the first floor. Interiors were brightened with mirrors. Sometimes tall pier-glasses hung between the windows. The hardy perennial, walnut, survived: for example, in the leather-seated chairs in the back parlour. But mahogany also appeared, notably in the several tables. In the dining room, the chairs had mahogany frames.[131] The fortunes of a second family, the St Legers, ennobled as Viscounts Doneraile, revived after the death in 1750 of the insane third viscount. Architects were called in to remodel Doneraile House, on the south side of Dublin and close to the Kildare's newly built *hôtel*. By 1753, the Doneraile property was being furnished. In the house, the arrangements evident in the Ingoldsbys' residence, more than two decades earlier, still prevailed. On the ground floor, the street parlour remained important. The feeling was heavier. The ten chairs were of mahogany, not with caned seats, but overstuffed with green damask. A vivid 'Turkey' carpet covered the floor. A purple marble table, supplied by David Sheehan for £15 in 1750, was conspicuous.[132] About the Ingoldsbys' pictures we are ignorant, since they were not included in the sale. At Doneraile House, the street parlour was decorated with sixteen prints in gilt frames. In the principal reception room, the first-floor drawing room, thirteen 'pictures' are laconically listed. On the ground floor, a passage – as in the Ingoldsby house – led to the 'back eating parlour'. There marble and mahogany were again

29. Anon, *View of Howth Castle, Co. Dublin, c.* 1740. Houses proved to be increasingly popular subjects with painters, as well as housing many of their paintings.

much in evidence. Sheehan had made an 'Egyptian' marble sideboard for £12 18s. 4d.[133] Four mahogany eating tables catered to the diners who might throng the house. Mahogany re-appeared elsewhere in the main rooms. More personal was a picture of the County Cork seat, Doneraile Court, placed over the chimney-piece in the viscount's dressing-room. A bust of Lord Shannon on the front stairs proclaimed political affiliations. Fewer goods shipped in by the East India Company were displayed. Chinoiserie survived in Lady Doneraile's dressing-room in the shape of a 'small India cabinet and frame' (or stand).

How, increasingly, a smart Dublin house was stuffed with necessities and 'neednots' can be glimpsed from the house taken by Viscount Conyngham (formerly Henry Conyngham), inheritor of Slane. In 1766, Conyngham purchased the remaining nineteen and a half years' lease on a property in Park Street, north of the river and close to Phoenix Park. For this he paid £400 as entry fine to a Dublin 'gentleman'. Thereafter, the annual rent would be £26. The house, built only in 1762 by Murtagh Lacy, came furnished. As such it represented what Lacy felt a grandee would expect or perhaps the minimum he could hope to supply, not Conyng-ham's tastes. Motley objects were jumbled into the place. 'The street bed chamber', for exam-ple, contained a bed of 'green English moreen', a Chinese cabinet with painted glass doors, mahogany desk and dressing-table, and eight modest rush-bottomed chairs. As in other Dublin houses of pretension, the dining room was arranged to impress.

The Park Street house had never before been inhabited by a functioning family, and the dining room was given over to other uses. The large mahogany dining table was pushed out into the hall and in its place a bulky sofa, eight upholstered chairs and two stools reposed. A large 'Scotch' carpet covered the floor. This dining room mainly made its impact through devices favoured in other Dublin buildings: a large oval pier-glass in a gilt frame, a pair of lacquered double sconces, a painting in a gold frame and another thirty-four glazed prints, also framed in gilt. Two gilded figures of Shakespeare and Rubens perched on gilt brackets.[134] More pictures – two small Dutch paintings and another forty-three glazed prints – adorned the staircase.

The house in Park Street was arranged much as the Ingoldsbys' and Donerailes' town houses. The street parlour had a Turkey carpet, eight carved mahogany chairs, protected with case-covers of check patterned cloth. As yet only blinds shielded the windows. A pier-glass, in gilt frame, hung above a mahogany pier table. In the back parlour, the ten chairs, the seats covered with horsehair, sideboard and knife box were all of mahogany. Another pier-glass, this time with a black frame, cheered the room. This, perhaps, picked up the motif of the lacquered pair of dumb waiters. The back room was also consecrated to eating. To meet the diners' needs a speciality from the Dublin cutlers Asgill – knives and forks with distinctive handles of ivory stained green – were sheathed in their cases.[135] Another novelty was a 'bamboo cistern and bandeazer'. The copious china, much of it oriental, silver (150 ounces) and sixty drinking glasses of varying sizes suggested that the house had been equipped and was hired by Conyngham for lavish entertaining.[136]

## V

The standards of decorating and furnishing in the permanent pads of aristocrats and squires in Dublin could not easily be achieved by those who merely roosted in the capital for the season. Hiring lodgings for a term of months or by the week exposed visitors to the tricks of landlords and landladies, who, thanks to mounting demand, by the 1730s were in a commanding position. What then was procured by tenants and lodgers obviously varied according to means, length and purpose of stay and the extent to which they expected regularly to be in the capital. The country squires French and Edgeworth rented houses in Dublin shortly after their marriages. Each, once elected to parliament, could expect to use the base at least every second winter. In practice, the lure of the winter season continued year by year regardless of whether the lord-lieutenant was in residence and parliament in session.[137] In the cases of both French and Edgeworth, they gave up their town establishments before they relinquished seats in the Commons. They did so because their families' needs had altered with their wives' illnesses and the needs of maturing children. Families at the level of the Edgeworths and Frenches bought extensively from Dublin craftworkers and shopkeepers. On occasion, they spent on a single marble chimney-piece what it was thought sufficed to support a labourer for a year.[138]

Hundreds rather than thousands commanded the income of squires and members of parliament like Edgeworth or French. This fact alone kept most from frequent and lavish embellishment of their homes. Moreover, some of the prospering gentlemen ignored the latest fashions. A satirist imagined 'the squire's habitation' as devoted largely to field sports. The muddy paws and fleas of dogs left their marks. 'Caps, hats, whips, great coats' were dumped on the chairs. 'The good family' of the owner was 'neither by fashions nor by seasons changed'.[139] While some who could afford material delights abstained, others, seemingly without the means to buy extensively, strained to do so. Unfortunately, few accounts and inventories relate to the professionals and middling sorts, let alone to the poor. At best, rare individuals from the middle station have left clues about their possessions. During the 1740s, the Limerick farmer and agent Nicholas Peacock added to his. He used general merchants in Limerick, the offerings at local markets and fairs, two brief trips to Dublin, and occasional auctions of the effects of grandees in his neighbourhood. Incentives to enlarge his household holdings, as indeed to extend his modest dwelling, included the availability of alluring commodities, especially in the shops of Limerick or at the auctions, regular contact with gentry like the Quins, Burys, Hartstonges and Widenhams, the wishes of a new wife, and the wants of a young family. In addition, it is possible that Peacock, on the margins of gentility, tried to refashion his house to accord with his social aspirations.

Peacock, when single, lived in an altogether humbler manner than his employers. He paid tax for only two hearths, suggesting a simple one-storeyed house, perhaps thatched with reeds from the nearby Shannon's banks.[140] Outbuildings and offices catered to his farm and lodged the servants. Other than to buy himself pewter spoons and a knife and fork, Peacock's chief weakness was to amass linen.[141] In 1742, an itinerant cooper and his son mended all Peacock's wooden vessels, except the powdering butt and meal tub.[142] The repairs may have extended to kitchen and household utensils. Certainly, Peacock was fond of his treen. In the spring of 1743 he recorded the gift from his sister of a small wooden bowl.[143] In the same year, he bought directly from a turner a consignment of wooden dishes: three large, four 'a size less', three small ones, eleven bowls, three punchbowls, eighteen new trenchers and some older pieces. Peacock promptly marked them as his, perhaps by branding.[144] Again, some items may have been for agricultural tasks, but more were for personal use. As yet, ceramics had not entered Peacock's home, whatever he encountered *chez* Hartstonge, Bury and Quin. During the same period, limited repairs and additions were made to larger items. Tim Calahan was the preferred carpenter. He devised a new rail for the tester of Peacock's bed, put locks on chests, mended chairs and closets and made gates.[145] This work was done on the spot and paid partly in kind, with oats.

Peacock passed the summer of 1743 at Court, his employers' nearby house. In his absence, he commissioned Cyprian Purcell to make a dresser, for 1s. 8d., and paid him for 'flowering my room', presumably whitewashing it.[146] Purcell would recur. With the enforced versatility required of craftsmen in the countryside, Purcell was consulted by Peacock about how to repair his clock. This novelty had cost Peacock 2s. 8½d.: a modest sum which suggested a rudimentary mechanism. For whatever reason, Peacock could not make it go. Nor could Purcell.[147] The latter proved more deft in fabricating a case for glasses and repairing the bedsteads.[148] Later in the decade, after Peacock had married, Purcell constructed the frame for a table.[149] More ambitiously, in 1746, the craftsman had furnished a plan 'of the house and orchard': a sign perhaps of extensions and improvements prompted by Peacock's marriage. Peacock and Purcell travelled together to Limerick city to buy the timber required to start the work.[150] Purcell stayed on friendly terms with Peacock, who even bought him a pair of red breeches.[151] Purcell may have been essentially an estate carpenter or simply a jack-of-all-trades, but he was on dining terms with the Peacocks.[152]

Goods continued to reach this Limerick homestead by a variety of routes. Peacock's sister presented him with a table. By 1743, he was buying new furniture. Six chairs from James Madden cost eight pence each. A new cupboard came from Daniel O'Brien.[153] The same summer, a sale nearby in Rathkeale afforded fresh chances of purchases. Some of the buys – two chairs, table and 'alphabet' [pigeon holes] – were on behalf of his employer, Price Hartstonge. However, the prints that he also bought, for 5s. 6d., may have ended up in Peacock's own cabin.[154] Peacock was close enough to the shopping mecca of Limerick to visit it often.[155] Yet he obtained surprisingly few of his household durables there. In 1750, four chairs were purchased in the city. At four shillings each they cost much more than those made at Kildimo, and suggest how his wife was altering their habits.[156] She seems also to have introduced tea-drinking with the attendant utensils into their house. Peacock's bride, Catherine Chapman, belonged to a family of gentlemen farmers on the borders of Cork and Limerick. Her status as well as gender may have made her eager to embellish her husband's modest house. Entertaining was elaborated. When a bachelor, he had usually visited others. Now, he and his wife exchanged visits with kinsfolk and neighbours. The hospitality obliged a wider choice of comestibles and the means to serve them appropriately.

In general, these furnishings cost, and may therefore have mattered, less to Peacock than his own clothes. However, three acquisitions did bulk large. The clock caused trouble until a neighbour wangled it. Similarly, Peacock's pocket watch became the centre of an incident in which a servant was accused of purloining it. In the event, the menial was unjustly accused. The precious article was discovered in the pocket of Peacock's breeches. Sense of time passing, calibrated by timepieces, separated Peacock from most with whom he dealt as agent, and brought him closer to his employers among the gentry. Sophistication in this respect was of a piece with his purchases of books and newspapers, and the introspection signified by his keeping of a terse diary. A third object beyond the means and imaginations of most of his neighbours arrived in 1745. Mrs Hartstonge presented Peacock with a large silver cup.[157] It is possible that it formed a discreet payment for earlier services, and so was quickly traded for cash.[158]

Peacock, in adding to his possessions, may have reflected how his neighbours among the squirearchy chose to live. Although occasionally at sea in a world where forms had to be completed, legal procedures observed and the distant state's demands obeyed, he cannot be regarded simply as a slavish imitator of what his acknowledged superiors did. The problem in assessing how those outside the landed élites arranged their homes is that most for whom any traces survive were connected with the squirearchy, commonly as suppliers of services. Peacock, essentially an agent, was an intermediary, ideally placed both to pick up the new-fangled and to be acclimatized to older and indigenous ways. Other householders in south Munster during the mid-eighteenth century, whose homes can be reconstructed, also straddled several worlds. Lucas, a contemporary of Peacock, living at the family farm outside Corofin, north of Limerick city, dwelt in a modest manner. His parents initiated minor improvements and repairs to the house. It was the scene of neighbourly entertainments. But how it was furnished is unclear.[159]

Most for whom some evidence of their possessions has survived belonged either to the landed or the professions and trades. At Bandon, the dispersal of the goods of an esquire, Boyle Travers, allowed others of similar rank to snap up trifles. Among those who bought at the Travers auction were Dr Leadbetter and members of the gentry. The willingness of the latter to buy miscellaneous goods at local sales, sometimes even of their tenants' possessions, again cautions against supposing that the prosperous bought only the sparklingly new. In 1768, Captain Bernard of Castle Bernard, the largest estate in the environs of Bandon, purchased delft, butter plates and linen from the property of a Dunmanway clothier, Benjamin Hayes.[160] Dr Leadbetter, in buying ivory and black-hafted knives and forks or 'two yellow jugs', was not acquiring essentials for his own establishment, but objects which for whatever reason appealed to his fancy. At the same time, his wife bought on her own account: eleven delft plates for 2s. 11d. Mrs Leadbetter was among over a dozen women who bid successfully for lots, mainly small quantities of glass and crockery rather than substantial furniture. Mrs Harris was able to acquire two pairs of the Travers' window curtains for 5s. 5d., and Mrs Bermingham a kitchen range. The social or marital standing and incomes of these women are not always clear. Yet, it is noteworthy that they bid confidently at this and other auctions, such as Benjamin Greene's at Cappoquin in 1734. Indeed, women bought at an auction of Sir John Perceval's furniture in County Cork in the mid-1680s.[161]

In the same locality, the Reverend Robert McClelland, curate of Kilbrogan since 1737, could be regarded in background and culture as of the quality. The clergy by virtue of education knew other environments, notably Dublin, where, by the mid-eighteenth century, most had been educated. Furthermore, they were widely viewed as agents through whom civility and politeness were to be disseminated across the Irish hinterlands. How they lived mattered. It could reflect well or ill on their sacerdotal function, and on the English and Protestant interests which they personified. They were, in addition, expected to set an example to their parishioners.[162] McClelland's worldly estate was valued in 1761 at a substantial £870 12s. The furnishings of his house constituted less than 18 per cent of this wealth. Nevertheless, they spoke of elegance and comfort. True to his calling, the cleric owned nearly 300 books, 'mostly printed sermons and divinity'. These amounted to slightly less than 10 per cent by value of the contents. Impressive too was the silver. When McClelland's silver watch – less costly than Peacock's – is included, the silver constituted about 16 per cent of the value of his household goods. McClelland also owned a small amount, both in quantity and value (sixteen shillings), of 'French plate': a coffee pot, three sugar casters and a pair of salt cellars. This tends to confirm the supposition that the imported did not seriously challenge the home-produced. Also swingeing duties deterred all but the most affluent from buying non-Irish silver.[163]

Quantities of glass – decanters and drinking vessels – were owned, but constituted less than 1 per cent of the total value. The McClellands were equally well provided with porcelain. They owned at least three dozen cups and saucers of 'burned china', as well as eighteen less highly regarded blue-and-white cups and saucers. By this date, porcelain could be supplied by English or continental manufacturers, often in imitation of the designs and fineness of the oriental originals. In aggregate not as valuable as the silver, nevertheless this choice china amounted to about 6 per cent of the total worth of his effects. Earthenware for kitchen and servants' use, in contrast, was assessed at only £1. Some impression of the look of the curate's house comes from his pictures. Separately itemized are '1 landscape, 1 patchwork hanging for a room' at £1. Another sixteen pictures, 'glazed and framed', were valued at £2 4s. These may well have been prints. They can be contrasted with the two large pictures and single landscape together reckoned at £8 16s. In all, about 8 per cent of the portable wealth was tied up in these pictures. To them can be added a curiosity of the house which the appraisers were probably at a loss to value accurately. Twelve plaster-of-Paris statues perched on fourteen brackets, seemingly with two flower-pots, and made an odd decoration.[164] More conventionally precious was a tortoiseshell cabinet, perhaps with brass mounts and inlaid with semi-precious stones. Alone it was valued at £3 10s.[165]

It is difficult confidently to contrast the look of the curate of Kilbrogan's house with that of peers' and squires' residences. McClelland apparently lacked the grandeur of mahogany and other imported woods and the most opulent textiles. However, it could be that Mrs McClelland and other legatees had removed coveted pieces before the inventory was taken. Moreover, unusual objects, such as the cabinet and plaster statuettes, resembled objects cherished by grandees in Dublin. The comfort in which the financially secure clergy of the established Church lived was demonstrated by the possessions of the Reverend Arthur Herbert in 1760. Herbert, of Currens in County Kerry, belonged to a dynasty which had exploited its kinship with the absent owners of much land in the area. The Kerry Herberts became important landowners in their own right.[166] The clergyman rented two substantial holdings, paying in all an annual £147 in rent. His farms were stocked with cattle and sheep. Herbert lived with refinement, much of it achieved – on credit – through a Catholic shopkeeper in Tralee. Silver, mostly for use at the tea and dinner tables, featured among his possessions. By value, it constituted almost 12 per cent of what was sold at Currens after Herbert's death. In addition, a few items, such as a silver tankard, were kept by his widow. Herbert's furniture was a mixture of mahogany, oak and (occasionally) yew, a local wood. Ceramics seem universally to have been the humbler delft, not porcelain. Sentiment dictated that a 'large family table' and some family pictures stay in the house. Hints of Herbert's lettered calling may be detected in a few pamphlets and books which were auctioned. Fifteen 'old' French books were left to a kinsman. Those who purchased at the Currens sale were all men, in contrast to the bidders at McClelland's or Greene's dispersals. Herbert's linen was sent to Killarney to be sold. Herbert was prosperous enough to settle a yearly £100 on his heir for maintenance until he came of age. Two sons, indeed, were dispatched to the college at Kilkenny, and one of them subsequently was returned to the Irish parliament. This branch of the Herberts, both by pedigree and avocation, could be regarded as typical of the élite of Protestant Ireland. Judging by his manner of life, with a 'butler' and an account with a wine merchant, Parson Herbert did not rely solely on his clerical stipend. His parsonage was not sparsely furnished, but, on the terse documentation from the auction, had not surrendered to the latest crazes of Dublin and London.[167]

The ways of life of the clergy shaded into the refinement of the gentry. Professionals differed as to how close to this sort of amplitude they approached. Dr John McKeogh, perhaps a Catholic, lived in the diocese of Killaloe. Evidence of his calling – that of a country practitioner – came from his horses, a bookcase with some books and an alarming 'oak chest for anatomy'. Signs of the hospitality that he dispensed appeared in a horn snuff box, wine glasses, two punchbowls, knives, forks and teapot. Pewter still predominated, but he had built up a modest store of silver before he died in 1751.[168] John Bentley operated as an apothecary in Cork. As such he stocked a daunting selection of drugs, herbs and elixirs. Panaceas, prophylactics and placebos were sought by all, but obviously the well-to-do found it easiest to give full rein to their quest for health. Bentley owned books, 'dispensaries' and 'pharmacopeias', from which he could concoct his cures. Vital to the mystique which surrounded his calling were the 'old books', which the appraisers spotted. Bentley's goods, auctioned in 1760, suggested physical ease. He possessed in abundance the essentials for tea- and coffee-drinking and other types of hospitality. Patterned either with snakes or dragons, his porcelain again may have been the exotic prototypes from the east or the equally vivid copies now flooding into Irish ports from English and European factories. Like most outside the plutocracy, Bentley had pewter for everyday use (sixty-seven pounds of it). But he did not lack silver. If his two silver watches are also included (each sold for £3 15s.), then about 11.5 per cent of the value of his effects lay in the silverwares. His rooms were notable for their looking-glasses and chimney-pieces, and may have been papered. But the sums for which the chimney-pieces were sold – 3s. 6d. and 5s. – suggested modesty, akin to that of Dublin lodgings rather than to the splendour of the marble ordered by the country squires. Bentley's best tables were made of mahogany. Any caller would have noticed numerous pictures. 'The character of King William', selling for 1s. 7½d., was probably an engraving. Forty-three more were lotted in large bundles, and sold for smallish sums (ten shillings, ten shillings and four shillings). They too can be presumed to have been prints. Auctioned separately was a 'landscape'. On its own, it fetched three shillings. Inexpensive when new, these images were resold cheaply and thus could add interest to the houses of even the middling kind.

Bentley the apothecary exemplified the multifarious occupations in the larger towns. The custom of curates, mariners, the cabinet makers, a limner and respectable spinsters and widows enriched him. But how exactly his house was arranged, whether separate spaces were consecrated to work and domesticity, is impossible to know. Bentley's house, as with many others in towns, was divided into his own quarters and rooms rented to two lodgers. Around the city, Bentley owned no fewer than forty-seven houses. These, too, he leased. The yearly rents amounted to £218. This income assured him, even without his professional earnings, of a competence comparable to that of lowlier squires and decently circumstanced clerics. It allowed him to surround himself with material trappings, but in settings that may still have been cramped and combining multiple functions.[169] It can safely be assumed that although Bentley and his two lodgers lived in the same premises in the centre of Cork, he had more possessions and more space in which to display them than did his tenants.

Health, which Bentley promised to preserve or restore, was sought by all. Those – professionals and traders – who catered to this need, especially in towns, could flourish. In the seventeenth century, and perhaps in the next, it enabled Catholics to live in comfort.[170] Other services also enriched suppliers, and so allowed them to live stylishly. Deportment was widely regarded as a route to physical well-being and (some contended) to moral health. Equally, a correct carriage commanded entry into polite society. A course of instruction could cost what a labourer earned over a year. In George II's Cork, Lawrence Delamain met this demand.[171] His success as a teacher of dancing enabled him to live well in the city and be accounted a gentleman. His refined style could be justified as essential to woo clients. He taught in his own house close to the Church of Ireland cathedral of St Finbarre. Delamain reassured exigent customers by creating a setting which resembled (or surpassed) their own homes in the city and county. An arbiter of true refinement, he needed the right stage. In the Delamain house, most money was spent on the front and back parlours. The former contained a mahogany dining table, a marble table, a card table, chairs with leather seats, and brass fittings for wall lights. More of the same were found in the back room. This, in the configuration common to many town houses, was equipped for refreshments. Tea caddy and bread basket were openly displayed; enclosed in 'the buffet' was a mass of silver, glass and china. The appropriate look was also enshrined in seventeen glazed prints on the walls. Here, in a house which doubled as business premises, it makes sense to distinguish between public and domestic spaces. Whether pupils penetrated into the dining room, or whether this was reserved for other types of visitor, is unsure. The absence of the dining table (instead it was in the front parlour) may mean that this room, cleared of clutter, was where the neophytes danced. Again, the dining room was contrived to impress, mainly through another twenty-six glazed prints. There, no doubt in place of honour, was Mrs Delamain's portrait. Mrs Delamain had a gold watch; her husband, the customary silver. More prints decorated the upstairs bedrooms. No more than Bentley the apothecary did Delamain support himself exclusively by his trade. He, too, was a *rentier*. His portfolio of local properties yielded a notional £125 p.a. What proportion of his annual revenues this formed is difficult to ascertain. At his death he was owed £136 14s. 7½d. by ninety-two pupils. Accounts were normally tendered quarterly, but not always paid promptly: £136 may not have been his income for an average quarter of the year.[172]

## VII

Servicing the well-to-do enriched some lawyers, doctors, agents, merchants and craftsmen. Capable of creating the demand that they then satisfied, it is often assumed that their own lives lacked refinement. In so far as they used their riches, it was to escape from the constricted and uncouth urban environment and to ape their betters, found traditionally among the landed. Few grew rich solely from servicing landowners. Nor is it always obvious that the ambition of all who had done well in the towns was to set up as country squires. Furthermore, the modes of housing, diet, dress and furnishing favoured by the town-dwellers were not invariably feeble copies of life in the country house. The inhabitants of towns, specially the ports, were ideally situated to learn and practise the latest fashions. Towns were designed as havens of urbanity. In late-seventeenth- and eighteenth-century Ireland, they were uniquely situated first to receive and then to spread the attitudes and accessories of gentility.

In analysing the way in which urban traders and notables lived, often the physical boundary between manufacture and trading on the one hand and the domestic on the other is blurred, if not imperceptible. Merchants in Restoration Ireland, both in Dublin and outports like Cork, Kinsale and Youghal, possessed numerous articles that would grace the seats of the important. Whether they were merely the stock in trade or the household furnishings of the owners cannot now be decided. Just as the deliberately polite were differentiating themselves through the ways in which their houses were organized and furnished, so in the content, service and even times of meals they also varied from the practice of the labouring orders. The growing availability of goods, and especially the proliferation of cheaper editions of the rare, undermined any attempt to limit access to material delights. What aimed to impress could also intimidate. As interiors became more crowded with objects, so life in them presented worse hazards. The proliferation of silver, china and furniture posed conundrums for those unversed in their uses. But their proper employment could be learnt, as could the right responses to the images on the walls or the music performed. Goods could, but did not invariably, mark off the wealthy from the modest and poor. In the right hands, they separated the truly genteel or virtuous from the rich but boorish. A vulgar parade of goods did not deceive the discerning.[173]

Despite the readier availability of more diversified artefacts, often in cheapened versions, the provinces sometimes lagged behind Dublin. In 1755, the impending visit of the lord-lieutenant to Youghal uncovered the lack of a suitable coffee-pot in the town. Since, from the 1690s, if not earlier, it had been possible to buy such an object in Cork, it was probably a silver pot rather than the homely tin or pewter that was wanted.[174] Nearly a century earlier, traders in Munster ports, such as Samuel Hayman and William Hovell, handled an increasing variety of imports and local commodities. The inventory of the Waterford merchant Skiddy showed that – even before 1641 – the successful supplier kept some of the novelties which he handled to adorn his own home. The same was true of Hayman at Youghal or David Johnston in Dublin during the 1670s. The retailers, keen to stimulate demand among their customers, developed a powerful feel for fashion.[175]

In Hayman's house at Youghal, his pewter outweighed silver. But his 127 ounces of silver surpassed the pewter in value. Indeed, among the household goods it even outstripped his stock of linen. Hayman kept gold coin to the value of £40 and silver worth £200 in his desk. More clearly, the Turkey-work of chair seats and covers, together with colourful table-carpets, signalled opulence.[176] In succeeding generations, the Haymans, strongly linked with western England, adopted other cultural idioms. Literature and music interested them.[177] Hovell, a near contemporary of Hayman in Cork city, kept for himself some of the commodities in which he traded. Hovell and his wife ensured that their household linen was of the best. An income estimated at £320 in 1689 put Hovell on a par with the middling gentry. He adopted some of their habits, even to the extent of hunting.[178] How ambivalently wealthy merchants regarded the ways of their landed clients was indicated by Daniel Mussenden in George II's Belfast. Mussenden was the leading merchant of the port. He retained his Presbyterian affiliations, which may have served as a brake on his inclinations to consumerism. He was scornful of a son and heir eager to enter the gentry of the county. The father also witheringly exposed some of the failings of the locally important at moments of political and economic crisis. Mussenden continued to direct his business and to live over the shop. But he was not immune from the pressures to diversify. Having bought a country estate – at Larchfield in County Down – he relished its embellishment. He purchased coach, silver, furniture from northern England and Dublin, and stone urns from the English west country with which to adorn the *cour d'honneur*.[179]

Religious beliefs may have curbed Mussenden's wholehearted exploitation of what his money might buy. Among dissenters the wish to pass as civil and respectable sometimes set up a tension with scriptural injunctions towards asceticism. Another from Ulster, John Black, sent money to a son and daughter-in-law, on condition that they bought 'useful and not vain-glorying furniture in their houses'.[180] Rare evidence about the possessions of country-dwellers is distorted not just because those whose goods justified the compiling of an inventory for probate were a minority within the population. In 1749, *The Reformer* starkly depicted the material privations of the majority of the population. 'A pot, a stool, a few wooden vessels and a broken bottle' were alleged to be their sole furnishings.[181] The sparseness of material life is graphically conveyed by the records of the effects left by members of the Quaker meeting of Ballyhagan in County Armagh.[182] Pared to the core, these domestic settings in their simplicity reflected a conscious choice as well as straitened lives. It also told of differences in expectations of and opportunities for display in the countryside. Nevertheless, even among the Ulster Friends, just as wealth and standing varied, so too did possessions. William Richardson, 'farmer', of Loughall in County Armagh, the most prosperous among a sample of fewer than a score, had moveable effects valued at £150 in 1716. They included livestock and equipment for making linen. His embrace of changing standards is suggested by the designation of a 'parlour' rather than the 'low' or 'back' rooms more often mentioned in his neighbours' homes.[183] Similarly, his ready money and wearing apparel were valued at £20; most others from the meeting had their clothing appraised at £3 or less. Despite the pretension of Richardson's house, spaces were not yet reserved for single functions. The parlour still contained the most valuable piece of furniture – a bed. Also, there were a large oval table and a clock, although the latter was 'much out of order'. Closest to Richardson in means was John Brownloe of Tullymore (County Armagh). In 1724, his goods were valued at £110. The interior of his dwelling accommodated staircase, where a clock stood, parlour, children's room and 'blue room'.[184]

Beds and chairs, together with the implements of spinning, weaving, cooking, brewing, cheesemaking and husbandry were ubiquitous. Beds differed in value and quality, the humblest – of 'chaff' or straw – reserved for the servants or 'lads'.[185] Seating, too, used a hierarchy of materials. Richardson owned both oak and rushed chairs. In 1735, appraisers distinguished between half a dozen 'fine' oak chairs and half a dozen 'coarser', as well as six of rush.[186] Timepieces were as yet rare. Richardson possessed a second-hand watch in addition to the apparently defunct clock. Uniquely in the group, Robert Greer from County Tyrone owned a silver watch. Greer in 1730, with a bleachyard, seems to have been in a more substantial way of business than most neighbouring Quakers. He alone had accumulated silver cutlery rather than the pewter, brass and treen found in the other households. In this, he might be felt to disregard the injunctions against ostentation and to be adopting the worldly ways of the city.[187] Value, intrinsic and associational, was attached to objects. Jacob Pearson in 1698 bequeathed to each of his daughters one bed and a pewter dish perhaps because he had little else to give. John Anderson, whose substance was valued at £37 14s. 6d., willed to his wife not only the conjugal bed in which he was lying and dying, but an 'ark' [meal bin] and 'a chest which formerly was hers'.[188] These Quakers, despite their modest circumstances, owned and esteemed books. Through them knowledge of their characteristic beliefs and of their denominational history was increased.[189] In contrast, three items already important to the genteel in metropolitan locations – knives and forks (in addition to the common spoons), drinking glasses and earthenware – were seldom noticed among the Armagh Quakers. Sometimes, the generalized descriptions, of (for example) 'trenchers', may have hidden these articles. John Scott of Kilmore (County Armagh) was unusual in having in 1729 nine 'earthen' dishes, together with a large pile of trenchers. It is possible that he ran some sort of public house.[190]

In a group enjoined to restraint in worldly goods, differences nevertheless developed. The records of Quaker possessions show the more general trend for the traders in towns, and especially in Dublin, to own more than their equivalents in the countryside. In the provinces, craftsmen and shopkeepers proliferated. At Nenagh, Birr and Edenderry in the 1720s, or in Ulster later in the century, traders remained general merchants not specialists. Their stocks rapidly diversified, but it could never satisfy the households of the well-to-do, who still repaired to Dublin and beyond.[191] There, specialists – both artificers and sellers – multiplied. Signs of the dominance of Dublin wholesalers and retailers included the business of Alderman William Stowell. When Stowell died in 1701, more than 500 clients had accounts with his well-stocked ironmongery. Stowell imported wares from England and Holland, as well as selling local manufactures.[192] In a similar way of business and of eminence comparable to Stowell were John and Daniel Molyneux.[193] On Cork Hill, near Dublin Castle, a pedestrian in 1711 would pass several periwig-makers, two toyshops, milliners, gunsmiths, a woollen draper, makers of pattens, shoes and razors, a brasier, a pewterer and a shop which vended gold and silver lace.[194] Advertisements emphasized the range and smartness of what they stocked. By the 1730s, the columns of the Dublin newspapers were filled with tempting notices of goods on sale in the capital.

Traders in Dublin adopted some of the possessions which they made and sold to others. David Johnston during Charles II's reign, illustrates this participation by those outside the landed orders in the consumerism. Johnston, a freeman of the city, imported goods. At the same time, he dealt in any country commodities which offered a profit. He sold to the titled. He himself owned a formidable battery of pewter, brass, treen, iron and earthenware, much of it for a lavishly appointed kitchen. Another component in his valuables was his linen, to which, in common with both country gentlemen and careful housewives, he attached great importance. Johnston's substance was also tied up in silver. He prized two 'Venus' glasses. Possibly these were *façon de venise*, in the Venetian style, rather than decorated with figures of Venus.[195] Johnston's willingness to sink some part of his assets in material comforts was repeated by two of his contemporaries in Dublin. George Craford was described as a gun-smith. In addition, he traded in cloth. He owned several properties in the capital. He also acquired showy silver tankards and cups. Otherwise, when his property was appraised in 1690, the bulk of his worth – £315 3s. 2¼d. – was in gold and silver coin. The household goods were valued at a lowly £24 1s. 10d.[196] A similar, although hazier, picture comes from the will of Craford's neighbour, John Barlow. A bricklayer, Barlow dabbled in other enterprises. Profiting from the growth of Dublin since the 1650s, he also accumulated silver.[197]

By the early eighteenth century, more beams, although feeble and flickering, can be shone into Dublin dwellings. John Pearson, a weaver, living in Francis Street in the Liberties, was in a sufficient way of trade to keep an apprentice. Pearson employed others to weave for him, probably expensive broadcloths, and may have imported other textiles. His living quarters were relatively modest: parlour, kitchen, chamber and cellar. The weaving seems to have been done elsewhere: in the garret of a house owned by his brother-in-law. In value, the furnishings constituted only a small amount of his substance, most of which was tied up in his stock and equipment. Pearson was, moreover, a Quaker, and so deliberately moderated his surroundings.[198]

By the end of the seventeenth century, the Irish Quakers were dismayed by the zest with which some of the Friends were running after the consumerism of the times. Injunctions against elaborate carved furniture, highly decorated interiors and ornate dress were often repeated.[199] In general, the commands seem to have deterred Quakers from hanging pictures on their walls, but they did not prevent the use of costly and imported woods or the accumulation of silver and decorative ceramics. Pearson's effects implied solidity but hardly austerity. His tables and chairs were fashioned from oak. Pewter, brass and wood were used for cooking and eating. Nearby, another Quaker, John North, a ribbon weaver, lived in much the same manner. The total valuation of his estate – at £576 13s. 4¼d. – was about £100 lower than Pearson's. In so far as a difference in character can be detected, North's was the more elaborately furnished house. He possessed numerous cane chairs, several looking-glasses, an escritoire, a clock in an oak case and, perhaps most revealingly, not just fifty-seven pounds of pewter but another fifty-seven ounces of silver and a silver watch. A third member of the aristocracy of textile workers and of the well-to-do Dublin Friends was the clothier Joseph Deane. His trade was conducted from a shop fronting the street. Otherwise his family divided its time between a well-appointed kitchen and 'the street room upstairs', which served as the main bedroom. Others slept in the garrets above. Despite the somewhat rudimentary demarcations of spaces, with the world of work barely separated from conjugal life, Deane exuded substance. Like North, he owned clock, watch, punchbowl, pewter and silver.

The chimney-piece in Deane's upstairs chamber was valued at twelve shillings. The marble chimney-pieces ordered in Dublin and sent down to Edgeworthstown and Monivea or across to Squire Price in Flintshire cost anything from £3 10s. to £5. Evidently the likes of Deane went for the cheaper version: simpler and fashioned from less costly materials than Kilkenny or imported marble. Even so, rather than emphasizing how palely this fixture resembled its equivalent in the rooms of the grand, it is more notable that a clothier should adopt, albeit at cut-price, this attribute. It denoted civility, if not gentility. A marble 'hearth-stone' also featured among the ornaments of the larger parlour in the house of an eighteenth-century dissenting pastor in Cork city.[200] Fixed hearths and properly built chimneys had long been interpreted in Ireland as a badge of difference between native Irish and the anglicized. In Deane's kitchen, a second feature announced a practice that can be found in numerous houses with an increasing volume of wares. An alcove shelved the earthenware. Maybe fitted with doors, it protected these precious articles; or, if the doors were left open or had never been affixed, the crockery pleased the eye with its colours and patterns. In County Cork, the earthenware of Mrs Peard was visible so as to please her visitors.[201]

In the Dublin of the 1720s and 1730s, curriers, bricklayers, cordwainers and tallow-chandlers lived with comforts akin to those of the quality rather than the proletariat. Housing and contents were ways in which the respectable and genteel lifted themselves above neighbours and employees. If imitation of acknowledged social betters sometimes explained the habits, other considerations also came into play. The wishes of spouse and children seem often to have prompted extra purchases. Also, as has been argued, traders in the ports were ideally placed to observe and even set fashions. Nicholas Carter, who died in 1733, was another bricklayer, and as such active in the expansion of Dublin. In his own quarters, he was surrounded by mainly oak furniture, not the showier walnut or mahogany. His oak bedstead, standing in the street room, was hung with brown serge curtains. This drabness was remote from the sheen of the damask and moreen preferred by the modish. Yet, Carter sank some of his wealth into improving how he lived. A 'new house parlour' was tacked onto his old premises. Here, among the sober oak, was a walnut desk. Furthermore, in the dining room – he was elevated enough to have a separate dining room – was a large oval table, also of walnut. He owned silver. In a modest way, Carter had been implicated in property development. When he died, he was engaged in constructing two houses on College Green. In these projects he had collaborated with grander figures, such as Sir William Fownes, Dr Marmaduke Coghill and Thomas Hewlett (perhaps the same who had advised Malone on his Westmeath house). Carter, conversing with these setters of style, might be assumed to have picked up their outlook. Conventional interpretation would have it that the cultivated like Coghill and Fownes turned to the likes of Carter for nothing except artisanal skills. For their part, the craftsmen learnt polite taste from their betters. In actuality, greater reciprocity may have marked the dealings of the self-appointed arbiters of taste, such as Coghill, with the craftworkers. Master craftsmen, insisting on what was practicable but keen to demonstrate their virtuosity, helped to determine what was erected. In this, they could display a discriminating fancy or taste, improved by handling imports, seeing engravings and pattern books and by themselves travelling.[202]

Joseph Gill, on first arriving in Ireland from the north of England, worked in the construction industry. His master was Benjamin Crawley, who subsequently oversaw Flower's Castle Durrow. In time, Gill quit building and set up as something akin to a builder's provider, with premises in Dublin. Although active in the Quaker movement, he amassed artefacts. Since he dealt in a wide variety of timber, he was beguiled into using the exotic – walnut, olive and even cedar – for his own furniture. A rare item of 'Irish oak' was also identified in his rooms after he died in 1741. Fine porcelain for tea, coffee and chocolate, pewter and silver were also bought. Gill, knowledgeable about timbers and their values, was careful in what he left to whom. To his wife went his horse chaise, a silver cup and his own 'walnut tree desk'. For his son, William Gill, were reserved the 'largest oval dining table standing in the lobby' and 'my large oak desk with drawers'.[203] The exactness of the descriptions, repeated in the instructions about the legacies of silver, may have been no more than a precaution to prevent disputes or mistakes. It could also argue a familiarity with these objects, used and seen daily in enclosed and intimate settings. They were capable of giving pleasure, and were then handed down to others in the hope that they would continue to do so. Affection may have arisen for no other reason than that artefacts embodied wealth. Silver could be converted into cash most easily. Pewter also had a resale value. Wooden furniture, china, indeed all the bric a brac and lumber cluttering rooms, were saleable through auctions and second-hand dealers. Gill, like others, reserved some pieces from a future executors' sale. By doing so, he invested them with a value which was as much sentimental, associational and even aesthetic as ruthlessly fiscal.

Gill, a stalwart of the Dublin Quakers, did not blatantly break the group's ban on superfluities. However, in common with prosperous contemporaries outside the community of Friends, he treated what others might dismiss as 'neednots' as essentials. His walls were apparently bare, save for modest mirrors and a barometer or 'weather glass'. Three maps and three prints did not too strikingly transgress. Maps were to be found in other Quaker homes. Those in the cordwainer Jonathan Fletcher's Meath Street home, of Ireland and Portobello (the latter also occurred in the 1750 Antrim inventory), were of a piece with an interior crammed with mahogany, walnut, 'fashionable' rush chairs, a clock valued at five guineas and his watch worth an estimated £5 14s. Fletcher owned two porcelain tea sets, decanters, a dozen ivory-handled knives and forks and a silver salver worth £3 3s. 2d.[204] The examples of Fletcher and Gill warn that a cryptic description such as 'cordwainer' could mask a man who kept his household in a comfort and fashion unknown to some who were accorded the styles of 'gentleman' or 'gentlewoman'. But how many cordwainers or bricklayers, even in Dublin, could maintain the style of a Fletcher or Carter must be questioned.

The congregation of a single parish or one Quaker meeting included people of discrepant circumstances. Mary Thackeray, an illiterate widow, belonged to the same community as Gill and Fletcher. She had a little to bequeath. Accordingly, in 1727, her son, Abner Thackeray, received her bed with its furniture, a chest of drawers, a looking-glass, an oak table and the oak case for a close stool. The daughter, Ruth Thackeray, had to be satisfied with her mother's smoothing iron, its heaters and box, together with 'my best green say apron'. The widow's woollen clothes went to two women, probably her granddaughters. Mrs Thackeray may have been left in the same condition as many widows, with the use and furnishings of a single chamber in the former matrimonial home. This at least gave her something. Another widow in her Quaker community, Mary Kelly, of Marrowbone Lane, was possessed at her death in 1731 of household goods valued at £26 2s. 11¼d. However, her executors concluded that, 'her wearing apparel being but of very small value', it could be bestowed on poor children. Perhaps Mrs Kelly had come down in the world. Her house was ample, with nine taxable hearths. She may have filled it with lodgers, in which case most were heavily in arrear with their rents.[205] A third widow, Smith, not a Quaker, lived in a house called the 'Hen Bin' in Dublin's Turnpike Alley until 1708. There she seems to have had the use of two rooms, in which her most solid possessions were a press bed and a chest.[206]

Meagre, too, was what John Brookes, a 'gentleman' of Mallow, left to his daughter in 1721. In addition to an annual £4, she was to have two new milking cows, a 'case' or chest of drawers, a looking-glass and one silver spoon.[207] Equal modesty was evident in the last dispositions of a Mallow widow. She had been a shopkeeper, who eked out her business by letting rooms to a wig-maker. She bequeathed to her daughter all her shop goods, the beds and bedding. There were also six pewter plates and three pewter dishes, but no silver. The only precious metal at her disposal was her wedding ring. This too would pass to the daughter or, if she preferred, £1 in lieu.[208] Widows and single women often struggled to maintain a household of their own. The lucky were properly provided for in the wills of parents, siblings or spouses. Frequently, they found it troublesome to secure that to which they were legally entitled. They appealed to the charitable. The unassuming could subsist on £5 to £10 annually. But such an income bought only a room or two, and few possessions.[209] At this level, access to the entrancing worlds of goods was restricted or vicarious. An incongruous object, a gift, bequest or theft, might even so enliven otherwise dreary interiors. A cheap engraving, a cracked piece of pottery or porcelain, a garish handkerchief or bright buttons delighted.

Throughout the seventeenth century, although the numbers of prosperous Catholics dwindled, some lived with the same appurtenances as their Protestant neighbours. The economic ratchet tightened, so that during the first half of the eighteenth century, few Catholics are recorded as owning objects thought to connote respectability and gentility.[210] Without substantial numbers of inventories, it is hazardous to compare the numbers and types of goods in seventeenth- and eighteenth-century Ireland with England or north America at the same time. Dublin and its hinterlands had more in common with London in population, wealth and proximity to sources of fashionable design than with (for example) Philadelphia, let alone Williamsburg. Indeed, in the Stuarts' and Hanoverians' kingdoms, the spending power of Dubliners was second only to that of Londoners. Beyond the populous capitals, resources were sparser. Critics suggested that Ireland contained too many, and inappropriate and imported, things, and not enough people. This view is not supported by all the evidence reviewed here. Nevertheless, it does alert us to the fact that the increasing variety and costs of artefacts alarmed the prudent and patriotic. Income and credit were the most obvious determinants of who bought what. Among those with money to spare, what then was accounted a necessity rather than a luxury varied, even when fashion decreed what was essential to the smart. Moreover, as has been suggested, it was possible to acquire prestigious articles at cut prices. Locally made copies, smuggling, theft, bequests, the second-hand and the auctions all brought the desirable and unusual into unexpected settings. In addition, choice was exercised. Whim and entreaties of friends and relations directed purchasers into acts that neither reason nor utility could justify. Delight needs to be remembered as a motive in modest, even more than in lavish, accumulations of material objects. Some rooms in Irish houses looked like their grandest counterparts in Britain thanks to these impulses; others resembled the spare interiors of the humble, whether in Britain or colonial north America.[211]

Chapter 4

# Goods

*I*

In 1712, the archbishop of Dublin, William King, planned to buy a set of silver plates. To this end, he consulted acquaintances – Lady Beresford and Major-General Richard Gorges – whose judgement he trusted. King needed the service for the expansive hospitality which he dispensed in Dublin. Guests were entertained at several tables, each of which had to be set with four, five or even nine silver dishes. The archbishop expressed himself happy to buy second-hand, and was prepared to pay up to £400. At first, he intended to make the purchase in London. However, having reflected on the price and the hazards of transporting the plate across the sea, he decided instead to direct his custom towards Dublin.[1] As in most matters, King had firm opinions about what he liked. Buying at a moment when patriotic feelings ran high against France, he derided the French style even in silver. He was content to follow the design of what he had seen on Gorges's table, 'only plain about the edges without furbelows'.[2] The fickleness of fashion, King supposed, would work to his advantage. He would pick up cheaply what had been discarded as old-fashioned. But he could not resist fulminating against 'the vanity [which] hath prevailed with many of the nobility of Great Britain, to fall into the French mode'.[3] Archbishop King became an increasingly strident champion of all things Irish, and, prefiguring other patriots, extended this attitude to goods. At the same time, King, aware of his public responsibilities as prelate and often a lord justice, cared about cutting the appropriate figure. Dishes arranged on the table rather than ranged on a buffet in themselves betokened the spread of French ideas about serving food.[4]

William King was a bachelor with an unusual sensitivity to locale and nation. Rich, he could purchase much that was beyond the means of even the country squire. Regularly in England – London, Bath, King's Weston – he observed changing fashions. Books formed his principal indulgence. His priorities hardly typified those of the cultivated in early-eighteenth-century Ireland. Yet his activities illustrate several themes important in the quickening consumerism of Protestant Ireland. Translated from the see of Derry to Dublin in 1703, he required greater show. This display spoke equally of public and private responsibilities. King also tried, more strenuously than most contemporaries, to balance a desire to buy Irish with an anxiety to adopt the correct modes. Once re-established in Dublin, the archbishop bought extensively in the city. Some articles were made in the kingdom; others had been imported. Mrs Viner varnished an escritoire and eighteen chairs; Gaskill supplied twenty chairs for the dining room; Elers provided a tea-table and tea-cistern. Mrs Scriven's bill for wooden furniture totalled £48.[5] Expensive, too, were the repeating clock from Tuton (£10) and one for the staircase at £6.[6] Rose sold him looking-glasses and sconces for £38. China came from Lisle; a case of new knives from Colman, whose principal skill was as an upholsterer. Sheriff, the joiner, made napkin presses, tables and two bedsteads. Sisson panelled some of the apartments, earning £40 for his services. Ward was paid £5 for 'plede' [plaid] for the window curtains of the dining room. More startling was the £100 spent with Smith for damask. Fabrics were also bought from Latouche. For new silver, the archbishop turned to his kinsman, David King. A sum of £110 was disbursed on a tea-kettle, sconces and other items.[7]

Archbishop King was an accurate gauge of what the fashionable should possess. Despite an incurable grumpiness, he relished the splendour of his position. His entertainments reflected novel commodities and ideas. By consulting friends, the archbishop reminded how the material setting of life not only catered to but was itself an element in refined sociability. As well as the massy silver, he purchased 'china dishes for the dessert': probably early imports from China. But for the finale of elaborate meals he also needed 'glass servers for the dessert'. Soon glass cruets were wanted. By 1721, jelly glasses were added.[8] Needs multiplied further, so that, by the middle of the century, other refined householders owned glasses for syllabub, sweetmeats and champagne, as well as the more familiar vessels for wine, ale, cider and water. In 1755, Squire Edgeworth acquired glass salvers (tazzae), on which to stand the glasses for dessert and a 'cut-orange glass', which often formed the centre of a display on the table.[9] Decanters, mugs, tumblers, some 'flowered', wine glasses and butter boats, all of glass, were among the effects of Boyle Travers, a squire in County Cork, by the middle of the eighteenth century.[10] How guests – or for that matter servants – reacted is not recorded. The seemingly endless complication of the accoutrements of sociability scattered more mines across already hazardous fields. Learning the correct use of, let alone cleaning, the utensils gave them a rather different meaning from that read into them by King or the other purchasers. Those, sometimes on the verge of starving, who broke or stole articles viewed the accessories of the grand in a mundane or mercenary way: as assets to be cashed in or unwonted complications. No doubt, some owners were chiefly interested in possessing what was widely known to have cost much. However, to conclude that this was the sole motive, of – for example – Archbishop King runs the risk of ignoring other, perhaps irrational, feelings. Without clear evidence, investigations of motives behind many acquisitions must remain inconclusive.

Three threads in the record of his acquisitions are worth disentangling: the activity of local producers; the increase in paintings and prints on walls; and the ownership of silver. Occasional references reveal that furniture was shipped into Ireland. Daniel Mussenden from Belfast exploited his commercial contacts in Liverpool to acquire Lancashire chairs for customers in Ulster and for himself. In 1755, his supplier disarmingly admitted 'that the man that made them and myself has quite forgot the pattern'. However, Mussenden was assured that the thirty-two low-backed and two high-backed Windsor chairs, shipped to Belfast, were 'the very newest fashion'.[11] James Coghill, brother of Marmaduke, and like him both a government functionary and discerning buyer, asked to have tables made after a model he had espied in Craven House in London.[12] It was both awkward and risky to ship articles across the Irish Sea. Sometimes, prototypes were imported so that the design could be reproduced in Ireland. Easier was the shipment of the costly woods which gave greater *éclat* to what was made in Ireland. Also, engravings, sketches and even recollections of objects allowed the speedy adoption and adaptation of what was in high regard elsewhere. Customers, on the basis of what they had seen in the houses of neighbours in the countryside, in smarter Dublin or London establishments or on travels in continental Europe, might tell craftsmen exactly what they wanted.[13]

Veneer, colour and look appealed to the fancy of patrons. The rarity of the woods used and the virtuosity of the fashioning determined what owners paid for different pieces of furniture. In 1743, Nicholas Peacock paid a modest eight pence each for six chairs for his bachelor pad; once married, and procuring seat furniture from Limerick, he paid four shillings each for four chairs.[14] In another league were the twenty chairs supplied by Gaskill for Archbishop King's Dublin dining room. They cost £9. They had to be worthy of the plate and china, as well as the food itself, with which the prelate regaled his guests.[15] Also highly esteemed were the products of William Scriven, used by the archbishop. He had earlier been employed by Sir John Temple to make furniture for his new seat of Palmerston. There, Scriven's most important commission was a set of ten cane-bottomed chairs for the 'drawing-room', which cost Temple £11 10s. in 1683. They were valued so highly that Temple planned to ship them to the safety of England in 1688.[16] That Scriven was at the top of his trade is also indicated by his supplying Dublin Castle during the viceroyalty of the second duke of Ormonde.[17] A few years later Mrs Scriven sold Richard Fitzpatrick, soon to be Lord Gowran, a dozen cane chairs with upholstered squab seats to drop in, for £6 5s. 2d. For Fitzpatrick, as for others like King, there were cheaper alternatives. Twelve rush-bottom chairs were to be had from Joseph Twinbok for £2 18s. 1d.[18] When, in 1710, the Veseys were tricking out their recently acquired country seat at Abbey Leix, chairs were sought in Dublin. They were destined for what already was known smartly as 'the drawing room', rather than a homely 'parlour'.[19] Probably these were the dozen red chairs with rushed seats and another dozen black ones procured from Abraham Reyner. The first set cost a reasonable £1 6s.; the second, £1 4s. Much more expensive and so presumably grander were

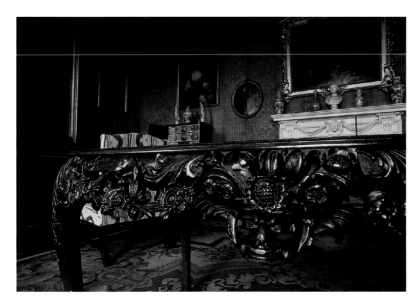

30. Irish mahogany centre table, *c.* 1750.

those bought by the Veseys from Edward Verdon in 1719. The dozen were priced at £5 8s. The suite was completed with two elbow chairs with caned seats, which cost £1 16s.[20]

It was easy enough to distinguish between different qualities of furnishings. In 1723, the effects of Richard Vigors at Burgage included a dozen elegant 'cane chairs', valued at £1 10s.; another dozen 'wainscoat' chairs, worth twelve shillings; and sixteen 'rush bottom chairs', also worth (in all) twelve shillings. The first were perhaps made of walnut; the second probably of oak or from a cheaper wood.[21] Similarly at the Percevals' Lohort, ten walnut 'Marlborough' chairs were noted in the 'withdrawing room' and another eight of walnut with 'French feet' in the principal bedchamber. These were easily distinguished from pieces made of mahogany, beech, yew and pine.[22] Customers discriminated between what might be fashioned on the estate or in the house and what should come from Dublin. Lord St George in Galway admitted that although his local carpenter could fashion seats, 'he could get none there that could make the frames'.[23] From County Down, Mrs Hill ordered a dozen cane-seated chairs, their backs to be 'as most fashionable'. She was uncertain whether to choose 'right Dutch' ones, which she preferred, or 'handsome cane chairs with cushions'. Having made up her mind, she then worried whether they 'may be done as neatly in the country as they ought'.[24] Earlier, her spouse, Michael Hill had enquired about the likely cost of a pair of walnut cabinets if made in the capital. He jibbed at the estimates. However, he did order a dozen cane-bottomed chairs in Dublin, the backs to be 'as most fashionable'.[25]

Provincials in Ireland usually looked to Dublin for what could not be found in the locality. Mussenden in mid-eighteenth-century County Down procured a set of chairs in Lancashire, but much for his residences came from Dublin sources.[26] So, too, did wooden furniture supplied to a trader in Donaghadee, some of which – to the value of £69 – was then shipped to a laird in the south-west of Scotland.[27] The usual pattern of the provinces being subordinated to the capital was occasionally reversed. Bishop Francis Hutchinson in Dublin for the meeting of parliament in 1733 had chairs brought down from County Down. This may have been to stop a gap in inadequately furnished lodgings.[28] As the bishop and his family settled in, they ordered seat furniture and other items from Dublin makers. But Hutchinson's tastes seemed reticent beside those of some of his colleagues and may explain his contentment with the country-made.[29]

Such was the demand within Ireland for wooden furniture that, by the 1720s, opportunist proprietors, like Thomas Watson Wentworth in the south-east and Oliver St George in the midlands, were having the timber from their woodlands converted into prefabricated components – splats, spindles, turned legs – for chairs.[30] In addition, operators within Ireland copied patterns introduced from elsewhere: Dublin craftsmen, what had been shipped in from overseas; provincials, models seen in Dublin.[31] In north Cork early in the eighteenth century, the Percevals' agent reported the arrival of an excellent craftsman from England.[32] At Castle Durrow in 1719, Morogh Og Boylan was paid for making a dozen chairs.[33] In 1741, another local contracted to make for £3, two dozen rush-bottomed chairs, 'to uphold staunch and firm in their joints, &c. for seven years to come, being well used'.[34] In the same house, John Coltsman, responsible for some architectural features, made shelves and a dresser in the kitchen.[35] By 1747, however, the household was importing chairs.[36] The Annesleys divided their time between a mansion in County Down and a Dublin house. While in Dublin in 1762 they bought from assorted suppliers. John Cavan made a desk and other 'articles of mahogany'. Margaret Shaw, in contrast, simply furnished a tallboy – for £4 2s. – and a small oak desk, at £1 8s. 6d. Again different grades of chair were wanted: a dozen with rush seats cost two shillings each; another dozen, for a son's rooms in Trinity College, were 4s. 6d. apiece.[37] A different strategy was revealed when the Annesleys exchanged a dining table with the prominent Dublin cabinet-maker, Kirchhoffer. It seems that some families only in Dublin seasonally but needing to entertain, hired large tables.[38]

## II

The availability of fashionable foreign woods, together with the latest patterns, allowed furniture makers, particularly in Dublin, to supply much of the local demand. Moreover, they developed their own stylistic quirks which appealed to the fancy of their customers.[39] Less successful in satisfying the home market were the manufacturers of ceramics. Pottery, other than utilitarian wares potted and fired in Irish kilns, had traditionally been imported. By the mid-seventeenth century, the new range and readier availability of ceramics, especially from the orient, fuelled demand. Massive jars, and gaudily patterned and glazed pots, gave magnificence to aristocratic interiors, such as the Ormondes' and Orrerys', in Restoration Ireland.[40] The use of these articles, whether for the service of meals or simply as ornament, spread. Delight as well as convention attracted the wife of a baronet from County Cork, Elizabeth Freke, to these novelties. Aghast that her house at Rathbarry had been denuded by an avaricious sister-in-law, she sought decorative as well as useful possessions. 'Bare walls' distressed Elizabeth Freke, so that she was delighted to be presented with 'a fine tortoiseshell cabinet' for the best chamber, 'with several pieces of fine china for it'. Soon 'five great jars for my best chamber' were added. In the event Elizabeth Freke furnished a house in Norfolk rather than the County Cork residence in her preferred idiom. Nevertheless, she and her family, moving often between Ireland and England, suggested the ease with which new fashions in décor could spread.[41]

Just as silver was frequently emblazoned with the armorials of the owner, so too were the fine wares from China. The custom of decorating with the crests and coats of arms of the westerners who had bespoken the wares spread quickly from continental Europe and Britain into Ireland. The first service to appear in Ireland, it has been suggested, was that of Sir John Stanley at Grangegorman, about 1720. An early retailer in Dublin, John Philip Elers, was connected both with the East India Company's agents in London and the Staffordshire pottery manufacturers, and may have been a route along which the unfamiliar travelled to Ireland.[42] By 1755 a set, 'all of burnished china with Lord Grandison's crest', was recorded at Dromana.[43]

Makers in western Europe and England quickly imitated what was marketed by the East India Company, often on cheaper faiences. The exotic, thanks to price and rarity, retained its cachet, and continued to sell at a premium, as the separate catalogue largely devoted to these wares in the Ingoldsbys' sale attested.[44] The earthenwares, nevertheless, met a growing demand. Once more, patriots lamented how this taste, coupled with that for numerous other imports, unbalanced Irish trade and impoverished the kingdom.[45] Opportunists, rather than Irish patriots, spotted the chance to cash in on a seemingly lucrative market. Entrepreneurs and technicians united to set up potteries. Towards the end of the 1690s, a venture began in Belfast. It exploited local clay and capital, drew in expertise from Britain and aimed explicitly at a domestic market but – clandestinely – at exporting, particularly to north America. Its success was limited, and seldom displaced British, continental or oriental dishes. Among those seeking the cheap, the Irish products could not compete against the imported.[46]

Others in Ireland hoped to succeed where the Belfast enterprise had failed. Efforts shifted to Dublin. The lord-lieutenant, Dorset, and the Dublin Society encouraged home industries. During the 1750s, Henry Delamain produced tin-glazed pottery. Said to sell 30 per cent cheaper than its imported competitors from Britain, the Low Countries and

31. Irish delft platter,
*c.* 1760.

France, it enjoyed a brief vogue. In 1749, Richard Edgeworth noted the purchase of a dozen 'Irish' earthenware plates. With a basket in which to transport them they cost 5s. 10d.[47] Edgeworth's subsequent purchases of pottery did not specify whether or not it was of local manufacture.[48] In 1758, a household in County Cavan bought 'a set' of Delamain ware, for £6 8s. 4d. Five years later, the well-travelled Balfours recorded their purchase of 'Delamain's ware'.[49] Within a decade Dublin wares had fallen prey to the lighter and more durable creamwares pioneered by Wedgwood in Staffordshire and soon on sale in Dublin.[50] Delamain was accused of unloading defective wares onto the unsuspecting.[51] Belief that demand existed tempted others in the provinces – at Doneraile, Rostrevor, Limerick and again in Belfast – to try this manufacture. All found business as precarious as Delamain had.[52]

The popularity of ceramics owed much to the growing elaboration of meals among the assertively polite. Both contents and service became more complicated, and necessitated more articles: utensils for tea and coffee, even in varying sizes. The truly elegant required different cups for chocolate and custards. Thus, a single household might possess four separate sets of teacups and saucers, two teapots of oriental porcelain and another three of coarser and probably European stoneware.[53] The price of the beverages, and of the equipment for their preparation and service, confined them to the prosperous and polite. One household in 1719 invested in the paraphernalia: tea-table, silver spoons, six cups for green tea, six cups and saucers for bohea tea, and the tea itself, which came in canisters. The

32. Irish delft plate from a service made by Delamain for the duke of Dorset, *c.* 1753.

investment amounted to more than £9.[54] In 1709, Jonathan Swift acquired six cups and then, in 1733, six blue-and-white cups with handles. It is impossible to know where they had been manufactured. Uncertainties about the availability of these elegant articles obliged one customer in Dublin to seek a replacement teapot from London.[55] The abundant porcelain among the Ingoldsbys' effects may indicate a household in which, with two daughters, female taste predominated. In the same circle, Molly Burton, returning from England to Ireland, carried with her four china dishes intended as a present for another woman.[56] Richard Edgeworth, shortly after his marriage, bought a tea-kettle for his wife. The acquisition might be regarded as necessary to the genteel society that she now inhabited as 'the new setting' of her diamond ring.[57] 'Tea-rooms' were mentioned in Dublin and country houses of the 1730s.[58] The rituals of the tea-table were not ones from which men were excluded or shrank. The cultivated bishop of Elphin, Simon Digby, deployed the necessary equipment in his country houses at Abbert and Lacken (both in Connacht).[59] During the 1740s, Dean Delany, an ardent promoter of civility, chattered to the lord-lieutenant over tea and coffee. Katherine Conolly, desirous of male company, had these beverages served every afternoon at 5 p.m.[60] On occasion, they coexisted with intoxicants. A visitor to Cootehill in 1717 reported that she and the company had supped heartily, then drank tea until two in the morning. The menfolk were inebriated and serenaded the ladies, one of whom concluded that 'the night closed with the breaking of windows and such like sprightly effects of tea and claret'.[61]

33. H. D. Hamilton, 'Tinker', 1760. The itinerant artificer mended a multiplicity of metal wares and, as in the case of Edgeworth's household, might repair damaged pieces of pottery and porcelain.

At a more modest level, Peacock in County Limerick, having married, invested in teapot and slop-bowl (costing in all one shilling) and then a fortnight later, bought a pound of tea.[62] In 1750, he spent 5s. 3d. on the tea and 1s. 8d. on the teacups.[63] Also in the provinces, the sale in 1734 of Benjamin Greene's possessions at Cappoquin in County Waterford included consignments of 'china' and 'delft'. The usefulness of tea-wares, tureens and soup plates was obvious. Less so was that of other items, such as a cracked china bowl or six small delft plates, all damaged. Despite these flaws, the bowl fetched a shilling, and the six plates attracted a bid of three shillings.[64] The faults may have been minor, not rendering the dishes useless. Furthermore, it was possible to repair pots with metal rivets inserted by tinkers. In the mid-eighteenth century, Squire Edgeworth had his punchbowl and other ceramics 'stuck' by Laurence Connor or 'hooped' by a visiting tinker, Francis Dignan.[65] It may be that the patterns and colours of these objects made them decorative enough to be desired, even if they could no longer be used. The second duchess of Ormonde's closet in Dublin Castle contained a large china dish which had been broken and mended.[66]

Ceramics, like textiles, bewitched through their look. Busy men confessed to a weakness.[67] Moses Leathes used the opportunities of military service in the Low Countries to supply others with the wares imported by the Dutch East India Company. He worried that because the slop bowl and sugar basin did not match the rest of a tea-set procured for his brother, William Leathes, 'they would not be liked'. Leathes, indeed, declared that he was unwilling 'for my own credit to send you what should not be esteemed and liked'.[68] An acquaintance in London procured from a 'china man', two dishes to complete a service for Lord Athenry. Chichester Fortescue scoured the shops of Paris on behalf of a friend in Ireland. Fortescue confessed that he 'never withstood so much temptation as in that shop'.[69] During the 1750s, one of the Smythes informed his kinsman at Barbavilla of what was available at the Dublin retailer. Two samples from the stock of Rouen faience were despatched to Westmeath. Neither matched what was already at Barbavilla, which their owner adjudged 'are much the prettiest of all'.[70] Bishop Synge of Elphin was equally concerned with questions of colour and design, not durability or even cost, when he wanted more Rouen ware. About to entertain his

34. H. D. Hamilton, 'Coarse Earthen Ware', 1760. Hamilton's drawing tells of the variety of useful wares, many of them made in Ireland rather than being imported, and how they were vended in the streets of Dublin.

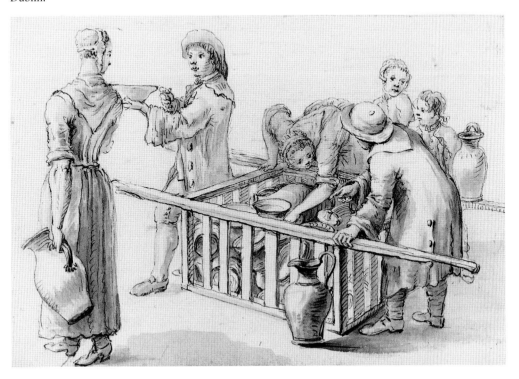

clergy at Elphin after the visitation, he bombarded his adolescent daughter in Dublin with instructions. The bishop was worried about the harlequin effect that the dishes might make, with some painted with blue borders and others with green and yellow. Told what was stocked in the Dublin shops, Synge responded grouchily, 'it is odds I shall not like them; and I'll shift with what I have'. He wanted 'strong and lively colours', even 'glaring'. The 'faintness' of a previous service had displeased him. He resigned himself at Elphin to having 'a motley show with blue dishes and other coloured plates'.[71] Especially in the 1740s and 1750s, the liking for Rouen ware exemplified the enthusiasm in Ireland for French style, to the despair of the Irish patriots.[72] In the end, only war against France stopped the trade.[73]

Producers struggled to please often idiosyncratic purchasers. Individually plates and dishes were of low value and bulky, but, as ballast on longer journeys, they were worth importing into Ireland.[74] High dues gave locals hopes that they might undercut overseas competitors. But the foreign never lost its savour. Between 1748 and 1750, utilitarian earthenwares valued at over £5,000 had been imported into Ireland.[75] The craving was sometimes satisfied opportunistically. Those close to the coast could equip themselves with eye-catching fabrics, ceramics or other novelties. In 1673, the arrival in Kinsale of a rich East India fleet was reported excitedly.[76] Wrecks were plundered and goods run ashore. Sometimes this salvage could be bought licitly. In Queen Anne's reign, a cargo of muslins, silks, bohea tea and china from a vessel wrecked off the Kerry coast was sold in Dublin.[77] More often what was removed from distressed ships caused controversy. In 1758, two East Indiamen put into Kinsale when one sprang a leak. From the distant north of County Cork, it was reported that 'most of the women are gone or have sent . . . to get great bargains of china and other fine neednots'. Fashionable emulation was blamed. 'A house is not thought to be furnished that has not a parcel of jars and images of china in it'.[78] In 1758, it was claimed that 'most of the running cash of the country' was carried off, and 'people of fashion' were left 'very low in cash' owing to regular purchases of contraband in Galway, Kinsale and Limerick.[79]

Porcelain, if manufactured outside Britain, was liable to pay duty, and so attracted the interest of the customs.[80] The officers regularly intervened, but smuggling continued.[81] At Kinsale in 1756, East Indiamen returning to England again attracted a great concourse by day and night. Guards were set to stop the cargo being pillaged, but they did not deter purchasers. In Cork as a result, it was noted, 'never such a sight of fine and coarse china ware' and 'fine, rich silks'.[82] Despite the seizures by customs officers, temptation was not to be resisted. Within a couple of months, the appearance of the familiar craft stimulated the same feverish demand. A lawyer in the town, Counsellor Verling, was accused of abetting the smugglers and impeding the revenue officers.[83] Widow Stammers in Bandon had china seized from her premises.[84] What was impounded was then sold by 'inch of candle' at auctions.[85] Whether bought legally or illegally, the lustrous delights bewitched buyers into spending more than they could afford. In Cork during 1756 it was concluded that 'a multitude of rich and poor laid out so much from one time to another that this city is merely drained out of cash'.[86] The port of Cork continued to supply the discerning. In 1769 it witnessed large auctions of 'ornamental china supposed to be sent here by the India Company'. In 1775, the arrival of an East Indiaman was announced. Its cargo, mostly silks and china, was thought to include few curiosities worthy of an aristo-crat's mansion. By then, the market seemed satiated, and the goods sold cheaply.[87]

Seizures were dispersed most regularly in Dublin. Already, in 1692, expensive trifles were auctioned publicly.[88] Even inland towns saw such sales. At Mullingar, they were skilfully timed to coincide with the assizes.[89] Specialists also aimed at this market. The Smythes from Bar-bavilla in Westmeath patronized 'Mrs Mary that keeps the earthenware shop' in Dublin.[90] In 1737, Richard Edgeworth bought china in Dublin from Mrs Elers. Her name, shared with one of the innovators in the Staffordshire potteries, suggests an early link between the English factories and Irish outlets. These would be strengthened in the 1750s, when at least three Eng-lish manufacturers had agencies in Dublin.[91] In 1742, Claude Duplain advertised fine earth-enwares, along with many other decorative novelties, which he had imported from France and was retailing from his Dublin shop. The Conollys dealt with him.[92] The following year, James White at 'the China shop' in Dublin's Fishamble Street, proclaimed the large quantities of ceramics which he had recently received from abroad. Among them were 'great variety of mandarins, china jars and bakers, with all kinds of china images and toys'. Not to be outdone, William Newton, also in Dublin, touted his 'large parcel of chinaware of the newest patterns'. In addition, he offered, 'several fine old pieces of china', reminding that already the antique as well as new was esteemed.[93] These advertisements revealed the ingenuity of suppliers in stimulating as well as meeting demand. In 1710, Lady Vesey at Abbey Leix had 'china work' sent on approval from Dublin, for 'her ladyship to pitch upon which [she] thinks fit'. The female retailer 'will take them again, if her ladyship does not like them'.[94]

The auction of Lady Brandon's property on St Stephen's Green, and the admiring gasps at the array of porcelain laid out for view, confirmed an enthusiasm for these gewgaws.[95] Sales in south Munster showed how the wares from the local ports had been dispersed into smart houses, and then, on the death of owners, passed to others. The Cork city apothe-cary Bentley had much 'china', including a basin described as 'dragon china' and a bowl referred to as 'snake china'. No, doubt these terms denoted the decoration: oriental in inspiration but not necessarily in the fabrication.[96] China for the Fermanagh mansion of Castlecoole was bought new at high prices and also at auction.[97] With the ready availabil-ity of a multiplicity of vivid artefacts, grandees struggled to show their pre-eminent taste. In 1755, Lord Grandison's seat at Dromana had ornaments such as white figures of a shep-herd and shepherdess, possibly from Bow or a German manufactory. The Grandisons, too, had an oriental armorial service, and the more everyday products of Rouen.[98] The lordly Taylors of Headfort set themselves apart in the ceramics stakes by buying for £107 a serv-ice of 'finest Saxon painted ware', presumably from Meissen or Dresden.[99] Early in the 1760s, the Annesleys used several suppliers in Dublin, one of whom – Mary Owen – sold them both 'flintware', probably imported porcelain, and the more utilitarian delft.[100] Acquisitions like the Taylors' dazzled through splendour and size. Ships captains and traders, especially if they dealt with the Baltic and North Sea ports, surreptitiously introduced smaller treasures into Ireland.[101]

Glass resembled ceramics in being a commodity of relatively low value, bulky, and awkward to ship into Ireland. It had clear utilitarian applications as glazing for windows of houses built in the recommended English styles. Settlers, such as Lord Cork, obliged to import window glass from England (often from Bristol), explored how local alternatives could be encouraged. Before 1641, several landowners, including Cork and Parsons at Birr, considered the possibilities which promised both profit to themselves and their tenants and a useful product.[102] Yet, a century later window glass was still procured from England or Holland.[103] At the same time, the manufacture of bottle and drinking glass began. The fanciful might contend, as with porcelain or pottery plates, that drink, like food, tasted better from elegant vessels. More clearly, glasses, even if not etched, painted or faceted, delighted guests and onlookers when they caught and refracted light. As a result, they became an element in display. By the 1670s, glassmakers were at work in Dublin. At first, they could hardly compete against the imports.[104] Wholesalers who, in the seventeenth century, deliberately appealed to aesthetic considerations, were disappointed. George Macartney in Belfast, eager to unload a batch of glasses, arranged to exhibit them in such a way as to entrance customers. The ploy failed.[105] The profits from a local glass industry were perhaps not as great as the proponents alleged: less even than from Irish potteries. However, it was a venture which again mesmerized patriots. In the same way that new types of furniture, silver and china were invented, so glass catered to different drinks and demands. The resultant glitter increased the dazzle of interiors. But the impact was achieved economically. The Bandon clergyman, McClelland, owned much glass, but in value it amounted to no more than 1 per cent of his effects. Special value attached to specific pieces, as to ceramic curiosities. At the Balfours' Dublin sale, a startlingly high price – nine shillings – was bid by Sir Laurence Parsons for a glass engraved with the inscription, 'To the Glorious Memory', commemorating William III.[106] However, this was an exception. Otherwise, only the imported Venetian or Venetian-style glass (*façon de venise*) was highly prized by its Irish owners, and then more commonly in the seventeenth than in the eighteenth century.[107]

## III

Many utensils fashioned from glass or china could also be made from silver. The last material was not only more durable, it better retained value. However, this very attribute made it prone to theft. Servants from whose safe-keeping silver vanished had their wages docked. In 1721 Sarah Kelly was, by some abstruse reckoning, made to pay a third part (five shillings) of the value of a spoon which she had lost.[108] Francis Kelly, a servant of Mrs Townley Balfour, was charged fifteen shillings for two spoons which disappeared while in his care.[109] In extreme cases, losses would be advertised in the newspapers and the thieves pursued. Archbishop King hoped to recover his stolen silver – and linen – in this way.[110] Edmund Walsh, convicted of stealing a silver spoon from a County Clare squire, was one of many sentenced to be transported.[111] In County Dublin, John Doyle was ordered to the American colonies for seven years, having removed, among other articles, four silver spoons valued at £1 3s. from Thomas Beaumont. Luke Gardiner, a Dublin plutocrat, was alleged to have lost a silver toothpick and a fork (valued at five shillings) to Catherine Stroud. Lord Kingsland, meanwhile, had been robbed of a silver spoon worth fifteen shillings. A spoon stolen from the Smythes of Barbavilla was reported to have turned up in the neighbouring county of Cavan. It was to be identified by the smith who made it, the engraver of its decoration being dead.[112] Engraving, especially with the crest and arms of the owner, assisted identification and recovery.[113] It also increased the show it made when displayed in buffets or on sideboards.

In County Dublin during the early 1740s, Robert Morehouse was relieved of a silver teaspoon said to be worth one shilling. Morehouse had also lost clothing. This was typical of recorded robberies in and around Dublin during the decade. Opportunist thieves were faced with much clothing and cloth, which although of lower value, were of more general use and therefore readily disposed.[114] Most daring of all among these thefts were those by Rose Madden (*alias* Singleton) and Elizabeth Murphy in the mid-1740s. The pair purloined silver from Dublin Castle. But the booty was merely part of a haul which included a looking-glass, pewter, bedding and clothing.[115] Indeed, of almost 100 separate thefts in the city of Dublin which came to court between 1742 and 1749, only seven involved silver or other precious metals.[116] Among household goods stolen, pewter and brass featured more often than silver: a preponderance which accurately reflected the materials in daily use.[117]

The County Limerick agent and farmer, Peacock, favoured wood and pewter for his household wares. In this, he resembled a hospitable 'old Irish gentleman' in the midlands, whose 'sideboard was not plate, but wood'.[118] Peacock recorded buying pewter spoons, as well as a knife and fork (of unspecified materials). At the local auctions, he also picked up pewter plates. These he subsequently exchanged in Limerick city for new ones.[119] Pewter, like silver, kept an intrinsic value, and could be refashioned to take account of altered tastes. Before marriage widened Peacock's horizons, only one piece of silver came his way. This was a covered cup presented to him by a grateful employer.[120] Such gifts had become a recognized way to thank employees or acquaintances.[121] Objects such as the cup given to Peacock, if displayed, impressed visitors and reminded of powerful connections. Their value went beyond its worth as bullion or scrap. For others, such presents had a more prosaic meaning. They could, when necessary, be converted into cash.[122] After Peacock was initiated into tea-drinking by his wife, he needed teaspoons. In 1748, he bought six in Limerick, paying the supplier – a general merchant not a silversmith – in instalments. Less than two years later, Peacock traded in the

35. Silver spoon, Cork, 1700. Spoons, of assorted sizes, were the commonest utensils to be fashioned from silver.

purchase.[123] Also in 1748, the christening of a son justified festivities, for which a punch ladle was purchased. The low price indicated that this was not of silver, but some base metal, pottery or even bone.[124]

Peacock's limited experience of silver reminded that it remained beyond the reach of most, even when they hankered after gentility. Yet, his modest home boasted a silver cup out of keeping with its surroundings. Its presence warned how silver entered houses by sundry routes – gifts, legacies or even pilfering – and was not always an accurate sign of income or status of the owner.[125] The silver teaspoons, which he returned to the Limerick retailer, denoted a politeness to which contemporaries sneaking into the gentry aspired. Their return suggested it was as yet a mode that could be followed or abandoned as occasion dictated. Gilbert Tarleton of Killeigh in King's County hovered between the status of gentleman and squire. He owned a dozen silver spoons. In 1739, he divided them between his two sons.[126] Another edging into gentility, Gilbert Kennedy, a Presbyterian minister at Tullylish in County Down, by 1745 had acquired a little silver. Six spoons were duly left to a son who had become a doctor.[127] John Brookes, 'a gentleman' of Mallow, bequeathed one silver spoon, together with two cows and a couple of articles of furniture to a daughter in 1721. Spoons were by far the most common utensils to be fashioned from silver. And among them, by the 1780s, the smallest – teaspoons – were the favourites. These preferences resembled those observed in Stuart England, where even the modest might own silver spoons. Ceramics were still preferred for the larger utensils like coffee-pots and teapots. Similarly the taste for eating off gold or silver plates rarely survived the availability of cheaper and more practical porcelain and pottery.[128]

Individuals and institutions gratified the useful with gifts of silver. In 1656, the incumbent lord deputy, Henry Cromwell, was to have a piece of plate from Dublin corporation to commemorate the baptism of his son.[129] In 1662, the municipality, listing with the prevailing wind, spent £350 on a gold cup and gold freedom box for the new viceroy, Ormond.[130] Meanwhile, in County Cork, the corporation of Youghal, anxious to enlist Lord Orrery's aid in forthcoming struggles, in 1661 presented him with 'a pair of fair silver candlesticks, a tankard and a dozen plates'.[131] Isolated gestures soon hardened into conventions. At Christmas in 1665, Lord Drogheda donated a large silver bowl, perhaps for punch, to the corporation of Drogheda.[132] In 1690, a Captain Ponel expressed his thanks to the town of Youghal, where he had been stationed during the recent war, by presenting its corporation with a silver punch-bowl. Holding three noggins, it was to be drained at the several feasts during the civic year.[133] A few years later, the Goldsmiths' Company of Dublin spent £10 on a piece of silver to acknowledge special services. In 1709, the Dublin Weavers' Company, in a quest to defend its privileges, rewarded the lord mayor of Dublin in the same way.[134] Joseph Damer moaned that he had served Christ's Hospital as its Irish agent without proper recompense for more than thirty years. Soon he was gratified with a handsome silver covered cup.[135] The normally par-simonious Lord Burlington ordered his Irish agent to spend £25 on a piece of silver to be presented to the wife of a local functionary.[136] The absentee Chief Remembrancer, Lord Palmerston, thanked his industrious subordinates by ordering gifts of silver for them.[137] In 1728, the trustees of the Linen Board rewarded Ruth Hillary for weaving a length of linen of 'extraordinary fineness', by presenting her with a piece of silver worth £5.[138] The corporation at Newry, delighted with the stimulus from the recently completed canal, spent twenty guineas on a punchbowl and silver ladle. These were presented in 1742 to Captain Gilbert who had managed the project.[139] Soon afterwards, the reformer and demagogue Charles Lucas was to receive either a gold signet ring or an engraved silver box from his own guild of barber sur-geons, for 'attempting to revive the ancient, most excellent constitution' of the city of Dublin.[140]

Freedom of corporations, conferred on perambulating grandees, topical heroes and local worthies, came in chased and wrought boxes: silver for most; gold for the exceptional.[141] Orders for these boxes made regular work for local craftsmen, as in Galway, Kilkenny and Kinsale, and so became another method through which civic pride could be expressed and benefits kept in the locality.[142] In 1684, when Sir Richard Kearney was granted the freedom of the Dublin Merchants' Company, it was recorded that this was the first time that it had been presented in a gold box.[143] John Brown, squire and agent at Rathkeale, so cherished the box which his great-grandfather had received from Limerick corporation that he decreed it should remain in the family in perpetuity. Corporations used silver regalia for their rituals. The most usual were the maces carried before the chief magistrate on public occasions. That for Dublin in 1663 cost £8 13s. 6d.[144] Insignia proliferated. Water bailiffs in coastal towns like Cork, Kinsale and Waterford received miniature silver replicas of oars to denote their offices.[145] Municipal corporations in investing their ceremonies with greater dignity followed where guilds had led. In 1674, the foremost guild of Dublin, the Merchants', commanded that its 'small plate' be converted into two large drinking cups, presumably for communal ritu-als. The Goldsmiths' Company bespoke two silver trumpets in 1701.[146] Six years later, the

Merchants' Guild had a leading Dublin silversmith, Alderman Thomas Bolton, fashion for it a monteith, which was valued at £60.[147]

Even greater was the use made of silver by the churches. Scripture and the canons of the church stipulated the use of precious metals for communion vessels. In seventeenth- and eighteenth-century Ireland it was not always practicable to obey. Poverty coupled with the clandestine nature of Catholic worship frustrated such arrangements. Nevertheless, the pious frequently gave communion plate to their churches. Accidents of survival, notably the institutional continuity of the churches, probably explain why silver made to accompany worship now forms the largest category of artefacts to survive from the seventeenth century.[148] Plate displayed on the altar, much of it engraved with the names of benefactors and their armorials, kept in remembrance the locally powerful.[149]

The place of precious metals in religious and civic rituals removed it from the everyday. The favoured might occasionally drink from silver cups and tankards, or be proceeded through the streets with the symbols of authority, just as their robes marked them as superior. However, the generality of the parishioners or freemen, on the regular occasions for commensality, were fobbed off with cheaper materials. Corporations, knowing the rate of theft and breakages, provided coarse wares for their feasts. At Kinsale, the forks wielded by the guests were of pewter.[150] These distinctions, with the more valuable and prestigious materials reserved for an élite, reproduced those in private houses. At Castle Durrow, for example, the Flowers stocked their kitchen with much pewter. It was used there in the preparation of food, and also by the servants. Some was bought in Dublin; much had been imported into Ireland, usually from England.[151]

By the eighteenth century, it may be that among the genteel, silver was ousting pewter, brass, tin or wood in the reception rooms. Before that metals other than silver contrived to make a brilliant figure. In 1673, the Youghal merchant Hayman owned 158 pounds of pewter as against 127 ounces of silver. He also possessed brass candlesticks and other utensils.[152] Hayman's contemporary, the Dublin trader Johnston, had pewter and brass in greater plenty than his precious hoard of silver.[153] The buttery of Bishop Thomas Hackett's house in County Down contained a few silver articles. But he was content with pewter for candlesticks, snuffers and plates. Among the pewter trenchers, it was possible to distinguish the 'fine' from the 'worse sort'.[154] Base metals did not vanish from grand establishments. When Lady Peyton's possessions in Dublin were listed early in the 1690s, pewter not silver abounded. The best was ornamented with her arms. The store included two 'rings': precursors presumably of the silver dish rings of the next century. Similarly, Archbishop King had his pewter engraved with his cipher.[155] In 1741, Squire Marsh's property included 90 pounds of English pewter and another 47 pounds of Irish.[156] Pewter vessels retained their value. They could be repaired or refashioned by pewterers and tinmen. Also, they were in demand at auctions.[157]

36. Kildare toilet service by David Guillaume, 1720–2. The sumptuous service, commissioned to celebrate the birth of an heir to the Kildares, came from one of the leading London makers.

Some anatomists of eighteenth-century Ireland rebuked its Protestant leaders for amassing silver.[158] In 1736, the unfailingly feline Orrery observed that Lord Kildare 'makes a much greater show of his plate than of his virtues'.[159] It is true that the Kildares had trumpeted re-entry into Irish Protestant society with commissions for grandiose silver services, as well as by building spectacularly in County Kildare and Dublin.[160] In the Dublin house of a Nugent, another aristocratic family, a 'sideboard of plate' in the back parlour was valued at £60: perhaps 30 per cent of the total worth of the Nugents' effects.[161] Lord Orrery's forbear, the first earl, had prized his silver.[162] Sometimes, these collections were ostentations. Yet, in the absence of other secure investments in Ireland, silver was a sensible purchase. Precious metalwork could be turned into cash. The return could disappoint, since the costs of fashioning would rarely be reimbursed, at least until the taste for the antique supplanted the craving for the new.[163] However, the slow development of banking in Ireland, together with recurrent bank failures before 1760, may have encouraged the wealthy in Ireland to prefer accumulations of silver longer than their counterparts in England.[164] In communities where coin was often scarce and confusingly varied in origins and value, silver constituted a currency. During the 1680s, the future Viscount Rosse twice pawned a silver watch to gain some ready cash.[165] Rosse's contemporary, Sir John Temple, invested some of his profits from the law and office in Charles II's Dublin in silver: it served him as currency when he was driven from the kingdom in 1688. Returned to England, he quickly raised £200 by trading in items.[166] Even more spectacular was the sale on behalf of Ormonde of unwanted silver to the leading Dublin silversmith in 1707. Ormonde received £277. He may have been shedding some of the magnificence that had surrounded him as lord-lieutenant, but he was also trying to reduce his ducal debts.[167] More modestly, an improvident widow, Jane Mussenden, raised money by pawning inherited silver in 1715.[168] Similarly, John Winslow secured an advance of £44 from his silver 'in pledge'.[169]

Rational choices go some way to explaining why the well-to-do accumulated silver. Production of silver within Ireland, measured by the weight assayed in Dublin, grew greatly. In 1696–7, 25,000 ounces had been submitted to the assay masters. Already, by 1708–9, the total had risen to 45,000 ounces. By the 1780s, it amounted to 84,200 ounces.[170] Massive and highly wrought pieces remained rare in comparison with the ubiquitous flatware used for eating meals and taking tea or coffee. Changing social and domestic habits may account for a shift away from heavy tankards and other drinking vessels to those consecrated to non-alcoholic drinks and convivial meals by the early eighteenth century.[171] The intrinsic value of the metal, combined with associations, necessitated care. Wary owners, such as Archbishop King, Bishop Synge and Squire Edgeworth, especially when away from home, stored their plate in the bank.[172] In the countryside, silver was secreted in hiding places.[173] Usually it was intended to be handled and seen. Stamped with the marks of the maker and place of manufacture, pieces could also be engraved to denote who owned it. These signs aided recognition if articles went astray and when they were bequeathed to legatees.

Some articles, arriving in a family as part of the dowry of a wife, left the house when she willed them to her particular friends or kindred. In 1628, Francis Aungier, Lord Longford, distinguished between what he had accumulated and what his bride had brought. A silver tankard which she had carried over from England, together with a silver cup presented to her by Lord Grandison, returned to her to be disposed of as she chose.[174] More than a century later, Elizabeth Parsons at Birr distributed much that she had brought with her on her marriage. All the plate decorated with a squirrel or with the arms of the St Georges, Lady Parsons's own family, would descend to Elizabeth Gore.[175] Thanks to inheritance, valuables could travel along the byways through collaterals of the family. Conventional enough was the bequest of plate by the widow Avis Cary of Redcastle in Donegal to her son. The silver had belonged to his father and grandfather. In 1710, Henry Hart of Muff in the same county intended all the silver marked with the Beresford arms for his wife.[176] Alderman Singleton, a rich worthy of Drogheda, designed all his plate for his widow, saving only that marked 'E. P.' which was to go to a son.[177] In like manner, Anne Trevor, having been married into two leading Irish Protestant dynasties, the Hills and Brodricks, distinguished carefully when bequeathing silver. To her grandson, Wills Hill, Lord Hillsborough, she left the silver, engraved with the Hills' armorials, which she had had before her second marriage. To the eldest grandson also went a silver basin and ewer emblazoned with her father Trevor's arms.[178]

Women could remember close friendships through legacies of silver, as of jewellery.[179] In 1716, Mary Pomeroy of Cork willed to her 'friend', Frances French, a pair of candlesticks with snuffers and the accompanying stand.[180] Jane Bulkeley in the Dublin of the 1720s attended meticulously to the disposal of her silver within her female circle.[181] The Knox heiress from Dungannon, Mary St George, left particular articles to kinswomen in Ireland. 'Sister Echlin' received a silver toilet set. Her companion, Mrs Jane Bowes, was given £200 in cash and 'my silver cup and cover with a viscount's coronet on it'. This was not part of the collection that Mrs St George and her husband had assembled but rather a legacy. Mrs St George's gold watch went to an Irish peeress, Lady Tyrawley; her jewels and diamonds to Miss Betty Knox, evidently a relation. Lady Tyrawley had already benefited from the generosity of the dowager Lady Blessington, who left her in addition to £100 a silver tea-kettle and lamp, silver warming-pan and other silver.[182] The rest of Mary St George's plate and furniture went to her cousin, Thomas Knox. If not immediately converted into cash, it, like the donor's corpse, had to be returned to Ireland to begin a new career there.[183] Later in the century, the redoubtable Lady Arbella Denny favoured other women with bibelots and silver.[184]

Another who devoted care to the distribution of her silver was one of the Conyngham sisters. Jane Conyngham, originally from Donegal, had married the pious functionary James Bonnell. But once widowed in 1699, she soon removed permanently to England. By the time she died in 1745, her collection probably consisted chiefly of pieces acquired in London. A particular prize was 'the wrought silver cup and cover', presented to her by the non-juror Robert Nelson. It was bequeathed to a kinsman, originally from Ireland, but long resident in London. However, the beneficiary was childless. Mrs Bonnell stipulated that the recipient, Ralph Smythe, 'would leave a charge that it may be preserved in the family'. In consequence it came to the Smythes in Westmeath where it long remained. Other items went directly to relations still in Ireland. Katherine Conolly was to have a silver chocolate pot (she was addicted to chocolate), a silver bell and a miniature of James Bonnell set in gold. To a second sister, Jane Bonnell willed a silver saucepan, which had been fashioned from a cup belonging to their father. The testator also decreed that this sister should in turn bequeath two salvers and the smallest of her three coffee-pots to her own daughter. Another woman in Ireland received two silver tea canisters and the middle-sized coffee-pot. Henry Lupton was to have a standish which he had himself given to Mrs Bonnell.[185] The requests, if implemented, warn of how quickly lines of descent were confused and how objects moved across the seas.

Bequests of silver, although welcomed as tokens of regard and for their monetary value, were not always treated as sacred. Early in the 1680s, the widow of the first Lord Orrery unsentimentally disposed of 3,700 ounces left to her by her husband. The limited market in Ireland then for silver made her opt to sell in England.[186] In 1741 Mrs Edgeworth inherited motley silver from an aunt. Much was taken promptly to Dublin silversmiths, who either engraved it with Mrs Edgeworth's own heraldic bearings or refashioned it into smarter and more useful wares.[187] Similar lack of sentiment was noted when Lord Barrymore expired in 1748. Much silver was carted away from Castleyons, the ancestral seat, in defiance of the expectation that it would 'be left as an heirloom'.[188]

Associations did often endear silver to its owners. The Dublin doctor Thomas Kingsbury treasured a pair of silver salt cellars because they were a gift from a squire in north Wales.[189] Other pieces reflected the preferences of purchasers. Archbishop King stipulated a plain style for his silver plates. Lady Crosbie cautioned her son in Dublin that his father, Sir Maurice Crosbie, would insist that a new pair of candlesticks match those already at Ardfert.[190] As well as aesthetics, patriotism came into play. King had considered buying in England, but on grounds of economy rather than anti-English feeling, turned to Dublin makers. Duties on imported plate were prohibitive. William Conolly, the future Speaker, was not inhibited by patriotic impulses from ordering silver from England in 1716.[191] Any sense that Irish work was inferior was contradicted by the speed and skill with which local smiths adopted the styles currently in vogue or invented their own distinctive designs. In 1755, diplomacy may have inclined the viceroy, Hartington, to order £274 of silver from Calderwood in Dublin.[192] But Hartington could be confident that the products would be of high quality and in high style. Earlier, in 1718, Thomas Medlycott, prospering in Dublin as a revenue commissioner but also a member of the Westminster parliament, decided to ship over from England his plate, 'most of it English made' and valued at £600. He was accustomed to treating guests, 'all 4 and 4', by removing one set of plates and substituting others for the next course. Once the silver had been unpacked, he had some melted down and refashioned, so turning 'some of his English plates into plates here'. The new wares were duly assayed with the Irish harp.[193] In contrast, other would-be dictators of taste in Dublin ordered their silver from the foremost English makers. Blayney Townley Balfour had an *épergne* from London. It weighed 141 ounces and cost £49 7s.[194] Early in the 1740s, George Wickes in London supplied Joseph Leeson with an '*épergne compleat*', as part of an order which set Leeson back £1,839.[195] A few years before, Bishop Robert Howard, in London on business, commissioned a finely chased waiter, a 'neat chased tureen' and a bread basket from London specialists.

## V

Men and women interested themselves equally in the look and fate of their silver. As with other possessions, it is usually difficult to ascertain how much was bought in Ireland, whether locally or in Dublin, and in England. Also, for those whose year was divided between the countryside and the capital, it is rarely clear what was kept where, or what was moved between the separate residences. The buying of the St Georges revealed the extent to which desiderata could be procured in either London or Dublin. Moreover, their commissions tell how taste was affected by seeing pieces belonging to others. Oliver St George avoided the lot of most younger sons, which he was, by marrying Mary Knox, the heiress of Thomas Knox from Dungannon in County Tyrone. In 1729, St George was thought to enjoy an annual income of £2,500.[196] He sat in the Irish House of Commons where, in 1720, he was an active promoter of the scheme for a national bank. But by the mid-1720s, he and his wife had elected to live primarily in London, with the result that first the Roscommon and then their Dublin house was put under wraps. Even before the St Georges turned themselves into absentees from Ireland, they had spent enjoyable periods in England. Shopping had been one pastime, and silver one of their favourite buys. During a London spree in 1716, the couple spent £234, mainly on clothes and textiles.[197] The St Georges had been familiar with London since 1703. Over the succeeding years, they bought silver from the leading craftsmen there. They patronized many of the most accomplished makers, especially the Huguenots who had flooded into the city: Aveline, Courtauld, Guillaume, Harache, Tanquaray, Platel.[198] Others from Ireland went to the same smiths. In 1708, the earl of Meath had secured a stunning wine cistern and fountain from Guillaume.[199]

So long as the St Georges divided their time between the two capitals, they spread their patronage. In Dublin, too, Huguenot craftsmen had settled, and some of them – Peter Gervais, David Rominieu and a mysterious Dutch goldsmith in Skinner Row – enjoyed the St Georges' custom.[200] Others such as John Phillips, also in Skinner Row, and the ubiquitous Thomas Bolton, were used.[201] The St Georges generally described what they wanted. Sometimes orders were based on what they had seen in the houses of their acquaintances. A bowl commissioned from Rominieu in Dublin was to match a silver teapot and to be 'in imitation of Lady Mountjoy's'.[202] In similar vein, Lady Vesey, wife of the future bishop of Ossory, commanded that old silver be recycled into a chafing dish 'such as Mrs. Pool had'. Others merely asked that articles be 'fashionable'.[203] The St Georges specified that a set of silver sconces bespoken from David Guillaume in London was to copy the pattern of Major Cadogan's.[204] The instructions troubled even the superlative Guillaume, and completion of the sconces was delayed.[205] Problems also arose when the patrons instructed the Dublin maker Gervais, whom they often employed, to make an *étui* and its contents after the pattern of Mrs St George's gold toothpick case. 'But he not being able to do it', St George had to have the order completed in London.[206] By the end of the 1720s, the St Georges had settled more or less permanently in London's Grosvenor Square. They interested themselves little in what Dublin could furnish. One of their last purchases, a colossal pair of ice-pails for £64 12s. 11d., was commanded from Guillaume.[207] Ice-pails told of raffish parties in the British metropolis. As yet these gross receptacles chilled wine, and were not *glacières* for frozen desserts. Only in 1758 did the acute O'Hara remark how ices had displaced custards at viceregal bashes in Dublin Castle. Crazes that gripped London, and the goods that catered to them, customarily took time to reach Dublin. While the smart in London were cooled by ices, their counterparts in Dublin still guzzled custards.[208]

St George was pilloried for spending no more than two months in Ireland whence his revenues came. His elder brother, Lord St George, criticized how the absentee squeezed his tenants in order to support his luxury. Such strictures suggest the husband decided how his wife's fortune should be spent. Moreover, outstanding bills from tradesmen and other creditors were addressed to Oliver St George. This encouraged an impression that he, not his wife, was the profligate. Other evidence hints that both enjoyed spending. When she married, Mary Knox was reputed to be well educated and 'a very sensible woman'.[209] It was also predicted that the heiress, '(match when she will) may think of nothing less than London or Dublin to spend her days in for the future'.[210] Her dissatisfaction with rural Ireland may have led the couple to remove to London, where her money sustained a giddy round. Heiresses, especially when endowed with a strong will as well as money, bent spouses to their desires. It was predicted that another from Ulster with a handsome competency (said to be £5,000 p.a.), Lady Betty Cromwell, would reform Lord Kingston. The peer was permanently sozzled, 'the effects of which too much appear in his complexion'. In the event, Lady Betty's fortune underwrote the rather different 'extravagance' of Edward Southwell and Vanbrugh's remodelling of King's Weston.[211] Oliver St George lost heavily in the South Sea Bubble. By the time of his death in 1731, much of his plate and other valuables had been impounded.[212] Mary St George, when widowed, did not return to Ireland. Only after her death did her body and many of her valuables come back.

The St Georges' taste for silver was shared by Sir Thomas Taylor. Owner of a 'great house' in the Smithfield development in Dublin and a country house outside Kells in County Meath, Taylor became a baronet and his descendants were ennobled. Taylor did not disclose how he split his collection of silver between town and country.[213] In 1715, he cryptically listed the 'plate belonging to my closet'. Already it was a rich array. As well as silver teapot and spirit lamp, coffee-pot and punchbowl, there were shaving basin, ewer and wash-ball case. By 1728, the total weighed 2,529 ounces and was valued at nearly £620. Taylor had been buying systematically since 1700, mostly from the foremost Dublin makers: Abraham Voisin, Thomas Bolton, Joseph and Thomas Walker, and Thomas Sutton. In 1710, the substantial commission for a silver tea-kettle, or pot with lamp, had gone to a London maker.[214] However, in 1719, when he

37. Silver soup tureen and cover by Thomas Walker, Dublin, 1751. Here grandeur and fine craftsmanship were supplied by a Dublin silversmith.

bought a second tea-kettle and lamp (perhaps a replacement), it was made by Alderman Bolton in Dublin, at approaching four times the cost of the earlier London version. In 1725, he noted that he had bought a dozen spoons: six were English, and cost £2 18s. 10d.; the other six, Irish, for £2 11s. By 1729, Taylor's ambitions (and purse) swelled even larger. His guests, when need arose, would dine off silver plates. From John Gregory were bought eight graduated silver dishes. They cost over £104. But this was as nothing to the forty-two silver plates which Taylor had from Thomas Walker in 1728 for £230. This did not satiate Taylor's appetite. He could not resist the chances to buy what was being sold from other estates: Michael Fleming's and, in 1735, John Wade's. From Wade's executors he purchased two dozen plates and two dishes for £164 8s. The willingness to buy what other grandees had discarded had been shown earlier by both Archbishop King and Oliver St George. In 1717, the latter had spent £69 15s. on a dozen silver plates formerly owned by the lord justice, Lord Galway. The armorials of Galway were erased and St George's substituted.[215] In 1741, Lord Castle Durrow, having bought a dozen plates in London, had the armorials of the previous owner polished out.[216]

The growing complexity in the service of refreshments and meals stimulated new utensils. Taylor was quick to acquire them. By 1715 he had two 'silver rings to set dishes on'.[217] He continued to buy novelties fashioned by the Dublin silversmiths to satisfy the refined: an orange strainer, for punch, in 1730; a butter boat in 1737; and a bread basket in 1740.[218] These acquisitions paralleled those of Robert Howard, another from a family which, like the Taylors, ventured on European tours, but remained deeply rooted in Protestant Ireland. Robert Howard confidently combined an exemplary hospitality at Elphin, of which he was bishop, with a cultivated life in his Dublin town house and the development of a family estate at

Shelton Abbey in Wicklow. In 1738, he spent £181 on silver with Ann Craig and John Neville in London.[219] In the event, by trading in old-fashioned wares and some scrap gold, he reduced considerably what he had to pay. Notable among the bishop's purchases were 'a fine chased waiter', which weighed more than 200 ounces and cost £75 3s. 6d. A 'neat chased tureen' weighed 129 ounces and cost £51 16s.; a chased bread basket of 65 ounces was bought for £34. Howard was keen to imprint his ownership. The smiths had to engrave his arms 'in a fine large compartment' and 'carved a curious border around the table[t]'.[220] These commissions were inseparable from the style of hospitality which assiduous bishops felt obliged to adopt. Archbishop King did not stint in his display of plate. Charles Carr, recently consecrated bishop of Killaloe, spent almost £170 with a leading Dublin silversmith. Thereby Carr may have confirmed the belief of some contemporaries that he was better fitted for the coffee-house than the episcopate.[221]

Another bishop confirms the impression of how readily the order adopted the elegancies of polite living, in which silver utensils were essential. Simon Digby, the bishop of Elphin, in his declining years after 1714, preferred his two country houses – Abbert in County Roscommon and Lacken in County Galway – to the town and attendance at the House of Lords. In Connacht, abundantly stocked libraries in both houses and his preoccupation with painting miniatures eased the eremitic existence. But whether or not the bishop shunned society and secreted himself to read or paint in his closet, the rest of his family maintained hospitality. The battery of silver kept in the country included tea equipages, salvers and much flatware. In Dublin, Bishop Digby had two silver flagons, possibly for liturgical use, and a toilet set, but little that betokened regular and grand entertaining. A modish country life, implied by the abundant silver, is further evoked by 'the drawing room' at Abbert. Walnut and lacquer predominated. Conspicuous was the 'Indian tea table with china'. Many similar objects crowded the drawing room of the second house, Lacken. An executors' auction at Lacken allowed the redistribution of some of this booty. More of it was carried off by the children, notably by the heir, John Digby, who soon set up elegantly on his own account at Landenstown in County Kildare.[222]

Families like the Digbys, Howards and Taylors emerged, blinking, from the shadowy world of mid-seventeenth-century office-holding and the lettered professions. The Taylors, in the accustomed manner of wealthy Irish Protestants, soon divided their time between the capital and County Meath. The Taylors' upward ascent took in county offices, membership of parliament, a baronetcy and eventually a peerage, grand tourism and the construction and fitting of a modern mansion near Kells.[223] By 1727, measured by weight, Taylor's plate, although dazzling, did not match what seventeenth-century magnificoes had deployed. Lord Longford in the 1620s had silver both for display and for use at his table. In his will he mentioned a 'plain white silver set and trencher set ordinarily used at table'. Equally useful and noteworthy were a silver pepper box and sugar caster. Then, too, there were silver spoons, porringer and cover and a ewer and basin.[224] In the 1660s, the state kept by grandees in Dublin for parliament and council meetings is apparent from inventories of Lord Kildare's plate and the magnificence adopted by Lord Cork.[225] A listing of the Ormondes' silver in 1705 recorded 7,377 ounces. This did not comprehend all that they possessed, scattered across the two kingdoms.[226] More strictly contemporary with Taylor was Earl Grandison. In the 1730s, he decided to reside at his mansion of Dromana on the River Blackwater in County Waterford. Flurries of excitement shook the house. Furniture might be ordered locally, but most of the 4,654 ounces of silver arrived with the earl.[227]

The state in which a peer or a bishop lived could hardly be emulated by a mere squire or gentleman, unless they had unusual resources and ingenuity. Three examples show how those who sat in parliament under the early Hanoverians also built up collections of silver. By 1737, Cornelius O'Callaghan, a member of parliament, landowner, active farmer and barrister, had both the incentives and the means to adopt the elegancies of modern living. However, he did not blind guests with a blaze of silver plate, either in his country house of Bantire in County Tipperary or in his Dublin quarters. Certain articles belonged in the Tipperary seat; others were kept in Dublin. At Bantire, almost all ornamented the table – a large two-handled cup and cover, four salvers, three sugar casters, two salt cellars, two candlesticks and a few smaller pieces – rather than being for individual use. In Dublin were found twelve spoons, four salt cellars, a teapot, and a coffee-pot and stand. These dispositions implied the prevalence of tea- and coffee-drinking in the city rather than among country neighbours.[228]

Another squire with a seat in parliament was Jeffrey Paull. His estates lay in Counties Carlow and Waterford. In 1729, he distinguished between 'tea plate', 'chamber plate' and 'table plate'. In addition to the elaborate necessities for serving tea and coffee, the principal pieces for the chamber were a toilet service complete with silver-framed mirror. Among the array for meals – the 'table plate' – were a marrow spoon and two 'rings for dishes'.[229] These presumably resembled the devices that Taylor had also bought. Paull did not specify where these articles were used: in countryside or city. It is possible that some were transported to Dublin for his relatively short stays while he attended the Commons.

Comparable in rank and income to Paull was the proprietor of Edgeworthstown, Richard Edgeworth, who was elected to the Commons in 1737. Silver featured in Edgeworth's domestic economy and sociable exchanges. His buying began early. Lodging with the kinsfolk in Dublin, in 1725 he presented them with a silver plate from Philip Kinnersley, a local silversmith. It was clearly a weighty item, since it cost Edgeworth £4 4s. 6d.[230] Later in the same year, Edgeworth presented another kinswoman with a pair of candlesticks, also fashioned by Kinnersley.[231] Once he was married and housekeeping on his own account, needs multiplied. In 1733, the birth of his first child led promptly to the purchase, again from Kinnersley, of a silver spoon to feed it.[232] The expenditure – of nine shillings – and the ease with which it fitted into Edgeworth's monthly budget could be contrasted with Peacock's temporary

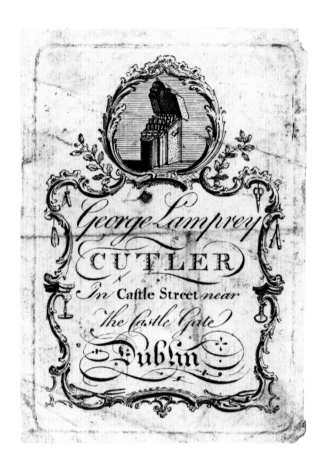

38. Advertisement of George Lamprey, cutler, Dublin.

acquisition of six teaspoons. Edgeworth added steadily to his stocks, returning often to Kinnersley. Most orders spoke of the rites of the table.[233]

The Edgeworths' holdings of silver were enlarged in 1743. A connection of Mrs Edgeworth, Mrs Dowling, left her a generous 226 ounces. This bequest – valued at £64 12s. 8d. – arrived opportunely, since it coincided with Edgeworth's year as sheriff. The office carried onerous obligations to entertain. The Dowling legacy, which also included £15-worth of gold plate, was quickly annexed. The inherited pieces were soon stamped with the new ownership. Knives, forks, salvers, casters, candlesticks and snuff-dish were sent to the Dublin smiths Pineau and Noah Vialas, to be engraved with the Edgeworths' armorials.[234] Generous as it was, the gift had to be augmented. A dozen silver-handled knives and forks were bought from Mrs Anne Walker. These too were engraved with the Edgeworth crest and arms, and a shagreen case made for them.[235]

Thereafter, only occasional additions were wanted. A coffee-pot came from Walsh for £7 in 1755. This, too, was quickly emblazoned with the Edgeworth heraldry.[236] Also in the 1750s, the Dublin speciality of cutlery with ivory handles stained green had reached the Edgeworth household. Two sets were acquired from Hewetson.[237] A dozen dessert spoons bought in 1759 again attested to the demands of polite society.[238] Another novelty was 'a French plate cross': a device to raise dishes from the surface of the table and keep them warm – a rival (perhaps) to the dish rings which had appeared among Taylor's plate as early as 1715.[239] Edgeworth used both. One of his last recorded purchases, in 1769, was a chased silver dish ring for £5 17s. from James Warren.[240] (These articles, or something with the same name, were shipped from London to Virginia in 1728.[241]) Edgeworth also used silver to gratify others. His son's schoolmaster at Drogheda was presented with a pair of silver coasters as a token of appreciation for his care of the boy.[242]

Silver was possessed by others outside the select covey of peers, bishops and members of parliament regularly in Dublin. Unfortunately, because no series of wills or probate inventories survive, only stray instances can be offered. Traders, both in the capital and the provinces, valued and used it. Country clergymen in Counties Cork and Kerry owned the silver utensils associated with tea- and coffee-drinking and the service of elegant meals. In addition, some of the accessories of writing – pen-case and sand box – were fashioned from silver. Dogs and even the falcons of the Cosbies of Ardfert in Kerry were adorned with silver collars.[243] In a number of provincial residences, between 10 and 16 per cent of the value of the contents resided in the silver.[244] It is seldom clear how these modest collections had been formed. Some objects were inherited, and special care was taken to ensure that in future generations they remained within the family.[245] More were bought, but whether locally or on visits to Dublin or England is unclear. In the eighteenth century, a few towns outside Dublin – Cork, Kinsale, Limerick and Galway – supported silversmiths.

Corporations used them, but private customers are harder to identify. In County Galway, the Blakes of Ballyglunin sometimes bought locally. At the same time, they patronized some of the best suppliers in Dublin: D'Oliers, the goldsmiths and jewellers; Michael Walsh for silver. In 1762, Blake, marooned in the country, asked others to procure for him in Dublin a salver and butter boat, and to have them engraved with his armorials. Yet, from a hawker in Galway, four spoons were bought. Moreover, an established silversmith in Galway, Andrews, made Blake a cream ewer, sugar basin and tongs. The Blakes, uniquely among those customers considered, were Catholics. Galway was an area where a Catholic gentry managed to survive in some numbers throughout the eighteenth century.[246] Blake bought regularly in the west of Ireland. 'A service of flint', probably hard-paste porcelain from continental Europe, was shipped in through Limerick. Other goods came from nearby auctions. Excluded from political life, Blake was not drawn to Dublin by parliamentary sessions. Yet the capital exerted its magnetism over him as much as over his Protestant neighbours, like French of Monivea. For many of the most substantial household purchases – mahogany dining tables and chairs as well as massive silver – Blake relied on Dublin.[247] In the rare cases in which Catholics still commanded ample incomes, they acquired the same articles as their

Protestant contemporaries. Others striving for respectability in straitened circumstances treasured the odd and precious possession.[248] Catholic bishops handed silver snuff-boxes, watches, a tobacco box, candlesticks and even a silver sundial to legatees. Archbishop Patrick Fitzsimons of Dublin, dying in 1733, commanded that a nephew and niece who inherited his plate should emblazon it with his coat of arms.[249]

For most, outside a few thousand of the well-to-do, monotony of diet matched modesty of possessions. Yet, as has been stressed, possessions arrived adventitiously. Also, purchasers did not always choose to buy what, in retrospect, might seem most necessary. Then, too, the numbers in the middling ranks, with annual incomes between £5 and £20, increased, amounting perhaps to 30 per cent of the population by the end of the eighteenth century.[250] Sadly, those whose effects were inventoried after they had died were seldom drawn from this larger group. As a result, the degree to which they contented themselves with low-priced versions of the modish, opting for earthenware rather than imported porcelain, deal not walnut or mahogany, treen, horn and tin rather than pewter and silver can only be guessed. It is improbable that all the 280,000 pieces of earthenware and glass shipped into Ireland from England between 1692 and 1695 were destined for the houses of magnificoes.[251] Individually the articles were worth little. Even so, the cook of Robert French was tempted in 1748 to make off from Monivea with seventeen delft plates, presumably in the hope of selling them. If he succeeded, then he helped redistribute notable artefacts.[252] In the same way, the total of 28,000 silver teaspoons assayed in Dublin in 1788 suggested that this utensil of polite society was reaching some of modest circumstances.[253] Lady Theodosia Crosbie, habituated as the daughter of an earl to elegant appurtenances, instantly spotted that the teapot from which worthy townspeople in Limerick poured her tea was fashioned from pewter not silver. Equally noteworthy, but not remarked by Lady Theodosia, was the fact that the provincial traders had adopted the strange and costly brew.[254]

# Chapter 5

# Pictures

*I*

Tables, chairs, beds, together with the equipment for cooking, eating and drinking, as much as shelter and clothing, could be justified as essentials for living. Paintings, in contrast, had no such utility. Some saw them as aids to devotion; others reviled them as idolatrous. By the end of the seventeenth century sophisticates, notably Lord Shaftesbury, contended that paintings represented and could communicate moral truths, and so were devices through which virtue could be learnt. On these grounds, the acquisition of pictures was recommended as a route to, and not just an accessory of, civility and gentility. By 1730, one astute observer in Dublin distinguished between routine portraiture, 'the skill to trace some faint resemblance of the face', and the virtuosi whose brushes revealed 'the secret soul . . . at once to paint the face and mind'.[1] If a few used arguments of this kind to excuse their purchases, more bought pictures for mundane reasons. Paintings and engravings, in common with other household objects, were treasured for their associations. Typically, they depicted ancestors, patrons, allies, friends and family. They could keep in remembrance the absent and departed. Like other possessions, they impressed visitors. The grandeur of connections, such as the Ormondes' with the Tudors or the Southwells' with the Medici of Florence, were proclaimed. Especially when displayed in ornately carved frames, the canvases were conspicuous in interiors. Increasingly, too, convention approved this kind of display. By the early eighteenth century, paintings and prints were promoted to give fashionable rooms a lighter and more varied feel, whether in the viceregal drawing room at Dublin Castle or in private houses.

Painted and printed images adorned eighteenth-century Ireland more widely than has usually been supposed. Grumpy tourists evoked sparse interiors; satirists conjured a rather different scene. Canvases, 'daub'd many an age ago', hung over doors. Otherwise, 'connoisseurs of art' had to satisfy themselves with torn landscapes, 'showing dim towers by time or broad-sword hacked/ Black fields and trees with frame and glazing cracked'.[2] In 1756, there were paraded Sir Bubble Buyall, Lady Squeeze, Formal 'a connoisseur', Rattlehead, a picture dealer, and Busy, a clergyman. Buyall, 'a man of large means', had created a museum 'of all the patched, exploded, dear, unauthentic pieces that have for these many years been imported' into Ireland. Lady Squeeze haunted auctions in the hope of bargains. Formal was accounted 'extremely well bred in the rust and mildews of antiquity'. These were types evidently familiar from the Dublin of the day. So, too, was the speculator in 'the refuse and trash of all auctions abroad', who then disposed of the wares in Ireland. A cleric was included: a reminder that this group was disproportionately important in Protestant Ireland in dictating taste and supporting improvements, which encompassed architecture, design and painting.[3] Indeed, it was a Church of Ireland clergyman, Matthew Pilkington, who compiled the first biographical dictionary of artists in English. He advised his patron, Charles Cobbe, archbishop of Dublin, on his collection and also bought on his own account. As such Pilkington may have been the caricaturist's model for the Reverend Mr Buyall.[4]

Notable in these jibes was the assumption that the market for pictures in Ireland was buoyant. As with other commodities, suppliers cashed in. Jobbing painters toured the provinces, seeking recommendations and commissions. The shrewd imported paintings and engravings. In time, opportunists arranged auctions of fine and applied art. Commercial impulses converged with philosophical disquisitions to popularize the ownership of pictures. Perhaps because it was such a recent development, it served as a butt for comedy. A steady growth of interest can be traced from the seventeenth century. Odd paintings are mentioned before 1641: Lovell's Adam and Eve in County Cork; the group of ten owned by Skiddy, the Waterford merchant.[5] In the Dublin house of Francis Barker, a gentleman, were to be found in 1639 four small pictures of Dives and Lazarus. These were reckoned to be worth in all three shillings. More valuable was a single 'large new picture in a frame', estimated at £1 10s. Barker owned another pair of framed paintings.[6] James Conran possessed one 'old picture', valued at sixpence; the three in Sarah Darworthy's Dublin chamber were thought to be worth 3s. 4d. each.[7] Two other Dublin establishments of the time – perhaps inns – were decorated with pictures: four unframed but on canvas; and a set of twelve Roman emperors.[8]

Thereafter, the clearest urge was to have likenesses taken, either to display in the sitter's home or to present to others. An example was set by the Ormondes. At their principal seat, Kilkenny Castle, spaces were created – notably the gallery and duchess's closet – where paintings could be displayed.[9] Largely through portraiture, this ducal house could exhibit its pedigree, with images of ancestors going back into past centuries, its grand connections, notably with Anne Boleyn and so with her daughter, Queen Elizabeth, its loyalty, through portraits of the Stuarts, and its weighty patrons and allies, such as Wentworth or other knights of the garter and officers of state at the court of Charles II. The Ormonds also flattered their dependants with depictions of themselves. In 1647, Ormond had the young Lely paint his portrait so that it could be given to his close collaborator, Sir Thomas Wharton.[10] Ormond even presented his likeness to the abbess of a convent in Flanders.[11] The Butlers also used journeys, sometimes not altogether propitious, to enlarge their collections. During 1647, the future first duke in transit for exile had John Hoskins of London paint him in miniature.[12] At this juncture, travel, whether enforced or voluntary, was felt to allow access to the best artists. In 1657, the Ormonds' heir, Ossory, warned that his mother was stranded in Ireland, 'where I fear she will not find any person so skilful in painting as would produce a picture fitting to send' to a respected follower. Ossory hoped to procure his own and his younger brother's portrait in Orléans.[13] The Ormonds were not, apparently, obsessive enough about collecting to instruct dealers to seek out rarities for them. Rather they took what was readily available. Even so, in deciding which of the wares on offer in the London or continental art markets should be bought, they exercised choice.[14]

Others agreed that the available in London, if inferior to what continental Europe boasted, surpassed the limited wares of Dublin. In 1683, Viscount Massareene, putting together a collection of family portraits, worried that Ireland lacked 'workmen that are good artists'. He warned, 'it is not fit to copy them till a good hand . . . be found'.[15] Massareene intended 'that every one of my three children shall have such a picture [of himself, in viscount's robes] at length'. To this end, he went to Lely, then at the height of his fame. Massareene approved the image of his daughter as 'perfectly finished'. The frames (carved and gilded) were procured in England and enhanced the rich effect. For a copy of his own portrait and one of his son, Massareene paid Lely £60.[16] Massareene, having only lately inherited his Irish dignity and property from an uncle, was tenuously linked with the kingdom. As a result he may have disparaged what could be done there. Others, equally wealthy and well travelled, contented themselves with Dublin productions. During the 1650s, as he increased in prosperity, William Petty distributed his portrait – perhaps in miniatures. They came from 'Desmidres' in Dublin, and cost £3.[17] Petty affected to despise 'pictures, models or old manuscripts', and to concern himself only with things of the mind or of practical use.[18] This self-denial did not extend to portraiture. As well as patronizing adepts in London, such as Lely, he used the current favourite in the Dublin of the 1670s and 1680s: Thomas Pooley. Petty defied custom by being depicted '*en déshabille* . . . in a beard of 31 days growth and in my own hair and without a periwig and in the simplest habit imaginable'. This intimate image was to be kept in a private place.[19] Nor did Sir John Perceval, keen to introduce the latest style into County Cork, disdain Pooley as his portraitist.[20] Another in Dublin, the cultivated lawyer Sir John Temple in 1679 paid a modest £9 for portraits of two of his daughters, together with the frames. These were copied and then presented to other relations.[21] Earlier, in a display of the courtliness needed to thrive in the snake-pit of official Dublin, Temple procured a portrait of the new lord-lieutenant, Essex.[22]

Demand in Dublin, both from residents and country visitors, supported a handful of painters. They were organized into a guild, one of twenty-four then in the city.[23] The arrangement reminded of the current uncertainty about the status of painting, viewed by most as a

39. Jonas Blaymires, *North Prospect of the Cathedral Church of St Patrick in Dublin, c.* 1738. One of Blaymires's architectural studies, intended to illustrate a new edition of Sir James Ware's writings on Irish antiquities.

craft not a profession or branch of liberal learning. Furthermore, the painters, yoked together with cutlers, usually turned their brushes to whatever work was wanted. Among their number were several heraldic painters, including Aaron Crossly, whose staples were tricking out showy funerals.[24] In each generation, the capital sustained one or two artists who monopolized the most fashionable and profitable commissions. Pooley was followed by Gandy, Latham, Slaughter and Hunter. By the end of the seventeenth century, a wider spread across the island of a moderate prosperity and new modes of self-expression made more work for portraitists. In County Down, Samuel Waring illustrated these trends. Waring had toured Europe, as has been seen, buying prints if not paintings in Rome. Moreover, he had prepared for the trip by conning treatises on art and architecture. Back in Ulster, he was deferred to by neighbours on account of these experiences and his superior 'fancy'.[25] In 1699, paintings became available in his own locality. An itinerant, Joachim Croger (or Crocker) portrayed the

Warings and some of their neighbours. A spirit of enterprise – or desperation – had first brought Croger from continental Europe to Dublin, and then impelled him north. He was said to be 'much employed about Portadown and is like to have much employment in this country'. Having painted fifteen pictures in the vicinity of Lurgan, he had only three canvases left.[26] He charged £3 for each.[27] Conceivably, Croger had been encountered by the young Waring while on his travels and then tempted to try his luck, first in Dublin and then in the north-east. Croger's portraits pleased. Arthur Brownlow, after dinner at Waringstown, pronounced the pictures, 'the best drawn to the like that ever he saw'. The only worry was whether the colour would 'hold'. To this end, Waring, like numerous contemporaries, collected recipes for varnishing and cleaning canvases. He had frames made in Dublin.[28] Meanwhile in western Ulster during the same decade, the bishop of Derry, William King, had his housekeeper, Judith Jemmett, painted by 'Mr. Lafort'. This commission cost only £1 10s.[29] King knew Dublin well and still visited the capital regularly, so contacts there may have secured the painting.

Family portraits remained the staple. In this, it can be argued, Irish tastes resembled those in late-seventeenth- and eighteenth-century north America.[30] Portraiture was the act of artistic patronage most commonly undertaken by both aristocratic and more modest families. In 1693, a clergyman in Wexford sent his own portrait to a sister in Wales. Self-deprecatingly, he wrote, 'how the limner performed the part, I am no competent judge of, yet I am apt to believe he is not inferior in skill to him who drew my cousin's'.[31] The quest for commissions tempted the adventurous into the countryside. Again, these painting tours resembled the devices by which artists in the English provinces and colonial America found work.[32] In 1739, de la Nauze, a 'face painter' from Dublin, was working at the house of James Cuffe in County Mayo.[33] By 1742, it was reported from the city of Derry that a painter, 'Delenes', had been in the district for six months. He charged six guineas for a half-length, and three for a head. During his stay, he had earned £200. The dean had paid £50 to have members of his family depicted.[34]

These successes in securing commissions encouraged the hopeful to believe that there was money to be made in provincial Ireland from painting. Edward Owen, member of a gentry family from Anglesey, took up painting professionally. He trained under Thomas Gibson in London, but failed to break into the artistic world there and returned to Wales. Examples of his skill were dispatched to a relation at Tuam.[35] This recipient enthused, 'that no piece that has been drawn is more admired by every body than your picture is. It is liked by critics that understand painting'. Tempted by such a reception, Owen tried his luck in Ireland, but evidently did not conquer. His kinswoman was no doubt fantasizing when she alleged that, had Owen stayed, he would have been assured of '500 guineas and good acquaintance, with a thousand welcomes'.[36] What was revealed was another circle of the cultivated, probably headed by the Church of Ireland clergy, this time in rural Galway. In this respect, the network of potential patrons, and what they wanted, closely resembled that in Owen's native Wales.[37]

However, the provincials in both places were pernickety. Another artist, Jonas Blaymires, who toured Ireland during the 1730s and hoped to sell his pictures to clerical households, found his antiquarian and topographical sketches scorned.[38]

The realization that artistic skills could enrich the possessor reconciled parents to such a career. The Southwells' agent at Downpatrick, John Trotter, was more than happy when a son evinced these talents, since 'a good painter may get good bread'. The younger John Trotter, said to have 'a genius that way' and 'liked by many of the Dublin Society', was to study for two years in Rome under the Society's patronage.[39] Often, as in the case of Trotter, talent opened the door to a life away from Ireland. The ambitious doubted whether their abilities would be recognized and rewarded as they wished in Ireland. However, it was not exclusively an Irish delusion to imagine that fortune awaited those who painted and sculpted in metropolises other than their own.[40] *Noblesse oblige* probably induced the Ormonds in 1680 to arrange the apprenticeship of Benjamin Ferrers, the deaf and dumb son of a gentleman, to a landscape painter, Henry Wagoner in England. The Ormonds owned landscapes by Wagoner.[41] Early in the eighteenth century a member of a Kilkenny family developed his artistic talents in the exotic location of Surat, south of Bombay, under the auspices of the East India Company. He portrayed functionaries of the Company, but was soon killed by the climate.[42] Another from the same family, Christopher Hewetson, an alumnus of Kilkenny College, later established himself as a leading sculptor in Rome.[43] More commonly, those born in Ireland, frustrated in their quest for work, removed to London or Bath.[44] A few – Hugh Howard and Charles Jervas – flourished. Moreover, they kept their Irish links in repair. Sometimes, as in Howard's case, they painted grandees and friends when they revisited Dublin.[45] Others included visiting Irish among their sitters in London. With some, ambitions exceeded accomplishment. William 'Blarney' Thompson acquired his first artistic tastes from paintings brought back from his European travels by Archdeacon James Smythe. Thompson's father served the Smythes of Westmeath as agent. Thereby the boy was introduced into a wider circle of those who owned and had opinions about art. The boy's first essays as a copyist were sent to a brother of the archdeacon living in London to be evaluated. A 'Mr Gavan, . . . a critic that way', was asked to point out faults, 'for the young man's amendment'. The comments were copious. The advice of the Londoners, while not entirely negative, cautioned against the boy removing to England.[46] The advice was ignored. Thompson was apprenticed, seemingly to Richard Wilson and Hogarth. Even so, the amateurs from the Smythe circle advised him, 'as yet not to paint in colours till he has learnt to design and strike out well, for ill habit at first contracted is not so easily laid aside'. The counsel availed little: Thompson ended bathetically in a paupers' prison.[47]

Just as the prosperous selected from a range of foreign, British and Irish goods, so when it came to paintings many enjoyed a similar choice. Those, like Petty and the Percevals, posting regularly between England and Ireland, used painters in both kingdoms. In 1715, the Veseys, while in England, purchased a pair of canvases from Mr Charlton for £15. These were destined for Abbey Leix.[48] The squire of Edgeworthstown, when in Bath, had its leading portraitist, William Hoare, portray his wife. The canvas cost ten guineas. Since Hoare charged thirty guineas for other of his portraits, the fee suggested a modest format and perhaps the cheaper medium of pastel.[49] Lady Mary O'Hara, wife of a Sligo squire, was painted in London by Allan Ramsay. The price was fifteen guineas.[50] Peter Ludlow, a Meath swell, soon to be ennobled, went to Joshua Reynolds, as did Lord Bellamont.[51] The Wards from County Down were patronizing the London painter Francis Cotes in the 1760s.[52] Travellers on the continent had long availed themselves of what was on offer locally. The sons of the first duke of Ormond turned to artists in Orléans. Later William Leathes in the Low Countries arranged for kinsfolk and acquaintances to be portrayed.[53] One of the Cunninghams in Ireland procured '4 little pictures done in miniature' from Bordeaux. Judged to be 'well done', they miscarried on their voyage via Rotterdam to Ireland, and had to be painted afresh.[54] Earnest grand tourists had themselves portrayed by the favourites in Rome and Venice. Several – Joseph Leeson, Joseph Henry of Straffan, James Stewart of Killymoon and Lord Charlemont – used Pompeo Batoni.[55]

Opportunity and price usually determined what was painted for the Protestants of Ireland. Of Pooley in the 1680s, it was said that he never charged less than £20. He billed Dublin corporation for £60 when he painted the new monarchs, William III and Mary II.[56] Portraits commissioned to hang in the hall of the Royal Hospital at Kilmainham in Queen Anne's reign cost £10 or £16. When John Michael Wright sought commissions in Ireland, he charged only £10 per head.[57] This was what Hugh Howard had charged Archbishop William King for his portrait.[58] However, two portraits commissioned in 1734 by the lord-lieutenant, Dorset, from Francis Bindon each (with frame) cost over £26. One was destined for the Royal Hospital. By 1740, James Worsdale, visiting from England, charged the viceroy, Devonshire, £45 10s. for the latter's portrait to be hung at Kilmainham. A second image of Devonshire by Worsdale cost only thirty guineas, presumably because more modest in its dimensions.[59] Between 1747 and 1751, a Fermanagh notable, Margetson Armar, made payments to Bindon of £50, perhaps for two pictures and another £21 14s. for his wife's portrait.[60] The Cobbe family at Donabate, north of Dublin, patronized assorted artists. A portrait of Sir Richard Levinge by Holland, who also painted Archbishop King, cost £6 18s. in 1723. Two years later, a double portrait of two boys cost £23 15s.

Considerably cheaper were portraits from Simon Pine in the 1750s (£2 16s. 10½d.) and – in 1765 – from Strickland Lowry, at £4 11s. and £9 2s.[61] By the 1790s, Thomas Robinson, also active as a portraitist in Ulster, demanded £20 for a full-length study, £10 for a half-length and £4 for a head.[62] These prices did not mark any great increase over the century. Always, price varied according to size and medium. The ovals, showing head and shoulders, painted by Croger, being more modest in conception, were to be had more cheaply. The adolescent

Patience Boleyn – who later married Robert Howard – had her picture 'drawn' about 1705, at a cost of £2 6s. (The frame cost a further 12s. 6d.[63]) Elinor O'Hara was charged £6 18s. and £5 15s. for two portraits. The second, completed in 1731, was by Carlton.[64] During the 1750s, not the least of Thomas Hickey's attractions, other than being well known in Dublin as 'the confectioner's son', was his willingness to draw likenesses of worthies in black and white chalk, for which, once glazed and framed, he charged a mere twenty-six shillings. This talented beginner, it appeared, would do for the women; men had to be portrayed by the better established Rupert Barber. These were modest sums when compared with the 100 to 200 guineas commanded by Gainsborough, or 200 by Reynolds. Indeed, even when Katherine Conolly's sister Jane Bonnell was painted in London by John Smibert, she was charged twelve guineas.[65]

Clients generally evaluated what they had ordered by verisimilitude to subject. In Connacht, Ellen Dunne valued the picture which she had been sent from Wales chiefly as a representation of an old friend. In gratitude, she wrote, 'when I am most thoughtful I can sit with pleasure to look at you, for it is all I shall see of you while I live . . . '[66] Mary Jones delighted in a portrait of a brother, being 'the likest I ever saw of anybody'.[67] Archbishop King was relieved that images of himself that he had dispatched to London resembled him enough 'to be known to my friends'.[68] Moses Leathes accounted portraits of his two nephews, executed by one of the best artists in Antwerp, 'well done and very like'.[69] In 1733, Lord Palmerston told his nephew, Flower, that a portrait of William Pulteney was ready to go to Castle Durrow, 'a half length, very like him and well done'.[70] Measured by this yardstick, London as well as Dublin artists were sometimes faulted. In 1735, Dr Marmaduke Coghill was unhappy about the way in which his head and body had been joined. He also hoped that a very recent honour, his installation as chancellor of the Irish exchequer, could be shown by the robes in which he was depicted.[71] However, the aesthetic Edward Southwell, to whom the commission had been deputed, chose to have Coghill portrayed in a brown velvet coat, 'that I may have it the sooner'. Southwell wrote of the painting, 'it is very like and looks kindly and affectionately upon me'.[72] Yet, Southwell returned the painting to the artist, Charles Jervas, originally from Ireland, 'for one stroke more of his pencil'.[73] Jervas had presumably made preliminary sketches of Coghill when in Ireland the previous year, which he worked up on his return to London.[74]

Hugh Howard, another Irish portraitist working in London, was found wanting. Sir Justinian Isham roared, 'pray tell Mr. Howard that I can't think the picture he has drawn of you is anything like'.[75] During the 1740s, a portrait of the lord chancellor, Jocelyn, was criticized by his son on pedantic grounds.[76] Others beheld those whom they loved, rendered in pigments, more appreciatively. When Katherine Conolly sought a portrait of a recently dead favourite, Frank Burton, she appealed to her niece by marriage in England, because 'no body can have a better fancy in all these things than you have'.[77] When Burton's portrait arrived, Mrs Conolly was moved to tears. Friends felt this effect was therapeutic; others praised the picture as the 'prettiest' they had ever seen. It was widely exhibited in the exacting Castletown circle. 'Every one I showed it to today admires the seeing of it'.[78] The pains of temporary separation as well as of death were dulled by contemplating the painted image of the absent. A Scotswoman, having removed to Ulster, was cheered to find that a visiting kinswoman resembled ancestral portraits. Catherine Bagshawe, stranded in Ireland while her husband soldiered in the East Indies, consoled herself by writing long letters, reading and rereading his less frequent replies, imagining herself as a character in a novel such as Richardson's *Sir Charles Grandison*, and mooning over Colonel Bagshawe's portrait. 'Your dear picture shall be my study which I have pinned opposite my bed'.[79]

Family feeling surrounded images of the absent and dead. Characteristic of this sentiment was the request from Elizabeth Cooke, when in Dublin during 1726, that two favourite portraits of relations be sent to her from Kilkenny.[80] Earlier, Lady Petty instructed a kinsman in Ireland to take special care of portraits of her dead husband and son.[81] Sir Donough O'Brien pestered Lord Thomond for portraits of the latter and his wife, which 'you were pleased to promise me to complete what I have of the family'.[82] In 1733, a connection in Cardiff appealed to William Flower, head of the Irish branch, for a portrait now in Ireland. Flower was told 'the picture, not being a piece belonging to your family, can be of no value to you but would be of uncommon [value] to me, I not having a picture of his'.[83] Within Flower's circle, portraits were swapped, and copies commissioned. At Castle Durrow, Richard Carver was set to work to copy a half-length portrait by Lely.[84] In 1736, Sir William Fownes, on taking over his family home, paid 'Mr. Browne' to tidy up ancestral portraits.[85] Mary Jones was gratified to receive family pictures from her grander sister, Katherine Conolly. However, one was so pitted that it could not even be copied.[86] Women may have been especially receptive to the sentimental resonances of portraits. Occasionally they were in a position to commission paintings on their own account. Elinor O'Hara, after her husband had died, not only supervised the construction of new house and gardens, but sat twice for her portrait in Dublin.[87]

Within some families, paintings came to be regarded as hereditary appurtenances. The same concern about their disposition was shown in wills as towards prized silver and furnishings. In this spirit, both Sir James Ware and Thomas Flower attended meticulously to the fate of the portraits of parents, ancestors and benefactors.[88] Henry Dalway, originally from County Antrim, ensured that an aunt would receive a particular portrait of him after his death.[89] When houses were sold, paintings were often exempted from the auctions. Indeed, wills sometimes specified that portraits were to be regarded as 'heirlooms' and not to be removed from the settings for which originally they had been commissioned.[90] In Dublin, the uncle charged with the care of the infant heir of the Balfours bought sundry items when the contents of the family house on St Stephen's Green were auctioned. These included eighteen family pictures, for which £19 3s. 6d. was given.[91] The eldest of the Smythes, without children

40. Philip Hussey, *Master Edward O'Brien*, 1746.

of his own, decided to give to a younger brother four pictures 'which I value and esteem, which I also entreat you to accept and keep for my sake and transmit with your estate to your son and his heirs male for ever'. In the event, the dampness of the intended destination – Barbavilla in Westmeath – conspired against the gift. Two of the pictures had to be returned to England for restoration. The donor, meanwhile, stated that he had another thirty or forty paintings in his possession.[92] George Conyngham, a proprietor in County Londonderry, decreed that his own portrait (by Lowry) should descend to a daughter, while the paintings (by Kneller) of William III and Mary II were to go to his heir and so remain in the family seat of Springhill. At the start of George III's reign, when Lord Abercorn inherited the house and contents of a relation in Dublin, he decided to keep any family portraits, 'that I may, if I please, keep them from falling into a stranger's hands'.[93] Paintings possessed monetary as well as associational value. In 1737, one Dubliner, hunting for some missing family portraits, discovered that they had been pawned by a poorer relation for 11s. 6d.[94]

On occasion, tender emotions were satisfied by miniatures. Set in gold, jewelled or finely engraved frames, they were too small and fragile to figure prominently in decorative schemes.

41. John Lewis, *Ann Dobbyn*, *c.* 1750. As the popularity of portraiture grew, so children became favourite subjects.

Instead, they were contemplated privately.[95] The Kildare squire John Digby of Landenstown used a trip to London in 1733 to have the currently fashionable enameller Christian Zincke set miniatures of family members in gold.[96] In the Petty family, three miniatures were prized. In part this was for their high monetary value. At £35 and £30 each, they were more costly than most contemporary canvases. Much of the worth consisted of their gold frames. Their importance led to their being kept in an ebony cabinet inlaid with precious stones.[97] Personal memorials went beyond images to objects, especially rings, which incorporated hair belonging to a dead relation or friend. Several in Katherine Conolly's circle adopted this mode of commemoration. While Molly Burton was sitting for hers, to be framed in gold and presented to a relation, a kinswoman tartly remarked, 'those who flatter comes best off'.[98] Mrs Conolly, ever watchful for tricks, feared lest crooked jewellers substitute threads from frayed collars for the human hair.[99] Also in Dublin, Penelope Ford, after her brother had died in England, begged for the 'pictures in miniature, which I must own I value more than all the other toys, as they are pictures of the family and I believe very good ones'.[100] The sentimental appeal of such imagery was occasionally exploited. A 'picture locket' had been exchanged in one generation for a piece of mourning jewellery incorporating hair. A following generation wanted instead the portrait miniature. Its current owner was urged to consider 'whether more than it is worth will not be more service to her'.[101] Despite the popularity of the genre, it was reported that Dublin contained only two miniaturists in 1737. Because of this scarcity, they demanded an extortionate five guineas to copy an old portrait.[102]

Copies multiplied popular images and images of the would-be popular. In addition, they enabled enthusiasts to complete their sets of ancestors in the manner of a game of happy families. In the same way as a building or silver, portraits embodied the continuities and connections of a dynasty. Institutional collections through which a longer history could be communicated were first made in Ireland at the Royal Hospital and Trinity College. In Dublin, some guilds and – in time – the corporation assembled portraits of their governors. In a similar mode, but constricted by space and money, the library of Maule's charitable foundation in Cork was embellished with portraits of two benefactors, Brigadier-General Stearne and Captain William Maule, the founder's dead brother.[103] More unexpectedly the Incorporated Society paid £3 3s. 11d. for a 'picture' to hang in the newly founded Castledermot School near Dublin. It may have been a tribute to the benefactor, Lord Kildare.[104] Individuals' collections remained domestic. In the seventeenth century, the only conspicuous exception was the gallery amassed by the Ormondes. Since the family had a strong role in the public life of Ireland, serving fives times as lord-lieutenant between 1641 and 1713, their paintings had a public dimension. Some were taken from their private residences to the state's buildings which they – temporarily – inhabited. Those (the bulk) left at Kilkenny were kept in galleries and closets to which the favoured had entry.[105]

By the eighteenth century, more individuals were forming collections. One avid buyer was Richard Edgeworth. This squire, having laboured hard to recover and restore his inheritance in County Longford, familiarized himself with the annals of his forbears. With this awareness came a wish to house and equip his family fittingly. He valued ceramics and silver, but paintings more. From the 1720s, he bought pictures with Edgeworth associations. In the main, these were portraits of relations. At a sale of a sister's goods he bought one for £2, which, at least temporarily, was hung in the back parlour of the Dublin house.[106] In 1732, he secured a likeness of his kinswoman, Lady Edgeworth, for £2.[107] Other portraits – of his father, mother, sister and a cousin – were cleaned and reframed. In 1738, shortly after his election to parliament, Edgeworth himself sat for 'Mr. Browne, the limner'.[108] While in Bath, he had Hoare paint his wife.[109] Back in Ireland, he turned to Philip Hussey in Dublin for his own portrait: a half-length.[110] At the same time, he gave Hussey, the pre-eminent portraitist of the day, other work. He repaired portraits of Edgeworth's parents, and copied that of another relation.[111] In 1758, Edgeworth paid Hussey to come down to County Longford to paint versions of several family portraits at Lissard, the seat of a senior branch of the Edgeworths. Hussey's charges were small: £2 5s. 6d. This was about what a leading barrister could earn as a single fee and considerably less than a fashionable physician expected for his attendance.[112] Meanwhile, the squire had secured from Kinsale images of his maternal ancestors. These, too, were to be touched up by the versatile Hussey.[113] Edgeworth recorded the purchase of few other works of art. In 1748, he had a watercolour of a landscape by Wilkinson sent down from Dublin. Otherwise, books and the embellishment of house and grounds seemingly interested the owner of Edgeworthstown more.[114]

42. Katherine Coote, 'A prospect of Cootehill taken from ye dressing room', *c.* 1745.

The market and craze for painting commended it as a pastime to members of the Protestant élite. In the 1680s, it was reported that Captain Aungier, a connection of Lord Longford, was diverting a country house party with experiments in painting.[115] 'Mr Pewley', perhaps Thomas Pooley, was recommended for a post as gentleman of the lord-lieutenant's bedchamber because he was 'ingenious in painting'.[116] The young Charles O'Hara in 1730 took lessons in painting from 'Mr Brown' – probably the same who painted Edgeworth – in Dublin. The tuition, requiring an entrance fee of £1 3s. and then a further £4 12s., was more expensive than O'Hara's dancing lessons.[117] The esteem in respectable quarters for painting as an accomplishment was also shown by Simon Digby, successively bishop of Limerick and Elphin. A chaplain of the first duke of Ormond, Digby notoriously owed his mitre to his facility with pen and brush. He portrayed his patron and many of his family.[118] Indeed, when he died in 1720, Bishop Digby's closets were bulging with miniatures, some in oil, many watercolours.[119] Digby's interests were shared. Descendants proved discriminating patrons and purchasers.[120] Jervas, who painted the bishop and his wife, may have learnt his own techniques initially from this patron.[121] Digby saw to it that his daughters learnt to draw and paint. By 1711, the girls were rumoured to surpass their father.[122] By that time, it was no longer strange to find women who painted. Among the effects bequeathed by Thomas Flower of Finglas in 1700 were some small paintings by his mother.[123] Mrs Price, wife of an official at Dublin Castle, had stocked her closet there with artist's equipment.[124] In 1720, the surveyor-general and architect, Thomas Burgh, wrote dotingly of a daughter 'representing by landskip those countries which before she described in verse'.[125] Lucy Dopping, sister of the versatile

43. Susannah Drury, *The west prospect of the Giants Causway in the county of Antrim in the kingdom of Ireland*, engraved 1744. Drury attracted fame through her gouaches, executed at the remote spot, and subsequently engraved and widely disseminated.

Hugh Howard, hoped that her daughters would learn to paint.[126] Richard Edgeworth equipped a favourite daughter with the materials for drawing, and hired a master, Henry Brooke, to instruct her.[127] In the city of Limerick by 1767, a stationer stocked 'books of designs for drawing, with pencils and shell colours'.[128] Often, it seemed, the skill arose from a wish to draw designs for elaborate needlework: a female art much praised.[129]

Amateurs who showed talent were tempted to make money from it. Particularly for girls, without many respectable ways of earning a livelihood, art offered the hope of deliverance from penury. Susannah Drury who was celebrated in 1741 for her views of the Giant's Causway, subsequently engraved, was the sister of a Dublin miniaturist. In addition, and more significantly, it was reported that she was 'a young gentlewoman'. She was commended as 'a modest and well behaved young woman', as much as for her draughtsmanship. Although awarded a premium by the Dublin Society for her work, it is unlikely that she earned handsomely.[130] Similarly, Laetitia Bushe strove to avoid social derogation by turning her skills with pencil and brush to profit. Through her talents, she preserved a precarious gentility, welcomed into the houses of the cultivated, but without making a paying career.[131] A precedent had been set by Henrietta Dering, who supplemented her and her husband's meagre income by portraying members of the wider family, which included the precious and precocious Southwells and Percevals.[132]

The sense that this was a strategy by which women could achieve some independence, not always or primarily financial, persisted. Lady Arbella Denny, whose activities sometimes crossed the conventional boundaries of gender, responded to sights as a painter might. Returning from a ride around the northern fringe of Dublin Bay, she struggled to communicate the beauties that she had seen. She concluded, 'I think I have found a pretty spot for the painter to stand on to take his view for the picture', and herself sketched the place.[133] An aggressive improver, Lady Arbella left to a favourite, Arbella Caldwell, drawing instruments and two guineas with which 'to buy pencils to improve her taste in drawing landscape'.[134] As in architecture, so in painting, to learn the theory and how to judge the works was approved. But to become a devilling practitioner threatened to lower the adept to the status of craft-worker or mechanic.[135] In consequence, there was a reluctance to trade these artistic skills, although need reconciled some of gentle birth – Hugh Howard, Susannah Drury and Laetitia Bushe – to doing so.

## II

Supplying images of and for the propertied generated the most artistic effort in Stuart and Hanoverian Ireland. Demand might be sluggish (although not as slack as some contended), but it was increasing, and could be fostered. In Pennsylvania during the first half of the eighteenth century, it has been calculated that no more than 200 paintings may have been made. The colony, with a population which grew gradually from perhaps 5,000 to nearly 24,000 in 1760, resembled in size and demand the Protestant settlements of Munster or Ulster a century earlier. Dublin alone was populous and prosperous enough to give work to a larger body of artists and artificers than – as yet – could Philadelphia. Indeed, it offered a more rewarding (if exigent) environment than Wales.[136] In the Irish provinces, livings were harder to earn. Richard Carver, in addition to copying family portraits of the Flowers for Castle Durrow, painted a series of canvases to be placed over chimney-pieces and doors. He did similar work at Howth Castle for the St Lawrences. Carver's status as journeyman artificer was confirmed when he was obliged to paint the horse chaises and an oiled floorcloth, an important decorative feature in houses of pretension. This necessary versatility recalled that of journeymen painters in eighteenth-century Pennsylvania, Scotland and Wales.[137] Hussey not only painted originals and replicas for Edgeworth, but also dealt with framing these and other pictures. A few years later, Hussey was involved in the auction of works from the Antrim O'Haras' collection. Some he 'improved' for the auctioneer.[138] Earlier, Hugh Howard, well connected in Protestant Dublin, painted a series of portraits, some posthumous, of luminaries from Trinity College, where a brother was a fellow. Freed by a fortunate marriage from taxing his limited dexterity, he dabbled in dealing. He sniffed out occasional treasures in Irish houses, from which, could he but sell them outside Ireland, he might make a killing. In return, he channelled into Dublin furnishing pictures, many of them copies and some of dubious authenticity.

Awakening interest in trading in works of art was betokened by a grant in 1681 of the right to import them into Ireland.[139] As yet, those with the taste and money to acquire more than portraits could usually do so independently. Sir Robert Southwell personified this development. While in Italy, he had been painted 'by one Justo of Antwerp'. A souvenir of his time as emissary in Lisbon was a painting of a festival there. On later diplomatic missions in Brussels, he was portrayed: first in 1671, and then in 1673. In England, he patronized Lely and Kneller; in Ireland, he and his Perceval kinsmen used Pooley. As younger members of the family travelled, they too presented mementoes, notably three portraits of notables executed by Henry Tilson while in Rome during the 1680s.[140] By the 1690s, Southwell had permanently uprooted himself from Kinsale, and the collection was kept in his English residences. At most, the paintings influenced those in Ireland indirectly. Copies were made and sent to friends and dependants. Some within his family retained strong Irish connections, and when in Ireland might pontificate about art as well as politics. In addition, his Gloucestershire mansion, King's Weston, was a popular staging post for Irish on the ride home.[141]

The Ormondes, richer and seemingly more permanently rooted in Ireland, showed how international travels could assist in assembling an eclectic collection. The Ormondes' possessions, divided between England and Ireland, and between capitals and country residences, reflected their cosmopolitanism. Their commissions of portraits have already been mentioned. Of a different type was the purchase in 1686 of six sea battles from the Dutch marine painter van der Velde. Even here, family sentiment may have played a role. The duke's heir, Ossory, before his sudden and much lamented death in 1680, had fought in similar naval engagements. Initially the canvases were hung in 'the little supping room' in the Ormonds' London place.[142] In their turn, these scenes were copied on behalf of Lord Inchiquin, whose family had also participated in the naval warfare of Charles II's time.[143] Paradoxically, the many wars of the late seventeenth and eighteenth centuries increased the chances to raid strange cultures. Plunder from the campaigns included works of art, some of which found their way to Ireland. One of the drawings which Hugh Howard knew to be lurking in an Irish collection was a 'caricatura' owned by General Frederick Hamilton.[144] The general was also noted for the taste in which he had embellished his County Londonderry estate at Walworth.[145] It is likely that this veteran had come by the picture in the course of his soldiering abroad. Hamilton, indeed, even after he had retired to a respected place in Dublin society, maintained contact with former comrades. One at least, William Leathes, among other services, advised on and arranged purchases of fine and applied art in the Low Countries. Leathes, who had originated in County Down, reserved some of the best for himself or his brother, Moses Leathes, another high-ranking army officer. Neither of the Leathes brothers returned to live in Ireland. Their paintings (like Southwell's) were hung eventually in their English houses, and so might be thought to have little relevance to the tastes of Irish Protestants.[146] Yet, because Leathes acted as an artistic pander, he directed artefacts from the Low Countries to customers in Ireland. Within the United Provinces and Netherlands, he guided the ignorant and interested around the sights, and schooled them in what was currently fashionable. Relations who visited him in the Low Countries had their portraits painted locally and were fixed up with 'old masters'.[147]

Soldiering on the continent was merely one of several reasons why information among Irish Protestants about what was happening in Britain and in mainland Europe increased. The volume of grand tourists from Ireland also grew. Not just the swankiest peers and their heirs goggled at the wonders, and returned home with souvenirs, fond memories, debts and diseases. More modest gentry, such as Samuel Waring, joined the movement. Waring, if he lacked the resources to raid Italy or the Rhineland, recorded buying engravings directly from the artist in Rome. Once back in Ulster, his interest in improving both the outside and inside of his house testified to foreign experiences. Another not of enormous wealth whose Irish life reflected travel was James Smythe. Younger son of a bishop, unsure whether to become a soldier or cleric, he chose the second. In the first decade of the eighteenth century, he reached Rome. Some solid testimonies of the trip were sent back to his brother-in-law in Ireland, Thomas Burgh. They included architectural treatises. Smythe, first in north Antrim, then in Meath, recollected the youthful journey. It left him with a permanent appreciation of architecture, painting, prints and furniture. At best, he applied these insights sporadically.[148] These examples, as those of the squire of Stradbally, Pole Cosby, who rode deep into central Europe, or of the trainee doctors sent to qualify in France and the Low Countries, suggest that it was not just the exquisites like Joseph Leeson and Ralph Howard, or the spoilt brats, such as the younger Frank Burton, who benefited from a stay away from Ireland.

Travel to England, duller but more routine, gave more a chance to perfect and apply their aesthetic education. Samuel Molyneux noted paintings as well as buildings and gardens. At Hampton Court in 1713, he saw Verrio's murals of the Caesars and raved over their 'fine, glaring colours'. The Mantegna *Triumph* hardly had to be described because it had recently been engraved and published. Similarly the Raphael cartoons were familiar from many engraved reproductions. However, Molyneux was taken by their 'inconceivably lively' colours.[149] More to Molyneux's taste were a series of heads attributed to Titian. These, displayed at Windsor, were adjudged 'the best pictures I ever saw in my life'.[150] A generation later – in 1751 – Robert French took a leisurely tour of England with his wife. His comments often betrayed the cribs by then available to the ardent tourist. At the same time, although his reactions to Raphael cartoons or an altar-piece in Chester cathedral followed the published opinions, they were sights that French had sought out and seemed to relish. Their direct effect on his existence in

44. Sir Joshua Reynolds, *General John Guise*. Guise's collection, housed in London until the 1760s, was seen by visitors from Ireland.

Galway may have been minimal, since there was no opportunity to cram Monivea with Raphaels. Yet, in looking and buying – whether in England or Ireland – his standards of comparison had been enlarged.

Not all who traipsed around foreign spectacles were overawed. One sightseer, clearly proud of his judgement in artistic matters, was consulted by Colonel Lambart about the pictures with which he should decorate his London house. He was flattered that Lambart 'was pleased to approve my taste'.[151] But when the Irish visitor was introduced into the London sanctum of General Guise, the tourist was unexpectedly critical. Guise's collection was famed. Two supposed Michelangelos were dismissed as little better than primed canvases. Faced with the profusion, the tourist was resolutely unimpressed. He concluded, 'this shows what sort of people connoisseurs are, and that all their curiosities are to be valued only by the great warmth and ardency of their own fancies and imaginations'.[152] What is notable about the observer from Ireland was his educated sensibility. He responded positively to much that he saw, including the Cornaro collection at Northumberland House. He judged St Stephen's Wallbrook, the centrally planned and most baroque of Wren's city churches, as 'one of the finest pieces of

45. Anon, *The Connoisseur*. Avid collectors, including those in or from Ireland, were satirized for being gullible.

architecture in England of modern construction, being the epitome of the dome of St. Paul's'. Wren's cathedral prompted him to muse on 'the sublime taste and grandeur' evident in 'that glorious structure'.[153] Striking out on his own, he – like French before him – enthused over the altar-piece in Chester cathedral. It was a tapestry based on Raphael cartoons, and portrayed St Paul with the sorcerer, Elymas. It was admired for the masterly way in which the emotions were conveyed. Further, the rules of proportion were 'exactly observed both with regard to nature, architecture and perspective'.[154] In the case of this traveller (and of others), standards by which to judge had been learnt before leaving Ireland.

Trips to England, and further afield, allowed the educated of Ireland to test their knowledge and discrimination. They also encouraged commissions and purchases. The St Georges on their regular shopping expeditions to London bought paintings at auction. They included: a 'Venus and Adonis', optimistically attributed to Rubens, for which they had paid £9; a 'battle-piece' by Tillemans; and a Vanderboon landscape.[155] Similarly, Blayney Townley, who added the name Balfour on inheriting more estates in Ulster and Leinster, treated himself on English and French holidays. In London, he had himself painted by Hans Hysing, the Swedish painter popular at George II's court. A copy was made which was destined for Nathanael Clements in

Ireland. For the latter, Balfour was charged ten guineas.[156] Balfour was especially fond of the work of Bernard Lens, either the second or third of the prolific dynasty. One Lens had recently been in Dublin.[157] Balfour purchased two landscapes and another dozen landscape drawings (some of Shropshire) by this master. The twelve were modestly priced at £2 12s. Framing them cost £6 8s. 6d. Balfour shipped back to Ireland a miscellany: a woman's head, a Venus, 'Abraham's servant and Rebecca', two copies from 'Watt an Capers', 'a piece of Italian figures', and 'several prints'. Unusual among the portraits was one of Oliver Cromwell. In general, Irish Protestants preferred to hang the head of William III on their walls.[158] In all, Balfour spent £47 8s. on about fifty works. This outlay matched another £45 16s. on china, but was overshadowed by £87 3s. 4d. disbursed on silver, and paled beside £232 on clothes and linen for himself and another £295 for his wife's clothing and linen.[159] Back in Dublin, Balfour had quickly to take in hand the affairs of his orphaned nephew, Billy Balfour. The uncle's services included saving eighteen family paintings from the auctioneer's hammer.

Entrepreneurs gradually moved into this potentially lucrative art business. The licensee permitted to import and auction works of art in 1681 seems not to have availed himself of the privilege. Only in 1707 has the first public sale of pictures in Dublin been noted.[160] Soon George Felster and his wife were active. They ran a tavern with public rooms suited to a variety of meetings, and sold snuff. In 1707, Felster was called upon to value engravings in the drawing room of Dublin Castle which had belonged to the Ormondes before they were sold to Lord Inchiquin. The couple also imported paintings which they then auctioned on their premises. Offerings included landscapes, historical scenes and sea-pieces.[161] Another who exploited this market was Caspar Erck. 'Bred to trade', Erck had long been a figure of substance in the city of Dublin.[162] In 1754, he touted a job lot of 'most valuable pictures . . . by eminent masters'. Among the artists whose works (or suppositious works) were exposed for sale in Dublin were Rembrandt, Ostade, Snyders, Teniers, Hollar, Rusidael, Van Eyck, Van Dyck, Weenix, Wouvermans, Brill, Breughel, Mompert and Segers. Only Salvator Rosa and Carlo Maratti dented this northern supremacy. This was in keeping with the preferences of the day, both in Britain and Ireland.[163] Two notable collections in Ireland at the time, Bishop George Berkeley's at Cloyne and Bishop Thomas Barnard's of Derry, showed a similar preponderance of works from the Low Countries rather than Italy.[164]

Ninety-four lots were to be auctioned in Dublin on Erck's behalf. Whether the consigner had carefully gauged the market and imported the desirable, or simply included whatever was to hand, is difficult to decide. Erck may have been a target of the attack in 1756 on 'an inundation of ill pictures imported by knaves, with design to impose on the tasteless and unwary'.[165] A rudimentary analysis of the offerings indicates that landscapes predominated: in thirty-four of the ninety-four canvases. Genre scenes (12), religious (8) and classical subjects (7) followed in popularity. Battle-pieces (7) and sea scenes (3) also had a small following. Surprisingly few of the works were described simply as interiors, still lives or of flowers and fruit. Attributions were, no doubt, optimistic, even imaginative.[166]

The bare catalogue of Erck's auction tells nothing of what proved popular and expensive, or what failed to sell. Local artists, struggling to earn bread, lamented the preference among the well-to-do for the foreign. This inclination matched the craze, even among professed patriots, for imported commodities. Just as the concerned tried to counter these habits by raising standards of design and craftsmanship in textiles, pottery and metal-wares, so too the Dublin Society, the most powerful lever behind these moves, encouraged graphic artists and sculptors through its system of premiums.[167] Its initiatives hardly altered the prevalent tastes. The kind of customer to whom Erck's and other sales of imported rarities were intended to appeal was Earl Grandison. The survival of a copy of the printed catalogue of 1754 among Grandison's papers at Dromana, his home in County Waterford, at the very least shows that the peer was tempted by the bait.[168] Whether he was hooked is unknown. Much of what Erck vended at the Sick-Hall in Crow Street would not have been out of place at Dromana. There Lord Grandison mixed family pieces with portraits of assorted notables ranging from Charles I and Henrietta Maria to Mary, Queen of Scots, Oliver Cromwell, the duchess of Marlborough, the duchess of Cleveland (a mistress of Charles II), and the duke of Ormonde. In addition, he hung two large landscapes, conversation pieces and two 'small flower pieces', one of shells, the other of peaches. In a great house, such as Dromana, long in the possession of the same tribe, each successive generation deposited its sediment. Thus, the impressive marble hall, sometimes used for dining, was hung with eleven long panels of 'Indian paper pictures' – probably imported by the East India Company from Canton – and four smaller ones over the doors.[169]

Peers like the Grandisons did not monopolize collecting and connoisseurship. Nor were the Dublin auctions necessarily aimed principally at them. Later in the century, the English architect James Gandon might sniff that Ireland contained only four collections of any consequence. All were owned by peers: Farnham, Leinster, Londonderry and Charlemont.[170] This judgement took a highly restrictive view of what constituted a collection, and inevitably ignored those already broken up. Indeed, many impressive assemblages proved as evanescent as the mansions in which they were hung and the other goods with which the pictures made a striking *mise en scène*. Scattered and often fragmentary or cryptic evidence reveals rather more interest in collecting and indeed more interesting collections. These activities were in turn stimulated and satisfied by both high-minded educators and chancers. The first elevated the arts into forces for moral good, and arranged the different types of painting in a hierarchy of worth.[171] Under such tuition, knowledge and appreciation of art, as of architecture, became an essential in the preparation of any gentleman. It bred the pundit, the poseur and the gullible. How pictures were to be evaluated, because not obvious, had to be taught. The discriminating coveted the rare. Technical accomplishment, perceived realism, and the depth and refinement of the sentiments awakened were all extolled. By 1747 the undergraduate Burke could praise painting conventionally, because 'it greatly tends to the furtherance and improvement of virtue by putting before our eyes the most lively examples of the reward of it and the punishment of the contrary'.[172] Since the second half of the seventeenth century, the greater availability of paintings added a further field for the ambitious to negotiate. Some frankly abdicated any aesthetic judgment to others whose fancy could be trusted, such as Samuel Waring and Hugh Howard. Confronted with copies as well as originals, or with subjects which elicited worthy and unworthy emotions, the uninitiated struggled not to err. As Lord Shaftesbury wrote early in the eighteenth century, 'they would be soundly mortified themselves if, by such as they esteemed good judges, they should be found to have purchased by a wrong fancy or ill taste'.[173]

Within Irish Protestant society, a few formed collections for exemplary and moral purposes. From the south Munster setting of Cloyne, its bishop, Berkeley, spread 'the polite arts', with their ethical resonances, among his neighbours. At least one contemporary, the Dungarvan apothecary Charles Smith, equally bent on improving the people of Ireland, believed that Berkeley succeeded. Berkeley's elegant appointments, musical concerts and gallery of paintings proved 'an example so happy, that it has diffused itself into the adjacent gentlemen's houses'. Soon the neighbourhood pulsed with 'a pleasing emulation . . . to vie with each other in these kinds of performances'.[174] Moreover, the cultivated insisted that carefully selected collections facilitated sociability. This, when carefully managed, led towards virtue. Bishop Barnard of Derry in 1750 stocked his library with folios of engravings and drawings, with which he was pleased to entertain his friends. He had assembled 200 paintings, 'well preserved and in good order'. Typically, 'a day of *virtù*' in Barnard's company meant a morning of 'prints, drawings, pictures; in the evening, music'.[175] The animator of the Dublin Society, the Fermanagh landowner and parson Samuel Madden, used his paintings to create an ensemble at Manor Waterhouse. The hall was panelled with 'curiously carved' woodwork; the great parlour commanded views of the newly planted avenue and Lough Erne. Both rooms were 'almost covered with fine pieces of painting, several of which are originals by names famous in Europe'. Like Berkeley, Madden sponsored musical evenings. He also took upon himself the reinvigoration of the arts in Ireland, for which he was sometimes ridiculed.[176]

The tradition of bishops interesting themselves in aesthetics as well as religion and philosophy continued. Some, it seemed, cared more for the first than the second. Arthur Smythe, son of the cultivated bishop of Limerick, Thomas Smythe, travelled to Italy in the 1730s after graduating from Trinity College.[177] The father, while in Limerick, was credited with introducing more sophisticated tastes in furnishing. In turn, another of his sons, Charles Smythe, represented Limerick in parliament and patronized the architect Edward Lovett Pearce, who, through his uncle, General Thomas Pearce, was linked with the place.[178] Arthur Smythe collected Italian books on architecture, painting and antiquities while abroad. These were eventually left to Marsh's Library in Dublin, in the hope that more in the capital – notably among the clergy – might learn his enthusiasms.[179] Even before being shelved in a 'public library', the volumes may have been lent to the curious. It was not flattery alone which made the Reverend Matthew Pilkington, when he presented a copy of his own seminal dictionary of painters, congratulate Smythe on his elevated taste, having had in Italy 'an opportunity of surveying most of the works' of the famous artists.[180]

Clerics, although disproportionately important in enlightening Protestant Ireland, were not the only doers of good. Ripples spread from the modest but personable Waring. Discernment backed by riches helped to achieve a greater impact. In the 1740s, Peter Ludlow, a Meath landowner, was thought 'a very ingenious gentleman', not least because he was 'very musical and understands painting'. His house at Ardsallagh was said to contain some good paintings. In 1755, he had Reynolds paint his portrait.[181] Occasionally addicts from Ireland threatened to ruin themselves – and successors – through their passionate collecting. Sir John Perceval's campaign of cultural innovations in the County Cork of the 1680s was blamed for his debts of £10,000.[182] In 1741, Sir Richard Levinge playfully scolded Sir John Rawdon, the young heir of the Moira estate in County Down, 'I wish you would let me tie you up from buying pictures, which make more bubbles and ruin more young men than all other expenses'.[183] Rawdon, recently under the tutelage of Thomas Prior, Madden's collaborator in the Dublin Society, had been escorted around continental Europe.[184] Rawdon was not easily restrained. By 1742, he was said already to own 'more than would fill two large houses'. Greater discrimination was urged, 'for 'tis not the number but those of the best masters that are to be valued'.[185] Rawdon's love of music and painting was shared by his intended bride, herself a gifted amateur painter.[186]

By the mid-eighteenth century, the notion that true refinement consisted not in conspicuous display but in restraint was shared by some who policed Protestant Ireland. In this spirit, the affluent Bishop Synge of Elphin mocked the pretensions of brethren who trumpeted their rank by attaching brass mitres to the doors of their carriages. He might have been thinking of Lady Vesey, wife of the early-eighteenth-century bishop of Ossory. She had fussed not only about the door furniture but also the cloth lining of her new equipage.[187] Posturing over questions of taste was deplored. 'Fribbling lords, senseless bucks and mincing ladies' made easy targets.[188] Mrs Delany wrote witheringly of the follies of Lord Chief Justice Singleton and his *virtuoso epicuroso*, Bristowe. 'Like a conceited connoisseur', the duo did 'strange things'.[189]

Impostures and absurdities told of the extent to which a need for art had pervaded the thinking of most who aspired to gentility and to be of the quality. Awkwardly uniting the roles of mentor, monitor and merchant, Robert Howard offers a gauge of just how deeply felt was the need for art. Howard, son of a leading physician in late-seventeenth-century Dublin, was reared in a community already steeped in intellectual and artistic activities.[190] Education at Trinity College nurtured these interests. They were further developed through Lord Pembroke's rarefied viceregal court between 1705 and 1707. Howard kept in touch with one of Pembroke's equerries, Andrew Fountaine, who, once back in England, aided Howard's and his circle's collecting of medals, coins and engravings.[191] Publications, travel to England and beyond, and visitors to Ireland all refined Howard's incipient understanding. In 1707,

Howard was disappointed that busts recently arrived from Hamburg in Trinity College, where he was a fellow, although approved by Pembroke, 'don't take with the generality'.[192] Almost thirty years later, Howard, now a bishop, allowed that demand for works of art in Ireland had increased, but the levity with which they were judged had not lessened. Accordingly, he instructed his brother, the artist Hugh Howard, to send over from England a package of paintings, 'not of price but agreeable show, for we go no further here'.[193] During the intervening years, Robert Howard continued his aesthetic education. Also, with his brother, he became an intermediary as well as instructor. Some of what his sharp brother in London supplied, he kept for himself; more, he passed to others. By the 1710s, he already owned a painting of the Madonna, kept in his study: an unexpected insight into the devotions of this Church of Ireland divine, but not dissimilar to clerical tastes in later seventeenth-century England. Indeed the Ormondes had also hung holy pictures in conspicuous spots. A group of the Virgin, St John the Baptist and the infant Christ, after Titian, had been placed first in the London house and then over the chimney-piece in the drawing room at Kilkenny. The second duke kept a Correggio of the Virgin in his bedroom at Dublin Castle, having moved it there from the gallery at Kilkenny.[194]

In 1726, Robert Howard received from Hugh Howard, a good copy of a celebrated Guido Reni to hang over his chimney-piece. It probably adorned his Dublin house rather than the see house in remote Killala. With it arrived a Madonna after Luco Giordano.[195] In 1729, a consignment from London included a copy of a Madonna by Andrea del Sarto, two copies after Pellegrini, hunting scenes by Wootton and – the most expensive at £5 14s. – a version of a Gaspar Poussin landscape.[196] They were followed in 1733 by two framed views of ruins.[197] The bishop, more the merchant than the moral improver, confided to his brother, 'you know I have an eye to furniture in them. Not that [it] is my taste, but there are no judges here'.[198] The Howards knew that paintings, like books, textiles and silver, helped to furnish a room, and bought accordingly.[199] Moreover, the bishop, as agent and importer, offered services which complemented his recommendations of servants, tutors, lodgings and shops to associates and kindred. The Howard brothers, strategically positioned in London and Dublin, occupied a niche comparable to that of Cardinal Albani in the Rome of their day.

The pair supplied Dr Marmaduke Coghill, who was embellishing his handsome suburban mansion at Drumcondra. In return, it seems, Coghill made Howard a present of a Van Dyck.[200] The Howards' sister, Mrs Dorothea Dopping, had specific wants. Not only did she give the exact measurements for the required paintings, the three that she requested were not to be 'exceeding dear', but 'such kind of pictures as you sent to my brother last', which had then been passed on (or sold) to 'Mr.' Singleton (probably the future judge).[201] What was seen in other houses awakened the desire to own something similar. The calculating planted the noteworthy in the hope of exciting such responses. The disinterested, like Berkeley and Madden, then wished to exploit them for moral gain. The Howards, it seemed, chiefly sought financial profits. Hugh

46. Anon, *View of Mount Ievers, Co. Clare, c.* 1737. Mount Ievers remains little altered from the image painted onto the plaster above the chimney-piece in one of the rooms in the house. Some details of the elaborate gardens suggest aspiration rather than achievement.

Howard applied his own skills as a copyist. Copies were widely valued, enjoying prime places in royal collections.[202] Customers in Ireland – the Flowers, Veseys and Edgeworth – happily plugged holes in their sets of ancestors with replicas. In the 1750s and 1760s, Hussey did not turn down such work. Nor did Hugh Howard. Revisiting Ireland in 1710–11, he furnished Trinity College Dublin (an institution with which his family was closely associated) with portraits of notable alumni, some dead.[203] Hugh Howard, familiar also with the London and international art markets, conspired to remove the desirable from Ireland. In 1705, he enquired discreetly about a painting owned by Lord Longford. (The Aungiers had a precocious interest in painting.) Howard was discreet because he wanted to avoid 'alarming the owner, who don't know what a treasure they are possessed of'.[204] Howard was also haunted by the 'caricatura' owned by

General Hamilton; "'tis on paper', he remembered, 'of a little crooked painter, and is one of those ridiculous drawings which the Italians call *caricaturà*'. He schemed to borrow it in order to make a copy. But once he had it, the plan changed to selling it in London.[205] It is possible that Howard planned to return only a copy to Hamilton's heirs. Howard inhabited a murky region where valuable originals, copies and outright forgeries could be confused.

Most who bought pictures wanted them as decoration. About 1698, the Reverend John Chalenor was spending £1 on 'staircase pictures' for his house, in County Dublin.[206] This was the sort of request that the Howards strove to satisfy. The imported carried a premium, but by the early eighteenth century locals also satisfied the need. Murals offered an alternative to wooden panelling, lavish stucco and thick tapestries. Journeymen painters, the core of the Painter-Stainers' Company, could easily adjust from escutcheons, blazons and signs to decorating walls. William van der Hagen, having painted an altar-piece for St Michan's church in Dublin, graduated to private houses. In repute in the environs of Waterford, van der Hagen also catered to another taste growing among the propertied. He executed topographical set-pieces. These included a representation of the port of Waterford, for which he received £20 in 1736.[207] At the same time, individuals commissioned views of their residences. The Smythes, owners of Ballynatray, the Ievers of Mount Ievers, Cosby at Stradbally, Ingoldsby of Carton and Browne at Westport are known to have indulged this pleasant vanity.[208] After ancestors, and along with stallions and mares, town and house were objects of pride. The patronage of painting in Wales during the same period showed a similar pattern.[209] More disinterested was the antiquarianism or simple curiosity which encouraged some – like Susannah Drury – to depict sights around the country. One of the earliest recorded manifestations, prefiguring Drury, is Edwin Sandys, better remembered as an engraver but reputed an 'excellent artist' accomplished in 'designing and taking of views', who accompanied Samuel Foley, the bishop of Down and Connor, to the Giant's Causeway in 1693. Sandys's sketches were adjudged 'curious'.[210] Their purpose was to record a remote phenomenon which was exciting close attention and much theorizing.

## III

The wish to add interest and refinement to interiors was more economically achieved through engravings than by oils. In 1705, Mrs Jean Hall from Dublin begged her kinsman, William Leathes, currently in the United Provinces, to send her black-and-white prints, 'to make my little house fine'.[211] A veteran of the grand tour, the Reverend James Smythe, back in Ireland, stumbled on some prints which he adjudged 'tolerable, and would not be amiss in a chamber'.[212] The ease with which the right look could be achieved by a clever deployment of prints largely explains the frequency with which 'pictures' appear in eighteenth-century inventories and accounts. Just as with oil paintings, so too with engravings, the knowing distinguished between those fit for furniture and those worthy of a place in collectors' portfolios.[213] Bishop Robert Howard, in common with many in his ambit, knew this difference. Tutored first by Fountaine, and then by his brother, Hugh Howard, he built up a collection.[214] The quest for rare engravings could become obsessive. Bishop Howard's delicate palate was titillated when a kinsman, Sir Daniel Molyneux, wrote from Paris of the choice prints on sale there.[215]

By the second half of the seventeenth century, engravings allowed the sedentary to learn of distant buildings (ancient and modern) and the traveller to remember sites and sights seen earlier. Both impulses explained why Dr Jeremy Hall, cicerone to the sons of Irish peers, bequeathed his 'fair book of prints' to Trinity College in 1688. The volume, like five large maps of Rome and various French publications, also left to the university, had probably been acquired on the continent.[216] The illustrations either prepared the inquisitive for future sight-seeing or offered a vicarious grand tour. One alumnus of Dublin University trained for Italy by assembling a library of relevant publications. Waring, in Italy as companion of Ormond's grandson, lacked the means to buy and ship home original oils and marbles. However, he did inspect the studio of one revered engraver, 'Petro [Piero] Santo Bartoli'. Waring recalled that, 'we bought the tomb of Ovid, giving two crowns only for the sheets'. Thus, he carried home some modest evidence of the Roman holiday. 'Tho' dear, yet for the rarity and to oblige the author, Mr. Ballo, we could not do otherwise'.[217] At Waringstown, he attended minutely to the improvement of estate and house. As has been seen, the Warings were portrayed by Croger. Samuel Waring concerned himself with how the portraits should be framed. But he was equally insistent that the right frames surround a group of prints which made a decorative feature in the house. For the engravings, he secured seven frames of 'the best sort' with pear-wood mouldings, ten smaller ones, and another twenty-one (at 9d. each) for the 'common cuts'. In England, also, pearwood was commonly preferred for framing prints.[218] At this stage, Waring's printed gallery embraced the king and queen (each twice), the duchess of Ormond, the seven Church of England bishops who had defied James II, three 'Dutch humours', three landscapes, one simply 'Dutch school', 'a fountain', 'a well', and a 'noble Venetian'.[219]

Descriptions are too terse to convey much sense of their look or how they were arranged. Even so, several points are worth emphasizing. The Warings in provincial Ulster decorated a room with prints probably in advance of the endorsement of the practice by the Ormondes in the drawing room of Dublin Castle. Waring's engravings may not have been visually so imposing as the viceroy's. Nevertheless, the country squire independent of any lead from the Castle had adopted a fashion in furnishing. An inventory of Waringstown survives. Taken when Samuel Waring inherited the property from his father in 1703, it is silent about the presence of the engravings, and indeed of the Croger portraits. On the evidence of the inventory alone, it would be supposed that the house was devoid of pictures. At the very least, this omission – perhaps because the value of the pictures was reckoned to be low – reminds that as

often as inventories inform they can mislead. In time, Squire Waring's interests were trans-
mitted to descendants and neighbours: a development helped by the presence at Waringstown of his collections. *Grisailles* preserved at Waringstown show a little of how the
prints could be used. The pictures – of ambition and bravura – were executed in gouache by
an otherwise unknown member of the Warings' circle, Grace McNaghten. One copied an
engraving by Francois Vivares after a painting by Patel. Vivares, who had settled in London,
was (so it was recalled at Waringstown) 'generally called the French Claude'. Especially for
women, without other means of instruction, unsuspected worlds were revealed by prints.
Some whom Mary Delany took under her wing refined their skills and delighted their admirers by copying engravings painstakingly.

The sketchy information about the engravings at Waringstown at the turn of the seventeenth and eighteenth centuries suggests that portraits dominated, as in contemporary galleries of oils. The medium allowed the speedy and relatively inexpensive reproduction of
images of the famous and topical.[220] Depending on alignment, these could be the Jacobite
hero, the second duke of Ormonde, Speaker Conolly, Archbishop King or the sovereign himself.[221] Towards the end of the first duke of Ormond's life, in the 1680s, one hundred 'cuts' of
his portrait had been ordered, in London and at a cost of £7 10s.[222] In 1703, the elder Edward
Southwell was being consulted about which image of his father, Sir Robert, who had recently
died, should be engraved by John Smith. Pooley, who had recorded Southwell in oils, assisted
in the choice.[223] In the 1720s, Archbishop King wearily submitted to have his portrait taken so
that a plate could then be engraved and an edition printed. Soon enough he found fault with
the whole enterprise and countermanded it. 'It is more like an ill-shaped lion's face than
mine', he roared, 'and a most frightful figure.' To repair the damage inflicted by the incompe-
tent Wilkinson, he proposed having an edition of three hundred struck from a mezzotint
taken from one of his portraits in London.[224] A few years later, Mrs Conolly was pleased to
present printed copies of her late husband's portrait to some of her dependants.[225] Concurrently, Hugh Howard, with suspect reluctance, consented to an engraving of himself being
made and sold in London.[226] In 1736, a Dublin doctor was delighted with a parcel of prints of
the late queen, which he distributed among appreciative friends.[227] Family feeling was again
satisfied when the earl of Egmont dispatched from England to a distant cousin, a lawyer in
Dublin, engraved portraits of members of their family.[228] In the 1750s Richard Edgeworth
happily subscribed for an engraved image of the Prince of Wales. So much did he value it that
he had the jobbing painter, Hussey, look to its framing.[229] In Strickland Lowry's portrait of
the Bateson family, from County Down, painted early in the 1760s, prints of the king and
queen and the elder Pitt hang among oils of local views.[230]

Engravings spanned a wide spectrum. At one extreme were the desirable items for which
*cognoscenti* competed. At the other lay the flimsy images designed to stimulate devotions. In
1700, a shipment of miscellaneous goods into Limerick included ten dozen '*Agnus Dei* with-

out glass' and more glazed. These can be identified as religious prints, originating on the continent. So cheap were they – the 120 were valued at only one shilling for the lot – that they must have been destined, via fairs, patterns and markets, for the homes of the Catholic poor.[231] They introduced unfamiliar imagery into sparsely adorned interiors. Occasionally they can be detected earlier in the seventeenth century. Elizabeth Coach, an inhabitant of Dublin in the 1630s, owned not only a 'picture with frame' – at the date, a rarity – worth an estimated three shillings, but nine dozen small prints and a further two dozen 'great' ones. The quantity suggests commercial rather than personal exploitation of what may have been imported engravings, perhaps of a devotional character.[232] A stationer in Dublin, when making his will in 1663, mentioned sixty 'paper pictures'.[233] In 1683, a Catholic gentleman, John Grace of Brittas (County Tipperary), disposed of several pictures. They included the secular 'Pastoral', in his own chamber, representations of 'Senators and Singers' and of 'Our Saviour delivering the keys'. It is impossible to know whether these were painted or printed.[234] By 1750, the sacred site of Holy Cross in County Tipperary owned '6 old pictures on paper', presumably of religious subjects and possibly engraved.[235]

In 1741, Bridget Grady, an innkeeper in Cork, had among the contents of her premises, 'some framed pictures', which can be presumed to have been prints. Along with tables and chairs, delft dishes and pewter, Cork topers could now drink in a setting which included pictures. A century earlier this was also true of grander Dublin hostelries.[236] By the 1760s, in the Lawders' County Leitrim house were 'a hall picture' and the 'Prodigal Son'. The latter, depicting one episode in the Old Testament cycle, was appropriate in a family whose fortunes had been made over two generations by Church of Ireland clergyman. Again, the edifying subject was more likely to have been engraved than painted.[237] Equally full of incident and moral purpose were the engravings after Hogarth. Andrew Crotty, agent to south Munster notables, among his other services as an intermediary secured prints for acquaintances in Ireland.[238] At the same time, a Dublin attorney was delighted to receive a set of Hogarth's engravings of *The Rake's Progress.*[239] As in eighteenth-century Scotland, so in Ireland a variety of routes allowed popular images produced in London quickly to arrive.[240] In both Ireland and Scotland (and provincial England) auctions also circulated decorative imagery. At an Irish sale in 1749, seven prints of Hogarth's *Harlot's Progress* went for £1 10s.[241] A satirist in 1756 had a clergyman complain of his 'little lodge in the country . . . damnably unfurnished'. The dining room was adorned only by 'a vile map over the chimney, and the worst set of the harlot's progress in dale[deal] frames'.[242] Maybe, this was not entirely a caricature. It differed from the effect of Lord Chief Justice Whitshed's house at Stormanstown, on the northern margins of Dublin, which he willed to a brother. As well as the judge's best coach and four coach horses, the brother would receive 'the cuts, prints and maps' there.[243] Nor was Hogarth's series disdained by the titled. *The Rake's Progress* adorned Howth Castle, where a profusion of engravings decorated the walls. In County Fermanagh about 1750, Margetson Armar paid to have a set of Hogarth's works framed.[244]

Doubts have been raised about the social groups able to afford engravings in eighteenth-century England. Other than the cheap devotional imagery, the engravings discussed above were to be found in the houses of professionals, the quality and the gentry. A notable such as Archbishop King was happy enough to own '23 small pieces of mezzotints in frames', which cost only sixpence apiece.[245] Between 1748 and 1750, 'prints' worth £612 are known to have been shipped into Ireland. What the term signified – bundles of cheap images or the rarefied and valuable – is impossible to decide. So the volume of this recorded trade remains equally uncertain.[246] The upper end of this market tempted artistic entrepreneurs. Lord Perceval, the Irish peer resident in England, was inveigled into a venture to print high-quality images in colour. Perceval boasted to his brother in Dublin, 'there never was a more ingenious invention nor any good furniture so cheap'.[247] Thanks to the still powerful Perceval–Southwell axis in Ireland, subscriptions were collected there. Philip Perceval in Dublin had his new purchases framed, and thought 'they look very well, especially mixed with other pictures'. The series reproduced mainly Italian masters, although a Van Dyck of two boys was included. The investors hoped that the religious character of most prints would recommend them to Catholic Europe. In Ireland, this was not the intended market. Rather, the prints appealed to Perceval's cultivated acquaintances, like the member of parliament from the Blackwater valley, William Maynard.[248] Customers in Ireland valued the images as versions of respected but remote originals rather than as aids to religious contemplation. Dubliners, however, did not take to Van Dyke's children, finding them ill-proportioned.[249] In the event, the whole project soon collapsed.[250]

## IV

In 1734, sundry goods of Benjamin Greene were sold at Cappoquin in County Waterford. Greene, an 'esquire', typified settlers established in south Munster in the seventeenth century and how some had prospered.[251] The planters, close to ports and with relations still in England, quickly learnt what was afoot beyond the province. The Greene auction also disclosed the increasing diversification of material life for successful Protestants within Ireland. Among many possessions, Greene owned numerous pictures. This contrasted with the early, Spartan era of the Munster plantation, a century before, when few except the topping like Lord Cork possessed such artefacts. As striking as Greene's accumulation of art was its dispersal at the sale. At least twelve bidders bought his pictures.

A couple of the new owners can be identified as members of other settler families from the area (Arthur Boate and John Codmore). Others – Thomas Flin, Ambrose Murphy and Daniel Sheridan – bore names which implied (perhaps wrongly) ethnic origins and confessional affiliation different from the Protestant planters. The possibility that Irish Catholics were

buying raises the problem of whether they too were following the fashions in material culture which, although promoted by the English of Ireland as peculiar to themselves, were continental and often Catholic in origin. The seventeenth century was a more propitious time
than the eighteenth for Catholics in Ireland to assemble collections of paintings.[252] In 1633, a
Catholic preacher was said to have explained a theological point by using a painting.[253] Furthermore, during the brief revival of Catholic fortunes under James VII and II, notables commissioned portraits which betrayed a strong and fashionable French influence.[254] But by the
time that Greene's effects were dispersed, few Catholics had the money for such acquisitiveness. Maybe the circumspect who enjoyed a modest prosperity could pick up inexpensive lots
at auction. An alternative explanation is that Flin, Murphy and Sheridan were merchants
buying stock which in time would be sold to others of status similar to Squire Greene.
Another buyer was the 'Widow Funosey'. The only woman among the twelve named buyers,
she too may have been a trader. Equally, the two lots which she secured – including '4 element
pictures' for 3s. 3d. – appealed to her fancy and would embellish her own home. Presumably
they represented fire, water, earth and air. The low price suggested that they were engravings,
perhaps Dutch or in a Dutch style. In this case, as throughout Greene's large collection, the
printed and painted are well nigh impossible to distinguish. The volume is clear. At least 140
of Greene's 'pictures' were sold. Of these at least twenty-four were described as mezzotints.
Only rarely are the laconic descriptions elaborated. William Landergan bought a 'painted
land sketch' for 1s. 2d.; John Jones, another 'land sketch' for 2s. 1d.[255] Possibly they were
designed to be inserted above chimney-pieces or doorcases. Occasionally, the works are
called 'Dutch'. They may have been firmly labelled with their place of printing; more probably, they were genre scenes or interiors recognizably Dutch or in the Dutch idiom.[256]

Mrs Matthew Dwyer, dying in the western diocese of Killaloe in the eighteenth century,
was possessed of a picture of 'King Charles'. Whether the first or second of that name was not
specified. She had more than twenty-four pictures. Their low value, two shillings for the two
dozen, another 2s. 4d. for 'some pictures', implied that they were engravings. In contrast, 'a
glass picture', on its own reckoned at three shillings, might have been painted. The
respectability of Mrs Dwyer was confirmed by her ownership of a silver watch.[257] By 1780,
Robert Tickell, a mariner, who had lived in Cork city, radiated material brilliance. In addition
to those fundamentals of polite living – china tea-wares, silver, pewter, and seat furniture –
he possessed thirty-four glazed pictures and another five probably unframed.[258] Elsewhere in
the same city, pictures abounded. They were sold in bundles among the effects of the apothecary Bentley. The inviting appearance of Delamain's rooms near the Protestant cathedral
where he taught dancing owed much to his numerous prints.[259]

This decorative device frequently recurred, and linked the houses of urban professionals,
thought of by some as a pseudo-gentry, with those of the landed. Four examples suffice to
show the ubiquity of engravings in a variety of interiors. Stackallen, in County Meath, like

Castletown and Conyngham Hall, attested to the successes of the Ulster Protestants who had rallied early to William III and ridden to success with him. Stackallen's owner, Gustavus Hamilton, moved from north-western Ulster into the Pale, built a grand if stylistically old-fashioned house and collected a peerage, ending as Viscount Boyne, in final tribute to his part in that victory. By 1757 Stackallen was to be let. Its contents included family (and other) pictures. An air of shabby grandeur enveloped the place. In the Great Hall or 'saloon', the ten large walnut arm chairs were dismissed as 'of ancient make'. Similarly, if the large parlour boasted panels of Indian (i.e. Chinese) painted paper superficially like those at Dromana, at Stackallen they were written off as 'very ordinary'. Homage to the sovereigns whom Hamilton had helped to install on their thrones, William and Mary, was made in the drawing room. It took the now antiquated form of gilt leather hangings on two of the walls: on one side, ornamented with the heads of William and Mary, and on the other with Queen Anne. Elsewhere in the mansion was a full-length portrait of King Charles, probably the second. In 'Miss Hamilton's chamber', still decorated in an earlier manner with tapestry and a mirror in a 'large, old-fashioned frame', was one painting of Venus and Vulcan and another of Darby and Joan. None of these was thought to be valuable, with the best reckoned at only 5s. 5d.

In contrast to these low values, a set of eight mezzotints, which dominated the small parlour, was highly esteemed. They were a mixed bag. Some were Dutch narrative subjects, each valued at £1 10s. Others depicted historical events: the battle of Naseby (1645), reckoned at £1 1s. 8d.; the revolt of the fleet (in 1648); and the trial of Charles I in 1649. Outstanding in this group was one print which showed Lord Boyne, the builder of the house, beating the watch. This rarity, at £4, was surpassed only by a 'midnight conversation' in colours, worth an estimated £5. Another topical image from the time when the mansion was new was a print of the Tsar Peter. A later addition was a print of the firework display which had dazzled Dublin in 1748. Pictures had clearly mattered in the original design and arrangement of the house. Unusually among Irish mansions of the date, it had been equipped with a long gallery.[260] This seems to have functioned in part as a billiard room. It was also in some sense a picture gallery. Thirty-four heads, all but one framed, were still located there in 1757. They were likely to have been painted on canvas. Whatever they represented – classical heroes or contemporary worthies – the display mimicked similar assemblages made by English aristocrats, such as Clarendon in his London house in the 1660s or the Scottish duke of Lauderdale at Ham House. The spending priorities, at least in the minds of the valuers of 1757 and perhaps of the Hamiltons, are shown by comparing the £5 at which the pictures were appraised with the £24 5s. 6d. for the billiard equipment.[261]

At Howth Castle, seat of the St Lawrences, barons and then earls of Howth, a similar mixture of family portraits and engravings had been accumulated. By the 1740s, a portrait by Bindon of Dean Swift, a friend of Lord Howth, a portrait of the house itself and its sur-

47. John Lewis, *William St Lawrence with dog*, before 1749.

roundings on the northern fringe of Dublin Bay, and a mysterious 'sea triumph' had been added. Richard Carver, used by Flower at Castle Durrow, had painted canvases above doors. Yet, in the dining parlour, the principal decoration was six prints. Four represented 'morning', 'noon', 'evening' and 'night'. The others were 'Anne of Cleves' and 'Southwark Fair'. Lady Howth's dressing room was hung with seventeen glazed prints. But it was 'the arch' which had the densest concentration: ninety-nine pictures of different sizes. Most, if not all, were engravings. Here were to be found Hogarth's sequence; another of 'the liberal arts' and an eclectic selection of portraits ranging from Julius Caesar, through Raphael, to Montrose, Cardinal Fleury and Robert Boyle. The family, which had converted from Catholicism, possessed a crayon drawing of the Virgin Mary. Other connections were recalled by depictions of the siege of Buda by Joseph Harrath, a German artist.[262] In contrast with this profusion, the town house of the Howths – in the northside quarter of St Mary's Abbey – was bare of paintings and prints, other than a full-length of Lady Belfield. However, this may be no more than a result of the different purposes for which the inventories were taken, rather than a sign that the Castle, as the main seat, was thought to be the more appropriate location for pictures.[263]

From north Antrim, something can be retrieved of the style in which another peer lived. The MacDonnells, marquesses of Antrim, had long affected splendour. However, reverses meant that the contents of their houses were periodically scattered, obliging new generations to refurnish. By the 1750s, the MacDonnells had been assimilated to the religion and ways of Protestant Britain and Ireland. Yet archaisms survived. It was rumoured that the long train of followers who coshered on Antrim as he moved from house to house caused him to fire the hunting lodge at Ballymacgarry rather than face the dependants.[264] Whatever the reasons for the fire, goods – including many pictures – had been rescued. Antrim owned a portrait of Mary Queen of Scots, but this need not be interpreted as an icon of a continuing Jacobitism in a family which, until the recent past, had been noted for its affection towards the Stuarts.[265] The topical could be studied through a map of General Wade's roads across the Scottish highlands: the routes which had aided the suppression of the 1745 Jacobite rising. Neither a print of the fountain at Versailles nor another of the battle of Fontenoy betrayed leanings towards France rather than Britain. Alongside these were found a plan of an unnamed English engagement in the Mediterranean and a study of the Blue Squadron, a naval flotilla. The MacDonnells had also acquired one from the lately issued set of Hogarth's *Marriage à la Mode*. Other decorative prints included four views of Venice, half a dozen coloured landscape prints, thirteen pictures of cut paper (a vogue to which the Howths had also surrendered), a dozen flower pieces and a single 'radish' picture (possibly a minutely detailed Dutch study of fruit and vegetables). As with the formula adopted by Philip Perceval in his Dublin House, oils and prints mingled on the walls. Five coloured prints of stag hunting and several more of racehorses with their jockeys probably mirrored Antrim's enthusiasms most accurately.[266] Equine passions were translated into paint in other mansions. Naïve images celebrated Lord Meath's hounds at Kilruddery and those of the Pakenhams.[267] Some grandees, it was noted, treated their horses as well as – if not better than – their womenfolk, and were prepared to spend lavishly for portraits of thoroughbreds. The invented Lord Frolic voiced an interest in a Wootton canvas, on sale at fifty guineas, 'as he is in some sort a relation of your family'.[268]

The same mélange of old and new subjects, printed and painted, was visible in the Dublin house of the Nugents, a branch of the family whose head was earl of Westmeath. Some, but not all, had conformed to Protestantism. In the mid-eighteenth century, John Nugent owned a picture of Martin Luther. Indeed, the Protestant reformer hung in the dining room, along with eight family portraits, handsomely set in 'gilt and lacquered frames'. Nugent's widow, perhaps dissatisfied with the appraisal by two engaged in the decorators' business as 'upholders' or upholsterers, had five of the best pictures taken away and valued by an expert, 'Mr. Hamilton', who reckoned them at £6. Less highly considered were 'the four seasons, coloured', valued at eleven shillings, which, with two more family pictures decorated the parlour. In the hall and on the stairs hung five maps and prints of horses.[269]

Engravings added visual interest to assorted homes. Usually cheap, they could be picked up easily at the numerous auctions in town and country by the middle of the eighteenth century. It was calculated that they would depreciate rather than increase in value over time.[270] One of the few 'luxuries' that the austere bachelor Peacock allowed himself before his wife encouraged a more crowded domestic setting were some 'prints'. He bought them at a County Limerick sale in 1743 for 5s. 6d.[271] What they represented is unknown. As has been seen, they could range from crudely executed aids to religious devotion, disapproved of by rigid Protestants as tantamount to idolatry, through the common images of notables, to reproductions of famous oil paintings and complex compositions of classical mythology and history. Peacock used printed material, in the more conventionally noticed form of books and newspapers. Through his reading, he learnt of distant and sometimes fabulous events. How a daily viewing of engravings in his otherwise bare interior affected his imagination and perceptions of the world around him cannot be known. But for Peacock, as for others who framed and hung such materials in their homes, the act expressed choice, and not always enslavement to fashion. Prints, and indeed oil paintings, were simply one among an increasing choice of commodities on offer to householders in eighteenth-century Ireland, as across western Europe and north America.

In the modest parlour of an Ulster parson, one set of engravings was described: 'Alexander's battles'.[272] Their impact on the household cannot even be guessed. A rare inkling of the effects comes from the uses of prints made by Squire Waring. Patiently and expertly he copied the engraved plates of elevations and plans from *Vitruvius Britannicus* and publications on continental architecture. By doing so, he familiarized himself with the details of buildings, some of which he had once seen but others of which were unknown to him. He honed his skills as draughtsman and designer through close scrutiny of the prints. Others in the Warings's orbit, including women like Grace McNaghten, diverted themselves by rendering elaborate engravings in different mediums. How fine prints could continue education was also illustrated by another grand tourist after he had settled back into the Irish countryside. The Reverend James Smythe had shopped in Italy on behalf of the surveyor-general, Burgh. Later Smythe exchanged with his elder brother at Barbavilla an engraving of the great palace of Racconigi outside Turin designed by Guarini.

How far by circulating images of this type the Smythes went beyond amusing and informing themselves to shaping what they – and others in their neighbourhood – built is hard to surmise. It would be absurd to contend that knowledge of grandiloquent baroque structures in Italy and Central Europe affected the concept or scale of what squires and squarsons such as the Smythes erected in the Irish midlands. Nevertheless, such publications supplied a standard against which local and more modest creations could be checked. Also, they offered a

48. Barbavilla lacquer cabinet, *c.* 1735, made by a Dublin joiner to incorporate imported painted panels. Its design was influenced by Archdeacon James Smythe, who had travelled extensively in Europe.

grammar of correct design and proportions and a vocabulary of ornament which were more directly applied, as when Smythe advised the squire of Barbavilla on a architectonic cabinet which was being made for the house. The cabinet incorporated panels painted with landscapes. Another Smythe brother, living in London, imported three oil paintings from Holland, which were then shipped to Ireland. They depicted Old Testament scenes of Adam and Noah.[273] In another mid-eighteenth-century house, Lohort Castle (County Cork), residents and guests could scan prints of Venice, seven London churches, Westminster Abbey, Sir Thomas Robinson's seat at Rokeby and Astley's at Melton Constable in Norfolk, sometimes derided as the acme of ostentation and architectural ignorance. The owners of Lohort, the Percevals, long absent from the Cork estate, strove constantly to raise the artistic standards of Ireland. But it may be doubted whether the majority of agents, employees and tenants penetrated to the study or loft where the engravings hung.[274]

The presence within houses of prints and paintings could kindle enthusiasms among the impressionable. This was the intention – and so the justification – of the highfalutin such as Shaftesbury and Berkeley, who endowed paintings with moral power. Those who aspired to connoisseurship realized that it had to be learnt laboriously, like other genteel attributes. It involved a cerebral endeavour, not just a sensory response to visual stimuli. At the same time, the true gentleman risked demeaning himself if he became too well versed in the technical minutiae.[275] Contemporary conventions certainly recommended the acquisition of works of art, and the ability to assess them. Enthusiasts profited: in the case of Hugh Howard, financially. His brothers in Dublin, Robert and William Howard, made collections of, respectively, paintings and books. Robert Howard, near the start of his clerical and collecting career, regretted that few in Dublin shared his discriminating fancy. The busts imported into the university had not been much appreciated. By the 1740s, when Bishop Howard's heir, Ralph Howard, later to be ennobled as Viscount Wicklow, was in the college, a series of busts was introduced into the library as embellishment.[276]

At this moment, Howard, a young exquisite, was exhibiting the refinements hereditary in his family. Soon he would become an avid purchaser of paintings, sculpture and prints. His set of rooms in the college was expensively rejigged. Prominent were paintings. Twelve picture frames and another two, fashioned from pearwood and gilded, attested to the array at which the visitor could gawp.[277] These dispositions presaged Ralph Howard's deeper immersion in European art during a protracted tour. As well as plunder from Rome, he returned with modern canvases by Richard Wilson.[278] The young Howard had fallen in with a group from Ireland, including Lord Charlemont, Joseph Leeson and Joseph Henry, who egged each other on in the hunt for the rare.[279] Over three generations, the Howards had speculated and collected. The future Lord Wicklow outdid them all. Brought up to care about the arts, he was also trained to fulfil the public responsibilities entailed with his property.[280] In Wicklow, as in Waring, what might have begun as a necessary part of his education as a gentleman turned into a pleasure and, perhaps, an addiction. Many, habituated to the look and contents of their houses, deputed to others – agents, wives, kinsfolk – decisions about additions and alterations. Some, however, interested themselves in their surroundings and were constantly on the look out for refinements and novelties. Theorists, such as Shaftesbury and Chesterfield, warned against too minute a concern with the technicalities. 'They must only be the amusements, and not the business of a man of parts'.[281] Like so much advice, it was as often ignored as heeded.

Chapter 6

# Park and Garden

*I*

During the 1680s, Lord Meath's estate of Kilruddery in County Wicklow was improved. What most impressed one contemporary were the projected deer park, a paddock for colts, and the decoy for wildfowl. The last was accounted not just the best in Ireland, but in the three kingdoms. Almost as an afterthought, changes to the house itself were noted.[1] Similar priorities governed Edmund Malone's planned alterations to his Westmeath property early in the next century. Pleasure grounds, orchard and kitchen garden had all to be included. The pairing of house and park was a commonplace of seventeenth- and eighteenth-century design. Malone was told that 'some fundamentals' for a residence of any pretensions should strive for 'good shelter and agreeable prospect'.[2] Theorists and architects pontificated about the intimate relationship between a habitation and its setting; owners insisted on it. Early in the eighteenth century, Samuel Waring attended both to reordering of his County Down residence and to replanning and replanting his gardens. Grand neighbours inspected his plantation and were gratified by gifts of saplings. Proud of his nurseries for trees, he wrote a brief treatise on their cultivation. The tract, in contrast to his writings on architecture, was published in Ireland.[3]

Late-seventeenth- and eighteenth-century gardens have largely vanished. Kilruddery is a rare exception. The layout of demesnes and gardens, because so perishable, is now difficult to retrieve: more so than that of the adjoining mansions.[4] Sometimes it has been assumed too readily that the few plans of plantings represent what was achieved, and not ideal and unrealized schemes. An optimistic employee on the Cork holdings of the Percevals drew at least nine alternative schemes for the plantations around Lohort Castle. None was executed.[5] At the opposite pole from the overly imaginative reconstruction of what may have been planted is the repetition of strictures that Ireland resembled a wilderness. Typical of the second genre is a lament from the 1690s. It deplored, as tasting 'of the savage . . . an ancient estated family' dwelling in the country on their lands, 'yet without a tolerable habitation, without the decorums of gardens and pomaries [orchards]; without meadows and enclosed pastures; without

49. *Lohort Castle near Mallow*, Co. Cork, engraved by J. Toms, *c.* 1738. The regular plantings around this seat of the absent Perceval family, the earls of Egmont, show the extent to which even absentees reshaped the landscape.

the couverture and embellishment of quicks and trees; without in fine anything that may speak of a genteel and wise economy'.[6] This gloomy view represented the tendency of new-comers, first the Old and then the New English, to decry what their predecessors had (or had not) done. Equally, the displaced, Catholic Irish or Old English, belittled the negligence and greed of their supplanters. The tirade of the 1690s warns that parks and gardens, as much as housing, furnishing, dress and diet, were interpreted as evidence of how confessional, ethnic and social groups differed. Irish and English, Catholic and Protestant, Whigs and Tories, landowners and their tenants, even townspeople and country-dwellers were believed by some to have distinctive concerns. This belief meant that disafforestation or afforestation, campaigns of horticultural and agricultural improvement, choices of flowers, shrubs and trees, even the patterns in which they were set, and the fruit and vegetables grown for the table were read for signs of merit (or demerit) in their propagators.

Two themes intertwine in traditional accounts. Because little has survived intact from the Stuart and Hanoverian eras, theory and ideology have bulked disproportionately large in explaining landscapes. Of late, however, some have reinstated mundane considerations of use and cost as more important than symbolism in determining plantings.[7] These arguments are

50. Lohort Castle, Co. Cork.

relevant to any analysis of gardening and gardens in Ireland. If labour was cheap there, rentals and revenues were also meagre, and hardly allowed the generality of proprietors to engage in grandiose landscaping. Practical needs governed many arrangements. Gardens supplied the owners' table and local markets. Home farms were stocked with poultry and livestock, much of which fed the household. Seeming indulgences, such as duck decoys and canals, on which Lord Meath prided himself, were sources of foods to diversify the already rich diet of the prosperous.[8] Surpluses were sold to neighbours or in nearby towns, and thereby supplemented the earnings of the gardeners and keepers. Provisioning and profiteering passed easily into the need for recreation. Health, both bodily and moral, might be preserved by appropriate pastimes. Accordingly, estates were laid out to accommodate them, whether walking, riding, playing bowls, boating, fishing or hunting. Enthusiasts insisted that sport could not be separated from improvement. The racing of horses advertised successes in breeding, which – it was argued – would strengthen the puny beasts that worked the soil of Ireland. Stables and paddocks, like stockades for deer and coverts for foxes and birds, were incorporated into the ensemble of the proprietor.

The wish to make a figure influenced what was grown. To this end, novelties were imported from exotic climes in the seventeenth century. At Palmerston, close to Dublin, Sir John Temple cultivated oranges. The Rawdons of Moira in County Down sponsored plant-hunting expeditions to Jamaica and hoped to popularize the finds among dull neighbours. In 1707, it was reported that Sir Arthur Shaen of Kilmore near Athlone was 'most curious for gardening', and owned a greenhouse in which he raised the tender.[9] Delicacies such as melons and pineapples impressed neighbours with the skills and wealth of the proprietor. As presents, the produce gratified the recipient and puffed up the giver. In time, these exotics became more familiar – at least to the lordly – and attitudes towards them grew blasé. Sir James Caldwell, entertained at Castle Ward in 1772, although appreciative of the service and content of his meal, thought the pineapple not good and commented on how few peaches, grapes and figs were offered.[10] Fashion powered a competition to grow the unusual and the best. The widening availability of the imported and innovative generated a relentless quest for what would be accounted choice because unfamiliar.

It was easy enough for the landed to subscribe enthusiastically to the cult of improvement. James Corry, a Fermanagh squire, was one of many who thought his 'great improvements of building and planting', embracing houses, gardens, orchards and a large deer park, all well walled, 'of great advantage as well as ornament'.[11] The advantages, it was said, spread beyond the proprietor, and his or her heirs, to tenants and others in the neighbourhood. Improvers also aimed to increase the income and profits from estates. In implanting agricultural and technological change among tenants and neighbours, activists hoped to ease the payment of rents and in time allow them to be increased. Active improvers simultaneously met private and public obligations. They were praised for advancing the English and – from the later sixteenth century – Protestant interest, prosperity and civility. Not only were houses to be built according to the styles current in England or Scotland, they were to be adjoined by orchards, plantations and paddocks. Leases repeatedly enjoined these additions. They also stipulated that tenants should enclose portions of their holdings, normally with hedges and ditches. Benevolent proprietors furnished root stocks and saplings from their own nurseries, just as they permitted the favoured to have their stock inseminated by prize bulls, stallions and rams.

Eighteenth-century ramblers approved land that had been domesticated, especially if it looked like the cultivated meadows and cornfields of lowland Britain. At the same time, as travellers in Ireland admitted, much remained undone. When localized famines in the 1720s warned of how far the kingdom lagged behind Britain, efforts were redoubled. Parliament

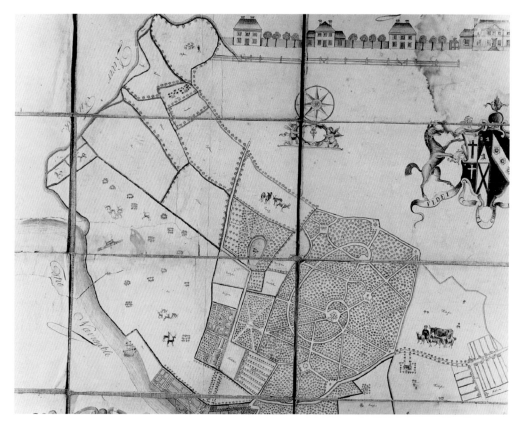

51. Henry Jones, *Plan of Dromana, Co. Waterford*, 1751. The elaborate reordering of the estate of the Earls Grandison near the precipitous banks of the lower reaches of the River Blackwater mixed formal and naturalistic plantings.

offered incentives. Institutions dedicated to improvement – notably the Dublin Society and the Physico-Historical Society – exhorted, instructed and rewarded. Gold medals and bounties cascaded over the public-spirited. Their achievements were celebrated in the press and in histories of individual counties. Publicity buffed up reputations: of Lord Grandison at Dromana, the Parsons of Parsonstown (later Birr), Robert French at Monivea and James Caldwell in County Fermanagh.[12]

The perception of danger from the Irish Catholics dwindled by the early eighteenth century. As a result, at least in the more settled regions of the island, house and park could be developed more adventurously. The first shed most defensive features; the second no longer needed to efface every trace of the indigenous and untamed. Slowly, rugged and unimproved landscapes came to be admired. Unadorned nature took longer to be appreciated in Ireland than in England, and never won over all. Yet, the fashions which seized the owners and plan-ners of gardens and parks in England touched the cosmopolitan of Ireland. The seventeenth-century predilection for rigid geometry and intricate plantings of evergreens, tortured into complex shapes, came to be dismissed as antiquated, and the natural to be prized.[13] Distant eminences were used as the foci of artificial prospects, as with the Sugar Loaf Mountain at Powerscourt or Nephin visible from the Cuffes' garden at Elm Hall in County Mayo.[14] Existing stretches of water – such as Lough Erne or the Rivers Liffey and Lee – were tapped in private parks.

Some sense of the alteration in attitudes can be retrieved from the ways in which water and timber were treated. The urge to drain, reclaim and divert did not vanish in the eighteenth century. Watery terrains and heavy rainfall faced many with the continuing problems of damp houses and flooded grounds. Nevertheless, and perhaps perversely, the modish introduced water into their parks. Rivers, streams, lakes and springs were channelled into fresh courses, cascades and fountains. Some were stocked with fish; others were turned into scenes for boating; a few were farmed with decoys for ducks. Water was no longer to be expelled.[15]

52. Jonathan Fisher, *A view of the lake of Killarney*, engraved by F. Vivares, 1770. Fisher brings out the contrast between the improved estate of Lord Kenmare, close to the lake, and the majesty of the mountains.

In a similar mood, trees, feverishly felled throughout the seventeenth century so that they should not harbour miscreants, had now to be replanted. A severe timber shortage made those that survived – such as the venerable oaks at Shillelagh – a precious commodity to be protected. Indeed, mature oak woods near Inistioge in County Kilkenny and at Dundrum were described as 'a mine above ground' or 'a growing treasure to posterity'.[16] At Shillelagh, after a period of neglect, a better appreciation of the value of the resource induced stricter care. The individual trees, if not yet talked to, were celebrated as 'the glory and ornament of the kingdom of Ireland'. Each was numbered; each had its characteristics minutely inventoried. In 1731, 2,150 'great trees' were valued at £8,317.[17] Younger trees, not fitted for the needs of the navy as knee-timbers, had commercial value. With the expanded demand for buildings and furniture, suitable wood was fashioned into prefabricated parts for joiners, chair-makers and builders. Bark was traded with tanners or shoemakers.[18] Once more, private gain and the public good converged.

Trees did not altogether cease to be associated with crime. Indeed, in some districts the situation approached that in mid-Wales during the same period, when disputes over timber most frequently embittered relations between tenants and landlords.[19] Wood reeves were hired by owners to protect their copses. Trespassers and thieves were prosecuted. The crimes, although regarded seriously, hardly equalled the alarm excited by the woodkernes, tories and raparees who had earlier lurked in the woods. War was waged against the poor who sought to strip and uproot the saplings and who let their beasts eat or trample the tender growths. Even in the seemingly untamed county of Kerry, depredations were as likely to be by merchants in Dingle with English names as by tanners of apparent Irish ancestry.[20] As in England and Scotland, venerable trees were invested with moral and even political connotations. In England, the reckless felling of woods was blamed on the Cromwellian usurpers of the 1650s. The despoliation of ancient oaks seemed to parallel the axe taken to Charles I. Replanting after 1660 (it has been suggested) denoted not just abundant land and thought for the future but aggressive loyalty to the restored monarchy. In Ireland, a willingness to invest in ample plantations of trees certainly spoke of wealth and farsightedness. It told too of confidence in a future in which Ireland under English tutelage enjoyed peace.[21]

From 1698, the Irish Parliament legislated to encourage tree-planting. Over the next century, seventeen statutes aimed to reward the planters and punish the destroyers.[22] Landowners could congratulate themselves that in establishing plantations and woodlands they were ornamenting their estates, shielding their houses, ensuring future profits, and helping the commonweal. As one agent exclaimed in 1755, woods were 'not only ornamental but useful and beneficial'. This was said of an estate the owner of which had zestfully felled much of the standing timber in the early seventeenth century on the grounds that it hid undesirables.[23] In the second half of the seventeenth century, the attitude spread from continental Europe, that

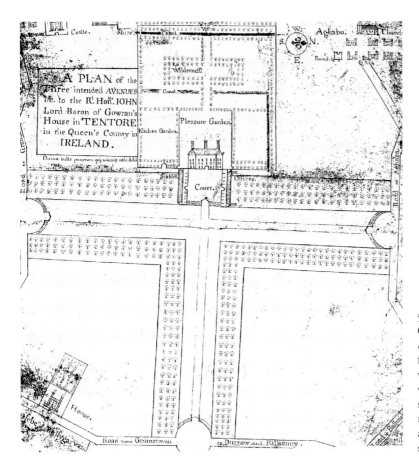

53. Plan of Tentore, Queen's County, *c.* 1715. The extreme formality required a variety of trees, which could be supplied from neighbouring estates and – gradually – by specialist nurseries.

the keen planter could parade his virtuosity. By introducing rarities, employing skilled foresters and arranging the timber in striking formations, aesthetic judgement as well as entrepreneurship was exhibited. At Larchfield in County Down, Daniel Mussenden, a leading merchant in Belfast, vowed to transform a raw setting. In 1734, he proposed to plant five or six acres with assorted trees, in 'some regular figure'. He chose an octagon, and set it with 8,000 trees. Six avenues or 'vistas', each twenty feet wide, radiated from a central clearing. Mussenden spent between £80 and £100.[24] This planting preceded the enlargement of the house at Larchfield by nearly a decade. It continued into the 1750s when sapling firs and ashes were shipped from Liverpool.[25]

The establishment of stands of timber accompanied gardening that yielded quicker results. Young plum trees – 'cloth of gold' – globe artichokes, pineapples and strawberries also arrived from England.[26] Mussenden, pleased with the results, resolved that henceforward he would devote himself to 'farming and improvement' as 'a very pleasant and

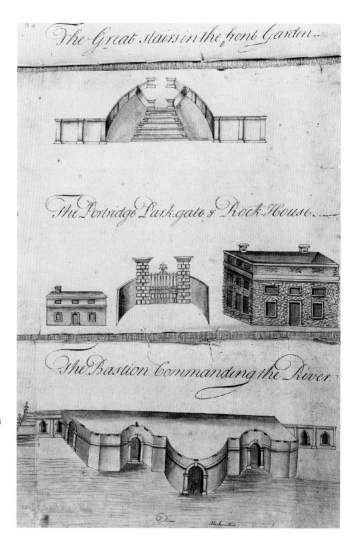

The handwritten labels on the drawing read:

*The Great stairs in the front Garden*

*The Portridge Park gate & Rock House*

*The Bastion Commanding the River*

54. Garden Buildings, Dromana, Co. Waterford, 1751. The ambition of the Grandisons' scheme is suggested by the number and substance of the pleasure buildings. The bastion added to the drama of the escarpment above the River Blackwater on which the estate was perched.

useful study'.[27] A religious man, he was aware of the ethical dimension. In future, the wood-lands would supply his tenants with cheap timber.[28] Similarly, the nurseries could furnish the fruit trees, which, under the terms of their leases, many tenants were obliged to intro-duce.[29] He constructed fish pond, watermill and bleach-green: amenities which might help humbler inhabitants of the area. In addition, he hoped through his exertions to diffuse a 'better spirit of husbandry' than currently prevailed among many of 'our landed gentlemen'. Only then would the ruinous shortages of corn in the kingdom be avoided.[30] Other ardent planters derived private pleasures while conferring public benefits from their investments. In Queen's County by the 1760s, a squirearchical family like the Weldons picnicked in their spinneys.[31]

## II

Scripture spurred some in Ireland, as in the rest of Europe, to enquire into the natural world. By understanding creation better, the enquirer apprehended the omnipotence and omniscience of the deity. Investigation of the multifarious works of nature was regarded by some not just as akin to, but in itself, an act of worship. An account of the Wicklow Mountains compiled in the late 1730s contended that they 'give the traveller a pleasing idea of the infinite power, greatness, majesty and goodness of the omnipotent creator, who formed these vast bodies out of nothing and still magnifies His own glory and goodness by rendering them useful to mankind'.[32] In similar vein, a curate from Lurgan in County Armagh, Richard Barton, was appointed by the Physico-Historical Society to investigate his county.[33] Barton succinctly argued that it was 'highly becoming a clergyman to interest himself in the phenomena of the natural world, which is the handywork of God, whose minister he is, and whose works are the objects of study'.[34] At the same time, the researches might yield practical benefits. The resources of the earth had been bestowed on humankind by a beneficent divinity. To survey and exploit them were religious obligations. Failure to do so – an omission of the allegedly lazy Irish Gaels – offended against the divine plan. Underdevelopment was traced to original sin, and the consequent expulsion from the Garden of Eden. Theology, both Catholic and Protestant, taught that sinful humans dwelt in an environment at once unfriendly and capable of reclamation. Accordingly, if an Edenic paradise could be recreated, it would enable the fallen to redeem themselves. An extreme application of these ideas, advanced by one Church of Ireland incumbent, asserted that bogs 'are not natural, but only excrescences and scabs of the body, occasioned by uncleanliness and sloth'.[35]

Nature, when left to its own devices, brought forth weeds and pests. Man in striving to correct this, reformed himself. By regaining control over unruly nature, sinners atoned. Nowhere in western Europe, it was argued, did the physical world so vividly reflect the consequences of these misdemeanours than the untamed uplands and pastoral peripheries of the British Isles and Ireland. Moreover, the supposed indolence of the indigenous Irish, when faced with the potential of their habitat, branded them as barbarians and blurred a vital distinction between men and beasts. Newer settlers were exhorted to make good the failures. Many were happy to do so since exertions were likely to bring immediate as well as future fruits. Ireland, in some of its regions and crops, was embarrassingly fecund. Indeed, rosy accounts portrayed the island as a pre-lapsarian idyll. Traps to ensnare reluctant immigrants were baited with evocations of ease and abundance. Throughout the seventeenth century, propagandists listed the numerous and bumper crops waiting to be plucked. On occasion, this very fertility tempted the newcomers to abandon the strenuous regime and opt for the easy habits of the locals. Fervent innovators derided what grew so readily, and advocated the cultivation of trickier crops. Simply to live on what fell unbidden into laps or mouths, it was thought, 'is no more than the beasts and birds do . . . The swine gathers and eats the fruits that fall under the trees, and understands not whence they are'.[36] The inhabitants of Ireland were not to wallow in plenty like brute beasts, but must strain after the taxing. The experimenters grappled with crops unsuited to the acid and sodden lands throughout much of the island. A few introductions answered high expectations, notably potatoes and flax. But many more, including some encouraged by the Dublin Society or its precursors – growing madder, rearing silkworms and popularizing broccoli – failed.[37] In 1760, the Dublin Society was encouraging John Smith, a County Dublin 'botanist', to cultivate madder, the roots of which made a lurid red dye. Apothecaries also used it. More than one hundred years earlier, Hartlib's friends had backed similar efforts. As in England, so in Ireland, higher prices in the 1750s and the importance of the dye to the textile industry revived interest in its culture. Again, in 1800, the Dublin Society sponsored the publication of a treatise on the plant.[38]

The Dublin Society, from its outset in 1731, linked natural history, husbandry, agriculture and gardening with 'manufacture or other branch of improvement' as objects of its collective endeavours.[39] Quickly, members compiled a catalogue of all books of husbandry and mechanic arts in English, Latin, French and Greek. At the same time, they were to collect information about the agriculture of France, Flanders, Holland, Germany, Poland and Italy. This ambitious programme hinted at a European network of correspondents, and linked the seventeenth-century intelligencers with the more formal societies across the continent in the eighteenth century.[40] By 1732, the Society was receiving information from Amsterdam.[41] In the following year, it had connected itself to a similar society in Scotland.[42] Immediately members directed their attention towards the culture of hops, woad and flax and towards new devices for winnowing.[43] The practical intentions of the organization were also revealed when an enquirer was dispatched on a mission to English hop-growing districts and when a nursery was established in Dublin.[44] Soon the group had its own gardener and supplier of seeds.[45] Indiscriminate enthusiasm for novelties led to equal attention for such diverse endeavours as introducing sumach trees (highly poisonous) from the orient and improving strains of turnips.

In the revamped Dublin Society after 1740, the plodding work of gardening and farming tended to be overshadowed by the schemes to encourage local manufactures.[46] The latter were calculated to grab public notice. Increasingly, the Society faced a conundrum common to other institutions with similar aims. It needed to sustain and expand support among well-to-do subscribers otherwise it would collapse. Yet, in order to realize its larger plans, it had to reach a wider constituency. Dispersing cheap tracts 'to every reader in the kingdom' was the intention: to bring 'practical and useful knowledge from the retirements of libraries and closets into the public view'. In particular, it was essential that 'the poorer sort, the husbandman and manufacturer' should be instructed.[47] The Society, notwithstanding this hope of broadening its appeal, relied on the proprietors, and especially its subscribing members, to diffuse its tidings through the countryside. Unashamedly it traded on vanity and greed as well as on patriotism. The absent or lethargic were tellingly contrasted to the active who improved lands, raised plantations, built houses, promoted husbandry and manufactures, thereby 'advancing private fortune and supporting the industrious poor'.[48]

The success of the Society is easier to trace among landowners than among their tenants. It fitted well with an existing view that gardening was 'an agreeable and useful diversion'.[49] Strange plants, some of which had been advertised by the Society, generally circulated in a restricted group. Sometimes, because gardeners were allowed to sell produce as an addition to their wages, rarities appeared at market. More commonly, baskets of succulent fruit and flavoursome vegetables in season (or preferably in advance of it) or (most gratifying) hot-house cultivars like melons and pineapples, would be dispatched to honoured neighbours. The servants who delivered them expected to be tipped handsomely.[50] The horticultural triumphs of the recently established proprietors of the seventeenth and eighteenth centuries may have built on indigenous Irish enthusiasm for vegetables and the skills of operatives recruited from the local populations. Appreciation of the delights native to the island was less frequently expressed than enthusiasm for imported crops and gardeners.[51] The prosperous enjoyed a more diversified diet as the varieties in cultivation multiplied. No more in eighteenth-century Ireland than in Scotland, Wales and Brittany did the food eaten by the bulk of the people alter.[52] The middling sorts, particularly in the environs of larger towns with well-supplied markets, were most likely to have a little money to buy the strange and tempting, in the same fashion as they experimented with furnishings and clothing.[53]

The feeling that Ireland lagged behind other European countries in the matter of gardening, no less than in prosperity, agriculture or intellectual exuberance, made the impatient look to notables to accelerate the pace of change. During the seventeenth century, first the grandees of Catholic Ireland and next their Protestant successors, such as the Ormondes at Kilkenny or Boyles at Lismore, Castlemartyr and Charleville, familiar with English and European developments, fostered the unfamiliar.[54] At Kilkenny, the Ormondes engaged a French gardener who devised spectacular fountains.[55] The Boyles regularly imported seeds and saplings from England. Some were planted in their own gardens; others in those of their agents and favoured tenants.[56] Successive lords-lieutenant also excited expectations that they would advance gardening. In the 1680s, Clarendon, under the influence of the leading pundit John Evelyn, vowed to improve the gardens at his official residences. By 1694, it was hoped that 'the gardener to the state', Harrison, would 'bring the most elegant cultivation of gardens and curious plants into fashion here'. Harrison, trained under Bobart in Oxford and encouraged by Lord Deputy Capel, was drowned before he could implant a better taste.[57] In this regard, as in so many others, viceroys from England disappointed. One, Devonshire, was warned by the gardener at Chapelizod of the neglect of the gardens. He was uninterested in initiating remedial action.[58]

It was left to the prosperous with a permanent interest in Ireland to test, record and innovate. One gripped by curiosity about the natural world was Sir Richard Bulkeley. He looked beyond his inherited property in County Dublin to the region, the whole island and indeed the globe. Bulkeley joined the Dublin Philosophical Society. Later enquirers would participate in the Dublin Society.[59] In Bulkeley's case, his odyssey would take him eventually to the wilder fringes of Protestant heterodoxy. The family seat at Old Bawn had been established by Sir Richard's forbear, an archbishop of Dublin. Another, William Bulkeley, wrote a treatise on orchards.[60] On inheriting in the 1680s, Sir Richard Bulkeley established extensive nurseries in which apples, quinces, cherries, apricots and walnuts grew.[61] Soon he tried grafts. But the entire enterprise was threatened by the Catholic resurgence in 1687. As a precaution, the trees were removed into an orchard protected – like the house itself – by a deep moat.[62] Once the Catholic threat had been repelled, Bulkeley returned to Old Bawn with renewed zeal. Recreation, speculation and experiment combined in his gardens. Frequent trips to England put him in touch with experts and suppliers. In Dublin, he joined the enquirers of the Philosophical Society, and eagerly shared talk of innovations and inventions. He discussed the topography and history of the area with neighbours. He staffed his household with Swiss, Palatines and a Huguenot, one of whom had trained as a *vigneron*. Bulkeley duly planted a vineyard, although he was pessimistic about the outcome.[63] He persevered with the fruit trees, if disappointed that the quinces bore few fruit. He wanted to introduce mulberries in order to set up a silk industry. These experiments paralleled those of entrepreneurs and improvers in England.[64] Frankly, Bulkeley acknowledged that his whim would prove, 'almost as much moment to philosophy tho' it do not succeed, as it will be to trade if it do'.[65]

More mundane, but perhaps more useful to the prevailing husbandry of the district, were Bulkeley's trials of different strains of meadow grass. His father had discovered that neither clover nor sainfoin suited the district. He also compelled tenants to sow hemp and flax-seed, whereby 'I shall greatly serve the public'.[66] He repeated the axiom learnt from the Oxford botanist Bobart, not to regard any plant as a weed.[67] In 1698, Bulkeley beseeched an English correspondent to let him know 'whether there are any new exotic trees, plants, flowers or seeds now in esteem or use there, and what they are'.[68] William King confessed that he stopped gardening on his own account in 1703 when moved from the bishopric of Derry to the archdiocese of Dublin. Having himself assembled a representative selection of books on natural history, he urged protégés and acquaintances to investigate the Irish manifestations of the subject more thoroughly.[69] The project was not new. From the 1650s through the 1680s and into the 1730s, the inquisitive pleaded for such an account. Once completed, it would prove the foundation for the better use of the untapped plenty of the island. County by county, Ireland was surveyed. But the accounts, dependent on local volunteers, varied wildly in detail and accuracy. All endorsed the creed of improvement and the common supposition that the Protestant settlers from Britain had engineered the main changes.

Archbishop King, as well as delving in the narrow compass of the garden, espied larger perspectives, bounded neither by Ireland and the British Isles nor by the terrestrial. King, bookish, high-minded and wearisomely patriotic, did not shun simpler horticultural delights. At Derry, he took part in exchanges with the gardeners of neighbouring notables, like Mrs Caulfield and Colonel Phillips.[70] Much was sent from suppliers in Dublin: asparagus and artichoke plants; willow salleys; seeds.[71] Other wants – earthenware pots and glass lights to protect the tender – seem to have been bought locally.[72] Once in Dublin, King may not have gardened on the same scale as in Derry, but at his residence of St Sepulchre's he had a 'pleasure garden', as well as vegetable plot. He continued to collect materials: trees from Queen Anne's gardener while in London on business; 'Dutch' box and laurel nearby in Dublin.[73] Ambitions were disclosed when – in 1709 – a 'Mr. Belfour' prepared a plan for King's 'new garden'.[74] Other clergy and laymen presented the archbishop with flowers 'to set in the garden'. The donors' gardeners were tipped for their trouble.[75] Maintaining the garden did not require unusual skill, if the yearly £4 paid to the gardener, Elias Roberts, is any sure guide. In Derry, he had paid Thomas Boodell double this sum. Plants and special equipment were more costly: glasses to straighten cucumbers cost King 19s. 6d. for a dozen.[76]

Ardent improvers diverted themselves with tasks which proclaimed virtuosity, and so raised their reputations in the neighbourhood. The pride of Samuel Waring in his nursery of infant trees was of a piece with his expertise in painting, architecture and fashionable living. Self- and family interest as much as disinterestedness urged these skills. In the 1690s, the Taylors of Headfort in County Meath introduced new kinds of pear trees in their gardens. Some were planted in the orchard, but others were situated in 'the pleasure garden' and near the summerhouse. These locations suggested that more than the fruit served at table was to be enjoyed. Skills of grafting and cultivation, even the beauty of blossom and ripening crop, might be admired.[77] In addition to Christian doctrine and patriotism, study of the classics approved such aptitudes. Cato and Cicero urged the propertied to civic activism. Reading Virgil conveyed an alternative message of the delights of rural seclusion. 'In philosophic or poetic ease/In still retreats, avoid the multitude'.[78] Some, such as Lord Broghill in 1659 or William Flower during the 1720s, surrendered to the Virgilian cult of retirement.[79] Usually it was a voluntary rather than an enforced exile. Flower amused himself in the country by erecting a new mansion and setting it in remodelled parkland. George Berkeley, once enthroned as bishop at Cloyne in 1734, concentrated on his palace and its grounds. Robert Howard confided how he had inspected the thick woodlands around Shelton Abbey on foot, adding 'you must know I can walk more than most bishops'. The opinionated Molesworth, entering old age, requested a seat to encircle the great elm at Breckdenstown, 'to sit and take the air upon'. He also pleaded that a bank of cowslips be protected.[80]

Many vigorous improvers alternated between the Ciceronian and Virgilian idioms. Flower never lived continuously at Castle Durrow. Instead, rustic life was enlivened by jaunts to

Dublin and England. Berkeley conceded that his improvements, like his collections, fulfilled their higher purposes only when shared.[81] Others who lavished much attention on their country properties thought similarly. Successive bishops at Elphin – Theophilus Bolton, Robert Howard and Edward Synge – were as keen to set an example on their demesnes as in their residences. They repeated the priorities of other prelates – William King at Derry, the elder Edward Synge in Tuam and John Stearne at Clogher – notable for the material and moral improvement of their dioceses.

## III

Most ventures into gardening were modest, have left few or no traces, and were as likely to come from dwellers in the town as in the countryside. Sensory pleasures, notably of taste, look and smell, not the advance of the common weal with consequent philosophical self-congratulation and financial profit, commonly resulted. Fruit, flowers and vegetables brought more immediate pleasures than slow-growing deciduous trees. Townspeople gardened as fervently as their cousins in the country. The beauty wrested from city soil might look meagre when set against the plantations on country estates. Yet, large urban plots gave the affluent abundant space to propagate and innovate. Samuel Desminières, member of a prominent Dublin dynasty of traders (originally from France), had roots of anemones, ranunculus and carnations shipped from Rotterdam in 1684.[82] Jonathan Swift as dean of St Patrick's, Bishop Edward Synge of Elphin in his adjacent town house, and Archbishop King (also in Dublin) cultivated enthusiastically.[83] During the 1670s, the quintessential city-dweller, Petty, had a garden at his St George's Lane residence which justified the employment of a gardener – a Huguenot, Bonnet – who would be poached by Lord Meath for his works at Kilruddery, south of the city.[84] Within Dublin's confines, the revenue commissioner, John Evelyn, was happy in 1694 to find a house of his own. Among its attractions was the opportunity for him to garden. Evelyn put into practice some of the ideas of his father, the elder John Evelyn, *the* pundit on all questions relating to gardens and trees. Similarly, in 1736, the Dublin physician Thomas Kingsbury was keen to retain a house close to St Stephen's Green, 'for the sake of the little garden'.[85] Less pleasing was the experience of a former fellow of Trinity, Caesar Williamson. Lodging in central Dublin during Charles II's reign, he was delighted to have the free use of an enclosed garden as part of the bargain with his landlord. Soon he discovered that others – 'men, beasts and laundresses' – enjoyed the same privilege.[86]

Estates in and around Dublin set and then surpassed standards in the nurture of rarities and in stylish landscaping. Visitors were impressed, as was intended, by what was achieved by the Allens at Stillorgan, at Howth Castle, by the Delanys at Delville, Lady Arbella Denny at Peacliff and Blackrock, the Molesworths of Breckdenstown and Nathaniel Clements around

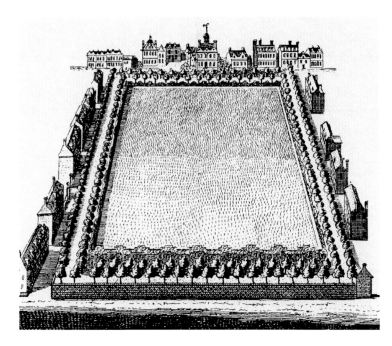

55. *Prospect of St Stephen's Green*, engraving from C. Brooking's map of Dublin, 1728. The large and carefully planted and regulated open space was regarded as an outstanding amenity and made the houses around the Green some of the most desirable in the capital.

the ranger's house in the Phoenix Park. In 1746, the last, was said to have 'the appearance of a living picture, or *camera obscura*, always changing and variegating the scene'.[87] Even the lofty Molesworth, proud of his own works, pressed his wife to view the Southwells' place at Clontarf, 'because they are well laid out and worthy of our imitation in due course'. The Southwells' achievements also appealed as 'very cheap and substantial'.[88] Between 1720 and 1770, Richard Edgeworth regularly visited fashionable gardens and improvements at Glasnevin and seaside Blackrock within reach of the city. Some of what he saw – for example the 'grotto' at Kinseally – might be imitated on his own Midlands estate.[89] At the same time, the bishop of Derry, William Nicolson, when in Dublin for parliament, refreshed himself by sauntering in Phoenix Park, inspecting Mrs Crofton's shell house or gasping at the cascade on Carter's grounds at Robertstown.[90]

Refugees from the stink of the city rejoiced in the bosky suburbs. One Dublin lady who rented rooms in the Dublin suburb of Templeogue, in order to refresh herself in the better air, insisted on having the right to walk in the garden 'at will' included in the weekly rent of fifteen shillings.[91] As towns, and especially the capital, grew more crowded, areas were set apart in which a semblance of the countryside could be reproduced. After 1660, Dublin corporation developed St Stephen's Green in the centre of the city. Alongside smart housing, a large central space was preserved. The green was enclosed, planted and policed. In the 1660s, limes were to be grown there. By the middle of the eighteenth century, mature elms had

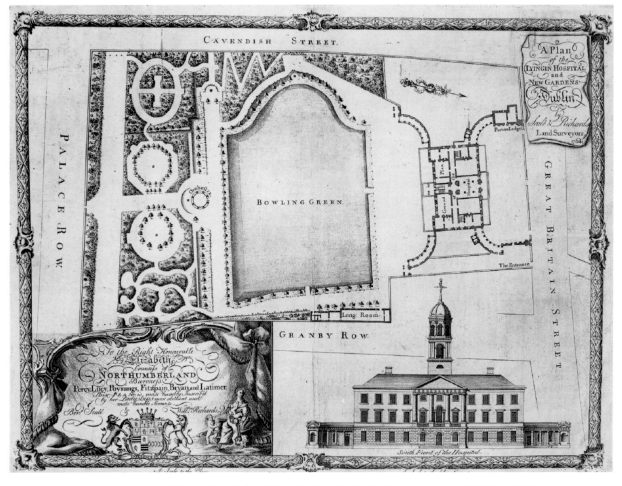

56. *A plan of the Lying-In Hospital and New Gardens, Dublin,* by Bernard Scalé and William Richards, 1764. Devised by the midwife Bartholomew Mosse, the maternity hospital was funded partly by the pleasure grounds, modelled after Ranelagh and Vauxhall in London.

grown too big, dripped water and shaded the pedestrians.[92] In another municipal initiative of 1766, 300 trees were planted along the canal to make it 'an agreeable walk'.[93] The craving for outdoor diversions prompted the entrepreneurial midwife Bartholomew Mosse to lay out gardens beside his Lying-In Hospital. They were an Irish answer to Ranelagh and Vauxhall, widely admired in London by visitors from Ireland. The pleasure grounds, like their English prototypes, raised money to finance the hospital. They were not, therefore, a place which all Dubliners could enter. Roomy suburban gardens, like Lady Arbella Denny's at Blackrock, were opened to the respectable. Upper servants judged whom to admit.

In the provinces, similar developments told of medical theories which advised escape from the foul air of dense quarters. Cork and Waterford acquired malls; at Derry and Limerick the city walls provided walks. These places were not so easily policed as enclosed and commercial gardens. Nevertheless, expectations about dress and demeanour may have deterred the uncouth and impolite. At Portarlington, the provision of hillside walks for the residents was inseparable from 'the great deal of society' in the town.[94] Other provincial boroughs had their bowling greens. That at Kinsale was reserved for the freemen and their consorts. By the middle of the eighteenth century, the green at Kilkenny was much patronized by 'the beau monde', who 'make a very handsome figure'. Equal *éclat* attached to the recreational centres of Dublin, such as the greens at Oxmantown and St Stephen's Green.[95] The new bishop of Derry was invited to his local bowling green in 1722.[96] By 1756, the condition of the bowling green at Strabane, 'now just a dirty common to the whole town', dismayed.[97] Bowling, like tennis, had once been 'a game for few but gentlemen'. In England, and perhaps in Ireland too, the exclusivity was lost in the eighteenth century.[98]

## IV

Gardens seldom answered a single need. They might speak of a wish to master unruly nature. In Irish contexts, they provided arenas where the English (or British) and Protestant could demonstrate the superiority of their concepts and techniques to the indigenes. While some fanatical gardeners competed, others collaborated. Information about and examples of better strains of pulses, cereals, animal feed and trees were exchanged happily. Public benefits were frequently promised, but – in the interim – simpler satisfactions resulted. Fine blooms, luscious fruits and unseasonable vegetables impressed recipients with the virtuosity and generosity of the donors. At the same time, rudimentary sensations of taste, smell and look were gratified. Flowers, in particular, were grown to be enjoyed. The Dublin merchant Desminières requested brightly coloured and highly perfumed varieties. Scented flowers, such as carnations, were among Archbishop King's favourites.[99] At Kilruddery by 1746, Lord Meath – or rather his gardeners – boasted nearly one hundred auricula seedlings of either English or Irish nurture and a further 690 in the collection.[100] Fownes at Woodstock, in addition to his ambitious plantings of trees, sought scarce auriculas.[101] Enthusiasts in the capital formed themselves into a Florists' Club, copied from similar groups in England. Conviviality and talk, sometimes with a political flavour, did not altogether edge out the competition to grow prize blooms. Chief among them were auriculas and carnations, which were toasted ritualistically.[102] Breeding prize specimens came to obsess as much as winning horse-races, cock-fights or even parliamentary elections.

Simple enjoyment united enthusiasts in town and country. The Reverend Peter Ward, exiled to a living remote in Donegal, amused himself by making a garden. Ward appealed to Squire Smythe at Barbavilla as 'a florist of public spirit'. He confided that at Culdaff he possessed a garden, 'which I would make as diverting to myself as I would because we do not abound with other diversions in the country'. 'Common' flowers thrived. Ward also sought 'some good flowers to make a figure among my neighbours'. What he craved was 'a very agreeable diversion in a place that needs it'.[103] He also asked Smythe to recommend a horticultural manual.[104] John Digby from Landenstown in County Kildare, always an indulgent parent and himself an enthusiastic plantsman, reported how his daughter had planted a plot, and begged more flower roots for it.[105] Female children were encouraged to garden. Indeed, it was felt that some aspects of gardening belonged particularly to women. Something of the appeal of the activity as instruction and refreshment is suggested by Lady Petty in 1685. She commanded her children's nurse not to neglect the Dublin garden in the early spring, and to 'get some flowers that will easily prosper'.[106] Agnes Hamilton reported how her garden at Caledon 'is now wondering sweet in its pride and much blown beauty', and contrasted its 'innocence and quiet' with the polluted city.[107] Most tellingly, at the Percevals' Burton in County Cork one area was designated 'my lady's flower garden', with a nearby 'pleasure house'.[108]

Since the garden furnished the table, the larder with preserves and the dispensary with herbal cures, it was seen as a part of housewifery, with which women properly dealt. But, as with so much else ordered for house and estate, men dominate the record of what was procured for the garden. They customarily kept the accounts, and thereby conceal what was initiated by wives, sisters and daughters. A rare glimpse of mutual interest is afforded by a meeting, or 'bower', of 'the most ancient and honourable institution of free gardeners' at Cashel in the later 1730s. Women presided, with men acting as stewards. The feminine orientation was emphasized further when the institution scheduled its festivities on the birthday of the queen. A 'splendid entertainment and ball', not horticultural feats, were noted. The officers of the army were also involved, and the society distributed charity to poor householders of the town.[109] Writers often ceded the flower garden to women.[110] That this was no fiction was shown by Mary Burgh, a sister of Squire Smythe of Barbavilla. She listed her wants and was duly sent lilies of the valley, sapling fig trees, carnations and artichokes.[111] Smythe, during absences in Dublin, entrusted oversight of the works at Barbavilla to his young wife, the former Barbara Ingoldsby, to whom, through its name, the project was dedicated. She attended both to details of the building and ornamentation of the mansion and to the arrangements in the gardens and plantations. As she confessed to her spouse, 'I am in more pain for this piece of management than any other you ever enjoined me to'. She worried lest the hot-beds overheat and bake the plants.[112] In this situation, it is impossible to determine whether the early schemes, with garish marigolds and

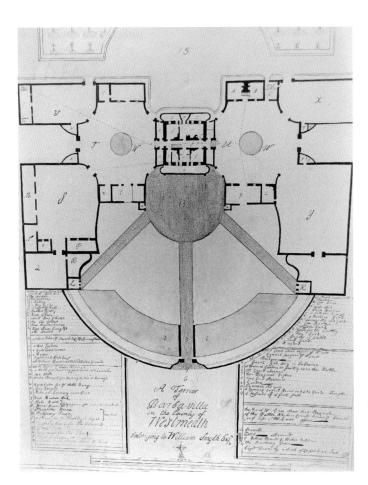

57. Plan of Barbavilla, Co. Westmeath, *c.* 1730. The way in which the Smythes' new house related to complicated gardens and grounds can be gauged from the contemporary plan.

nasturtiums close to the house, as well as the more sophisticated auriculas and carnations, represented the taste of William or of Barbara Smythe. Most plausibly, they shared the enterprise.[113]

Barbara Smythe reminds of the woman's part in gardening. She might affect diffidence, but, reared at Carton, she had been schooled in the latest fashions. She, no less than her husband, moved in the orbits of friends and kinsfolk conversant with the rare and remarkable. At the Smythes' social and economic level, knowledge of trees and plants belonged to the polite accomplishments which now ranged from dancing to darning, and from the Vitruvian tripos to the curl of a toupee. When William Smythe planned mansion and park he did not lack advice. One brother, the Reverend James Smythe, was not only an enthusiastic gardener but had travelled to Italy. The elder brother, a lawyer living in London, although deferring in matters of taste to his siblings still in Ireland, did not hesitate to send horticultural wants to Westmeath. The consignments ranged from saplings of elm, acorns of the red oak and beech mast, prized varieties of peach, fig and cherry to cauliflower and turnip seed.[114] Some died in transit or failed in the harsh conditions of Barbavilla. Varied sources were used: the gardeners of the grand and commercial nurserymen. More unexpected than the many avenues that brought plants and seeds into the Irish Midlands was the way in which expertise was gained by Smythe's own operatives. One, John Cooley, took himself to England, in order to pick up new skills. It may have been no more than an excuse for a jaunt, but Cooley put himself under the care of Alexander Home at Boreham. Home, 'the civilest gardener I ever knew', oversaw the gardens of both the Hoares (connections of the Irish Smythes) and Lord Salisbury.[115] There was a feeling that Cooley was aiming too high and that he would have done better to learn the secrets of the market gardeners. Reasonably enough, however, he insisted that he already knew enough of the nurture of vegetables.[116] Others, indeed, were reluctant to engage 'conceited' gardeners, fearful lest they dictate to their masters and mistresses.[117] Given the conventions of the times, it was the squire who was credited with and congratulated on the excellence of his plantations and improvements.[118] Smythe and his brothers turned for instruction to the revered manuals, such as John Evelyn's. But their achievements owed much to the labourers who levelled uneven ground and undulated the even terrain, to the women who weeded the beds and to the boys who scared off birds and poachers. At Barbavilla, Cooley and his colleagues ensured that the tender and strange survived.

As the bachelor King or the ardent Florists of the Dublin club revealed, men joined women and children in responding to scents and colours of garden flowers. Some collected rarities as they might precious medals and prints. Claudius Gilbert, a fellow of Trinity College, early in the eighteenth century acquired a volume of paintings on vellum of tulips. Most were Dutch, with vivid breaks likened to the plumage of parrots.[119] Tulips transfixed William Nicolson, lately arrived as bishop in Derry. He toured his diocese and the environs of Dublin.[120] In May 1722, he declared himself impressed by 'Mr. Blackhall's fine tulips'. Noggins of punch added to the enjoyment of his visit, and reminded how gardens had become occasions for, as well as locations of, sociability.[121] Bishop Edward Synge also cherished his flower borders. In them, although rarity remained a criterion for inclusion, smell and colour mattered. Accordingly, anemones, ranunculus and tulips were favoured. Synge laid down rules by which tulip bulbs when lifted should be separated into best, middling and breeders.[122] Some were gifts from Lord Meath. Others, 'those rascally tulips', discarded in Dublin, were sent to his see house in County Roscommon. The bishop reported, 'they are singly as bad as bad can be, but are so strong in their stems, the cups so large and the colours so lively, that altogether they make a very fine glare'. Even more gratifyingly, 'everybody views them with pleasure and surprise'.[123] Like the bright Rouen faience which he so painstakingly assembled for his table, the flowers impressed Synge's guests.

Gardens, even when modest and untouched by the latest vogue, satisfied and pleased. The reputation of a Waring or Synge owed much to their properties, and how they were proportioned, furnished and set. Pleasurable sensations abounded in gardens and parks. Gasps at the brilliance and perfume of the flowers, or the savour of strawberries and asparagus harvested from the garden, can still be sensed in the comments of a Synge or Waring.[124] If some were renowned for the excellence of their hounds, studs, herds or bleach-greens, others were praised for stands of timber, perfection of wall fruit and delicacy of hothouse produce. In 1714, Archbishop King thanked Lord Fitzwilliam for gifts from his Mount Merrion property on the southern fringe of Dublin. The offerings included melons, peaches, apricots and ripe almonds to rival those of France.[125] The proud proprietor able to distribute such presents swelled in repute. Conversely, it pained the likes of the Flowers at Castle Durrow to have to buy in nectarines, peaches and plums. The O'Haras from Sligo, throwing a lavish party in Dublin, were obliged to hire pineapples.[126] The skilled showed off. Bishop Synge sent melons to colleagues in the House of Lords and other worthies. As with gifts of game, there was a strict pecking order to ensure that the best went to the most important. Melons, more frequently than pineapples, bruited abroad the prowess of the cultivator.[127]

Simple indulgence of the appetites was disciplined, but not replaced, by the promptings of sociability, altruism and patriotism. The garden, long a symbol for the recovery of virtue, was turned into a site of feverish experimentation. Groups such as the Dublin Society followed preachers in elevating some forms of cultivation above others. Arable, tree-planting and flax-growing or fields of rape, clover and sainfoin grass were invested with a moral worth missing from 'lazy' pastoralism. Not all succumbed to the dogmas of the intolerant improvers. An orthodox manual such as Miller's *Gardening Dictionary* probably exerted greater influence than the Society's directives or indeed the injunctions of parliament.[128] Indeed, the popularity of the *Dictionary* made it the equivalent in Ireland of *La Maison Rustique* in the book-rooms of Breton nobles.[129] In 1735, the young Sir William Fownes, having recently inherited Woodstock in County Kilkenny, bought Miller's compendium for £1 5s.[130] As Fownes began strenuously to improve his estate, the book was studied.[131] Bishop Synge of Elphin also resorted to Miller's guide in 1750 as he improved his demesne in County Roscommon.[132] Another active on his country estate, Richard Edgeworth, swapped a flimsy 'Gardener's Calendar' for a copy of Miller's manual in 1734.[133] Such was the demand for the book that the squire of Gloster in County Offaly, Trevor Lloyd, had his copy stolen from his Dublin house.[134] Curiously, although the Dublin Society sponsored publications useful to horticulture and agriculture (many of them reprints), no manual composed explicitly for Irish conditions appeared. In contrast, John Reid's *Scots Gard'ner* had been published in 1683 and James Justice's *Scots Gardener's Director* in 1754.[135] But books, no matter how clear and how high in repute, could teach only so much.[136] Observation, experiment and experience were reckoned to be better instructors.

## V

Travel within and beyond Ireland introduced the discerning to novelties. The chance to tour for pleasure and instruction distinguished the few from the many and, in gardening as in philosophy, manners, dress, conduct and refinement, created an élite. Since money was usually the prerequisite for lengthy and leisurely peregrinations, it usually overlapped even if it was not exactly coterminous with the wealthier members of Irish Protestant society. One who took this course was the young Samuel Molyneux. The son of William Molyneux, progenitor of the Dublin Philosophical Society, he revived the club during Queen Anne's reign. In doing so he repeated the conviction of his father and other zealots that public good would attend the minute survey of Ireland's topography and history. Among other matters, Molyneux interested himself in horticultural innovations. He even owned a manuscript treatise on 'the raising, multiplying and planting of wild trees'.[137] After inspecting the remoter regions of Ireland, he journeyed through England in 1713. He applied aesthetics as well as utility to what he saw. Thus, he hailed Kensington Palace as the masterpiece of 'the new regular manner of greens and gravel gardening', but condemned the mode. He speculated that great men were attracted to the style because of their satisfaction 'in being able to force nature, and to make and finish a garden in a season'. Molyneux likened this contemporary craze to that for epigrams; he preferred the gardening equivalents of the epic and Pindaric ode. He sought variety in the garden, and longed for 'the beautiful scaravagie of noble grown trees in a wild wood'. For this reason he praised the Surrey gardens of Lord Halifax for embodying 'the true taste of beauty'. Halifax's planting 'has nothing saucy, and seems to endeavour rather to follow than to alter nature'. He instanced a hill planted with woods, in which vistas and 'innumerable private dark walks' had been cut.[138]

Molyneux, in applying the term 'scaravagie', revealed his familiarity with the writings (and even perhaps the talk) of another originally from Protestant Ireland, Sir William Temple. Nearly thirty years earlier, Temple, in *The Gardens of Epicurus*, had extolled irregularity in gardens under the garbled Chinese term of 'sharawadgi'. By 1713, Molyneux's preferences were in line with pundits such as the philosopher, Shaftesbury, and Addison in *The Spectator*.[139] Soon Molyneux ambled through northern Europe to Hanover. He then uprooted himself permanently from Ireland to make a successful career in England. Oversight of his Irish interests was necessarily deputed to others, and his enthusiasm for introducing the styles that he had admired elsewhere into his own estate, Castle Dillon in County Armagh, may have weakened.[140]

Other travellers from Ireland, seeing the same sights and hearing similar notions, did return to apply some to their holdings. Champions of anglicization and civility forwarded the causes through their plantations. Moral truths could also be learnt and communicated by carefully contrived gardens. Francis Hutcheson, an Ulsterman who laid some of the foundations of the Scottish enlightenment, saw gardens as the embodiment of beauty. The best offered 'uniformity amidst variety'. Specifically, he recounted the feelings aroused when 'that strict regularity in laying out of gardens in parterres, vistas, parallel walks' was 'neglected to obtain an imitation of nature even in some of its wildnesses'. These contrasts, Hutcheson maintained, pleased more than 'the more confined exactness of regular work'.[141]

Aesthetes and philosophers other than Hutcheson were pontificating about the proper forms for gardens.[142] Molyneux's comments implied a sharp awareness of the shift in taste away from geometric rigidity to more fluid schemes. The abandonment of rigid formalism for naturalism has sometimes been linked to Whig rather than Tory preferences. In particular, the works for the first Viscount Molesworth at Breckdenstown near Dublin have been proposed as both an aggressive assertion of his Whig views, with its rejection of 'French' artifice and absolutism, and a source of Hutcheson's aesthetics.[143] The strenuous superiority of Molesworth, his unconcealed contempt for most neighbours and their efforts, and the survival of evidence about what he achieved may give Breckdenstown an importance not appreciated by contemporaries, surrounded as they were by numerous improvements. Undoubtedly Molesworth engaged in projects which, through hydraulics as much as superlative stocks, would set a standard for less ambitious neighbours. Whatever impact the designs made, it was at best short-lived. By the mid-eighteenth century, verses praised Breckdenstown in entirely conventional idiom: 'where art and nature strongly vie', and 'promiscuous spread the fruits and flowers'.[144]

Breckdenstown, in its heyday, competed for notice with other ambitious schemes in the environs of Dublin and throughout the provinces. Among the latter, Castle Hamilton in County Cavan was approached by an avenue, nearly a mile long, of mature fir trees. Westwards from the front of the house opened a vista, two hundred feet wide and half a mile in length, framed by elms. To the south of the house was a parterre, which spoke of the survival of formality. But it was bordered by a wilderness, kitchen garden and 'fruiteries'. Four terraces descended to the lake. Here was sited a substantial banqueting house, and beyond lay the deer park. A commentator concluded that the ensemble was 'adorned by nature with such variety of landskips that it requireth not art to make it agreeable'. Nevertheless, art had been lavished on some parts of the grounds, especially those closest to the mansion.[145] Another Cavan seat, Thomas Fleming's Belvill, excited equal enthusiasm. It too used the setting by channelling the streams and pools into a 'variety of waterworks, terraces, diagonal walks, falls of water and dark walks'. A 'pleasure house' had a lower floor in the manner of a mock grotto, which opened onto a canal, perhaps to allow fishing. A gazebo was commended as a pattern for others.[146] Nearby, Florence Court, established by John Cole early in the eighteenth century, was noted chiefly for a situation of 'majestic wildness'. A deer park, two grand avenues of fir and elm, walks cut through the gardens told of human interventions. But the cascade and hanging gardens exploited the drama of nature.[147]

This blend of the tamed and untamed suited the terrain of Fermanagh and Cavan around the loughs and River Erne. It was adopted by Samuel Madden, a proprietor seen as the model for rural neighbours and colleagues in the Dublin Society. At Manor Waterhouse, Madden laid out pleasure gardens intersected with gravel paths. His notable collection of flowers and shrubs might reasonably be regarded as the counterpart of the gallery of paintings inside the house. Interior and grounds were brought together by inscriptions over doors which expatiated on the beauty of the setting. Various walks descended to 'a deep solemn glen'. Others were contrived as 'shady walks, terraces, recesses, labyrinths'. A wilderness and riverside walks added to the variety. At the centre of the wilderness was piled a pyramid of bones encircled by tombstones with 'curious' inscriptions. An admirer trilled, 'throughout all this wilderness, nature appears in her native beauty and charming wildness. The strokes of art are scattered with so loose and easy a hand as to serve only to display nature the more while they are scarce perceived themselves'.[148]

By the 1730s, the well informed followed the fashion for naturalism. In 1736, Sir William Fownes, having seen Europe, returned to his County Kilkenny inheritance. At Woodstock, he was coached by other officers of the sylvan taste police. One, Henry Brownrigg, was – like Fownes – a member of the Dublin Society. Brownrigg, conveniently at Orléans, procured plants from the best nurseryman in France for Woodstock. Brownrigg praised Fownes's recently engineered waterfall, 'so wild and natural', but counselled the planting of more cypresses, as best able to stimulate a contemplative feeling.[149] How new to Ireland was this evocation of mood by such plantings may be questioned. Archbishop Michael Boyle had paid for fifty cypresses for his new estate at Blessington early in the 1670s. At Lismore, during the 1680s, evergreens had been much in vogue. Fifty-seven cypress trees had been introduced there in 1688.[150] Comments on the trees around the residences of squires and gentlemen on the Wentworths' Shillelagh estate suggested that there too evergreens had been favoured in the 1690s.[151] Similarly, at Caledon, Agnes Hamilton and her husband strove to recreate the effects that she remembered from her Scottish home of Panmure. Early in the eighteenth century, she boasted that it had been achieved thanks to the maturing coppices and groves.[152] As with houses, so in the surrounding gardens and parks, discordant styles from varied dates might survive. Moreover, owners in one generation spent heavily to be *à la mode*; in the next, successors, either exhausted or indifferent, made do with what was there even if it was deemed old-fashioned.

The inclination to allow freer rein to nature never entirely conquered the liking for formality. Especially in the enclosures near the house, often stocked with flowers, fruit and vegetables, control was of the essence. In the 1730s, William Smythe of Barbavilla equipped his new mansion in Westmeath with an appropriate setting. Since the region was adjudged 'a bare country', tree-planting was a necessity. Indeed, it began before the works on the house itself.[153] Evergreens, such as holly, yew, myrtle and phyllera, were introduced. For the grander effects,

58. Turret or gazebo, Dromoland, Co. Clare. Natural prospects and reordered landscapes were savoured from viewing places, prospect houses and banqueting houses such as this building on the O'Briens' lands.

particularly the 'new groves' set out in 'quincunx order', oaks, elms and ash were used.[154] Utility, future profit, fashion, recreation and sensory pleasures all combined in an undertaking which retained such formal features as canal, bowling green, wall fruit and scented borders.[155]

## VI

The need to stock and tend gardens and parks supported specialists. The resulting commercialization paralleled what that in the clothing, furnishing and food trades. In the 1690s, the Veseys at Abbey Leix were supplied with seed from England.[156] By 1702, an agent of Sir Thomas Vesey dispatched from Dublin sundry vegetable and salad seeds, with 'a few of all sorts of lower seeds [of annuals] for the summer'. The Veseys already used a specialist near

# A CATALOGUE

## OF

## Garden SEEDS and Flower ROOTS,

d by *John Johnson*, Gardiner and Seedsman, at the *Orange-Tree* on *Corkhill, Dublin.*

**Seeds of Roots.**
...rasburgh Onion-Seed
Red *Spanish* Onion
White *Spanish* Onion
*London* Leek
Leek
...arrot
...e Carrot
...g Parsnep
...nera
...s, all sorts
...mbole
...

**Sallad Seeds.**
...don Radish
...ndwich Radish
...panish Radish
*Spanish* Radish
...e Lettice
...Lettice
...Lettice
...ttice
...ttice
Lettice-Seed
...ttice
...tice
...Lettice
...tice
...pinage
...pinage
...ch
...rach
...eet
...t
Beet
Endive
...aleree

Rocket
...n
...rn
...orrel
...orrel
...resses
Cresses
...av'd Cresses
...url'd Cresses

...hervil

Purslane

...arsley

...lad

...sparagus
...ver
...Cabbage
...tch Cabbage
...bbage
...bbage

...lewort strip'd
...avoy

...ellon
...ellon
...ellon
...cumber

---

Short Cucumber
Prickly Cucumber
Pompion
Gourd
Mekin
Symnel, all sorts
Calabash, all sorts.

**Pot-Herb Seeds.**
Endive
Succory
Borage
Buglos
Burnet
Blood-wort
Clary
*French* Sorrel
Double Marygold
Pot-Marjoram
Landebeef
Summer Savory
Columbine
Tansie
Nepp
*French* Mallows
Orach.

**Sweet-Herb Seeds.**
Thyme
Hyssop
Winter Savory
Sweet Marjoram
Sweet Basil, all sorts
Sweet Maudin
Rosemary
Lavender.
Baum.

**Physical Seeds.**
Cardus Benedictus
Scurvy-Grass
Angelica
Lovage
Smallage
Tobacco, all sorts
Dill
Common Fennel
*Italian* Fennel
Sweet Fennel
Caruawy
Cumin
Anise
Corriander
Gromewel
Henbane
Plantain
Nettle
Balsam
White Poppy
Cardamum
Gourd
Broom
Piony
Foenugreek
Flawort
Burdock
Elecampane
Daucus
Citrul
Worm-Seed
Rue
Goats Rue
Oclus Christi
Line Seed, or Flax Seed
Marshmallow
Mustard.

---

**Flower Seeds.**
Dutch Julyflowers
Stock Julyflowers
Bloody Wallflowers
*Bromton's* Stockflowers
White Wallflower
Matted Pink
Mountain Pink
Double strip'd Columbine
Double Larks-heel
Upright Larks-heel
Rose Larks-heel tipt
*African* Marygold
*French* Marygold
Snap-Dragon
Candy Tuft
Sweet Scabious
*Spanish* Scabious
Sweet Williams
*London* Pride
Capsicum Indicum
*Venus* Looking-Glass
*Venus* Navel-wort
*French* Honysuckles, all sorts
Lychnis, all sorts
Rose Campian
Noli me tangere, three sorts
Marvel of *Peru*
Nasturtium Indicum
Sweet Sultan, all sorts
Valerian, all sorts
Bellvidere
Everlasting Sunflower
Branch'd Sunflower
*Canterbury* Bell
Flos Adonis
Steeple Bellflower
Fox-Gloves
Ironcolour Fox-glove
Nigella Romana
Urtica Romana
Primrose Tree
Aramanthus, all colours
Aramanthus Tricolour
Love lieth bleeding
Princes Feather
Love Apple
Thorn Apple
Double Poppy strip'd
Double Holyhock
*Lobel's* Catch-fly
Monks Hood
Convulvulus Major
Convulvulus Minor
Bottles of all colours
Globe Thistle
Holy Thistle
Great blue Lupines
Small blue Lupines
Yellow Lupines
White Lupines
Everlasting Lupine
Scarlet Beans
Everlasting Pease
Dwarf Pease
Winged Pease
Purple Pease
Pearl Pease
Snails and Caterpillars
Horns and Hedgehogs
Sensible Plant
Humble Plant.
A scarlet Musk Pea from the *Indies*.

---

**Seeds of Ever-Green and Flowering-Trees.**
Cypress
Silver Fir
*Norway* Fir
*Scotch* Fir
Great Pine
Pinaster
Phillirea vera
Alaternus
Pyracantha
Arbutus
Arbor Indæ
Mazerian Berries
Cedar de Lebanon
Holly Berries
Myrtle Berries
Laurel Berries
Bay Berries
Juniper Berries
Yew Berries
Ever-green Oak-Acorns
Cork-Tree Acorns
Lime-Tree Seed
Cena Seed
Laburnum major
Laburnum minor
*Spanish* Broom Seed
Almonds
Chesnuts
Hornbeam Seed
Pistacia Nuts from the *Indies*
Apricock Stones.

**Sorts of Pease, Beans, &c.**
*Edwards's* Hotspur Pease
*Green's* Hotspur Pease
*Barnes's* Hotspur Pease
The *Indian* or *Marafat* Pea
Short Hotspur Pease
Long Hotspur Pease
*Sandwich* Pease
Crown Pease
*Windsor* Grey Pease
White Rouncival Pease
Grey Rouncival Pease
Blue Rouncival Pease
Green Rouncival Pease
Maple Rouncival Pease
Large white Sugar Pease
Small white Sugar Pease
Grey Sugar Pease
White Rose Pease
Grey Rose Pease
*Indian* Pease
Egg Pease
Sickle Pease
Gosper Beans
White Kidney Beans
Speckled Kidney Beans
Marble Beans
*Indian* Beans
*Windsor* Beans
*Sandwich* Beans
*Canterbury* Beans
Lentils.

**Seeds to improve Land.**
Clover Grass
Hop Clover cleans'd
Hop Clover in the Husk
Sain-foine
La lucern
*French* Furz

---

Dantzick Flax, or *East*-Country Flax.

**Flower Roots.**
All the kinds of Piccadee Ranuncules
All sorts of new double Anemonies
Tuberose Roots from *Italy*
Double white Tulip, all sorts
Double yellow Tulip
Double strip'd Tulip
Poppy Anemonies
Plain Auriculus, divers sorts
Double and strip'd Auriculus
Polyanthoes, all sorts
Irises, all sorts
Crown Imperials
Fraxinellas, all sorts
Hepatica's, double blue, and double peach Colour
Crocus's, all sorts
Narcissus, all sorts
Junquils, double and single
Piony's, all sorts
Fritillaria, all sorts
Hellebore, all sorts
Colchicums, all sorts
Cyclamen, Spring and Autumn
Bee Flower
Narcissus of *Constantinople*
Lillies, all sorts
Double white Lilly
Paper white Primroses
Lillies variegat. in the Leaf.

**Sorts of Choice Trees and Plants.**
Orange, strip'd and Hermophradite
Lemons
Cittrons
Pomgranate double flower
Mirtles, all sorts
Silver Mirtles
Silver Rosemary
Indian Fig
Oleander, red and white
Philirea, all sorts
Alaternus strip'd
Cytisus, Lunatus, & Secundus Clusii
Amomum Plinii
Hollies strip'd with yellow and with white
Hedghog Holly, and other Hollies strip'd, great Varieties
Laurestinus, both sorts
Laurel strip'd
Arbutus
Indian Juka, or *Adam's* Needle
Paliurs
Pyracantha
Terebinthus
Jucabea Marina
Horse Tongue Bay
Honey Tree
Olive Tree
Cedrus Libani
Barmudy
Passion Tree
Semper Vivens

---

Agnus Castus
The true Bay of Alexander
Arbor Judæ
Platanus Orientalis & Occidentalis
Cedar of *Virginia*
Tragacantha
Horse-Chesnut
Jessamines, *Spanish* yellow, *Persian* white, &c.
Cistus, all sorts
Marum Syriacum
Geranium noctu Olens
Jucca Peruana
Nightshade variegated
Mugworth variegated
Woodbine variegated
Althæa, purple, white, &c.

**Fruit-Trees.**
Dutch Goosberrys, the scarlet, smooth, and the scarlet hairy, and the large green hairy
Large *Dutch* white Corrines
Apples, divers sorts
Pears, divers sorts
Plums, divers sorts
Cherrys, several sorts
Quinces, all sorts
Medlers, all sorts
Figs, all sorts
Walnuts, all sorts
Grapes of several sorts
Peaches divers sorts
Apricocks, several sorts
Nectarins, all sorts
Strawberrys, all sorts
Rasberrys, all sorts
Mulberrys, both sorts.

**Trees for Walks.**
English Elms
Dutch Elms
Limes
Playns
Abealls
Horse-Chesnuts
Beach Trees
Horn Beam Plants.

**Flowering Trees and Shrubs.**
Roses, divers sorts
Syringos
Rose Elder
Double blossom Thorn
Glassenbury Thorn
Holy Thorn
Mirtle Leav'd Thorn

**Hardy Greens.**
Pyramid Hollys of all sorts variegated
Standard Hollys
Large Yews
Swedish Junipers
Bayes
Strip'd Fillerees
Laurestinus of all sorts
*Dutch* Box for Edging
Variegated Box.

*With many other Sorts.*

---

...nay be likewise there Accommodated with *Spades, Rakes, Hoes, Reels, Lines, Sheers, Sythes, Watering-Pots,* ...er *Sives, Pruning* and *Budding Knives*; *Artichokes, Asparagus, Colliflowers, Cabbage* and *Tarragan* Plants: All ...rts of Common *Garden-Pots*, proper for the use of *Gardiners*.

59. John Johnson, *A catalogue of garden seeds and flower roots.*

the New Gate in Dublin, 'that sells all sorts of garden seeds', and trusted him to send an apparently random selection.[157] However, it was said that no shop in Dublin could supply the Veseys with sainfoin or ryegrass seed.[158] By 1732, Sarah Johnson with her seed shop on Cork Hill in Dublin offered to furnish 'the best kind' of ranunculus, anemones, tulips and jonquils. In addition, she could supply 'seed' pomegranates and the popular early German hotspur pea.[159] Richard Edgeworth, regularly in Dublin and England, procured materials for his garden from the nurseries and seedsmen there. In common with landowners across the kingdom, he used Daniel Bullen in Dublin. In 1769, Bullen dispatched a variety of plants and seeds to Edgeworthstown.[160] Soon, the abundant choice available in Dublin attracted customers from north-western England. In the 1720s, the Senhouses of Netherhall in Cumberland bought most of their fruit trees from Dublin nurseries.[161] Customers were also attracted from north Wales.[162]

Much for the garden – as for the house – could be ordered off the peg from leading nurserymen and seedsmen. In the main these developments paralleled those in Scotland, although in some details lagging behind the northern kingdom.[163] Early in the eighteenth century, an enterprising seed merchant in Dublin issued a printed catalogue.[164] By the second half of the eighteenth century, horticulturalists multiplied in Dublin. Visitors inspected their stocks. The best – such as Landré near St Stephen's Green – provided staples and rarities. Peter Landré was importing fruit trees from England in 1714. He supplied the O'Haras in County Sligo with stocks of peaches, apricots, plums, pears and apples in 1720.[165] He offered the needs for different parts of an estate: from the flower garden to the grass seeds for lawns, banks, pastures and paddocks.[166] After he died in 1747, aged eighty, the business was continued by a nephew.[167] The Landrés' reputation was such that he secured orders from all provinces of the kingdom.[168] Godwin Swift, a revenue official exiled to west Cork, consoled himself by engaging on 'a little improvement' around his rented property near Skibbereen. To this end, he requested the dispatch of plants by 'honest' Landré in Dublin. His shopping list included bay trees, daphnes, mallows, hollyhocks, syringas and larch saplings as well as the ubiquitous auriculas and carnations.[169]

Nurseries and seed merchants also emerged in the provinces.[170] Some establishments were opened by enterprising landowners and their gardeners; others were independent commercial ventures. The O'Haras turned to a supplier in County Armagh for fir saplings. In addition, Elinor O'Hara, when in Dublin during the 1720s, picked up seeds of flowers that caught her fancy. Again the female interest in the decorative aspects of gardening is underlined.[171] Elsewhere, William Fennell, describing himself as a gardener with premises in Cork city, sold fruit trees as well as seeds. In addition, he boasted of the cascades, fountains and canals that he had created for Judge Bernard near Bandon. During the 1730s, Cornelius Kennedy kept retail outlets in both Kilkenny and Cork. In addition, he was prepared to advise on the spot and recommend gardeners to landowners. By 1756, Winifred Proven in Tuam retailed a wide range of vegetable and salad seeds, and enjoyed the custom of gentry from County Mayo.[172]

Exacting standards for gardens and plantations, like those in kitchens and stables, required expert suppliers and operators. The lordly, knowing that their own credit would be enhanced or depressed by their achievements in these spheres, engaged gardeners from Britain or further afield. George Mathew of Thomastown, in addition to advising others about their building projects, fussed about the surrounding gardens. He enquired after a gardener for Kean O'Hara. Mathew declined to press the man about his religion because he was persuaded of his excellence as nurseryman and kitchen gardener.[173] Molesworth, belittling almost all that he observed in Ireland, sneered at the ignorance and slovenliness of its gardeners.[174] He alleged that they neglected to record accurately the names of what they had planted. His complaints are contradicted by examples of others who took time to list species and yields, just as they noted names, ages, breeding seasons and progeny of hunters and bitches. Sir John Temple, when sending grafts and cuttings from Palmerston to an Ulster enthusiast, Sir Robert Colvill, instructed his gardener 'to make labels of the several kinds and to set down which of the pears and plums must be set against walls'.[175] Molesworth was so pessimistic about finding an adequate kitchen gardener in Ireland that he thought of seeking one in the Low Countries.[176] Henry Ingoldsby, owner of Carton, while in London engaged 'a thorough working gardener', skilled in pruning and raising trees.[177] From County Antrim in the 1720s, the Reverend James Smythe complained about the lack of a competent gardener, and turned for assistance to one of his other servants. When Smythe first removed to the Midlands, skilled help was again wanting.[178] Later, after 1749, when the ageing Smythe's gardener fell ill, his employer lamented the 'most horrid condition' of the garden.[179]

In County Longford, Richard Edgeworth at first relied for help on relations and neighbours. In 1737, he paid a kinsman's gardener 5s. 5d. for pruning his trees. Patient proprietors trained operatives for the garden as for the house. At Doneraile in County Cork, Hayes St Leger hired William Smith as a gardener in 1732. Smith was paid a yearly £10, together with grazing for a single horse. He evidently pleased. Within two years his salary was increased to £12. Eventually, in 1758, Smith graduated to be park-keeper at Doneraile, at an annual stipend of £15.[180] Running a rural establishment on the scale of the St Legers' required other outdoor specialists. A warrener doubled as a fowler, and was paid a modest £4 p.a. He was, however, allowed a house, garden and grazing for two cows in addition to two ferrets and nets needed for his work.[181] By the 1750s, the fowler received an annual £12. Better remunerated was the decoyman, whose skills could decide the success or failure of this prestigious sporting feature. In 1744, John Atkins, the St Legers' decoyman, received a yearly £15.[182]

A proficient gardener was treasured and, like competent cooks, housekeepers, coachmen and gamekeepers, might be cosseted and rewarded. The squire of Barbavilla, William Smythe, engaged a gardener recommended by another squire. The operator, James Houston, had trained with Landré, the Dublin nurseryman.[183] Houston demanded annual wages of twelve guineas, together with diet and lodging.[184] Edgeworth appreciated and rewarded the achievement of his gardener in raising early asparagus.[185] Gardeners were sometimes expected to possess more than manual dexterity as they escorted visitors around their plantations. Book-learning, the ability for example to comprehend Evelyn's *French Gardener* or other manuals, could be useful. In 1694, the viceregal gardener, Harrison, was approved as an excellent botanist with some understanding of natural history: at least 'enough for one of his rank'.[186] The note of condescension reminded that even the most skilled gardener was classed among the mechanics, labourers or upper servants.

In the Irish Midlands, an often harsh climate made gardening a challenge. Richard Edgeworth laboured first to retrieve and then to embellish his inheritance of Edgeworthstown. His efforts collapsed any clear boundaries between public and private activities. Reordering of the demesne, which bordered the small town of Edgeworthstown and the public highway, began soon after Edgeworth married. First, elms were planted in an avenue to give the approach to the house greater *éclat*. Flower and fruit gardens were restocked. Over the next thirty-five years, trees and shrubs were constantly added or replaced. Thereby shelter was offered to the house, which itself was enlarged and modernized early in the 1740s. The prospects from the mansion were diversified: in 1752, a vista was opened. An 'aha' or haha was dug. Later, serpentine walks were created – perhaps a sign of a dawning romanticism. Even at the close of his life, the squire was introducing more trees: horse and Spanish chestnuts and elms.[187] For all the evident activity, Edgeworth's heir wrote as dismissively of the garden as of his father's house. The son asserted that when he returned permanently to Edgeworthstown in 1782, he found a formal garden, 'in the original Dutch taste', modelled after the frontispiece in Miller's *Dictionary*.[188] In this way, later generations discounted what their forebears had accomplished.

'Outward improvements' still absorbed Squire Edgeworth in 1768. They necessitated decorative features, such as a 'chinese gate' into the front courtyard. Earlier, earthenware pots had been purchased. These probably lacked any decorative function: not so the stone plinth on which a sundial was mounted or the six stone jars in which vines were placed. These had come from a specialist near Bath, who furnished others in Ireland, like the Veseys at Abbey Leix, with ornamental and useful wares for their gardens. The Bath stone vases and baskets which adorned Abbey Leix may have served as prototypes for the articles which the thrusting proprietor of the Kilkenny marble works launched onto the Irish market.[189]

One of Edgeworth's final fancies was to erect a statue of a hermit. An element of realism was to clothe the figure in stockings and shoes. More practical were the brick-walled enclosures constructed at Edgeworthstown to shield sensitive plants and the matting to insulate them against unseasonable frosts. He was also trying to raise the arbutus, happier in the temperate south-west.[190] While planting for future generations, Edgeworth did not ignore

60. H. D. Hamilton, 'A green stall at the root market', 1760. Hamilton showed the demand for and availability of fresh vegetables, fruits and salad stuffs.

immediate wants. Wall and soft fruit remained concerns. In 1755, for example, he had planted a further twenty peach trees, eight nectarines, half a dozen apricots and a couple of figs.[191] Near the end of his life, he bought a treatise on the cultivation of peaches, hopeful that he might bring decades of experiment to perfection. As in other well-ordered establishments, the calendar was marked by the arrival of asparagus, cherries, strawberries and walnuts no less than by juicy spring lamb, 'green' (grass-fed) goose and oysters. Also, he regularly received gifts of delicacies from garden and park sent by neighbours: venison, teal, partridge, woodcock, snipe, eels, salmon, cherries and asparagus.[192]

In another bleak region, north Antrim, the Reverend James Smythe wrestled with nature. Convention, curiosity, boredom and greed inspired his gardening, first in Ulster and then in Meath. Smythe, like Squire Edgeworth, wanted produce for the table. He experimented with asparagus, celery and artichokes.[193] Onion seed, sent via Dublin, had been imported from Holland.[194] He grafted cherry and pear trees, some of which he sent south to his relations.[195] Perhaps inspired by publications from England and sponsored by the Dublin Society, Smythe developed a taste for home-grown fennel, said by him to make an excellent salad, and broccoli.[196] Removed to Kells as its archdeacon, he gardened methodically. He listed fruit trees – peaches, nectarines, pears, apricots, plums and cherries – growing against brick walls or in enclosures. Ten rows of gooseberries of different colours flanked his bowling-green. Some stocks came from England; more from neighbouring squires. Two plants particularly appealed to the archdeacon: the universally esteemed auriculas and cardamons. Smythe shared with other ardent cultivators the aim to raise a succession of fresh vegetables for as long a season as possible. New varieties of pea, bean, lettuce or cabbage were tried and compared for flavour with established favourites.[197] In this way, gardening fitted into the domestic economy and added to the pleasures of the table. Yet, seeming indulgences could be justified for their wider applications. Trials might in time improve yields, set standards for neighbours and tenants, raise rents and alleviate shortages of staple foods. In the case of Smythe, horticulture belonged to a culture moulded by education, travel and systematic observation of natural phenomena. Also, it endorsed a notion, circulated in print, that the Protestant clergy had special responsibilities in regard to understanding and exploiting nature.[198]

Smythe prized asparagus. Between 12 April and 7 June 1747 he recorded how many stems were cut. By mid-May, 5,416 stalks had been harvested. This bumper crop glutted the household. The taste for this vegetable verged on an addiction with Edgeworth. In 1755, the squire purchased 500 asparagus plants as well as seed from one Dublin supplier.[199] Some of the crops may have been presented to others, but it also seems likely that much was sold. Nicholas Peacock outside Limerick laid in a weighty 600 stalks of asparagus against festivities for the birth of a son.[200] These surpluses may have brought unfamiliar foods from the preserves of the gentry into the purlieus of the towns. Gardeners were allowed frequently to sell what was not required at their employers' tables. As a supplement to other earnings, the profits were not to be disdained. The gardener at Springhill in County Londonderry was to be paid from the sales of produce.[201] An agent and farmer in County Limerick sent a servant to sell plums in the nearby town, and thereby raised a useful 5s. 8d.[202] The absent owner of Palmerston, close to Dublin, decreed that 'people shall not be suffered to come in summer time to the garden to fruit'. Instead, the gardener was authorized to send it into the city 'and sell it all there'.[203] Formal agreements attested alike to the demand for seasonal produce and a growing commercialization.[204] While Carton was unoccupied, traders in Slane and Maynooth offered to buy the fruits from the gardens for a fixed sum.[205] A weaver and shoemaker from Waterford contracted to harvest the fruit from a country farm. Theirs was a modest enterprise: they paid an annual £4 15s. for the apples, pears and plums. Nevertheless, such devices brought the plenty of the countryside to townspeople.[206] In Dublin during the summer, street traders cried 'fine wall cherries, ripe wall-cherries – a penny a quart'. The lucky in Dublin, such as Samuel Waring, could have fruit sent from their own gardens. Commercial enterprise of the marketers brought seasonal fruits to more. Herb-women supplied prosperous households in Dublin.[207]

Other benefits were diffused beyond the limits of estates. The cultivation of apples and – less often – pears was frequently enjoined in leases. One fruit was cider, which, if drunk instead

61. H. D. Hamilton,
'Apples and pears', 1760.

of imported beverages, would fortify the Irish economy. It had always attracted fans, especially those who themselves, or whose ancestors, had known the drink outside Ireland. In 1744 orchards were recommended to one (absent) estate-owner for their beauty 'three times in the year: viz. in the spring, when in the blossom; in the harvest when the trees are full of golden and scarlet coloured apples; the third is at your table [in] a glass of good cider'.[208] Patriots like Madden within the Dublin Society wished to popularize it, which may explain its appearance at Trinity College in 1738.[209] For the Limerick agent Peacock, on the edge of gentility, cider, along with drams of spirits, was his preferred tipple. It was taken both with the squires and the less elevated of his neighbourhood.[210] In the same county, a morose Quaker surveyor sampled what was on offer at *The Cock* in Adare. He pronounced the cider the best ever. So great was the demand for the brew of the landlord, Lampard, that he bought £140 worth of fruit.[211] When not pressed into drinks, apples and pears, with their longer seasons, greater durability and ease of transport, appeared regularly at markets. Archbishop King had apples sent to him in Dublin from County Londonderry. Apple-women in Dublin did brisk business.[212] The potential value of fruit and vegetables justified the retention of green plots within the towns and the creation of new ones where food was grown, so stimulating in Ireland the market gardens that flourished around other large cities such as London and Edinburgh.[213]

62. H. D. Hamilton, 'Turnip porter', 1760.

In the sixteenth century, the diet of the Irish was thought to include cresses and roots. Salad stuffs were also in demand in the seventeenth century.[214] Sir William Petty in calculating the expenses of his household in the 1670s assumed that much would be bought at market: not only meat, poultry and fish, but fruit and vegetables. Unfortunately, by lumping the greengrocery with cheese, eggs, sugar, spices and oil, he made it impossible to ascertain the proportion of household spending devoted to these commodities. This mixture of goods accounted for 4.6 per cent of his annual spending in 1672.[215] The budget of a later Dublin resident, James Ware, recorded that 3.2 per cent of his expenditure in 1741 went on roots 'and garden stuff'. More costly was his indulgence in imported oranges and lemons, associated perhaps with the punch and cordials with which he refreshed guests. The fruit consumed 5.1 per cent of the annual budget. In 1744, total spending on 'garden stuff' amounted to 2.4 per cent, and on oranges, 2.1 per cent. Variations may be explained by abundance lowering prices or by Ware's longer absences from the capital. Ware certainly had a garden. Indeed, in 1741, 5.7 per cent of his outgoings went to it. But what it returned in terms of eatables is unknown.[216] These proportions differed little from the estimated expenditure of prosperous households in contemporary England.[217] How far the uncommon vegetables and fruit descended down the social and economic scales occupied by the Pettys and Wares is harder to ascertain. In general, access to and the ability (and willingness) to buy a more varied range of foods became a further mark of the civil and civilized.

Adventurous gardeners justified their preoccupations in terms of public benefits. More often these were said to guarantee stocks of staples than to vary the diet of the laborious and poor. Two exemplars of benevolence warn of its limited applications. Robert French, on inheriting Monivea, tackled the deficiencies of the grounds as well as of his house. He ordered trees – beech, larch, Scotch fir – from Dublin. Some were set in an avenue which would improve the approach to the mansion. In 1745, he employed seventy-three workmen on the project.[218] In 1754, he bought more firs – Scotch, Spanish and silver – and elms to create a 'sweep road' in front of the mansion. In the same year he was planting 'a broad walk'.[219] Sentiment led him to retain an avenue of beeches which had been established by his father. The same feeling also saved a silver fir, the gift of a great-uncle, which was transplanted in 1752 by his wife. In general, the notions of earlier generations were soon discarded as primitive and inferior, as in architecture, clothing and furnishings. Patrick French, Robert's parent, made a 'pleasure garden' and instituted potato-growing on boglands.[220] These features disappeared when the son created an avenue leading from the house into his township of Monivea. The woodland was further enlarged in 1765 with the introduction of more oaks, ash, firs, larch and beech. In common with other provident planters, French maintained two nurseries.[221] At the same time, he exploited family and friends to procure apple trees from Clonmel and cherry trees from Geashill. Sweet chestnuts and walnuts appeared. An experimental four peach stocks were acquired, but French seems not to have persisted with this venture, which – as has been seen – fascinated Edgeworth. Even pears and plums were few. Instead, hot-beds coddled the delicate.

In much of this activity, Robert French followed where his father had led. The latter bought glass for the hot frames and four 'cap glasses' to protect the tender. A glazier in Galway town supplied them.[222] Flowers were in demand, but so too were the humble cabbage and cauliflower. Like many another determined to learn, French equipped himself with Miller's *Gardener's Dictionary*.[223] He used the Dublin seedsman Bullen, and suppliers nearer to hand in Loughreagh, Ennis and Galway.[224] French's itch to improve led him, on the one hand, into efforts to drain the bog and redirect the river, and on the other to enclose and stock part of the river which ran through the demesne. In 1749, he introduced crayfish into the Monivea waters.[225] He planted a hopyard on some of the reclaimed bog, but when it failed he converted it into a kitchen garden and grew potatoes there.[226] He also tried new types of grass and fodder. He, and his guests, could relax after their – and the labourers' – exertions on the bowling-green. Curiosity not any real belief in the likelihood of success caused him to buy seeds of the massive cedars from Lord Pembroke's gardener at Wilton House in Wiltshire.[227]

French was famed for his promotion of flax-growing and linen-making among tenants. However, his own grounds less blatantly proclaimed utilitarianism. Even so, the intimate links between the demesne and the larger estate were confirmed when French took on as an apprentice gardener Tom Glenn, a product of the Charter School at Monivea, which French had enthusiastically supported.[228] This conventional linkage between material and moral betterment was emphasized when another busy landowner had a parcel of seeds and catechisms sent to his tenants.[229] John Digby of Landenstown, an uncle of Robert French, used house and garden less stridently for physical and moral betterment. Digby deprecatingly portrayed himself meandering about his estate with a volume of Milton in his hand. Tags from Spenser were inscribed on the lintels of garden temples. Happiness, he affirmed, was the proper object of the Christian: it resulted from works which advanced the public good and personal fulfilment. Digby's demesne, no less than the House of Commons, was a fitting place in which to exercise skills and perfect virtue.[230] This high-mindedness, so devotees like Digby argued, need not exclude full relish of the fruits of the earth.

Ryecourt in County Cork resounded to its energetic owner's projects. The proprietor, George Rye, was alarmed by the return of famine in the 1720s. With others, he investigated methods by which it might be prevented. Rye, more sceptical than many of his contemporaries, doubted whether the usual expedients, manuals and methods imported from England and continental Europe, would do the trick. Instead, the concerned must study what worked in Ireland, and disseminate the knowledge. Rye, in common with the like-minded in the Dublin Society and Physico-Historical Society, equated patriotism with such endeavours, 'it being my sentiment that the welfare of one's country is so noble a design that even to attempt it is praise-worthy'.[231] Rye's horizons, it may be supposed, were lengthened by study first at Dublin University and then at the London Inns of Court. Trained as a barrister, he reached the rank of colonel either through regular or militia service. He addressed other pressing problems, writing – for example – on the epidemic diseases of Cork city. Rye, 'a great improver in several branches of agriculture', typified a spirit which used the garden as a seedbed for practices and ideas with larger applications. They also yielded immediate pleasures.[232] Rye commanded his gardener to manure the flower beds with pulverized seashells. In consequence, he 'never saw better carnations or flowers fairer and larger than in that cold climate'. The mulch was then applied to ridges of potatoes, with equally satisfactory results. But the history of his estate warned how easily altruism might mutate. George Rye's heir, John Rye, was addicted to field sports. One result – improved breeds of hounds and horses – may have profited the locality. More immediately, the Muskerry Hunt gained.[233]

Much in gardening and silviculture was defended as helpful to the wider community. In practice, only two crops – the potato and flax – affected how large numbers lived. The role of benevolent or avaricious landowners in encouraging their cultivation is clearer with the second than the first. At the same time, although the evidence favours a minority of prosperous and methodical squires, there are occasional glimpses of how women, children, townspeople and the middling orders were affected by the greater variety of flowers, fruits and vegetables. It could be that artichokes, asparagus and even anchovies were more easily come by in mid-eighteenth-century Ireland than at any subsequent point until the close of the twentieth century. Few among the propertied questioned the reigning dogmas that improvement must help all within Ireland. Hume, surveying the Wentworths' holdings in Wicklow and Wexford, was one dissentient. He advised that the plantations of the 1690s, nearing maturity in the 1730s, be closely inspected. Doubting that much timber with commercial value had been raised, he admonished, 'don't let fine clipped hedges around pleasure gardens be surveyed, nor ornamental trees in avenues leading up to a gentleman's door'.[234] Another sceptic was Charles O'Hara, an active and thoughtful Sligo squire. Trying to reconcile the claims of the present and posterity, he admired the 'innocent simplicity' of his Sligo tenants. Yet, he approved strenuous measures to make them 'industrious and to preserve them'. The same measures would increase his rents and so finance his passion for the turf. In O'Hara's world, the stud book became as much a key to understanding the book of nature as treatises on flowers, fruits, flax and trees: *The Sportsman's Calendar* interested him as much as Miller's *Gardener's Dictionary*.[235] The O'Haras' Sligo estate echoed to several campaigns of improvement, the results of which were generally short-lived. O'Hara expressed qualms about the prevailing doctrine that lavish expenditure on the demesne bettered the whole neighbourhood. More clear-sighted than most of his contemporaries, he suspected that the changes flattered the self-esteem and improved the rentals of the owner.

O'Hara questioned conventional justifications for innovations in house, garden and estate. He analysed seismic shifts in the agrarian economy as landlords and tenants in the west responded to the pull of distant markets.[236] However, he ignored the effect on others of what he enjoyed himself. Even those with small plots and light purses experienced pleasures when they strolled along avenues, sampled strange foods and plucked seasonal flowers. Such sensations leave few imprints. The improved may have enjoyed the process less than the improvers. Without access to one's own land, there was no chance to put into effect the well-meaning directives. Among the wealthy, both women and children, customarily denied the enjoyment of property, were allowed a role in designing and tending beds. The majority of people, outside the palladium of property, had chances to refresh themselves through promenades and prospects which remained free. Even then, they were frequently expected to dress correctly to enjoy the first amenity. Otherwise, markets and street vendors touted both the commonplace and rare. But food gave only brief gratification. New – and some older – introductions were useless without the utensils with which to prepare and serve them or the ground in which to set them. In the end, the agreeably variegated but perishable produce of the earth appealed less to those with little to spend than the durable items of dress and adornment.

Chapter 7

# Sport

*I*

The diary of Ralph Howard (the future Lord Wicklow) disclosed that in 1748 he went to the races at Arklow, near his Shelton Abbey home in County Wicklow, and attended the associated ball. After Christmas there were more races and another dance. On Twelfth Night there was a football match. Howard spent £2 1s. on the event: probably for a prize rather than the price of watching. Later in the month, Howard awarded further prizes at a horse-race. During the next summer, more racing, this time at Kilcooly, attracted him.[1] Howard may have plunged into this hectic round, not so much because he adored the turf, but as part of his duties as high sheriff of his county. A successor in the post found himself and his family, 'being much gayer than we otherwise would have been. We had several balls and were invited everywhere up and down the country'.[2] In Howard's case, he was also building up an interest which eventually helped him into parliament as member for County Wicklow. He combined the sporting fixtures with a frenetic round of concerts, clubs and gatherings in Dublin. Soon he would quit his locality for an extended continental tour from which he would return with crates of paintings, engravings and statuary. There seemed no incongruity in Howard patronizing orderly country sports, the fashionable diversions of the city, and the haunts of the aesthete.[3]

Horse-races and hunting featured as prominently in the cycle of urban as of rustic pleasure. Yet the terms on which enthusiasts participated varied. The variations, although they could reflect temperament and locale, more frequently told of gender, confession and (most vitally) income. Among the well-to-do, commodious stables completed, and occasionally dwarfed, the family's residence. At Portmore in County Antrim early in Charles II's reign, Lord Conway gave precedence to the building of a new, circular stable.[4] At the same time, in south Munster, the second Lord Cork was content to squat in venerable buildings but accommodated his stud in modern quarters. Later, Bishop King at Derry had his stables ornamented with twelve columns as well as the essential mangers.[5] Visitors to the estates of the powerful were as likely to be dazzled by the improved strains of bloodstock, exotic plants and sporting amenities as by the modernity of house and furnishings. Owners rearranged parks into paddocks, rides, coverts and scrub to please whatever creature they aimed to kill.

The dominant presence in these ensembles and amusements were horses. Costly in themselves and in their keep, they required expert handlers and riders. Whether in the traces of a coach or on the racetrack, the beasts instantly advertised the judgement and standing of their owners. Possessing a nag differentiated the drudging majority from a fortunate few. Surprisingly, and on the basis of no more than personal observation, Sir William Petty announced in Charles II's reign that 'every man' now kept a pony to ride. The conclusion cannot easily be reconciled with another of Petty's pronouncements: that Ireland contained 100,000 horses.[6] Ownership of a mount immediately enlarged the circuit that could readily be travelled. Furthermore, by William III's reign, possession separated Catholics, legally prohibited from owning a horse worth more than £5, from their Protestant neighbours.[7] Horses, ever present for daily work and pleasure, featured in increasingly commercialized recreation. Accordingly, they lead the enquirer from secluded stable-yards and enclosures into public arenas. Most sport was gregarious rather than solitary. Even angling usually involved company.[8] Seventeenth- and eighteenth-century Ireland felt the same pressures – commercial and cultural – which elsewhere reserved prestigious pastimes for the few. Joining, let alone excelling, in competitive sports added to the occasions when a proper figure had to be maintained. It has been suggested on the basis of developments outside Ireland that urban recreations diverged more sharply from their rural equivalents, as also the amusements of the populace from those of the élite. In the Irish context, confession and ethnicity may have affected access to the diversions of the respectable.[9] There is, too, the question of how freely women participated in the pastimes.

Sporting fervour, especially when focused on horses, could be justified as altruism. An example was service by a stallion. This was represented as both a benefit and an honour which the affluent could bestow on peers and dependants.[10] The third earl of Cork, having recently come into his inheritance, was unhappy that his agents had put it about 'that 'tis a great favour to get a leap'. He wanted more of the tenants to have this boon: an attitude that varied the venerable notions of *noblesse oblige* or *droit de seigneur*.[11] The ability systematically and selectively to breed spoke of the time and resources to build, staff and maintain stables. The first earl of Orrery, was memorialized for 'His care to breed brave horses thou would'st ride/In peace for pleasure and in war for fight'.[12] In Ireland, unlike eighteenth-century Brittany, aristocrats did not have a legal monopoly over stud farms, but in practice only the affluent and leisured could engage in this activity, from which, some would contend, flowed public good. In 1699, a member of parliament, James Waller, had the wheeze that he could breed mares on an island confiscated from the defeated Jacobites. He hoped to inveigle grandees into cooperating, but there is no evidence that the project succeeded.[13] The private gains – in prestige as mounts won races, vaulted fences and gates, trotted through the city streets or ambled around the demesne – were clearer than any general improvement in Irish bloodstock. Money might be made from the enterprise, but the original investment was seldom recovered.

Throughout the seventeenth century, wars, starvation and disease depleted native stocks.[14] In 1666, it was suggested that Irish horses were so ill regarded that they sold at country markets for no more than 2s. 6d. Moreover, if not bought, they were left behind 'for the next comer, because they will not graze them'.[15] These jaundiced comments are in some measure confirmed by the low valuations put on many horses appraised in seventeenth-century Dublin.[16] Laments at the small size and paucity of native Irish horses (garrons and hobbies) prompted Essex, the lord-lieutenant between 1672 and 1677, to prod Charles II into directing a little of his passion for the turf towards Ireland. The king endowed prizes for the victors in races at the Curragh, a heath in County Kildare. This generosity stimulated competition among noble breeders, but did little to strengthen working horses.[17] The Curragh had long been the resort of the powerful from Dublin. In 1663, a member of Ormond's viceregal entourage announced his return from 'my Christmas gambols on the Curragh of Kildare, as hawking, hunting, coursing and horse-racing'. The festival took its tone from Ormond, whose craving for 'uninterrupted pleasures' embraced 'good weather, good hawks, much game and little business'.[18] In 1678, Ormond, again lord-lieutenant, looked forward to ten days of hunting and hawking on his lands around Kilkenny. In 1686, now aged seventy-six, he prepared regretfully to retire from field sports. He would console himself with a fruit garden.[19]

Already in 1670, official Dublin emptied and the affairs of state halted when the races were run at the Curragh.[20] Lord Massareene, a keen sportsman, gloated that steeds shipped over from Newmarket were easily beaten by the locally bred and trained, including his own. In two-horse races, the mounts of local notables were matched against each other. Passions were aroused; patriotism surrounded Irish steeds.[21] Massareene also revealed the presence of women among the onlookers. In 1683, the October races had been watched by 'many thousands of spectators and more coaches and ladies than I ever saw at a horse match, from whom our horses had so many good wishes before hand and acclamations after we won'. Massareene himself exhibited a yet more local pride when he carried the plate back to Antrim, 'where I hope it will abide'.[22] The magnetism of the Curragh among the governors of Ireland continued into the reign of Queen Anne.[23] The queen patronized the meeting to the tune of 100 guineas. Rules governed the races. They were to be confined to horses of Irish breeding, although in 1708 an exception was made for Lord Shelburne's 'Cricket', already in transit to Ireland.[24] The Curragh remained famous beyond Ireland.[25]

In the 1680s, landowners in County Down formed a society of horse breeders, which was promptly endorsed by the monarch. Intended to improve blood lines, the association served as a pretext for convivial assemblies and annual races.[26] It survived under intermittent vice-regal patronage.[27] By the mid-eighteenth century, its week of races at Downpatrick had become an important event in the social calendar of the county, and added to the attractions of the county town. Meanwhile, other race meetings multiplied. Corporations such as Youghal and Belturbet, as well as landed proprietors, offered plates and prizes, in bids to gain custom. Around 1710, groups of subscribers arranged meetings in Antrim and Fermanagh. At least two dozen were involved in the latter venture. Detailed regulations outlawed jostling and decreed 'fair play'. Non-subscribers were permitted to enter their mounts on payment of an entry fee of four guineas.[28] William Flower endowed a 'perpetual plate' for a race at Durrow in 1715. Only the fellow subscribers could compete. By 1731, twenty-two enthusiasts had contributed to the Youghal races.[29] At Mallow, the amenities of the spa were enhanced by horse-racing. In 1773, it was predicted that there would be a greater crowd at Mallow races 'than ever there was at the Curragh'.[30]

Sport was being promoted, formalized and sold to participants and spectators. Some of the vicious feuding of notables was diverted into less destructive contests on the turf. Nevertheless, intense loyalties were not only revealed but strengthened by the races, as the protagonists of particular owners or of separate localities urged on their favourites. At Youghal, confessional as well as geographical allegiances were aroused when Lord Galmoy challenged one of the Boyles – owners of much of the town – to a race. In 1727, the success in the same spot of a mount and jockey from distant Tipperary was resented.[31] Furthermore, the large wagers meant that more rode on the outcome of the contests than simple pride and reputation. For Henry French early in the 1750s posting between courses, a run of bad luck excused his inability to pay rent and debts. In 1753 he admitted that he had been left with only two guineas in his pocket after a disappointment at Lurgan. In the age-old cry of the addicted punter, French described how his fancy in the lead 'had at hollow all the world to nothing', only to stumble and injure itself.[32] Racecourses could themselves generate disorder. In 1711, the races run for a plate donated by Mervyn Archdall at Monea in County Fermanagh were so fiercely contested that they had to be reorganized.[33] The Mallow meeting in 1746 was enlivened by violence; two years later a young squire, heir to £1,200 p.a, was murdered at the Cashel meeting. The fixture at Rathkeale also provoked violence.[34]

Austere proprietors, such as Cox at Dunmanway and Caldwell in County Fermanagh, denied their tenants the conventional reward of horse-races on the rare days off. Landlords knew the dangers that might attend these recreations. In 1758, Lord Abercorn's agent stopped the townspeople of St Johnstown from relaxing with cock-fights and horse-racing. He lectured that 'an inch gained by honest industry was worth a yard otherwise, and that we did not want idle people at all'.[35] The local restrictions systematized a ban imposed by the Irish parliament in 1739, when all horse-races run for prizes worth less than £20 were to cease. The aim was clearly to end the numerous, more modest gatherings because they contributed 'greatly to promote and encourage idleness and debauchery among the farmers, artificers and day-labourers'. By gambling on the outcome, it was alleged, punters ruined their families. These prohibitions may have stimulated the quest for alternative and clandestine recreations. At least in theory, cock-fighting, dog matches and foot races were similarly restricted.[36] If some race meetings acquired a dangerous allure, many still enjoyed the backing and attracted the presence of the consciously polite. They were regarded as suitable recreations for respectable women.[37] One eighteenth-century commentator distinguished between 'great matches between noblemen and gentlemen, and plate matches', which were 'country business', and the meetings that sprang up in and around Dublin. Among the latter, the races at Crumlin were said to be haunted by 'jockeys, horse coursers, hostlers and farriers'. All, it was alleged, were intent on trickery. Whether in town or country, racing could prove a dangerous pursuit. 'Many an honest gentleman', it was remarked, 'hath been bubbled by it out of his whole estate'.[38]

Optimists and the desperate alike dreamt that horses of their breeding would triumph. Early in the eighteenth century, the impoverished Lord Bellew hoped that victory might save him. His sister-in-law, Lady Bellew, did not share his optimism. Bellew, a broken figure, all remnants of beauty gone and degenerated into 'a mere mope', schemed to sell steeds in France for £2,000. His sister-in-law wished him luck, but added, confusing the avian with the equine, 'all his geese are swans'. The genteel Misses Povey, fallen on hard times, banked on the sale of horses – their last substantial asset – to recover their fortunes. The sisters expected eighteen guineas from one horse to be sold at the autumn fair of Mullingar. They, like Bellew earlier, were disappointed.[39]

Racing triumphs advertised the excellence of particular stables and studs. Notionally, money could be made from the rearing as well as racing of horses. However, the examples of Bellew and the Poveys cautioned against extravagant dreams. The rich, like the second Lord Cork, gave away beasts. But Cork also traded. In 1662, he sold a black mare to Jack Jephson, the squire of Mallow, for £25; the next year, £40 in gold was paid by Lord Cavendish for a bay gelding; and in 1663, a grey went to Lord Roscommon, Cork's son-in-law, for £60. Roscommon financed the purchase through his winnings from Jephson on a wager over a game of bowls.[40] In 1665, Cork sold eighteen working horses to a single dealer.[41]

Sir Thomas Taylor at Headfort in County Meath attended assiduously to his stock, recording genealogies, couplings and births with as much care as others entered family events in their bibles. A contemporary felt that the choice of wife and horse posed equal difficulties.[42] At least in the naming of foals, there was greater freedom than in finding names for children. Speed, cunning, obstinacy and fidelity were hailed or hoped for.[43] Taylor put valuations on many of his breeding, but in practice few were sold. Instead, he presented acquaintances and neighbours with mounts. Thereby he added to the obligations which could eventually serve political purposes and be translated into votes. Other horses were used to draw his coach or for other tasks on the estate. If Taylor tried to total costs and profits of this enterprise, they have not survived. Many gains from horse breeding were not easily quantified: they included a ready supply of beasts for agriculture and recreation; admiring gasps at races, social gatherings or in the Dublin streets; the repute of doughty hunters or frisky fillies; even fame as a successful breeder, akin to that which attended those expert in propagating trees and shrubs. In short, horses could contribute to the figure made. However, they rarely made fortunes for their owners and breeders. The prices for the nine horses sold by Lord Drogheda during the 1750s ranged from 18s. 3d. to £8.[44] In 1723, eight horses belonging to Squire Vigors were appraised at £33 10s. for the lot.[45] The O'Haras from Sligo fared slightly better with the score that were sold on their behalf at Ballymote in 1731. The best fetched £13 10s.; the lowest, £1 14s.: the average price was £6 2s. 6d.[46] In 1730, the Paulls sold twenty-eight horses for £192 7s. 2d.: an average nearer £7 than £6.[47] The Limerick agent Nicholas Peacock was doing well when he sold a young black mare to his employer for six guineas. The horse was promptly lent to another local squire so that he could go to the Curragh.[48]

Horses differed greatly in purpose, power and value. Hunters and coach horses usually commanded the highest prices. In 1683, the coach 'cattle' of Sir Hans Hamilton had been valued at only £5 each. By 1770, four coach horses cost an official at Dublin Castle £113 15s.[49] In 1767, a St Leger was reported to have spent thirty-four guineas on a horse.[50] To ride a horse denoted prosperity, rank and – after 1695 – Protestantism.[51] Possessors had their circuits widened. But further distinctions arose. Number, colour and breeding all became indices of standing and income. The stylish sought blacks or bays to haul their carriages.[52] Temporary holders of public offices, particularly those – like Richard Edgeworth – who acted for a year as high sheriff in their county, borrowed coach horses and coachmen. Edgeworth gave £26 3s. 3d. for a bay horse in 1742: an expense that went with having his coach freshly painted with gold leaf.[53] Others, such as Michael Smythe of Portlick, challenging the established notables in Westmeath, fussed about sumptuous saddlery as well as their own clothes.[54]

The upkeep of stables with specialist staff added substantially to annual expenditure. At the end of the seventeenth century, advisers schemed to dock the spending of the second duke of Ormonde and his wife. In a yearly budget of £6,154, servants' wages fell to £700; their liveries and mounts to £209; and stables and coaches would take £500.[55] The percentage devoted to stables varied from establishment to establishment. Stables accounted for 3.5 per cent of Petty's spending in the 1680s, when he had all but abandoned Dublin. In the case of William King when bishop of Derry in the 1690s, stables amounted to 2.6 per cent of his yearly budget. Once he had been translated to Dublin, the total increased to 4.5 per cent. This reflected public duties as a lord justice and the greater show required in the city. Others, like Sir Cyril Wyche, also a lord justice, were conscious of having to make a striking figure with their equipages. But this was not exclusively a metropolitan trait. The first earl of Orrery in the 1670s, even after he had ceased to be lord president of Munster, expected to spend anything from £300 to £500 – 6 to 12 per cent of his yearly budget – on his stables and the liveries for the servants.[56]

Lord Justice Wyche, when he first bowled through the streets of Dublin in his coach, insisted on having horses that impressed. Six coach horses were considered the minimum to make the necessary impact. Each might cost £25.[57] Rochester, as lord-lieutenant in 1701, also agonized over whether his carriage horses would look handsome enough as they cantered through the capital.[58] During the 1690s, Evelyn realized that as a government functionary he must make the right impression and so incurred the expense of keeping a coach.[59] Coaches were costly. Those imported from England, once duty and carriage had been paid, might set their owner back by £100. Then they had to be maintained, driven and housed. In Dublin, residents usually owned a coach-house with accommodation for coachman, postillions and even grooms. In contrast, those up from the country or over from London had to rent stabling and places where the ostlers could sleep. Faced with these expenses, many only temporarily in Dublin did not travel with their own vehicles, but hired coaches and drivers once they had arrived in the capital. It was possible to buy second-hand. The younger Sir John Temple did so in 1667. He took over Colonel Edward Vernon's vehicle for £30. But simply to buy a single horse – from Lord Kingston – itself cost £20.[60]

Others made do with sedan chairs. For moving about congested thoroughfares, this made sense. Nevertheless, many in high stations insisted on a coach, with which came the expenses of horses and stabling. During the 1720s, thirty four-wheelers and thirty-seven lighter and cheaper two-wheelers were known to the authorities in the Dublin parish of St Michan. Since the population of the parish neared 20,000, this possession distinguished a favoured few from the mass.[61] Sir William Petty, in one of his speculations, thought that in the later seventeenth century, only 16,000 families in Ireland kept coach and saddle horses.[62] The rarity only spurred the grand to ensure that they had fitting equipages. It was noted approvingly that 200 coaches had attended the second duke of Ormonde when he arrived as lord-lieutenant. Moreover, thirty were drawn by six horses, and another forty by four.[63] So great was the crush of vehicles when the polite descended on St Andrew's Church for the annual concerts in aid of Mercer's Hospital, that the traffic had to be rerouted.[64] Some up from the country contributed to these traffic jams. In 1727, Lord St George travelled from Galway to Dublin for the winter season. He brought his coach and four black mares, black being still the most fashionable colour for coach horses. These were part of an establishment which included coachman, postillion, running footman, street footman, a manservant and a black butler.[65] The prestige associated with coach and horses led to them attending funerals. Even if the carriages were empty, their presence was regarded as a courtesy of the owner towards the deceased.[66] Yet, what some valued as a sign of prosperity and refinement, others condemned. The agent of the Orrery estates read (convincingly) the ownership of coaches by leading tenants as evidence of their profiteering at the expense of their absent landlord.[67]

More landowners were addicted to the breeding of horses than of rare trees. Equine interests could obsess, and occasionally ruin.[68] The O'Briens of Dromoland in County Clare

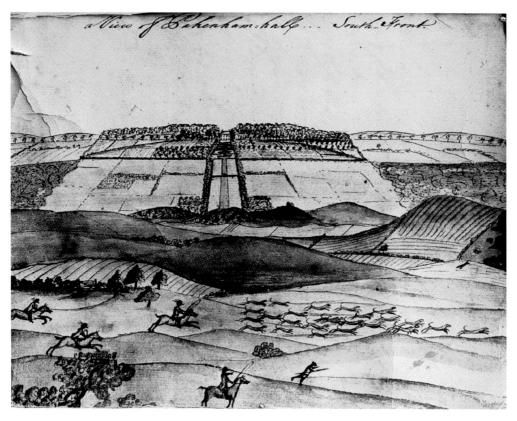

63. G. E. Pakenham, *Hunting outside Pakenham Hall*, 1736. Pakenham entered fully into the pleasures of the countryside (and Dublin), which evidently included the chase.

dedicated themselves to horses. In 1672, Henry O'Brien, a son of Lord Thomond, took care about who should have which horse from his stables after his death. A sliding scale of 'the next best' denoted O'Brien's evaluation of his relations and friends.[69] Sir Edward O'Brien brought the Dromoland branch of his family close to penury with his passion for the turf. The better to indulge it, he acquired a place, aptly named Jockey Hall, in County Kildare, close to the Curragh. At Dromoland, although stables figured prominently in O'Brien's improvements, it was not at the expense of a new mansion in the classical style and well-stocked gardens. In 1742, debts obliged him to offer for sale his entire stud, consisting of 'brood mares, colts and fillies of all ages'. In 1758, he candidly confessed that 'my sole amusement is my horses'. This, he contended, saved him from the addictions of cards, dice, whores and even hounds. Furthermore, the amusement and exercise of the horses prevented his health worsening.[70]

Most, even when they did not bet heavily, could not afford horses. Costly to buy, their feed, stabling and care consumed more money. Owners of racers faced particularly large bills. William Flower spent £2 1s. 5d. to send his 'Sultan' with a groom and jockey to race at the Curragh.[71] Win or lose, proud owners wanted to immortalize their favourites. By 1750, Lord Antrim had acquired five coloured prints of stag-hunting and several more of racehorses with their jockeys.[72] The year before, twenty-one engravings of racehorses were sold from an Irish house for 13s. 1½d.[73] The likenesses of Sir Edward O'Brien's champions were engraved. Trophies of the chase ornamented Howth Castle. Naïve images of the Kilruddery and Pakenham hounds were painted in the first half of the eighteenth century.[74] Sometimes, it was noted, the affluent treated their horses as well as – if not better than – their womenfolk, and were prepared to spend lavishly for portraits of thoroughbreds. The invented Lord Frolic was made to express an interest in a Wootton, on sale at fifty guineas, because the horse 'is in some sort a relation of your family'.[75] Later in the eighteenth century, fanatics such as O'Brien at Dromoland and his neighbour, Windham Quin, commissioned canvases of horses. Sir Ralph Gore's 'Othello' was another champion commemorated.[76]

Some extravagant in their stables and paddocks, such as Squire O'Hara and Lord Castle Durrow or – earlier – the second earl of Cork and his brother Orrery, could claim that in interesting themselves in horses, they assisted Irish agriculture. It is true that Lord Cork oversaw his kennels and stables with a vigilance that equalled his management of the whole estate. Recreation could not be separated from its more general welfare.[77] Stallions, hounds, setting dogs, spaniels and even a bloodhound were shipped from England. In 1656, a gelding purchased in Lincolnshire for £30 was sent over to County Cork. In 1662, he paid £100 for two from a horse-coper in London's Smithfield.[78] By 1671, he had an 'Arabian' horse in his park near Youghal.[79] Other animals were procured in Ireland. In his turn, Cork presented creatures to the important and useful: councillors in Dublin and the king's man, Ormond.[80] In 1660, he gave 'a young fine chestnut nag' of his own breeding to a son, and a black coach horse to a sister.[81] Cork showed off to visitors the paddocks outside Youghal where mares and foals grazed.[82] Cork's triumphs rested on the careful choice of employees for the stables and parks, as well as his personal superintendence. Owning property in England, he moved stock between the three kingdoms, so confusing and strengthening bloodlines.[83] In 1670, for example, six of his horses were sent from Youghal to England.[84]

The benefits of Cork's spending were clearest among a restricted circle of notables, kindred, neighbours and favoured tenants rather than among the generality of those living on his estates. Similar purposes were served by his second love – the deer park. During the 1650s, when the earl entertained the lord deputy, Henry Cromwell, to races run on the strand at Youghal, the earl was repairing and stocking his deer park at Lismore.[85] Soon, in 1661, he enclosed a new reserve nearer Youghal with a circumference of 8,500 perches.[86] A count in 1673 enumerated a hundred brace of fallow deer and another forty brace of red deer in the Lismore park. Stocks were to be replenished by twenty 'brave bucks' from Youghal. Later in the same year, the total of fallow deer was thought to have doubled.[87] Shelters were provided for the beasts.[88] Cork worried about encroachments. Interlopers were as likely to be presumptuous kinsmen and arrogant neighbours as indigent locals hunting for food or fuel. He intended that the right to ride and hunt on the precious sward should be accorded so as to honour the few, and not be devalued by too promiscuous resort. Worse threats arrived with the warfare of 1689 to 1691. The absent Cork procured a letter from the commander in chief to forbid any depredations on the park, but its effectiveness may be doubted.[89] Even in years of peace, such a large enclosure was impossible to police. In 1695, heavy losses of stock were reported, but without specifying whether it was through disease, marauding soldiers, poachers or the starving.[90]

The duke of Ormond and his sons similarly relished the chase. They too shared the enjoyment carefully with clients and rivals.[91] Meanwhile, Cork's younger brother, Orrery, eager to cut the right figure as lord president of Munster, bespoke a deer park at his new seat of Charleville. Other settlers already enjoyed this asset. At Mallow, the Jephsons possessed a herd of white deer: a curiosity both admired and envied.[92] Once the Orrerys deserted Charleville, the park was open to plunder. Tenants leased it. At first £70 was paid annually, but in 1692, the yearly rent dropped to £30: a sign of the decay of the reservation and the difficulty of finding a satisfactory custodian. The second tenant was required to maintain twenty pair of deer, but could also graze a few cattle. In the minds of some, such as the second Lord Cork, the presence of horses and cows was inimical to the good condition of parks. The lease for Charleville in 1692 also specified that head tenants from the nearby village should have the right to walk or ride through the grounds. Unless strictly monitored, this access might damage the sporting amenity.[93] As in so much else, whether in building, furnishing or the design of gardens, so even in the arrangement of deer parks, opinions changed. Cork's heir had nagged his grandfather to grass the park smoothly in order to improve the sport. He also worried that the privilege of hunting there had been granted too promiscuously. In 1698, the new earl declared unequivocally that he 'would refuse no gentleman of our country or neighbourhood a day or two's hunting', yet he was amazed at the freedom enjoyed by the likes of Judge Pyne and Lord Shannon, two local potentates. Cork realized that it was 'no small favour to a sportsman to have leave to hunt there', but worried about the type of dogs that some used.[94] Another in south Munster who used the right to hunt across his lands to strengthen political and social alliances was Alan Brodrick, in turn Speaker of the Commons and lord chancellor. In 1713, he assured his neighbour, Henry Boyle, eventually to succeed to Brodrick's role as the foremost politician of the region, that Boyle could hunt at Ballyannen whenever he chose, and 'turn out what deer you will'.[95]

Hunting had long responded and added to the nuances of society. Game laws, copied from England and continental Europe, restricted it to the wealthy and landed of Ireland.[96] From 1698, only those worth £40 p.a. (or more) were permitted to take a long list of game.[97]

Emparking and enclosing were costly in themselves, with the need to keep beasts in and pred-ators out.[98] Owners removed large tracts from regular cultivation, and in doing so proclaimed wealth and standing. Deer parks had to be staffed and watched.[99] The chase was also attended by rituals, which further complicated and stratified polite society.[100] Field sports, having long engendered rivalry, were integrated into arcane codes by which people were ranked and restrained. The nostalgic feared – on slender evidence – that novel notions of gentility were ending the easy bonhomie supposed once to have prevailed on the hunting field. By 1714, an aficionado of the chase was mourning its decline in Ireland.[101] The exequies were premature. Great parks, such as Ormonde's, Cork's and Orrery's decayed, but others replaced them. Around the Galtees by the middle of the eighteenth century, there were reputed to be twenty packs of buckhounds maintained by the owners of local deer parks.[102] Elsewhere, deer parks were created in the eighteenth century: for example, by Archbishop John Vesey at Holly-mount, in County Galway, and (later) by Archbishop Charles Cobbe on his Donabate hold-ings in County Dublin. A pamphleteer at much the same moment imagined a park encircled by a wall, nine feet in height, but nevertheless breached regularly by desperadoes.[103] At Baron-scourt in County Tyrone, the lowness of the enclosure explained the losses.[104] The absence of owners, either temporarily or permanently, could lead to their parks being invaded and wasted. Just as it often proved impossible to exclude trespassers, so those beneath the £40 p.a. threshold devised ways to evade the ban.

Deer, dead as much as alive, gave their owners a device with which to flatter. Lord Cork, with characteristic punctiliousness, fussed over who should receive portions of the carcass. Venison was regularly presented to equals and dependants. How much was given – whether an entire beast or merely a side – and which portions (the haunch was best) signified the standing of the beneficiary.[105] During his frequent absences from south Munster, Cork gave detailed orders as to who should receive gifts of venison.[106] Orrery's heir acknowledged that his father gave away more than was consumed in the household. Nevertheless, venison, together with other provender from the gardens, featured in the Orrerys' family menus.[107] Unashamed glee at being able to amaze guests at table by such viands was expressed by the bishop of Elphin in 1752. Bishop Synge waxed lyrical over 'a lordly haunch of venison which I reserved for a show and crack. I never saw the fellow. The largest dish I have scarce held it'. Earlier he had urged his daughter in Dublin to 'make a great figure with your haunch'.[108] Even decaying game was gratefully accepted. One agent reported to his master that he had duti-fully distributed wildfowl even though they were badly mangled and smelt vile.[109] Brigadier Edward Villiers, a neighbour of Lord Cork and Burlington, revealed that the latter's gift of venison stank, but acknowledged that 'your good intentions were the same'. Since the two had recently engaged in litigation against each other, Villiers may have written ironically. How-ever, during the warfare of 1689–91, the absent Cork and Burlington insisted that the officers of Villiers's regiment should be rewarded with cuts from his deer.[110]

Another courtesy was the gift of deer with which to stock new or replenish depleted parks. In 1656, Lord Cork dispatched forty does to the Connacht notable Sir Charles Coote. Fifty years later, Michael Beecher of Aughadown in the far west of County Cork was allowed a brace of bucks and four brace of does from the park at Lismore.[111] In time, hounds, partridge and pheasant were added to the courteous offerings, joining cuttings from plants, early fruit, collared pike, salted salmon and potted meats as social currency.[112] These exchanges were not always amicable. A haughty squarson stressed the distinction he conferred on his bishop by having a brace of scarce pheasant delivered to the episcopal table.[113] The second Lord Cork, towards the end of his life, resented the ambition of one neighbour, Lord Chief Justice Pyne, to enclose a deer park since it might encroach on Cork's. In the end, Cork used the courtesy of presenting Pyne with sixteen brace of deer to extort a promise that Pyne would not seek land from Cork's enclosure.[114] It was no chance that soon Pyne's son was active in parliament in promoting a bill to preserve deer.[115] The place of stock in neighbourly dealings, and the attendant opportunities to please or displease, are confirmed by Robert Molesworth. Fashioning an ambitious park in County Dublin, he expected a neighbour, Sir Walter Plunkett, to donate a few tench for a newly dug pond. Plunkett, an eccentric, demurred. Molesworth, exasperated at this 'incivility', not the sole fault which he detected among the Irish notabilities, told his wife, 'I had at any time buy rather than be obliged'.[116]

## II

Stag-hunting and horse-riding were not easily portrayed as public boons. Ridding Ireland of wolves could be. The need to exterminate vermin led in 1653 to the grant of forfeited lands in the barony of Dunboyne in Meath to Captain Edward Piers. In return, he was expected to keep three wolf dogs, a pair of English mastiffs and a pack of sixteen couple of hounds. In addition, he had to employ a huntsman and other helpers, and to organize hunts at least three times each month.[117] Whether because of exertions such as Piers's, or through human encroachment on the wolves' lairs, numbers dwindled, and with them the population of the celebrated wolf dogs, long prized as offerings to flatter the important and self-important. Even so, wolf-hounds were still being shipped from Connacht to English peers in the early eighteenth century. Within Ireland, Archbishop King was gratified to receive some.[118] New owners were warned about how much they cost to feed.[119]

Hares, foxes and otters were pursued instead of wolves. During the 1720s, William Nicolson of Derry developed a taste for trapping seals and hunting badgers. (At the same time he was having blasphemers branded.[120]) In 1713, the attorney-general reported that he was going into the countryside to hunt foxes.[121] That addict of the chase, Lord Cork, only once mentioned a wolf hunt: in 1662. Otherwise, he hunted bucks and stags or hawked.[122] Hawking, no less than the deer hunt, allowed the important to meet and relax. In 1656, Cork joined Lord Deputy Cromwell at Kilkenny for the sport.[123] Both Cork and Orrery employed a falconer.[124] Casts of falcons were secured and presented, like hounds and does, to fellow enthusiasts.[125] The relative merits of merlins and peregrine falcons were discussed obsessively.[126] In Derry, William King, while bishop, secured hawks from County Cavan and maintained a falconer.[127] In 1763, the Annesleys from County Down had their own fowler, as did the Pakenhams in Westmeath.[128]

Among the most valued services offered by acquaintances and agents, on a par with the recommendation of servants, tutors, lodgings and – maybe – wives, was the procuring of casts of falcons, wolf-, fox- and stag-hounds or setting dogs.[129] They were escorted across the kingdom and, indeed, across the seas. Kennels were replenished, and strains improved. Fleet greyhounds, hunting and setting dogs were all prized.[130] Beagles also appeared.[131] During the 1660s and 1670s, agents of Ormond scoured England for otter-hounds and beagles famed 'for tongues, speed, hunting, size and colour'.[132] The grandson of Ormond, Ossory, was willing and able to pay £6 and £10 for setting dogs in the 1680s.[133]

In this way, dogs joined horses as an object of competition. Peers like Cork and Burlington or Orrery were hardly to be outdone. The Boyles were constantly shipping bloodstock backwards and forwards across the Irish Sea in an effort to improve strains. In 1673, Thomas Parkes was paid a yearly £6 to look after Lord Cork and Burlington's hounds.[134] During the 1680s, another enthusiast, Lord Massareene, nursed his indifferent health in County Antrim and occupied himself with horse breeding. Also, he hunted sometimes 'with slow hounds'.[135] Hounds shipped from Waterford to Kilkenny on behalf of Bishop Thomas Vesey had presumably been imported.[136] In 1729, the Burlington agent had to confess to a disappointment with a gift from Henry Boyle of Castlemartyr. Of two hounds shipped over, the one that 'still had its castanets' [testicles] had died. The other 'qualified either for the seraglio or opera', having been gelded.[137] Local stocks were also replenished from continental Europe.[138] Later in the century, Patrick Savage of Portaferry (County Down) recorded the couplings and births among his hounds. Many came from neighbouring notables and squires. The prowess of particular dogs enhanced the reputation of their owners. Lord Jocelyn's 'Blueman' was renowned: 'a beautiful hound in shape and colour, and as good a one as ever was hunted'. His fame was even captured in verse.[139] Mastiffs were also prized. Extra expenses were incurred if the beasts bit, and their owners had then to compensate the bitten.[140] From South Wicklow came complaints about the pretensions of one tenant farmer who maintained a pack of fox-hounds, and, with his three sons, hunted at every opportunity. Soon, it was predicted, the cost and neglect of husbandry would ruin the farm.[141] By the eighteenth century, numerous private packs were kept. Stacpoole in County Clare kept thirty-three couple of hounds on his own account.[142] Nevertheless, there are hints that those who could preferred still to hunt stags. During the 1730s, the Bernards, living outside Bandon in County Cork,

64. ?Thomas Gibson, *Peter Browne of Kinturk, Co. Mayo, with an Irish wolfhound*. The wolfhound, admired for its prowess, made an excellent gift and companion.

65. Mary Delany, *Deer in the park at Delville, Co. Dublin*, 1748. Mrs Delany feared that, once she had given a name to each deer, she would be unable to have them killed or to eat them herself.

went to considerable lengths to procure deer from the parks of others in the vicinity, such as the Frekes and the Beechers. The Bernards employed a minion to 'catch' the foxes on the grounds. Lord Cork had done this earlier for his park at Lismore. Seemingly the animals were not chased.[143]

Alongside the zest to kill appeared an occasional inclination to conserve. Prey, once hunted, were petted. Mary Delany, having unwisely bestowed names on the deer at Delville, grew squeamish about eating them.[144] Squirrels, pine martens and then wolf cubs were tamed.[145] The ultimate transformation affected the eagle. This noble raptor was chained at Sir Richard Bulkeley's gate in County Dublin during the 1690s, and later outside Lord Trimlestown's castle in County Meath. Kept with the chickens, it was further demeaned by being fed on crows. As the landscape lost some of its menace, so did its inhabitants. The willingness to counterfeit wildernesses through domestic plantings had its counterpart in friendliness towards predators. This was captured in an episode recorded by a soldier, Adolphus Oughton, in 1740. With a local notable at Ballyshannon, he watched in fascination as a sea-eagle taught its eaglets how to fish and take lambs.[146] Unwittingly, by keeping grounds for sport, habitats were either saved or re-created.

Other rarities were cosseted. Singing birds, like canaries and finches, warbled in grand houses such as the Veseys' Abbey Leix. Squire Edgeworth was quick to buy his young daughter a pet bird. Parrots, such as Alicia Synge's 'Greeny', alternately amused and angered.[147] Bantams and ornamental fowl brought extra colour to the poultry yard, until stolen by foxes or opportunists.[148] Peacocks and peahens similarly brightened drab enclosures, but sometimes brought more pain than pleasure. At Waringstown, peacocks were banished from the garden when they ate cabbage plants and the tops of peas. Their former owner concluded that, 'they will oblige some gentry that wants them and are fond of them'.[149] Bishop Synge's peafowl, kept at Finglas, became targets first for dogs and than for vandals. He decided, 'not to trouble my head more about them'.[150] The affluent made pets of dogs. The yearly keep of the countess of Ossory's dog, Dorinda, amounted to £2: almost the same as that of a charity-school child.[151]

Love of sport was not limited to the countryside. Indeed, since most towns merged almost imperceptibly into their rural surroundings and even the largest retained substantial undeveloped areas, urban and rustic relaxations were hardly distinct. In the city of Cork, William Hovell, a grave merchant, confessed to a weakness for hunting. Hovell, thanks to his income, if not so obviously through culture, was amply qualified to take his place alongside country squires. By hunting he adopted a vital element in the culture of the quality.[152] By the eighteenth century, a new formality attended field sports. Again this did not debar townspeople, but rather those of modest means and, for that reason (among others) Catholics and – sometimes – women. Sportsmen banded together in hunts. Rituals sprang up around these associations. They included dances and assemblies in which women joined. Sports were being shifted into the world of politeness and civility. Gamekeepers and hunt servants had not only to dress respectably, but to behave decorously. Furthermore, they were warned against intruding 'themselves into such gentlemen's company at unseasonable times'. Advised not to resemble a butcher or ploughboy, they should instead aim, like the gardeners of the important, 'to look more genteel'.[153] Concurrently, horse-races were promoted as commercial entertainments like musical recitals. This stricter regulation may explain why at least one early-eighteenth-century commentator thought that manly sports were threatened. The lament belonged to a tradition of mourning the passing of old ways. Various reasons were offered. One interpretation saw the customary – and manly – pursuits as victims of recent English conquest and settlement. The newcomers not only supplanted Irish Catholic proprietors, but either outlawed or emasculated indigenous activities. Another contention was that the concurrent growth of urbanization and prosperity popularized supposedly polite but supine pastimes at the expense of the virile.

66. Member of the Westropp family, Co. Limerick, in riding habit. Women of standing and wealth shared in some of the excitements, if not all the conviviality, of field sports.

Undoubtedly the range of amusements offered by towns – and most conspicuously Dublin – increased. However, as we shall see, the devotees of field sports adapted to the changing atmosphere. So far as immigrants from Britain were concerned, they adopted country pastimes enthusiastically. An account of early-eighteenth-century Fermanagh had the new estate-owners 'hunting, hawking, riding, drinking, feasting and banqueting with each other', with a gusto that equalled that of their now displaced predecessors. To see this as a bid by insecure interlopers to embed themselves more securely in unfamiliar territory is to discount the ease and enjoyment with which they could follow activities which arose naturally from the terrain that they inhabited. With property came the possibility (and perhaps the responsibility) to engage in customary recreations.[154] Most Catholics had lost their lands by the end of the seventeenth century. The alacrity with which the lately established took over the sports hitherto played by the dispossessed irritated the latter. The irritation was aggravated by laws which prohibited most Catholics from the more prestigious recreations in which horses and weapons featured. Straitened resources also meant that, after the 1690s, few Catholics could bear the expenses of smart sporting life.[155] Even so, the severity of the bans enacted in 1695 was soon relaxed. If, as the laws decreed, Catholics were not to keep horses valued at £5 or more, then the incipient bloodstock industry would be stifled. Protestants appreciated the damage and agitated for a change. So, in 1713, it was agreed that Catholics could keep stud mares and stallions so long as they were under five years of age.[156] In any case, the threshold was high and may not in practice have inconvenienced Catholics seriously since the majority of horses were worth considerably less than £5.

While the statutes remained, they, like other restrictions on the Catholics, constituted a grievance. Sporadic drives to enforce them caused trouble. In 1737, a servant of Thomas Nugent, a 'gentleman of the best family and one of the best fortunes in County Westmeath', was apprehended as a poacher. Nugent protested that the underling – Michael Molloy – was his fowler. Nevertheless, Molloy, a Catholic, was imprisoned. Nugent retorted (accurately) that Molloy, as a servant of a gentleman, was not encompassed by the Game Laws. Despite the protestations, an officious justice of the peace, Arthur Rochfort, proceeded against first Molloy and then Nugent. There is some suggestion that Nugent's enthusiasm for sport led him to encroach on and even damage the grounds of neighbours, and that Molloy was prosecuted as an accessory of Nugent. In addition, Nugent's kinsman, Hugh Maguire, a Catholic on furlough from the imperial service, was drawn into the squabble, and indicted for carrying unlicensed arms. Rochfort's vendetta, arising from the feuding of leading families in the Midlands, was represented as a 'dispute between Protestant and papist'. Rochfort, by posing as a guardian of the endangered Protestant interest, secured the backing of the government in Dublin.[157] Country sports and the curtailing of rights to enjoy them brought home to once ascendant Catholics how much they had lost. In other societies, wealth controlled entry into the most esteemed pastimes; in Ireland, access was determined by both confession and money.

Laws alone did not restrict stag- and fox-hunting to the prosperous. Hunts, as they assumed greater formality, levied subscriptions. By 1780, members of the Ballylinan Hunt in County Kildare had to pay an entry fee of five guineas and then subscribe a further ten guineas annually. In addition, subscribers must kit themselves out in the uniform of the group and were expected to dine together, in their outfits, once each month. It comes as no surprise that the fourteen known subscribers were peers and leading squires of the locality.[158] The sociable dimension to the sport made these groups of hunters similar to the masonic lodges, knots of Friendly Brothers and more shadowy associations to which many enthusiastic sportsmen also belonged. The standardized dress and some of the ethos of the formal hunts resembled the soldiery, whether the regulars or the volunteers of the county militias.[159] Indeed, several hunts relied on an infusion of army officers stationed locally if they were to flourish. A patriotic purpose persisted. The improvement of Irish bloodstock had not been altogether forgotten. More immediately, in the case of the Ballylinan Hunt, the subscribers were to dress in cloth made in Ireland.

Some hunts strove to shake off the reputation for unruliness attaching to the sport. As early as 1714 efforts were made to curb excess at table once the chase was ended. One reformer, John Fleming in County Meath, resolved 'to proceed on a moderate plan'. He remembered how, formerly, he with his companions, 'our shamrocks we drowned in a bottle a man'. Henceforward, to prevent the exhausted sportsmen stupefying themselves, each would be limited to a single bottle, since 'intemperance wasteth what exercise gains'.[160] Not all abstained. The Kilruddery Hunt of 1744, the sport concluded, passed 'the rest of the day and the night/ In gay flowing bumpers and social delight'.[161] The mayhem associated with drunken huntsmen was suggested earlier when, in the Limerick of Queen Anne's reign, officers of the garrison mimicked a fox hunt. On this occasion the gentleman at bay was the hapless Tory bishop. Hunting symbolism was also adopted when, as at Athlone in 1685, targets for communal humiliation were identified with horned stags. The mockery of rough music was supplied by hunting horns.[162]

Hunting was defended on grounds of health and public utility. It was also championed as an antidote to sybaritic and effeminate recreations. The first printed account of Irish hunting, published in Belfast in 1714, opposed the masculine and aristocratic chase to the effete diversions of the city. The chief amusement of the stock city-dweller, 'Mr Townly', was the opera. It was roundly condemned by a devotee of the chase.[163] The sporting partisan introduced a false division between the metropolitan sophisticate and the simple country sportsman, comparable to Molesworth's between sedentary and well-travelled squires. It was repeated in the Dublin version of *The tricks of the town*, an English tract which was doctored for Irish readers in the middle of the century. The diatribe applauded country sports, like hawking, hunting, fishing and fowling as 'noble, manly and generous'.[164] Not only the grumpy Cork trader with his unexpected fondness for hunting, but cultivated grandees, such as the future Lord Wicklow, contradict this polarity.

Hunts often assembled in towns. Moreover, their supporters devised entertainments, usually scheduled in the assembly rooms of the larger boroughs, intended to frustrate riot and licence. By the 1760s much sociability attended the Antrim Hunt. It took over a ballroom recently erected at Ballymoney. The rules of the hunt stipulated that there should be dances on three nights weekly during the meeting, 'or oftener if the ladies please'.[165] In October 1764 came excited news of the County Down hunt. It had been together for a week and was accounted a 'numerous good meeting'. The hounds of two local grandees had excelled. 'Never a meeting so regular since the club began' was the verdict. The members of the hunt breakfasted at eight, dined at three, and took tea and coffee at six. With supper served at ten in the evening, the company were in bed by midnight. The courtesy of the huntsmen, notably towards women, was stressed.[166] Others commented on the presence of women at these events. In 1746, Thomas Wright, a visitor from England, was glutted with society. Near Lough Erne, he participated in a buck-hunt. The beast was pursued with French horn and 'many neighbouring gentlemen, who all dined on the side of the mountain under tents'. Notable on this occasion were a 'great many ladies'.[167] Back in 1739, an account of 'a famous hunting match' in County Antrim had also emphasized that there had been no intemperance.[168] During the 1760s, Anne Cooke, having married into the dynasty of sporting Weldons, active later in the Ballylinan Hunt, joined her husband and stepson at some, but not all, the race meetings of the locality.[169]

There survived raucous gatherings which women were unlikely to attend. Even in refined County Antrim, sportsmen would unbutton after a strenuous day with the hounds at a 'bachelors' dinner'.[170] At these less regulated events, men from differing social orders and maybe differing confessions mingled. In the 1740s, the penurious but genteel Edmund Spencer joined his patron Colonel Robert Oliver from Castle Oliver in County Limerick in buck-hunting. The exercise ended, Oliver moved to his 'villa' near Rathcormack to pass the winter in fox-hunting.[171] Oliver was accompanied by fourteen gentlemen who spent ten days hunting, supposedly, day and night.[172] 'A hunting club' flourished nearby at Liscarrol in 1745.[173] At much the same moment appeared the phenomenon of the 'five-bar gate gentleman', daring to the verge of foolhardiness in the field.[174] In 1755, Thomas Smythe of Drumcree in County Westmeath confessed how he had fallen in with a fox-hunting and fowling set. Smythe's confession suggested a measure of self-awareness and therefore the unlikelihood of his being seduced into excess. Indeed, he united these recreations with fashionably improving activities.[175] It is true that obsessed sportsmen, so far from improving, risked wrecking lands and fortunes. Heedless neighbours rode down ripening crops. Gamekeepers, grooms and huntsmen, in asserting their masters' interests, created or worsened feuds.[176] In 1739, one race between the nags of Lord Hillsborough and Dick Johnston, which preceded the hunting season in County Antrim, had as its consequence to entertain the company to 'as much meat and drink as could be destroyed' at a nearby inn. This was followed by hare-hunting with nineteen and a half couple of hounds.[177] The gruff, rough world of the stables and kennels had its counterpart in the ribaldry of the relaxing huntsmen. 'To dinner, my boys, was the word we obey/and jovial recount the exploits of the day'. In their cups, they sang catches which proclaimed their prowess in the chase. It could express local and even national attachments, as to St Paddy, 'with shamrocks exalted the badge of our saint'; equally it inspired reveries on the pudenda of fancied girls.[178] This association with excess made prim squires, such as Richard Edgeworth, abstain from the hunt. In turn, this abstention may partly account for the contempt in which he was held by more boisterous neighbours. However, Edgeworth did enjoy snipe shooting.[179]

Organized and impromptu shoots gradually altered the landscape. The quest for native species and the introduction of others, such as the partridge and pheasant, might encourage the preservation of their habitats. It also stimulated their simulation, with ponds, lakes, decoys, coverts and copses.[180] In the parklands and demesnes, the refinements of the house and the needs of sport met. Owners and their guests ambled around pleasure grounds and nurseries before viewing stables, plantations and improvements. From bowling on svelte greens, fishing the canals and ponds or boating on the lakes, it was a short step to riding, shooting and hunting. Just as repute enveloped householders who kept a good table and improved their lands, so the provision of and prowess in sports won plaudits. Sporting meetings functioned like other gatherings in being occasions when weighty matters could be aired. The important, notably English lords-lieutenant, who toured the provinces were honoured with races and hunts. In the uncertain 1650s, Henry Cromwell relaxed in south Munster. In return, he invited locals to hunt with him when in Dublin. On these occasions, the future of three nations was discussed. The Phoenix, surrounded by a park, was the most convenient venue.[181] Its continuing use for hunting bestowed mixed blessings on the neighbourhood. Would-be huntsmen engaged lodgings in the vicinity. However, the baying of hounds in the kennels disturbed the residents of nearby Arbour Hill. The intimacies of the sports field and of the subsequent conviviality eased the exchange of political information as much as of lore about breeds, bridles and brides. In 1755, a new lord-lieutenant, Hartington, was to be lured to the races near Hillsborough in County Down. The patron, Lord Hillsborough, promised not only 'good diversion', but 'a great meeting of the gentlemen of this and neighbouring counties'. At a political climacteric, Hartington would be able to observe 'their disposition with your own eyes, which is infinitely better than information'.[182] More prosaically, in 1730 John Blennerhasset invited Richard Baldwin to join him at nine the next morning for a hunt in County Kerry, during which a land deal could be finalized.[183]

Attempts to police recreations could never succeed completely in a society at once lightly governed and given to spontaneous revelry. Subscriptions excluded those of modest means; rituals usually debarred women. In any case, the expense of keeping hunters and hounds, the tips to hunt servants and the necessary kit increasingly reserved the smart hunts for a masculine minority. In 1714, it was reckoned that a pack of hounds with the proper handlers cost £40. By the 1780s, the expense had more than doubled.[184] Yet, humbler meets, free of the elaborations of the lordly, continued. In County Clare, the young farmer Lucas frequently coursed hares in the company of relations and neighbours. Already Twelfth Night after Christmas was consecrated to sport. Often, the bag was light but the exercise and company were appreciated.[185] Grander were the recreations open to Nicholas Peacock in the 1740s. As a connection and agent of the local gentry, he was invited to join their hunts.[186] He could do so because he kept a horse. Peacock had also to dress correctly for the occasion. Shortly before accepting an invitation from his 'master', Hartstonge, he bespoke a riding coat, waistcoat and whip.[187] Later he found himself spending on a 'bellyful of punch', and tipping the master of the pack and the huntsman.[188] Further glimpses into more modest recreations come from a junior army officer, Humphrey Thomson. Having lodged with the cultured in Kilkenny during the 1750s, Thomson moved to Donoughmore. Because soldiering was hardly arduous, he was able to pass many of his days in fishing, shooting and setting with dogs. 'It being a fine, sporting country and the farmers living well and hospitably and I living entirely in that style, was invited to every wedding and merry meeting in that neighbourhood', he recalled.[189] His experiences were shared by others quartered in the Irish provinces. Lieutenant Nicholas Delacherois, originally from Ulster, enjoyed 'a good deal of hunting, shooting, freedom of conversation' while stationed in the wilds of north Cork in 1770.[190] As well as being invited into the houses of the landed, feted at assemblies and solicited to assist the work of improvement, the officers joined in the country sports. For honoured guests, as for some of their hosts, these recreations were interspersed with the sedentary and cerebral pleasures of books, music and contemplation.

## III

Horse-racing, more than hunting, collapsed boundaries between town and country. It also involved those of divergent circumstances – economic, social and confessional. Race meetings multiplied. By the mid-eighteenth century, fixtures were advertised at seventy-two different locations; many more went unpublicized by the press.[191] Several were sited near Dublin: at Ringsend, possibly on the strand, Chapelizod and Crumlin.[192] Contemporaries distinguished between meetings graced or shunned by the respectable.[193] Sometimes all except subscribers were prevented from entering horses for the competition. But to restrict the spectators, even were it physically possible, would contradict the intentions behind these schemes. Races, attractive to the relentlessly polite, were not monopolized by them. Ancillary entertainments were designed to appeal to women and the avowedly refined. By these devices, a few meetings were raised into occasions which squires and their wives –

67. Bill head for Richard Singleton at 'The Fighting Cocks'. Cock-fighting engendered fierce rivalries, but, unlike horse races, seems to have remained a predominantly male passion.

Ralph Howard and the Weldons – happily patronized. Most, virtually hidden in the shadows, appealed more promiscuously. Even so, the terms on which the rich, the poor and the middling came differed. Owners, riders, punters, subscribers and spectators viewed the contests from varied perspectives. Races under royal, viceregal or aristocratic patronage were not the same as scratch gatherings. Yet, what place there was for the drones and drudges in these increasingly contrived and commercialized competitions can only be guessed. The numerous contests in obscure locations would yield no profits to the promoters unless more than the members of the élite – or indeed all the respectable Protestants – came. Few owned horses, especially racers and chasers; fewer still bred them. Many bet on their performance. Uneasiness about the propensity of rich and poor to gamble on the roll of the dice or a hand of cards suggests a reason why the popularity of horse-racing and cock-fighting troubled prigs and patriots. Escape from accumulating worries seemed to explain why Lord Bellew and the Misses Povey staked so much on horseflesh; escapism may suffice to account for the resort of so many of their social inferiors to the racetracks and cockpits.

In order to cater for the majority, cheaper replicas were fabricated: in recreation, no less than in clothing and furnishings. It was commonly complained that popular sports encouraged idleness, wasted money and provoked disorder. A cock-fight at Derry in 1750 coincided with horse-races. Punters from town and countryside were alleged to have lost heavily: John Hamilton, the squire of Munterloney, was reputedly poorer by £400.[194] During the winter of 1744, a bout between fighting cocks at Castlelyons lasted three days. The adversaries belonged to Mansergh, perhaps from Tipperary, and the heir to Castlelyons, Lord Buttevant. 'The wager was but small and that spent' by Buttevant, who had won. The victor was applauded because he 'behaved the whole time with a great deal of good humour'. A spectator noted, almost parenthetically, 'we drank hard'.[195] In England by the eighteenth century, cock-fighting, together with bear-baiting, was censured as 'an ancient barbarous sort of diversion', and confidently stated to be in decline. It may be provincial Ireland, like the remoter regions of Britain, was slower to reject the pastime.[196] Accounts of some bouts between fighting cocks emphasized the local loyalties of the contestants and their supporters. In 1741, a week-long contest between the 'gentlemen' of County Wicklow on the one side, and of Counties Meath and Dublin on the other, was advertised. The next year, another match between combatants from Leinster and Munster was announced.[197] Just who composed the teams and followers and how they were regarded – idlers and reprobates or better – are again unclear. In 1746, a peer like Lord Meath could still concern himself with the breeding of fighting cocks.[198] Taken together with Lord Barrymore's involvement in the sport, this evidence suggests a continuing enthusiasm among the important.

In 1755, a pamphleteer regretted that the linen-weavers, enjoying modest prosperity, had enough leisure to waste at 'fairs, patterns, races, cock-fightings and Holy Days observed in the popish church'.[199] Industry was not the unalloyed boon that had been predicted. It put money into the pockets of those bent on enjoyment. Wages were spent on pleasures which blurred the reassuring distinctions between the separate confessional communities.[200] Protestants were detected at entertainments which had been associated hitherto with the Catholics. It seemed that the ban on lowly sports enacted by parliament in 1739 was unenforceable. Before the passage of the law, disorders arising from sporting crowds can be glimpsed occasionally. During a panic over a rumoured Jacobite invasion in 1719, the Dublin government banned horse-races. It also stopped 'all tumultuous and numerous meetings under the pretence of foot-ball playing, hurling and commoning and other sports'.[201]

The official bans were extreme examples of unease about popular sports. The hostility extended to other gatherings, especially pilgrimages and patterns where Catholics congregated. Such apprehensions tended to confuse worries about the destructive potential of the lower sorts, sometimes lumped together as 'the mob', with long-standing anxiety about the behaviour and loyalty of the Irish Catholic majority. Indicative of these fears was the reflex of assuming that the more obviously popular recreations survived among and attracted the

Catholics.[202] In addition, these events tended to be noticed, and so stand a chance of being recorded, when matters went awry. In consequence, demotic entertainments were ineradicably linked with disorder. These quirks in the written evidence have led some later analysts to conclude that apparently impromptu contests, such as hurling and football, expressed a distinctive and indigenous culture, and amounted to acts of defiance against the new English Protestant order in Ireland.[203] Few of the documented games happened as spontaneously as elegiasts have supposed. Moreover, in the same way that the propertied moved into the recreations that had entertained their predecessors, so new proprietors patronized diversions that looked (to the sophisticated) coarse and unruly. Landowners as various as Richard Edgeworth and Pole Cosby supported football and hurling, just as they subsidized older forms of music making. Why, and the terms on which, they did so, elude us. Some would see such patronage as evidence of the insecurity of interlopers, striving desperately (and in the end unsuccessfully) to entrench themselves securely in local affections. No doubt an element of bread and circuses for the unsophisticated was present, although the lack of sophistication amongst the audience is more easily assumed than proved. Possibly less calculation and a more innocent quest for fun inspired their involvement.

Inseparable from many of the sporting fixtures were fairs, markets and patterns, which, with their stalls and booths, expected customers. They were also resorts for those with little or nothing to spend. Horses, dogs, fighting cocks, fowling pieces and even nets were beyond the purses of most. Yet there survived numerous opportunities to watch and bet while others raced. Inevitably what players, owners and subscribers felt differed from the experience of the casual spectator. With few exceptions, the respectable withdrew from arduous physical exertions, such as football and hurling, content instead to pay others to play.[204] Instead, the prosperous and powerful threw themselves into riding, hunting and shooting. Building and maintaining stables, lakes and coverts, grooming lush paddocks and parks, saddling pedigree chasers, putting up accomplished jockeys and putting on stylish clothes were privileges of a minority. In consequence, participation and prowess in the most highly regarded sports served to make – or enhance – a grand figure.

Chapter 8

# Dress

*I*

A voter in the County Clare election of 1745, supposedly a forty-shilling freeholder, was derided by other electors 'for his very mean appearance, which was so much worse than any yet produced that it seemed to engage every person's admiration . . . that he had neither a shirt nor a coat, nor a wig, but wore a dirty tattered nightcap'. Similar objections were levelled at a freeholder from Corofin, denounced as 'a common beggar', without a shirt to his back. This individual refuted detractors by revealing his shirt.[1] In the two incidents, dress was clearly equated with standing. The correct was regarded as a prerequisite for participating in public events, even a county election. This attitude had been demonstrated earlier, in 1685, when witnesses in court were dismissed as mere Irish labourers, 'scarce a cravat about their necks'.[2] It recurred later in the eighteenth century, as candidates in a keenly contested election in Cork dressed their humble supporters so that they could pass as freeholders. To achieve this, shops in Dublin were said to have been stripped of 'every coat, shirt, hat and wig, raiments and habilments of all kinds and of all sizes'.[3] Political opponents were ridiculed as likely to have their coats in pawn, to go without shirts in summer, and to lack brogues and stockings.[4]

Churchgoing, a more frequent occasion than county elections, also obliged worshippers to don decent garments. In 1760, it was reported from Sligo that children from the charity foundation wanted shoes and stockings, and so could not go to church.[5] The axiom that the respectable might be offended by the inadequately dressed lay behind the decision of the Protestant parish of St Michan in Dublin to pay for two sets of clothing for the poor widows whom it already relieved. These gifts would 'render their presence more sweet, clean and decent'.[6] Similar thinking obliged some unfortunates seeking admission to Lady Arbella Denny's refuge to borrow clothes from friends, in order to make the right impression.[7] The requirements taxed others. A mother prefaced a complaint about penury with lamentations about her inability to clothe a son. In 1726, it was said that George Reyler 'cannot appear in any family for want of suitable clothes'.[8] Equally, a visitor from County Mayo in the 1750s felt disabled from her customary social circuit – as well as from her devotions – by lacking money to dress fittingly.[9]

The concerned strove for the right look. Defenders of the established Protestant church insisted that its ministers should dress 'for order, gravity and decency'. Earlier governors of the Church were praised for recognizing 'what a vain, light humour was gotten into the world of changing fashion, habits and dresses every year'. In order to check it, standardized attire was sanctioned. Nevertheless, it was acknowledged that 'there are clothes fit for a man in several stations and actions of life'.[10] By 1720, the younger clergy could be mocked for sartorial vanity. Keen to engage their female parishioners, they 'could not preach with a ruffled band or a wig out of curl'. None relished doctrines 'that came not recommended with a scarf and a diamond ring'. At least one Dublin curate, Valentine Needham, took such details of dress and demeanour so seriously that he offended starchy superiors.[11] Military men had an equally delicate path to tread between excess and effacement. Uniforms were expensive (in the range of £40 for an officer), were to be had only from specialists in Dublin, and were subject to increasingly strict regulation. Officers scheduled to be transferred from the provinces to duty in Dublin fretted to know the details of their regimentals. Patterns submitted by the agent of the company had to be approved by the General Board of Officers in Dublin. Concern with the minutiae of silver or gold lacing and crossed belts earned the agent a reprimand. The functionary angrily denied that 'I could believe that frippery dress was proper'. On the contrary, 'I would always have troops dressed in a soldier-like way'. He might have added that the officers themselves had wanted gold rather than silver lace when in the capital.[12]

Finery disquieted in other circumstances. Demonstrators in the Blackwater valley in 1762, because arrayed 'in laced clothes and completely accoutred', were suspected of being Catholics returned from military service overseas.[13] Michael Smythe, squire of Portlick in Westmeath, aspiring to enter the House of Commons as member for Athlone, believed that victory depended on how he looked. His anxieties extended beyond his own rig at the assizes and quarter sessions to the bridle, saddlecloth and other furniture of his horse. Unsure of his own judgement or 'fancy' in these matters, Smythe deputed the choice to a more experienced relation: one, moreover, with readier access to the latest in Dublin. Here the provincial is found deferring to the metropolitan. Squire Smythe's campaign to enter parliament was rebuffed by better established families in his locality, who scoffed at his presumption – both social and sartorial – in challenging their supremacy. Others, nevertheless, conceded that Smythe lived and dressed in high style.[14] But Smythe, obsessed with his ambitions, confessed to impostures.[15] They seemed of a piece with the splendid attire that he sported, much of which had been selected for him by others. Subterfuges that elided or erased social distinctions alarmed. Excess in dress could be associated with overweening aims.[16] In the 1730s, a jaundiced agent in south Wicklow observed sardonically, 'every man who wears a good suit of clothes and rides a good horse is not the true industrious improving tenant', and listed numerous extravagances.[17] One remedy was to insist that the tenants seek self-sufficiency, in dress no less than in diet. If they grew and spun their own flax, a commendable taste for personal linen could be turned to more general benefit.[18]

Such episodes and comments showed that raiment, whether wig, coat or linen, indicated both rank and means. Efforts to ensure an exact fit of social standing with costume broke down in the face of the ingenuity of both producers and purchasers. Cheaper versions of the expensive, hitherto supposedly monopolized by the grand, were devised.[19] Sumptuary laws which confined particular textiles and garments to specific orders or occupations proved unenforceable in seventeenth-century Ireland. Only in restricted settings, such as municipal corporations, guilds, regiments, masonic lodges and institutions, could members be forced into the clothes tailored to their status. Subtle distinctions in wealth and discrimination were still conveyed through the cut, colour and texture of fabrics. Even what seemed merely uniforms, as in the local militias, excited competition. In a few contexts, common styles of dressing signalled shared principles. At the start of the new parliament of George II's reign in 1728, a group emerged among the novice members known as 'toopees'. The label, an observer explained, 'is not more than a particular kind of foretop which they have to their wigs, which they fancy denotes youth and smartness'. Soon it was transformed into an insult.[20] Twenty years later at a Dublin Castle reception, Lord Blessington preened himself in the gorgeous livery of the Prince of Wales. Blessington told Speaker Boyle that the prince had advised Boyle to dress in the same manner. Boyle, who prided himself on his plain country ways, retorted, 'he never wore a laced coat in his life'.[21]

Preferences in clothing and politics seldom fused so completely. However, the implications of dress went far beyond simple utility. Evolving ideas of civility and decency constantly changed attire. Bodies had alternately (or sometimes simultaneously) to be revealed and concealed. In Ireland, local variants of clothing conflicted with English expectations, and so acquired strong political and ideological significance. Laws banned the wearing of Irish costume, which was felt to smack of backwardness, even lasciviousness, and embodied the nomadism and bellicosity of the indigenes. The rebellion of the 1640s was said to have set back the adoption of English dress. The wearing of 'bands, ruffs, hats, cloaks, gowns, breeches, &c' was abandoned and instead 'kerchiefs, mantles, trousers, &c. and all Irish habit' were resumed.[22] By the beginning of the eighteenth century, exponents of English ways were offended by the ragged and dirty dress, or even the near nakedness, of the poor Irish.[23] Sometimes, the inquisitive were embarrassed to find that the unkempt and slatternly were penurious Protestants rather than (as expected) Catholics. Yet, feelings mounted against too slavish an embrace of alien, including English, ways. The draining of money from Ireland to pay for imported textiles and the wasting of money on extravagant outfits were added to the offences identified by Irish Protestant patriots.[24]

Repeated efforts were made to popularize the wearing of local manufactures. Viceroys and vicereines regularly decreed that nothing but Irish textiles should be sported at the state occasions in Dublin Castle. These injunctions were obeyed with seeming enthusiasm, but sometimes evaded with equal ingenuity.[25] As early as the 1660s, Ormond and his sons in their suits of Irish tweed cocked a snook at English legislators who were stunting Irish manufactures. In her turn, the second duchess of Ormonde while vicereine promoted local wear. The campaign was renewed during the 1740s. An onlooker in Dublin noted how many had arrived at a ball in the Castle in December 1745 dressed in Irish poplins. Lady Chesterfield, the consort of the lord-lieutenant, gave the signal with her ensemble. The craze briefly gripped smart Dublin. At another dance in honour of the Prince of Wales's birthday, everyone was arrayed 'in the manufacture of Ireland'. Patriotism, charity and high style ran conveniently together. Work was created for the distressed weavers of the capital.[26] In addition, it was reported that Irish textiles had been brought to 'vast perfection'. The fashion correspondent (an observant man) averred, 'a white or plain yellow poplin with coloured sprigs at a distance looks equal to a rich silk and sure comes much cheaper'.[27] Not all subscribed to these patriotic philippics. In 1681, Sir William Petty dismissed caustically plans to promote the export to England of Irish frieze (and whiskey). 'The truth is, 'tis a foolish design. There is better frieze and strong water to be had in England than here [in Dublin] and cheaper'.[28] Forty years later, a Dublin official, aware of 'a spirit among both sexes to wear stuff' of Irish manufacture, doubted that the 6,000 starving weavers were much helped.[29] Even Katherine Conolly, keen to stimulate home production, questioned the benefits. In 1731, she conceded that the newly arrived lord-lieutenant, Dorset, had ensured that the king's birthday was 'solemnized here in a grander manner than ever was known'. Mrs Conolly, in observing that the ladies wore 'the richest clothes ever . . . seen here', commented acidly, 'in the mean [time], the shopkeepers has the worst of it, for of many thousand pounds laid out, very few hundreds paid'.[30]

*Haute couture* was highly volatile. Novelty was at a premium. Catering to this fashion-conscious clientèle made work for a select company of craftworkers in Dublin. One *modiste,* Jane Gallagher, told of the stimulus to her business from the festivities at the Castle. In the summer of 1727 she had made twenty-five suits of clothes each week for three consecutive weeks, 'and her hurry is not over yet'.[31] Two years later, Mrs Gallagher was still inundated with orders, specifically for 30 October, 'when the ladies are to be very fine, most in Irish damasks and French silks trimmed'. The vicereine, Lady Carteret, had asked the ladies to wear only Irish damask, but seemingly there was not enough to supply all.[32] The wish to look stylish impeded the drives of well-intentioned viceroys to popularize Irish wares. Manufacturers in Ireland copied the latest. By 1748, what had been esteemed in the short reign of Lady Chesterfield was now shunned. Sprigged poplins were deemed 'old fashioned and worn by the lower kind of people'. Fabrics patterned all over 'are reckoned paltry, and are very little wore'.[33]

Jane Gallagher's popularity owed much to the speed with which she pirated the newest look from London. Her husband was employed by Oliver St George, an Irish landowner and member of parliament, who lived permanently in London. St George's wife, an Irish Protestant heiress, assisted Mrs Gallagher's industrial espionage. Through the post came patterns of mantua sleeves, cuffs and ruffles which would stamp the clothes being made in Dublin with high style.[34] Among Jane Gallagher's customers were the O'Haras, like the St Georges, associated with Connacht. This hints that her clientèle may have had a regional base, and that retailers and craftworkers fitted into networks formed by neighbours and kindred.[35] Mrs St George supplied the wife of a second of her husband's employees. The latter, Sarah Wilson, assured Mrs St George, 'the name of my having my patterns from your ladyship brings me more business than I could possibly expect if I had them from any other hand'.[36] The patriotic ladies, even when prepared to appear in Irish textiles, turned to London or Paris for the cut.

Ambivalence about the imported and home-produced added to the difficulties of viceroys and vicereines as they tried to reconcile a duty to advance English styles and to assist Irish manufactures. Too often the migrants in the Castle reminded of a dependency, in essence political but also cultural, under which many Irish Protestants chafed. Even those who professed devotion to English rule and rulers behaved with irritating inconsistency. They did not invariably reject what came from beyond Ireland, especially when it denoted high fashion. Thereby the stylish strengthened their claims to cultural leadership. A taste for the imported sometimes alternated but could also coexist with urges to buy the local.[37] During the 1720s, Katherine Conolly, wife of Speaker Conolly, not the vicereine, dictated tastes to the ladies of Dublin. In 1721, she organized an early expression of sympathy for the plight of the destitute Dublin weavers. She decreed that only suits of Irish stuff should be worn. Her sister confided, ''tis now the fashion for every body to wear stuff, but how long they will hold in that mind I cannot well tell. The ladies you know are given to change'.[38] When Mrs Conolly repeated her patriotic initiative, the counterpart of her husband's political exertions, she berated fickle fashion. 'It's strange that the people in England should be so fond of Irish things when here [in Dublin] they all run after English poplins to a degree of madness'.[39] She was unable to vanquish the craze for the 'modish' which had generally to be imported. A female acquaintance of Mrs Conolly voiced a common opinion: 'things . . . brought out of England . . . are 50 times prettier than anything we see in this town [Dublin]'.[40]

Katherine Conolly inadvertently endorsed the observations of Arthur Dobbs, a patriotic campaigner. Dobbs announced in 1729 – very much in the idiom of Mandeville, the contemporary English theorist – that women in Ireland 'are the spring that sets the whole machine of dress in motion'.[41] Female preferences, if for the foreign, would damage the Irish economy; a liking for the Irish-made would stimulate it.[42] Realists acknowledged that patriots, no matter how passionate, had no wish to be frumps. Local industries were accordingly encouraged to copy and create the vogues. By 1729, these initiatives were in their infancy, so that

Dobbs, despite his advocacy of protectionism for nascent Irish industries, was ready to exempt from any ban 'a few of the choicest of the British silks for birthdays and wedding suits'.[43] In 1717, a notable in Dublin waited impatiently for the arrival from London of his outfit for the coming celebrations of the king's birthday.[44]

Patriots eagerly espoused local industries, of which textiles promised to be one of the most lucrative. In England, during the seventeenth century, it was calculated that one-quarter of national income was spent on clothing and cloth.[45] There is no good reason to suppose that the proportion was lower in Ireland. In addition, successive interventions by jealous English parliament, which by 1699 had banned the export of Irish-made woollens, added weight to the making and use of the home produced. Immediately after the English prohibition, the city of Waterford petitioned to be compensated for the collapse of trade at its St John's tide market, hitherto devoted to the sale of Irish woollens.[46] The alarmism was, no doubt, exaggerated. The home market continued to sustain the textile industry which remained, after agriculture, the largest employer.[47] Its importance to places like Bandon, Carrick-on-Suir, Cork, Limerick and (above all) to Dublin could not be denied. Troublingly, demand fluctuated, particularly with the fortunes of agriculture. The public-spirited admonished their contemporaries to forsake the imported and instead patronize their own countrypeople as a way to invigorate sluggish demand. Notwithstanding the exhortations, between 1748 and 1750, imports into Ireland of old and new draperies were worth about £47,000; of cambrics, another £60,000; and of silks, over £35,000.[48] In 1750, it was reckoned that a quarter of Ireland's inhabitants used imported commodities. Of these, cloth and clothing, after tobacco, were the most valuable.[49] Zealots begged their compatriots to forswear the imported. The immediate target was what arrived from Britain. However, as France became both Britain's chief enemy and the principal source of allegedly frivolous fashions and luxuries, its commodities were singled out for attack. The taste for 'light, luxurious, expensive dress' was connected with 'a deep and dangerous scheme' of the French 'to oppress us by a sudden and strong invasion'.[50] Patriots in Hanoverian Ireland, insofar as they adopted an anti-French stance, became – sometimes unwittingly – supporters of Britain.


## II


Realists appreciated that those keen to put on the grand figure rarely jettisoned smartness in favour of a patriotic dowdiness. If Irish textiles were to command a profitable market within the kingdom, and even more so if they were to compete overseas where they were permitted, they needed to improve in style and quality. Linen became the prime target and proved the outstanding success. Yet there was interest in bettering the patterns, dyes and textures of other cloths. Linen, like most fabrics, was used for more than personal clothing. The same conventions which drove the genteel and respectable, and aspirants to gentility and respectability, to cultivate bodily hygiene and cleanliness, made them conscious of the desirability of domestic settings which exhibited greater refinement. Patrick Murphy, a Catholic from Kilkenny, was bequeathed abundant worldly goods, including precious metals. The family residence was furnished with bedding, 'and a great quantity of both loose and curious linen of all sorts, and all other ornaments and necessaries requisite'. Murphy, returned from a spell in mainland Europe, was maltreated by a malign uncle. Among the latter's offences was to 'set [the youth] to lie with one of the household servants who had a sheet or pair to lie in, which seemed unto him very black and nasty, after coming out of a cleanly living country'.[51] In similar mode, an army officer, probably with experience of serving overseas, complained of his accommodation in New Ross. At first he was refused sheets in which to sleep; then he was fobbed off with some already used by a beggar boy, dirtied and full of lice.[52]

Householders continued to measure their wealth in goods, of which linen – both personal and domestic – remained prominent. Textiles, because needed by all, were frequently stolen. The ease with which they could be unloaded hinted at the brisk traffic in the second-hand.[53] When linen was inventoried, appraisers or owners were quick to distinguish the commonplace, the rougher sheets suitable for the beds of servants, from the more refined.[54] At the same time, it is suggestive of the steady spread of exacting standards, which required more – and more varied – possessions, that some servants slept between linen sheets. The charter schools, rarely guilty of mollycoddling, prescribed precisely how often the sheets on pupils' beds were to be changed. In 1762, the interval was set at once a month: hardly a great victory for hygiene. It copied the practice of Mercer's Hospital in Dublin.[55] Committees of local worthies, often including women, oversaw the regulations. They uncovered but probably remedied only temporarily the failings of the schools.

Inmates of charitable institutions, such as the charity schools, were clothed. The Incorporated Society stipulated that each boy in its care should be allowed four shifts or shirts, which were to be changed once or twice weekly.[56] Its charges were provided with breeches, leather aprons and canvas smocks. In 1769, the Society raised the annual allowance for clothing each pupil from twenty to twenty-five shillings.[57] When pupils were sent out to make their own ways in the world, as apprentices or servants, they were often equipped with a suit of clothing. Since the outlay amounted to about 20 per cent of what provincial labourers spent in a year, the value of this subsidy in kind was great. The boon occasionally tempted desperate parents to enrol their offspring in the establishments. The newly clad then absconded.[58] By 1770, the problem was addressed directly when the central committee in Dublin stipulated that the Charter School children should henceforward wear a uniform, which 'will tend greatly to the discovery and recovery of any children who may happen to elope or be seduced'. The chosen garb was to be of stout but drab brown frieze.[59]

This circle of production and consumption was closed when the pupils of charitable foundations were put to work as weavers and spinners. In some places by delving in the plots adjoining the schools, the children raised the flax or hemp which in time would be converted by their colleagues into coarse fabrics. Local manufacturers might contract with the charter school committees to buy the labour of the inmates.[60] The pupils, parading regularly to church, usually wore clothes supplied by local tradespeople. The orders for garments, although humdrum, brought steady money to the preferred suppliers, as did contracts for books, utensils and simple furniture.[61] The fetish of respectable clothing, and of changing it frequently, gripped other philanthropic ventures. Supplicants at the door of Lady Arbella's Dublin asylum in the 1760s and 1770s felt that they had to present themselves decently clad. Some borrowed their attire; others risked rejection by appearing in ragged or foul gowns. Those admitted were liable to have their clothing burnt immediately if it offended the squeamish matron and founder. The charity made its charges don uniforms, then dressed the favoured 'to fit her for offering herself to be a servant in decent clothing', and sent the reformed back into the world in suitable attire. The right costume, in one case, cost £2 8s. 10½d.[62] In a cycle followed by other charities, the magdalens were expected to earn their keep by sewing and dressmaking. Some proved proficient seamstresses, making garments for their betters. In subsidized schools, female pupils were equipped to go as apprentices to mantua-makers, milliners and other branches of the clothing trades.[63] The benevolent handed out clothes. Lord Castle Durrow allowed William Budd, the local parish clerk, ten shillings to buy a coat in the grim year of 1740. The municipality of Kinsale helped one of its pensioners into a winter coat.[64] For functionaries of towns, courts, guilds and schools, not the least of the attractions of their places was the garb with which they were supplied.[65] Servants enjoyed a similar boon, bringing an occasional temptation to flee with their clothing.[66]

## III

The store set on accumulating an impressive stock of linen was shown by the Limerick agent Nicholas Peacock. More than once he itemized what he owned. In January 1744, he wrote in his journal, 'The Lord make me thankful . . . I have 8 tablecloths, 5 napkins, 7 new shirts, 7 a year old, and twelve old shirts, 24 stocks, 6 towels, 5 pairs of new sheets, a fine pair, a coarse pair and an old pair'. Two and a half years later, he again totted up his holdings and thanked God. Now there were eleven shirts, ten stocks, two waistcoats, three and a half pairs of fine pillow cases, seven handkerchiefs, twelve coloured handkerchiefs, thirteen nightcaps, twenty-three new towels, ten pairs of sheets, eight table cloths, five napkins and two coarse pillow cases. Peacock, on the margins of and keeping company with the gentry, embraced cleanliness. When away from home, he would sometimes return – or send a servant – to collect a clean shirt. Others listed their linen, seldom with quite the same self-congratulation that Peacock exuded.[67] One reason, in Peacock's and other cases, was that these possessions were their most valuable. Understandably, then, they wished to keep track of items which had to be sent to be washed or entrusted to servants. Losses, accidental or deliberate, inevitably occurred, but then errant washerwomen and valets could be called to account.[68]

Good management of the household entailed an adequate or even abundant supply of linen and other textiles. The reverse, for example with linen being spoiled by rats, often went with larger neglects.[69] Much of the plenty was displayed, not just on the bodies of the family and its servants as they ventured abroad, but in the house itself. As has been argued in chapter 3, throughout the seventeenth and into the eighteenth centuries interiors impressed chiefly through the richness of hangings and upholstery. More and different fabrics became available; fresh patterns and colours came into vogue. Tapestries might retreat as other coverings for walls advanced, but the primacy of textiles for furnishing remained. Indeed, the elaboration in the service and content of meals necessitated more napery. Householders like Katherine Conolly, who prided themselves on keeping a good table, included tablecloths and napkins of Irish linen in their brief. The cloths were woven in increasingly elaborate and often patriotic patterns, with harps and shamrocks. Not only did they advertise the civility of host and hostesses, they proclaimed Irish pride.[70] In 1724, a Dubliner was asked to seek out some fine linen in the town, 'for the honour of Ireland', to satisfy a commission from an absentee Irish peer.[71] Another recipient in England, having received consignments of linen from Dublin, announced, 'it wore extremely well, and did our manufacture some credit'.[72] The duke of Dorset, while lord-lieutenant, tried to boost the manufacture. Between 1734 and 1736, he and his wife spent more than £100 on linen from two Dublin merchants.[73] Within Ireland itself, prejudice against the local, on account either of its quality or design, took time to dispel. During the 1680s, the Cork trader William Hovell, perhaps at the behest of his wife, insisted on linen from Flanders.[74] Another from south Munster, Andrew Crotty, the foppish agent of the Boyles and O'Briens, ordered table linen for his aristocratic employers from Bruges. Crotty's own shirts and handkerchiefs came from the same source. Enslaved to refinement, he unfailingly carried a handkerchief, 'for tenderlies' – exaggerated gestures of sentiment.[75] Only occasionally were vanities in dress ridiculed as foppery rather than for being unpatriotic. The 19th earl of Kildare, 'an effeminate, puny, little man', was dismissed as 'extremely formal and delicate'. It was said that he would not remove his wedding gloves when he retired to the nuptial bed with his bride. He was also discovered in his 'syllabub' wig engaged in cut-paper-work: conventionally a diversion of women.[76]

By 1751, when the Synod of Ulster decided to reward its solicitor in London, table linen was deemed suitable. Naturally, it would be of Irish manufacture.[77] During the same decade, Squire Edgeworth ordered products from the lately established cambric factory at Dundalk. In 1756, he spent £6 5s. on a damask tablecloth and a dozen napkins.[78] Meanwhile, enterprising entrepreneurs in Ireland strove to improve the design and durability of the local wares. In County Down, the Warings had a table cloth woven with a scene of George II's coronation. Concurrently the Linen Board, an object of state subsidy, and the Dublin Society gave bounties to the innovative.[79] Many of these Irish fabrics were displayed in the rooms seen by guests. More intimate was the excellence of bed linen. Murphy's horror at being condemned to nasty linen has been mentioned already. A well-run household not only possessed an adequate store of domestic linen, but was presided over by women who ensured that it was properly made, laundered, starched, dried, stored and mended. Servants with particular skills with textiles, no less than those who could wash and refresh lace, dress wigs, shave masters or act as amanuenses, were cherished. Just as the articles were themselves costly, so too were the services of the specialists who could look after them well. Bachelors spent heavily to have their own linen washed carefully. Hence arose the need to list what they owned in order to keep track of it. In comparison, outer garments were cleaned only rarely, usually by specialists outside the household. The widow Elinor O'Hara had a variety of valuable garments – yellow damask, Venetian satin and silks – refreshed when she was in Dublin. Abigail Watson, in a more modest condition, having worn cloak and gown for the winter, sent them to be scoured and pressed.[80]

Although off-the-peg articles were becoming more easily available, especially in the specialized shops of Dublin, much – from the cloth itself to the piece of clothing – was custommade. Peacock had linen woven, shirts, trousers and coats cut out and sewn either by relations like his sister or by jobbing tailors. Lucas, a contemporary of Peacock in County Clare, noted how his mother had given eight lengths of her own cloth to a cousin for a coat. The diarist had a neighbour knit a pair of stockings for him. However, a coat for himself, costing £2 4s. 10d., was obtained in the nearby town of Ennis, as were a pair of red breeches.[81] Others bought materials in Dublin (or abroad), which were then made up according to preferred pattern by local operatives. The fashioning usually cost less than the fabric. Molly Moore, a young woman up in Dublin from Mayo, lavished £8 16s. 8d. on cloth, and then paid only £1 19s. 6d. to have it tailored.[82] Nevertheless, a realization was dawning that the crafting added to the value of the original material. What was sewn by family members, servants or itinerants no longer satisfied the smart. Tailors, seamstresses and mantua-makers varied in their skills no less than masons, carpenters and silversmiths. They charged accordingly.[83] Commercial operators never altogether supplanted dexterous needlewomen within the family. The sight of vivid patterns and dyes or the feel of rich textures tempted proficient women among the quality and the middling sort to try their hands at ambitious petticoats and handkerchiefs.[84]

Those unable to jaunt to Dublin, with its greater choice and higher prices, turned to fairs and markets or general merchants. From the early eighteenth century, the last proliferated in provincial towns.[85] By 1766, the shop and warehouse of Bryan Sheehy in Cork city beguiled with fabrics selected 'from the first makers in England and Ireland'. At Sheehy's were to be found the best 'superfine and refine' English cloths, bath rugs, beaver coatings, forest cloths, beaver druggets, marble cloth wiltons of the newest fashion, swan-skins, English striped flannels, English luterines for clergymen's gowns, the best English russels and callimancoes, the best English satins for gentlemen's wear, ginghams 'of the newest taste', English shalloons and anteloons, velverets cut and uncut, fustians, poplins, damasks and velvet. There were crapes and bombazines from Norwich. A few offerings were billed as of Irish origin, such as livery cloths, ratteens from Carrick-on-Suir, and Dublin camlets, damasks, stuffs and callimancoes.[86] Sheehy's range can be compared with what the Youghal trader Samuel Hayman stocked almost one hundred years earlier. In the intervening decades, the spending power of provincials had grown; so too had the assortment of goods available to them. Specialists appeared in larger towns like Cork and Limerick to cater to the demand. Yet, the perception persisted that it was only in Dublin that the latest and best were to be had. The belief receives support from the known stock of two Quaker merchants. John Pearson concentrated on the more durable cloths – denims, callimancoes, serges, shags and baize – needed for workaday dress. Some were woven on four looms in his garrets. He also stocked the broadcloth favoured for outer garments.[87] Joseph Deane, described as a 'clothier', kept a good selection of broadcloths, valued at £241. His trade enabled him to live in considerable comfort.[88] By 1740, Joseph Reymer, also in Dublin, could furnish a fine selection of cloths.[89] Later in the century, Philip Leonard, trading at the Dublin Corn Market, stocked 'all sorts of linen drapery', and listed sixteen separate types.[90] In the capital, too, were located the tailors, seamstresses and *modistes* capable of cutting and sewing the outfits to be worn at the Castle and other fashionable assemblies. At this level, there was some tendency to belittle the homespun and run after the imported. Both materials and styles which were thought to originate elsewhere, particularly in London or (better) Paris, were extolled.

Calculating merchants auctioned stuffs which they had imported. The sales of one leading Dublin mercer, Overstreet Grogan, generated lively interest. In 1761, Sarah Nugent was allowed £11 7s. 6d. to spend at one.[91] Goods salvaged from wrecked ships and impounded contraband were sold in the provinces from time to time. In Kerry in 1719, for example, there was excitement about a parcel of things 'useful for a family', including linen, rugs, blankets, quilts, shoes, stockings, hats, coarse broad clothes, kersies, druggets, serges, stuffs, calicoes, dursies and a few silks.[92] Both established and struggling producers resisted any who undercut them. In the port of Kinsale anger recurred over the hawkers and bummers who rowed out to the vessels in the harbour with 'jackets, breeches, stockings, several other sorts of goods, which are very ordinary and slightly made up'.[93] Cheaper versions of the fashionable reached outlying districts by other routes. A Galway woman may have voiced irony or simple delight when she reported to a grander neighbour, 'I am very fine in my new gown . . . and everyone is much pleased with it', although fashioned from cheaper poplin.[94]

68. Advertisement of Philip Leonard, linen draper, Dublin, which hints at the ever widening choice of types and qualities of cloth.

Those unable to afford entire new outfits each season might rejig the old with an astute purchase of accessories. The coloured handkerchief or apron were favourite devices to refresh the familiar. To match the light purses of servants and labourers, cut-price versions of the smart were produced. The humble – like their betters – did not always choose rationally when they decided how to spend their modest sums. The pleasure derived from the acquisition of new ribbon, handkerchief, apron or stockings is as easily overlooked as disparaged.[95] Female servants in the Vigors' household had money from their wages advanced so that they could buy handkerchiefs at Ballynakill fair. The 2s. 3d. that Mary Sindleton spent on a handkerchief in the 1720s represented about 3 per cent of her notional annual earnings of £4.[96] But the modest amounts available to the servants contrasted strikingly with the outlay on richer fabrics for the family itself. In England £9 was spent on a piece of chintz; several pounds were also paid for linen to make shifts for the Vigors children and diaper – a sort of linen – for household uses.[97]

Even in the matter of handkerchiefs, the wealthy enjoyed greater choice. Fancy as much as need governed these acquisitions. In 1740, Mrs Edgeworth was gratified with an embroidered handkerchief which cost £1 9s. 3d.[98] The wife of one of Lord Abercorn's agents was thanked for the present of a handkerchief for Lady Abercorn. The donor was assured that the gift 'is much admired', but was told – perhaps patronizingly – not to bother with more.[99] The need to cater to those with modest sums to spend stimulated the production of the appropriately priced. The stock of a Munster trader in the mid-eighteenth century revealed just how wide the selection had become. At the top end of his market were stamped cambric handkerchiefs at 2s. 9d. each, and silk ones retailing at 2s. 6d. But he also kept another fourteen types of silk handkerchief, ranging in price from 3s. 2d. to 11½d. Generally cheaper were the cotton versions which were to be had – in thirteen different qualities – at anything from 1s. 2½d. to 4d. The demand for such commodities was buoyant enough to allow the shopkeeper to specialize in cloth. His stock was valued at £238. His profits enabled him to accumulate 68 ounces of silver.[100]

Those in sharply divergent circumstances craved the odd striking article of dress. It was recognized that even the depressed charges of the Incorporated Society were not immune from desire. Recognizing this, its governors distributed five dozen straw hats as prizes to model pupils. Thereby, the directors hoped to foster and reward exemplary conduct.[101] The pervasiveness of the urge to spend on finery was further attested by a gossip in Waterford. In 1737, it was reported how a native of the city had returned after fifteen years in order to marry. Instead, the intending groom drowned himself. Before doing so, he had the sense to remove his shoes with silver buckles. If, as was rumoured, they had cost £10, they may well have been his most valuable possession.[102] Another tempted by the same gaudy accessory was a one-time servant and petty crook. The menial invested some of the proceeds of thieving in shoe buckles and so earned the name of Connor Buckley: a verbal play on his sparkling footwear.[103]

Indulgences of this sort dismayed rational reformers who wished to dictate how others should act and spend. Neither admonitions nor penalties corrected the inclination to buy the imported, the showy or the shoddy. Billy Smythe, an otherwise studious and sober student at Trinity College in the 1760s, illustrated the prevalence of the taste for the flashy. The youth conceded that the fellows of the college 'do not mind what sort of dress the young gentlemen wear, provided they have nothing red about them'.[104] Although Smythe denied any 'vanity and foppish in me', he was transfixed by a fad of the moment: gold twist buttons, and whinged to his father that he lacked the correct garb to go into Dublin gatherings. Faced with such whimsicality, some patriots resigned themselves to the fickleness of consumers and, adapting Mandeville's teaching, hoped that the cravings might aid the local economy.

The frequenters of polite society could reasonably contend that they had to dress for their parts. Some support for the belief that towns, and especially Dublin, demanded a smarter look comes from the relative proportions that wearing apparel constituted when effects were appraised. Captain Anthony Fitzgerald, as a naval commander in Cork, had a public position to maintain. In 1763, after he had died, his worldly goods were valued at £113 19s. ½d. His clothing amounted to £33 1s. 11d., or 30 per cent of the total. Another in the forces of the crown,

Colonel Samuel Bagshawe, calculated that he would spend about £42 annually on clothes. This allowed – modestly – for one new set of regimentals each year. In 1729, the uniform of a member of the Taylor family from Headfort in County Meath did cost £40.[105] Bagshawe reckoned that washing and mending would add another £6 10s. to his budget.[106] According to his estimate, about 17 per cent of his outgoings, excluding recurrent charges against his income, would be devoted to his apparel. The military felt strong pressures to appear in finery. Others without the excuse that they represented the monarch spent even more lavishly on their clothing. The annual expenses of a minor, William Balfour, were estimated at £142 13s. 6d. Of this sum a hefty 32 per cent went on dress. The boy's 'wearing clothes', costed at a yearly £22 7s., were separated from his linen, requiring another £10 18s. In addition, there would be his servants' liveries.[107] In comparison, country-dwellers in Ulster possessed clothes worth much less. Also, the homespun garments were thought to constitute a smaller proportion (scarcely 3 or 4 per cent) in the valuations of their owners' possessions.[108] Clothes might be cut to suit purses, but while it was practicable to shun apparently superfluous furnishings and artefacts, none could escape the need to dress.

## IV

Rites of passage called for costly garb. A standard was set that none in Ireland was likely to match when in 1685 Ossory, the heir to the kingdom's only dukedom, lavished £467 on his wedding clothes.[109] Throughout much of the seventeenth and eighteenth centuries, baptism and marriage were solemnized privately.[110] Privacy did not always preclude expensive celebrations. At their different levels, Richard Edgeworth, the squire, and Nicholas Peacock, the agent of the squire, bespoke finery for their wedding days. Although choice food and drink had to be supplied and tips given at christenings and nuptials, guests were not furnished with new clothes by their hosts.

   Dying often cost more than living. The splendour of obsequies varied, not just according to the standing and means of the deceased, but to religious temperament. The expense in the Dublin of the 1660s can be compared. The sum of £30 was spent on burying Elizabeth Vincent. The wedding of Adam Stokes, including a feast at *The Red House*, presumably an inn, was scarcely half the price of Mrs Vincent's funeral.[111] Testators sometimes forbade all vain pomps, even commanding that they be buried during the hours of darkness. Others asked that they be interred decently but without excessive display and cost. The careful stipulated the maximum to be spent.[112] 'Decency' was a subjective concept. The coffin and 'burial clothes' of a Dublin linen weaver, a Quaker, were priced at only £1 17s. 3¼d.[113] A culture of restraint was also evident in the burial of another Dublin Quaker, a tallow-chandler. The bill totalled less than £6.[114] In 1771, an inmate from the Magdalen Asylum was interred at St Kevin's in Dublin at a cost of 18s. 7½d. The charity provided a shift, a day cap and neck handkerchief in which to dress the corpse.[115] Landlords and employers sometimes paid for dependants to be buried. At Castle Durrow, the making of coffins for John Duigin and 'Jonathan' cost respectively 2s. and 2s. 6d.[116] This economy can be compared with what was disbursed – £52 13s. 2d. – on the funeral and attendant mourning when Jeffrey Flower, the schoolboy son of the owner of Castle Durrow, died.[117] Excess might, nevertheless, be criticized. In 1718, the burial of a Mrs Yates, *alias* 'Nanny Kent', financed by Lord Blessington, excited disapproval. Her coffin was covered with black velvet, lined with white quilted satin and furnished with silver hinges. All this betokened 'a person of quality', which the dead woman was not.[118]

Altogether more lavish was the public grief of Katherine Conolly for her husband, the Speaker. She adopted a vogue recently inaugurated by distributing to the mourners scarves not of the traditional crape or wool, but of Irish linen. Patriots and local traders alike approved the gesture. The practice, on a grandiose scale – 800 were handed out – and astutely publicized, spread. It may also have prolonged a funeral custom otherwise in danger of declining.[119] Again she followed convention by putting her entire household into mourning. Often those with foresight and resources anticipated this convention by assigning fixed sums in their wills for relations and servants to buy suits of mourning for close relations and servants. The Conollys had an unusually large establishment, but an unusually large income to match. Novel was the way in which the widow had her Dublin house hung with sombre material. Critics suspected that suppliers had tricked her into this extravagance; others explained it as further evidence of her disregard for contemporary etiquette and an ambition to arrogate to herself supremacy over Dublin's Protestant society. The censorious exclaimed, 'it does not belong to her to do what even a duchess could not have pretended to'.[120] It may have echoed the mourning for George I a couple of years before when some Dublin churches were draped in black.[121] As was feared, the costly habit spread. The Dublin house where Samuel Waring died in 1739 had two rooms and the entry hung with mourning, before his corpse was removed for burial in County Down. In 1745, the house of Lady Butler was similarly adorned with black cloth as part of the preparation for her funeral. The prosperous could afford such luxury.[122]

The elaborate heraldic funerals of earlier centuries did not disappear.[123] In the circle of the Southwells and Percevals of south Munster, care was lavished on interments. In 1670, the burial 'very handsomely' of a female member of the family had cost at least £225. In 1680, the Cork baronet Sir Philip Perceval was treated to the 'decentest and best of funerals that has been in that part of Munster this forty years'. It cost an estimated £700. On these occasions the local nobility and gentry were expected to greet the important corpse as they would have honoured the living person.[124] When the last earl of Thomond expired in 1741, it was rumoured that the funeral consumed an extravagant £1,000. 'But', a disappointed observer added, 'there was little show for the money'.[125] Customers were not always happy about the profiteering from the deaths of their kinsfolk. In the Parsons' family, straitened conditions owing to exile in the mid-seventeenth century recommended economy. Sir William Parsons wanted to be buried 'without charge or ceremony'. In the event his funeral – in England – was managed for £25, and those of two of his children for only £3 and £4.[126] By the eighteenth century, his namesake and successor ordered a private interment, without funeral sermon. The officiating cleric was to have a scarf; he and each bearer would also receive a pair of gloves.[127] In 1740, Sir Laurence Parsons quibbled over what he had been charged for escutcheons to adorn a bier.[128]

Few of substance entirely disregarded the conventions, even if they might think them vainglorious. William Smythe of Barbavilla decreed interment, 'without any funeral pomp very late in the night or very early in the morning', and to be carried on 'men's shoulders'.[129] Richard Edgeworth requested burial early in the morning, presumably to prevent any great confluence of the curious and so as to be performed 'very privately'. He, too, asked that six of his Protestant tenants should carry the coffin: the bearers, together with the minister, would be recompensed with hatbands and scarves.[130] Six years earlier, Edgeworth had seen to his wife's burial. In many particulars, it met contemporary expectations. There was a flurry of activity as he put himself, the servants and his children into sombre dress. An undertaker in Mullingar prepared the corpse for the vault. He then submitted a modest bill of £6 13s. 3d. for coffin, shroud and 'burial dress' for Mrs Edgeworth.[131] Linen scarves were presented to the two clergymen who conducted the service. Edgeworth ordered suitable mourning for his family and servants.[132] The requirements extended beyond clothes to the paper on which the bereaved wrote – he bought a quire of black-edged writing paper – and the wax with which letters were sealed.[133] His wife's death was also marked by a charitable dole to twenty poor people living near the Edgeworths.[134] This preference for helping the living more than the inert had been shown earlier in Edgeworth's spending. He had allowed his wife a generous £10 for mourning when an aunt died in 1740. But when she appeared at the wedding of a kinsman shortly afterwards, she was given £14 for her dress.[135] The same priorities granted Kitty White £9 11s. to buy mourning but £33 17s. to bedeck herself for the king's birthday celebrations in 1751.[136]

Funerals, whether discreet or ostentatious, were good for trade. The supply of painted hatchments and escutcheons to hang on hearse, house and church made work aplenty for herald-painters. They also added to the business of dealers in cloth. About 1740, Sir Laurence Parsons paid £20 19s. for escutcheons from a Dublin source. Six dozen were needed: the best – costing 7s. 6d. each – were painted on silk; the others, at 4s. 6d. each, were on glazed linen.[137] Conductors directed final journeys with aplomb.[138] Funeral processions distinguished between 'the higher rank', the 'middling station' and 'the lower rank'.[139] For Kean O'Hara's interment in County Sligo in 1719, escutcheons were supplied conveniently from Athlone and cost a mere £2.[140] The new stress on correct dress for the dead and living chiefly

69. H. D. Hamilton, 'An open hearse used at the funerals of the higher rank', 1760. In death, if not always in life, the hierarchies beloved of heralds and other conservatives were emphasized.

70. H. D. Hamilton, 'A hearse or sedan used at Cork for people of middling station', 1760.

71. H. D. Hamilton, 'A funeral procession of the lower rank', 1760.

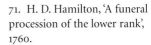

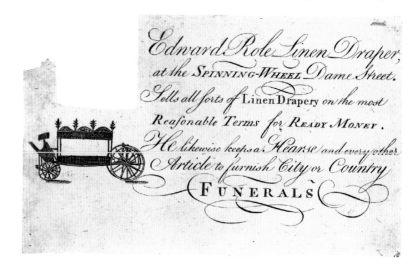

72. Trade card of E. Role, linen draper, Dublin, *c.* 1758. Funerals profited those able to dress the quick and the dead.

benefited the cloth trade. In parallel to English laws to encourage the woollen industry by insisting that cerements be of wool, an Irish statute of 1732 also commanded them. A proposal to make mandatory the use of linen had failed. Even so, one who advertised to undertake funerals in George II's reign was a Dublin linen draper.[141] The convention of following the hearse sombrely arrayed and, for those close to the dead person, to continue in this mode for weeks or months afterwards guaranteed orders for mercers, clothiers, tailors, seamstresses and mantua-makers. After 1727, the executors of Lord Doneraile found that the expenses of his shrouds, the embalmer, the coffin-maker and even the bills for food and alcohol were dwarfed by those from the cloth merchant. The last demanded nearly £172. The mercer provided suits for the servants and family and dressed the funeral coach and church. In addition, another supplier had made the cloaks for the horsemen and funereal horse furniture. Doneraile's coffin had cost nearly £30 and the brandy for the mourners under £10.[142] A similar division of expenditure had occurred when Kean O'Hara was buried in 1719. His Danzig oak coffin and hearse cost only £6, spirits for the mourners £15 11s. 8d., and ale a further £3 19s. 6d. Tobacco, pipes and candles required only modest sums. The Sligo merchant who had provided textiles sent the largest bill: of £78.[143]

An early indicator of the spread into polite Irish society of these codes was the mourning observed in Dublin after the death of the vicereine and local queen, the duchess of Ormond. This was soon followed by the more general mourning for Charles II.[144] The price of black cloth rose with Queen Mary II's death in 1694. An observer exclaimed, 'never was such mourning seen in this kingdom'. Churches as well as bodies were put into black.[145] After William III died in 1702, a woman in Dublin wailed, 'everybody has bought, that you can hardly get a glove or hood for money'. Some had everyday articles dyed. Those, 'without cloth by them, have to buy English', and at inflated prices.[146] By 1737, when the demise of Queen Caroline plunged smart Dublin into sable, the vain enquired impatiently how long this unbecoming colour would have to be worn. Lady Anne Conolly longed to cast off 'one's old rusty clothes'.[147] Those recently equipped with showy garments lamented that they could not now wear them. One remote in County Galway vowed to give a brocaded lutestring dress '2 or 3 wearings before the account comes from the court what they will mourn in'.[148] Those anxious to do the proper thing received strict orders about what to wear 'in such deep mourning'. From Waterford, Molly Mason commanded her brother in Dublin to have made a new suit, without buttons on the sleeves or pockets. She had already sent two pairs of 'weepers' (strips of white cloth to be sewn onto cuffs), six suitable cravats, three pairs of 'superlative' gloves and crepe.[149] She warned him, 'it is not fit for a man or your servant to make a weeper on a trimmed coat'. However, the Galway squire Robert French had weepers stitched onto his coat in 1744.[150] Cambric was bought on behalf of the younger Kean O'Hara to make weepers for his mourning after his father died.[151] Only the brave – or cussed – such as Mrs Delany defied the strict regulations in the upper reaches of society. In 1747, she and her husband followed 'the old mourning', being at 'a time of life to indulge the dictates of the heart more than the reigning fashions'.[152]

The unforeseen need of mourning clothes strained those on tight budgets. The thoughtful and well-to-do left money so that connections could kit themselves out appropriately. Sometimes, provision was generous. Henry Prittie of Kilboy bequeathed £50 each to children to equip themselves and their spouses after his death.[153] In County Tyrone, a squire, William Akie, bestowed £40 on his wife to buy black, and stipulated helpfully that the money should be paid within ten days.[154] Such sums far exceeded what even the most profligate could spend on a single outfit. John Croker, a Limerick landowner, allowed two of his sons £50 each to buy themselves mourning attire.[155] Anthony Alcock, left £20 by a relation, was able to put himself, a son and daughter into mourning.[156] Grace Kempston in 1723 allocated £10 to a son for the like purpose. It was remarked when mourners had not donned the appropriate gear.[157] If, on occasion, the generosity suggested surreptitious bequests to intimates, cash for 'mourning' was not a total fiction. Executors' accounts disclose much spent with clothiers and tailors.[158] Close relatives, servants and acquaintances were left with something more durable than a sore head and dyspepsia after an expansive wake and expensive baked meats.

Clothing itself, as well as money to buy it, often featured in the dispositions of the dying. Squire Edgeworth followed a common practice by willing most of his own apparel, except 'worked ruffles and laced clothes', to a manservant.[159] In 1720, Henry Dalway of County Antrim left to his old servant, James Bruce, a grey great coat trimmed with gold. The Tyrone squire, William Akie, divided his own clothes between two servants.[160] Robert Howard, bishop of Elphin, bequeathed all his clothes and £40 to his steward.[161] Others gave personal clothing to kinsfolk. William Neagle from Kinsale in 1712 passed all his woollen apparel except a black cloth suit and a cinnamon-coloured cloth coat to a relation.[162] A clergyman in late-seventeenth-century Tipperary thoughtfully left £2 p.a. to a kinsman 'in clothes if he needs it'.[163] The custom was found at all social and economic levels. Two Quaker widows in Dublin remembered kindred through legacies of clothing. Mary Kelly's apparel, 'being but a very small value, was given by consent of the legatees to clothe Susannah Jenkinson's children who very much wanted clothes'.[164] The clothing of Laetitia Reynolds, sheltered in the Magdalen Asylum, was returned to her mother after she had died.[165] Probably it was her only asset. Such gifts, of these apparently intimate articles, collapsed the sumptuary distinctions which money maintained long after laws had ceased to be enforceable. Notionally the humble could now assume a better look. This indeed was part of the liberty on which some Protestants in Ireland congratulated themselves. 'It is not the law that determines the fashion of my clothes, neither is it the gospel that cuts out my linen nor tells us what hat bands I must wear'.[166] But the freedom brought perils: the free dressed above their station and their purses. Not all the hand-me-downs were sported by the new owners: much must have been either recycled or sold.

Other legatees received money with which to purchase rings as keepsakes.[167] Squire Smythe of Barbavilla, despite his reticence over his interment, left ten guineas each to two friends and twenty guineas each to another pair in order to buy memorial rings. These were tokens of esteem and friendship.[168] Sometimes they would incorporate hair, even images of the dead person or messages, to bring them to perpetual recall. In 1739, Lady Parsons intended to present the officiating clergyman and her husband's Protestant tenants who bore her to the grave with mourning rings.[169] More promiscuous were gifts of scarves and hatbands to those who followed the hearse. Samuel Waring left orders that at his burial at Waringstown, forty-four of his tenants should receive hatbands and gloves. He also added a note, 'if any of the tenants' wives come or any widows that hold any land, they are to have gloves'. He also stipulated that the chief mourners were to wear mourning cloaks and precede the hearse. The garments – two dozen in all – were supplied from nearby Dromore, Lurgan and Newry.[170] In 1742, the burial of Mrs Isabella Balfour required, besides 'a fine coffin' (price £9 10s.), thirty-one cloaks, ten gowns, caps and staves, fine linen for twenty-one scarves, 'less fine linen' for thirty-three more scarves, fourteen hatbands for the servants, and another nineteen for the conductors. Hatbands were surprisingly expensive items, priced at five shillings each. Then there were gloves to be handed out. Four dozen of a superior quality and three dozen of an inferior grade for the men, and nine pairs for women.[171] Gloves were frequently distributed.[172] The Dublin Quaker John Pearson, a prosperous weaver, left to each of three personal friends a guinea with which to buy gloves.[173] Mourners presumably could wear them at less gloomy events than funerals. Yet, the material inducements to attend did not always succeed. In 1756, an agent in County Tyrone, although invited by card to a funeral, vowed that 'he wouldn't for the sake of a scarf attend a man whom he wouldn't visit in life'.[174]

73. H. D. Hamilton, 'Old cloaths to sell', 1760. Second-hand goods enabled humbler people to adopt the fashions of the grand, or simply to clothe themselves.

Death made extra work in unexpected quarters. Formal invitations to funerals were printed.[175] The cards were merely one element in increasingly complex arrangements overseen in Dublin by specialists. Undertakers, assisted by paid 'managers' and 'conductors', emerged in the eighteenth century and encroached on functions that heralds and clergy had previously monopolized. In the countryside, the doleful tasks still fell to agents and jacks-of-all-trades. Nicholas Peacock dealt with the interment of his employer and kinswoman, Alice Widenham, in 1742. He hastened into Limerick city to bespeak a coffin and to have a mourning suit made for himself. He also bought a pair of worsted stockings to complete his outfit. The following day, Mrs Widenham was 'taken out and carried to her long home'. Peacock helped to hand out scarves and gloves. The next day, he settled accounts with the glover and with the supplier of the hearse, and presented the bills to Mrs Widenham's executors.[176] The scale of the Widenham ceremony was clearly smaller than that of Speaker Conolly or even of Isabella Balfour. Indeed, in Peacock's own corner of Limerick, it was surpassed by the rites for two others from the Limerick quality a couple of years later. Peacock returned from one ceremony with scarf and hatband, and from the second with another hatband and gloves, valued not so much for themselves but as signifiers of his place in the local hierarchy.[177] The funerals, although distant from Dublin, in essentials obeyed the conventions of grander occasions in the capital. The speed with which Peacock procured the accessories suggested that the retailers of Limerick were well used to meeting demands for what must have been a staple of their livelihoods.[178] The stock of general traders in inland centres like Birr, Nenagh and Roscrea supports this view.[179] However, the ease of Peacock's task contrasted with the experiences of others in the environs of Limerick. The Lucases attended several funerals near Corofin during the harsh winter of 1741. They did not record carrying away any tangible souvenirs. For one burial, tobacco, boards, candles and pipes, but not gloves, scarves or hatbands, were ordered. In the event, only the tobacco arrived in time.[180] Again, the frank commercialization of death and grief profitably expanded the custom of the textile and haberdashery trades. In Limerick, a widow, Margaret Seymour, supplied all the necessaries 'for the decent solemnity of funerals in city or county, viz: hatchments, streamers, hearses, escutcheons, hangings, sconces, large and small cloth palls, cloaks, plumes, stands and tapers, death's heads for chapels, chased furniture for coffins, silvered or plain with inscription plates, figures of time, handles, letters assisted by the herald printer's office, Dublin'. By the early nineteenth century, a woollen draper and mercer in Sligo town could boast that carriages, 'funeral accommodations, coffin mountings, scarves and hat-bands', could be dispatched 'at a moment's notice'.[181]

## V

Peacock, joining in the rites of passage of his district, encountered increasingly rarefied conventions about dress, as about conduct, furnishings and hospitality. As a bachelor on the margin of genteel society, yet obliged by his agency to deal with numerous subordinates, he succumbed to the pressures. He had the resources both to amass an enviable stock of linen and to vest himself properly for different occasions. The prospect of hunting with his employer, Hartstonge, heir to a baronetcy, made Peacock bespeak a riding coat in Limerick. It was financed from the sale of sheep.[182] In November 1745, he summoned a tailor to make clothes for him at home. The following week, he rode over to Kilmallock to take part in an array of Lord Southwell's troop of militia, in which Peacock held a commission.[183] Civilians, swept along by the martial mood, enjoyed the finery in which they could strut and the masculine conviviality which, rather than military hardships, they sampled. The militia spurred

Peacock to preen. Already, his spending indicated attentiveness to his personal appearance. He bought cloth and clothes regularly from Limerick merchants; other garments he had made at home, by a sister or even – in the case of pair of linen drawers – by himself.[184]

Peacock's position brought him to events at which the homespun and home-made would not do. Of these, marriage was the most important. Preparations included the purchase in Limerick of blue cloth for his coat. At the same time he bought two fustian waistcoats, scarlet shag breeches and a hat. Selling sheep again paid for these goods.[185] Accessories, such as buttons, buckles and handkerchiefs, could be obtained from pedlars. Tailors in Limerick made the most important items.[186] In some instances, materials – mohair, sarsnet, canvas, buckram, thread and buttons – were bought in the city and then made up at home by itinerant tailors. One spent at least three days at Peacock's house in 1748, perhaps tailoring clothes for children and servants.[187] Serviceable materials might be re-used. A frieze (tweed) coat was cut up for a servant's waistcoat and breeches.[188] Marriage enlarged Peacock's social circuit, and this enlargement was reflected in his manner of living. He purchased more: furbelows for his wife; fabrics for the house; finery for himself. Linen spun and woven from his own flax served for curtains and bed-hangings: embellishments which his house had lacked before his marriage. More accoutrements came from the retailers and craftsmen of Limerick itself.[189]

In enlisting with the militia, Peacock entered an organization which visibly embodied not only the strength (or puniness) of Protestant Ireland, but also something of its origins in military conquest and its current ideologies.[190] The militiamen showed an unexpected sensitivity to colours. The gaudy regimentals of regular officers had long elicited admiring gasps. In 1745, when an emergency turned the militia from a paper into a physical force, its members had the chance to outdo the plumage of the regulars in the provincial garrisons. Commanders of the volunteers realized that, if they were to attract and retain troopers, they must lay baits. One inducement was subsidized entertainment. A second was the uniform. From the north of County Cork, the agent of the absentee earl of Egmont, titular commander of a militia band in 1745, reported the difficulties of persuading tenants to undergo training. Also, they wrangled over the colour and cut of their uniforms and the look and lacing of their hats. The men feared that, were they to wear the wrong colours, they might be mistaken for servants. They expected their commanders to pay for the outfits, so increasing the hidden subsidy that militia service offered to their indulgences. The transitory glory of the junior officers in the militia, drinking themselves under the table in taverns and parading in the churchyards and market squares of the neighbourhood, was lengthened when they appeared at assemblies in their regimentals.[191] This affectation, like the use of their ranks as titles of address, was a harmless vanity. It put them on a par (they hoped) with the professional soldiery, especially in the eyes of impressionable women. At the same time, buying the right rig no less than sparing time for the exercises restricted volunteering to the small contingent which could afford these sacrifices. The regulars set a furious pace hard for the amateurs to equal. Officers were expected to find their own costly clothing. The state supplied the rankers. Schemes to array the forces in Ireland with clothes manufactured there periodically cheered the Irish textile industry. However, the official orders rarely brought the steady profits which had been prophesied.[192]

Something of the same splendour attended the rituals of municipal corporations and trading guilds. The officers of boroughs were enjoined to appear properly habited, in the gowns appropriate to their degrees. Both on Sundays and at civic festivals, the functionaries were to be joined by the leaders and brethren of the individual guilds. In Dublin – and elsewhere – they were differentiated by special colours. Lurid scarves or sashes rather than complete costumes sufficed.[193] Modest freemen frequently remonstrated at the costs. With equal frequency, corporations reprimanded those who failed to comply with the codes for dressing.

## VI

Peacock found the cash to equip himself with new suits for the militia, hunting and marriage. In order to pass muster in polite gatherings, he bought extra clothes and accessories. Acquisitiveness in the matter of linen and care over surcoats stopped short of his head. He bought and wore wigs, but from the lowest end of the range. Throughout the 1740s, he customarily paid between six shillings and seven shillings and sixpence.[194] This price was similar to what an illiterate linen weaver in Dublin spent on his wig.[195] In eighteenth-century Ireland, wigs came at many prices: from about five shillings to twelve guineas. Richard, earl of Arran, one of the sons of the first duke of Ormond, paid £12 and £14 for his perruques.[196] In 1703, a squire from County Louth spent £9 on his.[197]

Ideas of politeness inhibited men from appearing in public in their own hair. By the end of the seventeenth century, the convention had spread into Ireland. Even servants had to wear wigs.[198] 'One-row' wigs might suffice. Traders cashed in. Materials – 'live' hair, hair docked from the dead or from horses and other beasts – partly determined price. But so, too, did style. This, as with clothes, altered with confusing frequency. A market in cast-off and revamped wigs developed.[199] Only the resolute refused to be rushed into constant buying, and clung to their favourites even when dismissed as outmoded. At public assemblies, particularly in Dublin, it was hard completely to ignore altering vogues. In Limerick, with its confluence of the important from the adjacent counties and the comings and goings of the port, recent modes would soon be known, and available. Peacock's stinginess in not going for a more upmarket version of the wig was of his choosing rather than forced on him by poverty.[200] Heavier demands were imposed by higher social station and a more conspicuous public role. Jonathan Swift settled for mid-price wigs. In 1709, he paid £2 10s.; in 1733, he bought two for £5 5s. 6d.[201] Edgeworth, while in London during the 1720s to read for the bar,

74. Miniature portrait of ?Sir Richard Ingoldsby,
*c.* 1705. The owner of Carton chose the most
fashionable and costly style of wig.

was prepared to spend five guineas on periwigs. They were cheaper than the full-bottomed wigs that had been *à la mode* at the end of the previous century.[202] Back in Dublin, Edgeworth went for a cheaper option at £4.[203] By 1739, he had adopted the simpler styles of tie-wig and bob-wig. The two were to be had from a Dublin peruke-maker for £6.[204] Later he returned to the same supplier for a bob-wig for which he paid £2 5s. 6d.[205] Staying in Bath during the 1740s, he favoured the newer mode of the brigade wig, to be had for two guineas.[206]

The differences in price were reflected in the look of wigs. The knowing identified costly imports and cut-price copies. Once committed to keep company with the bewigged, bills multiplied. Wigs, to look their best, had to be powdered and groomed. At rest, they were not to be tossed idly into a corner, but hung on a carpentered stand. Some wig-makers also supplied the ribbons with which to tie them and the 'frames' on which to arrange them in repose.[207] Edgeworth had a barber in the adjacent town of Edgeworthstown tend the wigs of his servants and shave himself. The scalp on which they sat also needed attention: shaved so that the hairpiece could sit snugly. He also had his head treated with brandy, perhaps to cure a condition like ringworm.[208] Traders responded to the needs of wearers ingeniously. Not only did they multiply economical versions to satisfy the likes of Peacock, they tried tricks. In

75. H. D. Hamilton, 'Perukes vampt and mended', 1760. Those of modest means evidently were enabled to adopt the necessary look.

Dublin, as in most sizeable boroughs, periwig-makers were overseen by trade guilds. The Dublin body tried to stamp out chicanery. In 1718, it waged war on those who abused the craft 'by mixing hairs cut off of several heads, together with those of different colours, mixing bleached hairs, horse hairs and live hairs together, and by giving false colours to hairs by dipping and dyeing'.[209] Sub-standard wigs were seized and guild officials who connived with brokers of old wigs were disciplined.[210] Customers suspected other deceits. The barrister Charles Caldwell, active in the official and legal worlds of the capital, deputed the choice of wigs to a colleague in London. Suavely Caldwell assured his correspondent, 'I know you are a man of taste, and therefore say nothing about fashion'. Even so, he expected value for money. In the event, the results displeased. Caldwell protested about the inferior quality and predicted that they would not last as long as Irish-made products. He raged, 'they have already lost all their curl'. Evidently the wig-maker had 'thought any hair good enough for an Irish chap'.[211]

Executing commissions at a distance on behalf of others always carried risks. James Waller, soon to be elected to the Irish parliament, entrusted nephews in London with his order. The 'long' wig was to be had of a named London maker, and should cost £5. Waller had sufficient faith in the perruquier to add, 'tell Mr. Parry the periwig is for me and I trust to himself for the goodness. If he will make it very good, you may exceed the £5 [by] five or ten shillings'. The second, short wig, was to be had from a different manufacturer, and ought to cost no more than thirty shillings.[212] Waller's sister, Lady Petty, was less pleased with the liberty taken by a servant in buying wigs for her children. She was outraged that thirty-five shillings rather than the customary thirty had been paid.[213] Nevertheless, the execution of commissions was a favour routinely asked and offered. Part of the hazard arose from the indecision; more came from the imprecision with which wants were described. In 1694, an agent in Cork complained to an acquaintance in Kerry that the latter had been 'short in your advice about the wig, in not saying whether a long one or a bob'.[214]

Wigs of Irish manufacture, like other goods, were not always despised as inferior to the foreign. An Irishman long resident in London bespoke a wig from Dublin. Instructions about colour, style ('tied up pretty full') and letting it 'lie in the pipes till I come' were precise. The result pleased, 'for it is not only good but cheap': it cost £1 17s.[215] Wigs from Dublin, if 'plain and natural', were also requested in Philadelphia, as yet unable to supply such refinements closer to hand.[216] In addition, Dublin was still valued as a source of gloves, linen for shirts and thread stockings. But the Irish wares were not always received uncritically. Kid gloves sent from a Dublin manufacturer, although 'very good looking', would have been more welcome 'had they been yellow . . . for white is too gay for me in the 42nd year of my life'.[217] Exiles from Ireland, if they continued to request specific articles from their homeland, were deluged with orders from kindred and acquaintances still in Ireland.[218] The errands involved the exchange of more than objects. Correspondents flattered their emissaries with talk of 'nice taste' and superior 'fancy'.[219]

Awkwardnesses over purchases were not all the fault of the contrariness of the wearer, with one desire giving way to another. Often, would-be purchasers struggled to find the right words to explain precisely what was wanted. In a time of rapid innovation in colours, patterns, textures and functions, the descriptive vocabulary lagged behind.[220] It was learnt only slowly – and often imperfectly – by customers.[221] Gradually, guides were offered through displays and advertisements, with their technical phraseology. The uncertainties hampered the successful discharge of orders. William Waring, the paterfamilias in County Down, when buying wigs, as in much else, relied on his son, at ease in both London and Dublin (as well as in continental Europe). The elder Waring knew what kind of periwig he wanted: 'I would not have too much hair in it, but a moderate one to come to my face and not to fly back'.[222] Other requests from the parent referred to what was worn 'by men of my age' or what he had seen on others of his acquaintances.[223] Three decades later, the bishop of Elphin asked his brother in London to send a hat, 'of the best sort, fit for my gravity'.[224] In 1771, another relation in Dublin was told 'I shall leave to your good taste to make choice of what you think proper'.[225]

76. Advertisements of Richard Smith, hatter, Armagh, and of James Winterscale, hatter, Sligo. By George III's reign, suppliers in the provinces were able to meet the demand for the essentials of clothing and furnishing valued by the respectable and would-be respectable.

Couched in such terms, the requests suggested unquestioning dependence on those of superior rank and judgement. They also implied deference of those in Ireland to those outside the kingdom. Diplomacy and courtesy certainly governed both the initial requests and their execution.[226] But on occasion, familiar relationships were re-ordered. Irish wares might be preferred to English ones. Seniors, such as Waring *père*, ceded authority to choose between articles to juniors. Similarly, social superiors, like the Hills of Hillsborough and Brownlows of Lurgan, deferred to Samuel Waring's aesthetic judgements.[227]

Goods extended and complicated not just the material but also the mental worlds of buyers and owners. Shopping, even for clothes, strengthened male power over female lives.[228] Men were entrusted with delicate errands on behalf of women.[229] Thomas Carleton, journeying from Ireland to England in 1678, was asked to buy a say apron for his mother and three pounds of combed wool for a sister.[230] Kean O'Hara in Dublin during the 1690s executed commissions for at least four women back in his native Sligo. Accordingly he bought lengths of silk, women's shoes, hoods and gloves.[231] The Clare farmer Lucas, on a sortie into Limerick, purchased a hat for his sister at home with money she had given him.[232] Sometimes, as when Toby Caulfield from County Sligo hunted throughout the city for women's shoes of a particular design, impatience or despair set in.[233] A few years later, Grace Waring was warned by a friend in Dublin that 'the laces are grown so very dear that I doubt you'll think me an ill market woman but I have bought some not unlike yours, tho not quite so good'. By the eighteenth century, wives and daughters frequently accompanied the head of the family on trips to Dublin. In consequence, they enjoyed opportunities to wonder at and succumb to the wares of the metropolis.[234] Anne Weldon, wife of a wealthy squire, confessed to spending two entire days shopping in Dublin during 1771.[235]

Even in the eighteenth century, men were more likely than women to visit Dublin on their own. This was also the situation with journeys to London or continental Europe. The itinerants were saddled with tasks. The extensive Smythe affinity from the Midlands often deputed commissions to a senior member, Ralph Smythe, long a London resident. Wants for garden, house and person were relayed to him. He confidently selected plants and seeds. More personal items caused greater bother. In the quest for pieces of silk and black lace hoods, he enlisted the women in the house where he had long lodged.[236] Despite the weightiness of these

77. H. D Hamilton, 'Hard Ware', 1760. Small items of haberdashery were hawked through Dublin and by pedlars in the provinces, allowing those of modest means, such as domestic servants, to acquire both decorative and useful objects.

matters, Smythe happily gratified his kindred still in Ireland. Some visited him, and relied on his guidance as to where best to locate the various desiderata that they sought on their own or their acquaintances' behalves.[237]

One costly purchase entrusted to him illustrates some of the strategies for shopping. Smythe's younger brother, William Smythe, the squire of Barbavilla, wanted a pair of diamond earrings for his daughter. Squire Smythe, a widower of more than ten years' standing, may have doted on his growing children like Richard Edgeworth and Bishop Edward Synge on theirs. Smythe turned to his brother in London to execute the commission. The latter reported, 'that I have seen several rings but none that I think he will like, tho some are very pretty, but when I am more at leisure I don't doubt but I shall be able soon to please a gentleman of his nice taste that way'.[238] True to his word, the elder Smythe went to a leading jeweller, Peter Webb. The last had the advantage of Irish origins. Confidence in Webb was increased because he was said to be related to Lady Coghill, prominent in Protestant Ireland. Smythe also knew others who dealt with him. Indeed, Webb was in demand to supply customers in Ireland. More importantly, since the commission would cost £90, the jeweller was esteemed 'an honest man in his way of dealing, which is a rarity'. The specification – presumably from Squire Smythe himself – was for 'three brilliants in each . . . and of a right good water'. Webb was able to complete the task within a fortnight. Ralph Smythe was well pleased with the result, 'which are brilliants transparent and really make a grand show'. They were duly packed in a shagreen case for careful dispatch to a relation in the Dublin Custom House. Nevertheless, Smythe worried lest his brother dislike the jewels, and so offered to replace them at his own expense if they did not please.[239]

The dutiful strove to bring back what had been bespoken. But often, failing to comprehend their orders or not finding an exact match, they improvised. In addition, they bought impulsively. So souvenirs filled their trunks. Gratefully received by wives, mothers, daughters, mistresses and termagants, these articles – textiles, jewellery, haberdashery, trinkets, bric-a-brac – represented men's ideas of what women's taste might or should be.[240] Women, because of their more constricted circuits, especially beyond Ireland, and their smaller budgets, had fewer chances to impose their tastes directly on the men around them. The constraints told of a patriarchy which relegated most women, other than widows and heiresses, to subordinate stations. Notwithstanding the economic, legal and cultural obstacles, women found ways to exercise choice as consumers.[241] Moreover, any analysis conceived entirely as calculation, emulation and deference may miss the innocence, impulsiveness and irrationality with which gaudy objects were acquired and exchanged. Chaos was predicted, 'if tradesmen, artificers and labourers should take it in their heads to turn fine gentlemen and pretend to mimic their betters'.[242] Typical of the contempt with which the modest purchases of the humble were held were the verses of a Church of Ireland minister in County Monaghan. The versifier expatiated on the cheap show of pleasure-seekers at a pattern in the 1760s. He noted striped linen dress, blue stockings, new pumps with buckles that had cost four pence, 'coarse black stockings', a 'one row wig', stays cast off by a mistress, a scarlet cloak, new cap and ribbons, 'bath-rug' coat, fresh ruffles, gloves, aprons, petticoats and handkerchiefs galore. Unintentionally, the availability of a wider selection of clothing at fairs and markets and through gifts was confirmed. So, too, were the qualms in the upper reaches of society when too many of the lowly acquired the accessories of refinement, albeit in cut-price versions. Clothing was more common as an object of extravagance and ostentation than flowers, trees, or even furnishings and housing. Whereas few had their own land and space in which to engage in memorable displays, all had bodies to dress.[243]

Chapter 9

# Dublin

*I*

In 1684, a resident boasted that Dublin had 'wonderfully increased in wealth, trade, splendour and civility' during the last twenty years.[1] In each generation and seemingly in every decade, similar impressions were recorded. About 1710, it was reckoned the fourth city in Europe, grown 'to a prodigious greatness and really magnificent'. Other reactions were more critical: ''tis a prodigy the covetousness that place grows to, so crowded with coaches and people and such a busy trading'.[2] The city's population, reckoned at perhaps 112,000 in 1744, rose to 140,000 by 1760. It also housed the densest concentration of Protestants – maybe 70,000 by the mid-eighteenth century.[3]

Dublin thrived because it performed many parts: seat of a viceregal court, parliament, government departments, the four central law courts and a university. Its port was the busiest in the kingdom; its schools and doctors were accounted among the best. Anxious husbands hired Dublin lodgings so that their wives could lie in with greater confidence. There corns could be cut and teeth be tended or – as one disgruntled patient had it – 'spoiled' by a 'French' surgeon.[4] Increasingly, its manufactures and shops acted as magnets. Provincials came to work, to learn, to relax, to buy, to intrigue and to whore. Dubliners fostered complex forms of regulation, employment and diversion. The unique character of the city was acknowledged when it was spoken of as a 'metropolis'.[5] On its side, Dublin demanded of both residents and visitors higher standards in housing, furnishings, clothes, deportment and recreations: in short, a grander figure. Anxieties accompanied the pleasures. Visitors made work for, but sometimes created tensions with, the permanent residents. As enthusiasts trilled anthems in celebration of Dublin, a ground bass warned of perils. The notorious risks of London – as of other cities – were easily detected in the Irish capital. As a result, Dublin served as a target for the killjoys who hymned rural simplicity.[6]

Physical expansion quickened from the later 1650s. Rapid growth aggravated problems: overcrowding and poverty for the Dubliners; scarcity of housing and higher rents for tran-

78. Francis Place, *View of Dublin*, 1699. Place, an English artist, visited Ireland between 1699 and 1700, and showed both the growth of Dublin and the survival of wooded and open spaces.

sients. What for many was a problem profited the entrepreneurial few. Property owners, including the municipality, Lord Aungier, Sir Humphrey Jervis, Joshua Dawson and Luke Gardiner, developed their holdings. Some developers simply leased a plot on which the lessee could build to his or her own specifications. Others offered a finished shell which the tenant had then to fill.[7] A few schemes, notably that of Dublin corporation around St Stephen's Green, were acclaimed and long attracted the wealthy.[8] Otherwise, particular quarters rose and fell in popularity. The increase in houses was quantified. In 1705, there were thought to be 7,369 in the city parishes; by 1718, 10,004; and in 1733, 11,718.[9]

Whatever efforts were made by speculators and proprietors to supply adequate lodgings, would-be lodgers moaned. Dublin abounded with housing of assorted vintages, types and prices. Notables inherited city properties from ancestors who had acquired them in the sixteenth and seventeenth centuries. First the dissolution of religious houses, next the confiscations from Catholic laypeople, and then the normal processes of selling and reselling meant that much of the city changed ownership. During the seventeenth century, both the long-established and newcomers, such as the Annesleys, Aungiers, Moores, Temples and Wares, invested profits from soldiering, office and trade in Dublin sites. The acquisitions were usually investments to secure a steady and growing revenue for the future rather than simply a town house. The long and generous terms on which the premises were often leased brought

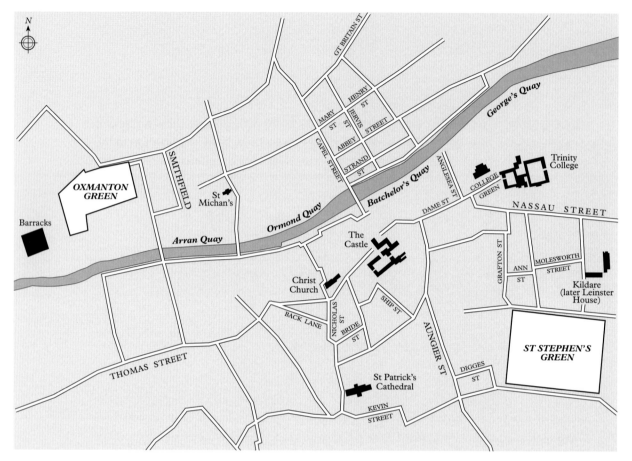

Map 1. Dublin streets.

the nominal owners relatively little by the end of the seventeenth century. This situation paralleled that on many rural estates where the head tenants, granted advantageous leases, did best. The Annesleys, advanced to be earls of Anglesey, having thrived in the official world of early Stuart Ireland, detached themselves from the kingdom by the end of the century. Late in the 1660s, Lord Anglesey was seeking a tenant for his spacious house near Trinity College. More typical of his family's substantial Dublin holdings were three houses, in Anglesey Street. Let in 1687 for £6 4s. 6d., by 1713 they were thought to be worth £70 to the lessee. Elsewhere, rents on the Angleseys' properties in cramped Back Lane and unfashionable St Nicholas Street ranged from a yearly £4 to £8.[10]

Once impressive premises were colonized by the indigent. One of the most striking was Cork House, centrally located near the Castle. The owner, Lord Cork, briefly revived the grand establishment when he was in Dublin to attend parliament and council in 1662–3. Thereafter, he had fewer reasons to be in the capital and, when need arose, could lodge with relations. Tenants were sought for Cork House. In 1669, Sir William Petty contemplated leasing it for £90 p.a, but in the end jibbed at paying the £100 demanded by the earl. Instead, the house, 'wonderfully gone to ruin', was divided among sundry traders.[11] Cork's younger brother, Orrery, without a permanent Dublin residence, but needing to be there immediately after Charles II's restoration, rented. In 1662, he took Thomas Court House from Lord Meath at a hefty annual rent of £300. Orrery was obliged to leave Meath free to use the great hall of the house in order to administer his liberty on the edge of the city.[12] The decline of once splendid houses, the building of replacements, and the quests for commodious lodgings and for profit remained constants of the Dublin scene.

Another prestigious property to slip from favour belonged to the Fownes family. Sir William Fownes was heavily involved in the corporate and institutional life of late-seventeenth-century Dublin.[13] His eminence was tellingly embodied in the 'Great House', near College Green. Residential fashions were altering. Soon, the Fownes tired of the city and favoured the salubrious suburb of Islandbridge and their County Kilkenny estate of Woodstock. The 'Great House' was let to a succession of tenants, of declining standing: a judge; the widow of a don at Trinity College; and – most sensationally – to Madame Violante, a famous rope-dancer, who performed there.[14] Its situation, once its charm, put off the important and affluent. By 1735, it was proposed to split the house, hemmed in with new buildings and disturbed by noisy schoolboys, into three units, and charge a total rent of £70.[15] Beset with the difficulties of finding satisfactory tenants, William Fownes's heir was warned, 'you will find . . . an estate in houses is the worst estate in the world'.[16] Not all agreed. New developments could enrich – not just entrepreneurs but also long-established landlords. The Hatches, overseeing the Dublin interests of the absent Temples, sponsored fresh schemes. No longer need the Temples worry that their down-at-heel premises, such as *The Cherry Tree*, functioned as a brothel. Fields were disappearing before rows of 'little villas', as at suburban Rathmines, which, so Henry Hatch boasted, 'is a pretty distance [from the city] for that use'.[17]

Although much was built, prospective tenants still grumbled about rents and facilities.[18] In 1677, Petty, probably the richest commoner in Ireland, bewailed the lack of a suitable house for himself and his family. He had earlier hoped to pay no more than £50 or £60 yearly. He compromised with a property that he hoped to improve. In particular, the pleasures of the garden could offset the inadequacies of the house itself. Also, like other husbands, he paid close attention to the needs and preferences of his wife and children. Often women insisted on greater comfort and convenience.[19] Few could afford to be as choosy as the Pettys. Their acquaintance, Robert Wood, like Petty a secretary to Lord Deputy Henry Cromwell during the 1650s, remained in Dublin as a schoolmaster after Charles II's return. Wood decided to take a property in the latest development of Smithfield. There a 'very neat convenient house' could be had for £41 p.a.[20] In London at the same time, speculative housing was also multi-plying. Some London houses might be rented for as little as £20 annually, but others rose to £40 or £60.[21] Dublin prices, when coupled with the other costs of living, meant – as will be seen – that many felt it was as chargeable to be there as in London. Economies were never-theless possible. At the end of the seventeenth century, the accountant-general James Bon-nell, although well-to-do, contented himself with a house in Strand Street, near the river, for which he paid a yearly £15.[22] Nearby was better-favoured Capel Street where dwelt Bonnell's kinsfolk, the Conollys, soon to be the successors of the Pettys as the wealthiest commoners in the kingdom. In 1730, modest premises in Capel Street were let at £29, £23 and £22 annually.[23] One was taken for a short term by a revenue collector from Belfast.[24] Richard Edgeworth, a squire from the Midlands, inherited premises in Capel Street. During the 1720s, while unmar-ried and training for the bar, he had no need of such a spacious house and so let it for £24 18s. yearly. He made do with lodgings, the cost of which equalled the rental income.[25] By the middle of the eighteenth century, it was assumed that a house in Dublin fit for the respectable could be had for £25 p.a.[26]

Meanwhile, perceptions sharpened as to what was suitable for whom. Dublin, despite its increasing size and population, remained intimate. Physical zoning according to rank and wealth of the inhabitants developed jerkily. More spacious accommodation on the fringes of the overcrowded centre and suburban settlements close to the sea beguiled some.[27] At the heart, offices, lodging houses, workshops, stables and shops nudged the houses of the impor-tant. Caesar Williamson, a quondam fellow of Trinity College, moved into scruffy quarters. The presence of a butcher's shop below his chamber, the hanging of washing in his patch of garden, and the racket from children all troubled him.[28]

The corporation in leasing its properties on College Green in 1747 differentiated 'good new' houses from the small, old and rickety. Annual rents in this prime location ranged from £28 to £12. Most tenants were tradespeople, such as a saddler, tailor and jeweller.[29] A few hung on in streets from which the tide of fashion had receded. Bishop Edward Synge persisted in living in Kevin Street, close to St Patrick's cathedral and Dublin Castle. The

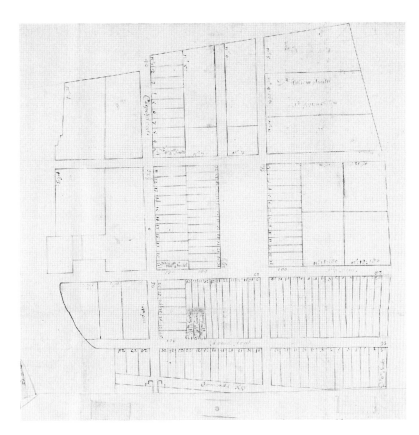

79. Plan of
Smithfield, Dublin,
1680. A development
on the north side of
the River Liffey that
attracted the
Smythes (later of
Barbavilla) and the
Taylors (later of
Headfort).

house was large, and the garden delighted him. However, he fretted over the disorders in the district, now largely deserted by those of his wealth and standing.[30] Some premises, either because of location or interior arrangements, were fit only for tradesmen or other inferiors. In 1721, a house lately occupied by a corporation notable was deemed appropriate as either coffee-house or lawyer's chamber.[31] At the start of George II's reign, a property in St Michan's parish, once occupied by Commissary Edward Butler, was transformed into a tavern. Walter Kennedy, living in part of the building, 'contrived a window by which he might get wine out of the tavern without going into it'.[32] By 1749, a property could be written off as in 'a very bad part of the town, such as [no] genteel person would reside in'. What was unacceptable to the genteel, nevertheless, was judged 'very fit for a tolerable tradesman'.[33] Part of the problem with this property was that it had only a narrow street frontage, although much space behind. Houses were now valued according to the width of their principal façades: a valuation also found in contemporary London.[34] In addition, the property had suffered from being divided between 'a pack of poor tradesmen'.[35] The same distinction between what might suffice for a tradesman and a gentleman was made explicitly in advertisements for houses to let as 'genteel' lodgings.[36] Numerous opportunists divided what they owned. In 1664, a house with eight hearths near St Patrick's cathedral was recorded as occupied by John Smith and his tenants.[37]

The available accommodation was severely strained at moments, such as the early 1660s and again after 1690, when the future settlement of the kingdom generated meetings of parliament, council and special commissions. The hopeful converged on Dublin. In 1697, with parliament in session, it was said that all lodgings in the city were full.[38] By 1700, house rents were alleged to have doubled in the previous two years. The increases were justified, in part, by improved design and workmanship. Sash windows had appeared: either an innovation introduced quickly from London or imported directly from the continent.[39] An official, arriving from England, was informed that a house on Arran Quay was available. Its remoteness from parliament was compensated by the good air and its closeness to the amenity of the bowling-green. Lord Limerick and Lord Mountjoy had recently chosen to lodge close to Oxmanton Green for the same reason. It was here, too, that Sir John Temple's heir stayed during the 1690s. The presence of a bishop in a nearby house was also considered a further draw, together with the local availability of stabling. No one mentioned one potential hazard of the area: the hounds giving tongue in the kennels in Phoenix Park.[40] The property, of two storeys with attics, was said to 'look fairly enough to the street for a Dublin house'. An alternative, more central in location, would be a house in the Aungier development of the 1670s. With two rooms to each floor and furnished except for linen, this could be Wyche's for £80 p.a. Alternatively, if he allowed the owner to retain the use of a chamber on the premises, the rent would drop to £70.[41]

In 1693, the younger John Evelyn arrived in Dublin to serve as a revenue commissioner: a job then worth £800 p.a. He shared the exacting standards of his cultivated parent, the diarist. Evelyn was startled by the expense of Dublin. In hired rooms, he felt gulled.[42] Soon, he rented his own house in Smithfield.[43] Not the least of its attractions was proximity to the Phoenix where the sickly Evelyn could ride. The house was soon filled with imported elegance. Musical evenings were staged. Also, Evelyn pottered in the garden.[44] Wyche and Evelyn, representing the English state in Ireland, may have exaggerated the importance of displaying their superiority by the way in which they lived. Visitors from England might insinuate elegance and comfort more tactfully. Temporary residents with their exacting standards were a godsend as tenants to properties that might otherwise be hard to let. At the end of William III's reign, a group of English officials brought to the city as special commissioners opted for the high style. They rented the modern mansion at Palmerston, just outside Dublin and overlooking the River Liffey, which the heirs of its builder, Sir John Temple, had vacated.[45] Soon it would be hired by another high office-holder, the judge and lord chancellor Sir Richard Cox.[46]

Office-holders strove to project a splendid figure. The trait was not unique to the immigrants from Britain. Denny Muschamp, a local and unabashed profiteer from the Williamite upheavals, searched for a better Dublin pad. Muschamp, the son-in-law of the primate and former lord chancellor, Michael Boyle, knew high society in both Ireland and England. In 1696, he inspected a house on the Aungier estate on offer at £400. Next he considered another property recently occupied by a judge. It, too, was available complete with contents, 'according to the catalogue which Mr Curtis gave me'. Muschamp haggled, willing to pay no more than £300.[47] A connection by marriage of Muschamp, Archbishop John Vesey of Tuam, baulked at the cost of a permanent house in the capital. In 1703, Vesey, conscious of being a prince of the Church of Ireland and active in the upper house of parliament, proposed to take lodgings for himself and family.[48] Numerous grandees from the provinces opted for the same course. New arrivals in town might take a chamber in an inn for a night or two; rooms in lodging houses by the week; or engage lodgings for a month or more. Others dossed down with relations and acquaintances. Unplanned, even enforced hospitality obliged householders to arrange rooms and furniture flexibly. Beds had to be set up and palliasses shaken out wherever there was room for the unexpected guest.

## II

Depending on funds and mood, Dublin – like London – delighted or appalled. Observers repeatedly compared the splendour of life there with the torpor or poverty of its hinterlands. A cleric just disembarked from England in 1703, was stunned by Dublin. However, he observed, 'if one was to live only in town, he would think we were the richest nation in the world'. He believed that the nobility and gentry would not be able long to sustain their show. Similar feelings led another to contend that those living in the capital, 'and have not seen the country, can scarce give credit to the monstrous barbarity of all parts of the country distant from them'.[49] Moralists and sensationalists warned of the hazards. All agreed about the expense. The methodical tried to quantify just what sums might be needed. Catherine O'Brien, contemplating retirement from London to Dublin for a winter, calculated that she would save £50 at most. Much more economical would be a spell in her box in distant County Clare.[50] Shortly before this, the archbishop of Dublin had averred that life in Dublin cost more than in London. In doing so, he was making a political point about how recent English laws had damaged the Irish economy and raised prices.[51]

In 1743, a judge recently arrived from England averred that it was a snare to assume that provisions were cheaper in Dublin than in London. House rents hardly differed and clothing was generally dearer, since the smart wore imported fabrics.[52] Within the capital, spending could clearly be adjusted to meet circumstances. However, cheeseparing was inimical to those for whom a stay in the city was inseparable from exhibiting and (they hoped) increasing their importance. Squires, especially if about to be or newly married, did not stint. Pole Cosby from Stradbally wintered in Dublin during 1739. He rented an entire house on Arran Quay for six months for £55. Its distance from the thronged centre where the Cosbys had lodged earlier may have indicated retrenchment. Otherwise, Squire Cosby saw to it that his party 'lived very handsomely'. He noted, 'we bought a great number of fine things, both for ourselves and the house'. He spent £80 on a coach, and maintained five liveried servants in addition to his own man. All was not indulgence. During the stay, his children's education was furthered. A daughter, for example, was taught to dance, sing and write.[53] Cosby, and so many others who established themselves briefly and expensively in the capital, relished its amusements and services. Dublin offered a diversity otherwise not available nearer than Bath or London.

Marriage justified lavish arrangements when provincials, like Cosby, Richard Edgeworth or Robert French, came to town. As bachelors, these same individuals, made do with lodgings. Preparing for a career or gasping for their inheritance, they restrained themselves. Edgeworth while a law student received an allowance of £60 p.a., from which he gave £20 to his sister for his accommodation and diet.[54]

Table 5.  Richard Edgeworth's expenses, 1721

| | |
|---|---:|
| Diet and lodging | £20 0s. 0d. |
| Clothes, books, 'necessaries' | £25 17s. 1d. |
| 'Pocket expenses' | £13 13s. 9d. |
| Total | £59 10s. 10d. |

In the capital, an overwhelmingly masculine society welcomed – and exploited – the unencumbered. A 'bagnio' catered to the unattached. Not, seemingly, a sleazy massage parlour, it may have prefigured the Turkish baths located on the quays later in the century and soothed the weary male.[55] Many meals were eaten in taverns, already developing a trade in food as well as in drink. Others were served in digs by the landlady's servants. After Christmas in 1723, the bachelor Edgeworth gave a supper party in his lodgings at which wine and rum were drunk, and for which he paid £1: the equivalent of what he normally paid for accommodation and diet for a fortnight.[56] Sir Thomas Vesey, the bishop of Ossory, forced from his country seat to the capital for the parliamentary session, entertained small numbers of friends over wine in his rooms.[57] Numerous other expenses mounted: for washing, the barber, entertainment, clothes. One visitor agreed with a barber to shave him three times weekly and to dress his wigs for a charge of one shilling.[58]

Dublin afforded single men with coin in their pockets (and indeed many married men) a richer selection of sociable rituals than did any country town. In 1684, an army officer from Connacht needing to be in Dublin was entertained by grand connections: sometimes in private houses, but also in taverns such as *The Rose*, *The Garter* and *The Feathers*.[59] By the late 1730s, Edgeworth, now a husband and father, in Dublin for meetings of parliament or other business, did not always keep the company of his young family. He still escaped to *The Rose* tavern, where former colleagues at the bar assembled regularly. Further sociability flowed when he met other members of parliament from his region. They coordinated coming measures in the House of Commons over dinner in hostelries.[60] In addition, Edgeworth was bidden to the entertainments of the important, such as the Speaker, lord chancellor, lord-lieutenant and the dowager countess of Kildare. Invitations from the grandees supplemented the constant visits between kindred, acquaintances and associates. Edgeworth's withdrawal from parliament after 1760 meant fewer invitations from the politically powerful.[61] Age, together with his responsibilities as a widower for his children, seems also to have ended his habit of dining with acquaintances and colleagues in Dublin inns. Hectic hospitality was widely regarded as a feature of the city. In 1763, an army officer disclosed, 'I have been but once in a tavern since we came here. We have always been feasting. I may say the people here keep great tables as ever I met with.' The largesse had its price. The officer complained that he was 'almost killed' by the plenty.[62] In addition, there were hidden expenses: vails for servants; wagers; hire of sedan chairs; and the need to shimmer.

The formal work of parliament, semi-state boards, corporations, guilds, vestries and the many voluntary bodies spilled over from official venues, such as the Parliament House, its committee rooms and the halls of the craft guilds. Sometimes colleagues met in private houses; coffee-houses were patronized too.[63] More commonly, inns were used. Dublin excelled all other places in Ireland in its tally of taverns, which ranged from the plush to dingy dives. In 1667, there were said to be 1,500 in the city.[64] The simpler ones provided tobacco and pipes (imported from Bristol); the more sophisticated, board games such as chess and draughts. Décor could be elaborate, and even themed.[65] Army officers were habituated to eating in public houses. Publicans competed fiercely for this profitable custom by selling viands. In 1742, Charles Carline, just removed from *The Prince of Wales* to *The Plume of Feathers* in Castle Street, tempted 'gentlemen' with 'the best of wines and nicest eating at reasonable rates'. Two or three dishes of meat would be on offer daily between 2 p.m. and 3 p.m.[66] In 1756, it was possible in Dublin to dine at the 'four-penny ordinary'.[67] By 1761, William Alcock, a squire from County Waterford, up in town, ate at the Chop House.[68] Tavern-keepers prepared food to be consumed off the premises. Edgeworth while in Dublin during 1759 had veal cutlets sent round to his lodgings. His son, when an undergraduate at Trinity College, ran up a bill with Martin Dillon, innkeeper, of £8 10s. 7½d. for victuals and wine carried to his college chamber.[69] These services recalled and surpassed Edgeworth's earlier patronage of the 'tart house' near Trinity College when in Dublin during the 1720s.[70] (It was apparently not a euphemism for a bordello, but the establishment of an expert pastry cook.) Strangers risked being tricked. In 1735, one visitor from Anglesey paid 3½d. for a little bread 'in a dirty eating house'.[71]

Business was often transacted in inns. Solid as well as liquid refreshments were supplied. So, too, were paper, ink and reading matter.[72] Committees which ran guilds, parishes and even the municipal corporation repaired to them.[73] Members of Dublin corporation over-seeing improvements to the harbour at Ringsend made this work a pretext for several excursions to the seaside. Five coaches ferried the party to *The Rose* near the quay. Matters were forwarded over a shoulder of mutton, ample libations of beer and wine, and tobacco. A week later the committee reconvened by the waterside. This time the worthies chose *The Exchequer*. Again five coaches were required. With fish, rabbits, beef, turkeys and ducks in addition to mutton, the fare was more festive, and the bill treble what had been spent on the previous outing. Subsequently these municipal worthies patronized *The Fleece* (twice) before returning to *The Rose* for a final working dinner of sausages, veal steaks, lamb fricasséed with oysters, chicken and mushrooms, salmon, venison and cheese.[74] The seaside setting had already established itself for boozy gatherings, ostensibly for business. Late in the 1670s grand jurors had assembled there to forward the work of the Irish admiralty court, assisted by dinner and drink.[75]

A sparse supply of public rooms obliged sundry groups to use the cheerful spaces in inns and coffee-houses. The functionaries of the Dublin parish of St Catherine's were accused of deciding the distribution of church pews in a local alehouse.[76] In 1684, Lord Meath's agent treated Dublin butchers at *The George* in a bid to persuade them to transfer their trade from the north side to Meath's new market. The host was mortified when the butchers insisted on drinking expensive sack rather than the expected (and cheaper) pot of ale.[77] Until a Linen Hall was built in the 1720s, cloth was bought and sold in the taverns of Thomas Street.[78] Howell Ellis was one among many men of the law who briefed attorneys and lawyers in Dublin inns. There, too, he purchased gold rings.[79] Another with negotiations to conclude joked how 'we dined at his expense at the tavern (for agents and slaves are always treated by masters and lords)'. The business finished, 'we sat very merrily from that time (viz. 4 after dinner) till 11, and no more business talked of'.[80] Members of masonic lodges, proliferating in Dublin from the 1720s, also assembled in inns.[81] Even the son – and evil genius – of Lord Lieutenant Dorset discussed political strategy in a tavern.[82]

A sense of what these premises afforded comes from *The Blackamoor's Head*, off the main street in St Michan's parish. It consisted of a large parlour, the windows of which looked into the principal thoroughfare, a second 'long' room, the kitchen, 'some drinking boxes that ran by the side of the kitchen', and then, beyond the kitchen, more private rooms which could be used by guests. The last presumably were the sorts of spaces in which the respectable would conclude deals rather than illicit liaisons.[83] Commodious premises offered bed as well as board. In 1727, the 'great inn' in Smithfield, *Tom of Lincoln*, advertised well-furnished lodgings for 5d. per night.[84] This might satisfy visitors for a short spell, especially when servants could be accommodated close by in cheaper rooms. In the 1760s, a squire and his son from Meath lodged at *The Raven* in Smithfield. If not bidden to dine with acquaintances and relations around the town, they also ate there.[85] The frequency with which individuals entered such establishments depended on gender, rank, income and stage in their lives. By the mid-eighteenth century, the provinces also abounded with 'carriers' inns' at which servants and their economical masters might stay.[86] A 'shebeen house' was to be distinguished from the more respectable alehouse in which courts leet and courts baron were held.[87]

Women, when travelling, were baited in inns, but seem not to have stayed in them in Dublin, except perhaps *in extremis.* Otherwise, women joined the Dublin scuffle. Wives sometimes prodded their spouses into metropolitan excursions, as in the cases of Edgeworth and French. Widows faced greater difficulties. Usually their income dropped and their circuits narrowed. Katherine Conolly, with £5,000 p.a. and houses in the city and country, was altogether exceptional. Her contemporary, Elinor O'Hara, widowed in 1719, alternated between County Sligo, her own kinsfolk at Thomastown in County Tipperary, Dublin and – perhaps to recover her declining health – Bristol and Bath. For Mrs O'Hara, Dublin meant regular losses at card parties, rarer forays to plays and musical concerts, measured donations to the poor and relentless shopping. The Widow O'Hara exhibited some of the same profligacy which seemed hereditary among the male members of the family. Coming herself from a dynasty – the Mathews – which could claim close kinship with the ducal house of Ormonde, she was part of a select company. She liked to impress. Accordingly she thought little of spending £60 on a repeating watch, £33 for a diamond buckle and an astonishing £100 to buy a set of stay buckles, set presumably with diamonds.[88] Dublin life was not cheaply bought by the likes of Mrs O'Hara. She calculated her keep in the capital for one period of twenty-eight weeks at £24 19s. 8¼d., lodgings at £13 3s. 6¼d., and the wages of a single man servant at £1 13s. 4d. Another, shorter spell in 1722 – of nineteen weeks – was thought to have cost £26 for basics of food and lodging.

More indicative of the self-effacement into which the widowed were – willy-nilly – forced was Mrs Conolly's sister, Mary Jones. She engaged her lodgings – in Great Britain Street, opposite *The London Apprentice* and not far from Katherine Conolly's luxurious establishment – by the year. There were other female lodgers in the place. Mary Jones gave up her maid, but retained a manservant. Washing she sent out to a former employee, and when unwell she engaged a 'nurse keeper'. Transport was arranged as needed. Mary Jones had been left an annuity of £200 by her husband, once a member of parliament.[89] Obviously this raised her far above the level of those having to subsist on £5 or £10 p.a. Also, she was subsidized, discreetly but sometimes humiliatingly, by her rich sister.

Other widows made similar adjustments. Elizabeth van Leuwen, relict of one of Dublin's leading physicians, was hustled off to the country when it was discovered that her husband had left little.[90] So, too, was Frances Crofton, ill-provided for in the will of her spouse. Mrs Crofton was told plainly by her eldest son that Dublin was an unsuitable place for her to live. On grounds of economy and in hopes of finding respectable supplements for her and her unmarried daughters, she was instructed to settle in a small town. Jean Mussenden, once widowed, tried various strategies to manage on the annual allowance of £50 granted by a more fortunate brother. In 1712, she took lodgings in the capital, and insisted that she did not live 'extravagantly, but as private as any one'.[91] Far from living 'handsomely' on this income, she was forced to pawn possessions to raise money. She could not decide whether it was more economical to engage lodgings by the year or keep house on her own account. Her brothers advised her to remove to the cheaper surroundings of Derry or Lisburn rather than remain in Dublin.[92] Mrs Mussenden, notwithstanding her problems, managed to travel to London and into Westmeath, where 'we live very great and the great greatest plenty I did ever see in my life'.[93] In the end, the constant shifting between locations led a brother to admonish her to 'fix somewhere and not be in perpetual travelling to no purpose'.[94]

Agnes Hamilton, when widowed, decided to quit her Tyrone house of Caledon for quarters in Dublin. One attraction was the presence of her two widowed sisters; another was the wish to further the education and then to arrange the marriage of a daughter and niece. During the previous thirty years, she had frequently visited the capital. Moreover, she had numerous acquaintances and relations there, so would not want for a congenial circle.[95] Katherine Howard, another relict of a successful doctor, escaped provincial exile. She seems to have enjoyed an annuity of £100. Mrs Howard let the Ship Street property which she had inherited for £36 p.a. and took lodgings at *The London Warehouse* in St Bride Street for £20 p.a.[96] Her new apartment consisted of three rooms on the first floor, 'a very good kitchen and cellar', and a pair of garrets. Once settled in, she professed herself delighted with 'the prettiest, clean, convenient lodgings in the whole city'. She furnished the apartment 'with my best things', selling 'the lumber', but not for the moment disposing of the rest, 'for they give nothing for old goods'.[97] The landlord and his wife added to the attractions of the new quarters. Katherine Howard found them, 'extreme quiet, civil people and as well pleased with me as I with them'. The couple travelled to London where they undertook commissions for their lodger. At first the widow confided that she was lonely in the evenings. Her son, studying law in London and similarly afflicted, was advised to keep a cat. The closeness to the church meant that she was saved from having to hire sedan chairs to carry her to services. As a widow with an adequate income, she savoured the sensations of the town. Although she attended public entertainments, such as concerts by the castrato Nicolini in 1711, family remained her prime focus and source of gossip.[98]

Women, heading households, either temporarily or permanently, acquired considerable power within Dublin society. Katherine Howard scaled down her establishment once widowed, but, thanks to her income, took firm control of her own affairs. Lady Arbella Denny was perhaps the most striking instance in the mid-eighteenth century. She dictated imperiously to relations and strangers alike how they should behave. Giddy kinswomen and the slapdash superintendent at the Dublin Foundling Hospital were lashed by her tongue.[99] She helped to popularize the seaside around Dublin Bay. Although she maintained two houses, she regretted that they were not bigger so that she could discharge all her familial obligations.[100] Relatively free to follow her own inclinations, thanks to status – the daughter of an earl and the widow of a member of parliament – she forthrightly expressed herself on such questions as comfort, hygiene, decorum and privacy. Anne Weldon as the daughter and heiress of a Dublin luminary also possessed the standing and means to participate fully in what the capital offered. She disliked the 'smoke and hurry' of Dublin, but conquered it sufficiently to spend long periods there in the 1760s. Links with family and others of similar standing supplied much of Mrs Weldon's company. In the absence of her husband, she organized the schooling of children and trips to the northern suburb of Clontarf, 'for them to bathe in the sea'.[101]

Women were thought to have special needs in housing. So Archbishop King supposed, as he hunted for suitable accommodation for the daughter of an old friend and colleague, Bishop Samuel Foley. The merits of an apartment of two first-floor rooms in the house of a clergyman's wife, 'a grave woman', in Bride Street included the absence of men from the house. Also, the lodgings, to be had for £25 yearly, were close to a new church – the same used by Mrs Howard.[102] Such apartments sometimes involved intimacies from which the sensitive shrank. Mrs Echlin fled from her lodgings after one night, 'there being a lodger over head who made a noise'.[103] Only the well-to-do could indulge these scruples. Most had less freedom to choose. In the early eighteenth century, Stephen Green had a central Dublin house in which ten tenants roomed. The two who leased cellars probably did not inhabit them but used them for storage. Among the lodgers were Mrs Reyna, with a chamber for which she paid £5 p.a., Mrs Owens, paying £3 yearly, and Mrs Vicars, who had one of the upper rooms overlooking the street at an annual rent of £3 5s. These tenants paid by the quarter, and were expected to give a month's notice of departure. Green's premises were a warren, in which both men and women dwelt. The back parlour was rented weekly, first by Mr Wordsworth at 2s. 1d. and then by a Mr Semple for one penny more. Mr Gavan was in the garret facing onto the street, at 11s. 6d. per quarter; in another garret was the tailor, Kardiff, paying £2 12s. p.a. In a back room lurked Gustavus McCance, finding £3 yearly. The most expensive accommodation was occupied by one McNamara. He had a first-floor room, looking over the street, together with the back kitchen. This cost an annual £6. Whether Green, the landlord, lived in the house is unknown.[104] Another lodging-house keeper, a tallow-chandler, Simon Todd, did reside with his family on the spot. During 1742, Todd shared his house on George's Quay with a retired boatman, once in the crew of the yacht which plied between Dublin and England, Mrs Elizabeth Ridley, and Thomas Keightley who, with his family, had arrived from England to work as the gardener at Powerscourt House.[105]

## III

Lucky householders with space to spare supplemented the household budget. In some cases, the need to add to exiguous earnings may have made them squeeze into a narrower compass than was comfortable. Living hugger-mugger, privacy was impossible. Tenants, in order to secure a room with a few tokens of respectability, must pay at least £2 p.a. Room rent in Dublin frequently exceeded this minimum, often by a considerable margin. Early in the 1760s, Charles O'Hara estimated that a country labourer could survive on £5 8s. 6½d. Almost a century before, Petty reckoned that a craftworker could earn £26 in a year. By 1749, £25 was cited as the cost of a respectable Dublin house.[106] Among the poorer sort, accommodation was likely to take at the very least 10 per cent of this wage. Indeed, the parlous condition of textile workers in the Dublin Liberties, 'pent up in single rooms with their whole families', by the 1750s was traced to the extortionate rents with which they were saddled.[107] In comparison, the prosperous, such as a French or Edgeworth, comfortable on yearly incomes from £800 to £1,500, were not burdened greatly by the costs of housing. Annual rents consumed maybe 2 or 3 per cent of their incomes. To the hire of houses had then to be added city dues like ministers' and lamp money and periodic cesses for parish expenses. More onerous were the requirements of fashionable establishments: elegant furnishings, servants and provisions. Then, too, the frenzy of commercialized fun could run away with funds. One resident planned how he 'could get out of Dublin from among my acquaintances, &c. and a place I am so well known in'. He schemed for a location where 'I could live more private and agreeable with my family'.[108]

If the straitened plotted escape from an expensive city, provincials dreamt of plunges into the Dublin season. This is better documented among notables who came for business and pleasure than among the immigrants desperate for a livelihood. The Cosbys of Stradbally, squires from the countryside, luxuriated in the metropolis, but had then to retrench with a spell in Bristol.[109] Dudley Cosby rented a furnished house on St Stephen's Green for six months during the winter of 1725. It cost £50. The purpose was to find a bride for the heir, Pole Cosby. The latter candidly confessed, 'so we, my f[ather], m[other] & sister went up to try and get a wife for me'. Once an acceptable partner was identified, the intending groom took 'handsome lodgings' in Capel Street. The parent, in preparation for his son's nuptials, also shifted across the river. He engaged another furnished house in Abbey Street at £10 monthly.[110] Five years later, the younger Cosby, now married and possessed of his estate, would return to Dublin for an extended visit.[111]

Another heir to a squire, John Pratt of Agher in County Meath, alighted in Dublin twice in 1745 and 1746. On the first trip, which lasted a month, Pratt stayed with relations.[112] Having recently been commissioned and mustered in the militia – the civilian response to the Jacobite uprising of 1745 – he paraded in his regimentals at a Dublin assembly the following winter. This was more decorous than the evening when he, in company with other officers, had drunk in a Meath hostelry 'to be sick'.[113] Pratt's month in the metropolis included hectic theatregoing. He saw at least four plays and attended two musical concerts.[114] He dined around the town, mainly in the ready-made society of his hosts and his family's kindred and acquaintances. He shopped enthusiastically. He bought clothes for himself and jewellery as presents for the people at home in Agher. A more serious side was shown when he purchased a tract on the sacraments, which he dutifully gave to his host on departure. The whole Dublin expedition cost £35 17s. 6d. Not having to pay for accommodation, Pratt could perhaps spend more freely. His second visit was more obviously linked with business. The main purpose was to sign his articles to be taken into training as a barrister. Dublin as yet lacked any institution devoted to legal education, so, in preparation for the obligatory spell at one of the London Inns, schemes of apprenticeship developed. The occasion was turned into a convivial one, of a type common in Dublin. It took place at *The Rose*, not in chambers. Pratt's bill for his share of the treat amounted to a hefty 13s.[115]

County Meath itself did not lack conviviality, much of it conducted in private houses, but sometimes *al fresco* and in taverns. Pratt, during his second Dublin stay, was taken by a friend from Meath to the latter's club, McClaughlin's. This, like the gathering of fellow professionals, was an amenity not to be found outside the city. Nor were such frequent and varied plays and assemblies. The same was true of shopping. Pratt bought clothes in his neighbourhood and sometimes had cloth tailored by a local. Yet, greater choice was to be found in Dublin. Not all were bewitched. Nicholas Peacock travelled from County Limerick twice in the 1740s. He came with the family which he served as agent and to which he was related. Peacock, unimpressed by Dublin, grumbled that he had bought only shoe buckles and a watch.[116]

Pratt was lucky to have connections in Dublin with whom he could lodge. Hospitality was frequently offered. Not to accept invitations, especially if they were tendered by agents and employees to their betters, caused offence. Mrs Esther Kingsbury, the widow of an eminent Dublin doctor, was mortified to learn that the son of the Welsh family for whom she and her husband had acted, had visited Dublin but not stayed with her.[117] Sir Cyril Wyche had also been importuned to confer favour on his Dublin agent by lodging with him.[118] Such invitations created obligations – as they were intended to. In the close confines of often crowded dwellings, quarrels erupted. A young woman, up from Mayo, frustrated by lack of money, railed against the relations with whom she was boarding. 'God forgive me, I hate them all, the dirty crew, from top to bottom'.[119]

Many visitors to Dublin found rooms for themselves. Billets might be advertised by a bill nailed to a door or in the newspapers.[120] Word of mouth recommended others. Accurate information about decent lodgings, in common with suggestions for servants and tutors, was greatly valued. In 1677, Ormond's secretary depended on another functionary already in the city to weigh up the relative attractions of different rooms.[121] So, too, more than fifty years later did Henry Boyle, the political leader of the Protestants of south Munster. Boyle, despite his importance in parliament, had neither the means nor the inclination to stay longer than he needed in Dublin. Architectural display was reserved for his own estate in County Cork. However, he needed a suitable base in the capital. In 1731, he was told of a house on Ormond Quay. It boasted a large dining room, important when so much business was transacted over the débris of the dinner table, a parlour, and a bedchamber with closet on the entrance floor. Upstairs were found another two bedrooms, with their closets and a dressing room. Above these were a panelled bedchamber supplied with its own closet and another room overlooking the (noisy?) street. Two attics were furnished with beds for the servants. The property was also well provided with offices: two kitchens, with piped water, two pantries, a wine cellar, stabling for six to ten horses, a coach house and a hundred loads of hay.[122]

Boyle was lucky to have an acquaintance willing to inspect possible Dublin quarters. In contrast, Major Henry Crofton rode up from the country to Dublin with his wife and two servants. The major lodged at an inn in Capel Street, and then scouted around for lodgings for the whole party.[123] In 1727, Samuel Waring found a house, ready furnished and close to Trinity College, 'after a deal of difficulty and consultations'.[124] Usually visitors of substance from the provinces had kindred and acquaintances in Dublin to whom they could turn, if not for temporary berths, then for advice.[125] The agent of the Maxwells of Finnebrogue (County Down) secured at auction the lease of a Dublin house (in Henry Street) for his employers.[126] The Smythes from Westmeath illustrate the problems of finding adequate accommodation in the city. The father of William Smythe of Barbavilla had taken a house in the original Jervis development of Smithfield early in the 1680s.[127] By the 1730s, that property had been abandoned, perhaps because no longer considered fit for the Smythes.[128] Squire Smythe resembled many of his social and economic level in liking or having to be in Dublin from time to time.[129] In 1735, he intended to bring up a party of three family members and a trio of servants. He was informed that a whole house could be rented for three months, at £10 per month. The rent included stabling for four horses and all wants except linen. First a friend went to look; then the friend's mother inspected the premises. She, 'not liking the window curtains in the parlour and dining room', demanded better. Even after these changes, the Smythes rejected the house.[130] Two years later, Smythe asked three women to find him a rented house. The best prospect seemed a house next door to one which the Smythes had previously hired, available at a weekly rate of £2 10s.[131] Just as women influenced the decision to take a Dublin house, so too their value in assessing accommodation and haggling over the price was widely appreciated. Indeed, in 1711, Archbishop King, looking for Dublin digs for a female dependant, confided, 'I will employ some woman to make the bargain, who may be more proper to beat the price than I can be.'[132]

Not even female forthrightness could reverse the trends of a growing and more affluent population which were inflating Dublin rents. Although Dublin resounded to new building,

80. Joseph Tudor, *A prospect of the city of Dublin*, 1753. In the half century since Place's panorama, the expansion of the city and the increase in churches and ambitious buildings were clear.

scarcity continued. About 1730, eleven new houses in Ann Street, between St Stephen's Green and Trinity College, had been snapped up immediately. The ground rents were low; they were available on leases for lives renewable for ever. Each consisted of four and a half storeys, which contained ten rooms and three closets. Rent of £30 p.a. was asked, but it was thought that the owner might settle for £26.[133] More than twenty years later, houses in the same vicinity were being 'taken by gentlemen and finished to their fancy'. Demand was so brisk that all had been let by Michaelmas of the same year.[134] In 1754, William Smythe was warned, 'no sooner a foundation . . . is laid but it is set, unless it be to wait for a greater offer', and he agreed that accommodation had become 'extravagantly dear'. Others suspected that the market was more volatile, especially during the alternate winters when parliament did not sit.[135] One consequence of the seemingly insatiable demand was that the Smythes' friends and agents in Dublin had to hunt for lodgings even more feverishly, 'every time they are wanted'. In 1751, Mary Ledwidge, who interviewed prospective servants and searched specialist shops on the Smythes' behalf, trudged around the possible addresses. Mary Ledwidge recommended a property opposite that of the Smythes' friend, John Digby of Landenstown. It possessed 'a good dining room and bed chamber'. The garrets, however, lacked fireplaces, and other rooms were partitioned. The landlady, Mrs Baker, claimed to have a good table-bed which she would set up in one of the rooms. In addition, she could provide china, tea-kettle and coffee-pot, but not cutlery, glass or linen. She required two pistoles a week (36s. 6d.).[136] Mary Ledwidge countered with an offer of thirty-five shillings. Alternative rooms were to be had at the same rent. In these, too, the shortage of beds led to a promise to put up temporary ones. A servant would be supplied to prepare the meat for table, but not china, knives, glasses or linen.[137]

Matters worsened. The next year, Mary Ledwidge trailed from end to end of Jervis Street, St Mary's Street and Abbey Street. All she found was a small house owned by an upholsterer in Capel Street. It had no coach house, would cost £3 weekly, and had to be taken for a minimum of three months. Savage, a second decorator and upholsterer in Capel Street, offered another house. Savage's had two parlours, its own dining room and a bedchamber, garrets, coach houses and stable. Mrs Ledwidge noticed, however, that the bed resembled 'a tent': not praise in her parlance. Yet another upholder, Moore, was prepared to let an entire house, which boasted 'a good handsome back parlour, salooned', for a weekly £2 10s. None of these landlords offered servants, kitchen equipment, cutlery, glass or linen. In the end, Mrs Ledwidge recommended one option as a 'much handsomer and cleverer house than Mr Savage's'.[138]

Other Dublin associates of Smythe pitched in with suggestions. Thomas Burgh from Oldtown in County Kildare, the son of the former surveyor-general, himself rented a house in Nassau Street near Trinity College for £80 p.a.[139] Burgh reported to Smythe on a small house in the recent north-side development of Sackville Street, close to the locale favoured by the Smythes. For the property, which had only two rooms on each floor, the builder demanded a down payment of £300 and an annual rent of £60. An alternative for the Smythes was an older property in the same area. The owner aimed to cash in on the boom by removing to the country and letting the central premises. His terms were said to be an entry fine of £140 and a yearly rent of £23. The house had only a pair of rooms on each floor. However, its attractions numbered a back parlour 'salooned' and so fitted for entertaining, good kitchens and yard, a 'pretty' garden, coach house, loft (where hay could be stored and the coachman might sleep) and stabling for four horses. Another draw was its proximity to the new St George's church, as well as to the older place of worship used by the Smythes when in town, St Mary's.[140] Smythe's cousin, an exacting judge, declared the property to be suitable and very cheap, 'considering how the value of houses are at present'.[141]

Buoyant demand for accommodation favoured Dubliners. Long-standing residents dreamt of cashing in. One greedy owner hoped to extort a fine of £600 and a high rent, 'as if all the inhabitants of the kingdom were coming to live here'. Nicholas Ogle had a house in Aungier Street, for which he paid £40 p.a. He had made the garden and built a coach house and stable. In 1753, he hoped to sell the remaining nineteen years of his lease for £200 and charge an annual rent of £60.[142] Mercenary motives seconded other imperatives. Edgeworth, like Smythe, chose to let a house in Capel Street that he had inherited and instead rent something at the better-favoured address of Grafton Street. Edgeworth paid an annual rent of £31. When, in 1744, he decided that the welfare of his family required removal to Bath, he sub-let the house at a yearly £40.[143] The modest profit hardly compensated for the inconvenience of having to engage lodgings when Edgeworth returned to Dublin. He posted between rooms in streets close to Grafton Street.[144] During the winter of 1755–6, when private and public affairs demanded his presence in the capital, Edgeworth was obliged to take a furnished house on the north side of the river, in Capel Street. It cost him £80 for seven months. To this was added the expense of extra stabling at *The Boot* inn.[145] Late in his life, Edgeworth, now a widower, was content with lodgings in York Street – back on the south side – with a landlady whom he knew of old. Again to a basic £12 for a stay of eight weeks had then to be added wages for the landlady's servant who prepared meals for Edgeworth.[146]

As provincials crowded into central quarters, sophisticates fled to the suburbs. The idea was gaining ground, planted by medical pundits and dealers in real estate, that living in the outskirts or by the sea helped health.[147] Wholesomeness was to be had on the edges of the city; even so, the smart and not so smart still preferred to be at the heart. Many grumbled about the trickery of landlords and the general expense and artificiality of the metropolis. Yet, while they repined, they scrimped and saved for a short draught of the elixir.[148] The attractive power of Dublin continued unabated. The multiplicity of its functions and services helped to explain its appeal. Also, provincials had more to spend, and more chose to spend it in the capital. By the 1750s, returns from agriculture subsidized the extravagances of substantial proprietors. Patriots and the public-spirited might decry the indulgences of the feckless, but came themselves in greater numbers and more frequently to the city, as parliament opposed the schemes of Dorset and Primate Stone. Housing scaled new heights as a few peers, led by Kildare, Tyrone and Powerscourt, constructed free-standing *hôtels* in prominent positions. However, most in Dublin still shifted with more cramped arrangements. Even so, the expectations of mere squires and the middling sorts about accommodation and diversions were heightened thanks to travel, talk, print and seeing what others had. The worry in the Smythes' circle about 'salooned' apartments, and how they were equipped, told of anxieties about comfort and appearances. More were wanting to live 'very genteel'.[149]

## IV

Temporary sojourners complained monotonously about the strains of Dublin life. They grumbled about the hurry, the vanities and how 'that grand parade would confuse my head exceedingly'.[150] The provident economized by alternating between quiet stays in provincial towns, such as Enniscorthy, Mountmellick, New Ross and Portarlington, and the frenzy of metropolitan life. Heavy obligations were not always shed outside Dublin. In the 1670s, Lord

Broghill, spendthrift heir to the earl of Orrery, was delighted to end the expense of maintaining a house of his own. But Broghill, as deputy for his father in the presidency of Munster, had a public position and so needed to impress. He entered into a complicated contract. In Limerick, Mrs Porson agreed to provide for the baron, his family and their servants: thirteen in all. For this service, Mrs Porson would charge an annual £300, and the Broghills were to be served dinner and a hot supper of meat for themselves. Their attendants, however, were denied the hot supper. The agreement required Broghill to furnish the lodgings, provide fire and candle, have his own servants clean it and wash the family's bed and personal linen. The landlady employed the cook and butler, equipped the kitchen and supplied beer. Broghill found his own wine. If more guests came, each would incur an extra charge of a shilling for each at every meal. Finally, should Lady Broghill consume excessive amounts of sugar and spice (as fine ladies were wont), further surcharges would be levied.[151] The Broghills' elaborate establishment was unusual outside the capital. For most, life away from the capital was managed more modestly. Around 1680, it was calculated that a family in County Waterford could get by on £8 p.a. The fare was not exactly Lenten. On three days each week, boiled meats such as bacon, beef or other viands from the markets would be eaten. The remainder of the week saw a diet of milk, butter, cheese and other seasonal foods, including fresh fish.[152] A later assessment – of 1750 – also from Munster suggested how much cheaper was life in the Irish countryside than in London, but offered no information about Dublin prices. Most butcher's meat was said to cost half what it did in London, with pork only a third of the price. Salmon, sold in London for thirty shillings could be bought for one shilling in Ireland. Lobsters, in contrast, were only half the price. The main exceptions to the generally happy situation for those in Ireland were soap and bread, both of which were reckoned to cost the same in both kingdoms. The comparisons suggested the variety on offer to the prosperous in fertile districts, but nothing of the costs of staples for the majority of the population.[153] Keeping house involved more than payments for diet. Some, unequal to the burden, gave up and instead boarded, either in provincial obscurity or in the meaner streets of the capital.[154]

The pressures to display and spend, whether in city or countryside, were felt unevenly. Those in public positions and obliged to go into public places experienced the heaviest. For this reason, government functionaries were liable to particularly onerous obligations. Sir Cyril Wyche, when housed in Dublin Castle towards the end of the seventeenth century, faced alarming expenses. He spent £17 10s. tipping the many servants at the Castle in the new year of 1682.[155] These minions expected to be gratified on St Patrick's Day and other holidays.[156] Wyche complied reluctantly, acknowledging that, 'if such matters be omitted, there is no comfortable being for anybody here in such an employment'.[157] Later, as a lord justice, Wyche needed to entertain lavishly. In 1693, he spent £123 17s. 2d. on a single month's housekeeping.[158] Regular attendants on the viceroy felt obliged to dress and live more splendidly than a private person or a provincial. Army officers attached to the lord-lieutenant as aides-de-camp constantly grumbled at the expenses.[159] Reluctant courtiers blamed the conventions of the Castle for their financial problems. However, it was the hectic round of Dublin which imposed the greatest strains. Only by retiring into obscurity was the costly sociability avoided.

Those permanently in Ireland were often better able to pace their spending than the transients desperate to flash brilliantly across the Dublin sky. During the 1660s, the younger Sir John Temple, a lawyer and office-holder, allowed his wife a monthly £10 for household expenses. Sir William Petty in the next decade aimed to retrench. He hoped to reduce his household from eleven members to four and to keep annual expenditure on it between £340 and £400.[160] By 1722, an ageing and straitened Lord Molesworth schemed to trim his household's monthly spending to £25.[161] Ten years later, Richard Edgeworth proposed to set aside £60 each month to cover his costs. He allocated a monthly £25 6s. 8d. to housekeeping, and gave it directly to his new wife, whose province this became.[162] In the 1740s, Mary Delany, wife of the cultivated and well-to-do dean of Down, Patrick Delany, was allowed £50 each month for housekeeping.[163] The problem with such figures is that the budgets seldom detailed precisely what was to be covered by the money. The Delanys, like the Edgeworths, shifted regularly between city and country. Records of expenditure of another household while in the capital – that of Sir Edward Bayly – show that it spent £103 on groceries over sixteen months. Bills for washing amounted to another £44. During a shorter period of six months, the same family disbursed over £61 for meat and fish in the Dublin markets.[164] The household of the bishop of Down and Connor, lodged temporarily in the capital, incurred extra expenses through such indulgences as the baking of two dozen mince-pies, four cheese cakes and a mutton pie on Christmas Eve of 1733.[165] The need to pay specialists again reminds of the additional work coming the way of Dubliners. But the extras guide uncertainly towards total costs of living in the capital. These uncertainties add to the obstacles in assessing just how expensive Dublin was, and how costs there compared with those elsewhere in Ireland, in England, and indeed in continental Europe. Scrupulous accountants tended to use different systems, and their records of spending seldom survive for long and continuous periods. As a result, a month in the country can rarely be compared with a month in Dublin (or London). Underlying expenses are often hidden. Also the size and composition of particular households are not easily gauged. Then, too, projections of expenditure did not always correspond with what actually was spent.

The last difficulty vitiates a calculation made by a Balfour in the second half of the eighteenth century. He expected to spend something over £900 in a year: a reasonable sum when set against likely annual receipts of £1,400.[166] One essential of Dublin life – a house – was relatively cheap, since Balfour benefited from a long lease on a property on the north side in Lower Abbey Street.[167] But Balfour's estimate made no allowances for running his country property in County Louth.[168] Nor did he anticipate the unexpected: medical attendance, births and deaths, educating children – whether at home with tutors, dancing-, singing-,

writing- and fencing-masters or at Drogheda, Kilkenny and Midleton. Dublin obliged charitable donations, as hospitals and other good causes abounded. Entertainments added further expense: tickets for musical concerts or plays generally cost 5s. 5d. or 3s. 3d. each.[169]
When the sociable visited private houses for parties, servants had to be tipped. Furthermore,
going into society brought unpredictable costs. Cards were a popular diversion and involved
both the profligate like Elinor O'Hara and the timid, such as Edgeworth, in regular losses.
They were played in both town and country houses. The austere denounced the diversion
as 'the refuge of bankrupt merchants, card-ruined noblemen, poor clergymen's widows and
half pay lieutenants'.[170] It did not deter the respectable, such as Edgeworth, from inducting
children into the mysteries. Losses, if individually modest, mounted into far from negligible sums.[171] Spending of this sort may have been lumped by Balfour under the vague heading of 'general housekeeping'. The obscure could avoid many of these indulgences, but for
those of the Balfours' standing such expenses were not optional but essential to uphold a fitting figure. In any case, Balfour had luxurious habits: he travelled widely in Europe, and
bought much while away. Disproportionately dear were those vanities of the smart in
Dublin: coach and horses, gargling claret, and burning in their grates only imported coal,
usually from Whitehaven.[172]

Table 6. Annual budget of the Balfour family[173]

| Heading | Annual expenditure | | | Percentage of total spending |
|---|---|---|---|---|
| | £ | s. | d. | |
| Servants' wages | 107 | 0 | 0 | 11.6 |
| Dublin house | 15 | 0 | 0 | 1.6 |
| Carriage taxes | 8 | 0 | 0 | 0.9 |
| Horses and stables | 120 | 0 | 0 | 13.0 |
| Soap and candles | 30 | 0 | 0 | 3.3 |
| Wax candles | 15 | 0 | 0 | 1.6 |
| Malt liquor for servants | 40 | 0 | 0 | 4.3 |
| Ale and cider | 11 | 7 | 6 | 1.2 |
| Wine | 45 | 10 | 0 | 5.0 |
| Coal | 75 | 0 | 0 | 8.2 |
| Travelling, shoeing horses, etc. | 45 | 10 | 0 | 5.0 |
| General housekeeping | 227 | 12 | 6 | 24.7 |
| Food | 180 | 0 | 0 | 19.6 |
| Total | 922 | 0 | 0 | |

Another who estimated his expenditure in Dublin was Samuel Bagshawe. An English army
officer posted to Ireland, Bagshawe, attending the lord-lieutenant and being quartered in
Dublin, felt that money flowed away. He puzzled how best to pare his expenses. Lodgings
were to be had, he believed, at £23 14s. 6d. for the year. To this charge were added food and

drink. Convention decreed that an officer breakfast at his own lodgings, then dine and sup at a tavern. Quickly another £74 10s. 5d. was added to the annual bill. Horses and servants were kept. The first cost an estimated £54 15s.; servants – two in town or one in the country – were calculated at £34 12s. 6d. Stylish dress was vital. As an army officer, what to others could be dispensed with as optional, was inescapable if Bagshawe were not to suffer any derogation. As often, the personal knocked any scheme sideways. Bagshawe had lost a leg. Without it, he spent more heavily on hiring coaches and sedan chairs. Notionally, he set aside £23 14s. 6d. p.a. for transport – the same sum as for his rooms. Bagshawe's annual expenses in Dublin exceeded his pay of about £230 by £104.[174] Any hope of retrenching was destroyed when he married. Immediately, his requirements changed and became costlier. In 1752, he took a house in Digges Street at £30 for a quarter.[175] By withdrawing from the capital, and indeed by serving overseas, money was saved. But back in Ireland, and from 1761, a member of its parliament, he could not avoid the burdens of metropolitan life.[176]

Records from other households in Dublin do not yield firm conclusions about relative costs of town and country, or even how spending varied month by month. The Wares, enriched by office in the seventeenth century, by the 1740s luxuriated on St Stephen's Green, still one of the best addresses in Dublin. There James Ware, *rentier* and townee, ran a curious and, no doubt, untypical bachelor house. He totted up spending for the (dear) year of 1741.[177]

Table 7. Expenses of James Ware, Dublin, 1741

| Heading | Annual expenditure | | | Percentage of total spending |
|---|---|---|---|---|
| | £ | s. | d. | |
| Food | 64 | 12 | 4 | 41.0 |
| Drink | 38 | 11 | 8 | 25.0 |
| Garden | 3 | 12 | 7 | 2.6 |
| Household goods | 17 | 5 | 1 | 10.9 |
| Repairs | 5 | 14 | 4½ | 3.8 |
| Coal | 8 | 3 | 9 | 5.1 |
| Candles | 2 | 14 | 10 | 1.9 |
| Soap | | 17 | 9 | 0.6 |
| Washerwoman, etc. | | 7 | 4 | 0.3 |
| Taxes | 3 | 8 | 5 | 1.9 |
| Servants' wages | 11 | 0 | 0 | 7.1 |
| Total | 156 | 0 | 7½ | |

The sum of £156 was not all Ware spent during 1741. He recorded, for example, an extra £25 4s. 6d. paid for fabric, and more to have it tailored.[178] Ware was not the hermit of St Stephen's Green. He was active in the Physico-Historical Society, serving as its secretary for Leinster. He was gathering the accessories of polite hospitality: coffee-pots and teapots, punchbowl, drinking and jelly glasses and china plates.[179] He was also a rich man, with a yearly income nearing £900. He could well afford exceptional outgoings. For the bachelor Ware, as for the married, one year's spending did not necessarily match that in the next. While country-dwellers like the Edgeworths, Frenches and Smythes decided whether or not to come to Dublin, Ware, the Dubliner, sauntered into the country or to England. Travelling varied what he spent. In 1742, he recorded £41 6s. 7½d. spent on food. Lower prices, after the shortages of 1741, explained some of the fall, but most resulted from Ware's being away from Dublin for three months. His expenses in 1742 totalled £104 12s. 4d.: a drop from the previous year.[180] Yet, on certain items – house furnishings and clothing – it had risen. Ware, meeting strangers, may have felt a need to impress by his appearance. Moreover, faced with novelties in the shops, he splashed out.[181] Ware's patterns of spending altered permanently when he removed to Bath, where he soon died. The St Stephen's Green residence passed to his younger brother, a clergyman. The Reverend Henry Ware had a young family and a church living in County Dublin. Both factors altered the way in which the family house was used, and – no doubt – the absolute and relative amounts spent under distinct headings. Unlike his elder brother, the cleric does not seem to have kept detailed accounts; if he did, they have not so far been found.

Fluctuations, arising from variations in the time passed in Dublin, can be observed in other families. The Galway squire Robert French noted spending anything from £668 to £6 8s. 9d. annually in Dublin between 1746 and 1774. The highest annual sum constituted 35.5 per cent of his total household spending for that year. It reflected French setting up house with his bride in Dublin. During the next four years, with the couple still eager to impress in the capital, Dublin life consumed between 21 and 27 per cent of the annual budget. Thereafter, the importance of Dublin to the Frenches diminished: at least as measured by the yardstick of spending.[182] Richard Edgeworth's expenditure in Dublin also varied absolutely and proportionately. He, like French, when newly married, spent heavily. In his first year of marriage (1733 to 1734), Edgeworth disbursed £1,074.[183] Thereafter totals fluctuated. An obsessive calculator, Edgeworth left a record of monthly spending, complete apparently to the last farthing. It reveals occasional expenses unique to the city – transport to and from parties and business, concerts, assemblies, plays and sensations – but others which had their equivalents in the countryside.

Dublin shopkeepers stocked and displayed an array of goods to entrap customers. Much was calculated to appeal to female fancies. Fathers, like Bishop Synge, Edgeworth and French, indulged daughters, just as earlier they had succumbed to the entreaties of spouses. On marrying in 1732, Edgeworth abandoned his nomadic life for a more settled – and costlier – one.[184] Edgeworth had inherited property in Dublin, but it did not suit him as a family house. He let it, perhaps for offices, and instead took a house on the south side of the city. An immediate sign of a new splendour were the liveries, including laced hats, of their servants.[185] He also acquired a coach. Imported from England, the freight alone cost £8 1s. (considerably more than a passage for a person) and customs duty added a further £6 19s. ½d. In addition, Edgeworth employed a porter to guard this valuable on the quay where it stood for nineteen nights.[186] In 1754, he bought a post-chaise. Costing £60, it came from a Dublin specialist, Archbold in Aungier Street.[187]

Dublin might be where the recently married Edgeworths chose to make the grand figure. But they did not forget County Longford. At first, they had to send for furniture from Edgeworthstown: a dozen chairs arrived in the spring of 1733. In the same manner, Bishop Hutchinson of Down and Connor had chairs sent from the country to Dublin.[188] Soon enough both the squire and the bishop were shopping for their country houses. This pattern persisted throughout Edgeworth's life. He bought an oak desk (price, £2 6s.) and a 'map-screen' (from Teague, an upholsterer) for 'my dining hall in the country'.[189] Silver and china were acquired, probably under his wife's direction. These goods, easily portable and valuable, were moved between city and country. With the Edgeworths, as with most others in eighteenth-century Ireland, it is impossible to know if particular items were reserved for urban or rural use. Embellishments, such as marble chimney-pieces, were transported from Dublin to the countryside. In 1749, Squire Edgeworth commanded a pair of brass-gilded scrolls, 'called mermaid arms', from Francis Booker, the leading Dublin dealer in mirrors, glass lamps and fittings. They too were destined for Edgeworthstown.[190] Towards the end of his life, Edgeworth, a widower, was still buying the new. In 1767, he procured a dozen of John Hewetson's distinctive ivory-handled knives and forks, with their handles stained green. Edgeworth's housekeeper bought china sauceboats, coffee cups and 'a shape for jelly for cream'. Fresh furniture was also ordered. Russell, a cabinetmaker in George's Lane, supplied eight 'parlour chairs', at a price of £1 for each.[191] Some purchases were intended for city use, but the majority were destined for Edgeworthstown. Provincials did not invariably think that what was bought in the capital surpassed what was to be had nearer at hand. Fairs, markets, local traders and craftsmen, workers on the estate and itinerants, and auctions in neighbouring houses all furnished country residences. Edgeworth turned to a clockmaker in Mullingar – Magennis. Not known from any surviving timepiece that he made, Magennis exemplifies the risk of overlooking and underestimating what the provinces were supplying.[192] If Dublin offered a wider choice than the Irish provinces, its goods might – in their turn – be eclipsed by the plenty of Bath, London, Paris and Rome.[193]

For the likes of an Edgeworth or a French, obliged to maintain bases in city and country, Dublin could prove costly. Edgeworthstown functioned as the dynamo driving a working estate. It was also the seat from which Edgeworth performed his local roles, as magistrate, high sheriff, turnpike trustee, member of parliament, landlord, patron and paterfamilias. Its very name and iconography associated it inextricably with the Edgeworths. Local obligations and ambitions forced Edgeworth into extravagances unthinkable in Dublin or England. When in the Irish capital, Edgeworth moved in several orbits: some professional, others regional and familial. But in the crowded city, although no nonentity, he was merely one of

81. William Jones, *View of Howth*, engraved by G. King, 1745. The setting of Dublin between mountains and sea afforded its inhabitants numerous opportunities for recreation.

many of similar condition. Again the ambivalences with which Dublin was viewed can be sensed. For some Dublin was an occasion of expense; for others, an escape from the claustrophobia and commitments of the rural scene.

Visitors departed, leaving the city to its permanent residents. They too savoured the modes and manners which they fashioned and sold to others. Edgeworth and French sampled the metropolitan pleasures invented by entrepreneurs. They relaxed in inns and at the bagnio, listened to concerts and plays, bought books, clothes, furniture and the services of doctors, tutors and lawyers. They paid to watch shows – of puppets, waxworks, automata and paintings. They inspected recently constructed grottos and gardens. The society inhabited by the substantial squire when in Dublin was composed of both permanent residents of the city and visitors like themselves. The migratory depended less than locals on the cycles of pleasure fabricated by parish, ward, guild, neighbourhood or municipality. Nor did they – at least if the example of the prissy Edgeworth is a reliable guide – surrender to all the commercialized entertainments devised by the ingenious to fleece strangers. He never, for example, mentioned going to horse-races, whether in town or country.

In the capital, those of modest means had more varied opportunities of employment and recreation than their counterparts elsewhere in the island. Satirists contended that the shopkeepers, craftworkers and artisans aspired to gentility and therefore were easily lured into spending on what was said to betoken sophistication. The tricks of the town, as catalogued by one sensationalist, appealed to the naïve anxious to assume the ways of their superiors.[194] Such an account, elaborating the deceits and depravities of Dublin, overlooked the unique satisfactions that it gave to its inhabitants. Numerous convivial, vocational, eleemosynary and improving societies overlapped. Some excluded on grounds of gender, income, standing or confession. They will be considered briefly in the final chapter. Nevertheless, Dublin offered – within Ireland – a unique diversity of avocations and recreations, which drew in, both absolutely and proportionately, more inhabitants. It was possible to skulk in the alleys and stews of the city. Any who ventured into its public places had to convey a fitting figure: at once a burden and a boon.

Chapter 10

# Going Abroad

*I*

Young Robert Southwell from Kinsale, touring western Europe early in the 1660s, sent home trophies.[1] One was an 'Italian' table, probably of marble or hard-stone.[2] The second souvenir was a Parmesan cheese. It was passed hastily from one suggested recipient to the next in an urgent game of pass-the-parcel.[3] In the first case, a few in Ireland sampled the strange vicariously; in the second, they tasted the foreign for themselves. The Southwells belonged to a family whose sense of itself and whose wider relationships were shaped and reshaped by frequent travel. In this they obeyed the urgings of another soon to be prominent in Protestant Ireland. Robert Molesworth regretted that too many 'gentlemen of Ireland' were obliged to manage their own lands. As a result, they seldom moved further than the fairs and markets of their locality. They read little and lacked chances to improve their 'natural parts'. In consequence, a gap opened between the sedentary, with a 'cramp'd and low education', and the mobile.[4]

Molesworth updated a view common in England throughout the seventeenth century. A particularly pungent expression of the opinion had it that 'upon his dunghill, the English gentleman is somewhat stubborn and churlish. Travel will sweeten him very much and breed in him courtesy, affability, respect and reservation'.[5] Contemporaries in Ireland agreed. In 1723, *The Gentleman Instructed*, revamped for Irish readers, lampooned the backwoodsman who 'confined his knowledge within the bounds of his own country'. To such, 'all the rest of the world was *terra incognita*'.[6] Ignorance could be remedied only by travel. Destinations differed; but even to go beyond the parish and barony into the county town, let alone to Dublin or London, could liberate.

Archbishop King, long a friend of the Southwells, argued that 'the true design of travelling . . . is not merely to satisfy curiosity of seeing variety, or learning the exercises that are proper for a complete gent'. To stare at the unfamiliar, the fault of the untravelled, was 'rude and unmannerly'. Instead, King wanted travellers to attempt a comparative ethnography. They should ponder why dress, customs and temperament varied across Europe. The answers, the archbishop hinted, lay in climate, ecology and history. Journeying might also suggest why Catholicism survived, and even flourished, in some countries. Above all, the tourist returned with a greater tolerance of divergences in behaviour. King predicted, 'you will not be apt to laugh or condemn what seems uncouth or awkward in any people'.[7] Not all agreed about the benefits of these excursions. The young might pick up irreligion and blasphemy. One father forbade his heir, on pain of disinheritance, to be educated overseas.[8]

Going abroad was recommended to the inhabitants of Ireland with many of the same arguments used throughout Europe and America. Fashion, curiosity or (most often) necessity impelled the Irish to travel. Many went in pursuit of trade, livelihoods or pleasure; fewer to perfect their education.[9] Gender also came into play. By 1728, an observer of the Dublin scene could comment, ''tis become a great fashion with us for our ladies to travel, and to do everything that is expensive'.[10] Increasingly, women accompanied husbands to Dublin or London.[11] Yet, even in George II's reign, it was still rare for them to venture further. Lady Arbella Denny, unusual in many of her attitudes and attributes, visited the Austrian Netherlands in the 1750s. Her party included others from Ireland, among them wives.[12] In the main, the daughters of the affluent were less likely than their brothers to be sent on a grand tour to finish their formation or equip themselves for a career. However, there is evidence that Spa, a halt on Lady Arbella's itinerary, had been attracting women since the early seventeenth century.[13]

Travel usually reflected – and then accentuated – economic, social and confessional differences. Enforced exile (the fate of many Catholics) or migration in search of subsistence (undertaken by poorer Protestants and Catholics from Ireland) produced feelings rather different from those of the rambler and pleasure-hunter. Reactions to Dublin, London and continental cities veered from rapture to repulsion. The expense, inconvenience or insults suffered in unfamiliar places deepened some travellers' affection for Ireland, or indeed for their favourite spot in Ireland. The bewitched shipped home to Ireland new ideas, tastes and commodities. Thereafter, the well-travelled saw themselves – and their Ireland – as part of a larger world encompassing Britain, western Europe and (sometimes) all civil and civilized peoples. Sometimes this was manifest in material objects – mementos of their tours; sometimes simply through ideas.

Two features of Ireland might be supposed to have propelled more of its inhabitants overseas. The political, legal and – in some measure – economic dependency of Ireland on England obliged the ambitious and aggrieved to congregate in London: the effective centre of power. In addition, repeated defeats doomed the Catholics of Ireland to subservience within their own country. Those unable to stomach the reversals or merely keen to escape the discriminations tried life elsewhere: in Catholic Europe, the West Indies and North America. A further characteristic of Ireland affected Catholics and Protestants alike. Its comparative underdevelopment prevented the kingdom supporting many in prosperity. The resulting

frustrations drove the restless and desperate to seek livelihoods away from Ireland. Sometimes, the uprooted, regardless of differing confession, endured the same dismal conditions
and followed similar itineraries. Occasionally, Catholics and Protestants, finding themselves
in the same spots overseas, were happy with one another's company. Sir George Lane (later
Viscount Lanesborough) recorded how, while a refugee at Charles II's court in the Spanish
Netherlands during the 1650s, he had been entertained with Lord Dillon and Lord and Lady
Taaffe, all Catholics. 'We are all civilly merry, and I was forced to trip about an Irish jig'.[14] The
contrived merrymaking was a product of extremity, and might not be repeated when the
exiles returned to Ireland.

More commonly, just as the reasons for exile differed, so too did destinations. Presbyterians headed for Scotland or the United Provinces; Catholics to places where their faith was
strong.[15] Irish Protestants did not avoid all Catholic territories, although war put France out
of bounds for long periods during the seventeenth and eighteenth centuries. Spain, a popular destination for Catholics from Ireland, beckoned to few others. Robert Black, of an Ulster
family, was unusual in starting his trip through the Low Countries, Germany, the Spanish
Netherlands, France and Italy at Cadiz.[16] Italy bewitched many.[17] Riders on the dusty trail
south to drink at the sources of classical civilization have tended to edge out the more sizeable contingents – from both Britain and Ireland – that opted for the cheaper and easier trip
to the Low Countries and northern Europe. Yet, the political and aesthetic impact of their
experiences equalled what could be gleaned from Italy. Many left Ireland permanently, dislodged by a malign political or economic atmosphere. Away from their homeland, the emi-
grants nevertheless preserved connections with it. The diaspora, both Catholic and
Protestant, and whether removed only to Britain, continental Europe or a distant hemi-
sphere, exerted strong influence over those still in Ireland. The absent, no less than the dead,
brooded powerfully over Irish communities. The exiles communicated notions, sent back
money and goods, and promoted overseas the idea and interests of their favourite Ireland.[18]
The privations and achievements of the uprooted have long attracted notice. Less regarded
have been the travellers, long-haul and short distance, who returned to Ireland.

*II*

Pedagogic theorists who extolled travel were gradually heard in seventeenth-century Ireland.
Before 1641, only a few sons of the wealthy, like the Boyles, followed their advice. A later Irish
voyager reminded prosaically, 'long journeys require long purses'.[19] The first earl of Cork allocated £500 for the year which two of his sons were to spend abroad. Soon the sum had to be
doubled. In 1678, the first duke of Ormond upbraided his grandson (and heir) who was run-

ning through £1,000 in a year at Orange. The youth, James Butler, had an entourage of governor and four servants, but no coach or horses.[20] The young Lord Roscommon subsisted more modestly at Caen. In the late 1650s, his annual expenses amounted to £300, rising to £400 when he enrolled at the academy.[21] In the next century, the leading Belfast trader, Daniel Mussenden, reckoned that his heir's stay in the Low Countries, lasting twenty-seven months, had cost upwards of £960.[22] Touring in this lavish style cost more than what all but a handful in Ireland had to live on for the entire year.[23] The curriculum for the Boyle boys when abroad ranged from book-learning to fencing, riding, dancing and playing tennis. Cork resembled other fathers in alternately raging at the extravagant price and wishing that his sons be equipped with 'anything that is fit for a young nobleman . . . for my honour and reputation, their own and yours [the governor's]'.[24] There were worries, too, about the libertinage encountered in Paris and Italy. So, for a season, the Boyle boys were sequestered in Geneva. Their parent was reassured that they neither imbibed Puritanism nor talked 'with Jesuits, friars, priests, or any other persons ill affected to their religion, king or state'.[25] The anxiety about the dangerous religious principles that might be picked up abroad intermittently agitated both the authorities and parents.[26] At the end of the seventeenth century, bans were imposed on Catholic training overseas in the hope of cutting the sinews which sustained Irish Catholicism. They failed.

The Boyles illustrate the truism that temperament determined what was learnt while abroad. Robert Boyle, the youthful philosopher, responded well to the opportunities, proving an apt linguist and keen on mathematics and fortification. His brother, Francis Boyle, future Viscount Shannon, benefited less. He fell in with others of similar outlook who thought 'that the greatest glory of a gentleman did consist of expending foolishly his money and in vanities . . . how many dogs he should keep, how many horses, how many fine bands, suits, ribbons, and how freely he would play and keep company'. Changes of scene, it was hoped, would cure these traits. The discipline of specific institutions, like the Accademia in Florence, was praised; sets of young milords camped in the vicinity were reckoned more or less vicious.[27] The Boyles' itineraries, determined first by the areas of fighting in Europe, were abbreviated as rebellions broke out in Ireland and England. The father's income was immediately reduced, and the boys returned to fight. Soon, the outcome of the warfare in the three kingdoms drove some Boyles, along with other Irish supporters of the defeated Stuarts, into temporary exile. Enforced stays in Normandy, the United Provinces and the Spanish Netherlands familiarized them with new places. The Boyles continued to believe in the advantages of travel for their male children. Also, they tapped the knowledge of a group of Protestant refugees who had settled in England and Ireland, but who maintained good connections across western Europe. Specialist governors and guides were emerging who pinioned the flighty to the discipline of foreign study and travel. Early in the 1660s, grandsons of the first earl of Cork headed for the

Spanish Netherlands in the care of Dr Jeremy Hall. During the 1680s, Hall returned to the same locale, now with members of the next generation of Boyles. In 1682, Hall reassured the kinsfolk of the young Lord Orrery that Paris abounded with suitable company. Lord Gormanston, Lady Longford, Lord and Lady Charlemont were there, together with 'several young Irish gentlemen'. The last included the sons of Lord Dungan of Clane, Sir Valentine Browne and Sir John Bedloe. Interestingly, Hall, in his eagerness to impress, did not differentiate Protestants from Catholics. More sinister to him and his employers in Ireland were 'the atheistical or debauched' of whatever religious denomination.[28]

Hall, sensing that his days as a tourist were closing, presented Trinity College with his guides to Rome, in the expectation that they could be used by new generations of Protestant travellers from Ireland. The itinerants would include more Boyles. Travel refined the artistic sensibilities of the head of the line, the third earl of Burlington (and fourth earl of Cork), a chief promoter of the Palladian revival. Because this aristocrat never visited Ireland, his journeying seemed irrelevant to the formation of Protestant Ireland. Yet, at least one of Burlington's companions, Isaac Gervais, returned from the continental tour to a church living on the earl's Irish estates. Gervais, if as his name suggested of Huguenot stock, continued the tradition – charitable and pragmatic – of the family employing Protestant fugitives from Catholic Europe. Gervais, living long in County Waterford, brought an unexpected perspective to his ministry in Munster.[29]

Meanwhile, another branch of the Boyles, the earls of Orrery, removed themselves permanently from their Irish estates. They, too, craved for Europe. In 1725, Charles Boyle, fourth earl, informed his agent in Ireland that he proposed withdrawing his son, Lord Boyle, from Oxford so that he could make 'those improvements in foreign countries which the time of his life will I think now soon require he should do'.[30] With a breathtaking naïveté, Orrery wondered if his Irish tenants might pay £300 towards the expected expenses. Not surprisingly, they would not. Father and son, already in Paris, were reduced to a 'penurious way of living, scarcely consistent with the character of a nobleman', and returned prematurely.[31] Orrery, a suspected Jacobite, envisaged something other than an innocent educational and recreational excursion.[32] His heir, Lord Boyle, later fifth earl of Orrery and (from 1753) fifth earl of Cork, once married to Margaret Hamilton, returned intermittently to Ireland. Improvements – especially of the demesne – were begun on his wife's ancestral estate of Caledon in County Tyrone. Economy, however, once more pushed the Cork and Orrerys overseas: between 1754 and 1755 to Italy.[33] The earl asserted that the gains from such experiences were not simply – or even primarily – aesthetic. He urged his compatriots 'to travel abroad, not to see fashions, but states, not to taste different wines, but different governments; not to compare laces and velvets, but laws and politics'. Exposure to other societies should convince all, he argued, 'that England is possessed of more freedom, justice and happiness than any other nation under heaven'.[34] In attributing education in liberty to foreign travel he echoed Archbishop King and Molesworth. The latter had contended that travellers would come to 'know experimentally the want of public liberty' in so many European states.[35] What Molesworth applauded, others deprecated. In 1737, Archbishop Boulter of Armagh feared that those who roamed abroad would be infected with republican principles and, on their return, might contrive to bring in 'a commonwealth'.[36]

Grand families turned to experts for guidance. The Butlers, like the Boyles, hired exiled Huguenots to lead sons safely around Europe.[37] Since trusty governors were hard to come by, 'it's a jewel if we light on a good one'.[38] In 1737, an Irish notable, Sir John Rawdon, needed a travel supervisor. An army captain had been approached, but demanded annual pay of £300.[39] Another military man, stationed in Ireland, so impressed the Fermanagh notable Sir John Caldwell that he was invited to accompany Caldwell's heir across Europe. He declined.[40] In the 1750s, when the Grandisons searched for a governor for their heir, few were expected to apply for the position, since it entailed being 'the slave of a silly woman and a teasing child'.[41] In these situations, the well-favoured, such as Dr Jeremy Hall, could pick and choose among prospective charges.

Another in constant demand was Sir Robert Southwell. By the 1690s, Southwell knew much of western Europe: first as educational tourist and then as ambassador. He saw to it that his own successors received a similar grounding. The elder Edward Southwell toured the Low Countries in 1691 and turned up in Paris in 1723; his son, the younger Edward Southwell, went to Hanover in 1726.[42] The upheavals of the mid-century coupled with the uncongenial Cromwellian regime first prompted the younger Robert Southwell to explore France and Italy in the later 1650s. Attentive and ambitious, he put his time to profitable uses. His family had old connections with the Medici, which he renewed in Florence. Moving on to Rome, the personable youth sought out the powerful. He recorded the table talk of cardinals, the exiled republican Algernon Sidney and expatriate Irish Catholics. Among the last group, he noted, 'my Lord Creagh would rather be buried on the highest mountain in Ireland than in St Peter's, such is his country's love'. Affection for a distant homeland suddenly united the two. Southwell bought extensively on his trips. Souvenirs of Italy, Portugal and the Spanish Netherlands were dispatched to the favoured, in Ireland and England, and into Southwell's English houses. The Grand Duke of Tuscany, blown off course by a gale, reciprocated and put in at Kinsale. The port, favoured as a deep and sheltered anchorage, saw numerous exotic arrivals, but the reigning Medici was out of the ordinary even by the cosmopolitan standards of Kinsale.[43]

Southwell traded on his reputation as a pundit. Intimate with the educational scene, he pontificated. He linked intending travellers with what they might need or otherwise miss. Moreover, the tales of travel, the best *auberge*, the quarters to be avoided, the tricks of the locals or the curiosities of the town, gave the Southwells more in common with others, such as Samuel Waring, whom they met in Ireland. Their shared experiences distanced them from the stay-at-homes. The cultural sophistication of the Southwells, Percevals, Butlers or Boyles arose from their wealth, and reminded of what it could buy: protracted absences from Ireland and excursions across the continent. These experiences accentuated differences within the Irish Protestant community expressed already and most tellingly by its leaders' frequent invisibility in the provinces. Yet, some of more modest means and more firmly grounded in local society enlarged their outlook by long expeditions. The Reverend Isaac Gervais was one; another, the Ulster squire Samuel Waring.

Heir to a County Down estate yielding about £600 p.a., Waring was picked to accompany the wayward Charles Butler, younger brother of the future second duke of Ormonde. Waring's tutors at Trinity College, where he had recently graduated, probably recommended him to their chancellor, Ormond, as a suitable companion for the latter's grandson. A Protestant refugee from Louis XIV's France, Maximilien Misson, dealt with the practicalities. Waring prepared with a seriousness which suggested that he was eager to gain as much as possible from his trip. Before departing, he furnished himself with the essential guides to Italy and the Low Countries and texts on architecture and painting. The party started at Brill and Leyden in the autumn of 1687. On paper, Waring freely expressed his opinions, or those that he picked up from his handbooks. He tried systematically to record and compare customs and appearances with what he knew from England and (more rarely) Ireland. Throughout his notebooks, he applied criteria, which elevated symmetrical and classical architecture above the Gothic. In Leyden, he noted, 'here are several good buildings worth the seeing'.[44] Much disappointed through its irregularity. In Bohemia, near Koninghof, he had espied 'nothing like a gentleman or a gentleman's house in all this country'. Diet and dress were all remarked, and sometimes criticized. Thanks to the standing of Butler, the itinerants were welcomed into the highest company: at Heidelberg, by the Elector. The ultimate destination was Italy. By December 1687, the band had reached Venice, whence they removed to Rome in the following spring. Already they were equipped with introductions to consuls and agents. In Venice, they had fallen in with English gentlemen, Sir Edward Bettison and Sir Uvedale Corbett, and their tutors; then with the Anglo-Irish peer Orrery and his Swiss tutor, Colladon.

Rome was used to grand tourists. Printed and personal guides coached the uncertain in the proper responses, some of which Waring, well primed, repeated. He mentioned the Altieri palace as 'looked on as the best piece of architecture of any palace of Rome'.[45] Other spectacles left him unmoved. He was mortified that the Roman spring, although so much more temperate than that in County Down, yielded 'no rarity of fruit'. Published accounts led the likes of Waring to expect the exotic, but only artichoke and asparagus pleased. Comparable disappointment was expressed later by a more exigent visitor from France.[46] In common with other visiting notables from Britain and Ireland (including Orrery), Waring and his companions were taken up by the genial and well-connected Cardinal Howard.[47] They were also hospitably treated by two 'of our Irish fathers', who showed them the shells and precious stones in San Columno. They also witnessed the exposition of relics. At St Peter's, 'excellent music' was heard.[48] Hosts at the Dominican friary at Monte Coelio in the ruins of Julian the Apostate's palace may have stereotyped their 'English' visitors by serving a hash of sweet-breads, followed by ribs of beef and two large plum puddings.[49] In this way, the Anglo-Irish Butler, the Irish Waring and the entirely English Corbett were all regarded as English. On a later occasion, Protestants from Ireland were delighted to be greeted in Paris because 'we were English, and from Ireland'.[50] Whether the travellers responded by suspending their distinctive senses of region, confession and ethnicity and by merging into an expatriate community of English speakers is uncertain.

The clearest impact on Waring of his Roman holiday was aesthetic. He inspected the antiquities and more modern curiosities; he looked into studios and shops. The painter Carlo 'Moral', 'the most famous painter in Rome', was visited, as was what remained of Kircher's studio, where the 'water inventions' fascinated Waring. With Lord Orrery, the party peeked into the sculpture shop of Pasquin on the Piazza Navona. Waring and his friends bought medals and engravings, and viewed the cabinet of Gian Pietro Bellori, antiquary to the pope and the exiled Queen Christina of Sweden.[51] On the homeward journey, the party dallied in northern Italy and the Spanish Netherlands. Waring, as well as noting the still unfinished Jesuit church in Brussels, toured the famous park at Angers. He was greatly struck by the 'most neatly kept evergreen hedges, the best of them that I have seen anywhere, running 20 feet high and not a foot over'. The topiary imitated rails and banisters. The water gardens and *jets d'eau* impressed less, owing to a lack of water.[52] The multiplicity of impressions crowding in on Waring were properly sorted only after he had returned to Ireland.

Some observations relating to building and gardening might be applied in and around his Irish estates. Others, such as discernment in painting, were less obviously utilitarian, but nevertheless elevated him among his neighbours. As he settled back into his life as a parliamentary squire, he shared recollections with others who had journeyed beyond Ireland and Britain. In Dublin during the 1690s he fell into the company of just such a voyager, who had compiled a description of the Rhine.[53] Waring amused himself by reworking and embellishing parts of his own written itinerary. In some places, he added coloured drawings.[54] In retrospect, he accounted the journey 'one of the chiefest and most satisfactory occurrences of my life', but reconciled himself to the fact that 'we shall take no more of these rambles for the future but in imagination'. Waring was not blind to the pretensions of some whom he had met. His taste for codifying extended to the tourists themselves. He identified six types. The first obsessively transcribed ancient inscriptions. A second marvelled at the beauty of the monuments themselves; the third gazed at paintings; a fourth was lost in admiration for 'the stupendous fabric' of the architecture; and a fifth gloried in the richness of all. Finally, the sixth 'blames his fancy and seems offended at so great an extravagance, judging God would be better pleased with less pomp and more simplicity of heart'.[55] In his own journals, Waring wavered between and frequently fused the distinct tendencies.

Two other legacies might affect Waring's future conduct in Ireland. While in Rome, he, like Southwell before him, talked with cardinals. He noted that one affable prince of the Church stated, 'that he had more kindness to his soul than to desire the popeship and told me that he never lived a happier life than when in a convent'. Waring was charmed by the cardinal's personality: 'his humour is very easy and as sweet [and] courteous, almost to a fault'.[56] Surprised, Waring had concluded, 'his cap [cardinal's hat] I really believe not so great a pleasure to him as it may be thought. His ways always of dwelling upon religion and making distinction is odd and would surprise a stranger. I am persuaded he does it only for discourse sake and drollery'. In addition, Waring entered Catholic churches in many cities, and saw the differences in worship. He also observed for himself the practices of Calvinists and Lutherans. In his subsequent public career in Ireland, Waring never emerged as a strident anti-Catholic. Nevertheless, one of the few books to survive from his library (which must have been voluminous) is a product of the popish scares of 1688–9, *A Collection of the Newest and Most Ingenious Poems, Songs, Catches, &c against Popery relating to the Times*.[57] He had probably bought it on the way back to Ulster after his continental tour. Waring's fortune in Ireland – like that of the Southwells and of most Irish Protestants – rested on the exclusion and dispossession of the local Catholics. Occasional social contacts with the latter, notably the Magennises, the former proprietors of much of the Warings' estate, continued into the 1690s, but apparently ceased thereafter. Away from Ireland, Waring and his kind mixed easily with Catholics, and suspended any open anti-Catholicism. Back in Ireland, they moved in an exclusively Protestant society.[58]

Political as well as confessional perceptions might be sharpened by foreign tours. In Rome, Waring was shown the Jesuit College. It boasted three large images depicting England, Scotland and Ireland. The last was already associated with the harp. But the figure, although allowed to hold a sceptre, wore no crown. The custodians of the house were questioned about this omission, odd since the pope had elevated Ireland into a kingdom. The priests replied that when Henry VIII assumed the title of king in 1541, the pope had refused to confirm it. Waring reported that among the Jesuits were several, 'who did not think fit to call the country a kingdom'. So, James VII and II was honoured in Rome as king of England or Great Britain, 'without mentioning Ireland'.[59] When Waring later sat in the Irish Commons, he would be reminded of the controversial status of Ireland in relation to England. A visual representation was hardly needed to bring home to Waring the contested issues of dependency or independence. Nevertheless, such incidents warned of how others saw Ireland and might provoke reflection – and outrage – among its inhabitants.

Strict guardians retained a preference for the traditional outposts of Protestantism such as Saumur or the United Provinces. Ormond hesitated to send overseas a ward, the young and impressionable Lord Courcy of Kinsale. Courcy, coming from a Catholic family, would 'be as much exposed to perversion in religion as in Ireland'. Indeed, the risks would be greater, 'by splendid sights and seeing mortifications, popish churches and churchmen'.[60] Gradually in the second half of the century the glamour of a Catholic country offset its perils. A university contemporary of Waring, St George Ashe, went to Vienna as secretary to the English envoy, Lord Paget. The intrepid Ashe drew parallels between the predicament of the empire threatened by the Turks and that of his co-religionists in Ireland during the viceroyalty of Tyrconnell. By the end of 1690, Ashe concluded that the 'Christian Turks', meaning the Catholics in Counties Meath and Kilkenny, 'are a great deal more barbarous than ours hereabouts, who keep their words almost invariably'.[61] During Passiontide in 1690, he confessed to a daily diet of 'religious puppet shows'. The temptation to scoff was countered by the grudging admission 'I never saw so glorious a sight'.[62] Later, when he was bishop of Clogher, any liking for the pageants of Vienna faded as he disparaged 'a patched motley religion, made up of inconsistencies, superstitions, mere mechanical exercises and theatrical representations'. The Catholic strategy, he concluded authoritatively, was to 'dazzle and amuse weak minds'. All the senses were gratified 'by a profusion of gaudy ornaments, splendid temples, exquisite statues and pictures, pompous processions, theatrical music, incense and perfumes'.[63]

Ashe derived other insights from his travels. In central Europe, he extended the network of scholarly contacts which he, and fellow members of the Dublin Philosophical Society, had established earlier in the 1680s. From Vienna, Ashe corresponded more easily with the learned in Germany, Italy and even Russia. He was given access to manuscripts in the imperial library. He described for the benefit of friends in Ireland the precious contents of the Schatzkammer.[64] He had manuscripts from Augsburg and Nuremberg as well as Vienna transcribed, and shared the transcripts with the interested. He collected rare medals to add to the collections of contemporaries at Trinity College. Tantalizingly, he reported on the unfamiliar music which he heard and sent back to Ireland some of the musical scores. True to the credo of the Philosophical Society, he investigated the relationship between musical harmonies and mathematics. Shortly after he had returned from this illuminating employment, Ashe was entrusted with the government of Trinity College and then successively (after 1695) of the dioceses of Cloyne and Clogher. In neither place was there much likelihood of performing the Viennese operas, one of which was sung by eunuchs.[65]

The sense of danger from too close an intimacy with Catholic Europe, although abating, did not vanish. In George I's reign, the brother of William Leathes worried about the prospect of his brother, as British envoy in Brussels, being denied regular Protestant services.[66] On his side, William Leathes gladly arranged for a nephew, Carteret Mussenden, to move from an academy in Tournai to one run by the Jesuits at Ghent.[67] By the eighteenth century, even fervent Protestants satisfied inquisitiveness by attending Catholic rites. James Smythe, the son of a Church of Ireland bishop and himself a future archdeacon, witnessed the ceremonies in

Rome during Holy Week in 1710. Smythe reported how the pontiff distributed palms to all pilgrims who kissed his toe, while he stood patiently 'to hear myself cursed and excommunicated among all the heretics'.[68] Earlier, sceptics reconciled themselves to kissing the pope's toe by treating it 'as a civil and usual compliment'.[69] The Italian churches were appreciated as rich settings of architecture, painting, sculpture and music. But there was, too, a more vulgar interest. Archbishop King warned against mocking what was strange. Instead, onlookers needed to think about the reasons for the survival of practices thought superstitious and idolatrous. The optimists believed that Protestant spectators, protected by faith and reason, could withstand a cult the blandishments of which operated primarily through the senses.

In this spirit, Pole Cosby, heir to Stradbally in Queen's County, while living in the United Provinces, sampled sundry religious services, including those of the French Catholic church. He excused the last as a means to improve his facility in the language: a familiar justification. He also contended that seeing the services deepened his antipathy to 'the ridiculous worship of the mass'. Cosby went regularly to the English church in Leyden. Although described as 'the Established Church', it was in essentials a Scottish Presbyterian kirk. The latitude which Cosby allowed himself in his religious devotions while on the continent contrasted with the narrow conformity which was demanded of his rank when at home in Ireland and which he willingly observed. At the same time, for Cosby to sample what was offered in the local mass-houses of Queen's County was no more thinkable than Waring venturing into Catholic churches in Ireland. In this particular, of religious behaviour and outlook, any weakening of prejudices while on the continent was reversed on returning to Ireland.

This, perhaps, does no more than state the obvious. Travellers from Ireland appreciated that neither Britain nor continental Europe (nor indeed America and India) were the same. What suited other places, if transplanted to Ireland, would not always thrive. During the 1750s, Lord Charlemont inspecting the Ottoman Empire was pleased by the toleration practised in the polymorphous state. Although he approved the Turks' *modus vivendi*, he stopped short of endorsing full civic rights for the Catholics of Ireland.[70] In the same way, courtesy or curiosity demanded attendance at sumptuous ceremonies or at cardinals' tables in Rome. It did not then follow that civility and politeness obliged Protestants, back in Ireland, to dine with the parish priest or junket to patterns. Only occasionally did shared cultivation and a common education overseas thaw the ice of the confessional moraines.

## III

The published list of those from Ireland who inscribed their names in the special volume maintained at the University of Padua in any single year seldom yields more than a quartet happy to be recorded as 'Hibernus'. The catalogue has its defects as a guide to those from Ireland who had travelled thus far. The peregrinations of notables from Ireland have occasionally been fleshed out: for example, those of the former Trinity don and future Irish bishop, George Berkeley, and the architect of the Irish Parliament, Edward Lovett Pearce. Berkeley reached Sicily, and then did time in Bermuda, before spreading enlightenment via artefacts, melodies and example in the Cork episcopal hamlet of Cloyne.[71] On the whole, the foreign experiences of the cultivated have been mined for explanations as to how they picked up both their polish and their prize possessions.[72] Many mundane journeys, whether of young heirs, adventurous traders or seasoned soldiers, are ignored, particularly if the voyagers never reached Italy. Others, who kicked their heels in the United Provinces or straggled along the Rhine, attract attention only when they arrive in the Catholic south.[73]

The routine traffic between northern Europe and Ireland was constant. During the 1660s, the undertakers of the textile factory at Chapelizod dispatched an observer to report on practices in Flanders.[74] Intending physicians, such as Victor Ferguson and Duncan Cumyng, headed for the medical faculty at Leyden.[75] Much that was encountered – religious worship, townscapes and landscapes – was familiar to the Protestants of Britain and Ireland. The sense of recognition was helped by the communities of immigrants settled in Ireland throughout the seventeenth century. A few from the Low Countries took up permanent residence, especially in Irish ports. Families like the Wybrants, Westenras and van Homrighs gained important places in the commerce and corporation of Dublin.[76] Trade between the north-western seaboard of Europe, Britain and Ireland was long established and valuable. It usually explained the first arrival of immigrants in Ireland. Trading, warfare, education and religion then sustained Irish links with the continent. Edward Stephens, originally from Cork, removed to Rotterdam.[77] The busy reformer from Cork, Henry Maule, obliged to settle the affairs of a soldier brother, sailed over to Maastricht. He used the visit to inspect charitable foundations, and – on his return – applied some of the lessons to his own venture in Shandon.[78] Lady Dunkellin, having retreated to Utrecht to retrieve her and her husband's affairs 'and not to be forgot', found the place dull. She pitied 'those who from our parts are sent hither for education'. She adjudged the discipline poor and the tutors not much better.[79] Vienna, which attracted St George Ashe, had earlier seen the adolescent Lord Roscommon. The Catholic earl of Carlingford served there as Charles II's ambassador.[80]

Regular shipping bound distant ports such as Hamburg to Ireland. Robert Molesworth when ambassador in Denmark relied on the bills of exchange on a Hamburg merchant to pay his expenses.[81] It was a Hamburg merchant, Stratford, who donated busts to his *alma mater*, Trinity College, in 1707.[82] In 1737 the owner of Birr, Laurence Parsons, staying in Hamburg, was much taken with the free port. He intended to remain for another three months before moving on, perhaps to Stockholm or Copenhagen. Earlier, Molesworth had one of his sons, Bisse Molesworth, spend time in Stockholm as secretary to the English ambassador.[83] Hamburg, cheaper than Holland, contained a 'vast deal of the best company'. At The Hague, in contrast, the society had been only 'so so'.[84] The leading Belfast merchant, Daniel Mussenden, had his correspondents in Hamburg and Bremen. They were utilized when Mussenden's son journeyed beyond Holland.[85]

Northerly journeys had political, ideological and cultural resonances which have hardly been investigated, such is the fixation with sunnier climes. The accession in swift sequence of William of Orange and the Elector of Hanover drew more from Ireland towards the northern destinations. The veneration of William as deliverer of the Protestants of Ireland extended to his wife, Mary II. The cult of Mary as careful housewife and deft needlewoman led to places associated with her, especially Het Loo, becoming Protestant shrines, to be visited by pilgrims from Ireland.[86] William and Mary, and through them the United Provinces, retained an allure among the Irish Protestants never rivalled by the Hanoverians and their consorts. Even so, prudence recommended that court be paid to the new dynasty. In 1711, William Smythe advised his brother, James Smythe, to add Berlin and Hanover to his itinerary.[87] Cosby was another from Protestant Ireland who arrived at Herrenhausen, the summer residence of the electoral court. Entry may have been helped by the pivotal position of Samuel Molyneux as secretary to the Prince of Wales, the future George II. Molyneux descended from and was related to many of the clerisy in Ireland. Casual tourism shaded into more purposeful political manoeuvring at Hanover. Alongside the potential gains of royal favour were cultural benefits.[88] The Low Countries and northern Europe were a more accessible source of paintings, artefacts, books and ideas than Italy or – for long periods – France.[89] Hamburg and other German cities, as well as the United Provinces, glutted the voracious with art and artefacts.[90]

Pole Cosby of Stradbally was dispatched to the Netherlands, thanks to his family's predilections towards Presbyterianism and Whiggery. On arrival, he exploited connections formed earlier by his father when soldiering and by Dublin Presbyterians. Young Cosby groped his way through this strange environment. At first, he dined at 'the English ordinary', where none but English, Scottish and Irish students ate. Feeling this segregation was contrary to the purpose for which he had come, he switched to the public ordinary. There he enjoyed 'conversing with people of all nations'. In the vacations, he rode deep into Germany and central Europe. Armed with letters of introduction 'to some top people at Hanover', he kissed the hands of George I and the Prince of Wales. In Berlin he was presented to George I's daughter, the queen of Prussia, and again kissed her hand, 'being subjects of England'. At least in memory (as frozen in his autobiography), and probably in actuality, Cosby tracked restlessly between a sense of himself as English and as Irish. In Munich, where he met several Irish Catholic priests, the hosts 'were joyful to see a countryman'. In the same way, at the Irish monastery in Prague, the inmates were 'as glad and full of joy to see us, as if we were their own kin'. Something of the homesickness which Southwell had discovered in Lord Creagh in Rome in 1660 afflicted the monks far from their homeland. Cosby happily partook of the conventual hospitality, but could not stifle the feelings of difference. Impressed by the monastic church, he wrote off the rest of the order's buildings as 'but ordinary and Irish all over, very dirty'. Nor was he prepared to suppress his opinion that the friendly priests were 'most extremely ignorant and very zealous of their superstitious religion'.[91]

Shortly after Cosby explored the continent, Robert Black, originally from Ulster, undertook a longer tour. Black in his responses repeated and expanded many of the themes evident in the accounts of Waring, Ashe and Cosby. He approved industry, modern classical buildings, order and cleanliness. Like Waring before him, Black prepared by studying classical architecture. He was severe on buildings, such as the Stadthuis of Amsterdam, which failed to use the classical orders correctly. Applying 'the established rules of that art', he censured the church of St Amand at Tournai, although of modern design, as 'not quite purified from the Gothic exuberance'. The Benedictine abbey in the same town pleased more, because 'a perfect piece of modern architecture' and 'the noble simplicity that is hereto observed far exceeds all the extravagance of ornaments to be met with in Gothic architecture'. By the same token, some Gothic structures were condemned. In Paris, the Palais Royale was a cluster of buildings 'as confused and irregular as can be imagined'. Notre Dame was dismissed 'as perfectly Gothic and clumsy: it is very dark by reason of the old painted glass windows full of cobwebs and is far from being kept with that neatness requisite for the first church of the kingdom'.[92]

Black borrowed descriptions and judgements of what he saw from the published handbooks. In Gouda, he revealed that 'little printed books' were given to travellers in order to identify the donors and subjects of the many stained glass windows in the church. Like numerous tourists, he was usually delighted to bump into others who spoke his language. Sometimes he discriminated between those from Ireland and from England, but both could be hailed as compatriots. At Bruges, he was charmed by his 'countryman', Nicholas Porter, who showed Black the 'utmost civilities', despite the lack of 'a recommendation or former acquaintance'. In Ostend, he was gratified by the 'extraordinary civility' with which he was treated by Patrick Sarsfield. Black was shown Dunkirk by 'a countryman', Captain Magee, an engineer as well as a military officer. At Bruges, Black was admitted 'by a worthy set of countrymen' into 'an ancient society, called of amity and concord'. This club was said to have been patronised by Charles II. It served as a social if not also a political focus for expatriates, but whether exclusively from Ireland or from Britain as well is undocumented. A trait that Black shared with some Protestants from Ulster was the feeling of being British, rather than English or Irish *tout court*. He judged Rotterdam 'more like a British colony than a Dutch city'. He liked Hamburg and Hanover, not least because in each he was welcomed fulsomely. At Hamburg, he had letters of introduction to an English trader, who entertained him at his country retreat in Holstein and introduced him to other English merchants of the steelyard. At the same time, he was civilly treated by locals, including 'Mynheer' Ankleman, a member of the ruling council. Black was impressed both by the look of the place and the manners of the people. A focus of polite sociability, it drew the landed from Holstein and Denmark to 'make a figure'. Hanover also extended hospitality to strangers, 'particularly English gentlemen that travel this way'. All were ranked 'my lords, as they think none other can undertake so expensive a journey'.[93]

The societies in these German cities were contrasted with that of Lille, equally magnetic to the pleasure-seekers from the surrounding region. Public concerts were held twice weekly, and it was possible to be introduced into assemblies of gentlemen and ladies. But, to Black's dismay, the chief recreation was gambling. Once in Paris, Black wished to avoid the exclusive company of the English speakers – like Cosby in the Netherlands – since the purpose of his three-month stay was to improve 'in the language and manners of the people'. Accordingly, he left an inn and lodged with a wig-maker near the Rue Monconseil. Thereby he hoped to avoid the 'course of debauchery with one another of whoring, drinking and other excesses'.[94] Successors from Ireland in Paris during the middle of the century were less disciplined. One herd of bucks, including Dick Boyle, Sir Ralph Gore, Tom Burgh, 'young Rochfort, Archdale and Kineer . . . went headlong in all the diversions of Paris, got fashionably disordered and all very sociably and with great unanimity took to their beds and underwent the grand mercurial course'.[95]

Black linked appearances with the prevalent political and religious systems in the places that he visited. Another from Ulster, William Leathes, ruminated as he shuttled between Bruges, Antwerp, Brussels and the United Provinces. Once the Austrians took over from the Spaniards as rulers of the Netherlands, Brussels stagnated. Leathes believed that the city could 'subsist but by a war or a court'. There were potential parallels with Dublin, but the Irish capital before the Union of 1801 never declined to the state where 'no strangers resort here as formerly, neither do the gentry of the country make a considerable figure, most retire to the country and leave the town desolate'.[96] Black felt that Louis XIV's exorbitant ambitions showed in towns within his territories. On the way to Hamburg, he observed 'that the peasants depending on absolute princes as we passed along are wretchedly poor and miserable, whereas the districts belonging to free states are well manured, the country cottages more cleanly and comfortable, and the people cheerful'. A pleasing brand of urbanity flourished in Hamburg, to which Irish Protestants in Ulster and elsewhere aspired. Late in the eighteenth century, a Cork gentleman, Thomas Ronayne, escaped from a Belgium overrun by the French to Hamburg. The free port, now praised as a spot 'where people enjoy liberty in the true sense of the word', had long exerted an attractive power.[97] In 1727, Black traced the prosperity and politeness of Hamburg's citizens to the city's republican constitution.[98] He disliked some Hanoverian possessions. Scenes in Oldenburg recalled indigenous Irish society. The peasants there 'live in cottages with hearth in the middle without a chimney, and the kitchen, bed-chamber, stable and hog sty all in one with a nasty confusion quite contrary to the delicacy of the Dutch'. Delmenhurst in the Duchy of Bremen, over which George II ruled, was written off as 'a poor nasty hole, excessively nasty with the dunghills under the window of their wretched huts which are without the least symmetry or contrivance'. Moreover, around Bremen he saw none of the country houses or improvements that should mark the approach to a city.

The spirit of enquiry in which Black reacted to the novel made him tolerate features which might have outraged him if encountered in Ireland. At Bremen, he observed that the principal church retained some pre-Reformation statuary. He explained these survivals on the grounds of 'the Lutherans not being so averse and bigoted against the ceremonies of that church as the Calvinists in Holland'. In Hamburg he was struck by the same phenomenon, and so asked his guide whether such images were part of the Protestant religion or not. He was told that 'they were indifferent and, since they had remained since popish times, that it was a pity to strip them of this gay furniture'.[99] In Dordrecht, he pondered a different problem. Its church retained bas-reliefs, 'some of them with heathen Roman history very improper in a Christian church'. Yet Black regretted that some of the best had been defaced, 'either through bigotry or ignorance'. While in Rotterdam, he also looked at the synagogue. On Sunday, he went to 'several churches', including one 'English' and two Presbyterian places of worship. At Frankfurt, Calvinists were not allowed a church within the city, but went beyond its confines to worship at a French reformed temple. The worshippers, whom Black joined, were adjudged 'polite people'. He was amazed when two hundred coaches arrived. Once in the Spanish Netherlands, he witnessed new religious observances. At Bruges, he saw the ceremony at which two English women took the veil. Elsewhere, he visited a Benedictine convent of Irish nuns, presided over by a member of the Arthur family from Limerick. Black wrote approvingly, that the abbess was 'a complete gentlewoman who showed us a great deal of civility'. At Tournai, the abbot of St Amand extended similar courtesies. Black recorded how he had been received 'with the greatest politeness and entertained . . . at his table with twenty dishes of the greatest delicacies besides a prodigal dessert of sweetmeats and plenty of the choicest wines'.[100] These, like the Roman feasts enjoyed by Waring, were experiences not open to Protestants in Ireland. In part, it was because of the circumspection with which the Catholic religious were obliged to act. Also, what in continental Europe might be justified as good manners or simple fact-finding, in Ireland still carried perils. Black was viewed within his own circle as an eminent and 'practicable virtuoso'. Others jotted down their observations, but Black's were extracted and studied by relations because 'moral and entertaining'.[101]

The Ulster Blacks personified a family in which trade, education and making a career united to plant members in Spain and France. John Black, after fifty-seven years near Bordeaux as an 'English' factor, returned to an estate in County Down.[102] There he resumed a place in local society, his austere Protestantism strengthened rather than diminished after long years among Catholics. His belief in the value of travel remained. Meeting an acquaintance from the neighbourhood who had served with the East India Company as a captain, he judged James Burnett 'greatly improved since I last saw him . . . by his seeing and knowing men and manners on his voyage round the Cape of Good Hope to Coromandel, Bengal, Fort St. George, &c.'[103]

By 1766, chances for Protestants from Ireland to travel had grown through service outside the kingdom in army, navy and colonial services. Stray references suggested that more travelled from Ireland into Europe than is often assumed. Robert Leslie, the son of an Ulster clergyman, turned up unexpectedly in Paris in 1715. Funds permitting, he intended to travel south.[104] Eleven years later, a future member of parliament for the University of Dublin, Dr John Ellwood, was in Montpellier, probably for his health, before pressing on to Rome.[105] A decade on, Henry Brownrigg appeared at Orléans. There, he executed orders with local nurserymen for his friends back in Ireland.[106] Other provincial towns in eighteenth-century France – Caen, Lyons, Montauban and Montpellier – attracted Irish Protestants.[107] After 1714, the Irish arrivals and departures in Brussels were watched. Some might be conspiring on behalf of the exiled Stuarts.[108] In 1722, it was reported that Lords Carlingford, Bellew, Fingall and an unnamed Irish Protestant peer had arrived, and that Captain Plunkett had returned from Spa. The following year the less ominous arrivals of James Caldwell and Compton Domville were noted.[109] These groups, not confessionally discrete, were clearly distinguished from 'the court' of Irish officers with whom Lord North and Grey consorted. Its members – Captain Bellew, Captain O'Farrell, Captain Macdonald, Mr Butler and Mr Power – were assumed to be Jacobites and 'wild geese', who soldiered for Catholic monarchs.[110] Meanwhile, those intending for the law and medicine studied outside Ireland. Trade carried others to distant places. Their experiences of the strange usually differed from the leisurely Italian journey of Butler and Waring. In turn, even when Irish Protestants found themselves in the same places as their Catholic compatriots, differences were effaced only temporarily: holiday romances seldom survived long after disembarking in the chillier environment of Protestant Ireland.

## IV

Going abroad and gaining fresh impressions need not always entail long voyages. Molesworth thought that to venture beyond the local market prised open closed minds. By that yardstick, the increasingly frequent forays of provincials not just to Dublin or London but to other places within Ireland and England conferred benefits. Again, these varied, partly with the destinations, but also according to the purposes and temperaments of the travellers. Some itinerants on their return understood better the idea and realities of England, Britain, the British and Hanoverian empires; others clung more tightly to their Irish identities. Lovers of liberty, critics of regalian rights and hedonists resulted.[111] Visitors marvelled and moaned.[112] Samuel

Molyneux, riding through England in 1713 en route for the continent, lamented the poor wine, which he charitably attributed to an embargo during the War of Spanish Succession. Irish pride also made him compare the quality of linen and roads in England badly with what he knew at home.[113] Proprietors and professionals of the social and economic level of a Molyneux shared much with Britons: confession, language, history and culture. At the same time, they did not feel altogether at ease. Numerous nuances reminded that they were outsiders. Robert French from County Galway in 1751 regarded the new Westminster Bridge as 'a noble building becoming the grandeur of the nation'. The view up river from Greenwich over the growing city provoked reflections on 'the grandeur, wealth and power of the nation'. At this moment, French's 'nation' embraced both Ireland and England. French, one of the English of Ireland, although his family had converted to Protestantism only a generation earlier, was comfortable enough in Georgian England. He saw much to commend on 'the most agreeable jaunt we had ever taken'.[114] But it did not take much wit to comprehend that the conditions of the two kingdoms differed markedly. Some English innovations, potentially, might be applied on his return to Monivea; others would not transplant successfully, like the seeds collected from the massive cedars at Lord Pembroke's Wilton House.[115]

In 1761, a Church of Ireland clergyman was one of many from Ireland who crowded into London at the time of George III's coronation.[116] Love of spectacle more than affection for Britain and its German monarch explained the influx. The cleric, like many another visitor, had introductions to London residents with Irish connections. At the Royal Exchange, where he had business, he hastened to the 'Irish walk'. There, one of the merchants invited him to dine with some fellow countrymen. 'The honour of Old Ireland' was several times invoked to justify expansiveness.[117] The visitor, when later entertained by Colonel Richard Lambart, heir to the earl of Cavan, remarked that the hospitality was 'in the Irish manner, with peace and plenty and a hearty welcome'. The festivities concluded with bottles of claret. Meeting English clergymen, 'of a very sober and self-denying spirit', he 'made a great reformation among them and infused so much of an Irish spirit that we now commonly drink our wine by the bottle'.[118] Pride in putting on the Irish was apparent in his mocking reference to the departure of his party from London, 'in as polite a manner as any travelling bog-trotters could for the honour of Old Ireland'.[119] This self-projection as 'a true Irishman' may have protected against mockery for accent and demeanour.[120] At times, this tourist seemed to pander to his hosts' unflattering notion of how the Irish cavorted.

Two Irish gentlemen wrote up their perambulation through England in 1752. Their Irishness, or (perhaps more accurately) their notion of themselves as the English of Ireland, was not obtruded. They were drawn to the pleasure gardens at Vauxhall, which they compared to the Elysian Fields. There, and at the rival Ranelagh Gardens, music was performed. At the second venue, Mrs Storer sang 'Ellen-a-Roon' in Irish, 'but with such clipping of the words that I was assured by one who well understood Irish that was she to sing it in Ireland it would be taken for some other dialect'. In fact, Elizabeth Storer was much in demand as a singer in Dublin.[121] Whatever criticism her accent excited among the knowing, in London the exoticism of the Irish language when coupled with the 'traditional' melody disarmed most auditors. No longer, it seemed, did the Irish language denote barbarism.[122] Fear of the wild Irish had by the mid-eighteenth century given way to mirth at their uncouthness.[123] 'Traditional' Irish airs and instruments were well liked in London.[124] The taste for Irish spectacles was also attested by an Ulster clergyman, Philip Skelton. He observed 'a wild Irishman' from County Antrim exhibited for money in London. Not alarming enough, the unfortunate had false beard and wings clipped to him.[125]

Language and dialect, smacking of exoticism, could be turned to profit in England. Yet, travellers from Ireland, anxious to succeed in polite society, worried about the ways that they dressed, behaved and spoke. Just as visitors from Ulster and Connacht were ridiculed by the metropolitan in Dublin, so travellers from Ireland were discomfited when they were mocked in strange cities.[126] Genteel Dubliners shunned sounds redolent of the remote. Unhappiness on this score testified to the spread of politeness into eighteenth-century Ireland. Accent and vocabulary were added to the many ways through which national affiliation was detected or expressed. Money could buy first the education to know the proper figure, and then the materials with which to construct it. Parents and children alike strove to shed their Irish intonations. One visitor to England admitted that, soon after he landed, 'I endeavoured to correct the brogue natural to our country'.[127] In north Antrim during the 1720s, the Reverend James Smythe feared for his daughter, Nancy. He concluded, 'it is impossible she can improve in this country except it be in the dialect of Scotland', and schemed to dispatch her to Dublin.[128] Bishop Synge of Elphin was equally determined that his daughter should not pick up the speech of servants. Whenever Alicia Synge's phonetic spelling betrayed Irish modulations, it was corrected.[129] Despite the precautions, the unwelcome accents were heard. Lucius O'Brien, from County Clare, enrolled at Hillsborough School in County Down, was lampooned for his 'country wretched twang'. The defect contracted in 'more early years', probably from servants, 'continues with very little amendment'.[130] Early in the 1750s, Bland at Blandsfort in Queen's County decided to transfer his nephews from a local school to one in Dublin, 'that they may lose the Irish brogue which they contract at country schools'. Later he explained that 'the Irish pronunciation . . . is very disagreeable to an English ear, and renders those . . . not well looked upon by the people here and held cheap in their opinion'. In short, according to Squire Bland, 'nothing appears so vulgar as the Irish twang'.[131]

Similar nervousness persuaded Richard Edgeworth to put his sons to school at Warwick. However, when the Edgeworths returned permanently to Ireland, the heir was moved to the prestigious academy at Drogheda. Now, the hapless Edgeworth boy was mocked for an accent which some took to be of Cumberland and others of Germany. Yet earlier, at Dr Lydiatt's in Warwick, he had been bullied and nicknamed 'Little Irish' for his brogue.[132] In 1758, a Belfast father was tempted to send his son to school in England, simply because 'the contracting early of a good accent and an agreeable manner of speaking' was essential if the youth were later to succeed at the bar.[133] At the humblest level, the Charter Schools worked to eradicate the brogue. An inspector at Primrose Grange towards the end of the century commended pupils on their facility in reading the Bible, 'tho not free from a disagreeable tone of voice'.[134] Back in 1721, when the leading Catholic lawyer Sir Toby Butler died at the age of seventy-eight, it was observed, 'his accent had a brogue 'tis true'. Already, maybe, such a feature was considered inappropriate or unusual.[135] Soon parental anxieties went beyond a simple distinction between intonations clearly English or Irish. An English employer thought an unsatisfactory maid servant 'to be Irish and inclined to popery'. These accusations were proved by the facts that 'she spoke the brogue strong, and owned she had lived a great deal in Ireland'.[136] Maria Gunning, one of two beauties from the Irish Midlands, even after she had become countess of Coventry and was adored in London drawing-rooms, was censured for her 'very vulgar accent', described as 'broad Irish'.[137]

In practice, attitudes, whether of the English towards the Irish or of Dubliners to provincials, were inconsistent. At Vauxhall, Irish airs sung by Mrs Storer enchanted English listeners. Moreover, the Irish sometimes retaliated. The Reverend John Chalenor, invited to preach at Holyhead, was astonished by the response. 'The Welsh brutes hearing him speak nothing but good English [the cleric had been born in Shropshire and educated at Dublin University] ran out of the church to the mirth of the beholders'.[138] Chalenor faced in unusually stark forms the hazards endured by most who sailed from Dublin to north Wales. On the western seaboard, the voyager arrived close to the second city of the Stuarts' and Hanoverians' empire. The disembarkation quays at Ringsend and Dun Laoghaire might sometimes be bleak, but they were only a short ride to the recognizable civilization of Dublin. Not so, landing on Anglesey, which was the prelude to a trek through rocky defiles and across treacherous sands and straits. Guides were essential and dangers real.[139] Those who opted to land at Parkgate found themselves in the unthreatening vicinity of Chester, but still faced the gruelling ride to London. In other parts of lowland England, such as the route from Cirencester to Oxford, a guide was needed.[140]

More than the terrain disconcerted itinerants from Ireland. In 1765, a touchy gentleman transplanted from Kerry to Yorkshire repined. 'Living here', he announced, 'is a most severe exile. I declare Iveragh is, by much, a more elegant place both for men and manners'. With a handful of exceptions, he had 'never met with a more complete set of brutes' than in northern England.[141] Scotland, particularly its remoter regions, charmed scarcely more. A reluctant member of the garrison at Fort William, used to the north of Ireland, felt that the local Scots were 'demons in human shape; they are utter strangers to both law and gospel'.[142] Oliver Goldsmith, uprooted from the Irish midlands, disliked 'this unfruitful country' of the Highlands, and saw 'no brook nor grove to cheer the stranger or make the inhabitants forget their poverty'.[143]

Travel between Britain and Ireland disclosed similarities and divergences. On the one side, it nourished anti-Irish feelings, which persisted into the eighteenth century. Some visitors from Ireland happily identified with an England where their forebears had originated. The dullness of Dublin was deprecated; the liveliness of London applauded.[144] Other travellers, less besotted with England, felt more strongly the sense of belonging to Ireland, albeit as the English of Ireland. Reactions usually reflected the reasons why and circumstances in which the travellers came. The troubles of the seventeenth century twice dislodged Irish Protestants. Refugees perched on the western seaboard where they had disembarked. During the spring of 1689, it was reported that 500 refugees from south Munster had sailed into Bristol and another 400 into Minehead.[145] Chester, Whitehaven and Ayr were other obvious shelters.[146] Many gravitated to London and its environs. There they formed a motley community.[147] The undoubted grandees, such as Ormond, Cork and Burlington, Blessington and Temple, knowing London well and well known there, were outnumbered by the obscure.[148] The emergency, as earlier that after 1641, swelled the numbers lobbying in London for alms, aid, military commissions and favours. Some 2,000 from Ireland, mostly poor women and children, were still stranded in England after 1690.[149]

Any sympathy for the plight of Irish Protestants quickly mutated into irritation at the way in which Ireland distracted attention and diverted money from – to the English – more urgent matters. In the immediate aftershock of the alleged massacres of Irish Protestants in 1641, survivors who escaped to England were assisted.[150] However, as outrage at maltreatment of fellow Protestants abated, so the fugitives from Ireland tended to be conflated with the Irish immigrants familiar in larger towns and westerly districts of Britain.[151] Already, the throng in an eastern suburb of London had earned it the sobriquet of 'Knockfergus'.[152] In time, the prospering with Irish links helped 'the poor and distressed Irish in London'. From 1704 an 'Irish Charitable Society' was active. Its directors and benefactors were noblemen and gentlemen, 'natives of Ireland', who found themselves – temporarily or habitually – in England. Although this Society was wound up in 1756, in the 1780s it was subsumed into a new London charity, the Benevolent Society of St Patrick.[153] Seasonal and longer-term movement from Ireland to Britain inevitably fluctuated in volume with the economic and political situation in the western kingdom. Numbers alarmed their English hosts. At Neston, the port of Chester, 120 women from Ireland were waiting to be repatriated in 1751. Another 200 were there in 1756. In 1758, an Irishman was to be returned from Cheshire to Kilcullen in County Kildare. So far from being isolated instances, 25,535 were recorded between 1750 and 1800 as having being rounded up and kept at the Neston house of correction before being shipped back to Ireland.[154]

Those who came as refugees or in search of work seldom cut a fine figure. A lucky few from Protestant Ireland thrived in England after 1660. But success in England could seldom be combined satisfactorily with continuing activism in Irish public affairs. Financing permanent establishments on both sides of the Irish Sea overtaxed even the wealthiest, as the Ormondes, Cork and Burlington and Conway discovered. Soon, most had to choose between living splendidly in Ireland or in England. Those like the Boyles, Temples, Cootes, Percevals and Southwells who opted for English lives did not forget Ireland, and not just as a vital source of their wealth. They bestirred themselves in the British parliament and at court to promote some measures and to block others.[155] They welcomed travellers from the old country. Visitors, by lodging with acquaintances from Ireland, saved money. The first earl of Orrery coshered on Lord Conway when in London in 1669.[156] During the crisis of 1689, Viscount Blessington, son and heir of the Irish Primate, Archbishop Boyle, lodged in Soho Square with the dowager countess of Mountrath.[157] Soon afterwards, Blessington's scheming brother-in-law, Denny Muschamp, was put up at Robert Molesworth's place off St James's Square.[158] While Molesworth was on an embassy to Denmark, his wife went to her Coote kinsfolk in their lodgings at St James's.[159] Another from the same circle, Richard Boyle, the ne'er-do-well son of the first Viscount Shannon, was accommodated by the countess of Portland in Pall Mall.[160] The habit continued into the next century and helped to sustain groups with a distinct Irish tone.[161]

It was not just the important from Ireland who had kindred or friends in London. In 1713, a young soldier from Dublin, John Fontaine, lodged at an inn in Pall Mall until he could discover the whereabouts of an uncle. Once the latter was located, Fontaine stayed in London for several months with members of his family and of the émigré Huguenot community.[162] After 1720, a young man from Ulster was taken to London by his father to sort out a legal imbroglio. They stayed with a grand acquaintance in Berkshire, who lent the visitors his coach to travel to London.[163] The Blacks kept a London house where members of the family from the north of Ireland, France and Spain could stay.[164] In 1762, Anne Weldon, arriving in London, headed for the lodgings of her friends from Ireland, the Caldwells. Once settled, she shared lodgings close to the Caldwells' apartment with other Irish intimates.[165] A fictitious account of visitors from Ireland in 1752 mentioned the travellers seeking directions in London, to 'where the Irish commonly set up'. In this case it was a hostelry, *The Three Cups* in Bread Street. Brandishing letters of introduction, another essential for the tourist, the trippers sought out fellow Irish, 'amongst whom I knew a few'.

There were clearly well-known pull-ins for the Irish away from home. The sightseers of 1752 tried an eating house run by an Irishman. On revealing their identities, 'we got the better fare'. Not only did this include French soup and goose, but excellent wine, which they had hardly tasted since berthing in England.[166] A lawyer from Dublin in 1752 lodged near The Strand in London. His landlord's name, 'Flin', hinted at an Irish origin.[167] In 1761, another visitor to London, 'seeing a group of Irishmen gossiping together, being at a loss I suppose where to dine, we joined them and listened to their chat'. This same tourist was outraged when he and a party of fellow countrymen were served inferior claret in a

London chophouse in 1761. He roundly told the publican, 'we belonged to the kingdom that knew the difference between good and bad claret'.[168]

When the young Edgeworth first came to London, he hired lodgings. Initially, he stayed at Mrs Norton's coffee-house. This billet was soon exchanged for accommodation *chez* Edward Carroll. Although less central in Paddington, the place was cheaper and perhaps, if as the landlord's name suggested an Irish association, more congenial.[169] Edgeworth, like Robert French, another trainee lawyer, passed some vacations in the countryside outside London, sharing with fellow students from Ireland, and ostensibly studying.[170] Would-be lawyers were the only vocational group in Ireland required to train in London. Over four hundred did so between 1688 and 1714.[171] Some physicians and surgeons sought instruction there, but it was on an individual footing. In any case, faculties in Scotland, France and the Low Countries were preferred. In London, Edgeworth consorted with others from Ireland.[172] He dined regularly with an uncle, typically in public houses.[173] In addition, he joined 'clubs', small groups which met in particular hostelries. Members of at least one, the Bull's Head, were reunited in Dublin a decade later.[174] He was also introduced to patrons of the Anglo-Irish community in England, such as Lord Burlington.[175] In later years, married and a parent, Edgeworth returned several times to England. However, London exercised no special fascination. His itineraries focused on Bath and Bristol, and placing sons at school in Worcester or Warwick and at college in Oxford.[176] The last task, not any compulsion to see George III's coronation – although he had witnessed the grandfather's in 1727 – dictated the English trip of 1761.[177]

Edgeworth's contemporary, Robert French of Monivea, when he toured England in 1751, returned to a London which – like Edgeworth – he had known earlier as a student at the Inns of Court. French noted what had changed since then. Not least, he had more money in his pocket and an appreciative bride. He could show off by showing her the sights. In all, the trip cost him £200. With a yearly income approaching £1,500 and the worst expenses of setting up house in Dublin completed, it was a permissible indulgence. Kinship was exploited.[178] An acquaintance in London furnished the Frenches with introductions for their visit to York; in Cambridge, their guide was another family connection. But, above all, the focus of their London stay was French's younger brother, the Reverend Digby French, already in the city. The itinerants on arrival went directly to the clergyman's lodgings.[179] In the same manner, the cleric who visited London in 1761 repaired initially to an inn in the city. Quickly he exchanged it for a 'very genteel apartment' near Bond Street, of two chambers with closet. This visitor, being gregarious, repeatedly fell in with company, much of it either firmly or tenuously linked with Ireland. Having arrived on 28 August, it was not until 7 September that he noted that he had dined at his lodgings for the first time.[180] Similarly, a young army officer from County Waterford when newly arrived in London put up at a tavern near Fleet Street. Then, having located a cousin who lived in the capital, the visitor was rescued from his lodgings and welcomed into the family home.[181]

Solidarity among 'the gentlemen of Ireland' in London was strongest when important measures were on the anvil. Crises impelled many from Ireland to the place where ultimate power over the kingdom was exercised. Even in more placid times, London was awash with Protestants from Ireland. Viscount Rosse grumbled to Ormonde in 1713, 'most of our young gentlemen are gone or going to London'.[182] Resignedly one Irish observer acknowledged, 'what is to be done will be done in London'.[183] Periodic efforts were made to organize the exiles. In 1715, when, with deft diplomacy, the Prince of Wales was installed as chancellor of Dublin University, gentlemen of Irish background were summoned. With forty or fifty in town, a decent show was predicted.[184] New regularity was given to otherwise erratic reunions by inventing an Irish Protestant festival. Formal commemoration of the 1641 uprising, introduced into Ireland in 1661, provided the occasion. By the eighteenth century, it was turned into a social event for expatriates. On 23 October 1713, after the London sermon 'for the gentlemen of our country', the worshippers repaired to the Pall Mall coffee-house and then dined together. It may be that enthusiasm for this form of celebration was at its height during the factious times of Queen Anne, and expressed the political affiliations of Irish Protestants.[185]

The foundation of charities in Ireland afforded Irish Protestants resident in England additional chances to meet. After 1733, a corresponding society was formed in London to assist the work of the Incorporated Society in Ireland. Its affairs were directed by a few stalwarts. They included absent proprietors, such as Viscount Blundell, the earl of Orrery, Edward Southwell, and sons of Lords Charlemont and Palmerston, who owed their wealth to Ireland. Unfamiliarity with the topography of the island may have caused the committee to purchase maps of the counties of Ireland in 1737.[186] Meetings were afforced by those passing through London: the bishop of Elphin, Robert Howard, sat at the board in 1737 and 1738. The new dean of Clogher, John Copping, also attended.[187] In 1741, it was resolved to compose a letter 'for such of the nobility and gentry of Ireland as are now in town', to solicit their help.[188] The Corresponding Society, like its counterpart in Dublin, raised funds through an annual sermon. Although preached usually by an English divine, the sermon provided a pretext for those with residual Irish links to congregate.[189] However, in 1742, the board of the Corresponding Society plaintively wished that 'their assemblies were more frequented, and that [the] gentlemen of Ireland who are now in this kingdom would show more favour'.[190]

The Irish in London during the eighteenth century never had the same focus for mutual support and recreation enjoyed by the Welsh, with their Societies of Cymmrodorion and Gwyneddigion, and a charity school in the capital run by the Honourable and Loyal Society of Ancient Britons. The Welsh resembled the Protestants from Ireland in wishing to advertise devotion to the new Hanoverian dynasty. Where Trinity College chose the Prince of Wales as its chancellor, the Ancient Britons acquired his wife as their patron.[191] English hosts often looked on the Irish much as they regarded the Welsh. In the century after 1660 attitudes switched from fear or contempt to affectionate mockery. Yet the cases of the two peoples were never identical, since Ireland with its geographical separation, confessional distinctiveness and continuing usefulness (at least potentially) to Britain's enemies posed the graver danger.[192]

## V

Large bills lessened the pleasures of London. Like Dublin, London required show. Pole Cosby on a visit to an uncle in Soho Square in 1723 remembered 'that the first thing I did was to deck myself out with fine clothes to make a good appearance, judging that I should be more taken notice of for it'. Those anxious to reduce costly obligations in Ireland by retreating to England succeeded only if they opted for provincial obscurity. The Cosbys subsequently veered between spells in England to recruit weakened finances and a frenetic plunge into the high life. Economy took them to York and Bristol.[193] Henry Ingoldsby, the heir to Carton, came to London after George I's accession. Ingoldsby, a Tory, found his political career blocked at home.[194] With about £1,200 p.a, he relished being 'a young Irish gentleman . . . in sweet London'. The charms, he confided, 'are not to be expressed'. He enjoined Irish acquaintants to spread the word, 'I neither keep a whore nor am I parted from my wife'. Soon, however, he admitted to being 'devilishly tired' of the metropolis.[195] Problems arose from a shortage of cash. In 1720, he had lost in the South Sea stock speculation. Also, remittances from Ireland disappointed.[196] By 1723, London lodgings secured through a Mr Shaw of the Dublin suburb of Artane did not please. The house had 'not [been] cleaned out for my reception'; a 'common porter' was sleeping in the sole bedroom. Since being vacated by the last tenant, Ingoldsby swore, ' 'twas never so much as swept out, but perfectly stinks, and the bed still in the dining room and the bill [advertising it was to let] on the door till we came in'. There was 'not one saucepan or pot in the whole house fit to be seen by Christians, all untinned and battered, and the bedding so dirty that it's impossible for us to lie in them'.[197]

Ingoldsby, the owner of a Dublin town house and Carton, was not accustomed to such squalor. Moreover, Shaw's house lay not in the fashionable West End, where the Ingoldsbys might have been expected to lodge, but in Queen's Square in Holborn. The housing, rapidly built by speculators, met a seemingly insatiable demand.[198] When Ingoldsby quit Shaw's place, worsted by the bugs, it was for an adjacent development off Red Lion Square.[199] This was remote from the fashionable squares and streets favoured by others from Ireland like Richard Waring, William Leathes, the St Georges or the Southwells. Despite the tribulations, Ingoldsby revelled in a round of 'operas, masquerades and plays'. He also spent on goods, including seeds and plants, which were to be shipped over to his Irish properties.[200] But, with debts mounting, marital relations strained if not severed and children dying, Ingoldsby soon denounced London as 'this villainous place'.[201] Ingoldsby's temperament rather than the city, 'this confounded extravagant place', was at fault.[202] After almost a decade of dissipation, he had neither the fervour nor the funds to continue. He abandoned London in order try to restore the foundations of the family in Ireland. He died before he could do so, leaving an inheritance so encumbered that the trustees sold it.[203]

The rake's progress of Ingoldsby could be matched by that of his contemporary, Williams Conyngham, also inheritor of a valuable estate in Leinster. Conyngham's extravagances took him to the European continent as well as to England. But he ended with much of his Irish property mortgaged to a consortium of London tradespeople. Conyngham had incurred many of his debts in London. Its temptations differed in scale rather than in essence from those of Dublin. Manuals that guided the uncertain as to how to behave in London or warned of the tricks of the town were readily adapted to Dublin. It was said that the better shopping in the English capital snared the unwary. However, it was never peculiarly Irish to take such baits. Furthermore, against every profligate St George or Townley Balfour can be set the careful from Ireland. French on his tour in 1751 divulged that he had spent a modest £41 on purchases and his wife, £23.[204] John Digby of Landenstown, in London during the 1730s, executed numerous commissions for those back in Ireland.[205] He also shopped energetically on his own account. Yet, there was no sense that he had overspent or wasted his estate.[206]

In contemporary legend, spendthrifts were balanced by the seekers of heiresses. Penurious Irish squires were said to flock to London in the hope of making not marring their fortunes. Occasional successes in this regard were lovingly studied. Tales of an Irishman, originally a stuff-weaver from Limerick, who had twice married dowagers in England, were cherished. Thereby he had come into money, which 'he let fly like a true Irishman in living hospitably and bringing his countrymen out of debts, gaols and scrapes'.[207] Wastrels undone by London are matched by the industrious, who, migrating from Ireland to London, prospered. Sons of William Waring, the County Down landlord, illustrate this exemplary theme. One flourished as a woollen draper; a second invested the profits from a good marriage and lengthy military service in a sumptuous London property.[208] Families from Ulster may have enjoyed special advantages when they moved into the British metropolis. Since the early seventeenth century, the London chartered trading companies had had a stake in the new Protestant plantation of the province. It did not always bring the predicted benefits. Nevertheless, it involved routine contacts between the province and London, with the possibility that agents, tenants and their offspring might be eased into positions in the city. Also, the permeable and unclear boundaries between the finances of the state, the exchequer and the revenue, and of the officers who handled them, together with the need for frequent communication between the London Treasury and its dependencies in Ireland, gave financial functionaries from Ireland the entrée into the banks and businesses of London.[209]

Shadowy worlds of work as well as of play drew many from Ireland to England. The merely laborious Irish in London (and elsewhere), because less sensational, and rarely as well documented as the profligates and adventurers, have mainly been overlooked – at least before the nineteenth century.[210] Dorothy Flanagan from County Roscommon claimed to have come from Connacht to Dublin and then on to London, 'all on foot'. Her mission was to beg exemption from the excise on ale and beer which she intended to sell.[211] Another absentee proprietor was impressed when a tenant walked all the way from Parkgate to London to plead not to be ejected from his farm. The landlord agreed to continue the walker in his tenancy as 'a reasonable indulgence for so long a journey'.[212] A woman purporting to be Mary Greatorex from County Waterford also turned up in London, to importune a connection for money.[213] Many more from Ireland are hard to spot, since, once they had settled into long residence, it was forgotten whence they had come. Those who alighted briefly have left more traces. William Smythe, obliged to be there to train as a barrister, likened the metropolis to Sodom. Women and music were its chief delights. So far from deriving great pleasure from 'good conversation . . . , there are so few, very few, to be met with in whose company I think myself safe from the prevailing follies and vices of the place', that he cowered in his lodgings. Smythe longed only to return to 'dear sweet Ireland and all the good company I left there'. Another transient, Henry Green, Archbishop King's steward, expressed a common reaction. 'We are all heartily tired of this very expensive place . . . I am of opinion if I get my foot on Irish ground once more, I shall never long to see old England again'.[214]

Green voiced the ambivalence felt by his employer. Just as Irish patriots berated absentees for neglecting their responsibilities in, and removing wealth from, Ireland, so they fulminated against the stampede to London and the apparently uncritical admiration of its modes and models. Archbishop King, on occasion a champion of overseas travel as a fundamental in education, jeered at Irish grandees besotted with the English capital.[215] Catholic Europe, it seemed, was tolerable, but not Protestant London. According to King, visitors from Ireland were held in low regard in London, living 'as it were out of the world there, and converse only in a very sneaking private way with one another, without making any figure or having any interest'. Warming to the theme, the archbishop spoke of 'a nobleman, that would appear with credit, reputation and splendour in his own country, sinketh there below the ordinary rate of gent'.[216] King's strictures were the more surprising as he himself frequented London (and Bath). On each trip, he directed to Dublin crates crammed with his purchases. Books were his principal indulgence, but he was not immune to pictures, prints and fabrics. In 1706, he returned from London with one of the most ostentatious imports: a new coach.[217] King's expenditure of £1,226 in 1709–10 overtopped that of abstemious squires like Edgeworth, French and Waring. The archbishop did not travel light. In 1716, his caravan consisted of sixteen horses, two chaplains and 'a proportionable retinue'.[218] King could afford it; he could also justify it since he appeared in London as representative of the Protestant Church – and maybe the Protestants – of Ireland.

King objected to the human traffic from Dublin to London, not only because it robbed the Irish capital of too many of its political and social leaders, but because the travellers abased themselves. King's sensitivity on this score arose from his awareness of how greatly Ireland was subordinated legally, constitutionally and economically to Britain. Others in Ireland shared his unease. Arthur Dobbs, for example, accepted that 'the great, the rich, the gay and young, who are easy in their circumstances, will always crowd to the circle of pleasure' in London. Dean Delany endorsed this view: money made in Ireland 'will always be spent in the seat of power and pleasure, and at the fountain-head of preferments and employments of all kinds'.[219] In King's eyes, between 1689 and 1720, an unwholesome cultural dependency had also deepened. This situation forced those from Ireland too often into the posture of entreaty. Indeed, King might feel that he himself had been manoeuvred into that ungainly position. Some of his protracted stays had been in pursuit of his claims as bishop of Derry against the London Companies and on behalf of the established Church of Ireland.[220] As in so many other questions of weight – the making of policy for Ireland or the distribution of offices there – these matters were decided in London, and usually in accordance with British not Irish priorities. King was mortified to see the judicial and legislative powers of the Irish Parliament, of which as a bishop he was a member, and the formal advisory role of the Irish privy council, on which again he sat, severely trimmed. Although he was invited to preach before Queen Anne, and respected in Britain as much as in Ireland as a man of learning, wealth and rank, the compliments availed little if the Irish interests which he strenuously – and tactlessly – upheld were set at naught. So, inconsistent as it might appear, remembering his own frequent appearances in London, Archbishop King condemned the Irish who flocked there.

## VI

Among Irish visitors to England, the popularity of London was rivalled by Bath. Spa waters were quaffed by valetudinarians from Ireland. First Tunbridge and Epsom, then Scarborough, Bath and Bristol were patronized. Some in Ulster crossed the sea to Moffat in Scotland to take its waters and improve their health.[221] In 1686, it was reported that three important members of the Dublin administration, 'all water drinkers', were at Tunbridge Wells.[222] Bath, more convenient for the southern and eastern ports of Ireland, was soon favoured by patients and the pleasure-bent. During the 1690s, a sickly daughter of the Warings tried its curative properties rather than those nearer home. She was joined by her mother. Their stay cost a substantial £108 12s. 4d.[223] In 1701, it was noted that the bishop of Raphoe was at Bath rather than in his diocese.[224] Thereafter Irish bishops were frequently to be found at the English springs.[225] William Conolly took his wife to Bath during the Tory ascendancy when his career was in the doldrums. Owen Wynne, a high-ranking soldier from County Sligo, was there at much the same season.[226] Sir Thomas and Lady Vesey, Tories, imbibed at Bath.[227] Often a stop at Bath preceded, or repaired the damage after, business and pleasure in London. Visitors as various as the eccentric invalid Sir Richard Bulkeley, Archbishop King, the egregious revenue official Brettridge Badham, and Richard Edgeworth drank at the springs.[228] The Dublin *rentier* James Ware, hitherto active in the philanthropic and improving societies of the capital, removed himself to Bath, where he died.[229]

To partake of the regime demanded money and leisure. The widowed Elinor O'Hara totalled her expenses for diet, candles and coal during a stay of twenty-three weeks at £17 5s.; on lodgings, £17 2s.; and for washing, another £4 2s. To these basics had to be added such items as the passage to sail back from Bristol to Dublin (£5 6s. 6d.) and her losses at cards (a further £9 6s. 6d.). Elinor O'Hara decked herself in a pearl necklace of four strings, for which she paid £11. She was introduced to the novelty of the sociable breakfast.[230] Soon Mrs O'Hara was followed to Bath by an extravagant son. He quickly ran up a bill of £30 with a landlady, who also lent him £65 in cash.[231] Richard Edgeworth's lodgings in Bath compared favourably in price with those he took for his family in Dublin. On the first visit, six weeks' board and lodging for all the Edgeworths cost £18. In 1753, Edgeworth paid £50 for a stay of nine months. A couple of years later, taking a house in Dublin's Capel Street for seven months set Edgeworth back £80.[232] Irish Protestants, such as Edgeworth, able to make the trip tended to be those already possessed of interests and connections in England. At Bath they participated in amusements which may have reminded simultaneously of their membership of polite society and of their Irishness. The diversions added to the expense: Edgeworth subscribed separately to the baths (two guineas for the season) and the coffee-house (a mere 2s. 6d.). As in Dublin and the Irish countryside, he had to bear frequent losses at cards. At Bath, he also followed convention by entertaining acquaintances to public breakfasts, and he appeared at such improving events as a lecture on the orrery.[233]

Towards the end of the seventeenth century, Bulkeley reported from Bath, 'here is a vast *monde* of quality'. All 'from the beggar to the duke' indulged in 'an universal ingurgitation of the waters'.[234] The Irish often gravitated towards one another. Some detected a strong Hibernian tone to the place. By 1717, the Irish were reputed to make 'a great show'.[235] Mary Delany, whose ailing husband – the dean of Down – sought a cure there, commented in 1757 'here are swarms of Hibernians'.[236] By 1761, a German observer of the Bath scene was delighted by the presence of many Catholic Irishmen. Educated on the continent, particularly in France and the Netherlands, these cosmopolitans helped render the resort 'especially pleasant to foreigners'. Not only could they speak foreign languages, but their civility contrasted with the chilliness of the English.[237] More permanent presences from Ireland were the immigrants who found work there, such as the chairmen. Robust, they acquired a reputation the reverse of refined.[238]

Bath did not enslave all. Expenses were high, tricks legion, and lodgings overpriced. Bishop Vesey, 'tired of this rotten place', longed to be back in Ireland. Meanwhile, a well-bred young woman from Ireland complained of being devoured by rats and mice in her lodgings.[239] But Bath and Bristol, despite their drawbacks, remained popular. One Protestant visitor from Ulster confided that he 'was getting into a very good acquaintance' at Bristol, although 'the plays, balls, public breakfasts, &c. far exceed the bounds of my finances'.[240] Another enthusiast from County Clare regarded Bristol as 'an enchanting town', with lodgings and houses fit for princes. The sickly believed themselves healed.[241] The Cosbys from Queen's County, although there to recoup their depleted finances, loved the shopping. At the great fair in the city, they bought seventy-eight separate parcels of goods.[242] The Hotwells at Bristol lured a fashionable crowd, but in general the place did not match Bath.[243] Only after 1750 were there signs of physical improvements which, it was hoped, would persuade the Bristolians 'that politeness is no ways incompatible with trade and commerce' and please exacting visitors.[244] Irish towns like Belfast, Kilkenny and Waterford had already achieved a happier balance between making and spending money.[245]

High costs negated the hopes of those who removed from Ireland to provincial England in order to save money. This motive drove Pole Cosby to exchange Stradbally for Bristol and maybe Edgeworth County Longford for Bath. Michael Smythe, squire of Portlick in Westmeath, ruined his finances and health in a vain bid to be elected to parliament. He and his wife were advised to retire 'to some cheap place where there is a good school and there live private in order to recover their affairs'. By 1741, the couple had established themselves at Bath.[246]

The knowledge that only a minority could afford to disport themselves outside Ireland – and that some of the travellers thereby overstretched themselves – emboldened entrepreneurs within the kingdom. In 1684, Bellon, a medical doctor enticed to Ireland by Ormond, expounded the God-given duty to tap natural resources. Specifically he outlined how the curative waters near the viceregal retreat at Chapelizod outside Dublin could be popularized. He proposed two rows of tents flanking a green, as 'suitable to the occasions of the more modest of the modest sex'. Bellon, mindful of continental and English resorts, recommended 'the divertisements of music, bowling, pins, lotteries, shooting . . . to disengage the mind from too serious or melancholic thoughts'.[247] Away from Dublin, the twin impulses of recreation and health popularized spas. By 1690, the mineral springs of County Wexford were being recommended to visitors from Wales, 'for several that have drunk of those do aver ours to be as good if not to exceed' those in Britain.[248] Already the lord deputy, Tyrconnell, had taken this advice and submitted to a régime of Wexford waters, fancied to surpass those of Tunbridge.[249] The effect was rather spoilt when the grumpy William King reported that all the lodging houses stank.[250]

Businessmen joined patriots to cry up Irish watering places. First, Castle Connell and Ballyspellan, next Mallow and Swanlinbar were promoted. In 1758, Dr John Rutty prefaced a published compendium with the rueful admission that he was unlikely to advance 'our own waters in opposition to the fashion, established with the growing luxury of the times, of preferring all foreign productions to our own'.[251] Through an elaborate analysis of the properties of the different springs, he sought to prove that many Irish sources were more efficacious than those of Bath, Bristol, Spa or Aix-les-Bains.[252] Even the relatively poor, such as a patient from Dr Steevens's Hospital in Dublin, journeyed to Swanlinbar and submitted to its regime for a month.[253] The humble, without the help of charity, could drink at their local springs and wells, many of which Rutty itemized.[254] As a Quaker, he stayed mum about their continuing religious associations. Much of what he described denoted the secularization as well as commercialization of older pilgrimages. A few sites succeeded in enticing a consciously respectable (and often Protestant clientèle) and from greater distances than could be walked by the dedicated pilgrim. By the 1690s, the Boyles' agent found it more convenient to try the cure at Castle Connell outside Limerick than posting over constantly to Bath.[255] Castle Connell was still popular in Rutty's time.[256] Ballyspellan, favoured by the smart Veseys in the 1720s, possessed a 'large dancing-room'. In 1732 it was reputed to be 'in great request'.[257] However, its location in a 'cold, mountainous tract' and the greater attractions of Kilkenny ended its short vogue.[258]

Longer in fashion among the polite and genteel were Mallow and Swanlinbar. Each offered a sociable programme which dimly reflected that of Bath. The owner of Mallow, Colonel Anthony Jephson, promoted its properties. Jephson, having built an assembly room, leased it to Mort Murphy. The latter scheduled a strenuous course of balls, ridottos, musical concerts and public breakfasts. The patrons were refreshed with the 'best teas, coffee, chocolate', and supplied with the Dublin newspapers twice weekly.[259] The initial gloss quickly dulled. A Quaker, staying at the spa for five days in 1753, praised the excellence of the hot wells, but added, 'notwithstanding all this, a mere shattered broken town, no repairs of the buildings that are scarcely able to keep up'.[260] The virtues of the Mallow waters had first been advertised by a Cork doctor in the 1720s. During the 1750s, the recourse of the likes of the Frenches from Monivea pushed up house rents.[261] Every evening they could take themselves to assemblies or balls in the long room. Races and a buck hunt added to the pleasures. In 1746, three plates worth £30 a piece and another three valued at £20 each were run. These races were reputed to draw a 'vast appearance' of ladies and gentlemen of fortune. Popular among the fanciers of the turf from Clare, Limerick and Cork, this regular event gave a more raffish feel to the society of Mallow. The feuds to which the local squirearchy was prone might disturb the races: both by the competition between the mounts and jockeys of rival owners and through the affrays that periodically erupted.[262]

Rakes may have been fewer at Swanlinbar in County Cavan. The Reverend Patrick Delany wrote in the summer of 1736 of the crowds, with 'three in a bed'. 'There were moreover about 14 or 15 tents on the banks of the lake mightily crowded', which sold whiskey and cold meats.[263] Yet, in 1742 John Digby knew nothing of the place when he enquired about its facilities on behalf of a daughter with a scorbutic disorder.[264] Within a few years, the baronet of Kells, Sir

Thomas Taylor, was in the habit of drinking its sulphurous waters.[265] In the summer of 1758 the Irish lord chancellor, John Bowes, left Dublin to drink at the Cavan spa.[266] Edgeworth, a devotee of Bath, found Swanlinbar handier. In 1767, as an elderly widower, he arrived with his daughter and a servant. A week's lodging and diet for his party cost £5.[267] The Edgeworths, believing in the efficacy of the Swanlinbar waters, stayed for four weeks. In 1769, Edgeworth returned for another three weeks, again with his daughter and now with four servants. The squire's weekly bill was pushed up from £5 to £6 6s. 10d. The party lodged with Beatty (or Batty), the entrepreneur who had developed the spa. Its attractions included public breakfasts and musical evenings in Batty's room at which healthy lemonade was served.[268] Edgeworth's sociable regime at Swanlinbar was interspersed – as earlier his stay in Bath – with jaunts to the curiosities of the neighbourhood.[269] The Cavan resort, with its rustic long room, only faintly echoed Bath, but it drew the genteel. Their affectations were soon satirized. Miss Clackitt, Miss Screech and Miss Pert, Lord Snuffle and Mrs Bumshuffle all jostling for the best seats may have been types or instantly recognizable as individuals to their contemporaries.[270]

Irish patriots, like Rutty, puffed the local. But, as with most other commodities, the foreign had an undeniable *réclame*. In any hierarchy, if Dublin ranked after London or Paris, so Mallow and Swanlinbar trailed behind Bath, Spa or Aix.[271] However, the Irish spa towns, although belittled, offered services and experiences not available in more constricted places. In addition, travel within Ireland was stimulated by medical pundits who espoused dipping in the sea and inland lakes as beneficial. Less advertised spots had their admirers. In the 1720s, Edward Crofton and his wife repaired to the midlands spa near Lissadorn; during the 1750s, the Blakes of Ballyglunin visited Mounttalbot spa.[272] As early as 1718, a Church of Ireland clergyman was bathing in the sea near Dublin; the mother of Laetitia Pilkington, the wife of a medical man, subjected her children to sea-bathing at Clontarf.[273] Rush, to the north of Dublin, was also favoured. In 1754, it was remarked, 'doctors, I think, begin to dislike this wholesome washing. It is more profitable to the patient than the physician'. However, it continued in repute during the 1760s and 1770s. Nancy Brabazon, daughter of a Connacht family, had a spell in Dublin where she not only learnt music and dancing, but was encouraged 'to take the air'. The regimen included forty-two days on which she paid 'the dipper' to plunge her into the briny.[274] Similarly, a daughter of the Annesleys had 'a bathing tub' to plunge her into Dublin Bay for a month.[275] The ailing Abercorn agent from Strabane repaired to Ballyshannon on the Donegal coast to stave off the grim reaper. Women and children particularly organized themselves (or were organized) to be by the seaside, often in the suburbs that sprang up along the eastern coast close to Dublin. The reluctance of the sickly Lord Charlemont to forego sea-bathing explained his absence from his Ulster estates. The elderly Lady Kildare by the 1770s could report other noblewomen floundering in Dublin Bay, and assumed that her own grandchildren missed their regular immersions at Blackrock.[276] Late in the century a Catholic bishop was drowned while bathing from Tramore on the Waterford coast.[277]

*A View of the Lake of Killarney taken from Macross Garden*
*1 Mangerton Mountain. 2 Toomish Mount.ⁿ 3 The Reeks. 4 Ross Castle. 5 Mountains over y̆ upper Lake.*

82. Mary Delany, *A view of the lake of Killarney taken from Mucross Garden, c.* 1748. The taste for the picturesque encouraged internal tourism and especially appreciation of the mountains and lakes around Killarney.

Local waters retained a following.[278] In some cases, ancient holy wells were incorporated into the cults of health and tourism. Indeed, an account in the mid-seventeenth century linked spas in Ireland with wondrous cures at places dedicated to Saints Patrick and Bride.[279] Protestants did not always shun the places revered by their Catholic servants, tenants and neighbours, but generally abstained from the patronal festivals at springs and wells as too riotous and redolent of superstition.[280] An inquisitive visitor from Presbyterian Monaghan late in the 1750s joined the thousands who flocked to St John's well outside Kilkenny on Midsummer's Eve. He scoffed at the supposed miracles and believed the Holy Ghost which descended at midnight to be a pigeon. The continuing hold on much of the population of traditional devotional centres for recreation was revealed by Nicholas Peacock. Living close to Patrickswell outside Limerick city, he allowed his servants to go to the regular patterns there. On these days, Peacock kept his own company, walking or reading. Among polite Protestants, not the least of the drawbacks were 'the confusion, drunkenness and noise always attending such meetings'.[281] When the genteel congregated around a watering hole, they usually sought physical rather than spiritual well-being. Astute promoters met these wants. A satirist implied that, in the concourse at Lough Derg during the 1770s, the wealthier Catholics paid the poor to be their proxies as pilgrims. Moreover, hardships were 'not a little aggravated by the sight of cold meats and wine given by the priests to such Protestant gentry as come hither out of curiosity'.[282]

While some well-known sacred sites felt a little of the commercialization of leisure, so too did the wilder reaches of the island. Greater security after 1715 slowly relaxed the Protestants of Ireland. Inaccessible regions were no longer feared as the sanctuaries of the savage. Slowly, recreational travel within Ireland acquired momentum. Coastal villages close to Dublin prospered. Addicts of sea-bathing and shell- and stone-collecting quartered the strands. By 1751, the fad 'made those in high life enquire for pebbles'. What was portrayed as 'an innocent frolic' was enlivened by competition as gentlemen tried to outdo one another in finding specimens fit to be polished by the lapidary.[283] Others, also touched by medical propaganda, sequestered themselves on mountainsides in the Mournes in order to drink goat's whey in the spring or crouched beside healing springs.[284] Not until the mid-eighteenth century did the untamed in the still dangerous south-west and north-west, such as the MacGillicuddys and

83. ?Laetitia Bushe, *A perspective view of Lower Lough Lene, Co. Kerry, c.* 1745. Laetitia Bushe, another woman praised as a painter, explored the dramatic hinterlands of County Kerry.

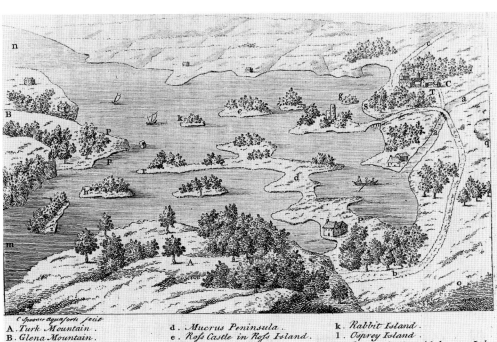

C. Spooner aquaforte fecit

| | | |
|---|---|---|
| A . *Turk Mountain* . | d . *Mucrus Peninsula* . | k . *Rabbit Island* . |
| B . *Glena Mountain* . | e . *Rofs Castle in Rofs Island* . | l . *Osprey Island* . |
| C . *Killarny Town* . | f . *Innisfallen* . | m . *Communication with the upper Lake* . |
| a . *Flesk River* . | g . *Otter Island* . | n . *The River Laun* . |
| b . *Road to Kenmare River* . | h . *Brickeen Island* . | o . *The foot of Mangerton Mountain* |
| c . *Road to Castle Island* . | i . *Dines Island* . | p . *Places of the best Echo* . |

the lakes of Killarney, bewitch the intrepid. In 1751, one advocate of internal tourism pleaded with 'every gentleman of fancy' to 'return after a summer's recreation with descriptions of beautiful rural scenes'.[285] Only then would the beauties of Ireland be painted and foreigners lured to the island. However, the inclination to ignore or even disparage the sights within Ireland was only slowly – and then never wholly – overcome.

Travel could as easily solidify as dissolve prejudices. Routes reflected money and motive. Members of the different confessional and ethnic communities sometimes ended at the same destination – Rome, Bath, Brussels or London – but did not respond in the same way to spectacles like the pope, Westminster Bridge or nuns taking the veil. Events closer to hand – fairs, markets, horse-races and the hurry of county towns during the assizes – did not mean the same to all who came. The prosperous were present as grand jurors, subscribers to hunts and concerts, shareholders in assembly rooms, patentees of markets and owners of horses and fighting cocks. The angle from which they looked on proceedings differed from that of the witnesses, defendants, jockeys, strollers, stragglers and corner-boys. Many of these events were heavy with possible menace. In part the threat arose from the prevalence of Catholics among the excluded and Protestants as participants. Crowds enjoying themselves modulated all too easily from exuberance to riot. The many who converged on popular spots were to be schooled in social pleasures and taught to spend. The danger remained that they might also pick up vicious or subversive notions. So, all travel, if only to the nearest market, fair or pattern, involved risks. Paradoxically, cities, celebrated as the seminaries of civility, harboured the worst temptations. Whether it was Dublin, London, Paris, Rome or Venice, each embodied 'liberty, pleasure and downright debauchery'.[286] Since venturing abroad assisted in the acquisition and refinement of social and moral virtues, it was integral to the English project for Ireland. Yet, its consequences could not always be predicted or controlled. The ambulant returned, sometimes hardened in their love of Ireland and antipathy to Britain (and further-flung parts), or enamoured of outlandish ideas, foods, objects and manners.

# Chapter 11

# Society

*I*

Few of the activities described in the preceding chapters were solitary ones. Houses, horses, dresses, dressers – and the wares on them – were all to be seen, admired, even envied. Domesticity and conjugality came to be cultivated, particularly among the prosperous and leisured. Yet, if these trends sharpened the division between public and private lives, the latter were not marked by any strenuous quest for privacy. In eighteenth-century Ireland, it was rare for any but the grandest houses to be organized so that the owner could be alone. Some pleasures, and the goods which ministered to them – books, prints, curiosities – were reserved for the select, who were honoured by being ushered into intimate cabinets and closets. Occasionally, the cult of rural retirement was extolled, but it did not amount to a wish for an eremitic existence. The important, such as Lord Broghill in the 1650s, William Flower in the 1720s and John Digby in the 1730s, weary with – or excluded from – public affairs retreated to their country estates. In Virgilian mode, they bustled about their plantations and paddocks, and enjoyed society, albeit a different one from Dublin's or London's.[1] They husbanded their energies (and their revenues), the better to parade through the metropolis.

Christian and classical writers taught the importance of public activism.[2] Those immured in the country soon chafed. One – in Roscommon – complained, 'I want the opportunities of conversation, speculations about many points, variety of manners, sentiments, books, antiquities, new sights, &c'.[3] Polite society in the county town of Kerry, Tralee, consisted of 'dancing, cards and sitting up'.[4] For want of livelier topics, the isolated wrote about the weather.[5] One provincial correspondent, having prattled on about trivia, stopped short. 'I am sick of the stuff I am forced to write for want of something more entertaining'.[6]

Society, passionately sought, was attended by strains. The diffident, keen to cut a dash, assembled the requirements. Clothes were widely seen as a principal need. Laurence Clayton bid to blind his colleagues on the magistrates' bench in County Cork by arraying his horse and himself 'very fine and sparkish'.[7] Clayton prefigured the exertions of Squire Smythe of

Portlick, battering against the parliamentary citadel in Westmeath occupied by rivals. Similar worries about looking fetching justified the prodigality of Anne Hill from Hillsborough and Pole Cosby of Stradbally. Mrs Hill confessed, 'I'm going to make a visit in a strange country, where I should be disgraced if I went as plain as I do at home'.[8] She sobbed, 'I can't appear where I am going without something more than white camlet . . . I hate myself in white'.[9] Meeting strangers in Germany spurred Cosby to bespeak a couple of smart suits 'and everything else that was handsome'. So splendid were the outfits that he remembered their colours and feel over thirty years later. Arriving in London, he changed his plumage on the principle that, by making 'a good appearance, judging that I should be more taken notice of for it'.[10] A country visitor to Dublin declared in 1759, without smart clothes it was impossible even to worship, let alone visit the respectable. It was well known that church was the place to see the fashions.[11] Even when visiting relations, extra effort was demanded to pass muster.[12]

Notables, well aware of what acquaintances and kindred in Britain sported, had the money to engage in similar displays. There are indications that those outside the social and economic élites were tempted by the cheaper versions of the bright and beautiful, especially in the particular of clothing. The purchases, irrational and unpatriotic to the minds of the austere, were intended for occasions when the finery could be admired rather than for moping in solitude. Most displayed themselves at patterns and fairs, promenades in open spaces and attendance at worship, not in the mêlée at Dublin Castle. Participants did not lack instructors. Just as dressmakers, tailors, mercers, perruquiers and vendors of gold and silver lace thrived, so too did the teachers of dancing, fencing, drawing and music. One dancing-master was so eminently respectable that he put his son into the holy ministry of the Church of Ireland. Others, like the famous Delamain in Cork, were highly respected in their local society.[13]

The spending of the literate and numerate eclipses the humbler transactions of an anonymous multitude. Reformers intended that all should join in commercialized consumption not simply (or primarily) because it yielded profits to the promoters, but because it advanced the cause of civility. In Ireland, by the end of the seventeenth century, this programme had become synonymous with the English and Protestant missions for Ireland. The gregariousness of the settlers was represented as good – morally as well as financially. It was contrasted with the caricature of how the indigenous Irish lived. Industrious Protestants were portrayed in busy towns, attracted by the opportunities to work and socialize, not huddling there for protection in an otherwise hostile environment. The indigenous Irish could not plausibly be represented as existing in solitude. Instead, they were depicted as dwelling in remote and inhospitable spots, inimical to the elegancies that the civilized now demanded and commanded. In so far as the picture had any truth, it was because many poor Irish were crammed into the shanty towns outside the walls of the hundred or so incorporated boroughs, into the makeshifts in the Dublin parishes and into clusters of cabins as a result of official action.

Champions of the English (or after 1707 British) Protestant order in Ireland accused the displaced Catholics of 'dissociability'.[14]

To live in society was deemed natural; solitude, unnatural. But professed Catholics were not the only group denied participation in the institutions and associations through which social as well as political virtues were learnt. Women and the Protestant poor were heavily restricted in their access. The excluded, by far the majority of the population, did not lack opportunities for sociability, but few have left legible traces. Diversions were more easily come by in town than in countryside, above all in Dublin (or London). Just as it is hard, indeed frequently impossible, to assess how far down the social and economic scales the materials of polite life descended, so too entertainments that were cheap, free or spontaneous blazed up and left no trace. In the course of the eighteenth century, social events became more contrived, commercial and – in their smartest forms – more expensive. Much of this activity was closed to all save communicant members of the Church of Ireland. Indeed, many organizations aimed at underpinning Protestant Ireland were male monopolies. Some levied entrance fees. In addition, expectations about dress and comportment kept out the humble. Only those able to put on the appropriate figure were full members of polite society. In response to the exclusions and in parallel to the cheap ribbons, aprons and stockings, boldly patterned pottery and striking engravings, there evolved cheaper and demotic forms of sociability – in the tavern, on the green, in the streets and at home.

Dublin enjoyed the most crowded calendar. Few events originated with or depended heavily on the temporary occupants of the Castle. Convivial circles overlapped, affording participants diversions which stretched from philanthropy to obscenity, from business and controversy into communal eating and drinking. Municipal and guild feasts were sometimes criticized because corporate funds were thought to be buying treats for the few. During the 1730s, Dublin guilds put limits on what their officers were to spend on parading around the town.[15] Yet, in the depressed 1720s, even the glum Archbishop King welcomed the jollifications for invigorating a sluggish economy.[16] The pageants were intended to solidify bonds fashioned from the shared history, privileges and residence of Dubliners. Simultaneously, they announced inequalities, even among members of these bodies, let alone among the non-members. Often the annual parades, awkwardly stage-managed, far from advertising harmony disrupted it. The freemen of Dublin numbered between 3,000 and 4,000. Some outsiders, notably the journeymen or day labourers, formed societies of their own. The main motives were to protect economic interests and care for the superannuated, widows and orphans. Simpler pleasures and the respectability conferred by regular meetings in their own hall and shared meals also appealed.[17] The mock heroics of skilled workers as, each year, they marched through the streets to a service, sermon, dinner and (sometimes) musical concert were affectionately described.[18] The sympathetic approved the activities as signs that the middling sort wanted only to imitate their betters in the corporation.[19] Others watched more nervously as subordinates filched yet more features of polite society, along with the replicas of dress, diet and furnishings. Nervy conservatives felt that social and economic demarcations were being blurred.

In Dublin, several societies of 'worthy gentlemen' celebrated Dean Swift's birthday in 1726. The programme concluded respectably with music in the Vicars' Hall after a religious service in St Patrick's cathedral.[20] More noticeable were the yearly scenes in Dublin on 4 November, the principal festival of the Irish Protestants. A bemused spectator wrote in 1761, 'we banquet with King William's ghost and every coach in Dublin parades round his statue, and every man is drunk to the memory of old glorious, by six'.[21] It was feared that 'Williamitism' might soon supplant Christianity as the prevailing cult in official Ireland.[22] Members of the university, of parliament, of masonic lodges and of charitable foundations regularly threaded through the narrow quarters of the capital. Frequently the crocodiles were preceded by distinctive symbols, wore insignia and heralded their approach with music. On occasion the conspicuous displays provoked the bystanders. In 1731, members of Trinity College proceeding to St Patrick's cathedral one Sunday in Lent were attacked. The students retaliated by arming themselves and henceforward marched to worship in a military manner. The assailants were readily – but perhaps wrongly – identified as 'a popish mob'. So, too, the rioters who disrupted theatrical performances in 1746 were assumed to be Jacobites and papists.[23]

The wish to proclaim *esprit de corps* by dining publicly and in a group was widely practised. In 1766, the Incorporated Society, in a bid to increase support, proposed a dinner at the *Phoenix* tavern close to the Castle. It was scheduled after its annual general meeting and fundraising sermon. The lord-lieutenant was to be invited, together with six peers and various members of parliament friendly to the Society. Shamelessly, the Society hoped thereby to increase attendance of grandees and so boost donations.[24] The problem was that the important had more calls on their time (and purses) than they could possibly meet. Worthy causes which involved concerted action, including shared meals, passed in and out of fashion. So, too, did the places where the meals were eaten. Groups shifted restlessly from tavern to tavern, hopeful perhaps of a better deal from the publican or greater liveliness. During the 1690s, the Weavers' Guild in the capital, lacking its own hall, conducted business in more than a dozen hostelries: *The Blue Posts, The Bunch of Grapes, The Cock, The Exchange, The Fleece, The Garter, The George, The Gun, The King's Head, The Leeds, The Lion, The Salutation,* and Mr Fox's and Mr Rooke's taverns. By 1703, the weavers had settled on Mr Leathley's establishment for the quarter-day dinner.[25] A second Dublin guild, that of St Audeon, had metamorphosed into a sociable group more concerned with mutual support than with trading. It too transacted its affairs in a variety of taverns: *The Bunch of Grapes, The Fleece, The Garter, The Rose* and *The Three Tuns.* It also borrowed the Carpenters' Hall for a meeting. Throughout the 1740s, the brethren ate their annual dinner on St Anne's day at *The Rose* in Dame

Street. By 1750 the event was shifted to the Custom House coffee-house: possibly a sign of changing habits among the substantial of the city.[26]

Rites of exclusion as much as inclusion, these jubilees were observed in corporate boroughs across the kingdom. The streets of the larger towns repeatedly resounded to groups *en fête*. In smaller places, landlords and agents, in efforts to inculcate the virtues of industry, devised pageants to reward and inspire their tenants. Ballyshannon, Belleek, Dunmanway and Kanturk witnessed rigged manifestations of the supposed unity of the tenants of the Caldwells, Coxes and Percevals.[27] Few, if any, were totally spontaneous; many revealed tensions within intimate communities. In a larger town, such as Limerick, Protestants of substance could join in the diversified associational life centred on the corporation itself, trading guilds, the Protestant cathedral and churches, and smaller clubs. Some groupings had distinctive political, vocational or confessional characteristics. Keeping out more than they included, they accentuated divisions – cultural, economic and ethnic – within the area. The most important, modelled on the Dublin Society, aimed to advance commerce and the arts in the city. Regular demonstrations of solidarity could have the opposite effect. Between 1747 and 1757, the Masons' Company, one of fourteen within Limerick, still had a vocational function and judged the quality of workmanship. Country-dwellers, like Henry Ievers of Mount Ievers, joined the Company.[28] Having no hall in which to meet, the fraternity shifted its regular assemblies around the private houses of the officers. Unity was proclaimed not only through oversight of their particular craft but on the days of civic rejoicing. In 1755, the impending visit of the lord-lieutenant brought orders that each guild should assist the mayor, sheriff and corporation in welcoming the dignitary in suitable state. The masons were to don blue scarves fringed with white. The reluctant were reassured that there would be future occasions to sport the accessories. The brethren were also exhorted to buy two standards which could be carried at the head of their phalanx. Forty-two members of the guild had appeared at one meeting, but no more than twenty-five were prepared to pay towards the banners.[29]

The descent of the viceroy on Limerick merely provoked extra display and rippled choppy waters. Annual celebrations in May and June already detonated trouble. Country people flooded into the city on the First of May and at Whitsun.[30] 'Many thousands' of labourers, cottiers and husbandmen, regimented according to their 'several degrees of agriculture', and armed with the appropriate props, processed. They clashed with craftworkers. The hectic season continued with state festivities such as the Prince of Wales's birthday. In these, as in other spectacles, soldiers of the garrison were to the fore. Each day they marched in formation to the Church of Ireland cathedral for a service. On red-letter days, the soldiery led by eighty-one officers paraded through the streets and then lined the city walls, which twice in the seventeenth century had seen a long defiance of English authority. In Limerick, as in other towns with large contingents of soldiers – Ballyshannon, Cork, Kinsale, Sligo and

Waterford – the military choreographed loyal pageants. During placid times, the garrisons brought valuable custom and thereby enriched locals. But, arrogant and assertive, all too often they introduced discord. Limerick had a long history of clashes between officers, churchmen and municipal functionaries. The paradox was that, notwithstanding the record of disorders, newly arrived officers were welcomed courteously, not least because they refreshed the stale company at drums and dances in the city.[31]

Fraternity was the ideal professed by such convivial groups. Necessarily more remained outside than inside these associations. The society generated by institutions – municipalities, trading companies, parish vestries and voluntary groups like the Incorporated Society – was fully open only to fortunate Protestants. Not all within the Protestant community were welcomed into the institutionalized sociability. Even those inside the organizations were graded. Cabals ran most of these bodies, and awarded themselves extra benefits. At communal festivities, such as civic and guild banquets, or treats provided by office-holders, landowners and would-be members of parliament, untutored tenants and freemen faced bewildering comestibles and utensils. Unequal in standing and income when they entered the fraternities, fresh inequalities arose from clumsiness in handling unfamiliar cutlery, crockery and foods. At shared meals, it was soon clear who was and was not habituated to eat with knives, forks and spoons, from pottery and porcelain rather than wood, tin or pewter, and familiar already with coffee, tea or claret. Moreover, the revellers, even when arrayed in a uniform, betrayed indigence and primitivism through the cut and colour of a coat, the quality and fashion of a wig or the look of a sword and mount.[32]

Communicant members of the established Church of Ireland, if male, enjoyed the largest choice of sociable gatherings. Those who sat through the annual dinners which followed the installation of sheriffs and mayors, ritual perambulations of boundaries, the Eastertide selection of parish officers for the coming year, or the auditing of churchwardens' accounts, were usually prosperous enough to participate in other, informal festivities. At Kildimo in County Limerick, members of the vestry dined off a shoulder of mutton in September, but at least one diner had frequent chances to enjoy such solid fare and company elsewhere.[33] Other celebratory meals, after the bishop's visitation, at the coming of age, marriage, inheritance or return home of a landowner, happened less predictably. A clergyman organized 'a great entertainment' after being ordained in Kildare cathedral in James II's reign.[34] In 1695, burgesses in the Wicklow borough of Blessington, having been selected, were given a good dinner.[35] Proctors for the diocese of Ossory were chosen in 1727 over 'a noble entertainment' at *The Star* in Kilkenny.[36] In 1763, when the church of St John in Dublin was to be rebuilt, parish worthies met the architect to study his plans in *The King's Arms*.[37] In the nearby parish of St Michan, measuring of bounds concluded with a dinner. Agents sometimes dispensed food and drink to encourage tenants and would-be tenants to bid boldly for leases.[38] Some condemned the practice as a cause of the economic retardation of Ireland. It was alleged that, when a poor sub-tenant complained to the landlord's agent, the latter was invited by the head tenant 'to drink a bottle of wine, makes his own story very good, while the poor undertenant standeth without in the cold and rain and dare not come in to justify his complaint'.[39] Auctioneers at country cants offered refreshments, so turning the sales into convivial occasions.[40] Those hoping to become burgesses of corporations and to be elected to parliament treated potential supporters. The recipients happily accepted the hospitality, becoming more exacting in what they expected and more sparing in their support.[41] Squires like Cosby and Weldon in Queen's County entertained neighbours and tenants – usually separately – on days important in their families' annals. The County Limerick agent Peacock was invited to companionable gatherings on his employer's birthday.[42] Further gatherings marked the passage of the liturgical and agricultural year, the rhythms of the neighbourhood and family or the unexpected.

## II

One development which told of the inclination towards society was the emergence of the club. In late-seventeenth- and eighteenth-century Ireland, where Protestants were still few and the cultivated even fewer, there was a tendency to herd together, both for safety and stimulus. 'Clubs' appeared in towns and countryside. They often arose when transients took meals in concert and divided the cost.[43] In rural areas, the clubs, such as those to which Flower of Castle Durrow and the bishop of Elphin were bidden, needed greater orchestration.[44] Mysterious, too, is the '26 club', to which the Paulls of Counties Carlow and Waterford subscribed in 1726. It may have been a group organized to contest a forthcoming election.[45] Effort and forewarning were required if the scattered inhabitants of a county were to gather. In some cases, shared political opinions and the wish to scheme may have inspired these select assemblies.[46] But the majority of clubs were probably inspired by no sinister motives. The urban and urbane, when deep in the provinces, missed the diversions of the town and especially the comradeship of the like-minded. They argued that socializing enabled rationality to develop and civility to flourish, and so introduced the ways of the city into the provinces.

The varied society enjoyed by the mobile and prosperous can be illustrated from what is known of the doings of some already encountered: John Pratt, Richard Edgeworth, Anne Cooke and Nicholas Peacock. In 1745, John Pratt, heir to an estate at Agher in County Meath, noted on 18 June that this was the first night on which he and his parents had dined alone for more than ten months.[47] Young Pratt, destined for the bar, plunged into the frenetic activity which his neighbourhood afforded. One focus was the church.[48] Another was running the county, with assizes at Mullingar and the quarter sessions in Trim. During the assizes, Pratt joined others in a 'club', or communal eating and drinking, for which he paid 4s. 6d. He was also invited to dine with the sheriff, a family friend.[49] Rebellion in Scotland during 1745 drew

Pratt into the militia. Service proved more strenuous socially than militarily. On 4 November, he joined his commander and others of the troop at a country tavern. Pratt admitted that he 'drank to be sick'.[50] Agricultural tasks further punctuated the year: lambs were castrated, a mare serviced, sheep shorn. Pleasure came from hearing the first cuckoo and eating the earliest lamb of the season.[51] Rabbits and hares were shot; fishing landed three dozen trout and six pike. Pratt hunted with Sheriff Rawdon's hounds.[52] During these expeditions, Pratt frequently dined or supped and sometimes slept at neighbours' houses. The magnificent establishment of the Rowleys at Summerhill and of the Rawdons at Branchhall were favourite stops.[53] In summer, the pace quickened. Pratt visited the Wesleys' Dangan and Garadice, owned by relations.[54] When away from home, he sometimes put up at an inn.[55] Fairs and markets further diversified the rural routine.[56]

At home in Meath, Pratt did not lack entertainment or commodities.[57] However, two trips to Dublin offered contrasts. In both capital and county, Pratt relaxed in taverns. The company was entirely male. So was that at a Dublin club, McClaughlin's, into which a chum from County Meath introduced him.[58] This amenity, together with the theatres which Pratt attended, was lacking in the countryside. Otherwise, urban and rustic sociability differed chiefly in the greater decorum of Dublin events. In Meath, many amusements, arising from the land, its needs and produce, smacked of the bucolic. At Clonymeath, shortly after the harvest was home, Billy Fitzsimons had a whole mutton roasted. Forty-seven people sat down at a single table to devour it.[59] The Pratts had obvious notables, such as Lord Galtrim and Sir Richard Levinge, to dine and sleep at their house at Agher.[60] On St Patrick's Day in 1746, the parish priest ate with the Pratts.[61] This gesture may tell of nothing more than a wish to maintain amicable relations with the local Catholics, from whom the Pratts' tenants, servants and labourers were recruited. At the same time, the invitation diluted the overwhelmingly Protestant character of the Pratts' guest lists. The clergy were the only Catholics, other than the occasional medical practitioner, whom ignorant Protestants might credit with education and a modicum of gentility, and so be welcomed.[62]

Pratt's companions in the tavern, at the hunt or at the assizes were men. Service in the militia and practice at the bar were activities from which women were debarred. Female guests were sometimes noted at table or in the house. One of Pratt's purchases in Dublin – earrings – spoke either of a romantic attachment or a commission from a female relative. Women impinged as well when Pratt had to sort out the effects of a sister who had died in Dublin. A similar pattern marked the activities of a kinsman and neighbour. Samuel Winter occupied a comparable stratum of Protestant society to the Pratts. The Winters, like the Pratts, discharged local offices as grand jurors, high sheriff, churchwardens and magistrates, rather than moving on the national stage.[63] An agreeably variegated company in the county was supplemented by forays into Dublin. Thither they went for education, preferment, professional services and relaxation. The Winters, in common with the Pratts, entertained and were themselves entertained frequently. They saw the wonders of their own district: Lord Belvedere's building on Lough Ennell and Lord Westmeath's improvements.[64] Dublin afforded spectacles, such as the riding of the city franchises and the lord-lieutenant's speeches to parliament.[65] Also, when in the capital, the Winters viewed novelties, notably the gardens of Lady Arbella Denny's seaside retreat at Blackrock and at Mosse's Lying-In Hospital.[66] In the country, the Winters – male and female – followed the accustomed rites of the season, which now included such commercial events as Trim races.[67]

The county of Meath, thanks to proximity to Dublin and the relative abundance of prosperous Protestants, possessed a vivacity and variety not always on offer in remoter regions. Yet, the steady spread of more sophisticated entertainments can be traced in Cavan in the 1750s and 1760s. There, the family of Joseph Story, archdeacon of Kilmore, based at Bingfield, regularly visited the town of Cavan. The Story children were instructed in writing and dancing. The new Terpsichorean prowess was exhibited at a series of assemblies organized by the dancing teachers of the town. By 1764, Jack Davis charged a subscription of £4 16s. 8d. for two years for the two adults of the family. Such fees made the events exclusive. Other diversions excited the town. In the summer of 1756 and again in December 1763, a touring troupe performed plays. In 1766, the Storys rode to Belturbet where the two daughters watched a military review. This was followed by an 'assembly', presumably with dancing. Another inducement for the Storys to stray further than their country seat was a 'club' which convened at Crossdoney, a smaller place than Cavan. Joseph Story noted modest disbursements (usually 6s. 6d. or 8s. 8d.) as his contribution to the proceedings. The Storys ranged beyond Cavan. Indeed, their familiarity with the amenities of more distant places – Dublin, England and continental Europe – may have created a wish for local equivalents. Their custom helped to sustain initiatives in Cavan, which, in turn, were patronised by neighbours with fewer chances to amuse themselves in distant spots.[68]

## III

Associational life and its attendant rituals usually excluded women.[69] Exceptions included the Incorporated Society, which drew ladies into local committees. Their task was to inspect particular charter schools. Lady Arbella Denny, with her Magdalen Asylum, was the first seriously to break into this male preserve: an achievement appropriately acknowledged with her election – the first of a woman – to membership of the Dublin Society. Earlier, when Katherine Conolly pricked her lady friends into strenuous sewing and embroidery, she was inventing through the sewing-bees a female equivalent of the panels and boards on which her husband, kinsmen and cronies sat. Women could not be magistrates, follow professions or join masonic lodges. But polite society in Dublin and provincial towns needed women alongside men. The

84. Lady Helena MacDonnell, embroidered bed coverlet, *c.* 1750. Women, especially in prosperous households, could demonstrate remarkable skills of organization, design and dexterity.

growing commercialization of leisure created more assemblies, concerts and entertainments in which women joined. Moreover, the confident, such as Katherine Conolly, Lady Arbella Denny and Mary Delany, arbitrated on social proprieties.[70] Before these developments, women had imprinted society, usually domestic or more restricted, with their own stamp. Their preferences, all too rarely recorded, affected how houses were furnished, decorated and used, and even when and in what style they were remodelled. In some cases, female wishes dictated how the year was divided between the country and town, or between Ireland and England.

Management of the household was conventionally regarded as the special province of women. They were not thereby sealed into a private world. Hospitality brought many into the homes of the prosperous and ensured that the work of hospitable women was appraised and applauded. Queen Mary II supplied one Ulsterman with a model. She complemented her husband, the deliverer of Protestant Ireland, with the excellence of her 'housewifery and industry'.[71] Novice housewives acquired their skills through informal networks of women or through formal apprenticeship. Miss Foley, the daughter of a bishop, was sent first to a female relation in County Sligo to learn the rudiments by observing her seniors. Later she was instructed by women in Dublin on how to run a household creditably.[72] Women swapped tips. At Katherine Conolly's elevated level, patterns and gossip were exchanged. Careful housekeepers jotted down the receipts and remedies of friends and guests. Eating well was a social pleasure. So, too, was preparing food. Recipe books compiled in the 1660s by Dorothy Parsons at Birr or Diana Twigge in early-eighteenth-century Limerick listed favourite dishes. Many were supplied by visitors, often other women. Dorothy Parsons collected much during her family's long stays in England: from relations and acquaintances, both female and male, as well as the decoctions of eminent doctors.[73] By comparison, Diana Twigge's collection was harvested from her almost entirely female friends in a smaller environment. Mrs Twigge, born and bred among the civic and clerical worthies of Limerick, wrote of instructions for making birch wine and a cure for gallstones, 'these two receipts were given my mama by Mrs. Story', probably the wife of the dean of the cathedral.[74] Olivia Elder from County London-derry evoked the multifarious tasks which fell to her: the chores of kitchen, brewhouse and farm. In addition, she was expected to show dexterity as a needlewoman. However she did not cower in the background. Her 'social circle' included visits to men, drinking tea and coffee, and conversation.[75]

Fitful beams are shone into female society in mid-eighteenth-century Ireland by the laconic diary of Anne Weldon. Only daughter and heiress of Sir Samuel Cooke, affluent patriot, former lord mayor and member of parliament for Dublin, she had been reared in a polite civic world. The daughter, like her mother, preferred a rural retreat near Lucan in County Dublin to the hubbub of Dublin.[76] However, she could not dodge public responsi-bilities, especially after she married (in 1762) William Weldon, a member of parliament and landowner in Queen's County.[77] Anne Weldon knew England as well as Ireland. In London, she headed for friends from Ireland.[78] In the Dublin of the 1760s, she followed circuits defined by her widowed mother and other family connections. In August 1767, Mrs Weldon noted that, although living in rooms just north of the river, she dined almost every day with her mother.[79] To her own family acquaintances, she added those of her husband, centred on two houses in Queen's County: Rahenderry and Sportland. In 1769, the Weldons took a Dublin house. Anne Weldon shared with her spouse some of the excitements of the town. They included a 'fancy ball' at the Castle on the eve of St Patrick's Day in 1770. To her fell much of the business of furnishing the house.[80] Metropolitan gaiety soon gave way to the cares of a country estate. There a brisk programme of recreation was followed. A horse-race at Shortland was preceded by a breakfast for such notables as Lord Jocelyn, the Burghs from Oldtown and Tom Conolly of Castletown. Mrs Weldon frequently accompanied her husband to these sports and on fishing expeditions.[81] Hunting and shooting, however, were reserved for men. Summer in the country favoured the *al fresco*: not just fishing, but picnics and even a dance in the 'wood house', a summer house.[82] Otherwise, what Anne Weldon chiefly remarked was the regular routine of churchgoing and supervising improvements at Rahenderry.[83]

Soon her husband departed to England.[84] In his absence, much again devolved on Anne Weldon: disposing of the lease of the Dublin property; closing up a country house; arranging sales of stock and furnishings. She reverted to a Dublin life, familiar since girlhood, in which she shopped, went to church, played cards, took tea and exchanged visits with the likes of Lady Arbella Denny, Lady Kildare and Lord and Lady Loftus of Rathfarnham Castle. This regimen contrasted with the oversight of a country mansion, with the worries over servants, redecoration, entertaining and the gardens. Whether in the capital or Queen's County, Anne Weldon's life was busy. In 1773, William Weldon died. The estate passed to his son by a first marriage, whose passion was field sports. Anne Weldon's diary ceased. Although she had shared much with her husband, and thrown herself into his ways, the couple were often apart. Even when together she was excluded from the camaraderie of the chase, the assizes and magistracy. Yet she readily retained and re-entered the society in which she was bred.[85]

Women with money, just as much as men, commanded a large and varied company. Modest, although far from poor, were the Peacocks, living near the banks of the Shannon in Limerick. Catherine Chapman, having married Nicholas Peacock in 1747, soon changed his ways. He did not forsake the predominantly male society connected with his work as an agent and on which he had depended as a bachelor. It was a circuit, moreover, which embraced country houses, the rural alehouses, fairs, markets, and the port of Limerick. The unmarried Peacock confessed occasionally that he had imbibed 'until drunk'. Some of these excesses were abetted by his future in-laws, minor gentry.[86] Peacock, living modestly on his own, suspected that he was visited at home not just for the pleasure of his person. In 1743, he was flabbergasted to discover, 'when I have drink, I find people come to drink it'. John Johnston and his son descended on Peacock and ate all his cheese.[87] In his solitary state, Peacock valued the companionship of his servants. On Christmas Day in 1745, he treated his 'little family' to a bowl of punch. Similarly, before he departed to be married, he gave them drink.[88] Notwithstanding these gestures, the physical proximity of the servants reminded Peacock of his loneliness, deemed unnatural by Christian and classical philosophies. He craved a partner with whom he could share confession and language as well as his bed. After he had found a mate, she soon introduced him to the newfangled (and costly) brew of tea. She perhaps persuaded him to play the host at home. The christening of children offered opportunities, but neighbours were invited to more than rites of passage. These invitations necessitated a larger house, more and better furnishings, and a bigger selection of comestibles. Catherine Peacock ensured that they made a fitting figure.[89]

The society inhabited and imagined by Catherine Peacock independent of her husband cannot be ascertained. He, not she, wrote a diary. In itself, this act reminded of the sparse provision of education and lower rates of literacy among women. Female neighbours attended her childbed.[90] The couple returned on visits to her relations. Nicholas Peacock went regularly into Limerick city. There he shopped, visited relations and transacted business. He never mentioned the pleasures that the genteel could buy there, and it seems safe to conclude they were beyond his ken and (probably) his purse. What Limerick, and other towns of its size, offered by the 1740s can be gauged from other comments. In 1751, an army officer stationed in Limerick reported that two public drums were held each week in the 'town house'.[91] Townspeople combined with landowners to open an assembly room. Societies directed to improve trade and masonic lodges also functioned. None impinged on Peacock.[92] Yet, the Peacocks, to judge from their possessions and habits, lived sociably and genteelly.

The amenities of mid-eighteenth-century Limerick existed in other provincial towns. Women sustained them. In Waterford, assemblies were policed by a director, on the model of Bath. The season ran throughout the winter. One November night it drew twenty-nine females.[93] In 1738, thirty-three ladies attended a ball in Waterford thrown by a local squire. Also present were officers from the garrison. Once the dance had ended, the men and women parted. The host repaired to a tavern with the military and remained there until eight in the next morning.[94] It was affirmed that the young women, although denied the all-night session, delighted in the *belle assemblée*. 'All young, sprightly, gay girls raised as high as music and champagne and much mirth could elevate them'.[95] In Kilkenny, too, 'the beau monde' included 'genteel female acquaintance'.[96]

Dancing- and music-masters also sponsored assemblies, as at Cavan: precursors of the shows of their pupils' proficiency by ballet-mistresses and line-dancers.[97] A new politeness was blossoming. In 1731, the corporation at Kilkenny had the assembly rooms ceiled and plastered the better to house respectable gatherings.[98] By the 1740s Cork boasted 'a good assembly room'; in the 1750s, Drogheda and Downpatrick, their weekly assemblies.[99] Earlier, in 1738, a description of Belfast lingered over the town house and exchange where the merchants congregated. A fine room had been constructed on the first floor, which accommodated the quarter sessions, meetings of the town council and fortnightly assemblies. There 'you shall see a fine appearance of ladies and gentlemen, so trade don't always spoil politeness'.[100] The developments were financed by investors, instructors and property owners. Price put the amusements beyond the reach of most. It was not simply the entry ticket, but the laborious business of learning fancy dance steps and being kitted out appropriately which put such pleasures beyond the generality. Even so, the provincial assemblies allowed town-dwellers to jostle against rustics, soldiers to mingle with civilians, and men to flirt with women.

## IV

Commercial sites of sociability proliferated outside Dublin from the 1720s. In the capital, meanwhile, outlets grew apace. Of several manifestations – theatres, assemblies, public gardens and coffee-houses – music must suffice to confront, if not to solve, various puzzles. More starkly than many other kinds of amusement it seemed (at least in some accounts) to have succumbed to pressures under which the imported ousted the indigenous, the artificial the impromptu, the commercial the free, and the contrivances of the élite the innocence of the populace. As in Scotland and Wales, written and printed airs supplemented and sometimes supplanted the oral. Unfamiliar instruments – violin, spinet, harpsichord – were introduced alongside indigenous pipes.[101] Music was played in the churches and theatres, at dances, state and civic festivities, and in private houses. In 1697, a new organ at St Patrick's cathedral was said to reproduce the sounds of kettle drums, trumpets, hautbois, flutes and fiddles, and to surpass any instrument in England.[102] Concert-going became a fashionable pastime.[103] Music was cunningly annexed to charity as concerts were staged regularly to raise funds for hospitals and poor prisoners. An aide-de-camp to the viceroy took tickets for Handel's Dublin début in 1741. *L'Allegro ed Il Penseroso* was given. 'A more numerous and polite audience than ever was seen upon the like occasion' was noted.[104]

These, too, were events over which women exercised little control, other than by appearing. Cost ensured that few but the notables of Protestant Ireland were admitted. Richard Edgeworth, Robert French and Ralph Howard wooed the opposite sex by taking them – and sometimes their chaperones – to concerts.[105] Married women also attended. Mary Delany, alive to the power of music as a moral force, condemned what she regarded as 'nonsense music' gaining ground on 'music of consequence' among Dubliners. After hearing *Messiah*, she stated with ineffable superiority, 'it adds greatly to the satisfaction of an entertainment to be seated by those who have the same relish for it we have ourselves'. She objected when a Dublin recital by Geminiani in 1760 was shortened so as to allow the ladies, headed by the vicereine, more time for dancing and cards.[106]

Music-making in Dublin, in order to subsidize charities, was turned into a commercial operation. Yet it remained possible to hear very different sorts of music, and in diverse contexts. The voluble Mary Delany personified this cultural promiscuity. She sneered at the ladies of the viceregal court with their short spans of concentration. Her own guests were regaled with apparently traditional Irish melodies rendered on the harp. Her husband, Dean Patrick Delany, acted as one of the midwives who brought into the light a published collection of 'traditional' music associated with the harpist Carolan.[107] Others of social standing comparable to the Delanys sampled a similar medley of music. Much was foreign, but some sounded traditional. In 1730, the mistress of Barbavilla, while in Dublin, heard Martin Clancy play the harp almost all evening in a private house.[108] Robert French, the Galway lawyer, subscribed to the Philharmonic Society in 1744, and took two tickets for a benefit performance of *Messiah* in Dublin later in the same year. He also bought a pair of seats for the annual concert in aid of Mercer's Hospital the following February. In 1748, he again heard *Messiah*.[109] How his interest continued is suggested by one of his most expensive purchases of the 1760s: a harpsichord for his daughter in County Galway. It cost £35.[110] Earlier, Squire Edgeworth had struck a deal with a leading Dublin instrument maker, Ferdinand Weber, to take a clavichord for his daughter at ten guineas, on condition that Weber would later exchange it for a harpsichord.[111] The Frenches and Edgeworths were of that small company which had sampled the music – and other wares – for sale in England, Dublin and the Irish countryside, and had the money to indulge in what they fancied.[112] Travel, perhaps most importantly to continental Europe, but even to England, extended appreciation of music.[113] Back in 1690, St George Ashe had been enraptured by the operas he heard in Vienna. Moreover, his learned circle in Dublin was interested in both the theory and practice of music.[114] Further hints at how these interests permeated respectable society came with the bequest of the Reverend Charles Baldwin of two of his best violins and his best six-stringed bass. The legatee was Lord Mornington who emerged at the end of George II's reign as the smartest virtuoso, occupying a place as musical arbiter in Protestant Dublin equivalent to that of the earl of Kelly in contemporary Edinburgh.[115]

Squire Edgeworth bought tickets for Dublin performances and the scores and libretti of Handel's operas and oratorios. The purchases continued interests evident when he was a law student in London during the 1720s.[116] He gave his children musical instruments, as well as lessons to play them and to sing.[117] Frequently – especially when in County Longford – he employed harpists, pipers and fiddlers. The performers were much in demand for festivals, notably the Christmas season, and at the time of the county assizes. One harper in particular – Brogan – was patronized by Edgeworth from the 1730s to 1760s.[118] Among other Protestant landowners there were similar signs of a taste for the archaic. In 1680, the Percevals in County Cork owned 'a large Irish harp', on which presumably 'Anthony's son, the old harper' performed whenever Sir Philip Perceval inclined that way.[119] Lord St George from County Galway was probably unique in his prowess on the pipes and the plaudits that he earned from a professional player.[120] More usual was the action of the Wynnes from County Sligo in paying a blind piper.[121] Other notables, thanks to their bounties, inspired compositions from Carolan.[122] Landlords, in backing local musicians, may have done no more than exhibit the propensity of the newly settled to take over the sports and recreations of their Irish and Catholic predecessors. Among newcomers, a passive acceptance of what had survived shaded into a drive more actively to revive what was disappearing. A Dublin curate, Matthew Pilkington, hailed Carolan and reversed the usual association of traditional music with cultural backwardness, incivility and dissociability. Pilkington argued that Carolan's playing would speed the reform of the Irish, 'their customs wild; their manners unpolite'.[123] Impulses to preserve and publish relics of the ancient Ireland, such as Pilkington's and the Delanys', arose as Protestant settlers relaxed. Just as untamed landscapes came to be appreciated, so too was the music thought to come from them.

While the curious searched out what survived from Ireland's past, the sophisticated aimed to correct current taste. The intended reforms paralleled those proposed in painting and building. In 1716, Philip Perceval, an office-holder in Dublin and brother of the absent Lord Perceval, planned to overhaul what was performed publicly in the capital. He wanted to 'bring music here to some perfection'.[124] Another stringent critic of the prevailing musical modes was a son of the meddlesome Lord Molesworth. Just as the Molesworths schemed to instil a proper appreciation of classical architecture by inducing the Italian Alessandro Galilei to work in Ireland and to amend Irish tastes in gardening, so music was to be advanced by luring Scarpetini to Ireland.[125] Designs like Perceval's and Molesworth's belonged to a more ambitious programme of ethical as well as aesthetic renovation. Delight in the correct in music, art and architecture led on to a proper awareness of the correct in public and private behaviour. But, grandiose schemes like Perceval's scored at best a limited success in popularizing 'better' modes.[126]

Music had long featured in the pageants of the grand, from the viceroy and the municipalities to regiments.[127] James II, on entering Dublin in 1689, was serenaded by pipers playing 'The king enjoys his own again'.[128] Music appealed widely. It could console the lonely, as when a young army officer learnt the German flute as an alternative to constant reading. Soldiers, defending their musical interests as 'a most bewitching study', claimed Frederick, the king of Prussia, as a model since he united prowess as a general and a flautist.[129] Music, when properly employed, guided the young towards correct deportment and equipped them for company. Accordingly, instruction was taken seriously by the polite and would-be polite.[130] Evenings in the houses of the respectable might typically include songs and tunes. Invariably these were events at which women were welcomed. During the 1680s, Alan Brodrick, a young barrister, wanting to please patrons and delight young ladies, grabbed the latest catch-books and learnt the newest airs from London. He begged for the unfamiliar, 'if the words be good and the air pleasing, and, the rather to comply with the females' fancies, it be pretty bawdy'.[131] John Evelyn won favour in Dublin Castle by introducing a lord justice to a talented singer.[132] Private parties often hinged on the making of music. Unfortunately we can only guess the differences in what the likes of Edgeworth heard when in the houses of his Dublin friends and when at home in Edgeworthstown. He listened to and bought the new, but, especially in County Longford, he hired instrumentalists whose skills and repertoire sounded more traditional. If newcomers, such as the Edgeworths, enjoyed some of the same airs as their predecessors, the coincidence in tastes need not be interpreted as a strategy of the recently arrived to hide insecurities and identify with their adopted country. Melody and tempo, no less than the bright hues of textiles, the fragrance from flowers and the savour of fresh foods, gave pleasure. Price and prestige played important parts in deciding what was performed on public stages. In private houses and in the open air, different considerations came into play and may have permitted greater diversity.

## V

Men and women, if able to afford seats and suitable dress, mingled at musical entertainments. Other outlets of sociability saw little or none of this mixing. Alongside the boards which managed the hospitals and ran their fund-raising events, improving endeavours proliferated. The schemes led to the formation of societies, among which the Dublin Society, the Incorporated Society and the Physico-Historical Society stood out. Originating in grim local conditions, the groups owed little to the initiative of English governors, although lords-lieutenant were quickly enrolled as patrons. The societies paralleled, occasionally imitated or were themselves imitated by the groups dedicated to improvement founded in early-Hanoverian Edinburgh and then in Aberdeen and Glasgow.[133] The associations were underpinned by conviviality as well as by altruism. So, too, were freemasonry and the anti-duelling societies: both solely male reserves.[134] Masonic lodges in Ireland are documented first in the Munster of the 1720s. Quickly they appeared elsewhere, conspicuously in Dublin.[135] The military were important to the formation and success of the lodges. In 1735, five of the thirty-six known lodges were based in regiments. Others flourished in towns with a large garrison or among army officers desperate for distractions. Isolated lodges in the provinces can be traced to the enthusiasm of a local landowner: Godfrey Wills at Willsgrove in Roscommon, Thomas Coote of Cootehill, and James Moore at Newport Pratt in Mayo.[136] In Cork and Dublin, thanks to larger populations of prosperous Protestant civilians, the soldiery may not have bulked so large in the membership.[137] The seventeen registered as members of the 'True Blue Lodge' of Belfast between 1748 and 1757 were all designated 'merchants', except for a single 'gentleman'.[138]

Different in intention were the Friendly Brothers of St Patrick. Emerging (or resurrected) at Athenry in County Galway in the early 1750s, the Friendly Brothers repudiated duelling and committed themselves to the peaceful resolution of disputes.[139] Their clubs, or 'knots', appealed to Dubliners. By 1754, they also existed in nineteen other places. The clubs offered an alternative to the excesses traditionally linked with the bored and rampant soldiery, and – ironically – became popular with officers serving in Ireland. The like-minded were emboldened to dissent from the martial values current among so many contemporaries, civilians as

85. Masonic jewel associated with
Elizabeth Aldworth. The rituals of
free masons and other clubs
demanded regalia and so stimulated
local production.

well as soldiers.[140] In their war against duelling, the brethren adopted the symbol of the
friendly mammal, the dolphin, as their own. Soon it would decorate the furnishings and
insignia that assisted their gatherings.[141] The knots, with their rites, drew in grandees, urban
professionals and traders.[142]

Early accounts of masonic ceremonies in the 1720s and 1730s lingered over the nobles who
participated. Peers – St George, Netterville and Mountjoy – often presided. A report published in the Dublin newspapers in 1739 revealed the presence of four peers as well as of
numerous members of parliament and squires at a gathering in *The Eagle* tavern in the city.[143]
Yet, the abundance of lodges in the capital – fourteen in 1735; sixteen by 1744 – testified to the
differing quarters, professional and vocational groupings and – perhaps – to the several confessions to which the separate lodges catered. A report of a procession of masons through the
Dublin streets, in or shortly after 1727, connects it with the annual parades of other crafts.[144]
Again, in 1761, 'the regular, registered, free and accepted masons' tagged along behind
journeymen wool-combers and weavers.[145] The popularity of the lodges in the capital was
indicated in 1744 not just by the total, but also by their meeting fortnightly. Moreover, their

visibility, clear from street parades, assemblies in public places and items in the press, recruited more. In 1725, a newspaper reported how about a hundred gentlemen proceeded by coach from *The Yellow Lion* in central Dublin to the King's Inns. There the company fell on 120 dishes of meat. Then the members of the lodge went as a group to the theatre, proclaiming their calling by wearing aprons.[146]

In the country, lodges convened only once a month. At first glance, the locations of the lodges – two each at Youghal and Limerick, others at Cork, Tallow in County Waterford and Newcastle in Limerick – coincided with areas of populous Protestant settlement. As yet, only two of the thirty-seven lodges were in Ulster: at Cootehill and Enniskillen. With

86. Invitation to Masonic Lodge 252, Cork. From the 1720s, south Munster and the city of Cork were centres of freemasonry.

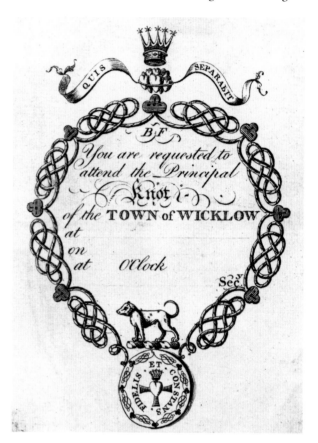

QUIS            SEPARABIT

B.F

*You are requested to attend the Principal Knot of the* TOWN of WICKLOW *at on at O'Clock*

Sec^y

FIDELIS · ET · CONSTANS

87. Invitation, Wicklow town knot of the Friendly Brothers of St Patrick. The Friendly Brothers originated as an anti-duelling society, and tended to attract respectable Protestants and townsmen.

few exceptions, landlords exerted scant influence over the organizations. Indeed, the majority of lodges may be seen as places where alternative orderings from those in landed society prevailed. In the early years, the professions of fraternity, shared with other brotherhoods like the guilds and corporations, may not have been altogether self-deluding. Masons did not shun publicity. At Youghal, the masons' festivities on St John's Day in 1743 followed the standard forms of civic jollity. Brethren walked the length of the port in pairs. Each sported around his neck a blue ribbon from which dangled a miniature set-square. After church, the company repaired to 'a house of entertainment'. The towns-people allegedly greeted the merrymaking with delight, saluting the masons from their windows and later displaying candles and lighting bonfires.[147] As with other occasions when spectators were expected to advertise their pleasure with illuminations, those who did not could become targets for displeasure. Publicity continued. The several lodges in Limerick were advertised, along with the city's other amenities.[148] In Cork, the different lodges of freemasons processed through the town. The route led from the Tholsel to the parish church of Shandon. After the obligatory 'excellent' sermon, the masons dined at *The Cork Arms*.[149]

Lodges and knots offered congenial company. The confraternities were further valued for their philanthropy. As the organizations expanded, they frequently functioned like the older trading guilds. In particular, they looked after their own when they stumbled into hard times. Sometimes, as at Coleraine in the 1750s, they relieved a larger community of the distressed and hungry.[150] Part secret fraternity, part benefit society, the lodges possessed strong convivial aspects.[151] One Dubliner showed how much he valued the meetings, and suggested why. Michael Wills, the son of a successful carpenter, emerged from the aristocracy of labour to take a place among the worthies of the capital. He continued and expanded the family firm, acting as contractor, architect and consultant.[152] Wills, a bachelor, belonged to both a 'Select' club and 'the Friendlies'. Indeed, he acted as treasurer to the Dublin knot of Friendly Brothers of St Patrick. The inn provided Wills with much of his social existence. It overlapped with fraternizing with the brethren of the knot. However, as in so many voluntary associations, interest fluctuated. In 1774, when Wills bespoke a dinner for twelve of his fraternity, only three turned up to eat it.[153]

The non-sectarian and egalitarian character of the masons and Friendly Brothers is sometimes stressed. Yet, the easy equality apparently upheld by continental lodges is not evident in the early accounts of masonic gatherings in Dublin. There, the titled were seated away from mere commoners.[154] In theory, Catholics might join Protestants at meetings, but it is unlikely that this happened in the eighteenth century.[155] Indeed, the opening of numerous lodges in Dublin may have given Catholic masons their own distinct venues. Public parades of masons, as of other groups, affronted some of the excluded. What happened in the secluded meetings cannot always be discerned, leading to suspicions of covert and sinister activities. How far the lodges strengthened or weakened the ideology and society of Protestant Ireland is a matter, in the main, of fruitless conjecture; clearer is what they added to the occasions for sociability.

Protestant masons, such as Wills, often belonged to other clubs, some with undisguised denominational and political aims. Youghal, a centre of early freemasonry, saw an equally precocious development of defensive Protestant associations. A Hanover Society was established in 1711. Copied from similar clubs in England, it was intended to challenge the current Tory hegemony, both locally and nationally.[156] Once the Hanoverians seemed secure on the throne, interest in and attendance at meetings waned. They revived whenever the Protestant state in Ireland looked to be endangered. In placid times, the club provided a pretext for periodic binges and summer cruises up the River Blackwater to local beauty spots. In 1779, the secretary minuted that there had been no business, 'but eating and drinking'.[157]

Comparable groups sprang up elsewhere. In the north of County Cork, the Loyal Protestant Association of Mallow was established in 1745. It was designed to co-ordinate resistance to any Jacobite invasion or Irish Catholic insurgency. Avowedly anti-Catholic, it required initiates to abjure the pope and pretender and renounce transubstantiation.[158] An initial burst of energy abated with the fears of invasion. Quickly the Mallow Loyal Association lost its pulling power. At first, it met fortnightly; by the summer of 1747, it convened only monthly. Discontinued later in 1747, it was resurrected briefly in 1755 when war with France renewed the possible threats to Protestant Ireland. Meetings in 1756 attracted only three or four members; in December 1758, none came to an advertised session.[159] By the 1770s, fears aroused by agrarian violence and politicization encouraged seemingly innocuous bodies such as the Anna Liffey Club of Kildare to assume a vigilante stance.[160] In Cork, members of the Boyne Society were reviewed at White's bowling-green on 4 November 1777: a sacred date for Irish Protestants. The following year, the societies of True Blues, Boyne, Aughrim, Union and Culloden marched gravely in their uniforms to church. It was remarked that this was the first public appearance in Cork of 'these sons of liberty'.[161]

The craze for volunteering gathered pace. Over the next few months, the splendidly arrayed volunteers would be seen in the public spaces of Cork and of other towns.[162] They drew in enthusiasts who had long been organized in convivial bands, which possessed sectarian and defensive potential. A Boyne Society existed in Dublin during the first half of the eighteenth century. It may have come into being to promote commemoration of the decisive victory of William over James through the erection of a monument near the battlefield. It also served as a gathering at which veterans could share their recollections of the engagement and enjoin watchfulness on the careless young. The lord-lieutenant briefly attended the festivities of the club at the Dublin Tholsel in 1737. No sooner had he left than proceedings degenerated into drunken harangues with duels only narrowly averted.[163] In the 1740s, Darby Clarke, who had seen action alongside William of Orange, was flattered to be the toast of Boyne and Enniskillen Clubs in Dublin. The former staged an 'elegant entertainment' attended by the viceroy, retiring lords justice, 'with numbers of nobility and gentry'. Clarke alone of the guests 'had the honour to be at the Battle of the Boyne'.[164] It was not difficult to imagine these raucous legionaries being transformed into a military corps during an emergency. Similarly, in the countryside, groups such as the Dettingen Club of 1743, the most recent in the north of County Cork, might acquire functions other than 'excess in drinking'.[165] Even associations, seemingly empty of any political or sectarian connotations, served as props of the Protestants' ascendancy. The Florists' Club, an exclusive body of well-heeled Dubliners and visiting notables, oversaw competitions to grow the finest auriculas and carnations. In summer, its members refreshed themselves with marine expeditions. Yet, in 1763, the club commanded its members to don orange cockades: already a colour and a gesture of political partisanship.[166] The Gardeners' Institute in Cashel, with its strong female participation and innocent pleasures, elaborated its events with military parades. Other bands of civilians pursuing knowledge and improvement upheld the Protestant cause. In 1757, the

88. Joseph Tudor, *Obelisk to William III beside the River Boyne, c.* 1745, engraved by J. Brooks. The Boyne Society may have been formed to campaign for this monument on the site of William III's victory over James II. The society continued as a convivial group dedicated to upholding and celebrating the Protestant interest in Ireland.

'Medico-Political' Society, investigating the antiquities and topography of Ireland, took issue with alternative Catholic interpretations. 'Jesuitical subterfuges' were detected, and must be challenged by the members of the learned society.[167]

What was implicit in many of these civil societies became explicit in one of the most common forms of association among men in Protestant Ireland: the militia. It cherished traditions about the origins and privations of Protestant settlements in Ireland. It satisfied the obligations which came with the privileges of citizenship: readiness to defend the state. It distinguished the Protestant citizens from their disenfranchised Catholic neighbours, who, in most cases, were legally banned from carrying swords, keeping firearms or owning horses. It also enabled the Irish Protestants to emulate the swagger of the regular soldiery. The British officers stationed throughout Ireland frequently prompted and led public demonstrations of loyalty to the ruling dynasty. They also dictated questions of style. As a result of their arrogance, the soldiery were viewed ambivalently. It had to be allowed that the regulars made 'a handsome sight' at arrays and rendezvous.[168] Troops at Limerick in 1752, were led by 'very top officers, dressed very rich and fine, making a great figure'.[169] Similarly, the officers, resplendent in their regimentals and exhaling the magic of distant places, were fêted at public and domestic gatherings. But the ease with which these visitors usurped social and sartorial leadership was envied and resented in some quarters. Irritated civilians responded by creating their own force – the militia – with its own pageantry.

The militiamen were ill equipped and poorly trained if required to halt an invasion or suppress insurrection – as was demonstrated embarrassingly in 1689 and 1760. However, as an exercise in sociability, the militia succeeded triumphantly. Men from assorted backgrounds – some like Pratt and Peacock met earlier – were swept along by the patriotic frenzy of the 1740s and mustered with their local militia regiments. The vanity of civilians, such as Henry Boyle, over their titles in the militia corps was laughed at. During the 1720s, Robert Wilson, a Dubliner of modest standing, secured a commission in the militia. He saw it as a useful addition to a quiverful of positions. Worried when he missed the first array, he hastened to dine with most of the troop. With calculation, he introduced himself to 'some of the best of them'.[170] With no invasion imminent, Wilson was unlikely to have to shift from play-acting to action. Commanders were often more eager than their subordinates to show their mettle during alerts.[171] Militia companies could proclaim the grandeur of their captains. In 1715, the absent Lord Perceval instructed his agent in County Cork 'to take care of my interest' by attending to the militia troop of Perceval's Protestant tenants. The absentee was desperate that his contingent should 'make as good a figure for number of men, horses, arms and servants as any in the country'.[172]

Perceval and his agent fussed over flags, drums and fifes and the colour and cut of uniforms. In fact, these seeming trivia obsessed the militiamen as well. In 1715, and again during the emergency of 1745–6, volunteers, drawn from the tenant farmers and modest traders, insisted that they wear blue, not red coats, since the latter were thought 'a badge of servile dependence'. The men expected to be treated at their commander's (and landlord's) expense. Dining together might be justified as a way to increase cohesiveness, but soon, when the panic ended, the troop declined into a select dining club. Its active members met at the Percevals' residence, Lohort Castle, where they were to sit on chairs emblazoned with their armorials. Similar priorities animated the active militiamen across the island. In County Down, communal feasts rather than rigorous drill were wanted. In Sligo, the local potentates, the Wynnes, were experienced regular soldiers. Owen Wynne directed some of his expertise into organizing the militia. Muskets were cleaned; officers entertained at hostelries; orange ribbon for cockades was purchased; so too were thirty-two hats, although the record is silent as to whether or not they were decked with gold or silver lace. The exertions made it reasonable to rejoice in a victory in which – at least vicariously – the Sligo volunteers had assisted. Accordingly, Wynne's biggest bill was for celebrating the victory at Culloden in 1746 and the birthday of the victor, Cumberland. Others in Ireland took equal satisfaction in these events, and Culloden Clubs were formed as another embodiment of Protestant solidarity and yet another outlet for sociability.[173]

## VI

Forms of sociability in Protestant Ireland could not be uncoupled from politics and ideology. Charles Lucas, a scourge of what he regarded as misgovernment in the Dublin of the 1740s, saw the importance of such societies to the cellular composition of the incumbent ascendancy. Indeed, Lucas's public prominence was rooted in one – a Dublin guild. His own experience, coupled with observation of his contemporaries, led him to urge the ambitious to cultivate 'an interest in some party or club, no matter with how little reason'.[174] It was then easier to launch into public affairs from such a secure base. Lucas's advice suggested that calculus drove many to join societies. At the same time, voluntary societies, like material goods, satisfied simpler instincts.

Food and drink occasioned and gave structure to gatherings, both formal and informal. Shared meals registered and, it was hoped, improved relationships. So the functionaries of the Church of Ireland vestries, the freemen of corporations, the brethren of guilds and subscribers to societies dined together at least once in the year. Toasts, drunken boasts and emulative consumption exposed and widened fissures among the ostensibly equal and like-minded. Less rigidly organized groups feasted more frequently. A lawyer recently removed to England asked to be remembered in Dublin by his 'friends of the dining club'.[175] Men such as Edgeworth or Pratt, finding themselves within company at the assizes, on the road and away from home, clubbed with others, so dividing the expense of evenings. Other occasions were rendered more congenial by shared food and drink. Bargains, sales and completed tasks were routinely sealed with drams. An agent, having 'softened' tenants 'with a glass of ale', discovered their real opinions.[176] Archbishop King saw to it that the men employed by his coach-maker were given drink when they delivered his new vehicle. Squire Edgeworth refreshed tenants who had laboured over his potatoes or saved the hay with tots of whiskey.[177] Many of these gestures were *d'haut en bas*, without the householder or customer being present when the rewards were distributed. In this particular, practice at Dublin Castle offered a model. Once the viceroy had entertained the important on the Protestant festival of 23 October (the anniversary of deliverance from the Catholic plot to seize the government), 'the common people' were allowed to carry away the broken meats that remained after the feast.[178] Bishop Hutchinson of Down and Connor, for example, allowed money to the poor and servants to drink the healths of Queen Caroline and other members of the royal family.[179] But sometimes, the donor did share the fun. The Limerick agent Peacock gave work-men dinner at the New Year in 1749.[180] Some of these sociable exchanges were between equals; others, not. Gifts also smoothed dealings between kindred, clients and patrons. Haunches of venison, runlets of whiskey, fruit cordials, braces of hares or snipe, baskets of cherries, straw-berries and raspberries, potted and collared meats or salted salmon, even melons from the hothouse, repaid favours and created obligations.[181] A seasonal glut could be unloaded con-veniently and flatteringly. The choice – cheeses, fish and fruit – themselves became reasons to meet, eat and celebrate. A group of professionals in Dublin assembled with some cere-mony to savour a cheese sent from Wales by an absent companion.[182]

The passage of each year was signalled by the first lamb or asparagus, a green (grass-fed) goose, the many berries and drupes of summer and the first potatoes of the new season.[183] These were delights to be shared, not to be consumed as a solitary vice by the glutton. Even gifts that had suffered in transit – putrid brawn, rotting game – were still prized as tokens of regard. In this spirit, the best from a batch of foetid preserves was given to a Dublin attorney, 'not that it could be used, but to show him your good designs'.[184]

Observation warned that the unthinking surrender to the appetites brought less welcome consequences. The quest for culinary excellence had 'erected the art of eating into no mean figure in the world'. At the smartest tables nothing arrived in its original form: eggs were shaped into cylinders; birds fashioned into beasts. Worse still, intemperate drinking ended in 'mad mirth, tenderless and sottish fondness, causeless quarrels, vain and wicked vaunts, open and avowed licentiousness'. Excesses, which might rend the fragile social fabric, were con-trasted with moderation. Even moralists were willing to allow 'social, temperate and innocent festivity'.[185]

In 1754, Peter Ievers was said to preside in a riverside Dublin pub over the 'ancient and numerous society' of cripples, blind and aged. The 'society', either a satire on the vogue for clubs or a cover for indulgence, confirmed the popularity of these organizations.[186] Benefits resulted. Company schooled participants in virtue and civility. It also introduced the socia-ble to the desirable and novel in dress, diet, talk and deportment. But to join fully in these enlightening associations took time and money. In addition, the paraphernalia of confes-sional tests and subscriptions restricted admission. The requirements placed most Catholics in Ireland at a disadvantage. The justification of the associations, that they civilized and anglicized, carried little conviction when the bulk of the Irish were shut out. Not only the poor, but women and the middling orders were debarred. Alternatives catered to the excluded. Many – from horse-races, through fairs, to religious patterns – were engineered to make money, but at least at prices lower than those for the entertainments of the élite. The proliferation of outlets for sociability may have widened the cultural gap between a prosper-ous, educated, smartly dressed and well-travelled few, and the majority in eighteenth-century

Ireland. But boundaries were not always clear or fixed. It was possible with determination and ingenuity to confuse or evade the discrete categories of gender, confession, town and country and even poor and rich.

The variety and availability of goods to those outside the self-proclaimed quality have been considered above. Much of the detail remains elusive. Even more obscure are attitudes of humbler consumers towards the commodities. Professionals and traders in Dublin and the large towns are found in possession of novelties, but rarely express their thoughts. One exception was Samuel Bryan, a Dublin skinner made good. He was of sufficient worth to serve as a grand juror for the city in the 1740s. Bryan was also a Protestant dissenter, an affiliation which inhibited too ready a relish for worldly goods. Bryan lectured a son who had emigrated to Philadelphia. In 1752, the younger Bryan was ordered to mix only with 'men of conversation and good manners'. The parent was outraged by reports that his offspring was 'taken up in boating on the river'. He commanded, 'away with boating'! But the ban was not absolute. Marine excursions were permitted, 'on business or on a party of pleasure with good company'. The senior Bryan, drawing on his own experience of Dublin rather than any understanding of customs in America, was prepared to sanction 'dancing, fencing, a glass of wine or punch'. In the respectable business worlds of Protestant Dublin such relaxations were tolerated; indeed, may have been essential to thrive there. Bryan, despite his strictures, was happy enough to receive specialities from the new world – preserved cranberries, cucumbers and peaches.[187]

The immediacy of physical pleasure, and doubts about its moral effects, disturbed another Protestant dissenter in Hanoverian Ireland. Joshua Wight, a Quaker surveyor, generally looked askance at the depravity around him in Munster. Yet he was not impervious to enjoyment. In 1755, he and other Friends arranged to picnic afloat in Cork harbour. In taking to the water, the Quakers joined others – Cork's own water club, the Youghal Hanover Society and the Dublin Florists – keen on this summer recreation.[188] Wight's party bought fish from a passing skiff and cooked it. 'We had very good and plenty of provisions', Wight acknowledged. 'All was very quiet and in moderation, and no superficiality of wantonness'. The Quaker diarist did not convey the smack of the swell against the boat, nor the sizzle and fragrance of the fish as it was fried. Even when escaping the baking brick dwellings of Cork in summertime, the grim Wight could not forget the follies of fallen humankind and the feckless Irish. On cue, as it were, his fears were corroborated. A drunk dived into the River Lee in a feat of bravado only to drown. In Wight's mind, the failings of the inebriate and of Ireland were one. Each supposed that it possessed greater strength than was the case. If the swimmer lacked the power to survive, so Ireland itself was succumbing to luxury. Protestants and Catholics gorged on what they could barely afford without heed for tomorrow.[189]

Wight, in common with fellow Quakers but unusually among his prospering contemporaries, valued restraint above show. Apart from those with religious scruples against ostentation, the discerning avowed that true distinction came from a moderate sampling of material plenty. The sententious decried the pleasure-lovers who, like the grasshoppers in scripture, glutted themselves 'with the luscious juices of spring and summer'. Self-restraint was easier for the rich and lofty, such as Bishop Howard and Bishop Synge, than for the straitened.[190] Worryingly, the vulgar too easily mistook moderation for meanness. In 1695, Archbishop Marsh averred, 'the common people judge by outward appearance'.[191] Equally, it could have been retorted that the more elevated were also guided, or misled, by externals. The look of individuals decided how they were ranked, and so added to the pressures to present an imposing figure. A further obstacle for those who urged voluntary self-effacement was that appearances were thought to connote inner qualities. As goods multiplied, true worth was harder to read from externals. With the proliferation of replicas, the look and manners of the civil and civilized could be counterfeited.

These hazards beset all societies undergoing economic change. In the eighteenth century, the processes stimulated debates on the enervating and stimulating impact of luxury: debates to which the concerned in Ireland contributed.[192] Reactions among the Irish were complicated by long-standing feelings about confession and ethnicity. In addition, patriots decried the adoration of the foreign. Until the eighteenth century, the inhabitants of Ireland had been pressed to adopt the attire, diet and housing of their supposedly more advanced neighbours, and congratulated when they did so. However, in the eighteenth century, what had previously been approved as aids to or signs of industry, integration and civility, was denounced. The ease with which inferiors were assuming the modes and manners of their betters no longer announced the welcome news that they had been assimilated to the standards of lowland Britain. Everywhere, those who essayed the grand figure threatened to collapse the fences between the social orders, with parvenus and the middling sort passing for the quality. In Ireland, further anxieties arose lest well-dressed, hard-working and polite Catholics be mistaken for Protestants. Larger and cheaper ranges of goods justified the worries. Nevertheless, money mainly determined styles of dress, furnishing, housing and demeanour. Rare Catholics – like the Bellews of Mount Bellew and Blakes of Ballyglunin – against the odds retained or acquired a modicum of wealth.[193] They snapped up objects identical to those coveted by their Protestant counterparts. The numbers of Catholics able to engage in expenditure of this sort remained small so long as property was owned overwhelmingly by Protestants. Because prosperous Catholics were few but poor Catholics abounded between the 1690s and 1780s, they were seldom accused of ostentation and excess. Instead, materialism, sometimes gross and destructive, was seen as the characteristic and a curse of the nascent Protestant ascendancy.[194]

# Notes

## Introduction

1. D. Dickson, *New foundations: Ireland, 1660–1800*, 2nd edn (Dublin, 2000), p. 111.

2. T. C. Barnard, 'The world of goods and County Offaly in the early eighteenth century', in T. O'Neill (ed.), *Offaly: history and society* (Dublin, 1998), pp. 371–92; P. Borsay and L. Boynton (eds), *Provincial towns in early modern England and Ireland: change, convergence and divergence*, Proceedings of the British Academy, 108 (2002); L. A. Clarkson and E. M. Crawford, *Feast and famine: a history of food and nutrition in Ireland 1500–1920* (Oxford, 2001), pp. 29–58; L. M. Cullen, T. C. Smout and A. Gibson, 'Wages and comparative development in Ireland and Scotland, 1585–1780', in R. Mitchison and P. Roebuck (eds), *Economy and society in Scotland and Ireland, 1500–1939* (Edinburgh, 1988), pp. 105–16.

3. C. O'Hara observations, NLI, Ms. 20,397; J. Osborne to Lord Orrery, undated [1680s], Petworth, Orrery Mss, general series, 27; Barnard, *New anatomy*, p. 282.

4. Clarkson and Crawford, *Feast and famine*, pp. 50–8; L. M. Cullen, *Anglo-Irish trade, 1660–1800* (Manchester, 1968), pp. 75–90, 216–20.

5. W. H. Crawford, 'A Ballymena business in the late eighteenth century', in J. Gray and W. McCann (eds), *An uncommon bookman: essays in memory of J. R. R. Adams* (Belfast, 1996), pp. 23–33; W. H. Crawford, 'The patron, or festival of St Kevin at the seven churches, Glendalough, County Wicklow, 1813', *Ulster Folklife*, xxxii (1986), pp. 38–46; D. Fitzgerald, Knight of Glin, 'Early Irish trade cards and other eighteenth-century ephemera', *Eighteenth-Century Ireland*, ii (1987), pp. 115–32; S. Foster, 'Going shopping in eighteenth-century Dublin', *Things*, iv (1996), pp. 32–61; S. Foster, 'Going shopping in Georgian Dublin: luxury goods and the negotiation of national identity', unpublished M.A. thesis, Royal College of Art and V & A (1995); S. Foster, 'Buying Irish: consumer nationalism in eighteenth-century Dublin', *History Today*, xlvii/6 (1997), pp. 44–51.

6. St G. Ashe, *A sermon preached before the Incorporated Society . . . 18 Feb. 1714/15* (London, 1715), p. 16; [R. Cox], *An essay for the conversion of the Irish* (Dublin, 1698), pp. 10–13; F. Hutchinson, *A letter to a member of parliament, concerning the imploying and providing for the poor* (Dublin, 1723), pp. 9–15.

7. P. Fagan, *Catholics in a Protestant country* (Dublin, 1998); J. Fenlon, 'French influence in late seventeenth-century portraits', *GPA Irish Arts Review Yearbook*, vi (1989–90), pp. 156–68; K. Harvey, *The Bellews of Mount Bellew: a Catholic gentry family in eighteenth-century Ireland* (Dublin, 1998); J. McDonnell, 'Art and patronage in the penal era', in *Maynooth College bicentenary exhibitions: Ecclesiastical art of the penal era* (Maynooth, 1995), pp. 1–51.

8. G. Kirkham, '"No more to be got from the cat but the skin": management, landholding and economic change in the Murray of Broughton estate, 1670–1775', in W. Nolan, L. Ronanyne and M. Dunlevy (eds), *Donegal: history and society* (Dublin, 1995), pp. 357–80; T. P. Power, *Land, politics and society in eighteenth-century Tipperary* (Oxford, 1993), p. 90; P. Roebuck, 'Rent movement, proprietorial incomes and

agricultural development, 1730–1830', in P. Roebuck (ed.), *Plantation to partition* (Belfast, 1981), pp. 82–101; P. Roebuck, 'Landlord indebtedness in the seventeenth and eighteenth centuries', in J. M. Goldstrom and L. A. Clarkson (eds), *Irish population, economy and society* (Oxford, 1981), pp. 138–53.

9. L. Baker-Jones, *Princes, privileges and power: the Tivyside gentry in the community* (Llandysul, 1999); D. W. Howell, *Patriarchs and parasites: the gentry of south-west Wales in the eighteenth century* (Cardiff, 1986); D. W. Howell, *The rural poor in eighteenth-century Wales* (Cardiff, 2000); B. Howells (ed.), *Early modern Pembrokeshire, 1536–1835* (Haverfordwest, 1987); M. Humphreys, *The crisis of community: Montgomeryshire, 1680–1815* (Cardiff, 1996); P. Jenkins, *The making of a ruling class: the Glamorgan gentry, 1640–1790* (Cambridge, 1983).

10. A. J. S. Gibson and T. C. Smout, *Prices, food and wages in Scotland, 1550–1780* (Cambridge, 1995); J. Gifford, *William Adam 1689–1748: a life and times of Scotland's universal architect* (Edinburgh, 1989); I. Gow, *The Scottish interior: Georgian and Victorian décor* (Edinburgh, 1992), pp. 6, 10–13; I. Gow and T. Clifford, *Duff House* (Edinburgh, 1995); D. Johnson, *Music and society in lowland Scotland in the eighteenth century* (London, 1972); J. Macaulay, *The classical country house in Scotland, 1660–1800* (London, 1987); S. Nenadic, 'Middle-rank consumers and domestic culture in Edinburgh and Glasgow, 1720–1840', *P & P*, clxv (1994), pp. 122–54; F. W. Robertson, *Early Scottish gardeners and their plants, 1650–1750* (East Linton, 2000); R. Scott-Moncrieff (ed.), *The household book of Lady Grisell Baillie, 1692–1733* (Edinburgh, 1911).

11. M. Bence-Jones, *Life in an Irish country house* (London, 1996); M. Girouard, *Life in the English country house* (New Haven and London, 1978); V. Pakenham, *The big house in Ireland* (London, n. d.); P. Somerville-Large, *The Irish country house: social history* (London, 1995). C. Maxwell, *Country and town in Ireland under the Georges*, 2nd edn (Dundalk, 1949); and E. MacLysaght, *Irish life in the seventeenth century*, 2nd edn (Shannon, 1969) provide much information and some insights.

12. Chesterfield to his son, 5 Dec. 1749, in B. Dobrée (ed.), *The letters of Philip Dormer Stanhope, 4th earl of Chesterfield*, 6 vols (London, 1932), iv, p. 1455.

13. L. B. Namier, *The structure of politics at the accession of George III*, 2nd edn (London, 1957), pp. 1–2; Johnston-Liik, *HIP*, iii, p. 12.

14. P. Camporesi, *Exotic brew: the art of living in the age of the enlightenment* (Oxford, 1998), pp. 148–9; R. Hoffman, *Princes of Ireland, planters of Maryland: a Carroll saga* (Chapel Hill and London, 2000); K. Lockridge, *The diary, and life, of William Byrd II of Virginia, 1674–1744* (Chapel Hill and London, 1987); A. Vickery, *The gentleman's daughter: women's lives in Georgian England* (New Haven and London, 1998).

15. M. Smythe to W. Smythe, 16 Feb. 1727[8], 15 May 1728, 21 July 1728, 2 Aug. 1728, 23 Feb. 1731[2], 30 Oct. 1731, 11 March 1731[2], NLI, PC 448.

16. M. Smythe to W. Smythe, 16 Feb. 1727[8], 9 March 1727[8], 6 and 21 July 1728, 2 Aug. 1728, 23 March 1729[30], 18 July 1730, 9 Sep. 1730, 30 Oct. 1731, 5 Jan. 1733[4], NLI, PC 448; L. Clayton to Sir J. Perceval, 15 March 1685[6], BL, Add. Ms. 46,962, f. 240.

17. Lord Palmerston to W. Flower, later Lord Castledurrow, 8 Oct. 1728, 30 April 1730, 16 Dec. 1731, 14 June 1744, NLI, Ms. 11,478; P. Ward to W. Smythe, 20 July [1721–30], NLI, PC 444; Legg (ed.), *Synge Letters*, pp. 115, 118, 180, 189, 201, 206, 213, 275, 295.

18. T. H. Breen, 'An empire of goods: the anglicization of colonial America', *Journal of British Studies*, xxv (1986), pp. 468–99; T. H. Breen, '"Baubles of Britain": the American and consumer revolutions of the eighteenth century', *P & P*, cxix (1988), pp. 73–104.

19. T. C. Barnard, 'Public and private uses of wealth in Ireland, *c.* 1660–1760', in J. R. Hill and C. Lennon (eds), *Luxury and austerity: historical studies, XXI* (Dublin, 1999), pp. 66–83; T. C. Barnard, 'Integration or separation? Hospitality and display in Protestant Ireland, *c.* 1660–1800', in L. Brockliss and D. Eastwood (eds), *A union of multiple identities: the British Isles, c. 1750–1850* (Manchester, 1997), pp. 127–46; P. H. Kelly, '"Industry and virtue versus luxury and corruption": Berkeley, Walpole and the South Sea Bubble crisis', *Eighteenth-Century Ireland*, vii (1992), pp. 57–74.

## 1 *The Viceroyalty*

1. Wyndham to Devonshire, 28 April 1737, Chatsworth, Devonshire letters, 243.0; A. P. I. Samuels (ed.), *The early life, correspondence and writings of the Rt. Hon. Edmund Burke, LL.D.* (Cambridge, 1923), p. 264.

2. S. Bagshawe to W. Bagshawe, 12 Nov. 1743, JRL, B 2/3/90. Cf. J. Copping to Sir H. Sloane, 15 Feb. 1741[2], BL, Sloane Ms. 4057, f. 109.

3. Lady Drogheda to T. Keightley, 16 March 1698[9], NLI, Inchiquin Mss, 978.

4. G. E. Howard, *The miscellaneous works, in verse and prose*, 3 vols (Dublin, 1782), i, p. xxxvi.

5. [H. Jones], *The bricklayer's poem. Presented to his excellency the Lord Lieutenant, on his arrival in this kingdom* (Dublin, 1745), p. 5.

6. Essex to Harbord, 21 April 1674, Bodleian, Add. Ms. C. 34, f. 90v.

7. C. Brady, *The chief governors: the rise and fall of reform government in Tudor Ireland, 1536–1588* (Cambridge, 1994); C. Brady, 'Court, castle and country: the framework of government in Tudor Ireland', in C. Brady and R. Gillespie (eds), *Natives and newcomers: essays on the making of Irish colonial society, 1534–1641* (Dublin, 1986), pp. 30, 43–8; S. G. Ellis, *Reform and revival: English government in Ireland, 1470–1534* (Woodbridge, 1986), pp. 12–31; H. Morgan, '"Over mighty officers": the Irish lord deputyship in the early modern British state', *History Ireland*, vii/4 (1999), pp. 17–21.

8. D. W. Hayton, 'The beginnings of the "undertaker system"', in T. Bartlett and D. W. Hayton (eds), *Penal era and golden age: essays in Irish history, 1690–1800* (Belfast, 1979), pp. 32–54; P. McNally, *Parties, patriots and undertakers: parliamentary politics in early Hanoverian Ireland* (Dublin, 1997).

9. J. Evelyn, jr. to J. Evelyn, 14 Jan. 1692[3], Christ Church, now BL, Evelyn Letters, f. 657.

10. W. Longueville to T. Hales, 15 Dec. 1685, Somerset CRO, DD/BR/ely, 3/11.

11. A. Hamilton to Lady Panmure, 28 Dec. 1700, NAS, GD 45/14/238, 77.

12. A. Hamilton to Lady Panmure, 29 Nov. [?1703], 10 May 1705, NAS, GD 45/15/238, 25, 75.

13. K. Conolly to C. Tickell, 2 Oct. 1724, Tickell Mss, private collection, Devon.

14. R. Howard to H. Howard, 25 April 1730, NLI, PC 227; cf. O. Gallagher to O. St George, 9 Jan. 1724[5], PRO, C 110/46, 313.

15. D. W. Hayton, 'Walpole and Ireland', in J. Black (ed.), *Britain in the age of Walpole* (Basingstoke, 1984), pp. 95–119.

16. C. Tickell to T. Tickell, undated [between 1725 and 1729], Tickell Mss, private collection, Devon; Bp. W. Nicolson to Abp. W. Wake, 6 June 1725, Christ Church, Wake Ms. 14/269.

17. R. Howard to H. Howard, 12 Oct. 1731, 2 and 13 Nov. 1731, 23 Dec. 1731, NLI, PC 227.

18. R. Howard to H. Howard, 15 July [1707], NLI, PC 227.

19. T. C. Barnard, 'Edmund Spencer, Edmund Spenser and the problems of Irish Protestants in the eighteenth century', in T. Barnard, *Irish Protestant ascents and descents, 1641–1770* (Dublin, 2003).

20. Bp. R. Howard to H. Howard, 13 Nov. 1731, NLI, PC 227; Lady A. Conolly to Lord Strafford, 31 Oct. [1733], IAA, box 76; Delany, *Autobiography*, 1st series, i, pp. 301, 308–9; *Dublin Gazette*, 666, 3–6 Nov. 1733; McParland, *Public architecture*, pp. 100–2.

21. A. Hamilton to Lady Panmure, 25 Jan. 1709[10], NAS, GD 45/15/238, 20.

22. O. Gallagher to O. St George, 9 Jan. 1724[5], PRO, C.110/46/313; H. Rose to Sir M. Crosbie, 21 Sep. 1731, NLI, Talbot–Crosbie Mss, folder 44; H. Boyle to Burlington, 17 Aug. 1731, Chatsworth letters, box 1720–36, 205.0.

23. Sir J. Temple, account book, s.d. 29 March 1687, Southampton UL, BR 7A/1.

24. W. Henry to Lord Hardwicke, 13 Oct. 1761, BL, Add. Ms. 35,596, f. 400.

25. Lady A. Conolly to Lord Strafford, 31 Oct. [1733], IAA, 97/84, box 76.

26. A. Hamilton to Lady Panmure, 18 July [1705], NAS, GD 45/15/238, 67.

27. Bp. R. Howard to H. Howard, 13 Sep. 1733, NLI, Ms. 12,149.

28. W. Longueville to T. Hales, 15 Sep. 1685, Somerset CRO, DD/BR/ely, 3/11.

29. S. Bagshawe to W. Bagshawe, 24 Nov. 1741, JRL, B 2/3/81.

30. A. J. Oughton, autobiography, NAM, Ms. 8808–36–1, p. 73.

31. S. Bagshawe to W. Bagshawe, 2 June 1743, JRL, B 2/3/88; Oughton, autobiography, NAM, Ms. 8808–36–1, pp. 65–7, 72.

32. S. Bagshawe, fragmentary journal, 1740–2, JRL, B 15/3/1; Oughton, autobiography, NAM, Ms. 8808–36–1, p. 72.

33. 'A catalogue of books to be sold at the Castle of Dublin . . . part of the library of Secretary Tickell deceased', *c.* 1729, Smythe of Barbavilla Mss, private collection, Berkshire; R. E. Tickell, *Thomas Tickell and the eighteenth-century poets (1685–1740)* (London, 1931).

34. McNally, *Parties, patriots and undertakers*, pp. 88–117.

35. R. Howard to H. Howard, 3 Jan. 1729[30], NLI, PC 227.

36. Capel to ?Nottingham, 5 July 1695, Nottingham UL, PW A 242; HMC, *Buccleuch Mss*, ii, part i, p. 209.

37. Carteret to Newcastle, 15 July 1725, PRO, SP 63/385, 281, 283; J. Pocklington to Abp. W. Wake, Christ Church, Wake Ms. 14, f. 260; Barnard, *New anatomy*, pp. 146–7.

38. Hartington to Mountcharles, 15 Nov. 1755, Chatsworth, Devonshire letters, box 1755, 260.183.

39. Bedford to N. Clements, received 30 Dec. 1760, TCD, Ms. 1742/79.

40. A. Clarke, *Prelude to Restoration in Ireland: the end of the Commonwealth, 1659–1660* (Cambridge, 1999), pp. 108–12; S. J. Connolly, *Religion, law and power: the making of Protestant Ireland* (Oxford, 1992), pp. 24–5.

41. Crown entry books, Co. Dublin, s.d. 24 Oct. 1745, 12 Dec. 1745, NA; *Dublin Gazette*, 975, 13–16 Feb. 1713[14].

42. Sir W. Petty to Lady Petty, 8 April 1684, Petty Papers, 5/126, now BL, Add. Ms.; J. Hall to dowager countess of Orrery, 8 April 1684, Petworth, Orrery Mss, general series, 30; *CARD*, v, p. 311; HMC, *Ormonde Mss*, new series, vii, 209–10, 220–1.

43. T. C. Barnard, 'The viceregal court in later seventeenth-century Ireland', in E. Cruickshanks (ed.), *The Stuart courts* (Stroud, 2000), pp. 256–65; J. L. J. Hughes, 'Dublin Castle in the seventeenth century: a topographical reconstruction', *Dublin Historical Record*, ii (1940), pp. 87, 90; R. Loeber; 'Rebuilding Dublin Castle: thirty critical years, 1661–1690', *Studies*, lxix (1980), pp. 45–68.

44. Essex to Shaftesbury, 8 March 1672[3], PRO, 30/24/50, 23.

45. J. Bold, *John Webb: architectural theory and practice in the seventeenth century* (Oxford, 1989), pp. 103–46; H. Colvin, J. M. Crook, K. Downes and J. Newman, *The History of the King's Works. V. 1660–1772* (London, 1976); M. Whinney, 'John Webb's drawings for Whitehall Palace', *Walpole Society*, xxxi (1945), pp. 45–107.

46. Loeber, *Architects*, pp. 26, 34–5, 84, 94, 112–13.

47. McParland, *Public architecture*.

48. H. Rose to Sir M. Crosbie, 21 and 23 Sep. 1731, NLI, Talbot–Crosbie Mss, folder 44.

49. Bp. R. Howard to H. Howard, 2 Nov. 1731, NLI, PC 227.

50. Ormond to Orrery, 14 Aug. 1678, Petworth, Orrery Mss, general series 29.

51. Inventories of hangings at Kilkenny, 13 July 1676, NLI, Ms. 2522/12 and 24; Ormonde inventories, 25 Aug. 1675, Oct. and Nov. 1684, NLI, Mss 2527/1; 2554; inventories of Ormond's goods in Dublin Castle, 21 March 1678[9], after 1705, and after 1713, NLI, Mss 2524, 2554; inventory of Kilkenny Castle, Dec. 1716, PRO, FEC1/876; J. Fenlon, 'Episodes of magnificence: the material worlds of the dukes of Ormonde', in Barnard and Fenlon (eds), *Dukes of Ormonde*, pp. 137–59.

52. Paintings returned from Dublin to Kilkenny, 24 July 1707, NLI, Ms. 2521, f. 212v.

53. Inventories of Ormond's goods in Dublin Castle, 21 March 1678[9] and after 1705, NLI, Mss 2521, 2554; Barnard, 'The viceregal court', pp. 256–65; Fenlon, 'Episodes of magnificence', pp. 137–59.

54. Sir W. Petty to Lady Petty, 10 Sep. 1681, 11 April 1682, Petty Papers, 5/85, 100a; Sir W. Petty to Mrs M. W., 12 March 1681[2], Petty Papers, 5/81; Lord E. Fitzmaurice, *Sir William Petty, 1623–1687* (London, 1895), p. 263; H. W. E. Petty-Fitzmaurice, marquess of Lansdowne (ed.), *The Petty–Southwell correspondence, 1676–1687* (London, 1928), p. 317.

55. J. Fenlon, 'The Ormonde inventories: a state apartment at Kilkenny Castle', in A. Bernelle (ed.), *Decantations: a tribute for Maurice Craig* (Dublin, 1992), pp. 47–59; J. Fenlon, 'The duchess's closet', *Bulletin of the Irish Georgian Society*, xxxvi (1994), pp. 30–47; J. Fenlon, 'The duchess of Ormonde's house at Dunmore, County Kilkenny', in J. Kirwan (ed.), *Kilkenny: studies in honour of Margaret M. Phelan* (Kilkenny, 1997), pp. 79–87.

56. Sir J. Temple, account book, s.d. 1 Aug. 1677, Southampton UL, BR 7A/1; Rochester to T. Keightley, 9 Feb. 1702[3], 16 June [1703], NLI, Inchiquin Mss, nos 2603–4; account of furniture and pewter purchased from Rochester, *c.* 1705, NLI, Ms. 2524; Ormonde's pewter, etc. appraised for Pembroke, *c.* 1707, NLI, Ms. 2521, f. 207.

57. T. MacCarthy, 'The Macarthy Mór', *Ulster's Office, 1552–1800* (Little Rock, 1996).

58. Sir R. Kearney's proposals, 1685, GO, Ms. 96, pp. 131–3; W. Hawkins, 'Manner of receiving the duke of Bolton', 26 March 1719, Marsh's Library, Ms. Z3.1.1, xx; notes by W. Hawkins, GO, Ms. 17, pp. 31–44, 77–8; T. Tickell, book of warrants and memoranda on ceremonial, House of Lords Record Office, Tickell Mss, iii, pp. 23, 33.

59. Abp. N. Marsh to T. Tenison, 10 April 1697, Lambeth Palace Library, Ms. 942/133.

60. Orders of 1701, 5 July 1711 and 30 Oct. 1713, GO, Ms. 96, pp. 141–2, 153, 161; order of 19 July 1716, House of Lords Record Office, Tickell Mss, iii, p. 39.

61. W. Stephens to J. Owen, 5 Nov. 1701, UCNW, Penrhos Mss, v, 557.

62. Fr White, Annals of Limerick, NLI, Ms. 2714, pp. 134–5.

63. Oughton, Autobiography, NAM, Ms. 8808–36–1, p. 66.

64. Sydney to Portland, 7 Nov. 1690, Nottingham UL, Pw A 1330.

65. Sir J. Ware, diary, BL, Add. Ms. 4784, ff. 243, 248v; Sir C. Porter to T. Coningsby, 23 April 1695, PRONI, D638/18/65; HMC, *Buccleuch Mss*, ii, part i, p. 209.

66. T. C. Barnard, 'The uses of 23 October 1641 and Irish Protestant celebrations', *EHR*, cvi (1991), pp. 889–920, reprinted in Barnard, *Irish Protestant ascents and descents*, pp. 111–42.

67. Rochester to T. Keightley, 29 Dec. 1702, 21 Jan. 1702[3], NLI, Inchiquin Mss, no. 2601.

68. R. Gwynne to Lord Tyrone, 27 Jan. 1676[7], private collection, Co. Waterford; A. Hamilton to Lady Panmure, 30 Nov. 1709, NAS, GD 45/15/238, 18; Abp. W. King, account book, 1700–15, 28 Feb. 1707[8], Feb. 1708[9], 1 March 1710[11], TCD, Ms. 751/2, ff. 193, 217, 265; Barnard, *New anatomy*, p. 154; HMC, *Egmont Mss*, ii, p. 25.

69. King account book, s.d. 15 March 1703[4], 19, 21 April 1704, 29 Nov. 1704, 16 March 1704[5], 27 April 1706, 28 Nov. 1706, 14 March 1706[7], 23 April 1708, 1 and 15 March 1710[11], TCD, Ms. 751/2, ff. 98, 100, 114, 120v, 148v, 163v, 171, 197, 266; ibid., 1715–23, s.d. 22 Nov. 1718, TCD, Ms. 751/3, f. 85.

70. R. Edgeworth, accounts, s.d. 31 Jan. 1756, 9 Feb. 1756, NLI, Ms. 1522, pp. 106, 108; account book of Bp. F. Hutchinson, s.d. 4 March 1733[4], PRONI, DIO 1/22/2.

71. R. Edgeworth, accounts, s.d. 12 Nov. 1755, NLI, Ms. 1522, p. 63.

72. P. Galloway, *The most illustrious order: the order of St Patrick and its knights* (London, 1999), pp. 11–13; L. L. Peck, 'Beyond the Pale: John Cusacke and the language of absolutism in early Stuart Britain', *HJ*, xli (1998), p. 141.

73. A.J. Guy (ed.), *Colonel Samuel Bagshawe and the army of George II*, Army Records Society (London, 1990), pp. 39–40. Delany, *Autobiography*, 1st series, ii, pp. 385–6; *The prelude to a levee; calculated for the meridian of the castle of Dublin* (Dublin, 1757), p. [9].

74. W. Crosbie to Sir M. Crosbie, 22 March 1745[6], NLI, Talbot–Crosbie Mss, folder 53.

75. W. Henry to Hardwicke, 13 Oct. 1761, BL, Add. Ms. 35,596, f. 400.

76. Lists of dinner guests, NLI, Mss. 1466–1470; J. Plukenett to H. Maxwell, 28 Feb. 1725[6], PRONI, D 1556/16/4/17.

77. C. Tickell to T. Tickell, n.d. [1725–9], Tickell Mss, private collection, Devon.

78. *The prelude to a levee*, pp. 13–15.

79. Halifax's journal, 1761–3, NLI, Ms. 8064.

80. Lady Carteret to C. Tickell, 28 Nov. 1731, Tickell Mss, private collection, Devon.

81. Dinner lists, s.d. 21 Jan. 1768, 23 Oct. 1769, NLI, Ms. 1470.

82. H. Caldwell to S. Bagshawe, 2 May 1752, JRL, B 2/3/341; Delany, *Autobiography*, 1st series, iii, p. 110.

83. C. O'Hara, journal, NLI, Ms. 20,389, 1 and 6, 28 Feb. 1758, 11 March, [10 May 1758].

84. C. O'Hara, journal, NLI, Ms. 20,389.

85. McParland, *Public architecture*, pp. 109–12.

86. Eyre to Rigby, 14 Aug. 1758; same to Major Rutter, 13 Sep. 1759, IAA, letter books of Thomas Eyre.

87. Estimates of A. J. Nevill, 9 Feb. 1749[50], PRONI, T 3019/1479 and 1489; McParland, *Public architecture*, pp. 103–5.

88. Minutes of Linen Board, PRO, 30/26/45, item 5; NA, Calendar of Departmental Correspondence, 24 July 1753, 16 May 1758.

89. N. Delacherois to D. Delacherois, 24 July 1757, NAM, Ms. 7805–63.

90. N. Delacherois to D. Delacherois, 22 Jan. 1770, NAM, Ms. 7805–63; cf. M. Ledwidge to ?R. Smythe, 20 Oct. 1767, NLI, PC 446.

91. *CJI*, viii, part ii, pp. cccclxi–cccclxiii; T. Bartlett, 'The Townsend viceroyalty, 1767–1772', in T. Bartlett and D. W. Hayton (eds), *Penal era and golden age: essays in eighteenth-century Irish history* (Belfast, 1979), pp. 88–112; M. J. Powell, 'The reform of the undertaker system: Anglo-Irish politics, 1750–1767', *IHS*, xxxi (1998), pp. 19–36.

92. Accounts of Dorset and Devonshire, 1730–41, Dublin Public Libraries, Gilbert Ms. 199; HMC, *Stopford–Sackville Mss*, i, pp. 166, 167.

93. Hartington to Devonshire, 21 May 1755, Chatsworth, Devonshire letters, box May–July 1755, 260.134; Conway to Sir R. Wilmot, 13 May 1755; T. Waite to Sir R. Wilmot, 13–15 May 1755, PRONI, T 3019/2610, 2611; J. Walton (ed.), '*The King's Business: letters on the administration of Ireland, 1740–1761, from the papers of Sir Robert Wilmot* (New York, 1996), pp. 110–11.

94. B. Fitzgerald (ed.), *Correspondence of Emily, Duchess of Leinster (1731–1814)*, i, (Dublin, 1949), p. 16.

95. H. Boyle to Hartington, 19 July 1755, Chatsworth, Devonshire letters, May–July 1755, 205.7.

96. Fitzgerald (ed.), *Correspondence of Emily, Duchess of Leinster*, i, p. 28.

97. C. Bagshawe to S. Bagshawe, 23 Sep. 1755, JRL, B2/3/25; E. Magennis, *The Irish political system, 1740–1765* (Dublin, 2000), pp. 93–109.

98. T. Kingsbury to Mrs A. Price, 22 May 1760, NLW, Puleston Ms. 3584D; Shannon to W. Crosbie, 26 Feb. 1761, NLI, Talbot–Crosbie Mss, folder 46.

99. Lord Broghill to Lord Dorset, 18 Dec. 1666, Kent Archives Office, Sackville Mss U 269, C 18/6; Rochester to T. Keightley, 18 June 1701, NLI, Inchiquin Mss 2598; E. Spencer to F. Price, 21 Jan. 1744[5], 7 Dec. 1745, NLW, Puleston Ms. 3580E; Delany, *Autobiography*, 1st series, ii, pp. 394, 400, 408, 414, 415; *Faithful memoirs of Ormonde* (London, 1732), p. 30; W. S. Lewis (ed.), *Correspondence of Horace Walpole*, 48 vols (New Haven, 1937–83), x, p. 1.

100. Draft statutes, 17 Aug. 1661, NA, M 2458/27. Cf. Bodleian, Carte Ms. 53, ff. 20–21v.

101. P. Francis, *Irish delftware: an illustrated history* (London, 2000), pp. 37, 38–9, 71, 131; plate 49; colour plates 7, 21; information from David Mitchell.

102. T. C. Barnard, 'A tale of three sisters: Katherine Conolly of Castletown', in Barnard, *Irish Protestant ascents and descents*, pp. 266–89.

103. McParland, *Public architecture*, p. 112.

104. C. O'Hara, journal, s.d. 6 Feb. 1758, 7 March 1758, NLI, Ms. 20,389.

105. C. O'Hara, journal, NLI, Ms. 20,389, 10/13.

106. HMC, *Stopford–Sackville Mss*, i, p. 170. For the rise of ices: E. David, *Harvest of the cold months: the social history of ice and ices* (London, 1994); R. Hildyard, 'Ice cream', in P. Glanville and H. Young (eds), *Elegant eating: four hundred years of dining in style* (London, 2002), pp. 86–8.

107. Rochester to T. Keightley, 7 June 1707, NLI, Inchiquin Mss, 2607; A. Hamilton to Lady Panmure, 10 May 1710, NAS, GD 45/14/438, 25.

108. T. Molyneux to H. Sloane, 7 Aug. 1707, BL, Sloane Ms. 4041, ff. 10–10v; R. Howard to Hugh Howard, 15 July [1707], 18 Sep. 1707, NLI, PC 227; S. Molyneux to unknown, 20 Dec. 1712, Southampton City Archives, D/M, 1/3, pp. 79–80; K. T. Hoppen, *The common scientist in the seventeenth century: a study of the Dublin Philosophical Society, 1683–1708* (London, 1970), pp. 192–3, 195; Ingamells, *Travellers*, pp. 376–7.

109. Lady Carteret to C. Tickell, 29 Sep. 1728, Tickell Mss, private collection, Devon.

110. *To his grace the duke of Ormond upon his leaving the government and kingdom of Ireland* (Dublin, [?1685]).

111. T. Caulfield to K. O'Hara, 15 June 1703, NLI, Ms. 20,388; W. Perceval to A. Charlet, 24 June 1703, Bodleian, Ballard Ms. 36, f. 24; *The congratulation humbly inscrib'd to his grace, the duke of Ormond* (London, 1712).

112. See, for example, the letters of Lady Carteret and her daughters to C. Tickell, Tickell Mss, private collection, Devon.

113. L. Duerloo, 'The court of the viceroy: Brussels and the Spanish Habsburg monarchy', paper delivered at Society of Antiquaries, 3 April 1998.

114. W. S. Clark, *The early Irish stage: the beginnings to 1720* (Oxford, 1955), pp. 44–94; A. Fletcher, *Drama, performance and polity in pre-Reformation Ireland* (Cork, 2000), pp. 240–50, 261–5.

115. Minute Book, 1736–72, s.d. 21 Dec. 1741, 24 Nov. 1743, 10 Nov. 1744, 14 Dec. 1745, 6 Dec. 1755, Mercer's Hospital, Dublin; D. Hunter, 'Audience for Handel', *Irish Musical Studies*, viii, forthcoming.

116. M. Craig, *Dublin, 1660–1860* (Dublin and London, 1952), pp. 13–17.

117. R. Loeber, 'Settlers' utilisation of the natural resources', in K. Hannigan and W. Nolan (eds), *Wicklow: history and society* (Dublin, 1994), pp. 267–73; T. C. Barnard, 'Land and the limits of loyalty: the second earl of Cork and first earl of Burlington (1612–98)', in T. Barnard and J. Clark (eds), *Lord Burlington: architecture, art and life* (London and Rio Grande, 1995), p. 191; above, pp. 235–6, 243–4.

118. Earl of Arran to W. Legge, 31 May 1665, Staffordshire CRO, Dartmouth Mss, D (W) 1778/1/1, 153; HMC, *Dartmouth Mss*, i, p. 11.

119. HMC, *Ormonde Mss*, iii, p. 357; M. Craig, 'New light on Jigginstown', *Ulster Journal of Archaeology*, xxxiii (1970), pp. 107–10; A. Vicars, 'Jigginstown Castle', *Journal of the County Kildare Archaeological Society*, i (1891–5), p. 19.

120. See above, pp. 233–4, 245–50.

121. T. C. Barnard, 'Scotland and Ireland in the later Stewart monarchy', in S. G. Ellis and S. Barber (eds), *Conquest and Union: fashioning a British state, 1485–1725* (Harlow, 1995), p. 256.

122. Accounts, Bodleian, Carte Ms. 53, f. 134.

123. Sir W. Petty to Lady Petty, 20 Nov. 1677, McGill UL, Osler Ms. 7612.

124. W. Robinson in RIA, Ms. 24 G 4/42; arrangements for Clarendon, 1685, Bodleian, Clarendon Ms. 88, ff. 171–80; Lord Sydney to T. Coningsby, PRONI, D 638/14/40; inventory of Dublin Castle, May 1693, NA, Wyche Mss, 2nd series, no. 142; inventory of Dublin Castle, 21 Dec. 1704, NLW, Puleston deeds, no. 6; establishment of Shrewsbury, 1713, RIA, Ms. 24 H. 22.

125. Essex to A. Capel, 16 June 1674, Bodleian, Add. Ms. C. 34, ff. 139v–140.

126. Account of Lord Hartington, 16 Sep.–14 Oct. 1755, Chatsworth, Devonshire Letters, 1755, box 260.418.

127. W. Smythe to R. Smythe, 2 Nov 1751, NLI, PC 445.

128. O. Gallagher to O. St George, 24 Feb. 1727[8], PRO, C 110/46/470.

129. R. Edgeworth, accounts, s.d. 22 Oct. 1733, NLI, Ms. 1510, p. 82.

130. *The prelude to a levee*, p. 14.

131. J. Le Hunte to C. Tickell, 2 Nov. 1758, Tickell Mss, private collection, Devon; Barnard, 'Katherine Conolly', pp. 266–89.

132. A. Stopford to C. Eustace, 6 July [?1723]; J. Le Hunte to C. Tickell, 9 Dec. 1758, Tickell Mss, private collection, Devon.

133. T. Mooney and F. White, 'The gentry's winter season', in D. Dickson (ed.), *The gorgeous mask: Dublin 1700–1850* (Dublin, 1987), pp. 1–16.

134. However, for evidence of basset being played at Dorset's court: Delany, *Autobiography*, 1st series, i, p. 290; *The Dublin Evening Post*, no. 147 (30 Oct.–3 Nov. 1733). It had certainly been played during the viceroyalty of the second duke of Ormonde. Inventory of Dublin Castle, *c.* 1705, NLI, Ms. 2524. Edgeworth bought basset cards in 1767: Edgeworth, accounts, s.d. 22 April 1767, NLI, Ms. 1533, p. 156. Barden's bill, 1752, NLI, Ms. 25,431.

135. J. Evelyn, jr. to J. Evelyn, 5 May 1694, Evelyn Letters, f. 667v, now BL, Add. Ms.

136. A. Hamilton to Lady Panmure, 22 Jan. [*c.* 1703], NAS, GD 45/14/238, 55.

137. 'A catalogue of books to be sold at the Castle of Dublin . . .', Smythe of Barbavilla Mss, private collection, Berkshire.

## 2 House

1. T. Hewlett to E. Malone, 15 Jan. 1714[15], Brabazon Mss, private collection, London, box III.

2. W. Perceval to K. O'Hara, 25 May 1718, NLI, Ms. 20,385; 'An essay on Sir Robert Maude's fine seat at Dundrum', BL, Egerton Ms. 846A, f. 163.

3. W. Perceval to K. O'Hara, 21 Nov. 1717, NLI, Ms. 20,385.

4. Sir E. Crofton to K. O'Hara, 6 Jan. 1718[19], NLI, Ms. 20,385.

5. G. Mathew to K. O'Hara, 25 Feb. 1718[19], NLI, Ms. 20,385; directions for payments by E. O'Hara, 1719–30, NLI, Ms. 36,373/1.

6. E. Richardson to T. Seele, 1 Feb. 1664[5], TCD, MUN P/1/469, 19.

7. 'Further observations on the state of Ireland', [1730s], BL, Add. Ms. 21,133, f. 70v; S. Madden, *Reflections and resolutions proper for the gentlemen of Ireland* (Dublin, 1738), pp. 10–11.

8. A. P. I. Samuels (ed.), *The early life, correspondence and writings of the Rt. Hon. Edmund Burke, LL.D.* (Cambridge, 1923), p. 315.

9. Bp. J. Evans to Abp. W. Wake, 7 May [1720], Christ Church, Wake Ms. 13/174.

10. A. Langford to E. Owen, 6 May [1738], UCNW, Penrhos Mss, i, 1087.

11. R. Cox, *An essay for the conversion of the Irish* (Dublin, 1698), pp. 10–13; J. Johnston, *Bishop Berkeley's Querist in historical perspective* (Dundalk, 1970), pp. 134–5; Madden, *Reflections and resolutions*, p. 11.

12. *Particulars relating to the life and character of the late Brockhill Newburgh, esq.* (n.p., 1761), pp. 12–13, 19.

13. M. Craig, *The architecture of Ireland from earliest times to 1880*, pbk edn (London, 1989), p. 186; B. de Breffni and R. ffolliott, *The houses of Ireland* (London, 1975), p. 100.

14. *Particulars relating to the life and character of the late Brockhill Newburgh, esq.*, p. 14.

15. Williams (ed.), *Correspondence of Swift*, iv, p. 519.

16. *Particulars relating to the life and character of the late Brockhill Newburgh, esq.*, pp. 13–14, 16–17, 20–1.

17. 'An essay on Sir Robert Maude's fine seat at Dundrum', BL, Egerton Ms. 846A, f. 163.

18. W. Henry, 'Hints towards a natural, typographical [sic] history of the Counties Sligo, Donegal, Fermanagh and Lough Erne', NA, M.2533, pp. 374, 464–5.

19. J. Summerson, 'The classical country house in eighteenth-century England', *Journal of the Royal Society of Arts*, cvii (1959), reprinted in J. Summerson, *The unromantic castle* (London, 1990), pp. 79–120.

20. Barnard, 'Cork settlers', pp. 322–33; R. Loeber, 'Irish country houses and castles of the late Caroline period: an unremembered past recaptured', *Quarterly Bulletin of the Irish Georgian Society*, xvi (1973), pp. 1–69.

21. M. Craig, *Classic Irish houses of the middle size* (London, 1976), p. 60; *Archaeological inventory of County Cork. I. West Cork* (Dublin, 1992), pp. 322–3.

22. Sir R. Southwell to Sir J. Perceval, 8 Feb. 1685[6], BL, Add. Ms. 46,962, f. 202v.

23. C. O'Brien to T. Burgh, before 18 Feb. 1717[18], NLI, Inchiquin Mss, 1830.

24. T. Burgh to C. O'Brien, 18 Feb. 1717[18], NLI, Inchiquin Mss, 1830.

25. J. Smythe to W. Smythe, 14 Dec. 1731, NLI, PC 449; Barnard, 'French of Monivea', pp. 271–96.

26. B. Crawley to ?W. Flower, 12 Dec. 1715, NLI, Ms. 11,481/1.

27. J. H. Gebbie, *An introduction to the Abercorn letters . . . 1736–1816* (Omagh, 1972), p. 260.

28. Delany, *Autobiography*, 1st series, ii, p. 513.

29. G. Hill, *An historical account of the plantation in Ulster at the commencement of the seventeenth century, 1601–1620* (Belfast, 1877); J. Barry, *Hillsborough: a parish in the Ulster plantation* (Belfast, 1965), pp. 45–50.

30. F. Lascelles to M. Ward, 6 May 1737, PRONI, D 2092/1/4, 138.

31. G. Worsley, 'The origins of the Gothic revival: a reappraisal', *TRHS*, 6th series, iii (1993), pp. 175–95; G. Worsley, *Classical architecture in Britain: the heroic age* (New Haven and London, 1995), pp. 105–50; H. M. Colvin, *Essays in English architectural history* (New Haven and London, 1999), pp. 217–44; E. McKellar, *The birth of modern London: the development and design of the city, 1660–1720* (Manchester, 1999), pp. 155–84.

32. See, for example: R. North, *Of building*, ed. H. M. Colvin and J. Newman (Oxford, 1981), pp. 3–6, 62, 93–4; Barnard, 'Cork settlers', pp. 322–33.

33. 'A descriptive account of the county of Kildare in 1682, by Thomas Monk', *Journal of the County Kildare Archaeological Society*, vi (1910), pp. 342–3; cf. the market house described in A. Locke to Lady Ardglass, 15 Sep. 1688 and undated, PRONI, D 970/1, pp. 18, 19.

34. C. E. B. Brett, *Court houses and market houses of the province of Ulster* (Belfast, 1973); C. Casey, 'Court houses, market houses and town halls of Leinster', unpublished M.A. thesis, University College, Dublin (1982).

35. Francis Boyle, Viscount Shannon, *Moral essays and discourses upon several subjects* (London, 1690), p. 61; G. S. Cotter, *Poems, consisting of odes, songs, pastorals, satyrs, etc*, 2 vols (Cork, 1788), i, pp. 133–87.

36. Memorial of 29 Oct. 1708, RD 2/124/326.

37. E. Malone to M. Brabazon, 9 June 1715, Barber Mss, private collection, London, box III.

38. E. Malone to M. Brabazon, 20 June 1724, Barber Mss, private collection, London, box III.

39. A Thomas Howlett subscribed to the third volume of *Vitruvius Britannicus* in 1725.

40. Memorials of 16 Sep. 1720, RD 32/46/18909; 10 Feb. 1720[1], RD 29/343/17910; 1 April 1725, RD 68/60/46992; Thrift list of Dublin freemen, s.d. 1720, Dublin City Archives. In 1731, a Thomas Hulet lived in Queen Street, Dublin: vestry book of St Paul's, Dublin, 1698–1750, RCB, P. 273/6.1, p. 84. There was also a Thomas Hewlett, 'gentleman', in St Michan's parish, where in 1729 and 1730 he served as churchwarden. Vestry Book, St Michan's, Dublin, 1724–60, RCB, P. 276/4.1, pp. 52, 63, 64, 73.

41. T. Hewlett to E. Malone, 15 Jan. 1714[15], Brabazon Mss, private collection, London, box III.

42. G. Boyd to C. Colclough, 8 March 1714[15], NLI, Ms. 29,766.

43. R. Smythe to W. Smythe, 1 Aug. 1730, Smythe of Barbavilla Mss, private collection, Berkshire; J. Smythe to W. Smythe, 20 Feb. 1733[4], NLI, PC 449; B. Span to W. Smythe, 3 June 1744, NLI, PC 449.

44. R. Edgeworth, accounts, s.d. 21 June 1736, 25 Jan. 1738[9], NLI, Mss 1511, p. 115; 1512, p. 154; Sir R. Levinge to W. Smythe, 7 Sep. 1733, NLI, PC 449.

45. C. Casey, 'Books and builders: a bibliographical approach to Irish eighteenth-century architecture', unpublished Ph.D. thesis, TCD, 2 vols (1991).

46. T. Lloyd to W. Harris, 3 Jan. 1746[7]; Bp. H. Maule to W. Harris, 1 Aug. 1748, Armagh Public Library, Papers of the Physico-Historical Society.

47. C. Casey, '*Miscelanea Structura Curiosa*: an early Georgian compendium of garden buildings', in *GPA Irish Arts Review Yearbook, 1990–1991*, pp. 85–91.

48. Edward Scott, *The new book of constitutions* (Dublin, 1751), pp. 7, 53–4, 69.

49. Scott, *New book of constitutions*, pp. 66–7, 69, 70.

50. Scott, *New book of constitutions*, pp. 119–20; L. Whyte, *Poems on various subjects* (Dublin, 1740), p. 189. In *CARD*, xi, p. 498, Wren is hailed as a mason.

51. Scott, *New book of constitutions*, subscription list; Casey, 'Books and builders', pp. 37, 50, 73–4.

52. T. C. Barnard, 'The cultures of eighteenth-century Irish towns', in P. Borsay and L. Proudfoot (eds), *Provincial towns in early modern England and Ireland; change, convergence and divergence*, Proceedings of the British Academy, cviii (2002), p. 222; P. Fagan, *Catholics in a Protestant country: the papist constituency in eighteenth-century Dublin* (Dublin, 1998), pp. 126–58; P. Mirala, 'The eighteenth-century masonic lodge as a social unit', *Ulster Folklife*, xliv (1998), pp. 60–8; above, pp. 361–5.

53. J. Hall to dowager countess of Orrery, 13 Feb. 1685[6], Petworth, Orrery Mss, general series, 30.

54. Loeber, *Architects*, pp. 66, 67.

55. Will of J. Hall, 5 March 1687[8], PRO, PROB 11/405, 100; Barnard, 'Cork settlers', pp. 341–2; Barnard, *New anatomy*, p. 209; M. Quane, 'Dr. Jeremy Hall Endowed Schools, Limerick', *North Munster Antiquarian Journal*, xi (1968), pp. 47–50; E. Wilson, 'Dr. Jeremiah Hall and his charities', *Transactions of the Halifax Antiquarian Society* (1956), pp. 1–10.

56. E. Chaney, *The evolution of the Grand Tour* (London, 1998); B. Redford, *Venice and the Grand Tour* (New Haven and London, 1996), pp. 28–31.

57. Notebook of S. Waring, PRONI, D 695/228.

58. M. Misson, *A new voyage to Italy*, 2 vols (London, 1695).

59. R. Lassels, *The voyage of Italy* (London, 1670), quoted in Redford, *Venice and the Grand Tour*, p. 12.

60. S. Waring to M. Misson, [*c.* 1699], private collection, Co. Down.

61. Barnard, 'What became of Waring?', pp. 189–99; PRONI, D 695/M/1; R. Gillespie, *Settlement and survival on an Ulster estate: the Brownlow leasebook, 1667–1711* (Belfast, 1988), p. xlix; D. W. Hayton (ed.), *Ireland after the Glorious Revolution* (Belfast, 1976), p. 229.

62. E. C. Nelson, '*A short treatise of firr-trees . . .* (Dublin, 1705) by Samuel Waring', *Archives of Natural History*, xix (1992), pp. 305–6.

63. S. Waring, notebook, PRONI, D 695/229, p. 25.

64. Paper of C. Bowen [1720s], NLI, Ms. 36,373/1; hearth tax receipts for Annagh, 2 July 1724, 10 Jan. 1746[7], NLI, Ms. 36,390/1.

65. Casey, 'Books and builders', pp. 113–14.

66. R. Woodley to P. Brett, 7 July 1718; R. Woodley to K. O'Hara, 29 Oct. 1718; W. Bowen to K. O'Hara, 29 Oct. 1718, 21 Feb. 1718[19], NLI, Ms. 20,385.

67. W. Waring to S. Waring, 8 March 1698[9], PRONI, D 695/67.

68. A. Hill to S. Waring, 1 Jan. 1707[8], 2 Oct. 1713, and undated [?Oct. 1713], private collection, Co. Down.

69. S. Waring to unknown, undated, after 1 Nov. 1728, and ? Oct. 1728, private collection, Co. Down.

70. C. Platt, *The great rebuildings of Tudor and Stuart England* (London, 1994); N. Cooper, *Houses of the gentry, 1480–1680* (New Haven and London, 1999).

71. Barnard, 'What became of Waring?', pp. 197–9, 203–12.

72. Surveyed in Craig, *The architecture of Ireland*, pp. 111–50, 177–99; Loeber, 'Irish country houses and castles of the late Caroline period: an unremembered past recaptured', pp. 1–70.

73. Barnard, 'Cork settlers', pp. 309–10; R. Cox, 'Regnum Corcagiense; or a description of the kingdom of Cork', ed. R. Day, *JCHAS*, 2nd series, viii (1902), pp. 89–97; D. Dickson, 'A description of Co. Cork, *c.* 1741', *JCHAS*, 2nd series, lxxvi (1971), pp. 152–5; S. P. Johnson (ed.), 'On a manuscript description of the city and county of Cork, *cir.* 1685, written by Sir Richard Cox', *JRSAI*, xxxii (1902), p. 363; C. Smith, *The antient and present state of the county and city of Cork*, 2 vols, 2nd edn (Dublin, 1774).

74. D. M. Beaumont, 'The gentry of the King's and Queen's Counties: Protestant landed society, 1690–1760', unpublished Ph.D. thesis, TCD, 2 vols (1999), i, p. 32.

75. R. Richey, 'Landed society in mid-eighteenth-century County Down', unpublished Ph.D. thesis, Queen's University Belfast (2000), pp. 4, 8.

76. C. O'Brien to J. Bonnell, 30 June [1709], NLI, PC 435.

77. Earl of Tyrone to W. Bucknor, 9 Feb. [1700], private collection, Co. Waterford; C. Smith, *The antient and present state of the county and city of Waterford* (Dublin, 1746), p. 105; M. Girouard, 'Curraghmore, Co. Waterford', *Country Life*, cxxxiii, 3440–2 (Feb. 1963), pp. 256–60, 308–11, 368–71; S. O'Reilly, *Irish houses and gardens* (London, 1998), pp. 140–9.

78. Elevation and plan of house and garden, Cloughmagherrycall, Co. Down, *c.* 1716, Oxon CRO, Annesley Mss, E/6/7/10D/48 and 49.

79. G. Taylor and A. Skinner, *Maps of the roads of Ireland, surveyed 1777* (London and Dublin, 1778); J. H. Andrews, 'Charles Vallancey and the map of Ireland', *Geographical Journal*, 132 (1966), pp. 50–9.

80. Cooper, *Houses of the gentry*, pp. 5–6.

81. Barnard, *New anatomy*, pp. 35–7.

82. F. McNamara to T. Carte, 30 July 1730, Bodleian, Carte Ms. 227, f. 83v.

83. Arran to W. Legge, 21 May 1665, Staffordshire CRO, D (W) 1778/I/i, 150; A. Owens to Lord Perceval, 2 Feb. 1740[1], BL, Add. Ms. 47,007, f. 7.

84. A. Clifton-Taylor, *The pattern of English building*, new edn (London, 1972); B. Harrison and B. Hutton, *Vernacular houses in north Yorkshire and Cleveland* (Edinburgh, 1984); R. Machin, *The houses of Yetminster* (Bristol, 1978); E. Mercer, *English vernacular houses: a study of traditional farmhouses and cottages* (London, 1975); P. Smith, *Houses of the Welsh countryside* (London, 1975); D. Portman, 'Vernacular building in the Oxford region', in C. W. Chalkin and M. A. Havinden (eds), *Rural change and urban growth* (London, 1974); Royal Commission on Historical Monuments, *Rural houses of West Yorkshire, 1400–1830* (London, 1986); idem, *Rural houses of the Lancashire Pennines, 1560–1760* (London, 1985); J. T. Smith, 'Lancashire and Cheshire houses: some problems of architectural and social history', *Archaeological Journal*, cxxvii (1970), pp. 156–81; J. T. Smith, *English houses, 1200–1800: the Hertfordshire evidence* (London, 1992); R. B. Wood-Jones, *Traditional domestic architecture of the Banbury region* (Manchester, 1963).

85. A. Gailey, *Rural houses in the north of Ireland* (Edinburgh, 1984). Also K. Danaher, *Ireland's traditional houses* (Dublin, 1993); P. Robinson, 'Vernacular housing in Ulster in the seventeenth century', *Ulster Folklife*, xxv (1979), pp. 1–28; P. Robinson, 'Urban vernacular housing in Newtonwards, County Down', *Folklife*, xvii (1979), pp. 20–38.

86. C. Smith, account of Tipperary, RIA, Ms. 24 G 9, pp. 284–5; Richard Barton, *A dialogue, concerning some things of importance to Ireland, particularly to the County of Ardmagh* (Dublin, 1751), sig. [A3], pp. 11, 15, 21–3.

87. J. A. Oughton, autobiography, NAM, Ms. 8808–36–1, p. 61.

88. 'Description and valuation of the late Lord Carleton's estate in East and West Carbery' [Co. Cork, 1728], NLI, PC 383.

89. J. Horn, *Adapting to a new world: English society in the seventeenth-century Chesapeake* (Chapel Hill and London, 1994), pp. 330, 427.

90. K. A. Lockridge, *The diary, and life, of William Byrd II of Virginia, 1674–1744* (Chapel Hill and London, 1987), pp. 53, 71, 123–4, 133–43. Cf. R. L. Bushman, *The refinement of America: persons, houses, cities* (New York, 1992), pp. 103–38.

91. D. B. Rutman and A. H. Rutman, *A place in time: Middlesex County, Virginia 1650–1750* (New York and London, 1984), pp. 211–22; L. B. Wright, *The first gentlemen of Virginia* (San Marino, 1940); D. Blake Smith, *Inside the great house: planter family life in eighteenth-century Chesapeake society* (Ithaca and London, 1980).

92. Bushman, *The refinement of America*, pp. 139–80; R. Hoffman, *Princes of Ireland, Planters of Maryland: a Carroll saga, 1500–1782* (Chapel Hill, 2000); Rhys Isaac, *The transformation of Virginia, 1740–1790*, new edn (Chapel Hill, 1999), pp. 34–40; Rutman and Rutman, *A place in time*, pp. 204–10, 216, 232–3.

93. R. Black, Travel journal, 1727–8, PRONI, T 1073/3.

94. Delany, *Autobiography*, 1st series, i, pp. 291–2.

95. D. Reading to H. Temple, 22 Oct. 1715, Southampton UL, BR 141/3/6; NLI, reports on private collections, no. 95; Barnard, *New anatomy*, pp. 150, 230–1.

96. Hume's report, NLI, Ms. 6054, p. 7.

97. Survey of Lord Malton's Irish lands, 1728, Sheffield City Libraries, WWM A 769, pp. 8, 11–12.

98. Hume's report, NLI, Ms. 6054, pp. 8, 16.

99. R. Purcell to Orrery, 24 Oct. 1754, Harvard UL, Ms. Eng. 218.19. The importance of coaches as a social and economic denominator is brought out in S. E. Whyman, *Sociability and power in later-Stuart England: the cultural worlds of the Verneys, 1660–1720* (Oxford, 1999), pp. 101–6.

100. T. C. Barnard, 'Land and the limits of loyalty: the second earl of Cork and first earl of Burlington (1612–98)', in T. Barnard and J. Clark (eds), *Lord Burlington: architecture, art and life* (London, 1995), pp. 167–99.

101. T. Barnard, 'Introduction', and J. Fenlon, 'Episodes of magnificence: the material worlds of the dukes of Ormonde', in Barnard and Fenlon (eds), *Dukes of Ormonde*, pp. 30–43, 137–60.

102. Barnard, 'Cork settlers', pp. 323–4.

103. Notebook of Sir J. Perceval, BL, Add. Ms. 47,113, f. 59.

104. Orrery to Sir R. Southwell, 16 July 1678, V & A, Orrery Mss 2, f. 19; P. M. Kerrigan, *Castles and fortifications in Ireland, 1485–1945* (Cork, 1995), pp. 99–100, 108–14; Loeber, *Architects*, pp. 25–9.

105. PRONI, D 2707/A1/11/23, [1731].

106. W. Boyle to H. Boyle, 27 Nov. 1718, PRONI, D 2707/A1/1, 3; A. Crotty to H. Boyle, 30 May 1727, PRONI, D 2707/A1/1, 8; J. Bourke to H. Boyle, 30 June 1729, PRONI, D 2707/A1/1, 18; A. Bucke to H. Boyle, PRONI, D 2707/A1/1, 46; D. Power *et al.*, *Archaeological inventory of County Cork. II. East and South Cork* (Dublin, 1994), p. 318; C. Smith, *Cork*, i, pp. 125–9.

107. M. Coghill to E. Southwell, 5 April 1733, BL, Add. Ms. 21,123, f.33.

108. Sir R. Southwell to G. Souden, 7 April 1696, NLI, Ms. 24,833.

109. Sylvia Collier, *Whitehaven, 1660–1800* (London, 1991).

110. G. Beard, *The work of Grinling Gibbons* (London, 1989), p. 55, plate 75; R. Loeber, 'Arnold Quellin's and Grinling Gibbons' monuments for Irish patrons', *Studies*, lxxii (1983), pp. 84–98.

111. Bp. J. Hartstonge to Abp. W. King, 30 May 1715, TCD, Mss 1995–2008/1653.

112. Inventory of King's Weston, 1690s, Yale University, Mellon Collection; K. Downes, 'The King's Weston book of drawings', *Architectural History*, 10 (1967), p. 27.

113. E. Southwell to M. Ward, 21 July 1734, PRONI, D 2092/1/4,97; McParland, *Public architecture*, pp. 165, 168, 169–71, plates 79–82, 204.

114. E. Southwell, tour journals, Beinecke Library, Yale University.

115. Barnard, 'Cork settlers', pp. 322, 329–31; Loeber, 'Irish country houses and castles of the late Caroline period', frontispiece and plate 8; R. Loeber, 'Early Irish architectural sketches in the Perceval/Egmont collection', in A. Bernelle (ed.), *Decantations: a tribute to Maurice Craig* (Dublin, 1992), pp. 110–20.

116. A. Hawksworth, bill, 1682, BL, Add. Ms. 47,052, f. 24.

117. J. Anderson, *A genealogical history of the house of Yvery*, 2 vols (London, 1742), ii, pp. 388, 393–4.

118. S. Molyneux to unknown, 20 Dec. 1712, 28 Feb. 1712[13], Southampton City Archives, D/M, 1/3, pp. 34, 39.

119. S. Molyneux to unknown, 28 Feb. 1712[13], Southhampton City Archives, D/M, 1/3, pp.105–6, 109–10.

120. S. Molyneux to unknown, 28 Feb. 1712 [13], Southhampton City Archives, D/M, 1/3, pp. 135–9.

121. S. Molyneux to unknown, 20 April 1713, Southhampton City Archives, D/M, 1/3, p. 159.

122. A. Nickson, account book, 1713–20, Sheffield City Archives, WWM A 759, p. 421; C. O'Brien to T. Burgh, before 18 Feb. 1717[18], NLI, Inchiquin Mss 1830.

123. Contract, 16 Sep. 1672, NLI, de Vesci Mss, J/19; HMC, *Ormonde Mss*, v, p. 292; vii, p. 110.

124. J. Smythe to W. Smythe, n.d. [*c.* 1750], NLI, PC 449; Loeber, *Architects*, pp. 31–9; E. McParland, 'The office of the surveyor-general in Ireland in the eighteenth century', *Architectural History*, xxxviii (1995), pp. 91–101; McParland, *Public architecture*, pp. 13–14, 83–4, 138, 140–1, 145–7.

125. M. Quane, 'Viscount Weymouth Grammar School, Carrickmacross', *JRSAI*, lxxxvi (1956), p. 39.

126. Stonework, etc. at Conyngham Hall, measured by J. Curle, 14 Feb. 1712[13], IAA, Castletown deposit, box 55; C. Casey and A. Rowan, *The Buildings of Ireland. North Leinster* (London, 1993), p. 156; A. Rowan, *North-West Ulster* (Harmondsworth, 1979), p. 176; Loeber, *Architects*, p. 44.

127. H. M. Colvin, *A biographical dictionary of British Architects, 1600–1840*, 3rd edn (New Haven and London, 1995), pp. 69–71; Colvin, *Essays in English architectural history*, pp. 217–44; H. M. Colvin, 'The Townsends of Oxford: a firm of Georgian master-masons and its accounts', *Georgian Group Journal*, x (2000), pp. 43–60; W. G. Hiscock, *A Christ Church miscellany* (Oxford, 1946), pp. 17–37.

128. Loeber, *Architects*, p. [117]; McParland, 'The office of surveyor-general', pp. 91–101.

129. H. M. Colvin, J. M. Crook, K. Downes and J. Newman, *History of the King's Works. V. 1660–1772* (London, 1976), pp. 3–116; Colvin, *Biographical dictionary*, pp. 69–71.

130. R. Woodley, receipt, 30 March 1720, NLI, Ms. 36,373/1

131. Joseph Gill, journal, 1674–1741, Friends' Historical Library, Dublin; J. Loveday, *Diary of a tour in 1732 through parts of England, Wales, Ireland and Scotland* (Edinburgh, 1890), p. 47.

132. de Breffni and ffolliott, *The houses of Ireland*, pp. 92–4; Beaumont, 'Gentry of King's and Queen's Counties', i, pp. 231–2; R. Loeber, 'Castle Durrow', *Quarterly Bulletin of the Irish Georgian Society*, xvi (1973), pp. 103–6; Loeber, *Architects*, p. 43.

133. W. Flower, agreement with B. Crawley, 6 Jan. 1714[15]; B. Crawley, proposals, ?Sep. 1715, NLI, Ms. 11,455/1 and 3.

134. W. Flower, agreement with J. Rudd, 10 Nov. 1716; W. Flower, contract with D. Phelan and W. Daley, 28 March 1715; B. Crawley to W. Flower, 18 Nov. 1717; bills of J. Coltsman, J. Owen, J. Rudd, B. Demave, T. Woods, P. Holohan, NLI, Ms. 11,455.

135. W. Perceval to K. O'Hara, 25 May 1718, NLI, Ms. 20,385.

136. J. Gill, journal, Friends' Historical Library, Dublin.

137. M. Wills, notebook, IAA, 81/88; C. Casey, 'Books and builders', i, pp. 148–63; C. Casey, '"De architectura": an Irish eighteenth-century gloss', *Architectural History*, xxxvii (1994), pp. 80–96.

138. J. Crofton to W. Smythe, 27 Dec. 1732, NLI, PC 436.

139. G. Wills to J. Crofton, 7 Sep. 1742, NLI, PC 436.

140. *Faulkner's Dublin Journal*, 28 June 1746; H. T. Crofton, *Crofton memoirs* (York, 1911), p. 114.

141. Elphin census, 1749, NA, Ms. 2466, f. 115.

142. J. Hicky to Lord Perceval, 18 Aug. 1740, 1 Jan. 1740[1], 22 Sep. 1741, 24 June 1746, BL, Add. Ms. 47,007, ff. 1, 5v, 15, 75.

143. Sir W. Petty to ?Sir G. Carteret, 26 Oct. 1666, McGill UL, Osler Ms. 7612; V. Gookin, *The great case of transplantation in Ireland discussed* (London, 1655), p. 17.

144. Bp. R. Howard to H. Howard, 3 June 1731, 16 May 1732, NLI, PC 227; W. Smythe to R. Smythe, 27 March 1731, Smythe of Barbavilla Mss, private collection, Berkshire.

145. Gebbie (ed.), *Abercorn letters*, p. 48.

146. Gebbie (ed.), *Abercorn letters*, pp. 42–3.

147. Bp. J. Stearne to Abp. W. King, 22 Jan. 1714[15], TCD, Mss 1995–2008/1574.

148. S. Pike to Lord Grandison, 15 March 1744[5], Villiers–Stuart Mss, Dromana, T 3131/C/7/27.

149. J. Coltsman, bills and receipts, 1715–17, Castle Durrow accounts, NLI, Mss 11,455; 11,469; account book for Castle Bernard, 1719–28, pp. 44, 71, 142, 168, Cork Archives Institute, Doherty Mss, U/137; R. Edgeworth, accounts, s.d. 12 June 1723, NLI, Ms. 1508, p. 69.

150. R. Edgeworth accounts, s.d. 1 June 1739, 18 Dec. 1740, NLI, Mss 1513, p. 23; 1514, p. 83; contract of J. Mulvihill and R. Wall with G. Brabazon, 29 May 1767, Barber Mss, private collection, London, box I.

151. H. Kelly to Lord Perceval, 24 Feb. 1740[1], 6 Nov. 1744, BL, Add. Ms. 47,007, ff. 9, 69.

152. N. Peacock, journal, s.d. 22 July–10 Nov. 1743, 28 and 29 May 1744, 9 Dec. 1744, 17 June 1745, 10 May 1746, 24 Dec. 1748, 7 March 1750[1], NLI, Ms. 16,091.

153. List of Irish MPs, 1713, BL, Add. Ms. 61,637A.

154. Daybook, Irish accounts, 1707–13, Sheffield City Archives, Strafford Mss, WWM A 758, pp. 150, 212.

155. Johnston-Liik, *HIP*, iii, pp. 305–7.

156. W. Wogan to E. Southwell, 17 Jan. 1716[17], 23 Feb. 1716[17], 21 Nov. 1717, BL, Add. Ms. 37,674, ff. 64, 78, 120; K. Severens, 'A new perspective on Georgian building practice: the rebuilding of St. Werburgh's Church, Dublin (1754–59)', *Bulletin of the Irish Georgian Society*, xxxv (1992–3), p. 3.

157. T. Burgh to W. Smythe, 30 Aug. 1720, NLI, PC 446.

158. T. Burgh, jr. to W. Smythe, 14 Aug. 1733, 18 April 1735, 20 Dec. 1740, NLI, PC 446.

159. T. Burgh to W. Smythe, 3 May 1726, NLI, PC 446.

160. [E. S. Pery, Viscount Limerick], *Letter from an Armenian in Ireland, to his friends at Trebisond* (London, 1757), p. 113.

161. Delany, *Autobiography*, 1st series, ii, p. 490.

162. Lady A. Conolly to Lord Strafford, 8 Nov. 1733, BL, Add. Ms. 22,228, ff. 90–90v.

163. Lady A. Conolly to Lord Strafford, 24 May [1734], BL, Add. Ms. 22,228, ff. 120v–121.

164. 'Autobiography of Pole Cosby, of Stradbally, Queen's County, 1703–1737(?)', *Journal of the County Kildare Archaeological Society*, v (1906), p. 91; *Memoirs of Richard Lovell Edgeworth, Esq.*, 2 vols (London, 1820), i, p. 331.

165. McParland, *Public architecture*, pp. 179–203.

166. G. Mathew to K. O'Hara, 25 Feb. 1718[19], NLI, Ms. 20,385.

167. W. Perceval to K. O'Hara, 21 Nov. 1717, NLI, Ms. 20,385.

168. W. Perceval to K. O'Hara, 3 April 1718, NLI, Ms. 20,385; T. Hewlett to E. Malone, 15 Jan. 1714[15], Barber Mss, private collection, London, box III.

169. George Berkeley commented, 'several [designs] have been made by several hands', G. Berkeley to Lord Perceval, 7 Sep. 1722, BL, Add. Ms. 47,029, f. 132v.

170. T. Barnard, *The abduction of a Limerick heiress: social and political relations in mid-eighteenth-century Ireland* (Dublin, 1998), pp. 15–17.

171. B. Smythe to W. Smythe, 20 Oct. 1730, Smythe of Barbavilla Mss, private collection, Berkshire; B. Smythe to W. Smythe, 20 and 24 Aug. 1730, 3 Sep. 1730, 24 and 27 Oct. 1730, 22 April [?1731], 'Sat. a.m.' [?1730], NLI, PC 448.

172. Abp. J. Vesey, journal, pp. 15, 42, NLI, de Vesci Mss, G /5.

173. Bp. T. Vesey, library list, NLI, de Vesci Mss, DH, T/2A; bill of S. Pepyat, 12 July 1707, NLI, de Vesci Mss, J/3.

174. W. Perceval to Sir T. Vesey, 14 May 1701, NLI, de Vesci Mss, J/3A; D. W. Hayton, 'The High Church party in the Irish Convocation, 1703–1713', in H. J. Real and H. Stover-Leidig (eds), *Reading Swift: papers from the 3rd Münster symposium on Jonathan Swift* (Munich, 1998), pp. 117–40.

175. Anderson, *House of Yvery*, ii, pp. 324–5.

176. W. Perceval to A. Charlet, 5 Feb. 1712[13], 20 Nov. 1718, Bodleian, Ballard Ms. 38, ff. 80, 107; W. Palliser to H. Dodwell, 19 Oct. 1697, 19 Jan. 1701[2]; W. Perceval to H. Dodwell, Ms. Eng. Lett. C. 28, ff. 34, 57, 64; W. Perceval to H. Dodwell, 2 Sep. 1704, 26 Feb. 1704[5], St Edmund Hall, Oxford, Ms. 9, pp. 95–110, 137–44; W. Palliser to W. Perceval, 22 Aug. 1702, PRONI, D 906/62.

177. H. M. Colvin, *Unbuilt Oxford* (New Haven and London, 1983), pp. 23–77.

178. W. Perceval to H. Dodwell, 10 July 1703, Bodleian, Ms. Eng. Lett. C. 28, f. 64; D. Pulteney to W. Perceval, 15 July 1712, new style, PRONI, D 906/61; W. Perceval to A. Charlet, 14 May 1713, Bodleian, Ballard Ms. 36, f. 82.

179. W. Perceval to Bp. T. Vesey, 8 Jan. 1714[15], 13 Sep. 1715, NLI, de Vesci Mss, J/3A; W. Perceval to A. Charlet, 21 April 1715, 1 Dec. 1715, 18 April 1717, 21 July 1717, 29 April 1719; Bodleian, Ballard Ms. 36, ff. 94v, 96, 102–3, 104, 108; Lord Perceval to W. Perceval, 3 March 1721[2]; W. Perceval to Lord Perceval, 14 April 1722, BL, Add. Ms. 47,029, ff. 109, 114v.

180. W. Perceval to Col. Foley, 4 Feb. 1732[3], PRONI, D 906/78; Minute Book, 1731–3, s.d. 24 Feb. 1731[2], 29 March 1733, RDS; Minute Book, 1733–41, s.d. 22 Nov. 1733, 14 Feb. 1733[4], RDS.

181. Minute Book, 1731–3, s.d. 14 Dec. 1732, RDS.

182. Barnard, 'Cork settlers', p. 320.

183. B. de Beffni, 'The building of the mansion at Blessington, 1672', *GPA Irish Arts Review Yearbook, 1988*, pp. 73–7; income of Abp. M. Boyle, 1671–2, NLI, de Vesci Mss, H/4.

184. G. Mathew to K. O'Hara, 15 Feb. 1717[18], NLI, Ms. 20,385.

185. W. Perceval to K. O'Hara, 3 April 1718, NLI, Ms. 20,385.

186. Beaumont, 'Gentry of King's and Queen's Counties', ii, p. 240.

187. W. Perceval to K. O'Hara, 29 June 1718, NLI, Ms. 20,385.

188. Bp. T. Godwin to Abp. W. Wake, 12 Sep. 1719, 25 May 1720, Christ Church, Wake Ms. 13/108, 176.

189. Account of Archdeacon D. Hearn with Abp. T. Bolton [1730s], PRONI, D 562/458; A. P. W. Malcomson, *Archbishop Charles Agar: churchmanship and politics in Ireland, 1760–1810* (Dublin, 2002), pp. 347–50.

190. B. Smythe to W. Smythe, 3 Sep. 1730, NLI, PC 448.

191. Taylors of Headfort, account book, NLI, Ms. 25,386, openings 46, 52, 54.

192. J. Smythe to W. Smythe, 15 Jan. 1730[1], NLI, PC 449.

193. M. Wills, 'Designs for private buildings on two, three, four, five and six rooms on a floor, and one of eight rooms', Royal Institute of British Architects, Ms. D3.

194. *CARD*, xi, p. 125.

195. W. Waring, 'An estimate of the charge I was at in building my house, etc', 19 April 1673, private collection, Co. Down.

196. Bp. J. Parry, contract with J. Middleton, J. Dowling and P. Hayden, 16 Sep. 1672, NLI, de Vesci Mss, J/19.

197. Gebbie (ed.), *Abercorn letters*, p. 89.

198. P. J. Jupp, 'Genevese exiles in County Waterford', *JCHAS*, lxxv (1970), p. 32

199. Petitions to Ormonde, 1703–7, RIA, Ms. 12 W 24, ff. 9, 26.

200. Visitation of diocese of Derry, *c.* 1730, RCB, Ms. GS 2/7/3/34, p. 15.

201. Revd J. Smythe to W. Smythe, 3 April 1730, NLI, PC 449.

202. Revd E. Ormsby to Bp. R. Howard, 1 March 1733[4], NLI, PC 227.

203. K. Benson to J. Bonnell, 4 July 1738, NLI, PC 435.

204. Gebbie (ed.), *Abercorn letters*, pp. 42–3.

205. M. E. Garnett, 'The great rebuilding and economic change in south Lonsdale, 1600–1730', *Transactions of the Historic Society of Lancashire and Cheshire*, cxxxvii (1987), p. 70.

206. Barnard, *New anatomy*, pp. 21–80.

207. Barnard, 'Cork settlers', pp. 321, 356, n. 49; R. G. Wilson and A. Mackley, *Creating paradise: the building of the English country house, 1660–1880* (London and New York, 2000), pp. 233–351.

208. M. Girouard, *Life in the French country house* (London, 2000), pp. 110–145, 265–294; J. Macaulay, *The classical country house in Scotland, 1660–1800* (London, 1987), pp. 27–142.

209. Bp. W. Nicolson to Abp. W. Wake, 3 May 1720, Christ Church, Wake Mss, 13, f. 172; Bp. H. Downes to Abp. W. Wake, 13 Sep. [1720], Christ Church, Wake Mss., 13, f. 198; J. Nichols (ed.), *Letters on various subjects . . . to and from William Nicolson, D.D.*, 2 vols (London, 1809), ii, pp. 529, 576; McParland, *Public architecture*, p. 19.

210. Delany, *Autobiography*, 1st series, iii, pp. 518, 525.

211. T. Smythe to R. Smythe, 31 Jan. 1756, NLI, PC 448.

212. M. Crofton to W. Smythe, 27 Dec. 1732, 18 April 1737, 18 May 1741, 21 Oct. 1741, NLI, PC 436; G. Swift to Sir W. Fownes, 16 May 1757, 30 June 1757, NLI, Ms. 3889/4 and 5; S. Burdy, *Life of Philip Skelton*, ed. N. Moore (Oxford, 1914), p. 118; Delany, *Autobiography*, 1st series, ii, p. 325; Legg (ed.), *Synge letters*, pp. 155–6, 440.

213. Bp. W. Nicolson to Abp. W. Wake, 13 July 1725, Christ Church, Wake Mss, 14, f. 275.

214. Notebook of John Thomson, *c.* 1698–1765, NLI, Ms. 3131, pp. 234, 260; NA, Elphin Census, 1749, NA, M 2466, f. 322.

215. *A just and true relation of Josias Bateman's concern* (n.p., *c.* 1732), p. 18; Barnard, *New Anatomy*, pp. 223–5.

216.   R. French, account book, NLI, Ms. 4918, pp. 2, 3, 7.

217.   T. C. Barnard, 'The worlds of a Galway squire: Robert French of Monivea, 1716–1779', in G. Moran and R. Gillespie (eds), *Galway: history and society* (Dublin, 1996), pp. 271–96; D. A. Cronin, *A Galway gentleman in the age of improvement: Robert French of Monivea, 1716–79* (Blackrock, 1995).

218.   D. Fitzgerald, Knight of Glin, 'Francis Bindon (*c.* 1690–1765)', *Quarterly Bulletin of the Irish Georgian Society*, x (1967), pp. 3–36.

219.   R. French, account book, NLI, Ms. 4918, p. 608.

220.   R. French, journal of a tour, 1751, NLI, Ms. 7375.

221.   R. Edgeworth, accounts, s.d. 19 Oct. 1734, NLI, Ms. 1510, p. 145.

222.   R. Edgeworth, accounts, s.d. 30 July 1753, NLI, Ms. 1520, p. 154; note on coat of arms, NLI, Ms. 1520, unpaginated.

223.   R. Edgeworth, accounts, s.d. 8 April 1755, NLI, Ms. 1521, p. 181.

224.   See above, pp. 162–3.

225.   R. Edgeworth, accounts, s.d. 18 July 1764, 8 and 16 Aug. 1764, 28 Nov. 1764, NLI, Ms. 1528, pp. 79, 86, 95, 145.

226.   R. Edgeworth, accounts, s. d. 25 Sep. 1767, NLI, Ms. 1533, p. 236.

227.   *Memoirs of Edgeworth*, i, p. 331.

228.   *Memoirs of Edgeworth*, i, p. 202.

229.   L. Baker-Jones, *Princelings, privileges and power: the Tivyside gentry in the community* (Llandysul, 1999), pp. 36–43; Barnard, *New anatomy*, pp. 58–65; D. W. Howell, *Patriarchs and parasites: the gentry of south-west Wales in the eighteenth century* (Cardiff, 1986), pp. 8–9; B. Howells (ed.), *Early Modern Pembrokeshire, 1536–1815* (Haverfordwest, 1987), pp. 299–308, 329–30; M. Humphreys, *The crisis of community: Montgomeryshire, 1680–1815* (Cardiff, 1996); G. Morgan, *A Welsh house and its family: the Vaughans of Trawsgoed* (Llandysul, 1997); G. Morgan (ed.), *Nanteos: a Welsh house and its families* (Llandysul, 2001); B. Phillips, *Peterwell: the history of a mansion and its infamous squire* (Aberystwyth, 1983); S. Pugsley, 'Landed society and the emergence of the country house in Tudor and early Stuart Devon', in T. Gray, M. Rowe and A. Erskine (eds), *Tudor and Stuart Devon: the common estate and the government* (Exeter, 1992), pp. 96–118; P. R. Roberts, 'The landed gentry in Merioneth, 1660–1832, with special reference to the estates of Hengwrt, Nannau, Rug and Ynysymaengwyn', unpublished M.A. thesis, University of Wales (1963).

230.   Palmerston to W. Flower, 30 April 1730, NLI, Ms. 11,478.

231.   Palmerston to W. Flower, 8 Oct. 1728, NLI, Ms. 11,478.

232.   Palmerston to W. Flower, 19 Aug. 1731, 16 Dec. 1731, 14 June 1744, NLI, Ms. 11,478.

233.   Williams (ed.), *Correspondence of Swift*, iii, p. 548.

234.   Palmerston to W. Flower, 8 Oct. 1728, NLI, Ms. 11,478.

235.   Palmerston to W. Flower, 30 April 1730, 19 Aug. 1731, NLI, Ms. 11,478; T. Jeffreys to Lord Castle Durrow, 2 Sep. 1735, NLI, Ms. 11,475/1; M. Coghill to E. Southwell, 20 Oct. 1733, BL, Add. Ms. 21,123, f. 63v; appointments diary of Lord Palmerston, Southampton UL, BR 3/110, s.d. 9 May 1738; Williams (ed.), *Correspondence of Swift*, v, pp. 1–2.

236.   H. Boyle to Burlington, 17 Aug. 1731, Chatsworth, Devonshire letters, 1720–36, 205.0; Williams (ed.), *Correspondence of Swift*, iv, 548.

237.   Beaumont, 'Gentry of King's and Queen's Counties', i, pp. 231–3; de Breffni and ffolliott, *The houses of Ireland*, pp. 92–4; Loeber, 'Castle Durrow', pp. 103–6.

238.   W. Perceval to K. O'Hara, 25 May 1718, NLI, Ms. 20,385.

239.   W. Cooley to Lord Perceval, 28 Jan. 1741[2], BL, Add. Ms. 47,007A, f. 25v.

240.   Contract with John Rudd, 4 Nov. 1726, NLI, 11,469.

241.   T. Burgh to ?W. Flower, 29 Oct. 1726, NLI, Ms. 11,481/9.

242.   Receipts of Demave, 19 Dec. 1715, 3 Jan. 1733 [4], 18 May 1742, 19 May 1743, NLI, Ms. 11,468/5.

243.   Receipt of 15 Nov. 1746, NLI, Ms. 11,468/5.

244.   J. Jellycum, bill, 12 Aug. 1747, NLI, Ms. 11,462/3.

245. J. Loughlan, accounts with the Flowers, 1715–50, NLI, Ms. 11,463.

246. G. Kirkham, ' "No more to be got from the cat but the skin": management, landholding and economic change in the Murray of Broughton estate, 1670–1755', in W. Nolan, L. Ronanyne and M. Dunlevy (eds), *Donegal: history and society* (Dublin, 1995), pp. 357–80; H. Meehan, 'The Conynghams of Slane and Mountcharles', *Donegal Annual*, li (1999), pp. 22–35.

247. Will of Henry Conyngham, 29 Aug. 1705, proved 27 Aug. 1706, NLI, PC 345, box 1.

248. Assignment of 1 Jan. 1703[4], Denbighshire Record Office, DD/BK/I, 228.

249. Casey and Rowan, *North Leinster*, p. 156; Rowan, *North-West Ulster*, p. 176; Quane, 'Viscount Weymouth Grammar School, Carrickmacross', p. 39.

250. Goods of Conyngham in executors' accounts, IAA, Castletown deposit, box 55.

251. 'Goods in dispute'; accounts for Conyngham Hall, 1710–11 and 1711–12; accounts for stable, etc. 13 Feb. 1712[13], W. Billing to W. Conolly, 17 Feb. 1712[13], stonework, etc. measured by J. Curle, 14 Feb. 1712[13], IAA, Castletown deposit, box 55.

252. Revd A. Hamilton to W. Conolly, 9 Sep. 1710, IAA, Castletown deposit, box 55.

253. Revd A. Hamilton to W. Conolly, 11 Nov. 1710, IAA, Castletown deposit, box 55; W. Conolly to T. Knox, 18 March 1711[12], IAA, Castletown deposit, box 55.

254. K. Conolly to J. Bonnell, 30 July 1721, NLI, PC 434; cf. C. Smith, *The antient and present state of the county of Kerry*, new edn (Dublin and Cork, 1979), pp. 258–9.

255. K. Conolly to J. Bonnell, 11 June 1719, NLI, PC 434.

256. C. Conyngham to J. Bonnell, 18 Feb. 1723[4], NLI, PC 435.

257. W. Conyngham to J. Bonnell, 23 Nov. 1726, NLI, PC 435.

258. Indenture of W. Conyngham, 5 April 1738, NLI, PC 345, box 1; mortgage of Slane to T. Stopford, 31 July 1756, NLI, PC 345, box 1.

259. K. Conolly to J. Bonnell, 2 Dec. 1735, 11 Jan. 1736[7], NLI, PC 434.

260. K. Conolly to J. Bonnell, 21 Nov. 1735, NLI, PC 434; M. Jones to J. Bonnell, 19 Aug [], NLI, PC 435.

261. K. Conolly to J.Bonnell, 4 and 16 Feb. 1736[7], NLI, PC 434.

262. R. Jones to J. Bonnell, 28 Oct. 1738, NLI, PC 435; C. Conyngham to J. Bonnell, [Oct. 1738], NLI, PC 435.

263. Conveyance from H. Conyngham, 16 July 1700, NLI, PC 346, box 1; declaration of W. Conyngham, 17 Feb. 1725[6], NLI, PC 346, box 1; will of W. Conyngham, 25 May 1734, NLI, PC 346, box 1; H. Conyngham to J. Bonnell, 5 April 1743, NLI, PC 435; marriage settlement of Col. H. Conyngham and E. Merrett, 17 Aug. 1744, NLI, PC 349, box 1.

264. GEC, *Complete peerage*, iii, 410.

265. Barnard, *Abduction of a Limerick heiress*, pp. 15–20.

266. Illustration of Carton in J. Harris, *The artist and the country house*, revised edn (London, 1985), pp. 98, 151, plate 166; D. Fitzgerald, Knight of Glin and E. Malins, *Lost demesnes* (London, 1976), figure 8.

267. M. Ledwidge to W. Smythe, 6 Jan. 1738[9], NLI, PC 436.

268. D. Griffin and C. Pegum, *Leinster House, 1744–2000* (Dublin, 2000).

269. S. O'Reilly, *Irish houses and gardens from the archives of* Country Life (London, 1998), p. 65. The fullest account is D. J. Griffin, 'Castletown, Co. Kildare: an architectural report', IAA, 2 vols (1994).

270. Sir R. Bulkeley to ?M. Lister, 24 June 1686, Bodleian, Ms. Lister 35, f. 121v; T. C. Barnard, 'A tale of three sisters: Katherine Conolly of Castletown', in Barnard, *Irish Protestant ascents and descents*, pp. 266–89.

271. Memo of 11 April 1723, IAA, Castletown deposit, box 76.

272. K. Conolly to C. Tickell, 28 Sep. 1728, Tickell Mss, private collection, Devon.

273. G. Berkeley to Lord Perceval, 7 Sep. 1722, BL, Add. Ms. 47,029, f. 132v.

274. J. Gifford, *William Adam, 1689–1748* (Edinburgh, 1989), pp. 150–5; T. Clifford and I. Gow, *Duff House* (Edinburgh, 1995), pp. 29–64; J. Harris, 'The architecture of the house', in A. Moore (ed.), *Houghton Hall: the prime minister, the empress and heritage* (London, 1996), pp. 20–4.

275. K. Conolly to J. Bonnell, 22 July 1732, NLI, PC 434.

276. A. Worth to J. Bonnell, 21 Aug. 1722, NLI, PC 435.

277. K. Conolly to C. Tickell, 28 Sep. 1728, Tickell Mss, private collection, Devon.

278. K. Conolly to J. Bonnell, 27 Nov. 1732, 24 April 1735, 14 May 1736, NLI, PC 434.

279. O. Gallagher to O. St George, 9 April 1730, 14 Nov. 1730; R. Wilson to O. St George, 17 April 1730, PRO, C 110/46, 724, 758, 783.

280. M. Jones to K. Conolly, 25 July [], NLI, PC 435.

281. M. Jones to J. Bonnell, 14 March [*c.* 1741?], NLI, PC 435/40.

282. M. Jones to J. Bonnell, 24 May [1741 or 1742], NLI, PC 435.

283. M. Jones to J. Bonnell, 14 March [1741?], 24 May [1741?], NLI, PC 435.

284. Lady Anne Conolly to Lord Strafford, 29 Jan. 1733[4], BL, Add. Ms. 22,228, f. 102v; Lord Mount Stewart, tour of Ireland, *c.* 1775, NLS, Ms. 9587, f. 62v; J. Howley, *The follies and garden buildings of Ireland* (New Haven and London, 1993), pp. 8, 11–14; W. Fitzgerald, 'Castletown and its owners', *Journal of the County Kildare Archaeological Society*, ii (1896–9), pp. 361–78.

285. R. Wilson to O. St George, 24 April 1730, PRO, C 110/46, 933; K. Conolly to J. Bonnell, 18 April 1730, NLI, PC 434.

286. Jean Hamilton to J. Bonnell, 16 Dec. 1731, NLI, PC, 435.

287. M. Jones to J. Bonnell, 27 Oct. [], NLI, PC 435.

288. F. Burton to J. Bonnell, 9 Dec. 1729, NLI, PC 435.

289. K. Conolly to J. Bonnell, 22 Jan. 1721[2], NLI, PC 434; K. Conolly to C. Tickell, 2 Oct. 1724, 19 Dec. 1724, 23 April 1729, Tickell Mss, private collection, Devon.

290. *The Compleat Gamester* (London, 1721), pp. 23–4; A. Hamilton to Lady Panmure, 10 May 1710, NAS, GD 45/14/238, 25; and above, p. 17.

291. M. Jones to J. Bonnell, 16 Oct. [1733?], 28 Feb. [1734?], NLI, PC 435.

292. M. Jones to J. Bonnell, 5 Jan. [], NLI, PC 435.

293. K. Conolly to J. Bonnell, 21 Dec. 1739, 15 Jan. 1739[40], NLI, PC 434.

294. Delany, *Autobiography*, 1st series, iii, p. 282.

295. Mrs C. Bagshawe to S. Bagshawe, 23 Sep. 1755, JRL, B2/3/25.

296. Hartington to Lady Burlington, 27 June 1755, same to Devonshire, 14 July 1755, Chatsworth, Devonshire letters, May–July 1755, 260.147, 260.153; T. Pakenham to Hartington, 4 Sep. 1755, Chatsworth, Devonshire letters, Aug.–Oct. 1755, 420.0; Mrs C. Bagshawe to S. Bagshawe, 23 Sep. 1755, JRL, B2/3/25.

297. James Bonnell to J. Strype, 14 Feb. 1694[5], 25 Jan. 1698[9], Cambridge UL, Add. Ms. 1/80, 85; Jane Bonnell to J. Strype, 13 June 1699, Cambridge UL, Add. Ms. 2/232; *The life and character of James Bonnell* (London, 1703).

298. T. Knox to A. Murray, 22 July 1704, 23 Nov. 1704, PRONI, D 2860/4/11 and 12.

299. R. Jones to W. Conolly, 1 Feb. 1704[5], 3 Oct. 1705; W. Conolly to R. Jones, 29 Oct. 1713, IAA, Castletown deposit, box 78.

300. M. Jones to J. Bonnell, 5 Feb.[], 9 Sep. [], NLI, PC 435.

301. M. Jones to J. Bonnell, 26 May [], NLI, PC 435.

302. M. Jones to J. Bonnell, 5 May [], 12 Aug. [], NLI, PC 435.

303. M. Jones to J. Bonnell, 13 Oct. [1738], 29 June [], NLI, PC 435.

304. M. Jones to J. Bonnell, 18 Dec.[], NLI, PC 435.

305. M. Jones to J. Bonnell, 11 May [1733 or 1734], NLI, PC 435.

306. K. Conolly to J. Bonnell, 2 Oct. 1736, NLI, PC 434.

307. K. Conolly to J. Bonnell, 2 Oct. 1736, 1 Aug. 1738, NLI, PC 434.

308. K. Conolly to Lady A. Conolly, 2 April 1747, IAA, Castletown deposit, box 76.

309. K. Conolly to J. Bonnell, 9 July 1742, NLI, PC 434.

310. K. Conolly to J. Bonnell, 17 Oct. 1738, NLI, PC 434.

311. M. Jones to J. Bonnell, 12 June 1741, NLI, PC 435.

312. M. Jones to J. Bonnell, 12 Oct. [], NLI, PC 435.

## 3 Interiors

1. Delany, *Autobiography*, 1st series, iii, p. 159.
2. Illustrated in D. Fitzgerald, Knight of Glin, *Irish furniture* (Dublin, 1978), pp. 6–7.
3. Will of George Wilde, 1 Nov. 1665, PRONI, T 808/14615.
4. I. M. Young, *300 years in Inishowen* (Belfast, 1929), p. 321.
5. Will of Joseph Gill, 22 Nov. 1741, Friends' Historical Library, Dublin, MM II L.2, pp. 133–4.
6. Will of Thomas Pearson, 25 Oct. 1753, Friends' Historical Library, MM II L.1, p. 26.
7. Young, *300 years in Inishowen*, p. 342.
8. W. P. Burke, *History of Clonmel* (Waterford, 1907), p. 330; P. Crossle, 'Some records of the Skerrett family', *Journal of the Galway Archaeological and Historical Society*, xv (1931–3), pp. 34–5, 59.
9. E. Peard to F. Price, *c.* 1740, NLW, Puleston Ms. 3579E.
10. J. Le Hunte to C. Tickell, 9 Dec. 1758, Tickell Mss, private collection, Devon.
11. J. Lenox to W. Lenox, 25 Sep. 1739, PRONI, D 1449/12/51.
12. Will of Arthur Beatty, 8 April 1741, PRONI, T 282C.
13. Ware account book, TCD, Ms. 10,528, f. 12v; R. Edgeworth, accounts, s.d. 6 April 1765, NLI, Ms. 1528, p. 207.
14. D. Cuffe to B. Pratt, 'Sat. Feb.' and 29 June 1757, NLI, Ms. 5245.
15. J. Alcock to A. Mason, 12 Oct. 1739, Dromana, Co. Waterford, Villiers–Stuart Mss, T 3131/B/5/11.
16. J. Leathes to W. Leathes, 19 March 1717[18], Suffolk CRO, Ipswich, de Mussenden–Leathes Mss, HA 403/1/6, 24.
17. J. Leathes to W. Leathes, 9 Oct. 1717, Suffolk CRO, Ipswich, de Mussenden–Leathes Mss, HA 403/1/6, 21.
18. J. Leathes to W. Leathes, 8 Oct. 1719, Suffolk CRO, Ipswich, de Mussenden–Leathes Mss, HA 403/1/6, 30; cf. M. Berg, 'New commodities, luxuries and their consumers in eighteenth-century England', in M. Berg and H. Clifford (eds), *Consumers and luxury: consumer culture in Europe, 1650–1850* (Manchester, 1999), pp. 63–85.
19. M. Finn, 'Men's things: masculine possession in the consumer revolution', *Social History*, xxv (2000), pp. 133–55.
20. Account of Lt G. Knox with Gen. H. Conygham, 1705, IAA, Castletown deposit, box 57.
21. L. Gardiner to N. Clements, 19 March 1744[5], TCD, Ms. 1741/15.
22. S. Waring, notebook, 'no. 3' reversed, PRONI, D 695/229; T. Caulfield to K. O'Hara, 9 Dec. 1703, NLI, Ms. 20,388; A. Caulfield to K. O'Hara, 28 Feb. 1703[4], NLI, Ms. 20,388; E. O'Hara to K. O'Hara, 17 May [?1717], NLI, Ms. 20,277; Barnard, 'What became of Waring?', p. 194.
23. J. Digby to W. Smythe, 21 April 1733, 25 Aug. 1733, NLI, PC 445.
24. Account book of Bp. F. Hutchinson, s.d. Nov. 1730, PRONI, DIO 1/22/2.
25. H. Dixon, *An introduction to Ulster architecture* (Belfast, 1975), pp. 39–40.
26. C. O'Brien to Sir D. O'Brien, 4 Feb. 1712[13], NLI, Inchiquin Mss, no. 957.
27. Inventory of Corofin, Co. Clare, 9 May 1718, NLI, Inchiquin Mss, no. 1804.
28. Sir J. Temple, account book, s.d. 11 and 14 May 1677, Southampton UL, BR 7A/1.
29. Sir A. Newcomen to Bp. A. Dopping, 7 June 1693, Armagh Public Library, Dopping Mss, 2/221.
30. P. Earle, *The making of the English middle class: business, society and family life in London, 1660–1730* (London, 1989), pp. 269–301; D. Levine and K. Wrightson, *The making of an industrial society: Whickham, 1560–1765* (Oxford, 1991), pp. 231–41; M. Overton, *A bibliography of British probate inventories* (Newcastle, 1983); C. Shammas, *The pre-industrial consumer in England and America* (Oxford, 1990); M. Spufford, 'The limitations of the probate inventory', in J. Chartres and D. Hey (eds), *English rural society, 1500–1800: essays in honour of Joan Thirsk* (Cambridge, 1990), pp. 139–74; L. Weatherill, *Consumer behaviour and material culture, 1660–1760* (London, 1988).
31. J. Bold, 'Privacy and the plan', in J. Bold and E. Chaney (eds), *English architecture: public and private* (London, 1993), pp. 107–20; N. Cooper, *Houses of the gentry* (New Haven and London, 1999), pp. 8–9,

273–5; M. Girouard, *Life in the English country house* (New Haven and London, 1978), pp. 119–62; L. Pollock, 'On the stage of the world: the concept of privacy among the élite of early modern England', in A. Wilson (ed.), *Rethinking social history: English society, 1570–1920 and its interpretation* (Manchester, 1993), pp. 78–96.

32.  S. Nenadic, 'Middle-rank consumers and domestic culture in Edinburgh and Glasgow, 1720–1840', *P & P*, cxlv (1994), pp. 122–56; L. Weatherill, 'A possession of one's own: women and consumer behaviour, 1640–1760', *Journal of British Studies*, xxv (1986), pp. 131–56; A. Vickery, *The gentleman's daughter: women's lives in Georgian England* (New Haven and London, 1998), p. 206.

33.  W. Billings to W. Conolly, 6 March 1710[11], IAA, Castletown deposit, box 55; Bp. F. Hutchinson, account book from 1729, s.d. 25 Feb. 1733[4], PRONI, DIO 1/22/2.

34.  Inventory of Col. Bourke, NA, Chancery Pleadings, unidentified material, box 36.

35.  Inventory of P. Marsh, 4 May 1741, NA, Chancery Pleadings, unidentified material, box 31.

36.  D. W. Howell, *Patriarchs and parasites* (Cardiff, 1986), p. 182; M. Humphreys, *The crisis of community: Montgomeryshire, 1680–1815* (Cardiff, 1996), p. 33. Also: M. Girouard, *Life in the French country house* (London, 2000); J. Horn, *Adapting to a new world: English society in seventeenth-cenury Chesapeake* (Chapel Hill and London, 1994), pp. 305–6; J. L. Lindsey, 'Pondering balance: the decorative arts of the Delaware Valley, 1680–1756', in Philadelphia Museum of Art, *Worldly goods: the arts of early Pennsylvania, 1680–1758* (Philadelphia, 1999), pp. 88–9.

37.  Household book from 1758, Carton, Mss of the duke of Leinster, Ramsden, Oxfordshire. Cf. L. G. Carr and L. S. Walsh, 'The planter's wife: the experience of white women in seventeenth-century Maryland', *William and Mary Quarterly*, 3rd series, xxxiv (1977), pp. 542–71; Horn, *Adapting to a new world*, p. 330; T. Meldrum, *Domestic service and gender, 1660–1750: life and work in the London household* (Harlow, 2000), pp. 71–100.

38.  Bp. H. Downes to Abp. W. Wake, 4 March 1723[4], Christ Church, Wake Mss, 14, f. 174.

39.  Barnard, *New anatomy*, pp. 73, 322; B. B. Butler, 'Lady Arbella Denny, 1707–1792', *Dublin Historical Record*, ix (1946–7), pp. 1–20.

40.  Lady A. Denny to Lady A. Crosbie, 25 Feb. 1755, NLI, Ms. 20,601.

41.  J. Hamilton to C. Eustace, 20 July 1718, 18 Nov. 1718, Tickell Mss, private collection, Devon.

42.  Depositions of A. Nash, *c.* 1745; C. Quinn, *c.* 1745; R. Madden, 1766, NLI, PC 438; T. C. Barnard, *The abduction of a Limerick heiress: social and political relationships in eighteenth-century Ireland* (Dublin, 1998), p. 34.

43.  J. Swift and T. Sheridan, *The Intelligencer*, ed. J. Woolley (Oxford, 1992), pp. 89–90.

44.  Richard Barton, *Farrago: or, miscellanies in verse and prose* (London, 1739), p. 82.

45.  P. Thornton, *Seventeenth-century interior decoration in England, France and Holland* (New Haven and London, 1978), pp. 107–225.

46.  Inventory of Cork House, Dublin, 16 Nov. 1645, Chatsworth, Lismore Ms. 28/4.

47.  Inventories of F. Barker, 29 March 1639; and T. Ottowell, 30 July 1639, BL, Add. Ms. 11,687, ff. 137v, 146v.

48.  Inventory of earl of Kildare's house in Dublin, 11 Dec. 1656, NLI, Ms.18,996.

49.  Kildare inventory, 26 May 1663, NLI, Ms. 18,996.

50.  'Testamentary records from Lettice Evoryna O'Hanlon of Orior', *The Irish Genealogist*, ii (1943–55), pp. 180–2.

51.  Inventory of Portlester, 16 April 1628, BL, Add. Charter, 13,340. Cf. Thornton, *Seventeenth-century interior decoration*, pp. 107–17.

52.  Inventory of Malby Brabazon, 9 Feb. 1637[8]; inventory of Sarah Brabazon, widow of Malby Brabazon, 23 Feb. 1657[8], Barber Mss, private collection, London, box III.

53.  B. Mac Cuarta, 'A planter's funeral, legacies and inventory: Sir Matthew De Renzy (1577–1634)', *JRSAI*, cxxvii (1997), pp. 18–33; B. Mac Cuarta, 'Sir John Moore's inventory, Croghan, King's County, 1636', *Journal of the County Kildare Archaeological Society*, xix (2000–1), pp. 206–17.

54. St J. D. Seymour, 'The household furniture of Castletown-Waller in 1642', *Journal of the North Munster Antiquarian Society*, i (1909–11), pp. 255–8.

55. R. Lockyer, *The life and political career of George Villiers, first duke of Buckingham, 1592–1628* (London, 1981), pp. 408–11.

56. H. MacDonnell, 'A seventeenth century inventory from Dunluce Castle, Co. Antrim', *JRSAI*, cxxii (1992), pp. 117–27.

57. B. Ó Dálaigh, 'A comparative study of the wills of the first and fourth earls of Thomond', *North Munster Antiquarian Journal*, xxxiv (1992), pp. 48–63.

58. J. C. Walton, 'The household effects of a Waterford merchant family in 1640', *JCHAS*, lxxxiii (1978), pp. 99–105.

59. Inventory of O. Weston, 23 Nov. 1638, BL, Add. Ms. 11,687, f. 125.

60. Inventory of S. Darworthy, 29 June 1639, BL, Add. Ms. 11,687, f. 145.

61. Inventories of A. Rookes, 21 Jan. 1638[9]; W. Cooper, 20 Feb. 1638[9]; H. Penn, 21 March 1638[9]; G. Hilliard, 7 May 1639, BL, Add. Ms. 11,687, ff. 128–9, 131–2, 139v–141v, 143–143v.

62. 'Abstracts of Wills', *Irish Ancestor*, ii (1970), p. 124.

63. E. A. B. Barnard and A. J. B. Wace, 'The Sheldon tapestry weavers and their work', *Archaeologia*, lxxviii (1928), pp. 255–314; W. Hefford, 'Prince behind the scenes', *Country Life*, 4 Oct. 1990, pp. 132–5; A. F. Kendrick, *Victoria and Albert Museum, Department of Textiles, catalogue of tapestries* (London, 1924); S. M. Levy, *An Elizabethan inheritance: the Hardwick Hall textiles* (London, 1998); C. Saumarez Smith, *Eighteenth-century decoration: design and the domestic interior in England* (London, 1993), pp. 23, 35, 66, 133–8; Thornton, *Seventeenth-century interior decoration*, pp. 107–9, 130–4; A. Wells-Cole, *Art and decoration in Elizabethan and Jacobean England* (New Haven and London, 1997), pp. 221–34.

64. Inventory of Dublin Castle, *c.* 1705, NLI, Ms. 2524; inventory of Kilkenny Castle, 1717; PRO, FEC 1/876, p. 5; J. Fenlon, *The Ormonde picture collection* (Dublin, 2001), pp. 31–2, figures 29 and 30, plate 33.

65. Lease of Chapelizod to C. Lovett, 17 July 1677, Southampton UL, BR /150; *A Memoir of Mistress Ann Fowkes (née Geale) . . . with some recollections of her family* (Dublin, 1892), pp. 26–7.

66. Minute book, Weavers' Company, 1734–60, s.d. 5 June 1739, RSAI; S. Derrick, *Letters written from Leverppole, Chester, Corke, the Lake of Killarney, Dublin . . .*, 2 vols (London, 1767), i, p. 95; A. K. Longfield, 'History of tapestry making in Ireland in the 17th and 18th centuries', *JRSAI*, lxviii (1938), pp. 91–9; A. K. Longfield, 'Some tapestry makers in Ireland', *Burlington Magazine*, lxxxv (1944), p. 250.

67. Goods sold from Damesgate, 19 June 1676, RIA, Ms. 24 G 1.

68. E. Pierce, accounts with Bp. T. Hackett, 1674–7, after 22 May 1676, PRONI, D 2056/1.

69. Will of Elizabeth, Lady Shelburne, 12 May 1706, BL, Add. Ms. 72,902.

70. Abp. W. King, account books, 1700–12, TCD, Ms. 751/2, f. 104; 1715–23, TCD, Ms. 751/3, f. 9.

71. Inventory of Revd R. Spence, *c.* 1730, TCD, Mss 1995–2008/2468(2).

72. Will of W. Whitshed, 3 March 1724[5], Marsh's Library, Ms. Z2.1.7, item 64.

73. M. Ward to J. Hamilton, 27 Aug. 1720, PRONI, D 2092/1/2, 35.

74. *A true copy of the last will and testament of George Clarke Esq; LL.D.* (London, 1737), pp. 21–2.

75. A. Wace, *The Marlborough tapestries at Blenheim Palace* (London, 1968).

76. Sir J. Temple, account book, s.d. 11 and 14 May 1677, 7 and 23 March 1683[4], Southampton UL, BR 7A/1.

77. Inventory of Rathcline, 10 April 1688, NLI, Ms. 8644/5.

78. For this work Haslehurst was to be paid at the rate of 2s. 6d. per yard, with 25 shillings for the chimney-piece. Sir J. Temple, account book, s.d. 19 March 1670[1], 29 Dec. 1671, Southampton UL, BR 7A/1.

79. Ibid., s.d. 18 May 1676, Southampton UL, BR 7A/1.

80. Inventory of Waringstown, 12 Oct. 1704, private collection, Co. Down.

81. Inventory of P. Dalton, *c.* 1748, NA, Chancery Pleadings, unidentified material, box 13.

82. Inventory of P. Marsh, 1741, NA, Chancery Pleadings, unidentified material, box 31.

83.   Inventory, Dublin Castle, 1705, NLI, Ms. 2524.

84.   Inventory, Dublin Castle, 1705, NLI, Ms. 2524; J. Fenlon, 'Episodes of magnificence: the material worlds of the dukes of Ormonde', in Barnard and Fenlon (eds), *Dukes of Ormonde*, pp. 137–59; Barnard, 'Introduction', in Barnard and Fenlon (eds), *Dukes of Ormonde*, pp. 36–7.

85.   Inventory of 1 May 1705, NLI, Ms. 2524; inventory of Dublin Castle [1707], NLI, Ms. 2521.

86.   Inventory of Kilrush, Co. Kilkenny, 7 July 1750, TCD, St George Mss, miscellaneous photocopy, 175/17.

87.   Will of M. Coghill, 23 March 1735[6], PRO, PROB, 11/695, 74; A. de L. Kirkpatrick, *Chronicles of the Kirkpatrick family* (London, n.d.), p. 19. For gilt leather, E. Koldeweij, 'The marketing of gilt-leather in seventeenth-century Holland', *Print Quarterly*, xiii (1996), pp. 136–48.

88.   Delany, *Autobiography*, 1st series, ii, pp. 308, 339; iii, p. 173; inventory of Revd R. Spence, 1 Sep. 1730, TCD, Mss. 1995–2008/2198, f. 4; D. M. Beaumont, 'The gentry of the King's and Queen's Counties: Protestant landed society, 1690–1760', unpublished Ph.D. thesis, TCD, 2 vols (1999), i, p. 243; R. ffolliott, 'Captain Balfour's auction 15th March, 1741–2', *Irish Ancestor*, xvi (1984), p. 23.

89.   *A catalogue of the household goods, of the late Henry Ingoldsby, esq. Deceas'd. To be sold by auction in Mary's-Street, on Monday the 29th. day of November, 1731 and to continue until the end of the week* (Dublin, 1731), pp. 5, 6.

90.   C. P. Curran, *Dublin decorative plasterwork of the seventeenth and eighteenth centuries* (London, 1967); J. McDonnell, *Irish eighteenth-century stuccowork and its European sources* (Dublin, 1991).

91.   Inventory of Killeen, 23 March 1735[6], NLI, Ms. 1678, printed in R. ffolliott, 'An inventory of Killeen Castle in 1735–6', *The Irish Ancestor*, ix (1977), pp. 102–7.

92.   A. K. Longfield, 'History of the Dublin wall-paper industry in the 18th century', *JRSAI*, lxxvii (1947), pp. 101–20. For its development elsewhere: E. A. Entwistle, *The book of wallpaper: a history and appreciation*, new edn (Bath, 1970); G. Saunders, *Wallpaper in interior decoration* (London, 2002); A. Wells-Cole, *Historic wall-hangings from Temple Newsam and other English houses* (Leeds, 1983).

93.   John Mansfield, bill, 4 Dec. 1747, NLI, Ms. 11,469/20; R. Edgeworth, accounts, s.d. 19 May 1749, 9 Aug. 1749, NLI, Ms. 1518, pp. 142, 170.

94.   R. Edgeworth, accounts, s.d. 12 Nov. 1742, 19 May 1749, 9 Aug. 1749, 8 May 1755, NLI, Mss. 1515, p. 203; 1518, pp. 142, 170; 1520, p. 190.

95.   Legg (ed.), *Synge Letters*, pp. 107, 154.

96.   Inventory of J. Bentley, 12 Dec. 1760, TCD, Ms. 2010–2015/388; Annesley family account book, 1761–6, s. d. 26 March 1764, PRONI, D 1854/8/17; S. R. Lowry-Corry, earl of Belmore, *The history of the Corry family of Castlecoole* (London and Dublin, 1891), pp. 268–9; 'Diary of Anne Cooke', *Journal of the County Kildare Archaeological Society*, viii (1915), p. 129.

97.   T. Eyre to R. Rigby, 7 June 1759, 7 and 10 July 1759, IAA, Eyre letterbook.

98.   *The Limerick directory* (Limerick, 1769), p. 7; Register of Bp. Foy's School, Waterford, RCB, Ms. 523.

99.   A. K. Longfield, 'Old wall papers in Ireland: some eighteenth- and nineteenth-century Chinese, French and English examples', *JRSAI*, lxxviii (1948), p. 158.

100.  M. Nichols to Mrs Fitzgerald, 7 March 170[?], 19 May 1710, NLI, de Vesci Mss, J/2; S. Butler to W. Crosbie, 5 Oct. 1757; E. Role to W. Crosbie, 15 Dec. 1757, NLI, Talbot–Crosbie Mss, folder 61.

101.  R. Edgeworth, accounts, s.d. 28 Sep. 1749, NLI, Ms. 1518, p. 169; Herbert, sale, 29 Oct. 1760, NA, M 1854 (iv); Castle Balfour auctions, Townley accounts, NLI, Ms. 9534, ff. 1–3; account of goods sold at Castle Balfour, 5 Oct. 1741, NLI, Ms. 10,279; sale of Revd R. McClelland's effects, 8 April 1761, TCD, Ms. 2010–2015/391.

102.  Spufford, 'The limitations of the probate inventory', pp. 139–74.

103.  L. Ford to Mrs Preston, 29 Feb. 1703[4], NLI, Ms. 17,726.

104.  List of plate weighed by T. Walker, 2 Feb. 1741[2], NLI, Ms. 10,279, Balfour Mss; goods valued by C. Coleman, [1742], NLI, Ms. 10,279; inventory of Lord Grandison's goods, April 1734, Dromana, Villiers–Stuart Mss, T 3131, C/3/2B.

105.	*A catalogue of the household goods, of the late Henry Ingoldsby, esq. . . . To be sold by auction in Mary's-Street, on Monday the 29th. day of November*, in NLI, PC 438.

106.	Memo for Denny Muschamp, *c.* 1672, NLI, de Vesci Mss, H/15.

107.	Sir J. Temple, account book, s.d. 1 Aug. 1677, 7 March 1683[4], Southampton UL, BR 7A/1.

108.	Abp. W. King, account book, 1700–12, TCD, Ms. 751/2, f. 262.

109.	Bp. J. Story account book, 1742–50, s.d. July 1742, Oct. 1742, Bingfield, Co. Cavan, Story Mss; Revd J. Story, account book from 1753, s.d. May 1766, Bingfield, Co. Cavan, Story Mss; O. Gallagher to O. St George, 9 Jan. 1724[5], PRO, C 110/46, 313; J. Smythe to W. Smythe, 17 and 31 March 1731[2], NLI, PC 449; W. Cooley to Lord Perceval, 28 Jan. 1741[2], BL, Add. Ms. 47,004A, f. 25v.

110.	E. Stafford to W. Conolly, before 6 March 1710[11], IAA, Castletown deposit, box 55.

111.	Valuations, *c.* 1740, letterbook of Revd F. Houston, PRONI, D 668/E/38.

112.	'Autobiography of Pole Cosby, of Stradbally, Queen's County, 1703–37 (?)', *Journal of the County Kildare Archaeological Society*, v (1906), p. 322. My emphasis.

113.	L. Payzant to Lord Perceval, 10 Dec. 1715, BL, Add. Ms. 46,966, f. 140; Paull, account book, NLI, Ms. 12,938, p. 39; B. Townley, executor's accounts, s.d. 7 Sep. 1741, 14 Oct. 1741, NLI, Mss. 9534, f. 1; 10,275; O'Hara notebook, s.d. 12, 18 and 26 Jan. 1764, PRONI, DIO/22/4A.

114.	O. Gallagher to O. St George, 10 Nov. 1724, PRO, C 110/46, 348.

115.	J. Smythe to W. Smythe, 17 March 1731[2], 31 March 1732, NLI, PC 449.

116.	H. Ingoldsby to W. Smythe, 30 July 1720, NLI, PC 445.

117.	N. Roche, 'Irish eighteenth-century looking glasses: makers, frames and glass', in B. Austen (ed.), *Irish furniture* (London, 2000), pp. 16–23.

118.	*A catalogue of the China ware and linen, of the late Henry Ingoldsby, Esq . . . to be sold by auction at his late house in Mary-Street, on Wednesday, the 8th. Day of December, 1731* (Dublin, 1731), copy in NLI, PC 438.

119.	D. S. Howard, 'Chinese armorial porcelain for Ireland', *Quarterly Bulletin of the Irish Georgian Society*, xix (1986), pp. 3–24.

120.	NLI, Ms. 9534, f. 64v.

121.	Charles Coleman, valuation of Mrs Isabella Balfour's goods at St Stephen's Green, Dublin, NLI, Ms. 9534, ff. 64v–72.

122.	H. Balfour's goods, sold at auction 15 March 1741[2], NLI, Ms. 10,279; ffolliott, 'Captain Balfour's auction', pp. 21–31.

123.	Barnard, *New anatomy*, pp. 73–4.

124.	Williams (ed.), *Correspondence of Swift*, iv, p. 220.

125.	Inventory of Sir Hans Hamilton, Hamilton's Bawn, Nov. 1682, PRONI, T 2741.

126.	This included leases, bonds, etc.

127.	Inventory of P. Marsh's house, 4 May 1741, NA, Chancery pleadings, unidentified materials, box 31.

128.	Inventory, Kilrush, Co. Kilkenny, 7 July 1750, TCD, St George Mss, miscellaneous photocopy, 175/17.

129.	Accounts of B. Townley, NLI, Mss 9534, ff. 1–2, 69, 70, 72; 10,275, s.d. 7 Sep. 1741, 14 Oct. 1741; 10,726/9; 10,279; ffolliott, 'Captain Balfour's auction', p. 31.

130.	Belmore, *History of the Corry family*, pp. 268–9.

131.	The Georgian Society, *Records of eighteenth-century domestic architecture and decoration in Dublin*, 5 vols (Dublin, 1909–13), iv, pp. 3–10; F. E. Ball, *Howth and its owners, being the fifth part of a history of County Dublin* (Dublin, 1917).

132.	Spufford, 'The limitations of the probate inventory', pp. 139–74.

133.	Sheehan may be the same craftsman who had been paid nine guineas for a marble chimney-piece and hearthstone for Fownes Court in 1738. He also supplied Castlecoole. Fownes, accounts for 1737–8, NLI, Ms. 8801/1; Belmore, *History of the Corry family*, pp. 248–9.

134.	T. Clayton, *The English print, 1688–1802* (New Haven and London, 1997), p. 108; J. H. Gebbie (ed.), *An introduction to the Abercorn letters* (Omagh, 1972), p. 78.

135. S. Foster, 'Going shopping in Georgian Dublin: luxury goods and the negotiation of national identity', unpublished M.A. thesis, Royal College of Art and V & A (1995), p. 83. For English examples of ivory handles stained green: P. Brown (ed.), *British cutlery: an illustrated history of design, evolution and use* (London, 2001), pp. 117, 120.

136. Lease between Roger Murray and Viscount Conyngham, 27 Oct. 1766, NLI, PC 346, box 1.

137. T. Mooney and F. White, 'The gentry's winter season', in D. Dickson (ed.), *The gorgeous mask: Dublin 1700–1850* (Dublin, 1987), pp. 1–16.

138. R. French, account book, NLI, Ms. 4918, pp. 121–34, 202–20; Barnard, 'French of Monivea', pp. 271–96.

139. G. S. Cotter, *Poems, consisting of odes, songs, pastorals, satyrs, etc*, 2 vols (Cork, 1788), i, pp. 133–54.

140. N. Peacock, journal, s.d 1 April 1740, 27 March 1745, 8 April 1747, 25 March 1748, 20 Feb. 1749[50], 7 April 1751, NLI, Ms. 16,091.

141. N. Peacock, journal, s.d. 10 March 1739[40], 1 Feb. 1741[2].

142. N. Peacock, journal, s.d. 8 May 1742.

143. N. Peacock, journal, s.d. 6 April 1743.

144. N. Peacock, journal, s.d. 25 and 28 Nov 1743, 1 Dec. 1743.

145. N. Peacock, journal, s.d. 22 Jan. 1741[2], 12 and 13 May 1742, 22 Dec. 1742.

146. N. Peacock, journal, s.d. 22 July–10 Nov. 1743.

147. N. Peacock, journal, s.d. 28 and 29 May 1744.

148. N. Peacock, journal, s.d. 9 Dec. 1744, 17 June 1745.

149. N. Peacock, journal, s.d. 24 Dec. 1748.

150. N. Peacock, journal, s.d. 10 and 16 May 1746.

151. N. Peacock, journal, s.d. 12 Aug. 1750.

152. N. Peacock, journal, s.d. 7 March 1750[1].

153. N. Peacock, journal, s.d. 10 Jan. 1742[3].

154. N. Peacock, journal, s.d. 23 and 24 May 1743.

155. A. Odell to J. Crone, 18 Dec. [?1767], Cork Archives Institute, Crone of Byblox Mss, PR 3, box 1.

156. N. Peacock, journal, s.d. 1 Aug. 1750, NLI, Ms. 16,091.

157. Ibid., s.d. 23 May–2 June 1745.

158. H. Clifford, 'A commerce with things: the value of precious metalwork in early modern England', in Berg and Clifford (eds), *Consumers and luxury*, pp. 151–2.

159. Lucas, journal, NLI, Ms. 14,101.

160. Inventory of B. Hayes, April 1768, Caulfield Mss, TCD, Ms. 2010–2015/404.

161. Inventory of B. Travers, undated, Caulfield Mss, TCD, Ms. 2010–2015/383; Barnard, 'Cork settlers', pp. 329–31.

162. T. C. Barnard, 'Improving clergymen, 1660–1760', in A. Ford, J. I. McGuire and K. Milne (eds), *As by law established: the Church of Ireland since the Reformation* (Dublin, 1995), pp. 136–51, 257–65, reprinted in Barnard, *Ascents and descents*, pp. 306–29.

163. Import figures from Robinson Mss, Gilbert Collection, Dublin Public Library.

164. Piercey in Dublin stocked 'vile statues and busts in plaster of Paris'. Gebbie (ed.), *Abercorn letters*, p. 78.

165. Inventory of Revd R. McClelland, 8 April 1761, TCD, Ms. 2010–2015/391; W. M. Brady, *Clerical records of Cork, Cloyne and Ross*, 3 vols (Dublin, 1863–4), iii, p. 220.

166. Barnard, *New anatomy*, pp. 227–8.

167. Accounts of Herbert's executors, 1760; book of executors' accounts, 1760, NA, M. 1854 (iv); Johnston-Liik, *HIP*, iv, p. 412.

168. Inventory of Dr J. McKeogh, 25 May 1751, BL, Add. Ms. 31,882, ff. 187–188v.

169. Inventory of J. Bentley, 12 Dec. 1760, TCD, Ms. 2010–2015/388.

170. Burke, *History of Clonmel*, p. 328.

171. *The Prelude to a Levee, calculated to the meridian of the Castle of Dublin* (Dublin, 1757), p. 17.

172. Inventory of L. Delamain, 20 Jan. 1763, TCD, Ms. 2010–2015/395.

173. D. Mitchell, 'The clerk's view' and I. Day, 'The honours of the table', in Brown (ed.), *British cutlery*, pp. 19–29, 32–41.

174. Unknown to W. Conner, 22 May 1755, Chatsworth, Lismore Ms. 36/138; P. Crofts to H. Owen, 30 Aug. [?1694], NLW, Powis Castle Correspondence, no. 715; Barnard, 'Cork settlers', pp. 330–1; J. Styles, 'Product innovation in early modern London', *P & P*, clxviii (2000), pp. 124–68.

175. G. Macartney to Capt. Nichols, 2 July 1679, 9 Aug. 1679, 26 May 1680, 19 Oct. 1680, 19 Jan. 1680[1], Macartney letterbook, 1679–81, Linen Hall Library, Belfast; W. Hovell, letters of 30 Nov. 1683, 7 March 1683[4], 27 July 1684, 19 Sep. 1684, 12 Dec. 1684, 26 May 1685, 8 Sep. 1685, 24 Aug. 1686, 23 Sep. 1686, Farmar Mss, private collection, Dublin; S. Smith to 'Laird' Broughton, 19 Dec. 1705, PRONI, D 2860/10/3; Barnard, 'Cork settlers', p. 336.

176. Inventory of S. Hayman, 8 July 1673, NLI, D 13351–13422/30; Barnard, 'Cork settlers', p. 345.

177. Notebook of George Hayman, Somerset CRO, DD/X/HYN 1; will of J. Hayman, 10 April 1777, NLI, D 13351–13422/46.

178. List of refugees from Ireland, 1689, TCD, Ms. 847; Barnard, 'Cork settlers', pp. 347–8.

179. W. Benson to D. Mussenden, 16 April 1755, PRONI, D 354/873; G. Johnston to D. Mussenden, 2 Aug. 1755, PRONI, D 354/742; accounts of D. Mussenden with W. Richardson, 2 and 15 June 1753, PRONI, D 354/597; Barnard, *New anatomy*, pp. 260–1, 268.

180. J. Black, 'Occurrences', s.d. 10 Nov. 1764, PRONI, T 1073/16.

181. A. P. I. Samuels (ed.), *The early life, correspondence and writings of the Rt. Hon. Edmund Burke, LL.D.*, (Cambridge, 1923), p. 315.

182. A. Gailey, 'The Ballyhagan inventories, 1716–1740' *Folk Life*, xv (1977), pp. 36–64; J. R. H. Greeves, 'The will book of Ballyhagan meeting of the Society of Friends', *The Irish Genealogist*, ii (1950), pp. 228–39.

183. A. Gailey, *Rural houses in the north of Ireland* (Edinburgh, 1984); P. Robinson, 'Vernacular housing in Ulster in the seventeenth century', *Ulster Folklife*, xxv (1979), pp. 1–28.

184. Wills and inventories of members of the Ballyhagan Quaker meeting, PRONI, T 1062/50.

185. Inventories of W. Stevenson, 3 May 1717; W. Allen, 19 Dec. 1717, PRONI, T 1062/ 35, 37; cf. C. Gilbert, *English vernacular furniture 1750–1900* (New Haven and London, 1991); C. Kinmonth, *Irish country furniture 1700–1950* (New Haven and London, 1993), pp. 150–71.

186. Will and inventories of W. Richardson, 3 May 1716, PRONI, T 1062/ 29–31.

187. Inventory of R. Greer, 3 Jan. 1730[1], PRONI, T 1062/ 92.

188. Wills and inventories of J. Pearson, [ ], Oct. 1698; W. Coats, 11 [ ] 1697; W. Mortan, 5 May 1708; J. Anderson, 20 Dec. 1718, PRONI, T 1062/ 8–11, 41–2.

189. Inventory of G. Weekliff, 17 Jan. 1718[19]; will and inventory of J. Williamson, 31 Jan. 1723[4]; inventory of R. Greer, 30 Jan. 1730[1], PRONI, T 1062/ 45, 46–9, 92.

190. Will and inventory of J. Scott, 9 March 1728[9], PRONI, T 1062/ 55–8.

191. Inventory of T. Egan, 3 May 1721, BL, Add. Ms. 31,881, ff. 295–6; wills and inventories of J. Pearson, 6 Feb. 1721[2]; J. Hiett, 25 Jan. 1723[4]; J. North, 2 Sep. 1724; J. Deane, 25 Oct. 1724, Friends' Historical Library, Dublin, MM III L.I, pp. 1–10; inventory of J. Eves, 16 June 1729; J. Boardman, 14 May 1741, Friends' Historical Library, Dublin, MM III L.I; Edenderry monthly meeting, wills and inventories, pp. 1–6, 18–20; inventory of D. Darrane, 27 Jan. 1743[4], BL, Add. Ms. 31,882, ff. 141–9; inventory of G. Roche, *c.* 1765, BL, Add. Ms. 19,868, ff. 177–8v; T. C. Barnard, 'The world of goods and County Offaly in the early eighteenth century', in T. O'Neill and W. Nolan (eds), *Offaly: history and society* (Dublin, 1998), pp. 371–92; W. H. Crawford, 'The patron, or festival of St. Kevin at the seven churches, Glendalough, County Wicklow, 1813', *Ulster Folklife*, xxxii (1986) pp. 38–46; W. H. Crawford, 'Provincial town life in the early nineteenth century: an artist's impression', in B. P. Kennedy and R. Gillespie (eds), *Ireland: art into history* (Dublin and Niwort, 1994), pp. 43–59; W. H. Crawford, 'A Ballymena business in the late eighteenth century', in J. Gray and W. McCann (eds), *An uncommon bookman: essays in memory of J. R. R. Adams* (Belfast, 1996), pp. 23–33.

192. Inventory of W. Stowell, 1701, NA, Chancery Pleadings, unidentified materials, box 14.

193. Barnard, *New anatomy*, pp. 268–9.

194. Dublin Public Libraries, Gilbert Ms. 195, p. 16.

195. D. Johnston, account book from 1669, Birr Castle Archives, Ms. A/16; Thrift list of Dublin freemen, Dublin City Archives. In the 1670s he gave £2 to the new King's Hospital, Monck Mason collections, III, part ii, Dublin Public Libraries, Gilbert Ms. 69, p. 380.

196. Will of G. Craford, 2 April 1690, Marsh's Library, Ms. Z2.1.7, item 78.

197. Will of J. Barlow, 8 Feb. 1688[9] Marsh's Library, Ms. Z2. 1.7, item 61.

198. Will of J. Pearson, 6 Feb. 1721[2], Friends' Historical Library, Dublin, MM III L.I, pp. 1–2.

199. *Memoirs of the life, religious experiences and labours . . . of James Gough* (Dublin, 1781), p. 106; R. Greaves, *Dublin's Merchant–Quaker: Anthony Sharp and the community of Friends, 1643–1707* (Stanford, 1998), pp. 209–11; *Some account of the life of Joseph Pike of Cork, . . . who died in the year 1729* (London, 1837), p. 66; M. Pointon, 'Quakerism and visual history, 1650–1800', *Art History*, 20 (1997), pp. 397–431.

200. Memo in Records of Princes' Street Presbyterian Church, Cork Archives Institute, U 87/3.

201. E. Peard to F. Price, *c.* 1740, NLW, Puleston Ms. 3579E.

202. Will and inventory of N. Carter, 1733, Friends' Historical Library, Dublin, MM II. L.II, pp. 80–3.

203. Will and inventory of J. Gill, 22 Nov. 1741, Friends' Historical Library, MM II L.II, pp. 127–45, 212–21; J. Gill, autobiography, 1674–1741, ibid.

204. Inventory of J. Fletcher, 30 Aug. 1745, Friends' Historical Library, Dublin, MM II. L.II, pp. 191–7.

205. Inventory of M. Kelly, 10 Sep. 1722; will of M. Thackeray, 29 Nov. 1728, Friends' Historical Library, Dublin, MM II. L.II, pp. 41, 47–8.

206. Inventory, 1 Feb. 1707[8], NLW, Puleston deeds, no. 631.

207. 'Mallow testamentary records', *Irish Ancestor*, i (1969), p. 52.

208. 'Mallow testamentary records', p. 55.

209. Barnard, *New anatomy*, pp. 77–8, 317.

210. Inventories of J. McKeogh, M. O Loghlen, M. Dwyer, 25 May 1751, Killaloe consistorial records, BL, Add. Mss 31,881, f. 75; 31,882, ff. 187–8, 205–6; Burke, *History of Clonmel*, pp. 328, 331; W. Carrigan, 'Catholic episcopal wills (province of Dublin)', *Archivium Hibernicum*, iv (1915), pp. 68, 75, 77, 87–8, 89–91; Crossle, 'Some records of the Skerrett family', pp. 34–6, 59; J. D. White, 'Extracts from original wills formerly preserved in the consistorial office, Cashel', *Journal of the Kilkenny and South East of Ireland Archaeological Society*, new series, ii (1858–9), p. 319.

211. R. L. Bushman, *The refinement of America: persons, houses, cities* (New York, 1992), pp. 5–138; C. Carson, 'The consumer revolution in colonial British America: why demand?', in C. Carson, R. Hoffman and P. J. Albert (eds), *Of consuming interests: the styles of life in the eighteenth century* (Charlottesville and London, 1994), pp. 483–697; R. Hoffman, *Princes of Ireland, Planters of Maryland: a Carroll saga, 1500–1782* (Chapel Hill, 2000), pp. 98–130; J. P. Horn, 'The bare necessities', *Historical Archaeology*, xxii (1988), pp. 74–91; Horn, *Adapting to a new world*, pp. 293–330; Lindsey, 'Pondering balance', pp. 69–120.

## 4 Goods

1. Abp. W. King to Lady Beresford, 16 Oct. 1712, 2 Dec. 1712; same to Maj.-Gen. R. Gorges, 8 Nov. 1712, 9 Dec. 1712, TCD, Ms. 750/4, pp. 56, 64, 76, 78.

2. Abp. W. King to Maj.-Gen. R. Gorges, 9 Dec. 1712, TCD, Ms. 750/4, p. 78.

3. Abp. W. King to Maj.-Gen. R. Gorges, 13 Nov. 1712, TCD, Ms. 750/4, p. 66.

4. M. Cock, 'The arrival of the dinner service', in P. Glanville (ed.), *Silver* (London, 1996), pp. 38–40.

5.  John Philip Elers was connected with an agent of the East India Company in London. G. Elliott, *John and David Elers and their contemporaries* (London, 1998), pp. 7, 9, 10, 38. Mrs Scriven continued the business of William Scriven, one of the foremost furniture-makers in late-seventeenth-century Dublin. M. Clark, 'Dublin piped water accounts, 1704/5', *Irish Genealogist*, ix (1994), p. 86.

6.  For Tuton, the clockmaker: W. G. Stuart, *Watch and clockmakers in Ireland*, ed. D. A. Boles (Dublin, 2000), p. 100. In 1714, Kean O'Hara paid £8 5s. for a clock from another Dublin maker, William Marshall. NLI, Ms. 36,365/3; Stuart, *Watch and clockmakers*, p. 64.

7.  Abp. W. King, account book, 1700–12, TCD, Ms. 751/2, ff. 80–100.

8.  Abp. W. King, account books, 1700–12, s. d. July 1709, Aug. 1710, TCD, Ms. 751/2, ff. 227v, 252; 1715–23, s.d. April 1721, TCD, Ms. 751/3, f. 143.

9.  Inventory of Lohort Castle, Co. Cork, 14 Oct. 1742, BL, Add. Ms. 47,004A, f. 74; inventory of L. Delamain, 20 Jan. 1763, TCD, Mss 2010–2015/395; R. Edgeworth, accounts, s.d. 10 Jan. 1755, 5 and 20 Nov. 1755, 6 May 1756, 17 May 1765, 16 Oct. 1767, Feb. 1768, NLI, Mss 1521, p. 172; 1522, pp. 61, 65, 140; 1528, p. 225; 1533, p. 245; 1534, p. 127; R. French, accounts, NLI, Ms. 4918, p. 202; inventory, Bp. R. Howard, 21 June 1740, NLI, PC 225; Lord Castle Durrow, bills for glass, 20 April 1748, 10 Aug. 1747, 20 April 1748, NLI, Ms. 11,468; *A catalogue of the household goods, of the late Henry Ingoldsby, Esq.* (Dublin, 1731), p. 8; R. ffolliott, 'Captain Balfour's auction 15th March 1741–2', *Irish Ancestor*, xvi (1984), p. 30.

10.  Inventory of B. Travers, TCD, Ms. 2010–2015/383.

11.  Account of D. Mussenden with W. Richardson, 2 June 1753; G. Johnston to D. Mussenden, 2 Aug. 1755, PRONI, D 354/597 and 742; C. Gilbert, *English vernacular furniture, 1750–1900* (New Haven and London, 1991), pp. 101–7.

12.  J. Coghill to J. Bonnell, 9 July 1726, NLI, PC 435.

13.  M. Ledwidge to W. Smythe, 8 March 1736[7], NLI, PC 436; ffolliott, 'Captain Balfour's auction', pp. 21–31; R. French, accounts, s.d. 26 June 1749, NLI, Ms. 4918, p. 205.

14.  N. Peacock, journal, s.d. 27 Jan. 1742[3], 1 Aug. 1750, NLI, Ms. 16,091.

15.  Abp. W. King, account book, 1700–12, TCD, Ms. 751/2, f. 88.

16.  Sir J. Temple, account book, s.d. 10 June 1673, 8 Dec. 1680, 16 Nov. 1683, 1686, 17 July 1688, 22 Sep. 1688, Southampton UL, BR 7A/1; Clark, 'Dublin piped water accounts, 1704/5', p. 86.

17.  Inventory, Dublin Castle, 1 May 1705, NLI, Ms. 2524.

18.  R. Fitzpatrick, account book, NLI, Ms. 3000, p. 62.

19.  M. Nichols to ?M. Fitzgerald, 10 July 1710, NLI, de Vesci Mss, J/1.

20.  Bills of A. Reyner, 1 Aug. 1710; and of E. Verdon, 22 Dec. 1719, NLI, de Vesci Mss, J/3.

21.  Inventory of R. Vigors, 12 Nov. 1723, NA, 1096/18/15.

22.  Inventory of Lohort Castle, 14 Oct. 1742, BL, Add. Ms. 47,004A, ff. 73–74v; H. Colvill to E. Brice, 26 May 1730, PRONI, D 116/16/7/8.

23.  O. Gallagher to O. St George, 30 July 1724, 22 Sep. 1724, PRO, C 110/46/332, 340.

24.  A. Trevor to G. Waring, 2 Oct. 1703, 17 Nov. 1703, private collection, Co. Down; cf. M. Hill to S. Waring, 26 and 31 July 1699, private collection, Co. Down.

25.  M. Hill to S. Waring, 26 and 31 July 1699, private collection, Co. Down.

26.  W. Benson to D. Mussenden, 16 April 1755, PRONI, D 354/873.

27.  Bills of J. Comack, 8 Nov. 1730; [*c.* 1732]; F. McCinn to A. Murray [1730/1], PRONI, D 2860/11/ 68, 75, 76.

28.  Bp. F. Hutchinson, account book, s.d. 1 Oct. 1733, PRONI, DIO 1/22/2.

29.  Bp. F. Hutchinson, account book, s.d. 1 and 29 Oct. 1733, 26 Nov. 1733, 31 Dec. 1733, PRONI, DIO 1/22/2.

30.  Daybook, Wentworths' Irish estate, s.d. 22 Nov. 1710, Sheffield City Libraries, WWM A 758, p. 234; accounts with T. Wentworth, 1707–13, Sheffield City Libraries, A 762, pp. 39–42; staff book, Wentworths' Irish estates, s.d. 1713–19, Sheffield City Libraries, A 763, pp. 39–43, 125–37; O. Gallagher to O. St George, 30 July 1724, 15 Aug. 1724, 17 Oct. 1724, 15 July 1725, 5 Aug. 1725, PRO, C 110/46, 332, 336, 346, 375–6, 379; O. Gallagher, timber account with O. St George, 1724, PRO, C, 110/46, 236.

31.  O. Gallagher to O. St George, 22 Sep. 1724, PRO, C 110/46, 340.

32.  W. Taylor to Sir J. Perceval, 5 and 28 Oct. 1703, BL, Add. Ms. 46,764A, ff. 34, 38; R. Oliver to L. Clayton, 22 March 1706[7], Surrey Local History Centre, Woking, Brodrick Mss, G 145/box 98/1.

33.  M. Og Boylan, receipt of 14 May 1719, NLI, Ms. 11,468.

34.  Contract with J. Onden (?), 25 June 1741, NLI, Ms. 11,468.

35.  NLI, Ms. 11,468/5. For Coltsman, see above, p. 48.

36.  Account, 13 Aug. 1747, NLI, Ms. 11,467; cf. Simon's bill, 4 Nov. 1732, NLI, Ms. 11,467.

37.  Annesley account book, 1761–6, s.d. 27 April 1762, 1 Oct. 1762, 6 Oct. 1763, 27 March 1764, PRONI, D 1854/8/17.

38.  PRONI, D 1854/8/17, s.d. 21 Dec. 1765. For the Kirchhoffers, see: D. Fitzgerald, Knight of Glin, *A directory of the Dublin furniture trade, 1752–1800* (Dublin, 1993), pp. 9–10; E. McCracken, *The Irish woods since Tudor times* (Newton Abbot, 1971), p. 130.

39.  D. Fitzgerald, Knight of Glin, *Irish furniture* (Dublin, 1978); D. Fitzgerald, Knight of Glin, 'Introduction', in Johnston Antiques, *An exhibition of Irish furniture*, (Dublin, 2000), pp. 1–11.

40.  Barnard, 'Cork settlers', pp. 330–1.

41.  R. A. Anselment (ed.), *The remembrances of Elizabeth Freke, 1671–1714*, Camden Society, 5th series, xviii (2001), pp. 47, 236, 237.

42.  R. Edwards, 'London potters, *c.* 1570–1710', *Journal of Ceramic History*, vi (1974), p. 62; Elliott, *John and David Elers and their contemporaries*, pp. 7, 9, 10, 38.

43.  Inventory, 12 Aug. 1755, Dromana, Villiers–Stuart Mss, T 3131/F/2/17.

44.  S. Richards, *Eighteenth-century ceramics: products for a civilised society* (Manchester, 1999); Hilary Young, *English porcelain, 1745–1795: its makers, design, marketing and consumption* (London, 1999), pp. 154–93.

45.  *The humble memorial of James Maculla, metalist, assay, and touch-master* (n.p., undated, ?1720s).

46.  P. Francis, 'The Belfast potthouse, Carrickfergus clay and the spread of the delftware industry', *Transactions of the English Ceramic Circle*, xv (1994), pp. 267–82; P. Francis, *Irish delftware: an illustrated history* (London, 2000), pp. 11–33.

47.  R. Edgeworth, accounts, s.d. 15 Dec. 1749, NLI, Ms. 1518, p. 190.

48.  R. Edgeworth, accounts, s.d. 10 and 26 March 1756, NLI, Ms. 1522, p. 121.

49.  J. Story, day book, s.d. Jan. 1758, Story Mss, Bingfield, Co. Cavan; Balfour accounts, s.d. 14 Sep. 1763, NLI, Ms. 10,276/9; cf. R. Meehan, 'Delamain pottery excavated from Dublin Castle', *GPA Irish Arts Review Yearbook* (1991–2), p. 154.

50.  M. Reynolds, 'Wedgwood in Dublin, 1772–1777', *Irish Arts Review*, 1, no. 2 (1984), pp. 36–8.

51.  T. Smythe to W. Smythe, 17 Feb. 1756, NLI, PC 448; Francis, *Irish delftware*, p. 55.

52.  Francis, *Irish delftware*, pp. 143–63; P. Francis, *A pottery by the Lagan: Irish creamware from the Downshire pottery, Belfast, 1787–c. 1806* (Belfast, 2001); C. Smith, *The antient and present state of the city and county of Cork*, 2nd edn, 2 vols (Dublin, 1774), i, p. 332.

53.  Inventory and accounts of W. Wynne, esq., NA, Chancery Pleadings, unidentified material, box 7.

54.  Edmonston's account, Jan. 1718[19], PRONI, D1618/8/8; bills of 21 Nov. 1743, 25 May 1744, 6 Aug. 1747, 5 Feb. 1747[8], 5 Aug. 1748, IAA, Castletown deposit, box 52; W. Conner to S. Bernard, 13 Nov. 1753, Cork Archives Institute, Doherty Mss, U/137; L. Clarkson, 'Hospitality, housekeeping and high living in eighteenth-century Ireland', in J. R. Hill and C. Lennon (eds), *Luxury and austerity: Historical Studies, XXI* (Dublin, 1999), p. 97; L. M. Cullen, *Anglo-Irish trade, 1660–1800* (Manchester, 1968), pp. 51, 77, 151–2.

55.  A. Hamilton to Lady Panmure, undated [*c.* 1700], NAS, GD 45/14/238, 79; J. Crofton to W. Smythe, 13 April 1733, NLI, PC 435; P. V. Thompson and D. J. Thompson (eds), *The account books of Jonathan Swift* (Newark and London, 1984), pp. 66, 164.

56.  R. Smythe to W. Smythe, 1 Aug. 1730, Smythe Mss, private collection, Berkshire.

57.  R. Edgeworth, accounts, s.d. 19 and 24 Nov. 1732, NLI, Ms. 1510, p. 34.

58.  R. ffolliott, 'An inventory of Killeen Castle, in 1735–6', *Irish Ancestor*, ix (1977), p. 103; Revd R. Spence, inventory, 1 Sep. 1730, TCD, Ms. 1995–2008/2198, f. 4.

59. Inventories of Bp. S. Digby, Lacken and Abbert, 1720, NLI, French of Monivea Mss, envelope 25.

60. Delany, *Autobiography*, 1st series, iii, p. 158.

61. A. Chetwood to C. Eustace, 14 May 1717, Tickell Mss, private collection, Devon.

62. N. Peacock, journal, s.d. 27 Jan. 1747[8], 10 Feb. 1747[8], 19 March 1749[50], NLI, Ms. 16,091.

63. Peacock, journal, s.d. 16 Nov. 1750, NLI, Ms. 16,091.

64. Inventory of B. Greene, 19 Jan. 1733[4], NA, Chancery Pleadings, unidentified material, box 6.

65. R. Edgeworth, account books, s.d. 6 Dec. 1748, 16 Oct. 1767, 4 Nov. 1768, NLI, Mss 1518, p. 75; 1533, p. 241; 1534, p. 235.

66. Inventory, after 1705, NLI, Ms. 2524.

67. E. Kowaleski-Wallace, *Consuming subjects: women, shopping and business in the eighteenth century* (New York, 1997), pp. 52–69.

68. M. Leathes to W. Leathes, 4 April 1713, n.s, Suffolk CRO, Ipswich, de Mussenden–Leathes Mss, HA 403/1/5, 60; M. Leathes to W. Leathes, 2 Dec. 1713, n.s, Suffolk CRO, Ipswich, de Mussenden–Leathes MSS, HA 403/1/1, 63.

69. F. Chichester to B. T. Balfour, 15 and 30 Dec. 1742; J. Pringle to B. T. Balfour, 25 Aug. 1750, NLI, Ms. 10, 367.

70. T. Smythe to W. Smythe, undated, NLI, PC 436/41.

71. Legg (ed.), *Synge letters*, pp. 294, 300, 303.

72. The Nugents in Dublin were one of several prominent families to possess a service from the factory. Eleven dishes, twenty-four plates, six of them cracked and several chopped, sold for £1 16s. Inventory of Nugent, *c.* 1749, NA, Chancery Pleadings, unidentified material, box 14; account book of the Blakes of Ballyglunin, NA, M. 6933/16, pp. 42–53; Barnard, 'French of Monivea', p. 39.

73. Francis, *Irish delftware*, p. 178.

74. Exports to Ireland, 1692–7, BL, Add. Ms. 20,710, ff. 16v–17, 40, 43v; Chester port book, 1703, PRO, E 190/1365/18; Chester port book, 1715, PRO, E 190/1388/1; Bristol port book, 1714, PRO, E 190/1771/1; list of vessels arriving in Cork, 25 Dec. 1706–3 Jan. 1706[7], National Maritime Museum, Greenwich, Southwell Mss, 18/139.

75. *A list of commodities imported into Ireland* (Dublin, 1752).

76. R. Booth to Mr Raworth, 23 Aug. 1673, Guildhall Library, Ms. 13830/12; list of shipping at Kinsale, 11 May 1704, National Maritime Museum, Greenwich, Southwell Mss, 18/207.

77. R. Hedges to J. Dawson, 8 Dec. 1707, Bodleian, Ms. Top. Ireland C. 2, extracted in *Analecta Hibernica*, i (1930), pp. 6–7.

78. J. Wight, journal, s.d. 20 July 1756, 4 Sep. 1756, Friends' Historical Library, Dublin.

79. E. Spencer to F. Price, 25 April 1758, NLW, Puleston Mss. 3580E.

80. Minutes of the Revenue Commissioners, s.d. 8 Jan. 1755, 1 Oct. 1757, 6 Oct. 1760, PRO, CUST 1/55, ff. 90v, 91v; 1/61, f. 67v; 1/65; f. 106; 5 Geo. II, c. 2; 7 Geo. II c. 2; Statutes, v, pp. 485–92.

81. Minutes of the Revenue Commissioners, s.d. 18 March 1760, PRO, CUST 1/64, f. 16v.

82. J. Wight, journal, s.d. 20 July 1756, Friends' Historical Library, Dublin.

83. Minutes of the Revenue Commissioners, s.d. 26 June 1756, PRO, CUST 1/59, f. 67v.

84. Minutes of the Revenue Commissioners, s.d. 9 May 1760, PRO, CUST 1/64, f. 93v.

85. Minutes of the Revenue Commissioners, s.d. 22 Sep. 1760, PRO, CUST 1/65, f. 60v.

86. J. Wight, journal, s.d. 4 Sep. 1756, Friends' Historical Library, Dublin.

87. F. Hodder to Lord Castlecomer, 29 January 1769, 24 July 1775, NLI, Ms. 35,561.

88. 'Goods to be disposed to sale by inch of candle at their Majestys' custom house, Dublin, 27 April 1693', Evelyn Mss, unbound.

89. J. Pratt, diary, s.d. 10 Oct. 1745, Cloverhill, Co. Cavan, Purdon Mss.

90. M. Ledwidge to W. Smythe, 8 April 1738, NLI, PC 446.

91. R. Edgeworth, accounts, s.d. 14 June 1737, NLI, Ms. 1512, p. 29; Francis, *Irish delftware*, p. 8; A. R. Mountfield, *The illustrated guide to Staffordshire salt-glazed stoneware* (London, 1971), pp. 1, 2, 5, 6, 10.

92. Bill of C. Duplain, IAA, Castletown deposit, box 52; *Faulkner's Dublin Journal*, 13–16 Feb. 1741[2].

93. *Faulkner's Dublin Journal*, 18–22 Oct. 1743. Some of these goods, including the mandarins, appeared at Howth Castle about this time. F. E. Ball, *Howth Castle and its owners, being the fifth part of a history of County Dublin* (Dublin, 1917), pp. 165–6.

94. M. Nichols to Mrs Fitzgerald, 7 March 170[?], 19 May 1710, NLI, de Vesci Mss, J/2.

95. J. Le Hunt to C. Tickell, 9 Dec. 1758, Tickell Mss, private collection, Devon.

96. Inventory of J. Bentley, 12 Dec. 1760, TCD, Ms. 2010–2015/388.

97. S. R. Lowry-Corry, earl of Belmore, *The history of the Corry family of Castlecoole* (London and Dublin, 1891), pp. 268–9.

98. Inventory of Dromana, 12 Aug. 1755, Dromana, Co. Waterford, Villiers–Stuart Mss, T 3131/F/2/17.

99. Bill, NLI, Headfort Mss, F/3/19; A. Cobbe, 'Musical instruments in eighteenth-century Newbridge', in A. Laing (ed.), *Clerics and connoisseurs: an Irish art collection through three centuries* (London, 2001), p. 73.

100. Annesley account book, 1761–6, s.d. 3 Dec. 1763, PRONI, D 1854/8/17.

101. Minutes of the Revenue Commissioners, s.d. 25 Jan. 1755, 19 June 1755, PRO, CUST 1/56, ff. 62, 64v–65, 69v.

102. M. Symner, answers to interrogatories of S. Hartlib, *c.* 1658, Sheffield UL, Hartlib Mss, lxii/45; G. Boate, *Ireland naturall history* (London, 1652), p. 141; T. C. Barnard, *Cromwellian Ireland* (Oxford, 1975), p. 39; T. L. Cooke, *The early history of the town of Birr, or Parsonstown* (Dublin, 1875), pp. 41–3; M. S. D. Westropp, 'Glassmaking in Ireland', *PRIA*, xix, section C (1911), pp. 34–5.

103. Cork and Burlington, accounts, 1672–4, s.d. 21 April 1672, NLI, Ms. 6273; accounts, 1684–91, s.d. 12 Dec. 1691, NLI, Ms. 6300; Bristol port books, 1714–15, PRO, E 1177/1; M. Ledwidge to W. Smythe, 29 Feb. 1743[4], NLI, PC 436; E. Hughes, *North country life in the eighteenth century. II. Cumberland and Westmorland, 1700–1830* (London, 1965), p. 53; Delany, *Autobiography*, 1st series, iii, p. 563.

104. P. Francis, 'The development of lead glass', *Apollo*, February (2000), pp. 47–53; N. Roche, 'Irish eighteenth-century looking glasses: makers, frames and glasses', in B. Austen (ed.), *Irish furniture* (London, 2000), pp. 20–1.

105. J. Agnew, *Belfast merchant families in the seventeenth century* (Dublin, 1996), p. 115; Francis, 'The development of lead glass', pp. 50–1.

106. ffolliott, 'Captain Balfour's auction', p. 30.

107. Account book of D. Johnston from 1669, Birr Castle Archive, Ms. A/16; St J. D. Seymour, 'The household furniture of Castletown-Waller in 1642', *Journal of the North Munster Antiquarian Society*, i (1909–11), p. 258; see above, pp. 87, 116–17.

108. Vigors account book from 1711, s.d. 7 June 1721, Carlow County Library, Vigors Mss.

109. B. T. Balfour accounts, s.d. 20 March 1744[5], NLI, Ms. 11,920.

110. Abp. W. King, account book, 1715–23, s.d. 25 Aug. 1718, Sep. 1718, TCD, Ms. 751/3, ff. 79, 81; R. Edgeworth, accounts, s.d. 29 Jan. 1736[7], NLI, Ms. 1511, p. 143.

111. RIA, Ms. 12 W 24, f. 48v.

112. M. Clarke to W. Smythe, 13 Feb. 1741[2], 12 March 1741[2], NLI, PC 447.

113. Anselment (ed.), *The remembrances of Elizabeth Freke*, p. 47.

114. NA, Crown entry books, County Dublin, 1741–2; ibid., 1742–3; ibid., 1744–5; and *passim*.

115. NA, Crown entry books, County Dublin, 1744–5; ibid., 1745–7. The accused women were acquitted.

116. NA, Crown entry books, County Dublin, 1742–9; J. Kelly (ed.), *Gallows speeches* (Dublin, 2001), pp. 114, 126.

117. Dublin inventories, 1638–9, BL, Add. Ms. 11,687, ff. 121–153v.

118. L. Whyte, *Poems on various subjects, serious and diverting* (Dublin, 1740), p. 70.

119. N. Peacock, journal, s.d. 10 March 1739[40], 1 Feb. 1741[2], 26 April 1744, 12 Sep. 1744, 15 Oct. 1744, NLI, Ms. 16,091.

120. N. Peacock, journal, s.d. 23 May–3 June 1745, NLI, Ms. 16,091.

121. G. Macartney to Sir J. Allen, 27 Sep. 1680, Macartney letterbook, 1679–81, Linen Hall Library, Belfast; Cork and Burlington to W. Congreve, 20 Dec. 1694, Chatsworth, Burlington letterbook, 1694–5; J. Damer to J. Reeves, 16 Jan. 1700[1], Guildhall Library, Ms. 13,823, f. 105; same to F. Brerewood, 28 March 1703, Guildhall Library, Ms. 13,830/1.

122. H. Clifford, 'A commerce with things: the value of precious metalwork in early modern England', in M. Berg and H. Clifford (eds), *Consumers and Luxury: consumer culture in Europe, 1650–1850* (Manchester, 1999), pp. 147–68, 151–2.

123. N. Peacock, journal, s.d. 28 Sep. 1748, 19 July 1750, NLI, Ms. 16,091. For two goldsmiths in Limerick in the 1670s, see part rental of Limerick, *c.* 1670, Petworth, Orrery Mss, general series, 15.

124. N. Peacock, journal, s.d. 4 May 1748, NLI, Ms. 16,091.

125. A. J. H. Sale, 'Ownership and use of silver in Gloucestershire, 1660–1740', *Transactions of the Bristol and Gloucestershire Archaeological Society*, cxiii (1995), pp. 121–49.

126. Will of Gilbert Tarleton, 'gent', 1739, NA, T 11639; RD 87/260/61544, lease of 21 and 22 April 1737; RD 104/440/73818, marriage settlement of John Tarleton and Barbara Mitchell, 25 Aug. 1740, Dorset CRO, D/SHC/81, rentals of Digbys of Geashill.

127. 'Abstracts of Wills', *Irish Ancestor*, ii (1970), p. 123.

128. A. FitzGerald and C. O'Brien, 'The production of silver in late-Georgian Dublin', *Irish Architectural and Decorative Studies*, iv (2001), pp. 9–47; P. Glanville, 'Spoons: the universal luxury', in Glanville (ed.), *Silver*, pp. 22–3.

129. *CARD*, iv, p. 93.

130. *CARD*, iv, p. 243.

131. L. Gosteloe to Lord Cork, 2 Jan. 1660[1], Chatsworth, Lismore Ms. 31/111.

132. T. Gogarty (ed.), *Council book of the corporation of Drogheda. I. 1649–1734* (Drogheda, 1915), p. 130.

133. R. Day (ed.), 'Cooke's Memoirs of Youghal, 1749', *JCHAS*, 2nd series, ix (1903), p. 57. It is illustrated in R. Caulfield (ed.), *The council book of the corporation of Youghal* (Guildford, 1878), plate 7.

134. Minute Book, Goldsmiths' Company, 1686–1731, s.d. 9 Oct. 1701, Assay Office, Dublin Castle; accounts for 1709–10, Masters' accounts, Weavers' Company, 1691–1714, RSAI, Dublin.

135. J. Damer to J. Reeves, 16 Jan. 1700[1], Guildhall Library, Ms. 13,823, f. 105; J. Damer to F. Brerewood, 28 March 1702, Guildhall Library, Ms. 13,830/1; copy of inscription on piece of plate sent to J. Damer, Guildhall Library, Ms. 13,830/2.

136. Cork and Burlington to W. Congreve, 20 Dec. 1694, Chatsworth, Burlington letterbook, 1694–5. The Belfast trader, George Macartney, gratified one of his principal contacts in Dublin by presenting the latter's wife with 'a good piece of plate'. G. Macartney to Sir J. Allen, 27 Sep. 1680, Linen Hall Library, Belfast, Macartney letterbook, 1679–81.

137. Palmerston to R. Roberts, 14 Aug. 1731, Southampton UL, BR, 2/7.

138. [James Corry], *Precedents and abstracts from the Journals of the trustees of the linen and hempen manufactures of Ireland* (Dublin, 1784), p. 97.

139. *Faulkner's Dublin Journal*, 16–20 Feb. 1741[2].

140. Minute Book of Barber-Surgeons' Company, TCD, Ms. 1447/8/1, f. 93.

141. For illustrations: J. Teahan, *Irish silver: recent acquisitions* (Dublin, 1981), p. 62 and plate 42; *Irish silver 1630–1820: Trinity College Dublin* (Dublin, 1971), pp. 55–6; R. Wyse Jackson, *Irish silver* (Cork and Dublin, 1972), plate 61.

142. Cork Freeman's Register, 1656–1741, s.d. 26 June 1685, 11 Aug. 1685, 18 Sep. 1686, 18 Oct. 1690, 15 April 1698, 27 July 1698, 10 July 1703, 20 Aug. 1703, 22 July 1708, 12 Sep. 1727, 3 March 1730[1], 28 July 1732, 2 June 1733, Cork Civic Museum, Fitzgerald Park, Cork; *CARD*, iv, p. 337, 398, 488; v, pp. 22, 54, 152, 376, 460, 475, 520; vi, pp. 34, 103, 129, 179–80, 186, 255, 259–60, 297, 338–9, 368–9, 380, 397, 412, 421, 497–8, 550; vii, pp. 4, 40–1, 167, 188, 280–1, 309, 344, 368, 476, 485, 496; R. Caulfield (ed.), *The council book of the corporation of the city of Cork* (Guildford, 1876), pp. 275, 279; Caulfield (ed.), *Council book of*

*Youghal*, pp. 436, 439; I. Delamer, 'Irish freedom boxes', *Proceedings of the Silver Society*, iv/2 (1983), pp. 18–23; Gogarty (ed.), *Drogheda*, pp. 249, 289, 291, 316, 320, 342, 374, 375; M. Mulcahy (ed.), *Calendar of Kinsale documents*, vi (Kinsale, 1998), p. 96; vii (Kinsale, 1998), pp. 9, 49, 51, 60: G. A. Hayes-McCoy, 'A Galway freedom box of 1771: with a note on corporate freedom', *Journal of the Galway Archaeological and Historical Society*, xix (1940–1), pp. 147–53; G. A. Hayes-McCoy, 'A relic of early Hanoverian rule in Galway', *Journal of the Galway Archaeological and Historical Society*, xxiii (1948–9), pp. 57–67; T. Sinsteden, 'A freedom box for "a hot whiffling puppy": Tighe family silver from Kilkenny', *Irish Arts Review Yearbook*, xvi (2000), pp. 139–41.

143. Transcripts of the documents of the Merchants' Guild, 1438–1824, s.d. 4 July 1684, Dublin Public Libraries, Gilbert Ms. 78, p. 169.

144. *CARD*, iv, pp. 281, 424, 440–1. For the Bandon mace of 1700: Teahan, *Irish silver*, plates 26–26d; T. Sweeney, *Irish Stuart silver: a catalogue raisonné* (Dublin, 1995), pp. 243–4. Also, Mulcahy (ed.), *Kinsale documents*, vii, p. 81; P. D. Vigors, 'Extracts from the old corporation books of New Ross, Co. Wexford', *JRSAI*, 5th series, xi (1901), p. 59.

145. Waterford corporation book, 1700–27, s.d. 30 June 1701; P. McSwiney, 'Georgian Kinsale: garrison and townsfolk', *JCHAS*, xliv (1939), p. 99 and plate ix; Sweeny, *Irish Stuart silver*, p. 244.

146. Minute Book, Goldsmiths' Company, 1686–1731, s.d. 9 May 1701, Assay Office, Dublin Castle.

147. Transcripts of the documents of the Merchants' Guild, 1438–1824, s.d. 12 Jan. 1673[4], 21 April 1707, Dublin Public Libraries, Gilbert Ms. 78, pp. 157, 179.

148. Sweeny, *Irish Stuart silver*, pp. 221–42; J. McDonnell, 'Art and patronage during the penal era', in Maynooth College, *Ecclesiastical art of the penal era* (Maynooth, 1995), pp. 3–51; typescript catalogue of Museum, Mullingar Cathedral, Westmeath.

149. St J. Seymour, *Church plate and parish records, diocese of Cashel and Emly* (Clonmel, 1930); C. A. Webster, *The church plate of the diocese of Cork, Cloyne and Ross* (Cork, 1909).

150. Bills of J. Curphy and J. Salmon, 10 Jan. 1760, NLI, Ms. 10,276/3; Mulcahy (ed.), *Kinsale documents*, iii, pp. 70, 77, 87; vi, pp. 41, 63, 65.

151. Abp. W. King, account book, 1700–12, s.d. 16 Aug. 1706, TCD, Ms. 751/2, f. 107; bill of J. Banfield, 2 July 1739; bill of D. Phelan, 13 June 1732, NLI, Ms. 11,467; bill of W. Hollis for exchange of pewter and making a dozen new plates, NLI, Ms. 11,468/6; list of pewter on back of E. Cooke to Mrs Sweet, 6 July 1727, Cooke Mss, Maidenhall, Co. Kilkenny.

152. Inventory of S. Hayman, 8 July 1673, NLI, D 13,351–13,422, item 31.

153. Account book of D. Johnston, from 1669, Birr Castle, Ms. A/16.

154. Notebook of steward of Bp. T. Hackett, s.d. 24 Aug. 1674, PRONI, D 2056/1.

155. List of pewter, 10 July 1691, NLI, Ms. 36,384; Abp. W. King, account book, s.d. 14 Sep. 1706, TCD, Ms. 751/2, f. 159.

156. Inventory of P. Marsh, 4 May 1741, NA, Chancery Pleadings, unidentified material, box 31.

157. J. Smith, accounts on behalf of Bp. Charles Carr, from 1716, PRONI, D 668/D/1, p. 19; bill of J. Maculla with A. Brabazon, 14 July 1721, Barber Mss, private collection, London, box III; account of things left in the St Georges' Dublin kitchen, July 1724, PRO, C 110/46, 228; bills of D. and W. Molyneux, 29 March 1743, 12 Dec. 1743; of F. Smith, 3 Oct. 1743; of Anne Ashley, 6 Aug. 1747; of E. Burroughs, 16 Dec. 1748, with W. Conolly, IAA, Castletown deposit, box 52; account book of Bp. F. Hutchinson, from 1729, s.d. 15 April 1734, 20 May 1734, PRONI, DIO 1/22/2; R. Edgeworth, accounts, s.d. 29 March 1765, NLI, Ms. 1528, p. 204.

158. S. Madden, *Reflections and resolutions proper for the gentlemen of Ireland* (Dublin, 1738), p. 63.

159. E. Boyle, countess of Cork and Orrery (ed.), *Orrery Papers*, 2 vols. (London, 1903), i, p. 183; *A letter from Sir Richard Cox, Bart. to Thomas Prior, Esq.* (Dublin, 1749), p. 45.

160. T. Schroder (ed.), *Heritage regained: silver from the Gilbert Collection* (London, 1998), pp. 36–7; E. Taylor, 'Silver for a countess's levée: the Kildare toilet service', *Irish Arts Review Yearbook*, xiv (1998), pp. 115–24.

161. Inventory of Nugent, 1749, NA, Chancery Pleadings, unidentified material, box 14.

162. Barnard, 'Cork settlers', pp. 327–31.

163. H. Clifford, 'A commerce with things', pp. 141–3, 156.

164. C. Carson, 'The consumer revolution in colonial British America: why demand?' in C. Carson, R. Hoffman and P. J. Albert (eds), *Of consuming interests: the styles of life in the eighteenth century* (Charlottesville and London, 1994), pp. 588–9; Clifford, 'A commerce with things', p. 151; L. M. Cullen, 'Landlords, bankers and merchants: the early Irish banking world, 1700–1820', *Hermathena*, cxxxv (1983), pp. 25–41; S. Quinn, 'Balances and goldsmith bankers: the co-ordination and control of inter-banker debt clearing in seventeenth-century London', in D. Mitchell (ed.), *Goldsmiths, silversmiths and bankers: innovation and the transfer of skill, 1550–1750* (Stroud, 1995), pp. 53–4.

165. Accounts of Viscount Rosse, 1680–1, s.d. 16 Jan. 1680[1], March 1680[1], Birr Castle, Ms. A/1/143.

166. Sir J. Temple, account book, f. 102, and s.d. 1 July 1675, 27 July 1678, 7 June 1687, Southampton UL, BR 7A/1.

167. Silver sold to T. Bolton, 29 July 1707, NLI, Ms. 2521, f. 212v.

168. J. Leathes to W. Leathes, 16 Feb. 1714[15], Suffolk CRO, Ipswich, de Mussenden–Leathes Mss, HA 403/1/6, 17.

169. Inventory of J. Winslow, *c.* 1724, NA, Chancery Pleadings, unidentified material, box 52; inventory of E. Davis, 12 Feb. 1746[7], TCD, Ms. 2012/129.

170. FitzGerald and O'Brien, 'The production of silver', pp. 9–47

171. Will of Sir J. Ware, 10 Aug. 1665, NLI, Ms. 115, f. 10.

172. Abp. W. King, account book, 1715–23, s.d. July 1716, Sep. 1718, TCD, Ms. 751/3, ff. 29, 81v; C. Naper to W. Smythe, 11 May 1740, NLI, PC 436; receipt, 1749, PRONI, D 619/12/A/95; Legg (ed.), *Synge letters*, pp. 87, 173, 265, 386, 488.

173. D. Lawder to Lord Brandon, 10 April 1762, TCD, Ms. 3821/248.

174. 'Testamentary records from Lettice Evoryna O'Hanlon of Orior', *Irish Genealogist*, ii (1943–55), pp. 180–2.

175. Will of 'Dame' Elizabeth Parsons, 26 Nov. 1739, Birr Castle, B/1/12.

176. I. M. Young, *300 years in Inishowen* (Belfast, 1929), pp. 332, 336.

177. Will of E. Singleton, 15 Aug. 1709, NLI, reports on private collections, no. 195, p. 1976.

178. Will of Anne, Viscountess Midleton, 10 July 1746, Denbighshire Record Office, DD/BK/I, 336.

179. M. Pointon, *Strategies for showing: women, possessions and representations in English visual culture, 1665–1800* (Oxford, 1997), pp. 32–49, 396–7; M. Pointon, 'Jewellery in eighteenth-century England', in M. Berg and H. Clifford (eds), *Consumers and luxury: consumer culture in Europe 1650–1850* (Manchester, 1999), pp. 120–42.

180. Will of Mary Pomeroy, 29 Feb. 1715[16], PRONI, T 2954/2/1.

181. Codicil to will of J. Bulkeley, 6 Aug. 1718, NLI, PC 435.

182. O. Gallagher to O. St George, 13 April 1725, PRO, C 110/46, 362.

183. Will of Mary St George, 18 Aug. 1746, PRONI, D 235/23.

184. B. B. Butler, 'Lady Arbella Denny, 1707–1792', *Dublin Historical Record*, ix (1946–7) p. 19.

185. 'Mrs Bonnell's disposition of plate', before 1745, 'Bonnell receipts', Smythe of Barbavilla Mss, private collection, Berkshire.

186. Barnard, 'Cork settlers', p. 327.

187. R. Edgeworth, account books, s.d. 9 and 10 May 1743, NLI, Ms. 1516, pp. 30, 31.

188. E. Spencer to F. Price, 29 May 1744, NLW, Puleston Ms. 3580E.

189. T. Kingsbury to F. Price, 19 Nov. 1743, NLW, Puleston Ms. 3584E.

190. Lady A. Crosbie to W. Crosbie, 6 Jan. 1732[3], NLI, Talbot–Crosbie Mss, folder 55.

191. NLI, report of private collections, no. 381 (Walker of Fonthill Abbey, Rathfarnham, Co. Dublin), p. 2716.

192. Bill of R. Calderwood, Chatsworth, Devonshire letters, 1755, box, 260.418.

193.  T. Medlycott to E. Southwell, 21 Jan. 1717[18], 30 March 1721, 12 May 1721, 3 Aug. 1721, BL, Add. Ms. 34,778, ff. 26v, 32, 44v, 82v.

194.  Balfour accounts, NLI, Ms. 11,922, ff. 64v, 99v. Captain Harry Balfour's silver, kept in his Dublin house, was valued in 1741 at £561, and constituted about 60 per cent of the worth of his possessions. NLI, Ms. 9534, ff. 69–70; 10, 279.

195.  V & A, Garrard Ledgers, George Wickes, 'Gentlemen's Ledgers 1740–1748', p. 65. I am grateful to Helen Clifford for this reference.

196.  [T. Prior], *A list of the absentees of Ireland* (Dublin, 1729), p. 7: rental of Dungannon, 1745 (worth £1,580 p.a.), PRONI, D 235/20.

197.  Bill of goods bought in England by O. St George, PRO, C 110/46, 195.

198.  Receipts and accounts, April 1700, 19 June 1700, 30 July 1703, 22 April 1710, 7 Oct. 1714, 11 and 30 April 1715, 13 May 1715, 21 and 30 Sep. 1715, 10 Oct. 1715 (bis), 21, 22 Oct. 1715 (bis), 28 April 1719, 9 June 1719, PRO, C 110/46, 125, 148, 149, 151–5, 165, 168, 169, 171–8, 213, 215, 899; D. Guillaume to O. St George, 9 July 1717, 14 Sep. 1717, PRO, C 110/46, 204–5, 210.

199.  These costly items did not long stay with the Meaths, but were acquired after 1715 by the Prince of Wales. J. F. Hayward, *Huguenot Silver in England, 1688–1727* (London, 1959), pp. 35, 37, 38, plates 23 and 27.

200.  Receipts and accounts, 10 July 1708, 20 Oct. 1708, 18 and 21 April 1718, and undated, PRO, C 110/46, 133, 136, 157–61, 180, 182v, 212, 226.

201.  List of silver, PRO, C 110/46, 179. For Bolton, see too: D. M. Beaumont, 'The Gentry of the King's and Queen's Counties: Protestant landed society, 1690–1760', unpublished Ph.D. thesis, TCD, 2 vols (1999), i, p. 244.

202.  Receipt for silver teapot, PRO, C 110/46/162.

203.  M. Nichols to Mrs Fitzgerald, 11 Aug. 1709, NLI, de Vesci Mss, J/8; A. Caulfield to K. O'Hara, 28 Feb. 1703[4], NLI, Ms. 20,388. A portrait of Mrs Pool by Garret Morphy was sold by de Vere in Dublin in July 2000.

204.  D. Guillaume to O. St George, 9 Aug. 1717, PRO, C 110/46/207. Cadogan had vestigial Irish links.

205.  D. Guillaume to O. St George, 9 July 1717; F. Fox to O. St George, 12 Sep. 1717, PRO, C 110/46/207, 204–5, 208.

206.  Contract with P. Gervais, 10 Feb. 1717[18], PRO, C 110/46, 198.

207.  Account, 28 March 1729, PRO, C 110/46, 225.

208.  C. O'Hara, journal, NLI, Ms. 20,389, 10/13. For the rise of ices: P. Camporesi, *Exotic brew: the art of living in the age of the enlightenment* (Oxford, 1998), pp. 70, 72, 121; E. David, *Harvest of the cold months: the social history of ice and ices* (London, 1994); R. Hildyard, 'Ice cream', in P. Glanville and H. Young (eds), *Elegant eating: four hundred years of dining in style* (London, 2002), pp. 86–8.

209.  T. Knox to Lady Anne Murray, 29 March 1700, PRONI, D 2860/4/7.

210.  T. Knox to J. Murray, 31 May 1700 PRONI, D 2860/4/8.

211.  R. Curtis to Lady Ardglass, 1 Sep. 1688, 20 Oct. 1689, PRONI, D 970/1, 24, 25; W. Fitzherbert to Lady Ardglass, 7 Sep. 1689, PRONI, D 970/1, 33; A. Hamilton to Lady Panmure, 7 Sep. 1697, NAS, GD 45/14/238, 14.

212.  Will of O. St George, proved, 7 May 1731, PRO, PROB 6/664/132.

213.  Barnard, *New anatomy*, p. 56; GEC, *Complete peerage*, vi, pp. 426–9; M. D. C. Bolton, *Headfort House* (Kells, [1999]).

214.  John Lund.

215.  List of plate, [1717], PRO, C 110/46, 139–40; receipt of 4 March 1716[17], PRO, C 110/46, 200; bills of Mrs Gerard, 23 May 1717, 29 June 1717, PRO, C 110/46, 201–2.

216.  Bill of John Briscoe, 25 April 1741, NLI, Ms. 11,467.

217.  The introduction of the distinctive Irish 'dish rings' is normally dated between 1732 and 1740: D. Bennett, *Collecting Irish silver* (London, 1984), p. 47; Wyse Jackson, *Irish silver*, p. 43; *Irish silver 1630–1820*,

p. 43; M. S. D. Westropp, *National Museum of Ireland. General Guide to the Art Collections. Metal work and silver* (Dublin, 1934), pp. 24–5.

218. Taylors of Headfort, account book, NLI, Ms. 25,386, openings 7, 54 (loose), 160, 161. For an illustration of an Irish lemon strainer of 1715: John Teahan, *National Museum of Ireland. Irish silver: a guide to the exhibition* (Dublin, 1979), plate 13a.

219. For a similarly massive piece by these same makers: Christie's, 19 Oct. 2001.

220. Bill of Ann Craig and John Neville with Bp. R. Howard [1738], NLI, PC 225. Cf. M. Dolley and E. George, 'A George II silver basket associated with Bishop Clayton of Clogher', *Clogher Record*, vii (1971–2), pp. 447–8.

221. J. Smith, accounts with Bp. C. Carr, from 1716, PRONI, D 668/D/1, p. 19. For criticism of Carr, Bp. E. Synge to Abp. W. Wake, 17 April 1716, Christ Church, Oxford, Wake Mss 12/37.

222. S. Digby, inventories of 1720, note of 18–19 April 1720, account of John Digby, 13 March 1722[3], NLI, French of Monivea Mss, envelope 26; memo of Patrick French [1720]; W. G. Strickland, *A dictionary of Irish artists*, 2 vols (Dublin and London, 1913), i, pp. 227–8.

223. C. Casey and A. Rowan, *The Buildings of Ireland. North Leinster* (London, 1993), pp. 313–17; Bolton, *Headfort House*.

224. 'Testamentary records from Lettice Evoryna O'Hanlon of Orior', pp. 180–2.

225. Kildare inventory, 26 May 1663, NLI, Ms. 18,996; R. Southwell to T. Southwell, 18 Nov. 1662, NUI, Cork, Boole Library, Kinsale manorial papers, 1662–1665, U/20.

226. List of plate, 4 Jan. 1689[90], BL, Add. Ms. 28,939, ff. 1–4; account of plate, 1 May 1705, NLI, Ms. 2524.

227. Grandison silver, Villiers–Stuart Mss, Dromana, T. 3131/F/2/5.

228. Inventory of Cornelius O'Callaghan, 1 Dec. 1737, South Tipperary Museum, Clonmel, Acc. 1985.65.

229. Paull account book, NLI, Ms. 12,938, at back.

230. R. Edgeworth, accounts, s.d. 23 Feb. 1724[5], NLI, Ms. 1508, p. 154.

231. R. Edgeworth, accounts, s.d. 13–14 July 1725, NLI, Ms. 1509, p. 25.

232. R. Edgeworth, accounts, s.d. 4 June 1733, NLI, Ms. 1510, p. 74.

233. R. Edgeworth, accounts, s.d. 8 March 1733[4], NLI, Ms. 1510, p. 102. For Kinnersley: Bennett, *Collecting Irish silver*, p. 147.

234. R. Edgeworth, accounts, s.d. 9 and 10 May 1743, NLI, Ms. 1516, note at back.

235. R. Edgeworth, accounts, s.d. 9 May 1743, NLI, Ms. 1516.

236. R. Edgeworth, accounts, s.d. 20 Nov. 1755, 1 Dec. 1755, NLI, Ms. 1516.

237. R. Edgeworth, accounts, s.d. 17 Nov. 1755, 11 Dec. 1755, 1 May 1758, 23 March 1767, 14 Feb. 1769, NLI, Ms. 1516.

238. R. Edgeworth, accounts, s.d. 4 May 1759, NLI, Ms. 1521, p. 71.

239. R. Edgeworth, accounts, s.d. May 1756, NLI, Ms. 1522, p. 140.

240. R. Edgeworth, accounts, s.d. 23 Dec. 1769, NLI, Ms. 1535, p. 288.

241. Carson, 'The consumer revolution in colonial British America: Why demand?', pp. 483–697, 600.

242. R. Edgeworth accounts, s.d. 6 Jan. 1758, NLI, Ms. 1524, p. 52.

243. Account of J. Williamson with C. O'Hara, 20 Nov. 1728, NLI, Ms. 36,365/5; M. Connor to Lord Brandon, 5 Aug. 1762, NLI, Talbot–Crosbie Mss, folder 67.

244. Accounts of Herbert's executors, 1760; book of executors' accounts, 1760, NA, M. 1854 (iv); inventories of J. Bentley, 12 Dec. 1760, Revd R. McClelland, 8 April 1761, L. Delamain, 20 Jan. 1763, TCD, Mss 2010–2015/391, 388, 395; inventory of Dr J. McKeogh, 25 May 1751, BL, Add. Ms. 31,882, ff. 187–188v.

245. Will of Sir James Ware, 10 Aug. 1665, NLI, Ms. 115, f. 10; will of Thomas Flower, 4 May 1700, Southampton UL, BR/138, B.91; will of J. Gill, 22 Nov. 1741, Friends' Historical Library, Dublin, MM II L.2, pp. 127–45, 212–21; memoir of J. Brown, Brown–Southwell Mss, Rathkeale.

246. P. Melvin, 'The Galway tribes as landowners and gentry', in G. Moran and R. Gillespie (eds), *Galway: history and society* (Dublin, 1996), pp. 324–30, 359.

247. Account book of the Blakes of Ballyglunin, NA, M. 6933/16, pp. 42–53.

248. Inventories from diocese of Killaloe, 18th century, Killaloe consistorial records, BL, Add. Mss. 31,881–2; W. P. Burke, *History of Clonmel* (Waterford, 1907), pp. 328, 330; P. Crossle, 'Some records of the Skerrett family', *Journal of the Galway Archaeological and Historical Society*, xv (1931–3), pp. 35–6, 49; J. D. White, 'Extracts from original wills formerly preserved in the consistorial office, Cashel', *Journal of the Kilkenny and South-East of Ireland Archaeological Society*, new series, ii (1858–9), p. 319.

249. W. Carrigan, 'Catholic episcopal wills (province of Dublin)', *Archivium Hibernicum*, iv (1915), pp. 68, 75, 77, 87, 89–90, 91.

250. D. Dickson, *New foundations: Ireland, 1660–1800* (Dublin, 1987), pp. 97–8.

251. Imports into Ireland from London and its outports, 1692–5, BL, Add. Ms. 20,710, ff. 16v–17.

252. R. French, account book, s.d. 28 Feb. 1747[8], NLI, Ms. 4919, f. 128v.

253. FitzGerald and O'Brien, 'The production of silver', pp. 39, 45.

254. Lady T. Crosbie to Lady A. Bligh [1746], PRONI, D 2092/1/6, printed in D. Fitzgerald, Knight of Glin, 'Three eighteenth-century letters of Lady Theodosia Crosbie's', *Journal of the Kerry Archaeological and Historical Society*, xvii (1984), pp. 76–8; Barnard, *New anatomy*, pp. 72–3.

## 5  Pictures

1. M. Pilkington, *Poems on several occasions* (Dublin, 1730), p. 51.

2. G. S. Cotter, *Poems, consisting of odes, songs, pastorals, satyrs, &c.* 2 vols (Cork, 1788), i, pp. 139–40.

3. Beaumont Brenan, *The painter's breakfast. A dramatick satyr* (Dublin, 1756); Crookshank and Glin, *Ireland's painters*, pp. 53–4.

4. B. Bryant, 'Matthew Pilkington and *The Gentleman's and Connoisseur's Dictionary of Painters* of 1770: a landmark in art history', in A. Laing (ed.), *Clerics and connoisseurs: the Rev. Matthew Pilkington, the Cobbe family and the fortunes of an Irish art collection through three centuries* (London, 2001), pp. 52–62.

5. Tholsel records, Dublin, BL, Add. Ms. 11,687; J. Walton, 'The household effects of a Waterford merchant family in 1640', *JCHAS*, lxxxiii (1978), pp. 99–105; 'Abstracts of wills', *Irish Ancestor*, ii (1970), p. 124.

6. Inventory of F. Barker, 29 March 1639, BL, Add. Ms. 11,687, f. 137v.

7. Inventories of J. Conran and Mrs S. Darworthy, BL, Add. Ms. 11,687, ff. 142v, 145.

8. Inventories of H. Penn, 21 March 1638, and G. Hilliard, 7 May 1639, BL, Add. Ms. 11,687, ff. 140v, 143–143v.

9. J. Fenlon, *The Ormonde picture collection* (Dublin, 2001).

10. Ormond accounts, Bodleian, Carte Ms. 30, f. 344v.

11. Bodleian, Carte Mss 30, f. 450; 213, ff. 526–7, quoted in R. Gillespie, 'The religion of the first duke of Ormond', in Barnard and Fenlon (eds), *Dukes of Ormonde*, p. 111.

12. Ormond accounts, Bodleian, Carte Ms. 30, f. 344v.

13. Ossory to G. Lane, 31 Oct. 1657, NLI, Ms. 8642/11.

14. T. C. Barnard, 'Introduction: the dukes of Ormonde' in Barnard and Fenlon (eds), *Dukes of Ormonde*, pp. 34–6; J. Fenlon, 'Episodes of magnificence: the material worlds of the dukes of Ormonde', ibid., pp. 144, 154–9; J. Fenlon, 'The duchess of Ormonde's house at Dunmore, County Kilkenny', in J. Kirwan (ed.), *Kilkenny: studies in honour of Margaret M. Phelan* (Kilkenny, 1997), p. 84.

15. Massareene to Newdegate, 8 Nov. 1683, 23 April 1684, Warwickshire CRO, CR 136, B 28.

16. Massareene to Newdegate, 6 Aug. 1679, 27 April 1682, 8 Nov. 1683, Warwickshire CRO, CR 136, B 281, C 284, C 285.

17. W. Petty, notebook, TCD, Ms. 2947, pp. 42, 54.

18. Sir W. Petty to unknown, 30 Dec. 1671, McGill UL, Osler Ms. 7612.

19. Sir W. Petty to Lady Petty, 10 Feb. 1677[8], McGill UL, Osler Ms. 7612; Sir W. Petty to Lady Petty, 5 June 1675, 3 June 1679, Petty papers, 5/28, 44; will of Lady Shelburne, 12 May 1706, BL, Add. Ms. 72,902.

20. HMC, *Egmont Diary*, iii, p. 366; Crookshank and Glin, *Painters of Ireland*, pp. 19, 21, plate 23; N. Figgis and B. Rooney, *Irish paintings in the National Gallery of Ireland, volume 1* (Dublin, 2001), i, pp. 389–93.

21. Account book of Sir J. Temple, s.d. 2 Jan. 1678[9], Southampton UL, BR 7A/1.

22. Account book of Sir J. Temple, s.d. 21 Oct. 1673, 16 Feb. 1675[6], 13 March 1683[4], Southampton UL, BR 7A/1.

23. J. Fenlon, 'The Painter Stainers Companies of Dublin and London, craftsmen and artists, 1670–1740', in J. Fenlon, N. Figgis and C. Marshall (eds), *New perspectives: studies in art history in honour of Anne Crookshank* (Dublin, 1987), pp. 101–8.

24. Barnard, *New anatomy*, pp. 44–5.

25. Barnard, 'What became of Waring?', pp. 185–212.

26. W. Waring to S. Waring, 25 Jan. 1698[99], PRONI, D 695/76.

27. S. Waring to W. Waring, 31 Oct. 1699, private collection, Co. Down; W. G. Strickland, *A dictionary of Irish artists*, 2 vols (Dublin and London, 1913), i, p. 233; W. A. Shaw (ed.), *Letters of denization and acts of naturalization for aliens in England*, Huguenot Society of London, xviii (Lymington, 1911), p. 243.

28. W. Waring to S. Waring, 8 March 1698[9], PRONI, D 695/69; S. Waring to W. Waring, 23 Nov. 1699, private collection, Co. Down.

29. Bp. W. King, account book, 1694–1700, TCD, Ms. 751/1, f. 53.

30. W. Craven, *Colonial American portraiture* (Cambridge, Mass., 1986); M. M. Lovell, 'Painters and their customers: aspects of art and money in eighteenth-century America', in C. Carson, R. Hoffman and P. J. Albert (eds), *Of consuming interests: the style of life in the eighteenth century* (Charlottesville and London, 1994), pp. 284–305; R. H. Saunders and E. G. Miles, *American colonial portraits, 1700–1776* (Washington, DC, 1987).

31. W. Owen to J. Owen, 24 Feb. 1692[3], UCNW, Penrhos Mss, I, 442.

32. L. Lippincott, *Selling art in Georgian London: the rise of Arthur Pond* (New Haven and London, 1983), pp. 36–8; Lovell, 'Painters and their customers', p. 295; J. D. Prown, *John Singleton Copley*, 2 vols (Cambridge, Mass., 1966), i, pp. 79–82.

33. J. Cuffe to Bp. H. Maule, 15 May 1739, Papers of the Physico-Historical Society, Armagh Public Library.

34. J. Lennox to W. Lennox, 10 Aug. 1742, PRONI, D 1449/12/51.

35. A. Langford to E. Owen, 6 May [1737 or 1738], 31 May [1737 or 1738], UCNW, Penrhos Mss, I, 1084, 1087; P. Lord, *The visual culture of Wales: imaging the nation* (Cardiff, 2000), pp. 75, 77–8.

36. E. Dunne to Mrs A. Owen, 26 Aug. 1735, UCNW, Penrhos Mss, I, 890.

37. Lord, *Imaging the nation*, pp. 75, 77–8.

38. J. Blaymires to W. Harris, 19 Jan. 1738[9], 28 April 1739, 16 May 1739, Papers of the Physico-Historical Society, Armagh Public Library.

39. J. Trotter to E. Southwell, 18 April 1757, BL, Add. Ms. 20,131, f. 127v; Crookshank and Glin, *Painters of Ireland*, p. 86; N. Figgis, 'Irish artists and society in eighteenth-century Rome', *Irish Arts Review*, iii/3 (1986), p. 28.

40. M. Craske, *Art in Europe, 1700–1830* (Oxford, 1997), pp. 28–67.

41. Inventory of St James's Square House, June 1685, NLI, Ms. 2522, 89; copy book of Ormond's letters, TCD, Ms. 10,721, ff. 88–9.

42. J. Spranger to J. Bonnell, 10 Jan. 1705[6], NLI, PC 435/1.

43. Figgis, 'Irish artists', p. 30; T. Hodgkinson, 'Christopher Hewetson, an Irish sculptor in Rome', *Walpole Society*, xxxiv (1952–4); B. de Breffni, 'Christopher Hewetson', *Irish Arts Review*, iii/3 (1986), pp. 52–75.

44. D. Alexander, 'The Dublin group: Irish mezzotint engravers in London, 1750–1775', *Quarterly Bulletin of the Irish Georgian Society*, xvi (1973), pp. 73–87; S. Sloman, 'Pickpocketing the rich', in *Pickpocketing the rich: portrait painting in Bath, 1720–1800* (Bath, 2002), pp. 12–13, 52.

45. Abp. W. King, account book, 1700–12, s.d. Dec. 1708, TCD, Ms. 751/2, f. 218; M. Wynne, 'Hugh Howard: Irish portrait painter', *Apollo*, xc (1969), pp. 314–17; A. Crookshank and D. Webb, *Paintings and sculptures in Trinity College Dublin* (Dublin, 1990), pp. 14, 27, 47, 72, 123, 138.

46. R. Smythe to W. Smythe, 20 Sep. 1746, 18 Oct. 1746, 5 April 1748, Smythe of Barbavilla Mss, private collection, Berkshire.

47.  R. Smythe to W. Smythe, 23 Jan. 1747[8], Smythe of Barbavilla Mss, private collection, Berkshire; W. Thompson to R. Smythe, 15 June 1754, 14 March 1778, n.d. [*c.* 1778], NLI, PC 448; Strickland, *Dictionary of Irish artists*, ii, pp. 446–7.

48.  Account of T. Fitzgerald, s.d. 30 Nov. 1715, NLI, de Vesci Mss, J/21.

49.  Edgeworth account book, s.d. 14 May 1754, NLI, Ms. 1521, p. 31; E. Newby, *William Hoare of Bath, R.A., 1707–1792* (Bath, 1990), p. 41; Sloman, 'Pickpocketing the rich', pp. 11, 36–43.

50.  O'Hara account book, s.d. 20 June 1759, NLI, Ms. 16,708, p. 36; A. Smart, *Allan Ramsay, 1713–1784* (Edinburgh, 1992), esp. pp. 25–7.

51.  N. Penny (ed.), *Reynolds* (London, 1986), pp. 186–7, plate 25.

52.  A. Upton to B. Ward, 11 April 1767, PRONI, D 2092/1/8, 117.

53.  M. Leathes to W. Leathes, 3 March 1704[5], 23 Aug. 1713, 18 Nov. 1713, 2, 13 and 19 Dec. 1713, 7 Feb. 1714 (?n.s.), 12 March 1714, 18 April 1714, 9 May 1714, de Mussenden–Leathes Mss, Suffolk CRO, Ipswich, HA/ 403/1/1, 3, 58, 59, 62–4, 66, 69–71, 74.

54.  J. Thorold to W. Cunningham, 14 Aug. 1737, 12 March 1738, n.s, 1 Oct. 1738, 8 Dec. 1738, Smythe of Barbavilla Mss, private collection, Berkshire, folder labelled 'Bonnell receipts'.

55.  S. Benedetti, *The Milltowns: a family reunion* (Dublin, 1997); E. P. Bowron, *Pompeo Batoni and his British patrons* (London, 1982), pp. 9, 27–8, 33, 36–7, 62–4, 66; C. O'Connor, *The pleasing hours: the grand tour of James Caulfield, first earl of Charlemont (1728–1799), traveller, connoisseur and patron of the arts* (Cork, 1999), p. 137; Ulster Museum, *James Stewart of Killymoon. An Irishman on the grand tour, 1766–1768* (Belfast, 1999); M. Wynne, 'The Milltowns as patrons: particularly concerning the picture-collecting of the first two earls', *Apollo*, xcix (1974), pp. 104–111.

56.  W. Cooper to Sir J. Perceval, 13 March 1685[6], BL, Add. Ms. 46,962, f. 236; *CARD*, vi, p. 58.

57.  *The notebooks of George Vertue*, Walpole Society, 6 vols (Oxford, 1930–47), iv, p. 120, quoted by Crookshank and Glin, *Painters of Ireland*, pp. 29–30.

58.  Abp. W. King, account books, 1700–12, s.d. Dec. 1708, TCD, Ms. 751/2, f. 218; 1715–23, s.d. June 1719, TCD, Ms. 751/3, f. 99.

59.  Accounts of Dorset and Devonshire, s.d. 21 July 1738, 24 April 1740, Dublin Public Libraries, Gilbert Ms. 199; R. Sandys to H. Boyle, 6 June 1741, PRONI, D 2707/A/1/11, 73; Crookshank and Glin, *Painters of Ireland*, pp. 46–51.

60.  Accounts of Dorset and Devonshire, 1730–41, Dublin Public Library, Gilbert Ms. 199, s.d. 4 May 1734; S. R. Lowry-Corry, earl of Belmore, *The history of the Corry family of Castlecoole* (London and Dublin, 1891), pp. 268–9.

61.  W. Laffan, '"Through Ancestral Patterns Dance": the Irish portraits at Newbridge House', in Laing (ed.), *Clerics and connoisseurs*, pp. 80–6.

62.  R. Richey, 'Landed society in mid-eighteenth-century County Down', unpublished Ph.D. thesis, Queen's University, Belfast (2000), p. 126.

63.  Accounts of Mary Leigh, *c.* 1705, p. 57, NLI, PC 225.

64.  Elinor O'Hara, account book, 1722–33, NLI, Ms. 36,387, pp. 25, 71.

65.  J. Le Hunte to C. Tickell, 2 Nov. 1758, 9 Dec. 1758, Tickell Mss, private collection, Devon; Crookshank and Glin, *Painters of Ireland*, pp. 72, 73, 75; A. Crookshank and D. Fitzgerald, Knight of Glin, *Irish portraits 1660–1860* (Dublin, 1969), pp. 54–5, 78; P. Caffrey, *John Comerford and the portrait miniature in Ireland, c. 1620–1850* (Dublin, 1999), p. 20; National College of Art and Design, *NCAD 250: drawings 1746–1996* (Dublin, ?1996), pp. 6–7; *Notebook of John Smibert*, Massachusetts Historical Society (Boston, Mass., 1969), p. 83.

66.  E. Dunne to Mrs A. Owen, 26 Aug. 1735, UCNW, Penrhos Mss, I, 890.

67.  M. Jones to J. Bonnell, 1 Dec. [*c.* 1735], NLI, PC 435.

68.  Abp. W. King to F. Annesley, 5 Oct. 1725, 26 Nov. 1725, 11 June 1726; same to Sir H. Sloane, 27 Nov. 1725, TCD, Ms. 750/8, 37, 53, 56, 103.

69.  M. Leathes to W. Leathes, 2 and 13 Dec. 1713, n.s, Suffolk CRO, Ipswich, de Mussenden–Leathes Mss, HA 403/1/1, 63, 66.
70.  Palmerston to W. Flower, 3 March 1732[3], NLI, Ms. 11,478.
71.  M. Coghill to E. Southwell, 27 Sep. 1735, 9 and 28 Oct. 1735, NLI, Ms. 875.
72.  E. Southwell to M. Coghill, 22 Feb. 1734[5], BL, Add. Ms. 21,123, f. 94.
73.  E. Southwell to M. Coghill, 19 March 1734[5], BL, Add. Ms. 21,123, f. 102v.
74.  Crookshank and Glin, *Painters of Ireland*, pp. 34–6.
75.  Wynne, 'Hugh Howard', p. 315.
76.  R. Jocelyn to R. Jocelyn, 31 Dec. 1744, PRONI, Mic.147/3.
77.  K. Conolly to Lady A. Conolly, 9 Feb. 1744[5], IAA, Castletown deposit, box 76.
78.  P. Cashel to Lady A. Conolly, 19 June [1745?], IAA, Castletown deposit, box 76.
79.  A. Hamilton to Lady Panmure, 25 May 1708, NAS, GD 45/14/238, 23; C. Bagshawe to S. Bagshawe, 1 Aug. 1755, 23 Sep. 1755, JRL, B 2/3/ 20, 25; Lady Caldwell to S. Bagshawe, [1755], JRL, B 2/3/277.
80.  E. Cooke to Mrs Sweet, 8 Oct. 1726, Cooke Mss, Maidenhall, Co. Kilkenny.
81.  Lady Petty to T. Waller, 16 Feb. 1674[5], BH 19/341, now BL, Add. Ms. 72,858.
82.  Lord Thomond to Sir D. O'Brien, 22 Oct. 1713; Sir D. O'Brien to Lord Thomond, 12 Nov. 1714, NLI, Inchiquin Mss, no. 908.
83.  E. Button to W. Flower, 5 June 1733, NLI, Ms. 11,475/1.
84.  Bill of Richard Carver, 22 July 1743 (or 1748), NLI, Ms. 11,469/12; F. E. Ball, *Howth and its owners, being the fifth part of a history of County Dublin* (Dublin, 1917), p. 134. For Carver, see E. Black, S. B. Black and W. A. Maguire (eds), *Dreams and traditions: 300 years of British and Irish painting from the collection of the Ulster Museum* (Belfast, 1997), pp. 56–7; Crookshank and Glin, *Painters of Ireland*, p. 111; Figgis and Rooney, *Irish paintings*, pp. 98–100.
85.  W. Fownes, accounts, 1735–6, s.d. 7 April 1736, NLI, Ms. 8801/1. Probably the same painter who portrayed Richard Edgeworth.
86.  M. Jones to J. Bonnell, 14 Nov. [*c.* 1735], NLI, PC 435.
87.  Elinor O'Hara, account book, 1722–33, NLI, Ms. 36,387/7, pp. 25, 71.
88.  Will of Sir J. Ware, 10 Aug. 1665, NLI, Ms. 115, f. 10; will of Thomas Flower, 4 May 1700, Southampton UL, BR/138, B.91.
89.  Will of Henry Dalway, 9 Dec. 1720, PRONI, D 1618/8/14.
90.  Memo by Patrick French on Bishop Simon Digby [*c.* 1720], NLI, French of Monivea papers, envelope 73; will of John Brown of Mount Brown, Co. Limerick, 17 Sep. 1803, Southwell–Brown Mss, Rathkeale, Co. Limerick, box 2, bundle 5(a); draft will of Daniel Mussenden, 18 June 1756, PRONI, D 354/166A.
91.  B.T. Balfour, accounts, NLI, Ms. 9534, f. 79v.
92.  R. Smythe to W. Smythe, 20 Feb. 1741[2], Smythe of Barbavilla Mss, private collection, Berkshire.
93.  Will of Mary Collis, 10 Nov. 1719, NLI, PC 223; J. H. Gebbie (ed.), *Introduction to the Abercorn letters* (Omagh, 1972), p. 284; M. Lenox-Conyngham, *An old Ulster house and the people who lived in it* (Dundalk, 1946), p. 44.
94.  T. Kingsbury to F. Price, 3 and 12 March 1736[7], 31 May 1737, NLW, Puleston Ms. 3584E, 34, 35, 40.
95.  For some early examples: Caffrey, *John Comerford and the portrait miniature in Ireland*, pp. 17–21.
96.  J. Digby to W. Smythe, 21 April 1733, NLI, PC 445; cf. P. Caffrey, *Treasures to hold: Irish and English miniatures 1650–1850* (Dublin, 2000), pp. 16–18, 46–8, 191–2; Caffrey, *John Comerford and the portrait miniature in Ireland*, p. 19.
97.  Inventory of goods delivered to Lady Petty, 22 May 1685; inventory of Sir W. Petty's goods, 16 Dec. 1687, BL, Add. Ms. 72,857/69, 173.
98.  M. Jones to J. Bonnell, 14 Oct. [*c.* 1738], NLI, PC 435.
99.  K. Conolly to J. Bonnell, 26 Aug. 1731, 30 Sep. 1731, NLI, PC 434.

100. P. Ford to Sir J. Hynde Cotton, 9 Jan. 1747[8], NLI, Ms. 17,726; cf. M. Clarke to R. Smythe, 26 Nov. 1763, NLI, PC 447.

101. R. Smythe to W. Smythe, 24 Jan. 1729[30], 7 March 1729[30], Smythe of Barbavilla Mss, private collection, Berkshire.

102. W. Perceval to Lord Perceval, 1 March 1736[7], BL, Add. Ms. 47,151, f. 287.

103. Lord Mount Stewart's tour, NLS, Ms. 9587, ff. 64, 66–7; Minute Book, Greencoat School, s.d. 12 Dec. 1720, St Mary's Church, Shandon, County Cork.

104. Account book of the Incorporated Society, 1733–78, TCD, Ms. 5419, p. 25; L. Whiteside, *A history of the King's Hospital*, 2nd edn (Dublin, 1985), p. 26.

105. Fenlon, *The Ormonde picture collection*.

106. R. Edgeworth, accounts, s.d. 6 March 1732[3], 30 June 1733, NLI, Ms. 1510, pp. 44, 76.

107. R. Edgeworth, accounts, s.d. 10 July 1732, NLI, Ms. 1510, p. 26.

108. R. Edgeworth, accounts, s.d. 7 and 15 March 1737[8], NLI, Ms. 1512, pp. 76, 77.

109. R. Edgeworth, accounts, s.d. 14 May 1754, NLI, Ms. 1521, p. 31; Evelyn Newby, *William Hoare of Bath* (Bath, 1990).

110. R. Edgeworth, accounts, s.d. 14 May 1754, 10 Oct. 1756, NLI, Mss 1521, 1522. For Hoare and Hussey, see Crookshank and Glin, *Painters of Ireland*, p. 44, plates 40, 45, 46.

111. R. Edgeworth, accounts, s.d. 10 Oct. 1756, 13 Dec. 1756, NLI, Ms. 1522, pp. 193, 205.

112. R. Edgeworth, accounts, s.d. 9 Aug. 1758, NLI, Ms. 1524, p. 152.

113. R. Edgeworth, accounts, s.d. 13 May 1756, 7 Feb. 1759, NLI, Mss 1522, p. 150; 1524, p. 249; Figgis and Rooney, *Irish paintings*, pp. 255–63.

114. R. Edgeworth, accounts, s.d. 12 May 1748, NLI, Ms. 1518, p. 29.

115. Katherine, Lady Perceval to Sir J. Perceval, 20 Feb. 1685[6], BL, Add. Ms. 46,962, ff. 221–2.

116. List of those unprovided for, [?1680s], NA, Wyche Ms, 2/161.

117. Elinor O'Hara, account book from 1719, s.d. 2 Oct. 1728, 30 Nov. 1730, NLI, Ms. 36,387/6.

118. An example is item seven in the inventory of Sir Robert Southwell's paintings, 'mainly at King's Weston, Gloucestershire, July 1695', Mellon Center for British Art, Yale University, Ms. 8.

119. Inventories of Bp. S. Digby, 1720, NLI, French of Monivea Mss, envelope 25; Caffrey, *John Comerford and the portrait miniature in Ireland*, p. 18; Strickland, *Painters of Ireland*, i, pp. 277–8.

120. Barnard, 'French of Monivea', pp. 274–5, 282–4.

121. Inventories of Bp. S. Digby, 1720, NLI, French of Monivea Mss, envelope 25; Caffrey, *John Comerford and the portrait miniature in Ireland*, p. 19.

122. W. Butler to Sir D. O'Brien, 2 May 1711, NLI, Inchiquin Mss, no. 2621.

123. Will of Thomas Flower, 4 May 1700, Southampton UL, BR/138, B. 91.

124. Inventory of J. Price, 21 Dec. 1704, NLW, Puleston deeds, no. 6.

125. T. Burgh to W. Smythe, 30 Aug. 1720, NLI, PC 446.

126. D. Dopping to H. Howard, 3 April 1731, NLI, PC 225.

127. R. Edgeworth, accounts, 8 April 1769, 2 Jan. 1770, NLI, Mss 1535, p. 154; 1536, p. 112; A. Crookshank and D. Fitzgerald, Knight of Glin, *The watercolours of Ireland* (London, 1994), p. 74; Figgis and Rooney, *Irish paintings*, pp. 90–1.

128. J. Ferrar, *An history of the city of Limerick* (Limerick, 1767), at end, unpaginated.

129. A. Hamilton to Lady Panmure, 28 Sep. 1692, 9 and 22 April [ ], 27 July [ ], NAS, GD 45/14/238, 4, 59, 62, 68.

130. J. Copping to Sir H. Sloane, 22 Aug. 1741, BL, Sloane Ms. 4057, ff. 68v–69.

131. Crookshank and Glin, *The watercolours of Ireland*, pp. 27–8, 30–1; S. J. Connolly, 'A woman's life in mid-eighteenth-century Ireland: the case of Letitia Bushe', *HJ*, xliii (2000), pp. 433–51.

132. Crookshank and Glin, *The watercolours of Ireland*, pp. 26–7, 29; W. Batson, *Henrietta Johnston* (Charleston, 1991); W. Laffan (ed.), *The sublime and the beautiful: Irish art 1700–1830* (London, 2001), figure 9.

133. Lady A. Denny to Lady Shelburne, 8 Oct. 1770, Bodleian, Ms. Lyell empt. 36.

134. B. B. Butler, 'Lady Arbella Denny, 1707–1792', *Dublin Historical Record*, ix (1946–7), p. 19.

135. K. Sloan, 'Industry from idleness? The rise of the amateur in the eighteenth century', in M. Rosenthal, C. Payne and S. Wilcox (eds), *Prospects for the nation: recent essays in British landscape* (New Haven and London, 1997), pp. 285–306; K. Sloan, 'Drawing – a polite recreation in eighteenth-century England', *Studies in Eighteenth-Century Culture*, xi (1982), pp. 217–40.

136. R. Saunders, 'The development of painting in early Pennsylvania', in Philadelphia Museum of Art, *Worldly goods: the arts of early Pennsylvania* (Philadelphia, 1999), pp. 53–61; Craven, *Colonial American portraiture*; Lord, *Imaging the nation*, pp. 50–78.

137. Bill of Richard Carver, 22 July 1743 (or 1748), NLI, Ms. 11,469/12.

138. E. O'Hara accounts, s.d. 19 Dec. 1763, 18 Jan. and 26 Jan. 1764, PRONI, DIO/22/4A.

139. Loeber, *Architects*, p. 109; D. Ormrod, 'The origins of the London art market, 1660–1730', in D. Ormrod and M. North (eds), *Art markets in Europe, 1400–1800* (Aldershot, 1998), pp. 169, 175; I. Pears, *The discovery of painting: the growth of interest in the arts in England, 1680–1768* (New Haven and London, 1988), esp. ch. 3.

140. Sir R. Southwell, inventory of paintings, July 1695, Mellon Center for British Art, Yale University, Ms. 8.

141. R. Cox to E. Southwell, 6 April 1704, 22 July 1704, BL, Add. Ms. 38,153, ff. 38, 70v.

142. Barnard, 'Introduction: the dukes of Ormonde', and Fenlon, 'Episodes of magnificence', in Barnard and Fenlon (eds), *Dukes of Ormonde*, pp. 36–7, 137–59; accounts of P. Pett, s.d. 6 Aug. 1686, 11 July 1687, NLI, Ms. 2535; inventory of St James's Square house, June 1685, NLI, Ms. 2522, 85; J. Graves, 'Extracts from the household expenses of James, earl of Ossory', *Transactions of the Kilkenny Archaeological Society*, i (1849–51), pp. 418–19.

143. List of pictures in Dublin Castle, *c.* 1705, NLI, Ms. 2524; Fenlon, 'Episodes of magnificence', pp. 148–9.

144. H. Howard to R. Howard, 2 Jan. 1734[5], 20 Nov. 1735, 4 Dec. 1735, NLI, PC 227.

145. Bp. W. Nicolson, journal, s.d. 15 May 1725, Cumbria County Library, Carlisle , notebook xxxvi.

146. W. Leathes to M. Leathes, [ ] June 1721, Suffolk CRO, Ipswich, de Mussenden–Leathes Mss, HA 403/1/5, 211; inventory of M. Leathes's house, Shalford, *c.* 1725, Suffolk CRO, Ipswich de Mussenden–Leathes Mss, HA 403/1/8; inventory of W. Leathes's house, Clarges Street, London, 15 July 1727, Suffolk CRO, Ipswich de Mussenden–Leathes Mss, HA 403/1/7; Barnard, 'What became of Waring?' pp. 205–6; J. H. Druery, *Historical and topographical notices of Great Yarmouth* (London, 1826), pp. 207–10; A. W. Moore, *Dutch and Flemish painting in Norfolk* (London, 1988), pp. 20–1, 72, 111–12; Christ Church Mansion, Ipswich, *The William Leathes Collection. Netherlandish old master paintings from Herringfleet Hall, Suffolk.*

147. M. Leathes to W. Leathes, 18 Nov. 1713, n.s., 13 Dec. 1713, n.s., 7 Feb. 1714, n.s, Suffolk CRO, Ipswich, de Mussenden–Leathes Mss, HA 403/1/1, 62, 66, 69.

148. J. Smythe to W. Smythe, 20 Feb. 1733[4], 17 Feb. 1737[8], 'Thursday, a.m.[1737/8?], NLI, PC 449/28; R. ffolliott, 'The furnishings of a Palladian house in 1742–3: Barbavilla, Co. Westmeath', *Irish Ancestor*, xi (1979), p. 87.

149. S. Molyneux to unknown, 14 Feb. 1712[13], Southampton City Archives, D/M, 1/3, pp. 83–5.

150. S. Molyneux to unknown, 28 Feb. 1712[13], Southampton City Archives, D/M, 1/3, p. 106.

151. 'Itinerarium Londinense', 1761, BL, Add. Ms. 27,951, f. 37v.

152. Ibid., ff. 64–64v. This account suggested that the paintings had suffered before they were willed to Christ Church and subjected to restoration in Oxford. J. Byam Shaw, *Paintings by old masters at Christ Church, Oxford* (London, 1967), pp. 5–9.

153. 'Itinerarium Londinense', 1761, BL, Add. Ms. 27,951, ff. 23, 27v.

154. Ibid, f. 69v; *The Chester guide* (Chester, 1782), p. 47; *The history of the cathedral church at Chester from its foundation to the present time* (London, 1793), pp. 100–1.

155. The five canvases had cost £23 12s. List of plate and pictures bought at auction, PRO, C 110/46, 141.

156. Balfour accounts, NLI, Ms. 11,922, f. 71.

157. K. Sloan, *'A noble art': Amateur artists and drawing masters* (London, 2000), pp. 111–13, 114–15; Caffrey, *John Comerford and the portrait miniature in Ireland*, pp. 20–1.

158. Inventory of Stackallen, NA, 1148/5/3; Lenox-Conyngham, *An Ulster house*, p. 44.

159. Balfour accounts, NLI, Ms. 11,922, ff. 64v, 71.

160. 'Goods still in Dublin Castle', 15 Oct. 1707, NLI, 2521, f. 210; *Dublin Gazette*, 22 July 1707; Crookshank and Glin, *Ireland's painters*, p. 52.

161. Accounts of St Thomas's watch committee, NA, M 4961; Abp. W. King, account book, 1715–1723, s.d. Nov. 1719, TCD, Ms. 751/3, f. 109. In 1715, George Felster was already importing 'English pictures', together with haberdashery and silk, into Dublin from Chester. The low valuation implies that they were prints. Chester port book, 1715, PRO, E 190/1388/1, f. 17v.

162. NA, Crown Entry Books, city of Dublin, 1748–9, s.d. 15 Feb 1748[9]; freeman of city of Dublin, 1748, Thrift list of freemen, Dublin City Archives; *CARD*, viii, pp. 323–4. The catalogue of the library of Erck's descendant is composed almost exclusively of books published after the merchant's death. *Catalogue of books being the libraries of the late Gasper Erck, esq. and another gentleman* ([Dublin, 1806]).

163. F. Haskell, 'The British as collectors', in G. Jackson-Stops (ed.), *The treasure houses of Britain: five hundred years of private patronage and art collecting* (New Haven and London), pp. 50–3; Bryant, 'Matthew Pilkington', p. 59; C. Sebag-Montefiore, 'Collecting in Ireland in the eighteenth century: the historic Cobbe collection in context', in Laing (ed.), *Clerics and connoisseurs*, p. 51.

164. C. Smith, *The antient and present state of the county of Cork*, 2nd edn, 2 vols (Dublin, 1774), i, p. 139; Delany, *Autobiography*, 1st series, ii, p. 625.

165. Brenan, *The painter's breakfast*, p. 1.

166. *A Catalogue of the remainder of the curious collection of original picture by the eminent masters; consigned to Caspar Erck merchant, with a great addition of most valuable pictures lately imported by him. To be sold by auction by Mr. Spring at the Sick-Hall in Crow Street, 4 March 1754* (Dublin, 1754).

167. W. Carey, *Some memoirs of the patronage and progress of the fine arts, in England and Ireland* (London, 1826), pp. 179–86; Crookshank and Glin, *Painters of Ireland*, pp. 69–82; National College of Art and Design, *Drawings 1746–1996*; J. Turpin, *A school of art in Dublin since the eighteenth century* (Dublin, 1995), pp. 1–55.

168. Villiers–Stuart Mss, Dromana, Co. Waterford, T 3131/F/2/16.

169. Inventory of Dromana, 12 Aug. 1755, Villiers–Stuart Mss, Dromana, Co. Waterford, T 3131/F/2/17.

170. T. J. Mulvany, *The life of James Gandon, Esq.* (London, 1846), p. 50. Cf. Lord Mount Stewart's tour, NLS, Ms. 9587, ff. 60v–61, 65, 70, 71.

171. L. Lipking, *The ordering of the arts in eighteenth-century England* (Princeton, 1970); L. Lippincott, 'Expanding on portraiture: the market, the public and the hierarchy of genres in eighteenth-century Britain', in A. Bermingham and J. Brewer (eds), *The consumption of culture, 1600–1800: image, object, text* (London, 1995), pp. 75–85.

172. A. P. I. Samuels (ed.), *The early life, correspondence and writings of the Rt. Hon. Edmund Burke, LL.D.* (Cambridge, 1923), p. 248.

173. B. Cowan, 'Arenas of connoisseurship: auctioning art in later Stuart England', in Ormrod and North (eds), *Art markets in Europe*, p. 161.

174. J. Johnston, *Bishop Berkeley's Querist in historical perspective* (Dundalk, 1970), pp. 130–1; Smith, *Cork*, i, p. 139. For Berkeley's lengthy tour of Italy (including Sicily), see E. Chaney, *The evolution of the grand tour* (London, 1998), pp. 314–76.

175. Delany, *Autobiography*, 1st series, ii, pp. 621, 625; iii, p. 52.

176. W. Henry, 'Hints towards a natural and typographical [sic] history of the Counties Sligo, Donegal, Fermanagh and Lough Erne', NA, M. 2533, pp. 464–5; Carey, *Memoirs of the patronage and progress of the fine arts*, pp. 180–2, 231–2; M. Dunlevy, 'Samuel Madden and the scheme for the encouragement of useful manufactures', in A. Bernelle (ed.), *Decantations: a tribute to Maurice Craig* (Dublin, 1992), pp.

21–8. For the later history of some of the paintings, see Crookshank and Webb, *Paintings and sculptures in Trinity College Dublin*, pp. 158–64.

177. J. Falvey, 'The Church of Ireland episcopate in the eighteenth century', unpublished M.A. thesis, University College, Cork (1995), appendix II, p. 148; Ingamells, *Travellers*, pp. 874–5.

178. Mss. History of Smythe family, pp. 211–21, Glin Castle, Co. Limerick; M. Lenihan, *Limerick: its history and antiquities* (Dublin, 1868), pp. 318, 331.

179. P. Bellori, *Descrizzione delle imagini dipinte de Rafaelle d'Urbino* (Rome, 1695), pressmark L.4.2.32; P. Bellori, *Le vite de' pittori, scultori et architetti moderni* (Rome, 1672), pressmark L.4.3.30; *Biblioteca Italiano o sia notizia de libri rari nella lingua Italiana* (Venice, 1736), pressmark L.4.3.31; F. Mura, *L'abcedario pittorico* (Bologna, 1736), pressmark L.4.3.25; A. Palladio, *I quattro libri* (Venice, 1581), pressmark L.4.2.31; G. P. G. Salodiano, *Di Alberto Durero pittore e geometra* (Venice, 1591), pressmark L.4.2.33.

180. M. Pilkington to Abp. A. Smyth, 29 March 1770, inserted in M. Pilkington, *The gentleman's and connoisseur's dictionary of painters* (London, 1770), Marsh's Library, Dublin, pressmark L.4.2.28.

181. Delany, *Autobiography*, 1st series, ii, pp. 320, 498; Penny (ed.), *Reynolds*, pp. 186–7.

182. J. Anderson, *A genealogical history of the house of Yvery*, 2 vols (London, 1742), ii, pp. 393–4.

183. Sir R. Levinge to Sir J. Rawdon, 2 Nov. 1741, PRONI, D/2924/1, p. 90.

184. Bp. R. Howard to H. Howard, 28 Nov. 1729, NLI, PC 227; D. Clarke, *Thomas Prior 1681–1751: founder of the Royal Dublin Society* (Dublin, 1951).

185. Sir R. Levinge to Sir J. Rawdon, 6 May 1742, PRONI, D/2924/1, p. 97; cf. Ingamells, *Travellers*, pp. 800–1.

186. HMC, *Egmont Diary*, iii, *1739–47*, p. 228; A. Cobbe and T. Friedman, 'James Gibbs and the design of Newbridge House', in Laing (ed.), *Clerics and connoisseurs*, p. 28; 'Catalogue of the historic Cobbe collection', ibid., pp. 93–5, 153–4; Sloan, 'A noble art', p. 70.

187. Lady Vesey to T. Fitzgerald, 7 March 170[?2]; T. Fitzgerald to Lady Vesey, 23 Nov. 1702, NLI, de Vesci Mss, J/2; Legg (ed.), *Synge letters*, p. 52.

188. Brenan, *The painter's breakfast*, pp. 5–6.

189. Delany, *Autobiography*, 1st series, ii, pp. 557, 567–8.

190. K. T. Hoppen, *The common scientist in the seventeenth century: a study of the Dublin Philosophical Society, 1683–1708* (London, 1970); [C. Molyneux], *An account of the family and descendants of Sir Thomas Molyneux* (Evesham, 1820); J. G. Simms, *William Molyneux of Dublin, 1656–1698* (Dublin, 1982).

191. Claudius Gilbert, one of the circle of Howard's contemporaries at Trinity and an ardent collector of medals and coins, had a copy of A. Fountaine, *Numismata Anglo-Saxonica & Anglo-Danica breviter illustrata* (Oxford, 1705): TCD, pressmark SS 2 19.

192. R. Howard to H. Howard, 18 Sep. 1707, NLI, PC 227; Abp. N. Marsh to T. Smith, 17 Sep. 1707, Bodleian, Smith Ms. 52, xxxiv.

193. R. Howard to H. Howard, 11 Jan. 1734[5], NLI, PC 227.

194. Draft will of Robert Howard, *c.* 1713, NLI, PC 225/1; Ormonde's pictures in Dublin Castle, after 1705, NLI, Ms. 2524; inventory of Dublin Castle, after 1713, NLI, Ms. 2521, f. 211; Ormrod, 'The origins of the London art market', pp. 169, 175.

195. H. Howard to R. Howard, 6 Sep. 1726, NLI, PC 227.

196. H. Howard to R. Howard, 11 March 1728[9], and bill, 1 April 1729, NLI, PC 227.

197. H. Howard to R. Howard, 29 Sep. 1733, 8 Nov. 1733, NLI, PC 227; R. Howard to H. Howard, 26 Oct. 1733, NLI, Ms. 12,149.

198. R. Howard to H. Howard, 3 June 1731, 11 Jan. 1734[5], NLI, PC 227.

199. T. C. Barnard, 'Learning, the learned and literacy in Ireland, 1650–1760', in T. Barnard, D. Ó Cróinín and K. Simms (eds), *'A Miracle of Learning': studies in Irish manuscripts and learning. Essays in honour of William O'Sullivan* (Aldershot, 1998), pp. 209–11.

200. H. Howard to R. Howard, 2 Jan. 1734[5], 20 Dec. 1735, NLI, PC 227; will of M. Coghill, 23 March 1735[6], PRO, PROB, 11/695, 74; Barnard, *New anatomy*, pp. 159, 164; A. de L. Kirkpatrick, *Chronicles of the Kirkpatrick family* (London, n.d.), p. 19.

201. D. Dopping to H. Howard, 8 Feb. 1731[2], NLI, PC 225.

202. F. Haskell and N. Penny, *Taste and the Antique* (New Haven and London, 1982), pp. 31–5, 42.

203. Wynne, 'Hugh Howard', pp. 314–17; Crookshank and Webb, *Paintings and sculpture in Trinity College Dublin*, pp. 14, 27, 47, 72, 123, 138.

204. R. Howard to H. Howard, 28 Feb. 1704[5], NLI, PC 227.

205. H. Howard to R. Howard, 17 April 1730, 2 Jan. 1734[5], 20 Nov. 1735, 4 Dec. 1735, NLI, PC 227.

206. D. Chalenor, 'The Rev. John Chalenor', *Irish Ancestor*, xvii (1985), p. 61.

207. J. Bradley, *Drogheda: its topography and medieval layout* (Drogheda, 1997), between pp. 16–17; A. Crookshank, 'Eighteenth-century alterations, improvements and furnishings in St. Michan's Church, Dublin', *Studies*, lxiv (1975), pp. 386–92; Crookshank and Glin, *Painters of Ireland*, pp. 55, 57–61; Crookshank and Glin, *Ireland's painters*, plate 66; J. Harris, *The artist and the country house*, 2nd edn (London, 1985), pp. 148–51; Laffan (ed.), *The sublime and the beautiful*, pp. 44–54.

208. *Irish houses and landscapes* (Belfast, 1963); Harris, *The artist and the country house*, p. 151.

209. Lord, *Imaging the nation*, pp. 50–96.

210. Sir R. Bulkeley to M. Lister, 22 July 1693, 13 April 1697, Bodleian, Lister Ms. 36, ff. 57, 182; *Philosophical Transactions*, xx (1698), pp. 209–23; Hoppen, *The common scientist*, p. 105; M. Pollard, *Dictionary of Members of the Dublin Book Trade, 1550–1800* (London, 2000), pp. 508–9.

211. J. Hall to W. Leathes, [10 May 1705], Suffolk CRO, Ipswich, HA 403/1/7, 14.

212. J. Smythe to W. Smythe, 15 Dec. 1730, NLI, PC 449/21.

213. D. Alexander, *The Dutch mezzotint and England in the seventeenth century* (London, 1977); A. Griffiths, *The print in Stuart Britain, 1603–1690* (London, 1998); S. Nenadic, 'Print collecting and popular culture in eighteenth-century Scotland', *History*, lxxxii (1997), pp. 209–11.

214. H. Howard to R. Howard, 28 Jan. 1728[9], NLI, PC 227.

215. D. Molyneux to R. Howard, 20 June 1736, NLI, PC 225.

216. Will of J. Hall, 5 March 1687[8], PRO, PROB 11/405, 100. Cf. his donations to the new buildings and especially for the embellishment of the new altar. TCD, Ms. 571, f. 4.

217. S. Waring, tour notebook, PRONI, D 695/226, p. [29]; T. Clayton, *The English print, 1688–1802* (New Haven and London, 1997), p. 45.

218. Clayton, *English print*, p. 118.

219. 'Paper of cuts', private collection, Co. Down.

220. Lovell, 'Painters and their customers', pp. 297–305; W. J. Shadwell, *American printmaking: the first 150 years* (Washington, DC, 1969), pp. 16–21.

221. R. Sharp, *The engraved record of the Jacobite movement* (Aldershot and Brookfield, 1996), pp. 56, 187–90; R. M. Elmes, *Catalogue of engraved Irish portraits* (Dublin, [1938]), p. 44.

222. Disbursements, after 1685, NLI, Ms. 2522, p. 178.

223. W. Wogan to E. Southwell, 3 July 1703, 30 Dec. 1703, BL, Add. Ms. 37,673, ff. 1v, 28; Elmes, *Catalogue of engraved Irish portraits*, p. 187.

224. Abp. W. King to F. Annesley, 8 March 1728[9], 3 April 1729, TCD, Ms. 750/9, 113–15.

225. Lady A. Conolly to Lord Strafford, 29 Jan. 1733[4], 26 Feb. 1733[4], BL, Add. Ms. 22,228, ff. 102, 110.

226. H. Howard to R. Howard, 3 Dec. 1737, NLI, PC 227.

227. T. Kingsbury to F. Price, 5 Oct. 1736, NLW, Puleston Ms. 3584E.

228. W. Perceval to Egmont, 16 Aug. 1748; Egmont to W. Perceval, 3 Nov. 1748, BL, Add. Ms. 47,008B, ff. 91, 99v.

229. Edgeworth account books, s.d. 28 May 1756, 8 June 1756, 8 Sep. 1756, NLI, Ms. 1522, pp. 150, 160, 180; cf. Clayton, *English print*, p. 174.

230. E. Black (ed.), *Museums and Galleries of Northern Ireland [Magni]. The catalogue* (Belfast, 2000), pp. 59, 281; Crookshank and Glin, *Painters of Ireland*, p. 40.

231. Dealings of P. Arthur and T. Mahon, 1700, NA, Chancery Pleadings, unidentified material, box 27.

232. Dublin City Archives, C1/J/2/2/110. The small prints were reckoned at 2s. per dozen; the larger at 4s. each dozen.

233. E. McC. Dix, 'An old Dublin stationer's will and inventory', *The Library*, 3rd series, ii (1911), p. 381; Pollard, *Dictionary of Members of the Dublin Book Trade*, p. 261.

234. J. D. White, 'Extracts from original wills formerly preserved in the consistorial office, Cashel', *Journal of the Kilkenny and South-East of Ireland Archaeological Society*, new series, ii (1858–9), p. 319.

235. C. O'Dwyer (ed.), 'Archbishop Butler's Visitation Book', *Archivium Hibernicum*, xxxiii (1975), p. 69.

236. Inventory of B. Grady, 6 Dec. 1741, TCD, Ms. 2010–2015, 371; cf. inventory of Edward Davis, innkeeper, 12 Feb. 1746[7], TCD, Ms. 2010–2015, 129.

237. Lawder of Bonnybegg, account book from 1759, s.d. 26 April 1768, PRONI, D 4123.

238. A. Crotty to Snow, 22 July 1729, Chatsworth, Crotty letter book, 1728–9.

239. J. Pickard to M. White, 29 June 1734; J. Pickard to S. White, 7 July 1736, Pickard letterbook, Dorset CRO, B/BLX, B18.

240. Nenadic, 'Print collecting', p. 205.

241. Goods sold, 27 Oct. 1749, NA, salvaged chancery pleadings, unidentified material, box 14; Nenadic, 'Print collecting', p. 208.

242. Brenan, *The painter's breakfast*, p. 7.

243. Will of W. Whitshed, 3 March 1724[5], Marsh's Library, Ms. Z2.17, item 64.

244. Ball, *Howth and its owners*, p. 165; Belmore, *History of the Corry family*, p. 269.

245. Abp. W. King, account book, 1700–12, s. d. 27 May 1706, TCD, Ms. 751/2, f. 153; E. E. C. Nicholson, 'Consumers and spectators: the public of the political print in eighteenth-century England', *History*, lxxxi (1996), pp. 5–21. For the social orders in Ireland, see Barnard, *New anatomy*, pp. 1–20.

246. *A list of commodities imported into Ireland* (Dublin, 1752).

247. Lord Perceval to P. Perceval, 2 Nov. 1721, BL, Add. Ms. 47,029, f. 79v.

248. Johnson-Liik, *HIP*, v, p. 233; McParland, *Public Architecture*, pp. 119, 187.

249. P. Perceval to Lord Perceval, 16 Oct. 1721, 14 Nov. 1721, 9 Jan. 1721[2], BL, Add. Ms. 47,029, ff. 74v, 87v, 95; Lord Perceval to P. Perceval, 30 Aug. 1721, 22 Jan. 1721[2], BL, Add. Ms. 47,029, ff. 69v, 96v.

250. Lord Perceval to P. Perceval, 27 March 1722, 7 March 1722[3], BL, Add. Ms. 47,029, ff. 110v, 158v–159; Clayton, *English print*, p. 71.

251. H. B. Swanzy and T. G. H. Green, *The family of Green of Youghal, Co. Cork* (n.p, 1902).

252. White, 'Extracts from original wills formerly preserved in the consistorial office, Cashel', p. 319.

253. M. B. Ní Mhurchadha, 'Contending neighbours: society in Fingal, 1603–60', unpublished Ph.D. thesis, NUI, Maynooth (2002), p. 312.

254. Jane Fenlon, 'French influence in late-seventeenth-century portraits', *Irish Arts Review Yearbook*, vi (1989–90), pp. 158–68.

255. It is tempting to speculate that this purchaser may have been the painter William van der Hagen, who worked in the vicinity.

256. Inventory of goods of B. Greene, 19 Jan. 1733[4], NA, salvaged Chancery Pleadings, box 6.

257. Inventory of Mrs M. Dwyer, BL, Add. Ms. 31,882, ff. 205–206v.

258. Inventory of R. Tickell, 25 Nov. 1780, TCD, Ms. 2012/132.

259. Inventory of J. Bentley, 12 Dec. 1760, TCD, Ms. 2010–2015/388; inventory of L. Delamain, 20 Jan. 1763, TCD, Ms. 2010–2015/395.

260. H. Howard to W. Howard, 21 May 1726, NLI, PC 227.

261. Conveyance and inventory of Stackallen from Richard Hamilton to John Fitzmaurice, 1 June 1757, NA, 1148/5/3; cf. A. Rowan and C. Casey, *The Buildings of Ireland. North Leinster* (London, 1993), pp. 485–7.

262. Ball, *Howth and its owners*, frontispiece and pp. 133–4, 164–6.

263. *Records of eighteenth-century domestic architecture*, iv, pp. 3–7.

264. J. A. Oughton, Memoir, NAM, Ms. 8808. 36.1, p. 52.

265. H. MacDonnell, 'A seventeenth-century inventory from Dunluce Castle, Co. Antrim', *JRSAI*, 122 (1992), pp. 117–27; H. MacDonnell, 'Jacobitism and the third and fourth earls of Antrim', *The Glynns*,

xiii (1985), pp. 50–3; J. H. Ohlmeyer, *Civil war and Restoration in three Stuart kingdoms: Randall Mac-Donnell, marquis of Antrim, 1609–1683* (Cambridge, 1993), pp. 61–5, 276.

266. Inventories of Ballymacgarry and Glenarm, 1 and 2 May 1750, PRONI, D. 2977/5/1/5/39.

267. *Irish houses and landscapes*, plate 3; Crookshank and Glin, *Painters of Ireland*, pp. 49, 74–5, 78–9; C. Maxwell, *Country and town in Ireland under the Georges*, 2nd edn (Dundalk, 1949), facing pp. 32–3; V. Pakenham, *The big house in Ireland* (London, 2000), p. 128.

268. Brenan, *The painter's breakfast*, p. 32.

269. Inventory by Richard Harford and Nicholas Higley, 14 Oct. 1749, NA, Chancery Pleadings, box 14. Higley is later recorded as an upholder on Lower Ormond Quay during the 1760s. D. Fitzgerald, Knight of Glin, *A directory of the Dublin furniture trade, 1752–1800* (Dublin, 1993), p. 9.

270. Revd F. Houston, inventory, [*c.* 1750], PRONI, D 668/E/38.

271. Peacock, journal, s.d. 24 May 1743, NLI, Ms. 16,091.

272. Revd F. Houston, inventory, [*c.* 1750], PRONI, D 668/E/38.

273. R. Smythe to W. Smythe, 10 May 1729, Smythe of Barbavilla Mss, private collection, Berkshire.

274. Inventory of Lohort, 14 Oct. 1742, BL, Add. Ms. 47,004A, f. 73.

275. M. Brownell, *The prime minister of taste* (New Haven and London, 2000), pp. 2–7.

276. Crookshank and Webb, *Paintings and sculptures in Trinity College Dublin*, p. 132.

277. Bill of Abraham Walker, 17 March 1743[4], NLI, PC 223(6).

278. B. Ford, 'Richard Wilson in Rome. 1. The Wicklow Wilsons', *Burlington Magazine*, xciv (Nov. 1952), pp. 307–13; D. H. Solkin, *Richard Wilson: the landscape of reaction* (London, 1982), pp. 179–81; Ingamells, *Travellers*, pp. 528–30.

279. O'Connor, *The pleasing hours*; M. McCarthy (ed.), *Lord Charlemont*, (Dublin, 2001).

280. R. Howard, account book, 1748–50, NLI, Ms. 1725; GEC, *Complete peerage*, xii, p. 622; Sothebys, *Catalogue of the choice collection of rare engravings and drawings formed by Hugh Howard at the commencement of the last century*, 12 Dec. 1883.

281. B. Dobrée (ed.), *Letters of Philip Dormer Stanhope, earl of Chesterfield*, 6 vols (London, 1932), iv, p. 1420.

## 6 Park and Garden

1. R. Dudley (ed.), 'The Cheney Letters, 1682–85', *IESH*, xxiii (1996), p. 111.

2. E. Malone to M. Brabazon, 9 Jan. 1715[16]; T. Hewlett to E. Malone, 15 Jan. 1714[15], Barber Mss, private collection, London, box III.

3. S. Waring, notebook 'From Basel to Flanders, 1688'; W. Waring to S. Waring, 13 and 21 Feb. 1696[7], 10 and 17 April 1697, 15 May 1697, 14 Aug. 1697, private collection, Co. Down; S. Waring, travel notebooks, PRONI, D 695/225–9; E. C. Nelson, 'A short treatise of firr-trees . . . (Dublin, 1705) by Samuel Waring', *Archives of Natural History*, xix (1992), pp. 305–6; Barnard, 'What became of Waring?', pp. 185–212.

4. Surveys, sometimes focused on periods earlier than that covered here, include: P. Bowe and K. Lamb, *A history of gardening in Ireland* (Dublin, 1995); D. Fitzgerald, Knight of Glin and E. Malins, *Lost demesnes* (London, 1976); R. Loeber, 'Irish country houses and castles of the late Caroline period: an unremembered past recaptured', *Quarterly Bulletin of the Irish Georgian Society*, xvi (1973), pp. 44–8 ; T. Reeves-Smyth, *Irish gardens and gardening before Cromwell*, Barryscourt Lectures, IV (Kinsale, 1999).

5. C. Hay to Lord Perceval, 1 July 1743, 23 Sep. 1743, 31 Oct. 1743, 3 Nov. 1743, 12 Feb. 1744[5], BL, Add. Ms. 47,007, ff. 97, 106v, 114, 118, 135–46, 154–5.

6. P. Kelly (ed.), 'The improvement of Ireland', *Analecta Hibernica*, 35 (1992), p. 70.

7. A. McRae, *God speed the plough: the representation of agrarian England, 1500–1660* (Cambridge, 1996), pp. 231–99; T. Williamson, *Polite landscapes: gardens and society in eighteenth-century England* (Baltimore, 1995), pp. 2–18; T. Williamson, 'Gardens and society in eighteenth-century England', in S. Lubar

and W. D. Kingery (eds), *History from things: essays on material culture* (Washington, DC and London, 1993), pp. 94–111.

8. J. Verdon, journal, p. 44, Cardiff Central Library, Ms. 4.370; Abp. W. King, account book, 1700–12, s.d. Aug. 1706, TCD, Ms. 751/2, f. 157; R. Molesworth to L. Molesworth, NLI, P 3752; account book of Lord Drogheda, s.d. 21 Aug. 1733, NLI, Ms. 9470; *CSP, Ireland, 1663–5*, pp. 569, 582, 637; Dudley (ed.), 'The Cheney letters', p. 111; J. B. Fox, 'Duck decoys in north County Cork', *Journal of the Mallow Field Club*, ii (1984), pp. 111–20; J. Garry, 'Townland survey of County Louth: supplementary note to the townland survey of Beaulieu', *Journal of the County Louth Archaeological Society*, xxii (1992), pp. 412–13; F. O'Kane, '"Mixing foreign trees with the natives": Irish demesne landscape in the eighteenth century', unpublished Ph.D. thesis, NUI, Dublin, 2 vols (1999), i, pp. 18–63; R. Payne-Gallwey, *The book of duck decoys: their construction, management, and history* (London, 1886), pp. 189–96.

9. John Keogh to S. Molyneux, 22 Dec 1707, Southampton City Archives, Molyneux Mss, D/M, 1/2, 27. Cf. Lady Powerscourt to dowager countess of Orrery, n.d. [1680s], Petworth, general series, 27; K. T. Hoppen, *The common scientist in the seventeenth century: a study of the Dublin Philosophical Society, 1683–1708* (London, 1970), pp. 32–3; R. Gillespie and G. Moran (eds), *Longford: essays in County Longford* (Dublin, 1991), pp. 207–9; E. C. Nelson, 'Sir Arthur Rawdon (1662–1695) of Moira: his life and letters, family and friends, and his Jamaican plants', *Proceedings and Reports of the Belfast Natural History and Philosophical Society*, 2nd series, x (1977–82), pp. 30–52.

10. W. Crosbie to Sir M. Crosbie, 8 Feb. 1757, NLI, Talbot–Crosbie Mss, folder 54; R. Edgeworth, accounts, s.d. 22 Aug. 1764, NLI, Ms. 1528, p. 90; W. H. G. Bagshawe, *The Bagshawes of Ford: a biographical pedigree* (London, 1886), pp. 326–7. For the repute of the pineapple elsewhere: P. Camporesi, *Exotic brew: the art of living in the age of enlightenment* (Oxford, 1998), pp. 85–6; D. D. C. Chambers, *The planters of the English landscape garden* (New Haven and London, 1993), p. 113.

11. S. R. Lowry-Corry, earl of Belmore, *The history of two Ulster manors* (London and Dublin, 1881), p. 164. Cf. T. Dolan, account of Fermanagh, *c.* 1719, NLI, Ms. 2085, p. 111.

12. Minute Book, 1741–6, s.d. 17 Feb. 1742[3], Nov. 1744, RDS; Kelly (ed.), 'Improvement of Ireland', pp. 62–84.

13. But, see: D. Jacques, 'The formal garden', in C. Ridgway and R. Williams (eds.), *Sir John Vanbrugh and landscape architecture in Baroque England, 1690–1730* (Stroud, 2000), pp. 31–48.

14. J. Cuffe to ?W. Harris, 14 Dec. 1738, Armagh Public Library, Papers of the Physico-Historical Society; J. Cuffe, account of Co. Mayo, p. 9, Armagh Public Library, Papers of the Physico-Historical Society.

15. Castle Bernard, account book, 1719–1728, pp. 68, 71, 165, Doherty Mss, Cork Archives Institute, U/137; 'An essay on Sir Robert Meade's fine seat at Dundrum', BL, Egerton Ms. 846A, f. 160; HMC, *Various Collections*, viii, pp. 274–6, 286, 291, 311.

16. E. Cooke to Sir W. Fownes, 15 Dec. 1724, NLI, Ms. 8801/5; 'An essay on Sir Robert Meade's fine seat at Dundrum', BL, Egerton Ms. 846A, f. 162; estimate of A. Brabazon's woods at Kelcarne, Co. Roscommon, 1 July 1724, valued at between £2,200 and £2,400. Barber Mss, private collection, London, box III; return of oak trees at Finnebrogue, Co. Down, 1774, PRONI, D 1556/16/16/10; 'Autobiography of Pole Cosby, of Stradbally, Queen's County, 1703–1737(?)', *Journal of the County Kildare Archaeological Society*, v (1906), p. 92.

17. Mr Swallow, observations of Lord Malton's woods, 1728; J. Lee, 'valuation of the woods in Ireland', 1731, Sheffield City Archives, WWM A 766, p. 9, A 770, pp. 32–46; cf. T. Pakenham, *Meetings with remarkable trees* (London, 2001).

18. Swallow, 'observations', Sheffield City Archives, WWM A 766, p. 11

19. M. Humphreys, *The crisis of community: Montgomeryshire, 1680–1815* (Cardiff, 1996), p. 145.

20. Papers relating of trespasses in Lord Shelburne's woods, *c.* 1697–1729, BL, Add. Ms. 72,903, ff. 29–90.

21. T. Williamson, 'Estate management and landscape design', in Ridgway and Williams (eds), *Vanbrugh and landscape architecture*, pp. 12–30; T. C. Smout (ed.), *Scottish woodland history* (Dalkeith, 1997). Cf. Kelly (ed.), 'Improvement of Ireland', pp. 73–7.

22.  E. McCracken, *The Irish woodlands since Tudor times: their distribution and exploitation* (Newton Abbott, 1971), p. 137; *Schemes from Ireland for the benefit of the body natural, ecclesiastical and politick* (Dublin, 1732), pp. 10–11.

23.  W. Conner to ?Sir W. Abdy, [ ] June 1755, Chatsworth, Conner letterbook.

24.  D. Mussenden to H. Mussenden, 25 May 1734; D. Mussenden to C. Leathes, formerly Mussenden, 12 April 1735, Suffolk CRO, Ipswich, de Mussenden–Leathes Mss, HA 403/1/11, 13, 14.

25.  G. Johnston to D. Mussenden, 7 Nov. 1757, PRONI, D 354/750.

26.  B. Grierson to D. Mussenden, 6 Sep. 1757, PRONI, D 354/680.

27.  D. Mussenden to H. Mussenden, 21 May 1737, Suffolk CRO, Ipswich, de Mussenden–Leathes Mss, HA 403/1/11, 15.

28.  D. Mussenden to H. Mussenden, 25 May 1734, Suffolk CRO, Ipswich, de Mussenden–Leathes Mss, HA 403/1/11, 13; H. Mussenden to D. Mussenden, 5 Nov. 1757, PRONI, D 354/1058.

29.  Sir R. Bulkeley to M. Lister, 15 Feb. 1693[4], Bodleian, Lister Ms. 36, f. 44v.

30.  D. Mussenden to H. Mussenden, 16 Jan. 1743[4], 9 Dec. 1754, 17 Feb. 1759, Suffolk CRO, Ipswich, de Mussenden–Leathes Mss, HA 403/1/11, 21, 22, 26.

31.  'Diary of Anne Cooke', *Journal of the Kildare Archaeological Society*, viii (1916), pp. 216–18.

32.  Hoey, account of Co. Wicklow, Armagh Public Library, Papers of the Physico-Historical Society.

33.  Revd R. Barton to Secretary of the Physico-Historical Society, 18 May 1745, Armagh Public Library, Papers of the Physico-Historical Society.

34.  R. Barton, *Lectures in natural philosophy* (Dublin, 1751), pp. 95n.*, 112–13.

35.  [W. Henry], *An appeal to the people of Ireland* (Dublin, 1747), pp. 8–9.

36.  R. Austen, *A dialogue, familiar discourse and conference between the husbandman and the fruit trees* (Oxford, 1676), sig. *4; J. Evelyn, *Kalendarium Hortense: or the gard'ners almanac* (London, 1664), p. 55; Leonard Meagher, *The mystery of husbandry* (London, 1697), pp. 1–3, 99, 138.

37.  S. Pullein, *Some hints intended to promote the culture of silk-worms in Ireland* (Dublin, 1750); S. Madden, *Reflections and resolutions proper for the gentlemen of Ireland* (Dublin, 1738), pp. 121–2; S. Switzer, *A compendious method for the raising of the Italian broccoli, Spanish cardoon, celeriac, finochi, and other foreign kitchen-vegetables*, 4th edn (London, 1729); M. Thick, '"Superior vegetables": greens and roots in London, 1660–1750', *Food, Culture and History*, i (1993), p. 142.

38.  M. Symner, 'Answers to Hartlib's "interrogatories"', *c.* 1658, Sheffield UL, Hartlib Mss, lxii (45); Minute Book, 1758–61, s.d. 13 March 1760, RDS; C. Smith, 'History of County Limerick', RIA, Ms. 24 G 9, pp. 43–5; T. C. Barnard, *Cromwellian Ireland: government and reform in Ireland, 1649–1660* (Oxford, 1975), p. 239; Joan Thirsk, *Alternative agriculture: a history from the Black Death to the present day* (Oxford, 1997), pp. 105–18.

39.  Minute Book, 1731–3, s.d. 18 Dec. 1731, RDS.

40.  Minute Book, s.d. 20 Jan. 1731[2], RDS.

41.  Minute Book, 1731–3, s.d. 8 June 1732, RDS.

42.  Minute Book, 1731–3, s.d. 21 June 1733, RDS.

43.  Minute Book, 1731–3, s.d. 14 Oct. 1731, 18 Dec. 1731, 6 and 13 Jan. 1731[2], RDS.

44.  Minute Book, 1731–3, s.d. 29 March 1733, 24 May 1733, RDS.

45.  Minute Book, 1733–41, s.d. 16 Jan. 1734[5], 7 Oct. 1738, 8 March 1738[9], 3 April 1740, RDS.

46.  Minute Book, 1741–6, s.d. 17 Nov. 1741, 11 Dec. 1741, 30 May 1745, RDS.

47.  *The Dublin Society's weekly observations* (Dublin, 1739), pp. 4–8.

48.  Ibid., pp. 27–8.

49.  R. Maxwell to E. Brice, 16 Nov. 1736, 23 Aug. 1737, PRONI, D 4718/L1.

50.  Lord Cork's accounts, s.d. 28 Dec. 1661, Chatsworth, Bolton Abbey Ms. 262; Lord Cork and Burlington's accounts, s.d. 31 July 1669, NLI, Ms. 6267; 1678–9, s.d. 26 June 1680, NLI, Ms. 6902; 1684–91, s.d. 31 Aug. 1685, NLI, Ms. 6300; R. Edgeworth, accounts, s.d. 16 July 1735, 3 and 7 Sep. 1736, NLI, Ms. 1511, pp. 55, 127.

51. Joan Thirsk, 'England's provinces. Did they serve or drive material London?', in L. C. Orlin (ed.), *Material London, ca. 1600* (Philadelphia, 2000), pp. 97–108.

52. J. Meyer, *La noblesse bretonne au xviiie siècle*, 2 vols (Paris, 1966), i, pp. 579, 585–6.

53. M. Thick, *The Neat House Gardens: early market gardening around London* (Totnes, 1998); E. Topham, *Letters from Edinburgh; written in the years 1774 and 1775* (London, 1776), pp. 227–8; A. J. Youngson, *The making of classical Edinburgh, 1750–1840* (Edinburgh, 1966), pp. 242–4.

54. T. C. Barnard, 'Gardening, diet and "improvement" in late-seventeenth century Ireland', in Barnard, *Irish Protestant ascents and descents* (Dublin, 2003), pp. 208–34.

55. Ossory to Ormond, 2 July [1664], Bodleian, Carte Ms. 220, f. 151; Glin and Malins, *Lost demesnes*, pp. 6–7; Loeber, 'Irish country houses and castles', p. 46.

56. A. Crotty to J. Coughlan, 1 March 1728[9], Chatsworth, Crotty letterbook, 1728–9.

57. Sir R. Bulkeley to M. Lister, 2 Nov. 1694, 17 Nov. 1696, Bodleian, Lister Ms. 36, ff. 105. 164.

58. M. Humphreys to Devonshire, 25 Nov. 1739, RIA, Ms. 12 F 50.

59. Sir R. Bulkeley to M. Lister, 24 June 1686, Bodleian, Lister Ms. 35, f. 121v; T. C. Barnard, 'Reforming Irish manners', reprinted in Barnard, *Irish Protestant ascents and descents*, pp. 143–78.

60. W. Bulkeley, 'The compleate orchard', Southampton City Archives, D/M, 4/20.

61. Sir R. Bulkeley to M. Lister, 3 and 24 June 1686, Bodleian, Lister Ms. 35, ff. 119, 121.

62. Sir R. Bulkeley, 19 March 1686[7], Bodleian, Lister Ms. 35, f. 116.

63. Sir R. Bulkeley, 1 July 1693, 10 and 25 Aug. 1693, 10 May 1694, Bodleian, Lister Ms. 36, ff. 55v, 61, 63, 95.

64. Thirsk, *Alternative agriculture*, pp. 118–30, 135–9.

65. Sir R. Bulkeley to M. Lister, 19 March 1686[7], Bodleian, Lister Ms. 35, f. 116.

66. Sir R. Bulkeley to M. Lister, 1 July 1693, Bodleian, Lister Ms. 36, f. 55; Sir R. Bulkeley to M. Lister, [*c.* 1694], Bodleian, Lister Ms. 3, ff. 50v, 51.

67. Sir R. Bulkeley to M. Lister, 1 July 1693, Bodleian, Lister Ms. 36, f. 55.

68. Sir R. Bulkeley to M. Lister, 10 Oct. 1698, Bodleian, Lister Ms. 36, f. 213v.

69. Abp. W. King to Sir H. Sloane, 27 Nov. 1725, TCD, Ms. 750/8, 56; Bp. W. King, account book, 1693–1700, s.d. June 1695, March 1696, Oct. 1696, TCD, Ms. 751/1, ff. 77, 96, 97, 116.

70. Bp. W. King, account book, 1693–1700, s.d. 16 July 1693, Nov. 1696, TCD, Ms. 751/1, ff. 16, 120.

71. Bp. W. King, account book, 1693–1700, s.d. March 1696, Oct. 1696, May 1697, Feb. 1697[8], April 1699, TCD, Ms. 751/1, ff. 96, 116, 138, 163, 200; King, account book, 1700–12, s.d. 3 March 1699[1700], TCD, Ms. 751/2, f. 2.

72. Bp. W. King, account book, 1693–1700, s.d. July 1695, June 1699, TCD, Ms. 751/1, ff. 77, 206.

73. Abp. W. King, account book, 1700–12, s.d. Sep. 1708, Oct. 1708, Jan. 1710[11], TCD, Ms. 751/2, ff. 207–9, 262.

74. Abp. W. King, account book, 1700–12, s.d. Jan. 1709[9], TCD, Ms. 751/2, f. 215. 'Belfour', the designer, might be Robert Belford who imported garden seeds through Chester in 1715, Chester port book, 1715, PRO, E 190/1388/1.

75. Abp. W. King, account book, 1700–12, s.d. April 1709, TCD, Ms. 751/2, f. 221; King, account book, s.d. June 1719, TCD, Ms. 751/3, f. 99.

76. Abp. W. King, account book, 1700–12, s.d. May 1709, Aug. 1709, Aug. 1710, TCD, Ms. 751/2, ff. 223, 229v, 252v. By 1719, Roberts's successor, Carter, earned £10 p.a. King, account book, s.d. Dec. 1719, TCD, Ms. 751/3, f. 111.

77. Miscellaneous accounts, 1 Dec. 1695, Headfort Mss, NLI, Ms. 25,300/1.

78. 'An essay on Sir Robert Meade's fine seat at Dundrum', BL, Egerton Ms. 846A, ff. 160–3.

79. T. Birch (ed.), *The state papers of John Thurloe*, 7 vols (London, 1742), vii, pp. 683–4; Williams (ed.), *Correspondence of Swift*, iii, p. 319, iv, pp. 547–9, 556.

80. Bp. R. Howard to H. Howard, 3 June 1731, 10 May 1732, NLI, PC 227; HMC, *Various Collections*, viii, pp. 275–6.

81. B. Rand (ed.), *Berkeley and Swift* (Cambridge, 1914), p. 57; Williams (ed.), *Correspondence of Swift*, v, p. 6.

82.  J. Buchanan to A. Russell, 20 Nov. 1684, NAS, RH 1/2/797.

83.  P. V. Thompson and D. J. Thompson (eds), *The account books of Jonathan Swift* (Newark and London, 1984), pp. 54, 69, 192; Legg (ed.), *Synge letters*, pp. 9, 26, 46, 50, 66, 124, 148, 184, 261, 266, 447–8.

84.  Sir W. Petty to Lady Petty, 27 March 1684, Petty Papers, 5/125; T. Dance to ?Waller, 28 Aug. 1686, Petty Papers, 17, 103.

85.  T. Kingsbury to F. Price, 5 Oct. 1736, NLW, Puleston Ms. 3584E.

86.  C. Williamson to Birde [draft], Caesar Williamson letterbook, p. 24, Marsh's Library, Ms. Z4.5.16.

87.  P. Donnellan to R. Liddell, 12 June 1746; T. Waite to E. Weston, 2 and 4 Aug. 1748, PRONI, T 3019/761, 1090, 1093.

88.  R. Molesworth to L. Molesworth, 29 Jan. 1718[19], NLI, microfilm, p. 3752; HMC, *Various Collections*, viii, pp. 275–6.

89.  R. Edgeworth, accounts, s.d. 20 July 1720, 19 Aug. 1721, 21 May 1725, 27 April 1769, 4 May 1769, NLI, Mss 1507, pp. 30, 42; 1509, p. 21; 1535, pp. 162, 164.

90.  Bp. W. Nicolson, diary, s.d. 11 and 24 Aug. 1719, 18 Sep. 1722, Cumbria County Library, Carlisle.

91.  H. F. Berry, 'Notes from the diary of a Dublin lady in the reign of George II', *JRSAI*, 5th series, viii (1898), p. 142.

92.  *CARD*, ix, pp. 217, 294; R. Dudley, 'St. Stephen's Green: the early years, 1664–1730', *Dublin Historical Record*, liii (2000), pp. 157–79.

93.  *CARD*, xi, p. 321; cf. 'Ant. Constitution', *A short and easy method of reducing the exorbitant pride and arrogance of the city of Dublin* (London, 1748), pp. 43–4.

94.  Lord Mount Stewart, tour journal, NLS, Ms. 9587, f. 63.

95.  G. Talbot to Lord Cork, 14 May 1663, Chatsworth, Lismore Ms. 33/20*; Cork and Burlington, account book, 1686–9, s.d. 2 March 1688[9], NLI, Ms. 6303; R. French, account book, s.d. 3 May 1749, NLI, Ms. 4919, p. 81; *CARD*, iv, p. 286; v, pp. 114, 321, 354; M. Mulcahy, *Calendar of Kinsale documents*, iii (Kinsale, 1994), pp. 101; vi (Kinsale, 1998), p. 5; *A tour through Ireland in several entertaining letters* (London, 1748), pp. 89, 180.

96.  Bp. W. Nicolson, diary, s.d. 6 June 1722, Cumbria County Library, Carlisle.

97.  J. H. Gebbie (ed.), *An introduction to the Abercorn letters* (Omagh, 1972), pp. 22, 50.

98.  *The tricks of the town laid open* (Dublin, *c.* 1750), pp. 34–5.

99.  Abp. W. King, account book, 1700–12, s.d. Nov. 1710, TCD, Ms. 751/2, f. 258.

100. Bowe and Lamb, *A history of gardening in Ireland*, p. 37, quoting earl of Meath, household accounts, Kilruddery House, Co. Wicklow, Ms. E/1/1.

101. R. Shiel to Sir W. Fownes, 25 July 1745, NLI, Ms. 8470; W. Waller to W. Smythe, 1 March 1745[6], NLI, PC 445.

102. Minute Book of the Dublin Florists' Society, RIA, Ms. 24 E 37; E. C. Nelson, 'The Dublin Florists' Club in the mid-eighteenth century', *Garden History*, x (1982), pp. 142–8; R. Duthie, 'English florists' societies and feasts in the seventeenth and first half of the eighteenth centuries', *Garden History*, x (1982), pp. 17–35; R. Duthie, 'Florists' societies and feasts after 1750', *Garden History*, xii (1984), pp. 9–38.

103. P. Ward to W. Smythe, 20 July [1721–30], NLI, PC 444.

104. P. Ward to W. Smythe, 1 May [1721–30], NLI, PC 444; J. B. Leslie, *Derry clergy and parishes* (Enniskillen, 1937), p. 61.

105. J. Digby to W. Smythe, 23 Jan. 1733[4], NLI, PC 445.

106. Lady Petty to A. and H. Petty, 14 Feb. 1684[5], BL, Add. Ms. 72,857/4.

107. A. Hamilton to Lady Panmure, 14 May 170[0], 10 May 1710, NAS, GD 45/14/238, 15, 25.

108. T. Smith, description of the park at Burton, Co. Cork, 1686, BL, Add. Ms. 47,052, f. 6.

109. *Pue's Occurrences*, 6 March 1736[7], 4 April 1738, 3 May 1738, 16 Sep. 1740, *Dublin Daily Advertiser*, 8 March 1737[?8].

110. Charles Evelyn, *The Lady's recreation: or, the third and last part of the Art of Gardening Improv'd* (London, 1717). Cf. J. Laurence, *The fruit-garden kalendar* (London, 1718), p. ii.

111. M. Burgh to W. Smythe, 24 Sep. 1743, 9 Nov. 1745, NLI, PC 446.

112. B. Smythe to W. Smythe, 6 April [1730–3], NLI, PC 448.

113. B. Smythe to W. Smythe, 24 April [?1733], NLI, PC 448; J. Cooley to W. Smythe, 9 Jan. 1731[2], 10 Jan. 1733[4], NLI, PC 436.

114. R. Smythe to W. Smythe, 14 June 1729, 22 Feb. 1730[1], 29 May 1731, 26 June 1731, Smythe of Barbavilla Mss, private collection, Berkshire.

115. R. Smythe to W. Smythe, 18 Dec. 1731, Smythe of Barbavilla Mss, private collection, Berkshire.

116. R. Smythe to W. Smythe, 24 April 1736, 15 May 1736, 23 Oct. 1736, Smythe of Barbavilla Mss, private collection, Berkshire.

117. Bp. E. Smythe to W. Smythe, 28 Aug. 1717, 11 Sep. 1717, NLI, PC 445.

118. R. Smythe to W. Smythe, 15 March 1734[5], 15 Dec. 1739, NLI, PC 445.

119. TCD, Ms. 985.

120. Bp. W. Nicolson, Diary, s.d. 24 Aug. 1719, 18 Sep. 1722, Cumbria County Library, Carlisle, Nicolson diaries, xxxiv, xxxvi; Bp. W. Nicolson, account book, 1723, s.d. 28 Oct. 1723, Cumbria County Library, Carlisle, Nicolson diaries, xxxiv, xxxvi.

121. Bp. W. Nicolson, diary, xxxvi, s.d. 26 May 1722, Cumbria County Library, Carlisle, Nicolson diaries, xxxvi.

122. Legg (ed.), *Synge letters*, pp. 115, 118, 180, 189, 201, 206, 213, 295. Cf. R. Molesworth to L. Molesworth, 28 March 1696, NLI, microfilm, p. 3752.

123. Legg (ed.), *Synge letters*, p. 275.

124. W. Waring to S. Waring, 19 June 1697, private collection, Co. Down; Legg (ed.), *Synge Letters*, pp. 34, 121, 180, 327.

125. W. O'Sullivan, 'Mount Merrion in 1714 – was there a stove house?', *Moorea*, iii (1984), p. 22. An English visitor complained in the 1690s about the impossibility of finding good fruit, despite the large gardens. J. Verdon, journal, p. 45, Cardiff Central Library, Ms. 4.370.

126. John Miller, bill, [1730s or 1740s], NLI, Ms. 11,467; N. Hickey, bill, 19 Oct. 1747, NLI, Ms 36,483/3.

127. E. Welch to Lord Brandon, 2 Oct. 1765, NLI, Talbot–Crosbie Mss, folder 69; R. Smythe to W. Smythe, 20 Sep. 1729, Smythe of Barbavilla Mss, private collection, Berkshire; Legg (ed.), *Synge letters*, pp. 72, 162, 441.

128. Philip Miller, *The gardeners dictionary* (London, 1731).

129. Meyer, *La noblesse bretonne*, i, pp. 581–2.

130. J. Dobbin to Sir W. Fownes, 30 Aug. 1735, NLI, Ms. 8802/4; account for 1735, NLI, Ms. 8801/1; also, catalogue of books at Lohort, Co. Cork, [17 Oct. 1742], BL, Add. Ms. 47,004A, f. 22.

131. J. Dobbin to Sir W. Fownes, 12 July 1735, 18 Sep. 1735, NLI, Ms. 8802/4; H. Brownrigg to Sir W. Fownes, 1 Jan. 1736, n.s., NLI, Ms. 8802/5.

132. Legg (ed.), *Synge letters*, p. 206.

133. Edgeworth account book, s.d. 31 Dec. 1733, 9 Feb. 1733[4], NLI, Ms. 1510, pp. 90, 94.

134. Crown Entry Books, Co. Dublin, 1745–7, NA.

135. F. W. Robertson, *Early Scottish gardeners and their plants, 1650–1750* (East Linton, 2000), pp. 194–5, 202–4.

136. In 1698, the Balfours of Townley Hall paid four shillings for *The English gardener*, s.d. 12 March 1697[8], NLI, Ms. 9536.

137. W. Bulkeley, 'The compleate orchard', Southampton City Archives, D/M, 4/20.

138. S. Molyneux to unknown, 14 Feb. 1712[13], Southampton City Archives, D/M, 1/3, 87–90.

139. H. Honour, *Chinoiserie: the vision of Cathay* (London, 1962), pp. 144–6.

140. Survey of Castle Dillon, *c.* 1705, Southampton City Archives, D/M, 2/1; C. E. B. Brett, *Buildings of County Armagh* (Belfast, 1999), pp. 109–10.

141. F. Hutcheson, *Essay on the nature and conduct of the passions* (Dublin, 1728), treatise 1, pp. 113–14.

142. N. Everett, *The Tory view of landscape* (New Haven and London, 1994); J. D. Hunt, *The figure in the landscape: poetry, painting and gardening during the eighteenth century* (Baltimore, 1977); J. D. Hunt and P. Willis (eds), *The genius of the place: the English landscape garden, 1620–1820* (London, 1975).

143. O'Kane, '"Mixing foreign trees with the natives"', pp. 18–63; Michael Brown, *Francis Hutcheson in Dublin, 1719–1730* (Dublin, 2002), pp. 25–50.

144. T. Mozeen, *A collection of miscellaneous essays* (London, 1762), pp. 57–8.

145. Account of County Cavan, pp. 8–9, Armagh Public Library, Papers of the Physico-Historical Society; cf. W. Henry, Account of Counties Sligo, Donegal, Fermanagh and Lough Erne, pp. 452–3, NA, M. 2533; C. S. King (ed.), *Henry's Upper Lough Erne in 1739* (Dublin, 1892), pp. 16–18.

146. Account of County Cavan, p. 11, Armagh Public Library, Papers of the Physico-Historical Society.

147. W. Henry, Account of Counties Sligo, Donegal, Fermanagh and Lough Erne, pp. 441–2, NA, M. 2533; A. Rowan, *The buildings of Ireland: north-west Ulster* (Harmondsworth, 1979), pp. 298–301.

148. W. Henry, Account of Counties Sligo, Donegal, Fermanagh and Lough Erne, pp. 464–5, NA, M. 2533.

149. H. Brownrigg to Sir W. Fownes, 1 Jan. 1736, n.s., NLI, Ms. 8801/5; Glin and Malins, *Lost demesnes*, pp. 19–20.

150. Abp. M. Boyle, accounts, *c.* 1672, NLI, de Vesci Mss, H/4; Cork and Burlington's accounts, 1684–91, s.d. 2 June 1688, NLI, Ms. 6300.

151. Hume, report, NLI, Ms. 6054, f. 115.

152. A. Hamilton to Lady Panmure, 20 Sep. 1703, 28 May 1708, 5 July 1712, 25 Aug. 1713, 15 Aug. [ ], NAS, GD 45/14/238, 17, 22, 27, 28/1, 36, 122.

153. J. Cooley to W. Smythe, 9 Feb. 1731[2], 10 and 25 Jan. 1733[4], NLI, PC 436; J. Thompson to W. Smythe, 8 Nov. 1746, NLI, PC 445.

154. J. Cooley to W. Smythe, 9 Feb. 1731[2], 25 Jan. 1733[4]; J. Thompson to W. Smythe, 8 Nov. 1746, NLI, PC 445.

155. E. Nugent to W. Smythe, 10 March [], NLI, PC 447; J. Cooley to W. Smythe, 29 Dec. 1742, 6 June 1758, NLI, PC 446.

156. Accounts with D. Muschamp, 1691–2, NLI, de Vesci Mss, H/2.

157. M. Nicols to Mrs Fitzgerald, 15 March [*c.* 1702], NLI, de Vesci Mss, J/5.

158. T. Fitzgerald to Sir T. Vesey, 6 April 1702; T. Fitzgerald to Capt. D. Green, 4 March 1703[4], NLI, de Vesci Mss, J/2; Sir T. Vesey to D. Green, 8 Nov. 1703, NLI, de Vesci Mss, J/5; bill for seeds [*c.* 1702], NLI, de Vesci Mss, J/3.

159. *Pue's Occurrences*, 7 Nov. 1733.

160. R. Edgeworth accounts, s.d. March 1769, 27 Oct. 1769, NLI, Ms. 1535, pp. 146, 261; R. French, accounts, NLI, Ms. 4918, p. 134; L. A. Clarkson and E. M. Crawford, *Feast and famine: a history of food and nutrition in Ireland, 1500–1920* (Oxford, 2001), p. 49.

161. E. Hughes, *North country life in the eighteenth century. II. Cumberland and Westmorland, 1700–1830* (London, 1965), p. 66.

162. W. Owen to J. Owen, 28 March 1687, 25 Aug. 1688, UCNW, Penrhos Mss, V, 436, 437; J. Fowles to E. Owen, 3 and 21 Feb. 1740[1], UCNW, Penrhos Mss, I, 1089, 1090; H. Owen and J. E. Griffith, 'The diary of William Bulkeley of Brynddu, Anglesey', *Transactions of the Anglesey Antiquarian Society and Field Club* (1931), pp. 51–2.

163. Robertson, *Early Scottish gardeners*, pp. 153–222.

164. J. H. Harvey and V. Kinane, 'The earliest known printed Irish seed catalogue', *Long Room*, xxxviii (1993), pp. 49–52.

165. List of trees sent, 2 Feb. 1719[20], NLI, Ms. 36,365/4.

166. C. Lyons to M. Brabazon, 21 March 1726[7], Barber Mss, private collection, London, box III.

167. Chester port book, 1715, PRO, E 190/1388/1, f. 18v; obituaries from Dublin newspapers, Leslie Mss, NLI, Ms. 2697.

168. Bills of O. Cosgrave with Sir T. Vesey, 28 March 1722, NLI, de Vesci Mss, J/3; C. Lyon to M. Brabazon, 21 March 1726[7], Barber Mss, private collection, London, box III; accounts of Bp. N. Forster, from 17 May 1726, TCD, Ms. 1995–2008/2182; NLI, Ms. 1593, s.d. 9 Dec. 1748; bills of O. and W. Cosgrave, 1733,

1742–3, 1749–50; bill of N. Austin, 1749, NLI, Ms. 11,467; receipt of O. Cosgrave, 14 April 1749, NLI, Ms. 11,468/3; McCracken, *The Irish woodlands since Tudor times*, pp. 138–41; Harvey and Kinane, 'The earliest known printed Irish seed catalogue', pp. 49–53.

169.   G. Swift to Sir W. Fownes, 18 Aug. 1757, NLI, Ms. 3889/8.

170.   Bills of John Jones, 9 Jan. 1737[8]; Mary Norton, 3 Jan 1737[8]; Henry McDonald, [1738], with Bp. R. Howard, NLI, PC 223 (6).

171.   Receipt of R. Barnes, 9 Oct. 1716, NLI, Ms. 36,387/3. Cf. receipt of W. Roe, [1720], NLI, Ms. 36,365/4; E. O'Hara, account book, 1722–33, p. 31, NLI, Ms. 36,387/7.

172.   Account book for Castle Bernard, 1719–28, p. 116, Cork Archives Institute, Doherty Mss, U/137; W. Proven, bill to J. Moor, 1755–6, Barber Mss, box I; *Pue's Occurrences*, s.d. 26 Dec. 1732, 20 Jan. 1738[9].

173.   G. Mathew to K. O'Hara, 15 Feb. 1717[18], NLI, Ms. 20,385.

174.   R. Molesworth to L. Molesworth, 14 March 1720[1], NLI, P 3752; HMC, *Various Collections*, viii, pp. 301–2.

175.   Sir J. Temple to Sir R. Colvill, 21 Jan. 1682[3], TCD, Ms. 1178, f. 11v.

176.   R. Molesworth to L. Molesworth, ?17 June 1718, NLI, P 3752; HMC, *Various Collections*, viii, pp. 274–5.

177.   H. Ingoldsby to W. Smythe, 20 April 1716, 8 Feb. 1723[4], NLI, PC 445.

178.   J. Smythe to W. Smythe, 17 Oct. 1723, 4 July 1732, NLI, PC 449.

179.   J. Smythe to W. Smythe, 24 May 1749, NLI, PC 449.

180.   H. St Leger, Servants' Book, NLI, Ms. 34,112/10, unfoliated.

181.   H. St Leger, Servants' Book, s.v. William Knowland, James Couch, 29 Sep. 1740, NLI, Ms. 34,112/10.

182.   H. St Leger, Servants' Book, s.v. John Atkins, Denis Duier, NLI, Ms. 34,112/10.

183.   J. Paull, certificate of 5 July 1753, NLI, PC 449.

184.   R. Butterfield to W. Smythe, 31 July 1753, 25 Aug. 1753, NLI, PC 449.

185.   R. Edgeworth, accounts, s.d. 17 March 1759, 17 March 1760, 17 March 1762, 18 March 1763, 17 March 1765, NLI, Mss 1524, p. 246; 1526, p. 98; 1527, p. 84; 1528, p. 157; 1529, p. 178.

186.   Sir R. Bulkeley to M. Lister, 10 May 1694, 2 Nov. 1694, Bodleian, Lister Ms. 36, ff. 95, 105.

187.   R. Edgeworth, accounts, 17 March 1738[9], 3 May 1740, 9 June 1742, 8 July 1742, 8 Feb. 1752, 29 Aug. 1767, June 1768, 12 Sep. 1768, NLI, Mss 1512, p. 64; 1514, p. 27; 1515, pp. 160, 171; 1533, p. 225; 1534, pp. 179, 182, 210. For another 'aha': 'An essay on Sir Robert Meade's fine seat at Dundrum', BL, Egerton Ms. 846A, f. 160v.

188.   *Memoirs of Richard Lovell Edgeworth, esq.*, 2 vols (London, 1821), ii, p. 7.

189.   Bill of T. Greenway, 5 June 1728, NLI, de Vesci Mss, J/3; R. Edgeworth, accounts, s.d. 5 Sep. 1754, NLI, Ms. 1521, p. 107; cf. J. C. J. Murphy, 'The Kilkenny marble works', *Old Kilkenny Review*, ii (1949), pp. 14–19.

190.   R. Edgeworth, accounts, 17 Oct. 1741, 17 Dec. 1755, 12 April 1758, NLI, Mss 1515, p. 67; 1522, p. 73; 1524, p. 81; for later concern, see C. Colvin and C. Nelson, '"Building castles of flowers": Maria Edgeworth as gardener', *Garden History*, xvi (1988), pp. 58–70.

191.   R. Edgeworth, accounts, s.d. 3 March 1741[2], 16 Feb. 1749[50], 17 Dec. 1755, NLI, Mss 1515, p. 106; 1518, p. 207; 1522, p. 73.

192.   R. Edgeworth, accounts, 25 May 1748, 15 Dec. 1755, 12 Nov. 1756, 19 and 22 Aug. 1764, 18 Aug. 1767, 22 May 1768, 17 June 1768, 9 July 1769, 30 Sep. 1769, NLI, Mss 1518, p. 31; 1522, pp. 72, 198; 1528, pp. 89, 90; 1533, p. 219; 1534, pp. 170, 181; 1535, pp. 210, 247.

193.   J. Smythe to W. Smythe, 17 Oct. 1723, 27 Feb. 1727[8], 12 April 1728, NLI, PC 449.

194.   J. Smythe to W. Smythe, 2 April 1725, NLI, PC 449.

195.   J. Smythe to W. Smythe, 2 April 1725, 4 Sep. 1727, NLI, PC 449.

196.   Switzer, *A compendious method for the raising of the Italian broccoli*; J. Smythe to W. Smythe, 21 Jan. 1728[9], 15 Nov. 1747, NLI, PC 449.

197.  D. Bullen, bill for seeds, 14 Feb. 1755, NLI, Ms. 10,276/3.

198.  John Lawrence, *The Clergy-man's recreation: shewing the pleasure and profit of the art of gardening* (London, 1716), sig. A3–[A4v].

199.  R. Edgeworth, accounts, s.d. 17 Dec. 1755, NLI, PC 1522, p. 73.

200.  J. Smythe, gardening notebook, NLI, PC 438; N. Peacock, journal, s.d. 6 May 1748, NLI, Ms. 16,091.

201.  Will of W. Conyngham, 20 Dec. 1720, PRONI, D 1449/1/33; N. Ogle to W. Smythe, 28 July 1753, NLI, PC 436; Sir J. Temple to H. Temple, 28 April 1696, 23 May 1696, 25 Aug. 1696, Temple Mss, Southampton UL, BR5/22, 4, 5, 13.

202.  N. Peacock, journal, s.d. 7 Sep. 1750, NLI, Ms. 16,091.

203.  Sir J. Temple to H. Temple, 14 and 28 Nov. 1696, Southampton UL, BR5/22, 18 and 20.

204.  W. Smythe to A. Blennerhasset, 28 Nov. 1739, NLI, PC 449; N. Ogle to W. Smythe, 28 July 1753, NLI, PC 436.

205.  J. Ebbs to W. Smythe, 18 and 29 June 1734, NLI, PC 449.

206.  Agreement of S. White with W. Smith and H. Richardson, 22 July 1734, NLI, Ms. 34,025/1; M. Mulcahy, *Calendar of Kinsale documents*, vi (Kinsale, 1998), p. 49.

207.  W. Waring to S. Waring, 25 July 1697, private collection, Co. Down; Abp. W. King, accounts, 1715–23, s.d. Aug. 1719, TCD, Ms. 751/3, f. 103; R. Edgeworth, accounts, s.d. 18 Aug. 1748, NLI, Ms. 1518, p. 52; G. W. Panter, 'Eighteenth-century Dublin street cries', *JRSAI*, liv (1924), p. 84; W. Laffan (ed.), *The Cries of Dublin drawn from the life by Hugh Douglas Hamilton, 1760* (Dublin, 2003), pp. 60–1, 100–1, 114–17, 146–9.

208.  C. Hay to Lord Perceval, 9 Oct. 1744, BL, Add. Ms. 47,007, f. 152.

209.  Cork and Burlington accounts, 1672–4, s.d. 14 Oct. 1672, NLI, Ms. 6273; minute books, 1731–3, s.d. 1 Nov. 1733; 1733–41, s.d. 28 Feb. 1733[4]; 1741–6, s.d. 24 Feb. 1742[3], RDS; Sir W. Petty to V. Greatorex, 7 Jan. 1667[8], McGill UL, Ms. 7612; Bursar's vouchers, 10 Feb. 1738[9], TCD, MUN P/4/ folder 42/9; R. Edgeworth, accounts, s.d. 17 May 1740, 25 Oct. 1768, NLI, Mss 1514, p. 33; 1534, p. 229; Barnard, 'Gardening, diet and "improvement"', pp. 73–4; Gebbie (ed.), *Abercorn letters*, p. 64; J. Johnston, *Bishop Berkeley's Querist in historical perspective* (Dundalk, 1970), p. 135; S. Madden, *Reflections and resolutions proper for the gentlemen of Ireland* (Dublin, 1738), pp. 45–7; Legg (ed.), *Synge letters*, pp. 114, 116, 124, 126, 141, 457.

210.  N. Peacock, journal, s.d. 14 July 1740, 19 April 1742, 20 July 1742, 30 Jan. 1742[3], 22 Nov. 1743, 16 and 17 Dec. 1743, 31 Jan. 1743[4], 15 March 1743[4], 10 May 1744, 7 Aug. 1744, 25 Nov. 1744, 1 Dec. 1744, 6 Jan. 1744[5], 25 Feb. 1745, 17 March 1745, 30 May 1748, 6 July 1748, 27 Sep. 1748, 23 Nov. 1748, 6 July 1750, 7 March 1750[1], 8 July 1751, NLI, Ms. 16,091.

211.  J. Wight, journal, s.d. 22 June 1752, Friends' Historical Library, Dublin.

212.  Accounts of J. Griffith, s.d. 17 April [1683], Sep. 1684, Marsh's Library, Ms. Z3.2.4, openings 2, 10; *CARD*, vi, p. 86.

213.  Thick, *The Neat House Gardens*; Youngson, *The making of Edinburgh*, pp. 242–4.

214.  Barnard, 'Gardening, diet and "improvement"', pp. 208–34; Clarkson and Crawford, *Feast and famine*, pp. 9–28; D. B. Quinn, *The Elizabethans and the Irish* (Ithaca, 1966), pp. 62–7.

215.  W. Petty, 'Proposal . . . to divide annual expenses of £1000 between household, coach, diet, clothes, servants, etc.', 2 Feb. 1671[2], BL, Add. Ms. 72,857/56.

216.  Ware, account book, TCD, Ms. 10,528, ff. 13, 15v, 19–21, 25.

217.  P. Earle, *The making of the English middle class: business, society and family life in London, 1660–1730* (London, 1989), pp. 269–81; Thick, '"Superior vegetables"', pp. 133–4.

218.  R. French, account book, s.v. 'avenues', NLI, Ms. 4918, p. 1; account book, s.d. 29 Nov. 1744, 9 March 1746[7], NLI, Ms. 4919, f. 77.

219.  R. French, account book, s.d. Feb. 1753, NLI, Ms. 4918, p. 245.

220.  Accounts of Theobald Butler with P. French, 1717–18, 1722, NLI, French of Monivea Mss, envelope 25.

221.  R. French, account book, s.v. 'planting', NLI, Ms. 4918, p. 504.

222. T. Butler, account book, payments to William Broadway, 1722, NLI, French of Monivea Mss, envelope 25.

223. R. French, account book, s.d. 15 Oct. 1744, 29 Nov. 1744, 7, 15, 19 and 25 March 1744[5], 11 April 1747, 2 Feb. 1747[8], NLI, Ms. 4919, ff. 64v, 65, 67, 75, 77, 79.

224. T. Butler, account book, 1722, NLI, French of Monivea Mss, envelope 25; R. French, account book, s.d. 1755, NLI, Ms. 4918, p. 134.

225. R. French, account book, s.v. 'gardens', NLI, Ms. 4918, pp. 244–7.

226. R. French, account book, s.v. 'hopyard in the bog', NLI, Ms. 4918, pp. 280–1.

227. R. French, journal of a tour, s.d. 5 July 1751, NLI, Ms. 7375; C. Hay to Lord Perceval, 13 May 1743, 1 July 1743, 5 Aug. 1743, BL, Add. Ms. 47,007, ff. 92, 97, 99; J. Stevenson, *Two centuries of life in Down, 1600–1800* (Belfast and Dublin, 1920), p. 449.

228. R. French, account book, s.v. 'gardener', NLI, Ms. 4918, p. 272.

229. A. Nickson, accounts with T. Wentworth, s.d. 24 Feb. 1713[14], 5 March 1713[14], Sheffield City Archives, WWM A 759, p. 383.

230. R. French to A. French, 3 Feb. 1736[7], J. Digby to A. French, 1 April 1737, NLI, Ms. 19,821; J. Digby to W. Smythe, 17 March 1736[7], 4 Dec. 1746, NLI, PC 445; account of J. Digby, TCD, Ms. 5096. Cf. M.-S. Rostvig, *The happy man: studies in the metamorphoses of a classical ideal* (Oslo, 1954); R. Mauri, *L'Idée de bonheur* (Paris, 1965); Johnston-Liik, *HIP*, iv, pp. 55–6.

231. [G. Rye], *Considerations on agriculture* (Dublin, 1730), pp. iii–xii, 6, 45–52; J. F. Collins, 'George Rye (1685–1735), his family and appreciation of his book *Considerations on agriculture*', *Bandon Historical Journal*, xvii (2001), pp. 39–55; C. Smith, *The antient and present state of the county of Cork*, 2nd edn, 2 vols (Dublin, 1774), i, p. 199.

232. *The Dublin Society's Weekly Observations* (Dublin, 1739), pp. 5–8.

233. Collins, 'George Rye', p. 40.

234. Hume, survey, NLI, Ms. 6054, ff. 8–9.

235. C. O'Hara, account book, pp. 46, 70, 84, 96, NLI, Ms. 16,708; fragmentary journal of C. O'Hara, NLI, Ms. 20,389/10/20.

236. C. O'Hara, reflections on Co. Sligo, *c.* 1760, NLI, Ms. 20,397; C. O'Hara to E. Burke, 10 Aug. 1762, printed in R. J. S. Hoffman (ed.), *Edmund Burke, New York agent with his letters to the New York assembly and . . . with Edmund Burke*, Memoirs of the American Philosophical Society, xli (Philadelphia, 1956), pp. 281–4; T. Bartlett, 'The O'Haras of Annaghmore, *c.* 1600–1800: survival and revival', *IESH*, ix (1982), 34–52.

## 7 Sport

1. R. Howard, account book, s.d. 17, 24 and 30 October 1748, 28 Dec. 1748, 6 and 20 Jan. 1748[9], NLI, Ms. 1725.

2. M. A. Simon to A. Black, 28 Aug. 1765, PRONI, T 1073/18.

3. R. Howard, account book, *passim*, NLI, Ms. 1725; records of Arklow Charter school, TCD, 5598, p. 2; GEC, *Complete peerage*, xii, part ii, p. 622; *HIP*, iv, pp. 444–6.

4. Loeber, *Architects*, pp. 60–1, 70–1; R. Loeber, 'Irish country houses and castles of the late Caroline period: an unremembered past recaptured', *Quarterly Bulletin of the Irish Georgian Society*, xvi (1973), p. 44.

5. Bp. W. King, account book, 1693–1700, s.d. Sep. 1695, TCD, Ms. 751/1, f. 82.

6. C. H. Hull (ed.), *Economic writings of Sir William Petty*, 2 vols (Cambridge, 1899), i, pp. 166, 175.

7. 7 Will. III c. 5; *Statutes*, iii, pp. 266–7.

8. 'Diary of Anne Cooke', *Journal of the County Kildare Archaeologcal Society*, viii (1915), pp. 126, 127, 451.

9.   Discussions include: S. J. Connolly, 'Ag Déanamh *Commanding*': élite responses to popular culture, 1660–1850', in J. S. Donnelly and K. A. Miller (eds), *Irish popular culture, 1650–1850* (Dublin, 1999), pp. 1–29; D. Fleming, 'Diversions of the people: sociability among the orders of eighteenth-century Ireland', *Eighteenth-Century Ireland*, xvii (2002), pp. 99–111; A. Harrison, *The Irish trickster* (Sheffield, 1989), pp. 98–101; K. Whelan, 'An underground gentry? Catholic middlemen in eighteenth-century Ireland', in K. Whelan, *The tree of liberty* (Cork, 1996), pp. 3–58.

10.  J. Loughlin, accounts, s.d. 25 March 1744, NLI, Ms. 11,463; N. Ogle to W. Smythe, 4 June 1740, NLI, PC 436; *CSP, Ireland, 1666–9*, pp. 95, 101.

11.  J. Malone to M. Brabazon, 10 July 1711, Barber Mss, private collection, London, box III; Cork and Burlington to W. Congreve, R. Power, D. Foulke and R. Bagge, 12 Jan. 1700[1], NLI, Ms. 13,227.

12.  T. B., *Minerva's check to the author, attempting to write an elegy upon the right honourable and much to be lamented Roger, first earl of Orrery* (London, 1680).

13.  J. Waller to E. Southwell, BL, Add. Ms. 38,151, f. 30–30v; P. Kelly (ed.), 'The improvement of Ireland', *Analecta Hibernica*, xxxv (1992), p. 67; J. Meyer, *La noblesse bretonne au xviiie siècle*, 2 vols (Paris, 1966), i, pp. 585–6. The lawyer and former M.P., Cornelius O'Callaghan kept eleven horses on Horse Island: O'Callaghan inventory, 1737, South Tipperary Museum, Clonmel, Acc. 1985. 63.

14.  R. Cooke to R. Power, 25 Dec. 1692, NLI, Ms. 13,243; C. Smith, History of County Clare, RIA, Ms. 24 G 9, p. 211.

15.  Lord Broghill to Lord Dorset, 19 Jan. 1665[6], Kent Archives Office, Sackville Mss, U 269, C 18/2.

16.  T. Barnard, 'Introduction', in T. Barnard and B. McCormack (eds), *The Dublin Tholsel records* (Dublin, forthcoming); R. A. Anselment (ed.), *The remembrances of Elizabeth Freke, 1671–1714*, Camden Society, 5th series, xviii (2001), p. 61; E. MacLysaght (ed.), *Calendar of the Orrery papers* (Dublin, 1941), p. 121.

17.  R. Molesworth to L. Molesworth, 24 May 1700, NLI, microfilm, p. 3752; J. Waller to E. Southwell, BL, Add. Ms. 38,151, f. 30–30v; R. Molesworth, *Some considerations for the promoting of agriculture and employing the poor* (Dublin, 1723), p. 26.

18.  E. Cooke to W. Legge, 10 Jan. 1662[3], Staffordshire CRO, Dartmouth Mss, D 1778/I/i, 110; HMC, *Dartmouth Mss*, i, p. 11; E. MacLysaght, *Irish life in the seventeenth century*, 2nd edn (Shannon, 1969), pp. 145–6.

19.  Ormond to Sir R. Southwell, 4 June 1678, BL, Add. Ms. 21,484, f. 33; Ormond to Sir R. Southwell, 18 Nov. 1686, V & A, Ormonde Mss, 3, f. 35.

20.  Sir W. Petty to Sir R. Southwell, 23 July 1670, BH, Petty Mss, 9/39, now BL, Add. 72,852; Sir W. Petty to J. Rutter, 14 March 1670[1], McGill UL, Osler Ms. 7612; W. Ellis to Sir C. Wyche, 17 Feb. 1683[4], NA, Wyche Mss, 1/1/38; Lady Petty to ?Charles Petty, 27 Sep. 1684, Petty Mss, BH, Petty Mss. 8/22, now BL, Add. Ms. 72,857; Sir W. Temple, 'An essay upon the advancement of trade in Ireland (written to Lord Essex), Dublin, 22 July 1673', in W. Temple, *Miscellanea* (London, 1684), pp. 132–6.

21.  Lord Delvin to A. Brabazon, 1 July 1713, Barber Mss, private collection, London, box I.

22.  Massareene to Newdigate, 8 Nov. 1683, Warwickshire CRO, CR 136/B 285. For racing at Lisburn in 1664, Lord Conway to Sir E. Dering, 13 April 1664, BL, Stowe Ms. 744, f. 74.

23.  Sir R. Cox to E. Southwell, 2 Oct. 1705, BL, Add. Ms. 38,163, f. 104.

24.  *Articles for the queen's plate of one hundred guineas value to be run for yearly, on the first Wednesday of October, on the Curragh of Kildare* ([Dublin, 1708]).

25.  A. Carpenter (ed.), *Verse in English from eighteenth-century Ireland* (Cork, 1998), pp. 312–13; *The London rake's garland* (Darlington, c. 1765), pp. 5–6.

26.  Letters patent of the corporation of County Down horse breeders, 29 March 1686, PRONI, T 411; accounts of Dorset and Devonshire, s.d. 1 April 1738, Dublin Public Library, Gilbert Ms. 199; certificate of Devonshire's freedom of the corporation, 4 April 1738, Chatsworth, Devonshire letters, 163.101. For evidence of earlier races in the area: *CSP, Ireland, 1666–9*, pp. 95, 101.

27.  Debts of 2nd duke of Ormonde, Dec. 1700, V & A, Ormonde Mss, 5, 17/1; J. Weller to Sir R. Wilmot, 1 Sep. 1747, PRONI, T 3019/940; Harrington to Lords Justice, 4 July 1749, PRONI, T 3019/1361; Harrington

to Lords of Treasury, 8 Feb. 1749[50], PRONI, T 3019/1477; George II to Harrington, 27 Feb. 1749[50], PRONI, T. 3019/1499.

28. 'Horse-racing in Antrim in 1710', *UJA*, vii (1901), p. 158; S. R. Lowry-Corry, earl of Belmore, *The history of two Ulster manors* (London and Dublin, 1881), pp. 168–9.

29. Articles of agreement, 1715, NLI, Flower Mss, D 20,238; R. Giles to T. Baker, 29 May 1719, NLI, Ms.13,254; petition to Lord Burlington, 1 May 1728, PRONI, D 2707/A1/1, 11B; E. Jones to H. Boyle, 8 Aug. 1731, PRONI, D 2707/A11/26.

30. D. Crone to J. Crone, 11 May 1773, Cork Archives Institute, Crone of Byblox Mss, PR3/ box 1.

31. Orrery to Ormond, 20 Dec. 1678, V & A, Orrery Mss, 2, f. 61v; M. Ronayne to Lord Grandison, 22 April 1729, 23 Sep. 1729, Dromana, Villiers–Stuart Mss, T 3131/C/5/7, 47; Barnard, 'Cork settlers', pp. 335–6; R. Caulfield (ed.), *The council book of the corporation of Youghal* (Guildford, 1878), pp. 365–6, 369–70, 436, 507; cf. Lady H. Boyle to Cork, 6 April [?1664], BL, Althorp Ms. B. 5; Cork and Burlington to H. Browne, 20 March 1682[3], BL, Althorp Ms. B. 7.

32. H. French to R. Bourke, 12 June 1753, 6 Sep. 1753, 2 Aug. 1754, NLI, Ms. 8475.

33. P. Livingstone, *The Fermanagh story* (Enniskillen, 1969), p. 121.

34. E. Spencer to F. Price, 24 June 1746, 13 Sep. 1748, NLW, Puleston Mss, 3580E; L. F. McNamara, 'The diary of an eighteenth-century Clare gentleman', *North Munster Antiquarian Journal*, xxii (1980), p. 38.

35. W. H. G. Bagshawe, *The Bagshawes of Ford: a biographical pedigree* (London, 1886), p. 335; *A letter from Sir Richard Cox, Bart. to Thomas Prior, Esq.* (Dublin, 1749), p. 6; S. Derrick, *Letters written from Leverppole, Chester, Corke, the Lake of Killarney, Dublin . . .*, 2 vols (London, 1767), i, pp. 97–8; J. H. Gebbie (ed.), *An introduction to the Abercorn letters* (Omagh, 1972), p. 58.

36. 13 Geo. II c. 8; *Statutes*, vi, pp. 506–14.

37. 'Diary of Anne Cooke', pp. 126, 127, 451; Delany, *Autobiography*, 1st series, iii, p. 136.

38. *The tricks of the town laid open* (Dublin, *c.* 1750), p. 40.

39. Lady Bellew to Lord Raby, 12 Oct. [1713], BL, Add. Ms. 22,228, f. 41; J. L. Naper to W. Smythe, 1 Dec. 1736, NLI, PC 436; S. Povey to W. Smythe, 6 Aug. 1748, 28 Sep. 1748, 26 Oct. 1748, NLI, PC 448; cf. Kelly (ed.), 'The improvement of Ireland', p. 67.

40. 2nd earl of Cork's diary, s.d. 13 Nov. 1662, 26 Feb. 1662[3], 31 Aug. 1663, Chatsworth, Lismore Mss.

41. 2nd earl of Cork's diary, s.d. 18 Sep. 1665, Chatsworth, Lismore Mss; Cork and Burlington to T. Forster, 25 July 1695, Chatsworth, Entry Book of Cork and Burlington's letters, 1695–6.

42. R. Smythe to A. Alcock, 4 July 1765, NLI, PC 436.

43. Names for horses and mares in Taylor notebook, NLI, Mss 25,431, 25,432.

44. Earl of Drogheda, accounts, NLI, Ms. 9470, p. 94.

45. Inventory of Sir Hans Hamilton, Nov. 1682, NA, T 2741; inventory of R. Vigors, 12 Nov. 1723, NA, 1096/18/15; accounts for John Congreve, s.d. 21 Nov. 1743, NA, 1079/5/1.

46. Auction of C. O'Hara's horses, 1 Nov. 1731, NLI, Ms. 36,390/2.

47. Paull, account book, NLI, Ms. 12,938, p. 38.

48. N. Peacock, journal, s.d. 4 Sep. 1749, NLI, Ms. 16,091.

49. Jackson accounts, TCD, Ms. 9218, f. 24v; R. Maxwell, accounts, s.d. 21 Nov. 1744, PRONI, D 1556/16/14/4; account from 30 Sep. 1757, s.d. 7 Nov. 1757, PRONI, D 1556/16/14/27; account, s.d. 25 April 1738, PRONI, D 1556/16/7/13; B. T. Balfour accounts, NLI, Ms. 10,276/2.

50. D. Crone to J. Crone, 6 June 1767, Cork Archives Institute, Crone of Byblox Mss, PR3/ box 1.

51. 7 Will. III c. 5; *Statutes*, iii, pp. 266–7.

52. Sir W. Petty to Lady Petty, 27 March 1684, Petty Papers, 5/125, now in BL, Add. Ms.

53. R. Edgeworth, accounts, s.d. 26 Jan. 1741[2], 16 Sep. 1742, NLI, Ms. 1515, pp. 94, 189.

54. M. Smythe to W. Smythe, 21 July 1728, 2 Aug. 1728, 30 Oct. 1731, 11 March 1731[2], NLI, PC 448; T. C. Barnard, 'Integration or separation? Hospitality and display in Protestant Ireland, *c.* 1660–1800' in L. Brockliss and D. Eastwood (eds), *A union of multiple identities: the British Isles, c. 1750–1850*

(Manchester, 1997), pp. 127–46; cf. 'The Kerry cavalcade', in Carpenter (ed.), *Verse in English from eighteenth-century Ireland* , pp. 241–3.

55. Proposed establishment for Ormonde, *c.* 1700, V & A, Ormonde Mss, 5, 45/1.

56. See Barnard, *New anatomy*, pp. 487–9, and sources cited there.

57. W. Ellis to Sir C. Wyche, 5 Nov. 1681, NA, Wyche Mss, 1st series, 1/1/35; Sir W. Petty to Lady Petty, 27 March 1684, Petty Papers, 5/125, now in BL, Add. Ms 72, 856.

58. Rochester to T. Keightley, 9 Aug. 1701, NLI, Inchiquin Mss, no. 2598.

59. Z. Sedgwick to J. Evelyn, 18 July 1692; J. Evelyn to J. Evelyn, senior, 26 March 1694, Evelyn Mss, formerly at Christ Church, now in BL.

60. Sir J. Temple, account book, s.d. 20 June 1667, 22 Oct. 1667, Southampton UL, BR 7A/1.

61. List of carriages in St Michan's parish, Dublin, [late 1720s], RCB, P. 276/12.1, p. 203; 'Autobiography of Pole Cosby, of Stradbally, Queen's County, 1703–1737 (?)', *Journal of the County Kildare Archaeological Society*, v (1906), p. 177.

62. Hull (ed.), *Economic writings of Sir William Petty*, i, p. 175.

63. A. Hamilton to Lady Panmure, 29 Nov. [?1703], NAS, GD 45/14/238, 75.

64. Minute Book, 1736–72, s.d. 18 Feb. 1739[40], 2 Dec. 1752, Mercer's Hospital, Dublin.

65. O. Gallagher to O. St George, 14 Dec. 1727, PRO, C 110/46, 528.

66. J. Warburton, bill for Mrs Balfour's funeral, 24 Feb. 1741[2], NLI, Ms. 10,276/7; Executors' accounts for Mrs E. Vincent's funeral, D. Johnston, account book from 1669, Birr Castle Archive, *c.* 1669, Ms. A/16.

67. R. Purcell to Lord Orrery, 24 Oct. 1754, Harvard UL, Orrery Mss, Ms. 218/19.

68. Hume, report on Lord Malton's estate, NLI, Ms. 6054, p. 115.

69. J. Ainsworth (ed.), *The Inchiquin manuscripts* (Dublin, 1961), p. 511; *CSP, Ireland, 1670*, p. 205; Mac-Lysaght, *Irish life in the seventeenth century*, p. 144.

70. L. F. McNamara, 'Some matters touching Dromoland: letters of father and son, 1758–59', *North Munster Antiquarian Journal*, xxviii (1986), pp. 63–70; D. O'Brien, *History of the O'Briens* (London, 1949), p. 214; K. Sheedy, *The horse in County Clare*, i (Dublin, 2001), pp. 5–8; G. Weir, *These my friends and forebears: the O'Briens of Dromoland* (Whitegate, 1991), pp. 57–77.

71. Flower accounts, s.d. 7 April 1728, 19 July 1728, 9 and 26 Sep. 1728, 14 March 1728[9], NLI, Mss 11,463; 11,469/22; O. B. Dilkes to H. Boyle, 27 March 1731, PRONI, D 2707/A/1/3, 3.

72. Inventories of Ballymacgarry and Glenarm, 1 and 2 May 1750, PRONI, D 2977/5/1/5/39.

73. Goods sold, 27 Oct. 1749, NA, salvaged chancery pleadings, box 14.

74. F. E. Ball, *Howth and its owners, being the fifth part of a history of County Dublin* (Dublin, 1917), pp. 133, 164; Crookshank and Glin, *Painters of Ireland*, pp. 49, 74–5, 78–9; *Irish houses and landscapes* (Belfast, 1963), plate 3; C. Maxwell, *Country and town in Ireland under the Georges*, 2nd edn (Dundalk, 1949), facing pp. 32–3; V. Pakenham, *The big house in Ireland* (London, 2000), p. 128.

75. B. Brenan, *The painter's breakfast. A dramatick satyr* (Dublin, 1756), p. 32.

76. Crookshank and Glin, *Ireland's painters*, pp. 79–82; N. Figgis and B. Rooney, *Irish paintings in the National Gallery of Ireland*, i (Dublin, 2001), pp. 401–5; Belmore, *History of two Ulster manors*, p. 229; 'Sir Edward O'Brien with *Miss Don*', reproduced on the cover of Sheedy, *The horse in County Clare*, i; cf. S. Deuchar, *Sporting art in eighteenth-century England: a social and political history* (New Haven and London, 1988).

77. Lord Cork, account book, s.d. 16 Dec. 1657, 9 and 20 Jan. 1657[8], 17 and 21 June 1658, 7 Sep. 1658, 7 May 1659, NLI, Ms. 6256; L. Gosteloe to Cork, 4 and 11 Jan. 1661[2], 29 March 1662, 7 May 1662, 7 June 1662; A. Richards to Cork, 1 March 1661[2], Chatsworth, Lismore Ms. 32/55, 59, 74, 84, 89, 101; abstract of Garret Roche's letters, s.d. 9 and 30 March 1671[2], 18 May 1672, 3 July 1672, 24 Sep. 1672, 31 May 1673, 18 June 1673, 6 and 17 Sep. 1673, 2 Dec. 1673, 25 March 1674, 6 Feb. 1674[5], 2 Oct 1675, 15 Sep. 1676, 22 Dec. 1677, 19 Jan. 1677[8], 1 June 1678, 25 Sep. 1678, NLI, Ms. 7177.

78. Lord Cork's diary, s.d. 7 June 1662, Chatsworth, Lismore Mss; Cork and Burlington to H. Browne, 21 March 1681[2], BL, Althorp Ms. B. 7.

79. Account book, s.d. 30 March 1654, Chatsworth, Bolton Abbey Ms. 275, p. 21; account book, s.d. 26 Nov. 1656, Chatsworth, Bolton Abbey Ms. 278, p. 25; Cork's diary, s.d. 30 April 1669, 18 Aug. 1671, Chatsworth, Lismore Mss; account book, s.d. 30 Oct. 1657, 2 Aug. 1658, 31 Jan. 1658[9], NLI, Ms. 6256; B Drew, accounts, s.d. 18 May 1674, NLI, Ms. 6273; accounts, s.d. 22 Sep. 1671, 30 March 1672, 4 May 1672, NLI, Ms. 6274; abstract of G. Roche's letters, s.d. 6 Oct. 1675, NLI, Ms. 7177; Cork and Burlington's accounts, s.d. 19 Oct. 1680, 2 Dec. 1680, NLI, Ms. 6902; account book, 1684–91, s.d. 15 May 1684, NLI, Ms. 6300; Cork and Burlington to W. Congreve, 8 Feb. 1693[4], Chatsworth, Lismore Ms. 34/53.

80. Lord Cork's diary, s.d. 7 Nov. 1655, 14 March 1660[1], 6 Jan. 1661[2], 24 May 1662, 21 Aug. 1665, Chatsworth, Lismore Mss.

81. Lord Cork's diary, s.d. 14 Sep. 1660, 30 Oct. 1667, Chatsworth, Lismore Mss; Thanet to Cork and Burlington, 1 July 1667, BL, Althorp Ms. B.5.

82. Lord Cork's diary, s.d. 22 Aug. 1661, 7 Oct. 1662, 12 June 1663, 19 Oct. 1663, 13 June 1665, 6 Sep. 1665, 17 Aug. 1666, Chatsworth, Lismore Mss.

83. For other examples, see: Chester port book, 1715, PRO, E 1990/1388/1.

84. Cork and Burlington, account book, 1669–71, s.d. 16 June 1670, NLI, Ms. 6267.

85. Lord Cork, diary, s.d. 3 Aug. 1658, Chatsworth, Lismore Mss; W. Gostelow, *Charles Stuart and Oliver Cromwell united* (London, 1655), pp. 82–3.

86. Lord Cork's diary, s.d. 6 Sep. 1661, 19 May 1671, Chatsworth, Lismore Mss.

87. Abstract of Garret Roches' letters, s.d. 2 Aug. 1673, 17 Dec. 1673, NLI, Ms. 7177.

88. Cork and Burlington's accounts, 1684–91, s.d. 22 Oct. 1686, 28 Nov. 1691, NLI, Ms. 6300; R. Bagg, accounts with Cork and Burlington, s.d. 8 Oct. 1692, NLI, Ms. 6903.

89. Cork and Burlington to W. Congreve, 18 Nov. 1690, NLI, Ms. 13,226.

90. Cork and Burlington, account book, 1669–71, s.d. 15 March 1670[1], NLI, Ms. 6267; abstract of G. Roche's letters, s.d. 20 July 1672, 25 July 1677, 8 Aug. 1677, 5 Sep. 1677, 1 June 1678, NLI, Ms. 7177; Cork and Burlington's accounts, 1686–91, s.d. 18 Oct. 1686, NLI, Ms. 6303; Cork and Burlington to W. Congreve, R. Power and D. Foulke, 27 May 1695, Chatsworth, Entry Book of Cork and Burlington's Letters, 1694–5; J. Waite to R. Musgrave and T. Baker, 3 May 1707, Chatsworth, Waite letterbook, 1706–8; D. Foulke to R. Musgrave, 19 Feb. 1709[10], NLI, Ms. 13,242.

91. Bp. W. King, account books, 1693–1700, s.d. July 1695, TCD, Ms. 751/1, f. 77; 1700–12, s.d. Aug. 1706, TCD, Ms. 751/2, f. 157.

92. M. D. Jephson, *An Anglo-Irish miscellany: some records of the Jephsons of Mallow* (Dublin, 1964), p. 34; S. P. Johnston (ed.), 'On a manuscript description of the city and county of Cork, *cir.* 1685, written by Sir Richard Cox', *JRSAI*, xxxii (1902), pp. 355–7, 362.

93. 'Memo of several particulars of late Lord Orrery', 25 March 1683, Petworth, Orrery Mss, general series, 13; lease to W. Sanders, 6 April 1692, Harvard UL, Orrery Mss, Ms. 218 22F.

94. 3rd Lord Cork to W. Congreve, 30 April 1698; 3rd Lord Cork to W. Congreve, R. Power, D. Foulke and R. Bagg, 12 Jan. 1700[1], NLI, Ms. 13,227.

95. A. Brodrick to H. Boyle, 9 June 1713, PRONI, D 2707/A1/1/1B.

96. Meyer, *La noblesse bretonne*, i, pp. 467–9.

97. 10 Will. III c. 8, abstracted in R. Bolton, *A justice of the peace for Ireland*, ed. M. Travers (Dublin, 1750), i, p. 270.

98. T. C. Barnard, 'Gardening, diet and "improvement" in later-seventeenth-century Ireland', *Journal of Garden History*, x (1990), p. 73; R. Loeber, 'Settlers' utilisation of the natural resources', in K. Hanigan and W. Nolan (eds), *Wicklow: history and society* (Dublin, 1994), pp. 267–73; P. Stamper, 'Woods

and parks', in G. Astill and A. Grant (eds), *The countryside of medieval England* (Oxford, 1988), pp. 128–48.

99.   J. Birrell, 'Deer and deer-farming in medieval England', *Agricultural History Review*, xl (1992), pp. 112–26.

100.  D. Beaver, 'The great deer massacre: animals, honor and communication in early modern England', *Journal of British Studies*, xxxviii (1999), pp. 187–216; R. B. Manning, *Hunters and poachers: a social and cultural history of unlawful hunting in England, 1485–1650* (Oxford, 1993); P. B. Munsche, *Gentlemen and poachers: the English game laws, 1671–1831* (Cambridge, 1981).

101.  A. Stringer, *The experienced huntsman* (Belfast, 1714, reprinted Dublin, 1780), p. 285.

102.  W. H. W. Wyndham-Quin, earl of Dunraven, *The fox hound in County Limerick* (Dublin and London, 1919), pp. 16, 69.

103.  J. Cuffe, account of Co. Mayo, etc, *c.* 1738, p. 5, Armagh Public Library, Papers of the Physico-Historical Society; *A genuine history of the family of the great negroes of G . . . , taken from an African manuscript in St. Sepulchre's Library, Dublin* (London, 1756), pp. 5–6; A. Laing (ed.), *Clerics and connoisseurs: the Rev. Matthew Pilkington, the Cobbe family and the fortunes of an Irish art collection through three centuries* (London, 2001), p. 68.

104.  Crown entry books, Co. Dublin, s.d. 10 Dec. 1744, NA; Gebbie (ed.), *Abercorn letters*, p. 33.

105.  Sir W. Petty to Lady Petty, 14 July 1679, 26 Aug. 1679, Petty Papers, 5/51, 57; A. Spurrett to J. Nettles, 21 Nov. 1704, Chatsworth, Spurrett letterbook, 1703–4; M. Ronayne to Lord Grandison, 23 Sep. 1726, Dromana, Villiers–Stuart Mss, T 3131/C/5/5; R. French to W. Smythe, 4 Jan. 1741[2], NLI, PC 449; J. Smythe to W. Smythe, 29 June 1747, NLI, PC 449; J. Harwood to L. Dillon, 23 Jan. 1759, NLI, Ms. 35,748/2; Barnard, *New anatomy*, pp. 208–38; Legg (ed.), *Synge letters*, pp. 63, 79; Beaver, 'The great deer massacre', pp. 193–5, 204.

106.  Abstract of Garret Roche's letters, s.d. 14 Aug. 1675, 8 Aug. 1677, NLI, Ms. 7177; Cork and Burlington to W. Congreve, 27 June 1691, 26 July 1692, 14 Aug. 1694, 31 Oct. 1695, 22 July 1697, NLI, Ms. 13,226; Cork and Burlington to W. Congreve, R. Power and D. Foulke, 1696; Cork and Burlington to R. Power, 18 July 1696, Chatsworth, Entry Book of Cork and Burlington's letters, 1695–6.

107.  Broghill to Dorset, 2 May 1673, 3 March 1673[4], Kent Archives Office, Sackville Mss, U269/C, 18/22, 25; Orrery household menus, Petworth, Orrery Mss, general series, 14; Orrery household menus, NLI, Ms. 34; Johnston (ed.), 'On a manuscript description of the city and county of Cork', p. 355; MacLysaght (ed.), *Orrery papers*, pp. 215–17.

108.  M. Mason to J. Mason, 12 and 15 Nov. 1737, Dromana, Villiers–Stuart Mss, T. 3131, B/1/21 and 24; Legg (ed.), *Synge letters*, pp. 79, 468–9.

109.  M. Ledwidge to W. Smythe, 22 Nov. 1742, NLI, PC 436.

110.  E. Villiers to Cork and Burlington, 2 Sep. 1691, NLI, Ms. 13,230; Cork and Burlington accounts, 1684–91, s.d. 17 Nov. 1684, 27 March 1685, 18 May 1685, NLI, Ms. 6300; Cork and Burlington to W. Congreve, 4 Oct. 1690, NLI, Ms. 13,226; Cork and Burlington to R. Power, 25 Jan. 1693[4], Chatsworth, Entry Book of Cork and Burlington's letters, 1693–4.

111.  Lord Cork's diary, s.d. 10 Sep. 1656, Chatsworth, Lismore Mss; J. Waite to R. Musgrave, 11 Jan. 1706[7]; J. Waite to R. Musgrave and T. Baker, 3 May 1707, Chatsworth, J. Waite letterbook, 1706–8; J. Waite to R. Musgrave, 31 Jan. 1709[10], Chatsworth, J. Waite letterbook, 1708–10.

112.  J. Smythe to W. Smythe, 3 Jan. 1732[3], NLI, PC 449; E. Mervyn to same, 21 Oct. 1741, NLI, PC 449; G. Dewers to W. Forward, 6 March 1743[4], NLI, PC 225.

113.  J. Smythe to W. Smythe, 3 Jan. 1732[3], NLI, PC 449.

114.  ?W. Congreve to Cork and Burlington, n.d. [before 25 July 1696]; Cork and Burlington to W. Congreve, 25 July 1696, 6 and 20 Oct. 1696, 24 and 26 Nov. 1696, Chatsworth, Lismore Ms. 34/100, 101, 113, 116, 118, 121.

115.  Johnston-Liik, *HIP*, vi, p. 135.

116.  R. Molesworth to L. Molesworth, 11 Nov. 1695, NLI, microfilm, p. 3752; J. Verdon, journal, p. 44, Cardiff Central Library, Ms. 4.370.

117. R. T. Dunlop, *Ireland under the Commonwealth*, 2 vols (Manchester, 1913), i, p. 192, n.1.

118. Lord Broghill to Lord Dorset, 20 Oct. 1665, 7 Jan. 1667[8], 26 May 1668, 24 Feb. 1668[9], Kent Archives Office, Sackville Mss, U/269, C18/1, 12, 14 and 15a; Fr J. Gibbins to Lord Howth, [?1697], NLI, reports on private collections, no. 140; Abp. W. King, account book, 1700–12, s.d. March 1699[1700], Aug. 1702, March 1711[12], TCD, Ms. 751/2, ff. 4, 60, 266v; HMC, *Dartmouth Mss*, iii, p. 115; MacLysaght (ed.), *Orrery papers*, p. 38; W. M., *Hesperi-neso-graphia: or a description of the western isle* (London, 1716), p. 3; Temple, 'An essay upon the advancement of trade', pp. 112–13.

119. F. Bellew to Lord Raby, 10 Oct. [1707], BL, Add. Ms. 22, 228, f. 36v.

120. Bp. W. Nicolson, diary, s. d. 31 May 1721, 13 and 29 July 1722, 12 June 1724, 13 Aug. 1725, Cumbria County Library, Carlisle.

121. HMC, *Egmont Mss*, ii, p. 5; R. G. A. Levinge, *Jottings of the Levinge family* (Dublin, 1877), p. 45.

122. Lord Cork's diary, s.d. 23, 26 and 30 July 1661, 3, 9, 12, 16 Aug. 1661, 20 Sep. 1661, 24 and 28 Oct. 1662, 17 and 27 Nov. 1662, 2 June 1663, 30 June 1666, 4 Sep. 1666, 8 Aug. 1671, Chatsworth, Lismore Mss.

123. Lord Cork's diary, s.d. 23 Sep. 1656, 10 Oct. 1662, Chatsworth Lismore Mss; Cork, account book, s.d. 17 Jan. 1658[9], NLI, Ms. 6256.

124. Lord Cork, account book, s.d. 9 Sep. 1658, NLI, Ms. 6256; Cork and Burlington's accounts, s.d. 30 May 1681, NLI, Ms. 6902; Cork and Burlington's accounts, 1684–1691, s.d. 7 Aug. 1686, NLI, Ms. 6300.

125. L. Gosteloe to Cork, 20 June 1663, Chatsworth, Lismore Ms. 33/52; Cork and Burlington's accounts, s.d. 15 June 1680, NLI, Ms. 6902; Cork and Burlington's accounts, 1684–91, s.d. 7 June 1686, NLI, Ms. 6300.

126. Sir J. Shaen to Lord Broghill, 14 June 1659, Petworth, Orrery Mss, general series, 26; Lord Anglesey to Lord Orrery, 23 Sep. 1665, Petworth, Orrery Mss, general series, 22; Lord Broghill to Lord Dorset, 7 Jan. 1667[8], 12 and 26 May 1668, 30 June 1668, Kent Archives Office, Sackville Mss, U 269, C 18/12–15; accounts of W. Cooper, 1664–71, p. 12, Petworth, Orrery Mss, general series, 17; Lord Orrery to unknown, Petworth, Orrery Mss, general series, 27; MacLysaght (ed.), *Orrery papers*, p. 122.

127. Bp. W. King, account book, 1693–1700, s.d. May 1693, Oct. 1693, Feb. 1693[4], May 1697, May 1699, Aug. 1699, TCD, Ms. 751/1, ff. 12, 14, 24, 36, 138, 204, 211.

128. Annesley, account book, 1761–6, s.d. 20 Oct. 1763, PRONI, D 1854/8/17; R. Edgeworth, accounts, s.d. 11 Oct. 1742, NLI, Ms. 1515, p. 194.

129. Lord Delvin to A. Brabazon, 1 July 1713, Barber Mss, private collection, London, box I; O. O'Mally to A. Brabazon, 14 May 1722, Barber Mss, private collection, London, box III; Lord Meath to A. Brabazon, 22 June 1722, Barber Mss, private collection, London, box III.

130. Arran to W. Legge, 6 May 1664, Staffordshire CRO, D (W), 1778/1/i, 133; D. Muschamp to T. Fitzgerald, 19 July 1695, NLI, de Vesci Mss, H/2; Ball, *Howth and its owners*, p. 120.

131. Sir P. Perceval, accounts, 1679, BL, Add. Ms. 47,037, f. 43; J. Stanley to L. Dillon, 14 Feb. 1761, NLI, Ms. 35,748/1.

132. F. Dodington to Ormond, 24 July 1664; E. Cooke to Ormond, 24 Aug. 1667, 9 Sep. 1667, Bodleian, Carte Ms. 215, ff. 56, 366, 376; Ossory to Ormond, 2 July [1664], Bodleian, Carte Ms. 220, f. 151.

133. Accounts of P. Pett, from 25 June 1685, s.d. 20 Sep. 1685, 13 Oct. 1686, NLI, Ms. 2535; A. Crotty to Henry Boyle, 8 May 1729, 22 Dec. 1729, PRONI, D 2707/ A1/11/10 and 20; bills, 7 Oct. 1759, 15 Nov. 1759, PRONI, Maxwell of Finnebrogue Mss, D 1556/16/14/30 and 39; Crown entry books, city of Dublin, 20 July 1747, NA; D. Bourke, earl of Mayo, and W. B. Boulton, *A history of the Kildare Hunt* (London, 1913), pp. 21–4, 27; E. F. Dease, *A complete history of the Westmeath Hunt from its foundation* (Dublin, 1898), pp. 3–4; Colin A. Lewis, *Hunting in Ireland: an historical and geographical analysis* (London, 1975), pp. 39–56; Wyndham-Quin, *Fox-hound in County Limerick*; 'Longford Papers', *Analecta Hibernica*, xv (Dublin, 1944), pp. 121–3.

134. Accounts, 1672–4, s.d. 1 Feb. 1672[3], 13 Dec. 1673, 17 July 1674, NLI, Ms. 6273; accounts of L. Gosteloe and G. Roche, s.d., 22 July 1678, 1 and 10 July 1678, 26 Aug. 1678, 22 and 24 Oct. 1678, 20 Jan. 1678[9], NLI, Ms. 6902.

135. Massareene to Newdegate, 20 Feb. 1687[8], Warwickshire CRO, CR 136/ B 289.

136. N. Cormick, account with Sir T. Vesey, May 1718, NLI, de Vesci Mss, J/21.

137. A. Crotty to H. Boyle, 22 Dec. 1730, PRONI, D 2707/A1/1/20.

138. M. MacEwan, *The Ryan family and the Scarteen hounds* (Wilton, 1989), pp. 22–3, 36–7.

139. P. Savage, 'The hound book', 1767–83, PRONI, D 552/B/3/1/170; Carpenter (ed.), *Verse in English from eighteenth-century Ireland*, p. 301.

140. R. Edgeworth, accounts, s.d. 8 Aug. 1740, 19 Dec. 1768, 31 Jan. 1769, NLI, Mss. 1514, p. 39; 1534, p. 249; 1535, p. 119.

141. Hume, report on Lord Malton's estate, NLI, Ms. 6054, p. 115.

142. J. Hore to R. Power, 29 Aug. 1703, NLI, Ms. 13,243; MacEwan, *The Ryan family and the Scarteen hounds*, pp. 36–7; McNamara, 'The diary of an eighteenth-century Clare gentleman', pp. 38, 39, 41.

143. Cork and Burlington, accounts, 1678–80, s.d. 21 and 28 April 1679, NLI, Ms. 6902; accounts, 1684–91, s.d. 11 Nov. 1684, NLI, Ms. 6300; Castle Bernard, account book, 1719–28, pp. 117, 145, 165, Cork Archives Institute, Doherty Mss, U/137.

144. Delany, *Autobiography*, 1st series, iii, pp. 15–16.

145. Lord Broghill to Lord Dorset, 26 May 1668, 24 Feb. 1668[9], 3 June 1673, Kent Archives Office, U/269, C18/14, 15a, 23; Legg (ed.), *Synge letters*, p. 200.

146. Sir R. Bulkeley to M. Lister, 1 July 1693, 28 Feb. 1699[1700], Bodleian, Lister Mss 3, f. 43; 36, f. 56; W. Peard to F. Price, 20 Jan. 1746[7], 26 Feb. 1746[7], 28 March 1747, 25 May 1747, NLW, Puleston Ms. 3580E; J. A. Oughton, autobiography, NAM, Ms. 8808–36–1, p. 48; *Memoirs of Richard Lovell Edgeworth, Esq.*, 2 vols (London, 1820), i, pp. 57–62.

147. R. Smith, account with Abp. M. Boyle, 1671, NLI, de Vesci Mss, H/4; R. Thomas to Abp. J. Vesey, 18 Aug. 1687, NLI, de Vesci Mss, G/7A; N. Cormick, account with Sir T. Vesey, s.d. 16 July 1725, NLI, de Vesci Mss, J/26; E. O'Hara, account for A. O'Hara, from April 1730, NLI, Ms. 36,387/6; R. Edgeworth, accounts, s.d. 17 Jan. 1742[3], NLI, Ms. 1515, p. 220; N. Peacock, journal, s.d. 4 April 1744, NLI, Ms. 16,091; Legg (ed.), *Synge letters*, pp. 184–5, 219.

148. *Dublin Gazette*, 15–19 Nov. 1709; Legg (ed.), *Synge letters*, pp. 431, 463.

149. W. Waring to S. Waring, 3 April 1697, private collection, Co. Down.

150. Legg (ed.), *Synge letters*, pp. 137, 140, 150, 172, 196, 216, 331, 332, 349, 350–1, 360, 394, 420, 438.

151. Accounts of P. Pett, from 25 June 1685, s.d. 7 Nov. 1685, NLI, Ms. 2535.

152. W. Hovell to unknown, 4 Sep. 1685, Farmar Mss, private collection, Dublin; Barnard, 'Cork settlers', p. 334.

153. Stringer, *The experienced huntsman*, pp. 45, 224.

154. T. Dolan, account of Co. Fermanagh, *c.* 1719, NLI, Ms. 2085, pp. 23–4.

155. 7 Will. III c. 5; 10 Will. III c. 8; 2 Anne c. 6; 6 Anne c. 6; 8 Anne c. 3; 2 Geo. I c. 10; 6 Geo. I c. 10; W. E. H. Lecky, *A history of Ireland in the eighteenth century*, 5 vols (London, 1916), i, p. 146; *Statutes*, iii, pp. 260–7, 487–96; iv, pp. 12–31, 121–5, 190–216, 342–9, 530–50.

156. 8 Anne c. 3, *Statutes*, iv, pp. 190–216; *CARD*, ix, pp. 192–3; P. Fagan, *The diocese of Meath in the eighteenth century* (Dublin, 2000), pp. 11–12; HMC, *Ormonde Mss*, ii, p. 475.

157. Case of Mr Nugent and Mr Maguire [1737], Chatsworth, Devonshire letters, 244.0 and 2; Lords Justice to Devonshire, 23 May 1737, Chatsworth, Devonshire letters, 244.1; Abp. H. Boulter to Devonshire, 7 June 1737, Chatsworth, Devonshire letters, 242.2; W. Smythe to T. [?Nugent], 27 Jan. 1738[9], NLI, PC 449.

158. Mayo and Boulton, *The Kildare Hunt*, pp. 49–52.

159. Nicholas Woulfe, 'The Granahan Hunt', 1758, printed in Sheedy, *The horse in County Clare*, i, pp. 189–90.

160. John Fleming, hunting song, 1766, NLI, Ms. 25,432; Stringer, *The experienced huntsman*, pp. 39–40, 50, 283.

161. 'The Kilruddery Hunt', originally in T. Mozeen, *A collection of miscellaneous essays* (London, 1762), pp. 33–6, reproduced in Maxwell, *Country and town in Ireland under the Georges*, pp. 33–5.

162. T. C. Barnard, 'Athlone, 1685; Limerick, 1710: religious riots or charivarias?', *Studia Hibernica*, xxvii (1993), pp. 61–75.

163. Stringer, *The experienced huntsman*, p. 285.

164. *The tricks of the town laid open*, p. 11.

165. A list of the hunt subscribers contained the names of forty-nine gentlemen. They were drawn from County Londonderry as well as Antrim, and from the boroughs of Belfast and Derry. J. B. Hamilton, *Ballymoney and District in the County of Antrim prior to the twentieth century* (Ballycastle, 1957), p. 69.

166. J. Clewlow to B. Ward, 22 Oct. 1764, PRONI, D 2092/1/8, 108; 'The transformation', in S. Burdy, *Ard-glass, or the ruined castles* (Dublin, 1802), pp. 79–85, extracted in Carpenter (ed.), *Verse in English from eighteenth-century Ireland*, pp. 526–9.

167. J. Buckley, 'The journal of Thomas Wright, author of *Louthiana* (1711–1786)', *County Louth Archaeological Journal*, ii (1908–11), p. 182.

168. W. Magill to Lord Antrim, 7 March 1738[9], PRONI, D 2977/5/1/5, 18A.

169. 'Diary of Anne Cooke', pp. 205, 207–8, 450–1.

170. A. Stewart to Sir A. Acheson, [ ] Oct. [1758], PRONI, D 1606/1/19.

171. E. Spencer to F. Price, 29 Sep. 1744, NLW, Puleston Ms. 3580E.

172. W. Peard to F. Price, 18 Dec. 1744, NLW, Puleston Ms. 3579E.

173. R. Purcell to Lord Perceval, 10 Sep. 1745, BL, Add. Ms. 47,001B, f. 131; E. Bolster, *A history of Mallow* (Cork, 1971), p. 59.

174. A. Cooke to W. Smythe, 26 May 1750, NLI, PC 449.

175. T. Smythe to R. Smythe, 11 Nov. 1755, 15 Dec. 1755, NLI, PC 448/38.

176. W. Thompson to W. Smythe, 1 April 1733, NLI, PC 445; affidavits of J. Brien and M. Dellaney, 20 April 1753, Surrey Local History Centre, Brodrick Mss, G 145/box 98/1; W. Thompson to W. Smythe, 1 April 1733, NLI, PC 445.

177. W. Magill to Lord Antrim, 7 March 1738[9], PRONI, D 2977/5/1/5, 18A.

178. Lists of hounds, stallions, mares and songs, *c.* 1750, Headfort Mss, NLI, Ms. 25,431; C. O'Hara, account book, pp. 46, 70, 84, NLI, Ms. 16,708; lists of hounds, from *c.* 1750, Doneraile Mss, NLI, Ms. 32,976/2, openings 275–9; 'The Kilruddery Hunt', in Mozeen, *A collection of miscellaneous essays*, pp. 33–6, and Maxwell, *Country and town in Ireland under the Georges*, pp. 33–5.

179. R. Edgeworth, accounts, s.d. 17 Nov. 1756, NLI, Ms. 1522, p. 200; J. Piers, libellous poem, NA, Dublin Crown Entry Books, city of Dublin, 1746–7, s.d. 1 Dec. 1746, 14 Feb.1746–7; *Memoirs of Richard Lovell Edgeworth*, i, pp. 67–8.

180. M. Symner, answers to interrogatories of S. Hartlib, *c.* 1658, Sheffield UL, Hartlib Mss, lxii/45; Ossory to Ormond, 27 Aug. 1664, Bodleian, Carte Ms. 220, f. 169v.

181. Lord Cork's diary, s.d. 15 Nov. 1656, 30 May 1665, Chatsworth, Lismore Mss; Ormond to Arran, 12 Feb. 1683[4], Bodleian, Carte Ms. 220, f. 17.

182. Hillsborough to Hartington, 7 July 1755, Chatsworth, Devonshire letters, box May–July 1755.

183. J. Blennerhasset to R. Baldwin, 17 July 1730, NLW, Powis Castle, letters, no. 909.

184. Stringer, *The experienced huntsman*, p. 282; Mayo and Boulton, *The Kildare Hunt*, p. 52.

185. Lucas, journal, s.d. 6 Jan. 1740[1], 31 March 1741, 17 June 1741, NLI, Ms. 14,101.

186. N. Peacock, journal, s.d. 12 Oct. 1744, 17 Nov. 1744, 10 Aug. 1745, 30 May 1748, 24 Oct. 1748, NLI, Ms. 16,091.

187. N. Peacock, journal, s.d. 18 Sep. 1744, NLI, Ms. 16,091.

188. N. Peacock, journal, s.d. 12 Oct. 1744, 10 Aug. 1745, 30 May 1748, NLI, Ms. 16,091.

189. H. Thomson, memoir, Bodleian, Ms. Eng. Hist. d. 155, ff. 38v–39.

190. N. Delacherois to D. Delacherois, 25 April 1770, NAM, Ms. 7805–63.

191. Maxwell, *Country and town in Ireland under the Georges*, p. 32.

192. M. Wills, account book, 8 Oct. 1755, 27 Nov. 1756, IAA, 81/88; *Dublin Courant*, 3–12 Aug. 1749.

193. P. Fagan, *The second city: portrait of Dublin, 1700–1760* (Dublin, 1986), pp. 74–5.

194. J. Colhoun to Abercorn, 25 May 1750, PRONI, T 2541, 1A/1/2/16.

195. W. Peard to F. Price, 31 Jan. 1743[4], NLW, Ms. 3579E; McNamara, 'The diary of an eighteenth-century gentleman', p. 30.

196. *The tricks of the town laid open*, pp. 41–2.

197. Fagan, *The second city*, pp. 75–6; *Dublin Courant*, 12–16 June 1744.

198. J. Vernon to Lord Meath, 1746, Kilruddery, Co. Wicklow, Meath papers, J/3/9/3.

199. *Remarks on the present state of the linnen-manufacture of this kingdom* (Dublin, 1755), p. 18.

200. P. Delany to M. Ward, 1 June 1746, PRONI, D 2092/1/7, 133.

201. *Dickson's Intelligencer*, 31 March 1719, quoted in É. Ó Ciardha, *The fatal attachment: Ireland and the Jacobite cause, 1685–1766* (Dublin, 2001), p. 188.

202. K. Danaher, *The year in Ireland* (Cork, 1972); A. Gailey, *Irish folk drama* (Cork, 1969); A. Harrison, *The Irish trickster* (Sheffield, 1989), pp. 87–101.

203. M. Concanen, *A match at football of an Irish champion* (London, 1721), partly printed in Carpenter (ed.), *Verse in English from eighteenth-century Ireland*, pp. 90–8; and discussed in Fagan, *The second city*, pp. 79–81. See, too: M. B. Ní Mhurchadha, 'Contending neighbours: society in Fingal, 1603–60', unpublished Ph.D. thesis, NUI, Maynooth (2002), pp. 228–39.

204. 'The excellent new songe, an excellent old tune, being the newest Cartown garland', private collection, Berkshire; H. Thomson, memoir, Bodleian, Ms. Eng. Hist. d. 155, ff. 38v–39; T. Dolan, account of Fermanagh, NLI, Ms. 2085, pp. 23–4; MacLysaght, *Irish life in the seventeenth century*, pp. 353–4; 'Autobiography of Pole Cosby , of Stradbally, Queen's County, 1703–1737 (?)', *Journal of the County Kildare Archaeological Society*, v (1906), pp. 179–80; Thady Lawler, *An apology for pipes and pipers* (n.p., *c.* 1730), p. 2; [Sydney Owenson], *Lady Morgan's Memoirs*, 2 vols (London, 1862), i, pp. 41–4.

## 8 Dress

1. Poll book, Co. Clare, 1745, TCD, Ms. 2059, f. 92v.

2. HMC, *Ormonde Mss*, new series, viii, p. 344.

3. *A dialogue between the Rev. B. O'S[ulliva]n and J[]s G[]g, the attorney* ([?Cork], 1790); *A new song on a late occasion* ([?Cork], 1790); *A new copy of verses in favour of Abraham Morris, esq.* ([Cork?], 1790).

4. *[ ] to the Rt H[onoura]ble. Ld. Vt K[ingsboroug]h* ([?Cork], 1790).

5. Accounts and roll, Primrose Grange Charter School, s.d. 20 Feb. 1760, TCD, Ms. 5646.

6. Poor Book, St Michan's, Dublin, 1723–34, RCB, P. 276/8.1, p. 105.

7. Register of inmates of Magdalen Asylum, from 1766, RCB, Ms. 551/1.1, nos 30, 44.

8. A. Reyler to ?M. Nugent, 12 April 1718, 8 March 1725[6], NA, M 3272.

9. M. Moore to M. Moore, [*c.* 1759]; M. Moore to J. Moore, 11 Dec. 1759, Barber Mss, private collection, London, box I.

10. W. King, 'Treatise against Presbyterians', TCD, Ms. 1042; 'Curate's address to the gown', in W. Young, notebook, TCD, Ms. 10,664, pp. 1–50.

11. *The right of precedence between phisicians and civilians enquir'd into* (Dublin, 1720), p. 22; Barnard, *New anatomy*, p. 84.

12. J. Adlecron to S. Bagshawe, 27 June 1752, JRL, B 2/2/5; W. Montgomery to D. Graeme, 12 and 14 Nov. 1767, 17 Dec. 1767, 21 Jan. 1768, NAS, GD 190/3/321, 17 (2), 18, 24(3); GD 190/3/322, 29; H. Calder to D. Graeme, 21 Nov. 1767, 26 Feb. 1768, 12 April 1768, NAS, GD 190/3/321, 20; GD 190/3/322, 47, 53; Barnard, *New anatomy*, pp. 186–7.

13. John Kirby to Samuel Bagshawe, 2 April 1762, JRL, B 15/1/38.

14. J. Mussenden to W. Leathes, 18 [ ] 1724, Suffolk CRO, Ipswich, de Mussenden–Leathes Mss, HA 403/1/6, 109.

15. For the same problem in England: A. Shepard, 'Manhood, credit and patriarchy in early modern England, *c.* 1580–1640', *P & P*, clxvii (2000), p. 89.

16. 'The Kerry Cavalcade', printed in A. Carpenter (ed.), *Verse in English from eighteenth-century Ireland* (Cork, 1998), pp. 241–3, also, pp. 405–6; Barnard, *New anatomy*, pp. 237–8; C. Smith, *The antient and present state of the county of Kerry* (Dublin, 1756), p. 101, n. q.

17. Hume, report on Lord Malton's Irish estates, NLI, Ms. 6054, f. 15.

18. P. Kelly (ed.), 'The improvement of Ireland', in *Analecta Hibernica*, xxxv (1992), pp. 59–61.

19. The essential guide remains M. Dunlevy, *Dress in Ireland* (London, 1989, reprinted Cork, 1999). Stimulating perspectives are also offered by B. Lemire, *Fashion's favourite: the cotton trade and the consumer in Britain, 1660–1800* (Oxford, 1991) and D. Roche, *The culture of clothing: dress and fashion in the 'ancien regime'* (Cambridge, 1994).

20. E. Cooke to unknown, 22 Feb. 1727[8], NLI, Ms. 8,802/11; A. Philips to T. Tickell, 21 Jan. 1728[9], Tickell Mss, private collection, Devon; *To the honourable House of Commons, &c. The humble petition of the footmen in and about the city of Dublin* (Dublin, 1732).

21. T. Waite to E. Weston, 23 Aug. 1748, PRONI, T 3019/1113.

22. Deposition of M. Clapham, TCD, Ms. 814, f. 79; D. B. Quinn, *The Elizabethans and Ireland* (Ithaca, 1966), pp. 91–105.

23. Bp. W. Nicolson to Abp. W. Wake, 24 June 1718, Christ Church, Wake Ms. 12/275.

24. A. Dobbs, *An essay on the trade and improvement of Ireland* (Dublin, 1729), pp. 46–7, 91–2, 95; J. Johnston, *Bishop Berkeley's Querist in historical perspective* (Dundalk, 1970), pp. 125–31, 135, 139; S. Madden, *Reflections and resolutions proper for the gentlemen of Ireland* (Dublin, 1738) pp. 36–9, 164, 175–6, 185–9; *A new excellent ballad on the present taste of Dublin* ([?Dublin], *c.* 1740).

25. W. S. Lewis (ed.), *Letters of Horace Walpole*, 48 vols (New Haven, 1937–83), x, p. 1.

26. E. Spencer to F. Price, 21 Jan. 1744[5], 7 Dec. 1745, NLW, Puleston Ms. 3580E; Delany, *Autobiography*, 1st series, ii, pp. 394, 400, 408, 414, 415.

27. E. Spencer to F. Price, 7 Dec. 1745, 24 Feb. 1745[6], NLW, Puleston Ms. 3580E.

28. Sir W. Petty to Lady Petty, 4 Oct. 1681, BH Petty Papers, 5/89.

29. T. Medlycott to E. Southwell, 3 April 1721, BL, Add. Ms. 34,778, f. 33.

30. K. Conolly to J. Bonnell, 3 Nov. 1731, NLI, PC 434/6.

31. O. Gallagher to O. St George, 13 July 1727, PRO, C 110/46/496.

32. O. Gallagher to O. St George, 25 Oct. 1729, PRO, C 110/46/729; cf. O. Gallagher to O. St George, 24 Feb. 1727[8], PRO, C 110/46/471.

33. E. Spencer to F. Price, 2, 4 and 16 Feb. 1747[8], NLW, Puleston Ms. 3580E.

34. O. Gallagher to O. St George, 30 Oct. 1725, 11 Dec. 1725, 23 Feb. 1726[7], 14 March 1726[7], 24 Feb. 1727[8], PRO, C 110/46/404, 406, 414, 419, 471.

35. E. O'Hara, account book, 1722–33, NLI, Ms. 36,387, p. 70; bill of J. Gallagher, 13 March 1733[4], NLI, Ms. 35,365/6.

36. S. Wilson to M. St George, 22 Aug. 1730; PRO, C 110/46/916; O. Gallagher to O. St George, 14 Jan. 1726[7], PRO, C. 110/46/410.

37. S. Foster, 'Buying Irish: consumer nationalism in eighteenth-century Dublin', *History Today*, xlvii/6 (1997), pp. 44–51.

38. J. Bulkeley to J. Bonnell, 4 April 1721, NLI, PC 435.

39. K. Conolly to J. Bonnell, 7 March 1740[1], NLI, PC 434.

40. Anne Hill to S. Waring, 7 Feb. 1703[4], 12 April 1704; Anne Hill to S. Waring, 21 April 1705, private collection, Co. Down.

41. Dobbs, *Essay*, p. 47.

42. N. Harte, 'The economics of clothing in the late seventeenth century', *Textile History*, xxii (1991), pp. 277–96.

43. Dobbs, *Essay*, p. 46.

44. T. Medlycott to E. Southwell, 20 May 1717, BL, Add. Ms. 34,778, f. 18.

45. Harte, 'The economics of clothing', pp. 277–91.

46. Petition of city of Waterford to Ormonde, 1703, RIA, Ms. 12 W 24, ff. 43v–44.

47. Barnard, *New anatomy*, pp. 283–5; L. A. Clarkson, 'The Carrick-on-Suir woollen industry in the eighteenth century', *IESH*, xvi (1989), pp. 23–41; W. H. Crawford, 'The creation and evolution of small towns in Ulster in the seventeenth and eighteenth centuries', in P. Borsay and L. Proudfoot (eds), *Provincial towns in early modern England and Ireland; change, convergence and divergence*, Proceedings of the British Academy, cviii (2002), pp. 97–120; D. Dickson, 'Inland city: reflections on eighteenth-century Kilkenny', in W. Nolan and K. Whelan (eds), *Kilkenny: history and society* (Dublin, 1990), pp. 340–2; J. McVeagh (ed.), *Richard Pococke's Irish tours* (Dublin, 1995), pp. 97, 103, 187, 195.

48. *A list of commodities imported into Ireland* (Dublin, 1752).

49. *A representation of the state of the trade of Ireland before the House of Lords in England* (Dublin, 1750), pp. 11–13.

50. P. Delany, *Sixteen discourses upon doctrines and duties* (London, 1754), pp. 316–17, 325–8.

51. Murphy notebook, NLI, Ms. 1505, pp. 29, 35; T. G. Fewer, 'The hearth money roll of 1665 . . . ', *Old Kilkenny Review*, liii (2001), p. 97.

52. *The true and impartial account of the proceedings between Mr. Samuel Smith, merchant in Ross, and Gaspert Labalme, major . . .* (n.p., 1698); *The works of Mary Davys*, 2 vols (London, 1725), i, pp. 277–80; Carpenter (ed.), *Verse in English from eighteenth-century Ireland*, pp. 135–7.

53. Abp. W. King, account book, 1700–12, s.d. 16 Dec. 1707, 26 Jan. 1709[10], TCD, Ms. 751/2, ff. 208; *The Dublin Intelligencer*, 13 Dec. 1707; Mercer's Hospital, Minute Book, 1736–72, s.d. 25 April 1739, 12 June 1742, Mercer's Hospital, Dublin; N. Ginsburg, 'Rags to riches: second-hand clothes, 1700–1978', *Costume*, xiv (1980), pp. 121–35; B. Lemire, 'Peddling fashion: salesmen, pawnbrokers, tailors, thieves and the second-hand clothes trade in England, *c.* 1700–1800', *Textile History*, xxii (1991), pp. 67–80; G. Walker, 'Women, theft and the world of stolen goods', in J. Kermode and G. Walker (eds), *Women, crime and the courts in early modern England* (London, 1994).

54. Inventory of M. Brabazon, 9 Feb. 1637[8], Barber Mss, private collection, London, box III; inventory of earl of Kildare's goods, 11 Dec. 1656, NLI, Ms. 18,966; linen delivered to Mr Wixted, 26 May 1663, NLI, Ms. 18,966; inventory of S. Brabazon, 23 Feb. 1657[8], Barber Mss, private collection, London, box III; inventory of Ormond's linen at Kilkenny, 25 Aug. 1675, NLI, Ms. 2552; linen left at Kilkenny, 10 July 1676, NLI, Ms. 2527, p. 70; Ormond's goods at Dublin Castle, 21 March 1678[9], NLI, Ms. 2554; inventory of Corofin, Co. Clare, 9 May 1718, NLI, Inchiquin Mss, no. 1804; K. O'Hara to E. O'Hara, 15 Oct. 1715, NLI, Ms. 20,278; The Georgian Society, *Records of eighteenth-century domestic architecture*, 5 vols (Dublin, 1909–13), iv, pp. 7–8.

55. Rules and orders of the Incorporated Society, 1735–79, s.d. 24 Nov. 1762, TCD, Ms. 5301, p. 47; Mercer's Hospital, Minute Book, 1736–72, s.d. 31 Dec. 1737, Mercer's Hospital, Dublin.

56. Rules and orders of the Incorporated Society, 1735–79, s.d. 29 July 1752, 13 March 1765, TCD, Ms. 5301, pp. 29, 51; accounts and roll, Primrose Grange Charter School, s.d. 14 July 1774, TCD, Ms. 5646.

57. Incorporated Society Board Book, 1761–75, s.d. 1 Nov. 1769, TCD, Ms. 5225, p. 169.

58. Account book of Incorporated Society, 1733–78, TCD, Ms. 5419, pp. 24, 38, 40v, 45v, 47, 66, 71v, 88v, 90v, 96v–97, 98, 110, 113v, 123v, 124v, 126, 143v; rules and orders of the Incorporated Society, 1735–79, s.d. 19 April 1749, 19 Aug. 1772, TCD, Ms. 5301, pp. 19, 64; register of Bishop Foy's School, Waterford, 1711–1902, s.d. 17 April 1740, RCB, Ms. 523.

59. Rules and orders of the Incorporated Society, 1735–79, s.d. 14 Feb. 1770, TCD, Ms. 5301, pp. 58–9.

60. Accounts and roll, Primrose Grange Charter School, s.d. 27 June 1757, 29 Oct. 1759, 16 Nov. 1759, 24 May 1760, 16 Oct 1760, 15 Dec. 1760, 11 Oct. 1762, TCD, Ms. 5646.

61. *A hymn to be sung by the charity children of St. Andrew's Dublin . . . 2 Feb. 1730/1* (Dublin, 1730[1]).

62. Register of Magdalen Asylum, RCB, Ms. 551/1.1, nos 1, 2, 3, 21, 30, 31, 34, 37, 44.

63. Register of Green Coat School, Cork, St Anne's Church, Shandon, County Cork; Register of Incorporated Society children, 1765–92, TCD, Ms. 5668; accounts and roll, Arklow Charter School, TCD, Ms. 5598; accounts and roll, Ballycastle Charter School, TCD, Ms. 5609; accounts and roll, Ardbraccan

Charter School, TCD, Ms. 5597; Order Book, Primrose Grange Charter School, Sligo, 1757–90, TCD, Ms. 5646.

64. Accounts of J. Loughlin, s.d. 25 March 1739; 25 March 1740, NLI, Ms. 11,463; M. Mulcahy (ed.), *Calendar of Kinsale documents*, vii (Kinsale, 1998), pp. 53, 80, 98.

65. Masters' Accounts, Weavers' Company, Dublin, 1691–1714, accounts for 1697–8, 1701–2, RSAI; Churchwardens' accounts, St Michan's, Dublin, 1723–61, s.d. Aug. 1724, 1735, RCB, P. 276/8/2, pp. 27, 157; Vestry Minute Book, St Michan's, Dublin, 1724–60, s.d. 5 Jan. 1735[6], RCB, P. 276/4/1, p. 148; Mercer's Hospital, Minute Book, 1736–72, s.d. 29 Nov. 1746, Mercer's Hospital, Dublin; accounts and roll, Primrose Grange Charter School, s.d. 19 Feb. 1759, TCD, Ms. 5646; *CARD*, vi, pp. 189, 208, 230, 500; vii, pp. 355, 514; M. Mulcahy (ed.), *Calendar of Kinsale documents*, ii (Kinsale, 1989), p. 76; vii, pp. 3, 45.

66. Ware, household accounts, after 8 Aug. 1769, TCD, Ms. 10, 528, f. 108.

67. 'Master's linen', D. Johnston, account book from 1669, Birr Castle, Ms. A/16; list of Lady Peyton's linen, [1690s], NLI, Ms. 36,384; Vigors family, account book, 1711–20, s.d. 24 Aug. 1717, 13 Dec. 1718, 4 Dec. 1719, Carlow County Library; W. Alcock, 1761, journal, TCD, Ms. 10,165, ff. 2–2v, 74v.

68. R. A. Ansalment (ed.), *The remembrances of Elizabeth Freke, 1671–1714*, Camden Society, 5th series, xviii (2001), p. 47.

69. Partial inventory, undated but 18th century, NA, Chancery Pleadings, uncatalogued salvaged material, box 44.

70. K. Conolly to J. Bonnell, 26 Aug. 1731, 26 Aug. 1734, 3 Dec. 1734, 28 Feb. 1736[7], 20 Sep. 1736, 24 Sep. 1739, 24 July 1740, NLI, PC 434; T. Kingsbury to F. Price, 3 and 17 July 1736, 5 April 1746, 24 Feb. 1746[7]; Mrs E. Kingsbury to Mrs A. Price, 17 Nov. 1753, 22 Dec. 1753, NLW, Puleston Ms. 3584E; Mrs E. Kingsbury to Mrs A. Price, 28 Oct. 1754, NLW, Puleston deeds, no. 656; D. J. Griffin, 'The building and furnishings of a Dublin townhouse in the eighteenth century', *Bulletin of the Irish Georgian Society*, xxxviii (1996–7), p. 39.

71. E. Cooke to Sir W. Fownes, 22 Aug. 1724, NLI, Ms. 8801/8.

72. H. Howard to R. Howard, 8 Oct. 1729, NLI, PC 227; S. Bagshawe to Mrs Bagshawe, 12 Sep. 1740, JRL, B 2/3/77.

73. Accounts of Dorset and Devonshire, 1730–41, s.d. 22 Nov. 1734, 20 July 1736, Dublin Public Libraries, Gilbert Mss 199; N. Clements to E. Weston, 21 May 1747, PRONI, T 3019/873. As Lord Steward of the royal household, Dorset switched orders for linen from Holland to Ireland. Information from David Mitchell.

74. W. Hovell to W. Goold, 9 July 1684, private collection, Dublin, Hovell letterbook, 1683–8.

75. A. Crotty to P. Gould, 23 Sep. 1726, Chatsworth, Crotty letterbooks.

76. Lady A. Conolly to Lord Strafford, 8 Nov. 1733, BL, Add. Ms. 22,228, f. 89v; John Carteret Pilkington, *The real story of John Carteret Pilkington* (London, 1760), p. 144.

77. *Records of the General Synod of Ulster from 1691–1820*, 3 vols (Belfast, 1897), ii, pp. 362, 372.

78. R. Edgeworth, accounts, s.d. 26 March 1756, NLI, Ms. 1522, p. 118.

79. E. Lewis, 'An eighteenth-century linen table cloth from Ireland', *Textile History*, xv (1984), pp. 235–44.

80. E. O'Hara, account book, 1722–33, NLI, Ms. 36,387/7; A. Watson to E. Carleton, 1 March 1751, NLI, Ms. 5928/13; E. Brice, executors' accounts, PRONI, D 1556 16/17/13; Roche, *The culture of clothing*, pp. 367–70.

81. Lucas, journal, s.d. 15 Jan. 1740[1], 18 Feb. 1740[1], 8 May 1741, NLI, Ms. 14,101.

82. Bill to M. Moore, 11 Aug. 1753, Barber Mss, private collection, London, box I; bill of C. Helson, 29 Aug. 1719, Barber Mss, private collection, London, box III; account of D. Lenihan with J. Adair, 1754–5, NLI, Ms. 21,601.

83. Executors' accounts, John Martin, NA, Chancery Pleadings, salvaged material, box 3.

84. A. Hamilton to Lady Panmure, 28 Sep. 1692, 23 Feb. 1692[3], 13 Jan. 1695[6], 25 Oct. 1714, 9 April [?1715], NAS, GD 45/15/238, 2, 4 , 8, 31, 59.

85.  Inventory of Terence Egan, Birr, Co. Offaly, 16 June 1721, BL, Add. Ms. 31,881, ff. 295–7; inventory of Joseph Eves, 16 June 1729, Friends' Historical Library, Dublin, MM II L.I, pp. 1–10; inventory of Daniel Darrane, Nenagh, Co. Tipperary, 27 Jan. 1743[4], BL, Add. Ms. 31,882, ff. 141–54; bill of J. Bourke to G. Brabazon, 1740–1, Barber Mss, private collection, London, box I; T. C. Barnard, 'The worlds of goods in Co. Offaly in the early eighteenth century', in T. P. O'Neill and W. Nolan (eds), *Offaly: history and society* (Dublin, 1998), pp. 371–92.

86.  Handbill of B. Sheehy, 23 Sep. 1766, TCD, Ms. 2012/306.

87.  Will of J. Pearson, 6 Feb. 1721[2], Friends' Historical Library, Dublin, MM II L. II.

88.  Will of J. Deane, 25 Oct. 1724, Friends' Historical Library, Dublin, MM II L. II, p. 8. Also, the wills and inventories of H. Brookfield, 30 Nov. 1728, J. Stevens, Dec. 1730, S. Watson, 3 Sep. 1731, Friends' Historical Library, Dublin, MM II L. II, pp. 53–4, 60–2, 65–9.

89.  Fragments from inventory of J. Reymer, NA, Chancery Pleadings, uncatalogued salvaged material, boxes 14, 17, 27, 52. Cf. bill for cloth from Eustace and Russell to Sir M. Crosbie, 20 March 1749[50], TCD, Ms. 3821/218.

90.  Trade card of P. Leonard, 33 Corn Market, Dublin, in Bodleian, Johnson collection, album 111, no. 100.

91.  Reynell account book, account with S. Nugent, s.d. 29 Oct. 1761, NLI, Ms. 5991; Legg (ed.), *Synge letters*, p. 304, and note 8.

92.  M. Fitzgerald to Sir M. Crosbie, 25 Feb. 1718[19], TCD, Ms. 3821/173.

93.  M. Mulcahy, *Calendar of Kinsale documents*, iii (Kinsale, 1994), pp. 13, 19, 27, 79.

94.  B. Lynch to M. Brabazon, n.d.[1720s], Barber Mss, private collection, London, box III.

95.  J. Anketell, 'On Stramore patron, Co. Monaghan', TCD. Ms. 10,664, pp. 79–85, partly printed in Carpenter (ed.), *Verse in English from eighteenth-century Ireland*, pp. 492–6.

96.  Vigors account book, 1711–24, s.d. 1 July 1720, 22 May 1723, 1 Jan. 1723[4], Vigors Mss, Carlow County Library, Carlow.

97.  Vigors account book, s.d., 23 July 1719, 23–24 Aug. [?1719], Vigors Mss, Carlow County Library, Carlow.

98.  R. Edgeworth, accounts, s.d. 10 March 1739[40], NLI, Ms. 1513, p. 83.

99.  J. H. Gebbie (ed.), *An introduction to the Abercorn letters* (Omagh, 1972), p. 266.

100.  Inventory of George Roche, n.d. (*c.* 1760), BL, Add. Ms. 19,868, ff. 177–178v.

101.  Rules and orders of the Incorporated Society, 1735–79, s.d. 2 March 1752, TCD, Ms. 5301, p. 28.

102.  M. Mason to J. Mason, 26 Nov. 1737, Dromana, Co. Waterford, Villiers–Stuart Mss, T 3131/B/1/27.

103.  B. Badham to ?H. Boyle, 7 Nov. 1731, PRONI, D 2707/A/1/11, 37.

104.  W. Smythe to R. Smythe, 7 April 1767, NLI, PC 446; S. R. Penny, *Smythe of Barbavilla: the history of an Anglo–Irish family* (Oxford, 1974), pp. 71–2.

105.  Taylor, account book, NLI, Ms. 25,386, opening 36.

106.  A. J. Guy (ed.), *Colonel Samuel Bagshawe and the army of George II, 1731–1762*, Army Records Society (London, 1990), pp. 94–5.

107.  W. C. Balfour, annual expenses, 1742–8, NLI, Ms. 10,277/1.

108.  Inventories of J. Scott, 9 March 1728[9]; J. Smith, 22 Oct. 1731, J. Brownlow, 7 June 1740, PRONI, T 1062/55–6, 68–9, 79–81.

109.  Bills, 1685, V & A, Ormonde Mss, 6, f. 27; T. C. Barnard, 'Integration or separation? Hospitality and display in Protestant Ireland, *c.* 1660–1800', in L. Brockliss and D. Eastwood (eds), *A union of multiple identities: the British Isles, c. 1750–1850* (Manchester, 1997), pp. 132–4.

110.  Abp. H. Boulter to Abp. W. Wake, 21 May 1726, Christ Church, Wake Ms. 14/264.

111.  D. Johnston, accounts as executor of Elizabeth Vincent and with A. Stokes, 1669, Birr Castle, Ms. A/16, account book from 1669.

112.  Will of J. Croker, 24 Sep. 1751, NA, T 7087; will of R. Gunning, 15 Aug. 1748, Northamptonshire CRO, G (H) III/1; will of Sir R. Newcomen, 17 Jan. 1734[5], PRONI, D 3168/1/2; will of R. Rochfort, 3 May 1726, PRONI, T 3468/1; will of R. Waring, 23 April 1761, PRONI, T 1023/59; W. P. Burke, *History of Clonmel* (Waterford, 1907), p. 330.

113. Inventory and executors' accounts of J. Burton, 13 Oct. 1737, Friends' Historical Library, Dublin, MM II L. II, p. 94.

114. Inventory and executors' accounts, N. Beeby, 30 June 1741, Friends' Historical Library, Dublin, MM II L. II, p. 188.

115. Register of Magdalen Asylum, RCB, Ms. 551/1.1, nos 28, 75.

116. Bills of J. Butler and P. Holohan, *c.* 1720–30, NLI, Ms. 11,469/2 and 3.

117. Accounts of J. Loughlin, 27 Nov 1730, NLI, Ms. 11,463/2.

118. H. Alcock to J. Mason, 14 June 1718, Dromana, Villiers–Stuart Mss, T 3131/B/1/9.

119. S. Bagshawe, journal, before 24 Nov. 1740, JRL, B 15/3/1; 'The autobiography of Pole Cosby of Stradbally, Queen's County, 1703–1737(?)', *Journal of the County Kildare Archaeological Society*, v (1906), p. 182; W. Hawkins, *The order of proceeding to the funeral of the Rt. Hon. William Conolly, esq.* (Dublin, [1729]); J. Trusler, *The tablet of memory* (Dublin, 1782), p. 175.

120. K. Conolly to J. Bonnell, 9 Dec. 1729, NLI, PC 434; J. Bulkeley to J. Bonnell, 13 Dec. 1729, 24 Jan. 1729[30]; T. Pierson to J. Bonnell, 30 Oct. 1729; F. Burton to J. Bonnell, 9 Nov. 1729, 9 and 13 Dec. 1729, 26 Jan. 1729[30], NLI, PC 435; O. Gallagher to O. St George, 4 Nov. 1729, PRO, C 110/46/733.

121. Vestry Book, St Michan's, Dublin, 1724–60, s.d. 23 April 1728, RCB, P276/4.1, p. 54; proctors' accounts, St Patrick's Cathedral, Dublin, 1718–35, s.d. 4 Aug. 1727, RCB, C. 2.1.10(1).

122. Executors' accounts for Lady Butler, 25 Feb. 1745[6], NA, Sarsfield–Vesey Mss, account no. 46; bill of A. Chapman, 1746, NA, Sarsfield–Vesey Mss, account no. 47; S. Waring, executors' accounts, 22 Dec. 1739, private collection, Co. Down.

123. Barnard, *New anatomy*, pp. 4–5; 'The autobiography of Pole Cosby of Stradbally', p. 181.

124. HMC, *Egmont Mss*, ii, pp. 20, 21, 23, 100–1.

125. J. Potter to R. Wilmot, 28 May 1741, PRONI, T 3019/385.

126. Will of Sir W. Parsons, proved, 28 Feb. 1650[1], PRO, PROB 11/215, 33; accounts of L. Parsons, Birr Castle, Ms. A/12.

127. Will of Sir W. Parsons, 18 Oct. 1733, Birr Castle, Ms. B/1/10.

128. L. Parsons to J. Acton, after Nov. 1739, Birr Castle, B/4/25.

129. Will of W. Smythe, 27 Aug. 1768, Smythe of Barbavilla Mss, private collection, Berkshire.

130. Will of R. Edgeworth, 20 March 1770, NA, T 5555.

131. R. Edgeworth, accounts, s.d. 21 and 29 Sep. 1764, NLI, Ms. 1528, pp. 105, 107; cf. s.d. 22 April 1720, NLI, Ms. 1507, p. 16.

132. R. Edgeworth, accounts, s.d. 21, 22 Sep. 1764, 7 and 25 Oct. 1764, NLI, Ms. 1528, pp. 105, 114, 122, 125.

133. R. Edgeworth, accounts, s.d. 22 Sep. 1764, NLI, Ms. 1528, p. 114.

134. R. Edgeworth, accounts, s.d. 23 Sep. 1764, NLI, Ms. 1528, p. 106.

135. R. Edgeworth accounts, s.d. 21 and 26 Jan. 1739[40], 5 March 1739[40], 3–4 May 1743, NLI, Mss. 1513, pp. 76, 77, 82; 1516, p. 29.

136. Executors' accounts for K. White, s.d. 1 April 1751, 18 Oct. 1751, NLI, Ms. 116, f. 24. Evidently the spending was justified since she was singled out for admiration. W. Smythe to R. Smythe, 2 Nov. 1751, NLI, PC 445.

137. L. Parsons to J. Acton, after Nov. 1739, Birr Castle, Co. Offaly, B/4/25; bill for funeral of J. Moore, 11 Aug. 1756, Barber Mss, private collection, London, box I.

138. E. Role to Sir M. Crosbie, 16 Dec. 1757, NLI, Talbot–Crosbie Mss, folder 61; trade card of Role, Bodleian, Johnson collection, album 111.

139. W. Laffan (ed.), *The Cries of Dublin drawn from the life by Hugh Douglas Hamilton, 1760* (Dublin, 2003), pp. 66–9, 184–5.

140. E. O'Hara, accounts, from 1 April 1719, NLI, Ms. 36,387/6.

141. 7 Geo. II c. 13; *Statutes*, vol. vi, p. 40; Dobbs, *Essay*, pp. 50, 91–2; trade advertisement, Bodleian, Johnson collection, album 111.

142. Bills for funeral of A. St Leger, Viscount Doneraile, July and Aug. 1727, NLI, Ms. 34,112/14.

143. E. O'Hara, accounts from 1 April 1719, NLI, Ms. 36,387/6; bill of M. Knox, 3 April 1719, NLI, Ms. 36,387/1.

144. Lady Petty to A. and H. Petty, 1 Nov. 1684, 14 Feb. 1684[5], BL, Add. Ms. 72,857/4, 23.

145. J. Evelyn to J. Evelyn, senior, 12 Jan. 1694[5], 26 Feb. 1694[5], Christ Church, Oxford, Evelyn Mss, now in BL; J. Bonnell to Bp. W. King, 19 Jan. 1694[5], TCD, Mss. 1995–2008/400; A. Hamilton to Lady Panmure, 10 March 1694[5], NAS, GD 45/14/238, 5; A. Spurrett to T. Baker, 28 March 1704, Chatsworth, letterbook of A. Spurrett, 1703–4; M. Supple to H. Boyle, 22 June 1727, PRONI, D 2707/A1/1/9. On the invention of mourning: L. Taylor, *Mourning dress: a costume and social history* (London, 1983).

146. F. Manley to G. Waring, 22 Nov. [1702], Anne Hill to G. Waring, 11 April 1705, private collection, Co. Down.

147. Lady Powerscourt to dowager countess of Orrery, 13 Aug. [?1685], Petworth, general series, 27; K. Conolly to J. Bonnell, 20 Dec. 1737, NLI, PC 434; Lady A. Conolly to unknown, 18 April 1738, BL, Add. Ms. 22,228, f. 162v.

148. C. Nolan to E. Nolan, n.d. [?1727], Barber Mss, private collection, London, box III.

149. M. Mason to J. Mason, 3, 5 and 10 Dec. 1737, Dromana, Villiers–Stuart Mss, T. 3131/B/1/31, 32, 34.

150. R. French, account book, s.d. 13 Dec. 1744, NLI, Ms. 4919, f. 65v.

151. E. O'Hara, accounts from 1 April 1719, NLI, Ms. 36,387/1.

152. M. Delany to unknown, 13 Oct. 1747, Newport Public Library, Gwent, Delany Mss, 2/167; Delany, *Autobiography*, 1st series, ii, pp. 476–8.

153. Will of H. Prittie, 15 Dec. 1737, NLI, Ms. 29,806/130; will of G. Johnston, 24 Oct. 1759, PRONI, D 3406/G/3.

154. Will of W. Akie, 6 Jan. 1732[3], PRONI, D 1618/8/16.

155. Will of J. Croker, 24 Sep. 1751, NA, T 7087; will of Grace Kempston, 9 May 1723, NLI, microfilm, p. 4529; cf. will of Elizabeth, Lady Parsons, 26 Nov. 1739, Birr Castle, Ms. B/1/12; will of Thomas Edwards, 29 March 1721, PRONI, D 1618/8/15.

156. A. Alcock to J. Mason, 28 Jan. 1717[18], Dromana, Villiers–Stuart Mss, T 3131/B/1/2.

157. J. Crosbie to D. Crosbie, 18 March 1713[14], TCD, Ms. 3821/159.

158. Paull, account books, s.d. 15 May 1717, NLI, Mss. 13,991, opening 6; 12,938, pp. 24, 25, 27; W. Piers to B. Pratt, 12 June 1750, NLI, Ms. 5245.

159. R. Edgeworth, will, 20 March 1770, NA, T 5555.

160. Will of H. Dalway, 9 Dec. 1720, PRONI, D 1618/8/14; will of W. Akie, 6 Jan. 1732[3], PRONI, D 1618/8/16.

161. Will of R. Howard, 13 Oct. 1736, NLI, PC 351(1).

162. Will of W. Neagle, 18 June 1712, TCD, Ms. 2014/228.

163. St J. D. Seymour (ed.), *Adventures and experiences of a seventeenth-century clergyman* (Dublin, 1909), p. 8.

164. Wills of Mary Thackeray, 29 Nov. 1728 and Mary Kelly, 19 Feb. 1730[1], Friends' Historical Library, Dublin, MM II L. II, pp. 41, 47.

165. Register of Magdalen Asylum, RCB, Ms. 551/1.1, no. 75.

166. R. Synge, sermon on Ephesians 5:5, *c.* 1683, Synge Mss, private collection, Greenwich.

167. N. Jones to G. Legge, [1670], Staffordshire CRO, Dartmouth Mss, D (W) 1778/I/i, 303; will of H. Dalway, 6 Jan. 1698[9], PRONI, D 1618/8/5; will of J. Wilson, 19 Feb. 1700[1], Southampton UL, BR/138/1; Burke, *History of Clonmel*, pp. 329, 340.

168. Will of W. Smythe, 27 Aug. 1768, Smythe of Barbavilla Mss, private collection, Berkshire.

169. Will of E. Parsons, 26 Nov. 1739, Birr Castle, Ms. B/1/12; Burke, *History of Clonmel*, p. 330.

170. Executors' accounts, 20 and 22 Dec. 1739; papers about S. Waring's funeral, Dec. 1739, private collection, Co. Down.

171. J. Warburton, bill for funeral of Mrs Isabella Balfour, 1742, NLI, Ms. 10,276/7.

172. Ten pairs of 'glazed' gloves for men were distributed at the funeral of Edward Brenan, about 1751. NA, Chancery Pleadings, salvaged material, box 1; 'Autobiography of Pole Cosby', p. 182.

173. Will of J. Pearson, 6 Feb. 1721[2], Friends' Historical Library, Dublin, MM II L. II.

174. Gebbie (ed.), *Abercorn letters*, p. 50.

175. Card for funeral of D. Byrne, Dublin, 24 Jan. 1683[4], RIA, broadsides collection, vol. 1, item 38; executors' accounts for R. Dalway, 10 May 1698, PRONI, D 1618/8/4.

176. N. Peacock, journal, s.d. 5, 6, 7, 8 October 1742, NLI, Ms. 16,091.

177. N. Peacock, journal, s.d. 15 Nov. 1743, 1 Aug. 1744, NLI, Ms. 16,091.

178. For the similarity with English practices: R. Houlbrooke, *Death, religion and the family in England, 1480–1750* (Oxford, 1998), pp. 248–94.

179. Barnard, 'The world of goods and County Offaly', pp. 371–92.

180. Lucas, journal, s.d. 18, 29 and 31 Jan. 1740[1], 3 and 22 Feb. 1740[1], NLI, Ms. 14,101.

181. R. Herbert, 'Limerick shop-signs of the eighteenth century', *North Munster Antiquarian Journal*, ii (1940), p. 160; advertisement of A. McKee, NLI, Ms. 36,365/1.

182. N. Peacock, journal, s.d. 18 Sep. 1744, 12 Oct. 1744, NLI, Ms. 16,091.

183. N. Peacock, journal, s.d. 16, 19, 24 and 25 Nov. 1745, NLI, Ms. 16,091.

184. N. Peacock, journal, s.d. 16 Feb. 1746[7], NLI, Ms. 16,091.

185. N. Peacock, journal, s.d. 18 and 20 April 1747, 9 May 1747, NLI, Ms. 16,091.

186. N. Peacock, journal, s.d. 19, 23 and 24 Oct. 1747, NLI, Ms. 16,091.

187. N. Peacock, journal, s.d. 8, 13–15 Dec. 1748, 5 July 1749, 18–19 Dec. 1749, 21 Jan. 1749[50], NLI, Ms. 16,091; B. Lemire, 'Developing consumerism and the ready-made clothing trade in Britain, 1750–1800', *Textile History*, xv (1984), pp. 21–38.

188. N. Peacock, journal, s.d. 21 Sep. 1741, NLI, Ms. 16,091.

189. N. Peacock, journal, s.d. 21 Jan. 1749[50], 24 April 1750, NLI, Ms. 16,091.

190. For his cornet's commission, N. Peacock, journal, s.d. 14 Dec. 1740, 8, 14 and 24 March 1743[4], NLI, Ms. 16,091.

191. J. Pratt, diary, s.d. 1 Feb. 1745[6], Cloverhill, Co. Cavan, Purdon Mss.

192. R. Lawrence to Ormond, received 30 Oct. 1668, Bodleian, Carte Ms. 36, f. 521; HMC, *Ormonde Mss*, n.s., iv, pp. 38–40; vii, p. 27; *A memoir of Mistress Ann Fowkes* (Dublin, 1892), pp. 26–7; W. Penn, *My Irish Journal, 1669–1670*, ed. I. Grubb (London, 1952), p. 22; R. Lawrence, *The interest of Ireland in its trade and wealth stated*, 2 vols (Dublin, 1682), ii, pp. 102–5.

193. *CARD*, xi, pp. 486–8.

194. N. Peacock, journal, s.d. 21 Oct. 1740, 22 July–10 Nov. 1743, 16 Dec. 1743, 19 April 1750, NLI, Ms. 16,091.

195. Inventory of J. Burton, 13 Oct. 1737, Friends' Historical Library, Dublin, MM II L. II, p. 95.

196. J. Vallancez, bill, 1678–81, Dorset CRO, D/FSI, box 222.

197. Balfour, account book, 1697–1710, s.d. 12 Oct. 1703, NLI, Ms. 9536.

198. Accounts, s.d. 7 Aug. 1713, Inchiquin Mss, NLI, Ms. 14,468; *Faulkner's Dublin Journal*, cxii, 17 May 1726.

199. Laffan (ed.), *The Cries of Dublin*, pp. 78–9.

200. N. Peacock, journal, s.d. 23 May 1745, 4 June 1745, NLI, Ms. 16,091.

201. P. V. Thompson and D. J. Thompson (eds), *The account books of Jonathan Swift* (Newark and London, 1984), pp. 71, 208.

202. Balfour, account book, s.d. 12 Oct. 1703, NLI, Ms. 9536.

203. R. Edgeworth, accounts, s.d. 30 Dec. 1724, 1 March 1726[7], NLI, Mss 1508, p. 148; 1509, p. 118.

204. R. Edgeworth, accounts, s.d. 28 Nov. 1739, NLI, Ms. 1513, p. 68

205. R. Edgeworth, accounts, s.d. 29 Sep. 1744, NLI, Ms. 1516, p. 134.

206. R. Edgeworth, accounts, s.d. 15 Sep. 1743, 5 Dec. 1743, 10 Feb. 1758, NLI, Mss. 1516, pp. 68, 76; 1524, p. 65.

207. Bill of C. Plunkett with C. O'Hara, 24 Dec. 1724, NLI, Ms. 35,365/5; inventory of Lohort Castle, 14 Oct. 1742, BL, Add. Ms. 47,004A, f. 73–73v.

208. R. Edgeworth, accounts, s.d. 1718, 1 Jan. 1719[20], 15 Feb. 1719[20], 14 March 1719[20], 15 Feb. 1721[2], 30 July 1723, 3 and 10 Nov. 1735, 17 Dec. 1735, 16 June 1743, NLI, Mss 1507, pp. 8, 15, 25, 26, 57; 1508, p. 73; 1511, pp. 68, 69, 73; 1516, p. 40.

209. Minute book of Guild of Barber Surgeons, 1703–57, s.d. 13 Oct. 1718, TCD, Ms. 1447/8/1, f. 30.

210. Minute book of Guild of Barber Surgeons, 1703–57, s.d. 24 Nov. 1720, 15 Jan. 1721[2], TCD, Ms. 1447/8/1, ff. 35, 36v.

211. C. Caldwell to J. Pickard, 13 June 1745, 27 May 1746, Dorset CRO, D/BLX/B17 & B19.

212. J. Waller to A. and H. Petty, [Aug. 1684], BL, Add. Ms. 72,857/16.

213. Lady Petty to A. and H. Petty, 19 Dec. 1684, BL, Add. Ms. 72,857/28.

214. C. Crofts to H. Owen, 1 Aug. 1694; account of C. Crofts with H. Owen, 1694, NLW, Powis Castle correspondence, nos 663, 726.

215. R. Smythe to W. Smythe, 31 Dec. 1713, 20 July 1714, Smythe of Barbavilla Ms, private collection, Berkshire.

216. K. A. Miller, A. Schrier, B. D. Boling and D. N. Doyle (eds), *Irish immigrants in the land of Canaan: letters and memoirs from colonial and revolutionary America, 1675–1815* (Oxford, 2003), p. 246.

217. R. Smythe to W. Smythe, 19 Nov. 1717, 31 May 1729, 20 Sep. 1729, 1 Nov. 1729, 21 Dec. 1729, 10 Feb. 1729[30], 30 May 1730, Smythe of Barbavilla Mss, private collection, Berkshire.

218. R. Smythe to W. Smythe, 5 April 1729, Smythe of Barbavilla Mss, private collection, Berkshire.

219. R. Smythe to W. Smythe, 13 and 27 Feb. 1730[1], 29 May 1731, 26 June 1731, Smythe of Barbavilla Mss, private collection, Berkshire.

220. J. Styles, 'Product innovation in early modern London', *P & P*, clxviii (2000), pp. 124–68.

221. Barnard, 'Integration or separation?', pp. 127–46.

222. W. Waring to S. Waring, 3 April 1697, 1 May 1697, private collection, Co. Down.

223. W. Waring to S. Waring, 20 Feb. 1696[7], private collection, Co. Down; T. Barnard, 'Public and private uses of wealth in Ireland, *c.* 1660–1760', in J. R. Hill and C. Lennon (eds), *Luxury and austerity: Historical Studies, XXI* (Dublin, 1999), pp. 73–4; Barnard, 'What became of Waring?', pp. 185–212.

224. Bp. R. Howard to H. Howard, 23 April 1731, NLI, PC 227.

225. T. Black to A. Black, 7 Oct. 1771, PRONI, T 1073/23.

226. T. Coningsby to C. Fox, 15 Sep. 1690, Dorset CRO, D/FSI, box 238, bundle 15.

227. Barnard, 'What became of Waring?', pp. 185–212.

228. T. H. Breen, 'An empire of goods: the anglicization of colonial America, 1690–1776', *Journal of British Studies*, xxv (1986), pp. 468–96; C. Campbell, 'Understanding traditional and modern patterns of consumption in eighteenth-century England: a character-action approach', in J. Brewer and R. Porter (eds), *Consumption and the world of goods* (London and New York, 1993), pp. 40–57; M. Finn, 'Men's things: masculine possession in the consumer revolution', *Social History*, xxv (2000), pp. 133–55.

229. R. Power to W. Congreve, 21 and 28 June 1694, Chatsworth, Lismore Ms. 34/64, 65.

230. Carleton notebook, s.d. 1678, NLI, Ms. 4715.

231. C. O'Hara, accounts from April 1690, NLI, Ms. 36,387/1.

232. Lucas, journal, s.d. 10 June 1741 NLI, Ms. 14,101.

233. Unknown to K. O'Hara, [1690s], NLI, Ms. 20,277; Revd T. Caulfield to K. O'Hara, 19 March 1702[3], 9 Dec. 1703, NLI, Ms. 20,388; A. Crosbie to W. Crosbie, 9 May 1746, TCD, Ms. 3821/214.

234. A. Hill to G. Waring, 21 April 1705, 28 May 1705, 6 Sep. 1705, private collection, Co. Down; A. Hamilton to Lady Panmure, [*c.* 1710], NAS, GD 45/14/238, 79; F. Manley to G. Waring, 29 Sep. [*c.* 1720], private collection, Co. Down; M. Ledwidge to R. Smythe, 19 Oct. 1765, 23 Nov. 1765, 26 Sep. 1765, NLI, PC 446.

235. E. Cooke to Mrs Sweet, 29 May 1726, 30 June 1729, 15 Jan. 1729[30], Cooke Mss, Maidenhall, Co. Kilkenny; 'The diary of Anne Cooke', *Journal of the County Kildare Archaeological Society*, viii (1916), p. 218.

236. R. Smythe to W. Smythe, 12 and 19 Aug. 1732, Smythe of Barbavilla Mss, private collection, Berkshire.

237. R. Smythe to W. Smythe, 10 Sep. 1737, 28 April 1739, 26 Sep. 1741, 20 Feb. 1741[2], 29 Sep. 1747, 3 Nov. 1747, Smythe of Barbavilla Mss, private collection, Berkshire; J. Digby to W. Smythe, 21 April 1733, 25 Aug. 1733, NLI, PC 445.

238. R. Smythe to W. Smythe, 13 Feb. 1730[1], Smythe of Barbavilla Mss, private collection, Berkshire.

239. R. Smythe to W. Smythe, 13 and 27 July 1749, Smythe of Barbavilla Mss, private collection, Berkshire. For Peter Webb, see PRO, C 108/248.

240. Finn, 'Men's things', pp. 133–55.
241. A. Vickery, 'Women and the world of goods: a Lancashire consumer and her possessions, 1751–81', in Brewer and Porter (eds), *Consumption and the world of goods*, pp. 274–81; L. Weatherill, 'A possession of one's own: women and consumer behaviour in England, 1660–1740', *Journal of British Studies*, xxv (1986), pp. 31–56.
242. *A letter to a member of parliament containing a proposal for bringing in a bill to revise, amend or repeal certain obsolete statutes, commonly called the ten commandments* (Dublin, 1738), p. 15; *The distress'd state of Ireland considered; more particularly in respect to the north in a letter to a friend* (n.p., 1740), pp. 14, 49.
243. Carpenter (ed.), *Verse in English from eighteenth-century Ireland*, pp. 492–6.

## 9  *Dublin*

1. W. Molyneux to J. Flamsteed, 8 April 1684, Southampton Civic Archives, Molyneux Papers, D/M, 1/1, f. 73v.
2. A. Hamilton to Lady Panmure, 22 April [*c.* 1705], 27 July [*c.* 1709], NAS, GD 45/14/238, 62, 68.
3. D. Dickson, 'The place of Dublin in the eighteenth-century Irish economy', in T. M. Devine and D. Dickson (eds), *Ireland and Scotland, 1600–1850* (Edinburgh, 1983), p. 179; P. Fagan, *Catholics in a Protestant country: the papist constituency in eighteenth-century Dublin* (Dublin, 1998), pp. 9–52.
4. J. Smythe to W. Smythe, 15 Jan. 1735[6], NLI, PC 449; R. Edgeworth, accounts, s.d. 16 Aug. 1743, 25 Feb. 1752, NLI, Mss 1515, pp. 63; 1519, p. 210.
5. *An examination of certain abuses, corruptions and enormities in the City of Dublin* (Dublin, 1732), p. 3; E. Lloyd, *A description of the city of Dublin* (Dublin, ?1732), sig. A2, p. 3; 'Philostelus', *A letter to the Right Honourable Sir Ralph Gore, Bart.* (Dublin, 1732), p. 14; John Long, *The golden fleece* (Dublin, 1762), p. 26.
6. *The tricks of the town laid open* (Dublin, *c.* 1750); A. Stringer, *The experienced huntsman* (Belfast, 1714, reprinted Dublin, 1780); *A dialogue between Dean Swift and Tho. Prior, esq.* (Dublin, 1753).
7. Plans of Jervis's development, TCD, Ms. 8556/70 and 73; N. T. Burke, 'Dublin 1600–1800: a study in urban morphogenesis', unpublished Ph.D. thesis, TCD (1972); P. Clark and R. Gillespie (eds), *Two Capitals: London and Dublin, 1500–1840,* Proceedings of the British Academy, cvii (2001); M. Craig, *Dublin, 1660–1860: a social and architectural history* (Dublin and London, 1952), pp. 3–68; L. M. Cullen, 'The growth of Dublin, 1600–1900: character and heritage', in F. A. A. Aalen and K. Whelan (eds), *Dublin: city and county: from prehistory to present* (Dublin, 1992), pp. 252–77; R. Dudley, 'St. Stephen's Green. The early years, 1664–1730', *Dublin Historical Record*, liii (2000), pp. 157–79; The Georgian Society, *Records of eighteenth-century domestic architecture and decoration in Dublin*, 5 vols (Dublin, 1909–13), ii, pp. 31–111.
8. Journal of J. Verdon, p. 36, Cardiff Central Library, Ms. 4.370; Craig, *Dublin, 1660–1860*, pp. 19–21.
9. Account of houses in the parishes of Dublin, 1701–5, TCD, Ms. 888/2, 262; 'houses in Dublin', 20 July 1719, BL, Add. Ms. 47,127; return of houses, 1733, Monck Mason collections, vol. iii, part i, Dublin Public Libraries, Gilbert Ms. 68, pp. 151–2; W. Petty, *The political anatomy of Ireland* (London, 1691), p. 117.
10. Sir W. Petty to J. Grant, 6 Nov. 1668, 22 Dec. 1668, McGill UL, Osler Ms. 7612; Annesley rental, 1712–20, Oxfordshire CRO, E6/7/E/3.
11. Sir W. Petty to Cork, 13 July 1669 and undated, McGill UL, Osler Ms. 7612; Cork and Burlington, miscellaneous rental, 1693, p. 2, Chatsworth, Lismore Mss; T. C. Barnard, 'Land and the limits of loyalty: the second earl of Cork and first earl of Burlington (1612–98)', in T. Barnard and J. Clark (eds), *Lord Burlington: architecture, art and life* (London, 1995), pp. 167–99.
12. E. MacLysaght (ed.), *Calendar of the Orrery Papers* (Dublin, 1941), p. 25; L. T. Stockwell, *Dublin theatres and theatre customs (1637–1820)* (Kingsport, 1938), p. 27.

13.  Williams (ed.), *Correspondence of Swift*, iv, pp. 65–70; Johnston-Liik, *HIP*, iv, pp. 232–3.

14.  Sir R. Cox to E. Southwell, BL, Add. Ms. 38,154, f. 41.

15.  Sir W. Fownes to W. Fownes, 19 March 1733[4], Cooke Mss, Maidenhall, Co. Kilkenny; J. Dobbin to Sir W. Fownes, 24 June 1735, 12 July 1735, 16 Aug. 1735, 27 Nov. 1735, NLI, Ms. 8802; accounts, 1736–7, 1737–8, NLI, Ms. 8801; Stockwell, *Dublin theatres and theatre customs*, pp. 46, 66–8.

16.  J. Dobbin to Sir W. Fownes, 24 June 1735, 12 July 1735, 16 Aug. 1735, 27 Nov. 1735, NLI, Ms. 8802.

17.  H. Temple, account book, 1712–21, Southampton UL, BR 2/2; H. Hatch to Lord Palmerston, 6 July 1728, 5 Dec. 1741, Southampton UL, Broadlands Mss, BR 142/1/1; BR 142/1/11; Palmerston to H. Hatch, 19 Nov. 1741, Southampton UL, BR 2/8; *The villa: or Glasnevin, a poem* (Dublin, 1754).

18.  Sir J. Temple to H. Temple, 30 Sep. 1697, Southampton UL, BR 5/22.

19.  Sir W. Petty to J. Grant, 6 Nov. 1668, 22 Dec. 1668; Sir W. Petty to Lady Petty, 8 Sep. 1677, 6 Oct. 1677, 16 Feb. 1677[8], McGill UL, Osler Ms. 7612. By 1674, after renewing the search, he was warned that a suitable residence would cost a yearly £80–90, together with an entry fine of perhaps £200. T. Waller to Bunworth, 17 Oct. 1674, BH, Petty Papers, 16, now BL, Add. Ms.; contributions to ministers' money, St Werburgh's, Dublin, 1661–5, RCB, P 326/27/3/42; 'Rental of landgable rents, City of Dublin, 1665', in *The fifty-seventh report of the deputy keeper of the public records . . . in Ireland* (Dublin, 1936), p. 561.

20.  R. Wood to Sir W. Petty, Petty Papers, 6, part ii/63, 64, now BL, Add. Ms; T. C. Barnard, *Cromwellian Ireland: English government and reform in Ireland, 1649–1660* (Oxford, 1975), pp. 244–5.

21.  E. McKellar, *The birth of modern London: the development and design of the city, 1660–1720* (Manchester, 1999), p. 66.

22.  James Bonnell to J. Strype, 14 Feb. 1694[5], 25 Jan. 1698[9], Cambridge UL, 1/80, 85; Jane Bonnell to J. Strype, 13 June 1699, Cambridge UL, 2/232; vestry book, St Mary's, Dublin, 1699–1739, RCB, P 277/7.1, p. 16; M. Clark, 'Dublin city pipe water accounts 1704/5', *Irish Genealogist*, ix (1994), p. 78.

23.  Account of O. Gallagher with O. St George, 1730, PRO, C 110/46, 629.

24.  O. Gallagher to O. St George, 19 Feb. 1729[30], PRO, C 110/46, 720.

25.  R. Edgeworth, accounts, s.d. 14 Aug. 1724, NLI, Ms. 1508, p. 117.

26.  R. Poekrich, *A third address to the gentlemen, clergy, freeholders and freemen of the City of Dublin* (Dublin, 1749), p. 7.

27.  Cess applotment book, St John's, Dublin, RCB, P 328/10.1; contributions to ministers' money, St Werburgh's, Dublin, 1661–5, RCB, P 326/27/3/42; G. S. Cary (ed.), 'Hearth money roll for Co. Dublin, 1664', *Journal of the County Kildare Archaeological Society*, x (1922–8), pp. 245–54; xi (1930–3), pp. 386–466; 'Rental of landgable rents, City of Dublin, 1665', pp. 528–63. Cf. M. J. Power, 'The social topography of Restoration London', in A. L. Beier and R. Finlay (eds), *The making of the metropolis: London, 1500–1700* (London, 1986), pp. 199–222; McKellar, *The birth of modern London*.

28.  C. Williamson to Birde [draft], Caesar Williamson letterbook, p. 24, Marsh's Library, Ms. Z4.5.16.

29.  *CARD*, ix, pp. 230–1.

30.  Legg (ed.), *Synge letters*, p. 295.

31.  *The Dublin Courant*, 566, 21 Oct. 1721, extracted in Christ Church, Wake Ms. 13/284.

32.  Observations on houses in St Michan's parish, Dublin, *c.* 1730, RCB, P 276/12.1, p. 46.

33.  E. Spencer to Mrs A. Price, 27 Nov. 1749, NLW, Puleston Ms. 3580E.

34.  R. North, *Of building*, ed. H. M. Colvin and J. Newman (Oxford, 1981), pp. 25–6.

35.  E. Spencer to Mrs A. Price, 27 Nov. 1749, NLW, Puleston Ms. 3580E.

36.  *Faulkner's Dublin Journal*, 8–11 March 1726[7], 25–29 July 1727; advertisement in Moore of Newport Pratt Mss, NLI, Ms. 5737.

37.  Cary (ed.), 'Hearth money roll for Co. Dublin, 1664', p. 422.

38.  Sir J. Temple to H. Temple, 30 Sep. 1697, Southampton UL, BR5/22.

39.  C. O'Brien to Sir C. Wyche, 25 April 1700, NA, Wyche Mss, 1/1/172; H. J. Louw, 'The origin of the sash-window', *Architectural History*, xxvi (1983), pp. 49–72.

40.  Papers relating to Arbour Hill, NA, M 2461/61 and 65.

41. C. O'Brien to Sir C. Wyche, 18 and 25 April 1700, 14 May 1700; Bp. W. Moreton to Sir C. Wyche, 16 May 1700, NA, Wyche letters, 1st series, 1/1/168, 172, 173, 174.

42. J. Evelyn to J. Evelyn, 27 March 1693, 26 March 1694; Z. Sedgwick to J. Evelyn, 18 July 1692, Evelyn Mss, formerly at Christ Church, now in BL.

43. T. Knox to J. Evelyn, 15 Sep. 1693, Evelyn Mss, formerly at Christ Church, now in BL.

44. J. Evelyn to J. Evelyn, 19 Sep. 1692, 5 May 1694, 27 May 1695, Evelyn Mss, formerly at Christ Church, now in BL.

45. J. Evelyn to J. Evelyn, 26 Oct. 1692, Evelyn Mss, formerly at Christ Church, now in BL; Sir J. Temple to H. Temple, 10 Sep. 1696, 22 Oct. 1696, 22 June 1697, 24 Aug. 1697, 5 Nov. 1697, 17 March 1697[8], Southampton UL, BR5/22, 14, 17, 30, 33, 39, 44; J. Isham to Sir J. Isham, 8 July 1701, Northamptonshire CRO, IC 2191.

46. F. E. Ball, *A history of County Dublin*, part iv (Dublin, 1906), p. 92; T. C. Barnard, 'Gardening, diet and "improvement" in later seventeenth-century Ireland', *Journal of Garden History*, x (1990), pp. 80–1.

47. D. Muschamp to T. Fitzgerald, 20 June 1696, 20 May 1697, NLI, de Vesci Mss, H/2.

48. Abp. J. Vesey to A. Vesey, 8 Aug. 1703, NA, Sarsfield–Vesey Mss, 53.

49. Bp. N. Wilson to Bp. W. Moreton of Kildare, 3 Nov. 1693, NA, Wyche Mss, 1/1/96; W. Perceval to A. Charlet, 24 June 1703, Bodleian, Ballard Ms. 36, f. 24; E. Nicholson, *A method of charity-schools* (Dublin, 1712), p. 28.

50. C. O'Brien to T. Keightley, 17 July 1705, NLI, Inchiquin Mss, no. 1155; C. O'Brien to J. Bonnell, 30 June [1709], NLI, PC 435; Bp. T. Godwin to Abp. W. Wake, 5 Nov. 1720, Christ Church, Wake Mss, 13/203; W. Yorke to Lord Hardwicke, 11 Oct. 1743, BL, Add. Ms. 35,587, f. 182v.

51. Abp. N. Marsh to T. Smith, 30 Aug. 1698, Bodleian, Smith Ms. 52, f. 67.

52. W. Yorke to Lord Hardwicke, 11 Oct. 1743, BL, Add. Ms. 35,587, f. 182v.

53. 'Autobiography of Pole Cosby, of Stradbally, Queen's County, 1703–37(?)', *Journal of the County Kildare Archaeological Society*, v (1906), p. 435.

54. S. Molloy, account with Sir E. Bayly, 1735–7, PRONI, D 619/12/A/16.

55. Letter of 18 Oct. 1736, Denbighshire RO, Ruthin, DD/BK/1/481; R. Edgeworth, accounts, s.d. Jan. 1724[5], 28 March 1769, NLI, Mss. 1508, p. 151; 1535, p. 149; 'Dr. Achmet', *The theory and uses of Baths* (Dublin, 1772).

56. R. Edgeworth, accounts, s.d. 2 Jan. 1720[1], 5 and 28 Dec. 1723, NLI, Mss 1507, p. 39; 1508, pp. 97, 99.

57. E. Scott, bill with Sir T. Vesey, 8 July 1723, NLI, de Vesci Mss, J/3.

58. H. Owen and J. E. Griffith, 'The diary of William Bulkeley of Brynddu, Anglesey', *Transactions of the Anglesey Antiquarian and Field Club* (1931), pp. 49–50.

59. B. Fletcher journal, 5–7, 13–15 Nov. 1684, private collection, Berkshire.

60. R. Edgeworth, accounts, s.d. 12 Nov. 1732, 7 and 28 Jan. 1732[3], 30 May 1733, 6, 13 and 16 Feb. 1733[4], 20 and 22 June 1734, 10 Feb. 1734[5], 17 March 1735[6], 9 Feb. 1736[7], 7 June 1737, 20 Feb. 1737[8], 3 and 16 Dec. 1739, 3, 10 and 11 Feb. 1739[40], 9 March 1739[40], 19 Nov. 1742, 18 Dec. 1749, 14, 17 and 27 Feb. 1752, 10 Dec. 1755, NLI, Mss 1510, pp. 33, 38, 39, 73, 94, 95, 129, 130; 1511, pp. 22, 84, 148; 1512, pp. 27, 74; 1513, pp. 69, 71, 78–9, 83; 1515, p. 210; 1518, p. 190; 1519, pp. 208, 209, 211; 1522, p. 72.

61. R. Edgeworth, accounts, s.d. 1 and 11 Feb. 1734[5], 22 June 1737, 7, 9, 15, 16 and 22 Nov. 1737, 28 Dec. 1737, 10 and 17 Nov. 1739, 4, 22 and 27 Dec. 1739, 1 Feb. 1739[40], 5 Dec. 1741, 1 Oct. 1744, 13 Feb. 1752, 30 Nov. 1755, 31 Jan. 1756, 26 Feb. 1756, 5 April 1756, 10 Nov. 1757, 31 Jan. 1758, 16 and 18 Nov. 1764, NLI, Mss 1511, pp. 20, 22; 1512, pp. 31, 59–61, 65; 1513, pp. 67, 69, 72–3, 78; 1515, pp. 79–80; 1516, p. 136; 1519, p. 208; 1522, pp. 67, 106, 110, 120; 1523, p. 177; 1524, p. 58; 1528, pp. 133, 136; Dublin Castle dinner guests, s.d. 31 Jan. 1756, NLI, Ms. 1466.

62. D. Hepburn to D. Graeme, 8 Feb. 1763, NAS, GD 190/3/319, 3.

63. R. Edgeworth, accounts, s.d. 4 Nov. 1719, 18 Dec. 1719, 21 May 1720, 12 Aug. 1720, 28 Nov. 1720, 26 Dec. 1720, 26 Jan. 1720[1], 31 July 1722, NLI, Mss 1507, pp. 23, 24, 29, 30, 33, 34, 35; 1508, p. 13.

64. *CARD*, iv, p. 418.

65. Inventories of A. Rookes, 14 Jan. 1638[9], 21 March 1638[9], BL, Add. Ms. 11,687, ff. 128–9, 139v–141. Cf. A. Maçzak, *Travel in early modern Europe* (Cambridge, 1995), pp. 68–9.

66. *Dublin Journal*, 13–16 Feb. 1741[2].

67. *A genuine history of the family of the great negroes of G . . . , taken from an African manuscript in St. Sepulchre's Library, Dublin* (London, 1756), p. 12.

68. Ware, account book, TCD, Ms. 10,165, ff. 160v–161.

69. R. Edgeworth, accounts, s.d. 8 Dec. 1759, NLI, Ms. 1525, p. 151; NA, M. 1504, p. 348.

70. R. Edgeworth, accounts, s.d. 21 March 1719[20], Sept. 1720, NLI, Ms. 1507, pp. 26, 31.

71. Owen and Griffith, 'The diary of William Bulkeley of Brynddu', p. 50.

72. R. Edgeworth, accounts, s.d. 17 July 1722, 26–27 Oct. 1722, Feb. 1722[3], NLI, Ms. 1508, pp. 12, 16, 38.

73. R. Ashenhurst to Sir J. Temple, 8 July 1698, Southampton UL, BR/150; letterbook of C. Caldwell, s.d. 22 Oct. 1744, PRO, CUST 112/10.

74. Accounts, 1705–6, NA, Monck Mason's notes on Dublin, M 2549/179–80.

75. Admiralty court proceedings, BL, Lansdowne Ms. 1228, ff. 38–56v.

76. Vestry Book, St Catherine's, Dublin, 1657–92, s.d. 21 June 1688, RCB, P 117/5/1.1.

77. R. Dudley (ed.), 'The Cheney Letters, 1682–85', *IESH*, xxiii (1996), p. 109.

78. *Some reasons humbly offered for establishing a yarn-market in the city of Dublin* (Dublin, 1736), pp. 3–4, 16.

79. H. Ellis, notebook, UCNW, Gwyneddon Ms. 18, pp. 31, 87.

80. E. Mathews to Mrs J. Hamilton, 13 Dec. 1726, Denbighshire RO, DD/BK/I, 478.

81. E. Scott, *The new book of constitutions* (Dublin, 1751).

82. Sir J. Caldwell to C. Bagshawe, 2 Feb. 1754, JRL, B 2/3/386.

83. Notes on houses in St Michan's parish, Dublin, *c.* 1730, RCB, P 276/12.1.

84. *Faulkner's Dublin Journal*, 15 Nov. 1727.

85. Winter of Agher, account book, s.d. 15 June 1762, 8 Oct. 1762, 2 Nov. 1762, NLI, Ms. 3855.

86. *A genuine history of the family of the great negroes of G . . . ,* p. 13.

87. S. Derrick, *Letters written from Leverppole, Chester, Corke, the Lake of Killarney, Dublin . . .,* 2 vols (London, 1767), i, pp. 52, 58–9, 80; ii, p. 6; *A genuine history of the family of the great negroes of G . . . ,* p. 4; J. McVeagh (ed.), *Richard Pococke's Irish tours* (Dublin, 1995), pp. 50, 58, 195.

88. E. O'Hara, account book, 1722–33, NLI, Ms. 36,387/7, *passim*, but especially pp. 20, 23, 24, 34; bill of P. Bertrand and W. Wiltshire with C. O'Hara, from 10 April 1741, NLI, Ms. 35,365/7. Bertrand and Wiltshire took from O'Hara diamonds worth nearly £140.

89. M. Jones to J. Bonnell, 11 Aug. 1733, 30 Jan. [], 5 Feb [ ], 24 April [ ], 25 July [*c.* 1735], NLI, PC 435.

90. A. C. Elias, jr. (ed.), *Memoirs of Laetitia Pilkington*, 2 vols (Athens, Ga. and London, 1997), i, pp. 77–9; ii, p. 465.

91. J. Mussenden to W. Leathes, 20 June 1712, Suffolk CRO, Ipswich, de Mussenden–Leathes Mss, HA 403/1/7, 46; draft will of W. Leathes, 12 Dec. 1717, Suffolk CRO, Ipswich, de Mussenden–Leathes Mss, HA 403/1/8, 257; J. Leathes to W. Leathes, 4 March 1718[19], Suffolk CRO, Ipswich, de Mussenden–Leathes Mss, HA 403/1/6, 26.

92. J. Mussenden to W. Leathes, 20 June 1712, Suffolk CRO, Ipswich, de Mussenden–Leathes Mss, HA 403/1/7, 46; J. Leathes to W. Leathes, 16 Feb. 1714[15], 2 Nov. 1717, Suffolk CRO, Ipswich, de Mussenden–Leathes Mss, HA 403/1/6, 17, 22.

93. J. Mussenden to W. Leathes, 18 [] 1724, 1 Jan. 1725[6], Suffolk CRO, Ipswich, de Mussenden–Leathes Mss, HA 403/1/6, 106, 109.

94. W. Leathes to J. Mussenden, 15 Jan. 1722[3], Suffolk CRO, Ipswich, de Mussenden–Leathes Mss, HA 403/1/5, 318.

95. A. Hamilton to Lady Panmure, 10 Aug. [*c.* 1721], 2 Jan. [*c.* 1722], 5 Jan. [*c.* 1722], NAS, GD 45/14/238, 49, 52, 82.

96. K. Howard to W. Howard, 19 Dec. 1710, 17 May 1711, 18 Aug. 1711, NLI, PC 227.

97. K. Howard to W. Howard, 18 Aug. 1711, NLI, PC 227.

98. K. Howard to W. Howard, 19 Feb. 1708[9], 19 Dec. 1711, 6 Oct. 1711, NLI, PC 227; B. Boydell, *A Dublin musical calendar* (Dublin, 1988), p. 34.

99. B. B. Butler, 'Lady Arbella Denny, 1707–1792', *Dublin Historical Record*, ix (1946–7), pp. 2–18.

100. Lady A. Denny to Lady A. Crosbie, 25 Feb. 1755, NLI, Ms. 20,601.

101. 'Diary of Anne Cooke', *Journal of the County Kildare Archaeological Society*, viii (1915), pp. 117–18.

102. Abp. W. King to Mrs Foley, 8 May 1711; Abp. W. King to Col. Edgeworth, 26 June 1711; Abp. W. King to Elizabeth Foley, 28 June 1711, TCD, Ms. 2531, pp. 334, 346, 347.

103. O. Gallagher to O. St George, 24 April 1725, PRO, C 110/46/364.

104. S. Green, notebook, 1719–37, PRONI, T 898/1.

105. Deposition of Simon Todd, 9 April 1742, PRO, ADM 1/3990.

106. C. O'Hara, calculations, *c.* 1760, NLI, Ms. 20,397; Barnard, *New anatomy*, p. 282; C. H. Hull (ed.), *Economic writings of Sir William Petty*, 2 vols (Cambridge, 1899), i, pp. 141–4.

107. Long, *The golden fleece*, pp. 22, 26–7.

108. R. Edwards to F. Price, 4 Aug. 1745, NLW, Puleston Ms. 3577E.

109. 'Autobiography of Pole Cosby', pp. 90, 175–6, 265–6, 316, 435; Barnard, *New anatomy*, pp. 9–11; D. M. Beaumont, 'An Irish gentleman in England – the travels of Pole Cosby, *c.* 1730–1735', *Journal of the British Archaeological Association*, cxlix (1996), pp. 37–54.

110. 'Autobiography of Pole Cosby', pp. 173, 175.

111. Return of parishioners, 7 Sep. 1730, Vestry Book, St Paul's, Dublin, 1698–1750, RCB, P 273/6/1, p. 77.

112. For the Donnellans, see Elias (ed.), *Memoirs of Laetitia Pilkington*, ii, pp. 382–4.

113. J. Pratt, journal, s.d. 4 Nov. 1745, 1 Feb. 1745[6], Cloverhill, Co. Cavan, Purdon Mss.

114. They were: *Theodosius*, or *The Force of Love*; *Tancred and Sigismunda*; *The Orphan*, or *Unhappy Marriage*; and *The Fair Penitent*, for which see: E. K. Sheldon, *Thomas Sheridan of Smock Alley* (Princeton, 1967), pp. 417, 448, 466–7, 469.

115. He is not recorded in E. Keane, P. B. Phair and T. U. Sadleir (eds), *King's Inns Admissions Papers, 1607–1867* (Dublin, 1982).

116. N. Peacock, journal, s.d. 1–4 May 1744, 23 May–2 June 1745, NLI, Ms. 16,091.

117. E. Kingsbury to A. Price, 27 June 1757, NLW, Puleston Ms. 3584E.

118. J. Pacey to Sir C. Wyche, 25 April 1700, 14 May 1700; Bp. W. Moreton to Sir C. Wyche, 16 May 1700, NA, Wyche Ms, 1/1/171, 173, 174; W. Thomas to W. Smythe, 21 Aug. 1727, NLI, PC 449.

119. M. Moore to J. Moore, 20 June 1758, Brabazon Mss, box I, private collection, London.

120. O. Gallagher to O. St George, 11 Feb. 1724[5], PRO, C 110/46, 321; notes on new houses in parish of St Michan, Dublin, *c.* 1730, RCB, P 276/12.1, pp. 50–1; *Faulkner's Dublin Journal*, 253, 30 Sep.–3 Oct. 1727; 270, 28–31 Oct. 1727.

121. HMC, *Ormonde Mss*, new series, iv, p. 27.

122. E. Fleming to H. Boyle, 9 June 1731, PRONI, D 2707/A1/11/23.

123. H. Crofton to W. Smythe, 19 Feb. 1731[2], NLI, PC 448.

124. S. Waring to J. Waring, 11 May 1727, private collection, Co. Down.

125. J. Smythe to W. Smythe, 18 Oct. 1716, 6 Feb. 1720[1], NLI, PC 449.

126. R. Hamilton, bill of costs with R. Maxwell, PRONI, D 1556/16/16/13.

127. Indenture of Sir J. Povey and H. Jervis, 28 June 1681, NLI, PC 438.

128. J. H. Gebbie (ed.), *An introduction to the Abercorn letters* (Omagh, 1972), pp. 16, 298.

129. Johnston-Liik, *HIP*, vi, pp. 299–300.

130. M. Clarke to W. Smythe, 25 Nov. 1735, 2 Dec. 1735, NLI, PC 447/6.

131. M. Clarke to W. Smythe, 8 Oct. 1737, 26 Nov. 1737, NLI, PC 447.

132. Abp. W. King to Mrs Ormsby, 8 May 1711, TCD Ms. 2531, p. 335.

133. Notes on new houses, *c.* 1730, RCB, P 276/12.1, pp. 50–1.

134. N. Ogle to W. Smythe, 28 July 1753, NLI, PC 436.

135. R. Butterfield to W. Smythe, 12 May 1753, NLI, PC 449; M. Clarke to W. Smythe, 15 and 19 Jan. 1754, NLI, PC 447; W. Smythe to unknown, 5 Sep. 1753, NLI, PC 449.

136. A. J. Guy (ed.), *Colonel Samuel Bagshawe and the army of George II*, Army Records Society (London, 1990), p. 95.

137. M. Ledwidge to W. Smythe, 1 Jan. 1753, 6 Jan. [1753?], NLI, PC 446.

138. M. Ledwidge to W. Smythe, 22 Jan. 1754, NLI, PC 446. For Savage as supplier of furnishings to French, R. French, accounts, NLI, Ms. 4918, p. 123.

139. T. Burgh to W. Smythe, 14 Oct. 1754, NLI, PC 446.

140. R. Butterfield to W. Smythe, 21 April 1753, NLI, PC 449.

141. R. Butterfield to W. Smythe, 12 May 1753, NLI, PC 449.

142. R. Butterfield to W. Smythe, 12 May 1753, NLI, PC 449; N. Ogle to W. Smythe, 28 July 1753, NLI, PC 436.

143. R. Edgeworth, accounts, s.d. 1749, 28 May 1756, 17 June 1756, NLI, Mss 1518, p. 153; 1522, pp. 160, 163.

144. R. Edgeworth, accounts, s.d. 10 July 1744, 6 Oct. 1744, 24 Nov. 1746, 7 March 1752, 18 Aug. 1753, NLI, Mss 1516, pp. 125, 137; 1517, p. 61; 1519, p. 212; 1520, p. 173.

145. R. Edgeworth, accounts, s.d. 15 April 1756, NLI, Ms. 1522, p. 125.

146. R. Edgeworth, accounts, s.d. 25 April 1755, 9 and 10 May 1769, NLI, Mss 1521, p. 187; 1535, p. 170.

147. 'Portrait of an English lady in Dublin in the late 18th century', NA, M 6810, pp. 8–9; Mrs E. Echlin to C. Tickell, 4 Jan. 1755, Tickell Mss, private collection, Devon; H. F. Berry, 'Notes from the diary of a Dublin lady in the reign of George II', *JRSAI*, 5th series, viii (1898), p. 142.

148. S. Povey to W. Smythe, 24 June 1758, 27 May 1760, NLI, PC 448; Lady Caldwell to S. Bagshawe, [1751], JRL, 2/3/244a; A. Caldwell to S. Bagshawe, 25 Feb. 1752, 14 March 1752, JRL, 2/3/247, 2/3/249; S. Bagshawe to Lady Caldwell, 22 Feb. 1752, JRL, 2/3/246.

149. M. Ledwidge to R. Smythe, 1 Sep. 1767, NLI, PC 446.

150. Lady Caldwell to S. Bagshawe, 10 March 1753, JRL, B 2/3/264; A. Caldwell to S. Bagshawe, 13 March 1759, JRL, B 2/3/290; E. Echlin to C. Tickell, [1761], Tickell Mss, private collection, Devon.

151. L. Beecher to Orrery, n.d. [*c.* 1670], Petworth, Orrery Mss, general series, 27; Broghill to Dorset, 3 March 1673[4], Kent Archives Office, Sackville Mss, U/269, C 18/25.

152. J. Osborne to Orrery, n.d. [*c.* 1680], Petworth, Orrery Mss, general series, 27.

153. Prices of living in Lohort, Co. Cork and London, 1746, BL, Add. Ms. 47,007, f. 77.

154. D. Muschamp to T. Fitzgerald, 9 April 1697, 8 July 1697, NLI, de Vesci Mss, H/2; S. Povey to W. Smythe, 6 Aug. 1748, 28 Sep. 1748, 26 Oct. 1748, NLI, PC 448; S. Bagshawe to Lady Caldwell, 22 Feb. 1752, JRL, 2/3/246; 'Autobiography of Pole Cosby', pp. 84–6, 264.

155. Sir C. Wyche, disbursements, 1682, NA, Wyche Mss, 2nd series, 132.

156. See above, pp. 9–10, 369–70.

157. W. Ellis to Sir C. Wyche, 26 June 1681, NA, Wyche Mss, 2nd series, 141.

158. Sir C. Wyche, accounts, 1–19 Sep. 1693, NA, Wyche Mss, 2nd series, 138.

159. S. Bagshawe to W. Bagshawe, 24 Nov. 1741, 2 June 1743, 27 Sep. 1743, JRL, B 2/3/81, 88, 89; S. Bagshawe, fragmentary autobiography, JRL, B 15/3/1; C. Ellison to H. Ellison, 13 July 1730, 15 Aug. 1730, 13 Aug. 1733, 14 Nov. 1733, 16 Feb. 1733[4], Tyne and Wear Archives, Newcastle, acc. 3419, Ellison Mss; Barnard, *New anatomy*, pp. 192–3.

160. Sir W. Petty to T. Waller, 9 Jan. 1671[2]; Lady Petty to T. Crookshank, 20 Jan. 1671[2]; note of expenses since 28 March 1671, McGill UL, Osler Ms. 7612; budget, 2 Feb. 1671[2], BL, Petty Papers, Add. Ms. 72,857/56.

161. R. Molesworth to L. Molesworth, 20 Oct. 1722, NLI, p. 3752.

162. R. Edgeworth, accounts, s.d. 31 May 1732, NLI, Ms. 1510, p. 9.

163. Delany, *Autobiography*, 1st series, iii, p. 530; HMC, *Egmont Diary*, iii, p. 301; Williams (ed.), *Correspondence of Swift*, iv, pp. 104, 135–6.

164. Bill of C. Birch, 26 March 1737; bill of S. Mulloy, 11 Dec. 1735; receipt of G. Wilde, 26 June 1746, PRONI, D 619/12/A/4, 14, 16, 43.

165. Bp. F. Hutchinson, account book from 1729, s.d. 24 Dec. 1733, PRONI, DIO 1/22/2.

166. Balfour Mss, NLI, Ms. 10,276/9.

167. NLI, Ms. 9534, f. 79v; Georgian Society, *Records of eighteenth-century domestic architecture*, iii, p. 83.

168. Balfour accounts and rentals, 1751, NLI, Ms. 10,275.

169. R. Edgeworth, accounts, s.d. 20 March 1724[5], 21 Dec. 1725, 14 and 19 Feb. 1732[3], 9 and 21 Dec. 1733, 19 Jan. 1733[4], 14 and 21 Dec. 1741, 24 Feb. 1752, 1 May 1752, 17 March 1766, 17 April 1769, NLI, Mss 1508, p. 157; 1509, p. 37; 1510, pp. 42, 88, 89, 93; 1515, p. 82; 1519, p. 210; 1520, p. 23; 1531, p. 227; 1535, p. 156.

170. *Letters from an Armenian in Ireland, to his friends at Trebisond, &c.* (London, 1757), pp. 90–1.

171. R. Edgeworth, accounts, s.d. 18 Dec. 1719, 18 Feb. 1719[20], 16 Oct. 1721, 20 Feb. 1722[3], 9 March 1722[3], 1 and 10 May 1725, 28 June 1734, 29 and 31 Jan. 1734[5], 1 Feb. 1734[5], 17 Jan. 1738[9], 3 April 1739, 3 Nov. 1739, 24 Nov. 1741, 10 Dec. 1742, 7 Jan. 1742[3], 20 May 1743, 13 Feb. 1744[5], 9 Jan. 1756, 9 Feb. 1756, 3 July 1764, 24 Oct. 1764, 14 Jan. 1768, 30 Nov. 1769, 28 Jan. 1770, NLI, Mss 1507, pp. 24, 26, 54; 1508, pp. 34, 35; 1509, p. 21; 1510, p. 132; 1511, p. 20; 1512, pp. 154, 166; 1513, p. 65; 1515, pp. 79, 213, 219; 1516, pp. 34, 152; 1522, pp. 102, 108; 1528, pp. 75, 125; 1534, p. 110; 1535, p. 274; 1536, p. 143.

172. Bp. F. Hutchinson, account book, s.d. 15 Oct. 1733, PRONI, DIO 1/1/22/2; Ware household book, TCD, Ms. 10,528, ff. 3v, 4v; R. Carey to T. Mahon, 3 Oct. 1761, NLI, Ms. 10,081/2; accounts of B. Townley Balfour, from Jan. 1763, NLI, Ms. 10,726/9; J. V. Beckett, *Coal and tobacco: the Lowthers and the economic development of West Cumberland, 1660–1760* (Cambridge, 1981), pp. 85–9; L. M. Cullen, *Anglo-Irish trade, 1660–1800* (Manchester, 1968), pp. 78–86; *A letter to a commissioner of the inland navigation concerning the Tyrone collieries* (Dublin, 1752); F. Seymour, *Remarks on the scheme for supplying Dublin with coals* (Belfast, 1729); A. W., *The clothier's letter to the inhabitants of the liberties* (Dublin, 1759), pp. 5–6.

173. Balfour, accounts, NLI, Ms. 10,276/9.

174. Guy (ed.), *Colonel Samuel Bagshawe*, pp. 94–6.

175. Receipt of 24 March 1752, JRL, B2/7/111.

176. Receipt of 8 April 1760, JRL, B2/7/117.

177. Ware, account book, TCD, Ms. 10,528, f. 13.

178. Ware, account book, f. 14v.

179. Ware, account book, ff. 15v, 19v–20v.

180. Ware, account book, f. 16v.

181. Ware, account book, ff. 18–18v.

182. R. French, accounts, NLI, Ms. 4918; Barnard, 'French of Monivea', pp. 280–4, 289, 296.

183. R. Edgeworth, accounts, NLI, Ms. 1510, p. 107.

184. R. Edgeworth, accounts, s.d. 14 June 1732, 7 July 1732, 23 Oct. 1732, 7 Nov. 1732, 2 Feb. 1732[3], NLI, Ms. 1510, pp. 20, 22, 30, 32, 41.

185. R. Edgeworth, accounts, s.d. 6 and 7 Dec. 1733, NLI, Ms. 1510, pp. 87, 88.

186. R. Edgeworth, accounts, s.d. 2 Jan. 1733[4], NLI, Ms. 1510, p. 91.

187. R. Edgeworth, accounts, s.d. 19 Dec. 1754, NLI, Ms. 1521, p. 133.

188. Bp. F. Hutchinson, account book from 1729, s.d. 1 Oct. 1733, PRONI, DIO 1/22/2.

189. R. Edgeworth, accounts, s.d. 8 March 1732[3], 17 Oct. 1733, 1 and 5 March 1733[4], NLI, Ms. 1510, pp. 45, 82, 98, 101.

190. R. Edgeworth, accounts, s.d. 18 May 1749, NLI, Ms. 1518, p. 140.

191. R. Edgeworth, accounts, s.d. 23 and 24 March 1767, 26 April 1767, 1 and 5 May 1767, Aug. 1767, 29 Aug. 1767, Sep. 1767, 21 Oct. 1767, NLI, Ms. 1533, pp. 144, 158, 162, 163, 200, 222, 225, 244, 250.

192. R. Edgeworth, accounts, 31 July 1758, NLI, Ms. 1524, p. 140. Magennis is not recorded in G. Fennell, *A list of Irish watch and clockmakers* (Dublin, 1963) or W. G. Stuart, *Watch and clockmakers in Ireland*, ed. D. A. Boles (Dublin, 2000).

193. T. C. Barnard, '"Grand Metropolis" or "Anus of the World": the cultural life of eighteenth-century Dublin', in Clark and Gillespie (eds), *Two capitals: London and Dublin, 1500–1840*, pp. 185–210; S.

Foster, 'Going shopping in Georgian Dublin: luxury goods and the negotiation of national identity', unpublished M.A. thesis, Royal College of Art and V & A (1995).

194.    *Tricks of the town laid open.*

## 10  Going Abroad

1.    R. Southwell, notebook, BL, Egerton Ms. 1632.

2.    Within a few years he was able to procure for his mother four pieces of 'counterfeit marble' (perhaps *pietra dura*) depicting flowers, fashioned by Italians in London. HMC, *Egmont Mss*, ii, p. 22.

3.    R. Southwell to T. Southwell, 1 Nov. 1661, 20 Dec. 1662, Kinsale Manorial Papers, 1662–5, Boole Library, NUI, Cork, Ms. U/20; Sir J. Perceval to R. Southwell, 22 Nov. 1661, BL, Add. Ms. 46,938, f. 148v.

4.    Robert, Viscount Molesworth, *Some considerations for the promoting of agriculture, and employing the poor* (Dublin, 1723), pp. 28–9.

5.    W. Higford, *Institutions or advice to his grandson* (London, 1658), pp. 83–4.

6.    [G. Hickes], *The gentleman instructed*, 9th edn (London and Dublin, 1723), p. 13.

7.    W. King to E. Southwell, 21 Jan. 1717[18], TCD, Ms. 2535, pp. 62–6; W. King to C. Domville, 3 Feb. 1717[18], TCD, Ms. 2535, pp. 73–5; W. King to S. Molyneux, 10 June 1713, TCD, Ms. 750/4, 164.

8.    *Schemes from Ireland for the benefit of the body natural, ecclesiastical and politick* (Dublin, 1732), p. 27; S. R. Lowry-Corry, earl of Belmore, *The history of two Ulster manors* (London and Dublin, 1881), p. 178.

9.    On the last theme: S. Warneke, *Images of the educational traveller in early modern England* (Leiden, New York and Cologne, 1995).

10.   J. Bulkeley to J. Bonnell, 9 April 1728, NLI, PC 435; A. Hamilton to Lady Panmure, 18 Sep. [*c.* 1710], 2 Jan. [*c.* 1720], NAS, GD 45/14/238, 37, 52.

11.   H. Ingoldsby to W. Smythe, 3 April 1716, 20 March 1716[17], NLI, PC 445; R. French, tour journal, 1751, NLI, Ms. 7375; 'Diary of Anne Cooke', *Journal of the County Kildare Archaeological Society*, viii (1915), pp. 107–8.

12.   Lady A. Denny to Lady A. Crosbie, n.d. [1751], NLI, Ms. 20,601; Cleone Knox (ed.), *The diary of a young lady of fashion in the year 1764–1765* (New York, 1926), p. 224; C. L. von Poellnitz, *Les amusements des eaux de Spa*, 2 vols (Amsterdam, 1734); Arthur Ponsonby, *Scottish and Irish diaries from the sixteenth to the nineteenth centuries* (London, 1927), pp. 148–52.

13.   J. Ghazvinian, '"A certain tickling humour": English travellers, 1560–1600', unpublished D.Phil. thesis, Oxford University (2003), pp. 252–4; B. Dolan, *Ladies of the Grand Tour: British women in pursuit of enlightenment and adventure in eighteenth-century Europe* (London, 2001), pp. 3–13.

14.   G. F. Warner (ed.), *The Nicholas papers*, III, Camden Society (London, 1897), p. 127.

15.   L. M. Cullen, 'The Irish diaspora of the seventeenth and eighteenth centuries', in N. Canny (ed.), *Europeans on the move* (Oxford, 1994), pp. 113–48; N. Genet-Rouffiac, 'The Irish Jacobite exile in France, 1692–1715', in Barnard and Fenlon (eds), *Dukes of Ormonde*, pp. 195–210; G. Henry, *The Irish military community in Spanish Flanders, 1586–1621* (Dublin, 1992); T. O'Connor (ed.), *The Irish in Europe, 1580–1815* (Dublin, 2001); T. O'Connor and M. A. Lyons (eds), *Irish migrants in Europe after Kinsale, 1602–1820* (Dublin, 2003); G. Rowland, *An army in exile: Louis XIV and the Irish forces of James II in France, 1691–1698*, The Royal Stuart Society, paper lx (2001); K. Schüller, *Die Beziehungen zwischen Spanien und Irland im 16. und 17. Jahrhundert: Diplomatie, Handel und die Soziale Integration Katholischer Exulanten* (Münster, 1999); R. A. Stradling, *The Spanish monarchy and the Irish mercenaries: the Wild Geese in Spain, 1618–1668* (Dublin, 1994).

16.   Robert Black, travel journal, 1727, PRONI, T 1073/2.

17.   M. A. Hickson, *Selections from Old Kerry records*, 2nd series (London, 1874), pp. 273–7, 291–2. More generally, C. M. S. Johns, 'The entrepôt of Europe: Rome in the eighteenth century', in E. P. Bowron and J. Richel (eds), *Art in Rome in the eighteenth century* (Philadelphia, 2000), pp. 17–45.

18. F. G. James, 'The Irish lobby in the early eighteenth century', *EHR*, lxxxi (1966), pp. 544–57; O' Connor (ed.), *The Irish in Europe*; K. A. Miller, A. Schrier, B. D. Boling and D. N. Doyle (eds), *Irish immigrants in the land of Canaan: letters and memoirs from colonial and revolutionary America, 1675–1815* (Oxford, 2003).

19. J. Smythe to W. Smythe, 14 June 1710, NLI, PC 449.

20. Ormond to Sir R. Southwell, 14 Aug. 1678, V & A, Ormonde Mss, 2, f. 7.

21. J. Hall to dowager countess of Orrery, 16 Dec. 1686, Petworth, Orrery Mss, general series, 30.

22. D. Mussenden to ?H. Mussenden, 6 [ ] 1742, Suffolk CRO, Ipswich, de Mussenden–Leathes Mss, HA 403/1/11, 20.

23. A. B. Grosart (ed.), *The Lismore papers*, 2nd series, 5 vols (London, 1887–8), iv, pp. 160–72.

24. Ibid., 2nd series, iv, pp. 166–7.

25. Ibid., 2nd series, iv, pp. 98, 100–1, 103, 113, 115.

26. Quotation in M. Braddick, *State formation in early modern England, c. 1550–1800* (Cambridge, 2000), p. 288.

27. Grosart (ed.), *Lismore papers*, 2nd series, iv, pp. 205–7, 232–6; R. E. W. Maddison, *The life of the honourable Robert Boyle, F.R.S.* (London, 1969), pp. 1–56.

28. J. Hall to dowager countess of Orrery, 4 Dec. 1682, Petworth, Orrery Mss, general series, 29.

29. J. Horner to Abp. W. Wake, 24 June 1725, Christ Church, Wake Ms. 14/272; I. Gervais to Lord Hartington, 5 Sep. 1755; I. Gervais to Sir A. Abdy, 6 Sep. 1755, Chatsworth, Devonshire letters, 387.1, 287.2; J. McVeagh (ed.), *Richard Pococke's Irish tours* (Dublin, 1995), pp. 101–2; W. H. Rennison, *Succession list of the bishops, cathedral and parochial clergy of the diocese of Waterford* (Waterford, [1920]), pp. 78, 126, 157, 162, 181, 206, 210.

30. Lord Orrery to B. Badham, 6 May 1725, NLI, Ms. 4177.

31. Lord Orrery to B. Badham, 20 Dec. 1725, NLI, Ms. 4177.

32. On Orrery's politics: L. Smith, 'The career of Charles Boyle, fourth earl of Orrery (1674–1731)', unpublished Ph.D. thesis, University of Edinburgh (1994).

33. D. Fitzgerald, Knight of Glin, and E. Malins, *Lost demesnes: Irish landscape gardening 1660–1845* (London, 1978), pp. 44–6; Ingamells, *Travellers*, pp. 241–2; A. Rowan, *North-west Ulster* (Harmondsworth, 1979), pp. 161–4.

34. John Boyle, earl of Cork and Orrery, *Letters from Italy in the years 1754 and 1755* (London, 1773), p. 246.

35. R. Molesworth, *An account of Denmark as it was in the year 1692* (London, 1694), sig. a2–c8v.

36. *Letters written by his excellency Hugh Boulter, D.D., Lord Primate of all Ireland*, 2 vols (Dublin, 1770), ii, p. 151.

37. Ormond to Sir R. Southwell, 14 and 19 Aug. 1678, 11 Sep. 1678, 21 Jan. 1678[9], 23 April 1679, 27 Sep. 1679, 8 Nov. 1679, V & A, Ormond Mss, 2, ff. 7, 9, 12, 33, 47, 63v, 65; HMC, *Ormonde Mss*, n.s., iv, pp. 168, 222–3, 261, 296, 449–51.

38. Sir R. Southwell to Sir W. King, 5 Oct. 1683; Sir W. King to Sir R. Southwell, 6 and 15 June 1684, NLI, Ms. 664.

39. E. Southwell to M. Coghill, 2 Aug. 1737, 8 Sep. 1737, NLI, Ms. 856; Ingamells, *Travellers*, p. 1016.

40. J. A. Oughton, autobiography, NAM, Ms. 8808–36–1, p. 46.

41. Delany, *Autobiography*, 1st series, iii, pp. 579, 581.

42. R. and E. Southwell, notebook, BL, Egerton Ms. 1628, ff. 2, 19v; R. Meade to E. Southwell, 15 Sep. 1723; E. Southwell to W. Bowler, BL, Add. Ms. 9714, ff. 155, 164; Ingamells, *Travellers*, p. 880.

43. R. Southwell, notebook, 1660–1, BL, Egerton Ms. 1632; R. and E. Southwell, notebook, 1659–99, BL, Egerton Ms. 1628; observations on R. Southwell's letters, 20 Aug. 1669, BL, Egerton Ms. 917, f. 37; commonplace book of Lord Perceval, BL, Add. Ms. 47,127, ff. 79v, 167v; E. Southwell, journals, 1695–1716, Beinecke Library, Yale UL; correspondence of E. Southwell, 1696, Koninklijke Bibliotheek, The Hague, Ms. 133 C.6; A. M. Crinò (ed.), *Un principe di Toscana in Inghilterra e in Irelanda nel 1669* (Rome, 1968),

pp. 4–9; D. Howarth, _Images of rule: art and politics in the English Renaissance, 1485–1649_ (Basingstoke, 1997), pp. 244–6; M. Webster, _Firenze e l'Inghilterra_ (Florence, 1971), no. 28.

44.  S. Waring, journal, PRONI, D 695/225, p. 7.
45.  S. Waring, journal, PRONI, D 695/225, p. 15.
46.  P. Camporesi, _Exotic brew: the art of living in the age of the enlightenment_ (Oxford, 1998), p. 148; C. Chard, 'The intensification of Italy: food, wine and the foreign in seventeenth-century travel writing', in _Food, Culture and History_, i (1993), pp. 95–116; C. Chard, _Pleasure and guilt on the Grand Tour: travel writing and imaginative geography, 1600–1830_ (Manchester, 1999), pp. 50–6.
47.  J. Hall to dowager countess of Orrery, 5 Nov. 1687, Petworth, Orrery Mss, general series, 30; E. MacLysaght (ed.), _Calendar of the Orrery papers_ (Dublin, 1941), pp. 344, 346.
48.  S. Waring, journal, PRONI, D 695/228, p. 47.
49.  S. Waring, journal, PRONI, D 695/228, p. 27.
50.  Sir D. Molyneux to Bp. R. Howard, 12 April 1736, new style, NLI, PC 227.
51.  S. Waring, journal, PRONI, D 695/226, pp. 26, [29]. For Bellori, see F. Haskell, _Patrons and painters: a study in the relations between Italian art and society in the age of the baroque_ (London, 1963), pp. 158–61.
52.  S. Waring, notebook, 'From Basel to Flanders', 1688, private collection, Co. Down.
53.  S. Waring to M. Misson, [1699], private collection, Co. Down.
54.  2 vols, London, 1695.
55.  S. Waring to M. Misson, [1699], private collection, Co. Down; Chard, _Pleasure and guilt on the Grand Tour_, pp. 14–23.
56.  S. Waring, journal, PRONI, D 695/226, p. 23.
57.  London, 1689.
58.  K. van Strien, _Touring the Low Countries: accounts of British travellers_ (Amsterdam, 1998), pp. 67, 137, 165, 346.
59.  S. Waring, journal, PRONI, D 695/228, p. 29; M. Misson, _A new voyage to Italy_, 2 vols (London, 1695), ii, part i, p. 177.
60.  Ormond to Sir R. Southwell, 19 Feb. 1680[1], V & A, Ormonde Mss, 2, f. 83; GEC, _Complete peerage_, vii, pp. 287–8.
61.  St G. Ashe to unknown, 18/28 Dec. 1690; St G. Ashe to A. St George and S. Lightburn, 9/19 Dec. 1690, TCD, St George Mss, photocopy, 175/1 and 3.
62.  St G. Ashe to ?H. St George, 16/26 March 1689[90], TCD, St George Mss, photocopy, 175/2.
63.  St G. Ashe, _A sermon preached to the Protestants of Ireland, now in London . . . October 23, 1712_ (London, 1712), pp. 12, 16. For another expression of this view: D. Molyneux to R. Howard, 28 May 1727, NLI, PC 225.
64.  R. Distelbeger, 'The Habsburg collections in the seventeenth century', in O. Impey and A. Macgregor (eds), _The origins of museums: the cabinet of curiosities in sixteenth- and seventeenth-century Europe_, 2nd edn (Thirsk, 2001), pp. 51–61; S. N. Pearce, _On collecting: an investigation into collecting in the European tradition_ (London, 1995), p. 109.
65.  St G. Ashe to H. Dodwell, 3/13 Feb. 1689[90], 6 Feb. 1691[2], 10 and 26 March 1691[2], Bodleian, Ms. Eng. Lett. C. 29, ff. 13, 14, 15–16, 17; St G. Ashe to ?H. St George, 16/26 March 1689[90]; St G. Ashe to Revd B. Scroggs, 1/11 Feb. 1690[1], TCD, St George Mss, photocopy, 175/2 and 6; Lord Capel to Abp. T. Tenison, 28 May 1695, NA, M 3036.
66.  J. Leathes to W. Leathes, 27 April 1720, Suffolk CRO, Ipswich, de Mussenden–Leathes Mss, HA 403/1/6, 32; W. Leathes to C. Delafaye, 30 Aug 1719, 6 Sep. 1719, PRO, SP 77/68, ff. 217–217v, 219v–220. See also, J. Hall to dowager countess of Orrery, 23 Dec. 1686, Petworth, Orrery Mss, general series, 30.
67.  M. Leathes to W. Leathes, 16 May 1714, 26 May 1714, [] May 1714, 9 June 1714, Suffolk CRO, Ipswich, de Mussenden–Leathes Mss, HA 403/1/1, 76, 78, 79, 80.
68.  J. Smythe to W. Smythe, 14 June 1710, NLI, PC 449.

69. F. Thompson to S. Waring, 16 Dec. 1687, private collection, Co. Down.

70. C. O'Connor, *The pleasing hours: the Grand Tour of James Caulfield, first earl of Charlemont (1728–1799)* (Cork, 1999), pp. 33, 53–4, 257–62.

71. E. Chaney, 'George Berkeley's grand tours: the immaterialist as connoisseur of art and architecture', in E. Chaney, *The evolution of the Grand Tour* (London, 1998), pp. 314–76.

72. N. Figgis, 'Irish artists and society in eighteenth-century Rome', *Irish Arts Review*, iii/3 (1985), pp. 28–36; N. Figgis, 'Irish landscapists in Rome, 1750–1780', *Irish Arts Review*, iv/4 (1987), pp. 60–5; M. Wynne, 'Members from Great Britain and Ireland of the Florentine Accademia', *Burlington Magazine* (August, 1990); M. Wynne, 'Some British diplomats, some grand tourists and some students from Great Britain and Ireland in Turin in the eighteenth century', *Studi Piemontesi*, xxv (1996), pp. 145–54; exhibition catalogue of James Stewart of Killymoon, Ulster Museum, Belfast, 1999.

73. Some, indeed, see travel to Italy as the defining element of the Grand Tour. Chard, *Pleasure and guilt on the Grand Tour*, pp. 14–15. Alternative perspectives are offered by C. D. van Strien, *British travellers in Holland during the Stuart period* (Leiden, 1993); van Strien, *Touring the Low Countries*.

74. R. Lawrence to Sir G. Lane, received 20 May 1668, Bodleian, Carte Ms. 36, f. 330; instructions from Lawrence to A. van Fornenbergh, received 20 May 1668, Bodleian, Carte Ms. 36, ff. 332–3; van Fornenbergh's reports, received 26 May and Sep. 1668, Bodleian, Carte Ms. 36, ff. 347–8, 497–8.

75. R. Black, travel journal, 1727, PRONI, T 1073/2; R. W. Innes Smith, *English-speaking students of medicine at the university of Leyden* (Edinburgh, 1932); E. Peacock, *Index to English speaking students who have graduated at Leyden University* (London, 1883); E. A. Underwood, *Boerhaave's men at Leyden and after* (Edinburgh, 1977), pp. 24–5, 189–90.

76. T. C. Barnard, *Cromwellian Ireland* (Oxford, 1975), pp. 56–8, 85–8, 235; E. J. Bok-Cleyndert and R. Loeber, 'Het geslacht Wybrants', *Jaarboek van het Central Bureau voor Genealogie en het Iconographisch Bureau*, xlvi (1992), pp. 75–114; R. Loeber, 'English and Irish sources for the history of Dutch economic activity in Ireland, 1600–89', *IESH*, viii (1981), pp. 70–85.

77. H. Maule to R. Stearne, 19 May 1718, Society for the Propagation of Christian Knowledge, ALB, 5620, now in Cambridge UL; [H. Maule], *Pietas Corcagiensis* (Cork, 1721); D. W. Hayton, 'Did Protestantism fail in early eighteenth-century Ireland? Charity schools and the enterprise of religious and social reformation, *c.* 1690–1730', in A. Ford, J. McGuire and K. Milne (eds), *As by law established: the Church of Ireland since the reformation* (Dublin, 1995), pp. 174–5.

78. H. Maule to R. Stearne, 19 May 1718, Society for the Propagation of Christian Knowledge, ALB, 5620, now in Cambridge UL; army list, 1715, PRO, WO 64/3, p. 19; [Maule], *Pietas Corcagiensis*, pp. 25, 27, 45, 54, 59, 72, 78, 81.

79. Lady Dunkellin to Archdeacon Taylor, 12 and 22 Jan. 1721[2], 2 March 1721[2], NLI, Ms. 25,430.

80. J. Hall to dowager countess of Orrery, 22 Nov. 1687, Petworth, Orrery Mss, general series, 30.

81. R. Molesworth to L. Molesworth, 7 Sep. 1692, NLI, microfilm, p. 3752.

82. R. Howard to H. Howard, 18 Sep. 1707, NLI, PC 227.

83. R. Molesworth to L. Molesworth, 8 Feb. 1719[20], NLI, microfilm, p. 3752; HMC, *Various Collections*, viii, p. 285.

84. L. Parsons to T. Lloyd, 31 May 1737, Birr Castle, B/4/5; R. Black, travel journal, 1727, PRONI, T 1073/2; F. Kopitzsch, *Grundzüge einer Sozialgeschichte der Aufklärung in Hamburg und Altona* (Hamburg, 1982); M. Lindemann, *Patriots and paupers* (New York, 1990), pp. 3–73; P. Weber, *On the road to rebellion: the United Irishmen and Hamburg, 1796–1803* (Dublin, 1993), pp. 19–24.

85. D. Mussenden to C. Leathes, 2 March 1740[1], Suffolk CRO, Ipswich, de Mussenden–Leathes Mss, HA 403/1/11, 17.

86. R. Black, travel journal, 1727, PRONI, T 1073/2; S. Madden, *Reflections and resolutions proper for the gentlemen of Ireland* (Dublin, 1738), p. 66; A. W. Vliegenthart, 'Het Loo', in *William and Mary and their house* (New York and London, 1979), pp. 43–6.

87. W. Smythe to J. Smythe, 3 May 1711, NLI, PC 449.

88. R. Black, travel journal, 1727, PRONI, T 1073/2; B. Arciszewska, 'A villa fit for a king: the role of Palladian architecture in the ascendancy of the House of Hanover under George I', *Revue d'Art Canadienne/Canadian Art Review*, xix (1992), pp. 41–58; U. Dann, *Hanover and Great Britain, 1740–1760* (Leicester, 1991); R. Hatton, *George I: elector and king* (London, 1978), pp. 48, 97–8, plate 7.

89. St G. Ashe to H. Dodwell, 3/13 Feb. 1689[90], 6 Feb. 1691[2], 10 March 1691[2], 4 April 1693, Bodleian, Ms. Eng. Lett. C. 29, ff. 13, 14, 15, 21; J. Flamsteed to W. Molyneux, 10 May 1690, Southampton Civic Archives, Molyneux Mss, D/M, 1/1; J. Bonnell to J. Strype, 22 Sep. 1692, Cambridge UL, Add. Ms. 1, 73.

90. T. Ketelsen, 'Art auctions in Germany during the eighteenth century', in M. North and D. Ormrod (eds), *Art markets in Europe, 1500–1800* (Aldershot, 1998), pp. 143–52.

91. 'Autobiography of Pole Cosby, of Stradbally, Queen's County, 1703–1737(?)', *Journal of the County Kildare Archaeological Society*, v (1906), pp. 94, 97–8; T. C. Barnard, 'Protestantism, ethnicity and Irish identities, 1660–1760', in T. Claydon and I. McBride (eds), *Protestantism and national identity: Britain and Ireland, c. 1650–1850* (Cambridge, 1998), pp. 220–1; Ghazvinian, 'English travellers, 1560–1600', p. 49.

92. R. Black, travel journals, 1727–8, PRONI, T. 1073/2 and 3.

93. R. Black, travel journals, 1727, PRONI, T 1073/2.

94. R. Black, travel journals, 1727–8, PRONI, T 1073/3.

95. R. Fitzgerald to Sir M. Crosbie, 5/16 April 1751, NLI, Talbot–Crosbie Mss, folder 47.

96. W. Leathes to G. Tilson, 19 June 1717, PRO, SP 77/67, 242–3.

97. T. Ronayne to T. Sarsfield, 24 July 1798, Cork Archives Institute, U 372, folder 2.

98. R. Black, travel journals, 1727, PRONI, T 1073/2.

99. R. Black, travel journals, 1727, PRONI, T 1073/2.

100. R. Black, travel journals, 1727, PRONI, T 1073/3; Chard, *Pleasure and guilt on the Grand Tour*, pp. 50–6.

101. J. Black to A. Black [1762], PRONI, T 1073/13. On the conventions, J. Black, *The English abroad: the Grand Tour in the eighteenth century* (Stroud, 1992), pp. 213–37.

102. J. Black, 'Occurrences', s.d. 14 June 1763, 2 April 1765, 7 Oct. 1765, PRONI, T 1073/16.

103. J. Black, 'Occurrences', s.d. 14 May 1766, PRONI, T 1073/16.

104. R. Leslie to C. Campbell, 9 July 1715, Denbighshire CRO, Ruthin, DD/BK/I, 510.

105. Palmerston to D. Reading, 23 Nov. 1725, Southampton UL, BR 2/4; R. Howard to H. Howard, 20 March 1728[9], NLI, PC 227. An image of Ellwood is reproduced in J. Caffrey, *John Comerford and the portrait miniature in Ireland, c. 1620–1850* (Kilkenny, 1999), p. 19.

106. H. Brownrigg to Sir W. Fownes, 1 Jan. 1736, n.s., NLI, Ms. 8802/5.

107. R. Fitzgerald to Sir M. Crosbie, 11 Sep. 1742, 19 Jan. 1750[1], 5/16 April 1751, NLI, Talbot–Crosbie Mss, folders 47, 59; John Thomson, notebook, *c.* 1698–1765, NLI, Ms. 3131.

108. M. Leathes to W. Leathes, 25 Jan. 1715, n.s., Suffolk CRO, Ipswich, de Mussenden–Leathes Mss, HA 403/1/1, 101.

109. R. Daniel to W. Leathes, 11 July 1722, 3 Oct. 1722, 22 Dec. 1723, Suffolk CRO, Ipswich, de Mussenden–Leathes Mss, HA 403/1/3, 326, 339, 374; Abp. W. King to C. Domville, 3 Feb. 1717[18], TCD, Ms. 2535/75, pp. 73–5; R. Smythe to W. Smythe, 14 Feb. 1740[1], Smythe of Barbavilla Mss, private collection, Berkshire; H. F. Brown, *Inglesi e Scozzesi all' Università di Padova dell' anno 1618 sino al 1765* (Venice, 1921), p. 199; Ingamells, *Travellers*, p. 305.

110. R. Daniel to W. Leathes, 29 Nov. 1724, Suffolk CRO, Ipswich, de Mussenden–Leathes Mss, HA 403/1/3, 440.

111. Molesworth, *Some considerations for the promoting of agriculture*, pp. 28–9; D. W. Hayton, 'From barbarian to burlesque: English images of the Irish, c. 1660–1750', *IESH*, xv (1988), pp. 5–31; D. W. Hayton, 'Anglo-Irish attitudes: changing perceptions of national identity among the Protestant Ascendancy in Ireland, ca. 1690–1750', *Studies in Eighteenth-Century Culture*, xvii (1987), pp. 145–57.

112. 'Itinerarium Londinense', BL, Add. Ms. 27,951, ff. 22v, 24v, 25v, 31v, 41v, 57, 62v, 65.

113. Letterbook of S. Molyneux, 1712–13, Southampton Civic Archives, D/M, 1/3, pp. 31–2.

114. R. French, tour journal, 1751, NLI, Ms. 7375.

115. R. French, tour journal, s.d. 5 July 1751, NLI, Ms. 7375.

116. 'Itinerarium Londinense', BL, Add. Ms. 27,951, f. 24; M. Clarke to R. Smythe, 5 Sep. 1761, NLI, PC 447; Dowager Lady Caldwell to S. Bagshawe, [ ] Oct. 1761, JRL, B 2/3/307; E. Echlin to C. Tickell, 1761, Tickell Mss, private collection, Devon; T. G. H. Green (ed.), 'Diary of journeys to London from the south of Ireland in 1761 and 1762', *The Antiquary*, xxxvi (1900), pp. 343–4; 'Diary of Anne Cooke', pp. 107–8.

117. 'Itinerarium Londinense', BL, Add. Ms. 27,951, ff. 24v, 25v.

118. 'Itinerarium Londinense', BL, Add. Ms. 27,951,, ff. 28, 31v, 61v.

119. 'Itinerarium Londinense', BL, Add. Ms. 27,951,, f. 65.

120. 'Itinerarium Londinense', BL, Add. Ms. 27,951, ff. 22v, 35.

121. B. Boydell, *A Dublin musical calendar* (Dublin, 1988), pp. 290–1, 299; Delany, *Autobiography*, 1st series, ii, p. 415.

122. T. C. Barnard, 'Protestants and the Irish language, *c.* 1675–1725', *Journal of Ecclesiastical History*, xliv (1993), pp. 243–72.

123. Hayton, 'From barbarian to burlesque', pp. 5–31; Hayton, 'Anglo-Irish attitudes', pp. 145–57.

124. S. Donnelly, 'The Irish harp in England, 1590–1690', *Ceol*, i and ii (1984), p. 61; S. Donnelly, 'A Cork musician at the early Stuart court: Daniel Duff O'Cahill (*c.* 1580–*c.* 1660), "The Queen's Harper"', *JCHAS*, cv (2000), p. 18.

125. S. Burdy, *The life of Philip Skelton*, ed. N. Moore (Oxford, 1914), pp. 103–4.

126. *A dialogue between a secretary of state and a Connaught squire, or a satyr* (Dublin, 1714); James Kow, *The humble remonstrance of the five-foot-highians* (Dublin, reprinted London, 1733).

127. H. Huth (ed.), *Narrative of the journey of an Irish gentleman through England in the year 1752* (London, 1869), pp. 30, 70–2, 94–6, 103, 156.

128. J. Smythe to W. Smythe, 24 May 1728, NLI, PC 449.

129. Legg (ed.), *Synge letters*, pp. 122, 198.

130. L. F. McNamara, 'Some matters touching Dromoland: letters of father and son, 1758–59', *North Munster Antiquarian Journal*, xxviii (1986), p. 65.

131. Bland to Debrisay, 1751, and 4 Jan. 1753, quoted in D. M. Beaumont, 'The gentry of the King's and Queen's Counties: Protestant landed society, 1690–1760', unpublished Ph.D. thesis, 2 vols, TCD (1999), i, pp. 156–7.

132. *Memoirs of Richard Lovell Edgeworth, esq.*, 2 vols (London, 1821), i, pp. 50, 62.

133. W. Mussenden to ?H. Mussenden, 21 Sep. 1758, Suffolk CRO, Ipswich, de Mussenden–Leathes Mss, HA 403/1/11, 1.

134. Incorporated Society, TCD, Ms. 5466, 6 Jan. 1788; cf. Thomas Sheridan, *A complete dictionary of the English language*, 2nd edn (London, 1789), introduction.

135. *An elegy on the very much lamented death of Sir Toby Buttler, Knight* ([Dublin, 1721]); *A true and faithful account of the entry and reception of three extraordinary Irish ambassadors* (London, 1716), p. 20.

136. A. Saville (ed.), *Secret comment: the diaries of Gertrude Savile 1721–1757*, Thoroton Society of Nottinghamshire and Kingsbridge History Society (1997), p. 293.

137. W. S. Lewis (ed.), *Letters of Horace Walpole*, 48 vols (New Haven, 1937–83), ix, p. 185; xx, p. 324.

138. D. Chalenor, 'The Rev. John Chalenor', *Irish Ancestor*, xvii (1985), p. 60.

139. Abp. W. King, account books, s.d. 10 June 1710, TCD, Ms. 751/2, f. 246; F. Gwyn to 'brother', 24 July 1703, Cardiff Central Library, Ms. 2. 1037; Abp. W. King to R. King, 13 April 1706, TCD, Mss 1995–2008/1204; E. Southwell to Lord Finch, 30 Oct. 1715, Leicestershire CRO, Finch Mss, box 4950; R. Edgeworth, accounts, s.d. 17 Jan. 1724[5], NLI, Ms. 1508, p. 150; 'Sawney McCleaver', *Ireland in tears, or, a letter to St Andrew's eldest daughter's youngest son* (London, 1755), p. 47; Green (ed.), 'Diary of journeys to London from the south of Ireland', p. 368.

140. Abp. W. King, account books, TCD, Ms. 751/2, f. 243v; R. Edgeworth, accounts, s.d. 17 Jan. 1724[5], NLI, Ms. 1508, p. 150; Cork and Burlington accounts; journal of W. Burton [Conyngham], RIA, Ms. 12 F 15, p. 11.

141.  M. Herbert to A. Herbert, 26 Sep. 1765, NA, M 1857.

142.  W. Montgomery to M. Ward, 23 Nov. 1742, PRONI, D 2092/1/5, 135.

143.  O. Goldsmith to R. Bryanston, 26 Sep. 1753, Mss of Crozier and Sons, solicitors, Dublin, microfilm in NLI; another version printed in K. C. Balderston (ed.), *The collected letters of Oliver Goldsmith* (Cambridge, 1928), pp. 21–2.

144.  Abp. W. King to E. Southwell, 17 Jan. 1707[8], NLI, Ms. 2055; Abp. W. King to Lady Carteret, 14 Aug. 1728, TCD, Ms. 750/9, 92; R. Jocelyn, the younger, to J. Pickard, 12 July [1740], Dorset CRO, D/BLX/B13.

145.  Sir R. Southwell to ?Ormond, 16 April 1687, BL, Add. Ms. 38,153, f. 1; R. Cox to E. Southwell, 14 Sep. 1714, BL, Add. Ms. 38,157, f. 123v; St Martin's, Minehead, Churchwardens' accounts, Somerset CRO, DP M St M 4/1/1; newsletter from Bristol, 9 April 1689, Bristol RO, Ms. 12964(1), 6; R. Caulfield (ed.), *Autobiography of the Rt. Hon. Sir Richard Cox, Bart.* (London, 1860), p. 15; Barnard, 'Cork settlers', pp. 314–15.

146.  T. Twigge to J. Owen, 27 March 1689, 18 Aug. 1689, 15 Sep. 1690, UCNW, Penrhos Mss, v, 590, 591, 593; will of Revd A. Osborne, 13 Feb. 1689[90], NAS, GD 1/521/24.

147.  List of those who fled from Ireland, TCD, Ms. 847; Abp. J. Vesey, journal, NLI, de Vesci Mss, G/5, pp. 7–22; *Animadversions on the proposal for sending back the nobility and gentry of Ireland* (London, 1690); *Sr St John Brodrick's Vindication of himself* (London, 1690); [R. Bulkeley], *The proposal for sending back the nobility and gentry of Ireland* (London, 1690); R. Caulfield (ed.), *Journal of the Very Rev. Rowland Davies*, Camden Society (London, 1857).

148.  Sir J. Temple, account book, 17 Jan. 1688[9], Southampton UL, BR 7A/1 S. W. Singer (ed.), *The correspondence of Henry Hyde, earl of Clarendon*, 2 vols (London, 1828), ii, pp. 187, 195, 205, 212, 226, 238–45, 247, 268, 271, 273–4, 278, 281, 282, 286, 288, 290, 292; *Sr St John Brodrick's Vindication*, pp. 4–14; Bulkeley, *Proposal*, pp. 7–13.

149.  RIA, broadsides, 3 B 53–56/337.

150.  John Wilson (ed.), *Buckingham contributions for Ireland, 1642*, Buckinghamshire Record Society, xxi (1983).

151.  K. M. Noonan, '"The cruel pressure of an enraged barbarous people": Irish and English identity in seventeenth-century policy and propaganda', *HJ*, xli (1998), p. 170, n. 90.

152.  HMC, *Salisbury Mss*, xvii, pp. 448–9, quoted in P. Fitzgerald, '"Like crickets to the crevice of a brewhouse": poor Irish migrants in England, 1560–1640', in P. O'Sullivan (ed.), *Patterns of migration* (Leicester, London and New York, 1992), p. 25.

153.  *The Benevolent Society of St Patrick: its history and objects* (n.p., *c.* 1910), in Bodleian, Johnson collection, charitable societies, box 3; Peter Clark, *British clubs and societies 1580–1800: the origins of an associational world* (Oxford, 2000), pp. 299–300.

154.  G. W. Place, 'The repatriation of Irish vagrants from Cheshire, 1750–1815', *Journal of the Cheshire Archaeological Society*, lxviii (1986), pp. 125, 137; G. W. Place, *The rise and fall of Parkgate, passenger port for Ireland 1686–1815*, Chetham Society, 3rd series, xxxviii (1994), pp. 172–86.

155.  H. Petty to J. Waller, 8 May 1697, BL, Add. Ms. 72,902; F. G. James, 'The Irish lobby in the early eighteenth century', *EHR*, lxxxi (1966), pp. 554; J. T. Rogers, *A complete collection of Protests of the Lords*, 3 vols (Oxford, 1875), i, p. 32.

156.  St J. Brodrick to Lord Orrery, 13 July 1669, Petworth, Orrery Mss, general series, 28.

157.  Abp. M. Boyle to Lord Blessington, 15 and 22 Nov. 1690, Bodleian, Rawlinson Ms. C. 984, ff. 85–86b.

158.  D. Muschamp to T. Fitzgerald, 20 March 1696[7], NLI, de Vesci Mss, H/2.

159.  R. Molesworth to L. Molesworth, 8 July 1689, NLI, Clements Mss, microfilm, p. 3752.

160.  Viscount Shannon to R. Boyle, undated [*c.* 1672], NLI, de Vesci Mss, H/35.

161.  E. Southwell to Lord Nottingham, 30 Sep. 1707, Leicestershire CRO, Finch Mss, box 4950; P. Wemyss to Sir T. Vesey, 17 Dec. 1728, NLI, de Vesci Mss, J/23; A. Crotty to H. Boyle, 9 Feb. 1727[8], PRONI, Shannon Mss, D 2707/A1/11/7A.

162. E. P. Alexander (ed.), *Journal of John Fontaine; an Irish Huguenot son in Spain and Virginia, 1710–1719* (Williamsburg, 1972), p. 44.

163. E. T. Martin (ed.), *The Ash Mss, written in the year 1735, by Lieut.-Col. Thomas Ash* (Belfast, 1890), p. 19.

164. J. Black, 'Occurrences', PRONI, T 1073/16, pp. 4–5.

165. 'Diary of Anne Cooke', p. 107.

166. Huth (ed.), *Narrative of the journey of an Irish gentleman*, pp. 82–3, 125.

167. W. Perceval to Lord Egmont, ? 29 March 1752, BL, Add. Ms. 47,008B, f. 150.

168. 'Itinerarium Londinense', BL, Add. Ms. 27,951, ff. 38v, 57.

169. R. Edgeworth, accounts, s.d. 31 Aug. 1724, 31 Dec. 1724, 23 Feb. 1724[5], NLI, Ms. 1508, pp. 138, 148, [185].

170. R. Edgeworth, accounts, s.d. 18 and 27 May 1727, NLI, Ms. 1509, pp. 148, 149; R. French to W. Smythe, 29 May 1712, NLI, PC 447.

171. Barnard, *New anatomy*, pp. 113–28; D. Lemmings, *Gentlemen and barristers: the Inns of Court and the English Bar, 1680–1730* (Oxford, 1990), p. 18, n. 26.

172. R. French to W. Smythe, 24 Oct. 1713, NLI, PC 447; T. C. Barnard, 'The uses of 23 October 1641 and Irish Protestant celebrations', *EHR*, cvi (1991), pp. 889–920.

173. R. Edgeworth, accounts, s.d. 13 Oct. 1724, 11 Feb. 1726[7], 11 July 1727, 22 Sep. 1727, 11 Oct, 1727, NLI, Mss 1508, p. 142; 1509, pp. 115, 155, 164, 168.

174. R. Edgeworth, accounts, s.d. 26 Jan. 1726[7], 5 Feb. 1726[7], 1 March 1726[7], 27 April 1727, 1 May 1727, 2 Aug. 1727, NLI, Ms. 1509, pp. 112, 118, 124, 145, 158; cf. R. French, account book, NLI, Ms. 4919, f. 64v.

175. R. Edgeworth, accounts, s.d. 28 Aug. 1724, NLI, Ms 1508, p. 137.

176. R. Edgeworth, accounts, s.d. 27, 29 and 30 Aug. 1753, NLI, Ms. 1520, p. 177.

177. R. Edgeworth, accounts, s.d. 6 Sep. 1727, 10 and 11 Oct. 1727, 7 and 10 Sep. 1761, 10, 11 and 12 Oct. 1761, NLI, Mss 1509, pp. 163, 168, 187; 1527, pp. 164, 173–4.

178. J. Carswell and L. A. Dralle (eds), *The political journal of George Bubb Doddington* (Oxford, 1965), pp. xiii–xiv.

179. R. French, journal, 1751, NLI, Ms. 7375.

180. 'Itinerarium Londinense', BL, Add. Ms. 27,951, ff. 22, 23v, 40.

181. Green (ed.), 'Diary of journeys to London from the south of Ireland', pp. 342–4.

182. Lord Rosse to Ormonde, 16 Oct. 1713, Birr Castle, Co. Offaly, Ms. B/2/2.

183. L. Roberts to H. Temple, 17 Feb. 1721[2], Southampton UL, BR 140/5.

184. R. Howard to Abp. W. King, 31 March 1716, 10 April 1716, TCD, Ms. 1995–2008/ 1763, 1768.

185. St G. Ashe, *A sermon preached to the Protestants of Ireland, now in London, at the parish-church of St Clement Dane. October 23, 1712* (London, 1712); John Dane, *The Reformation protected by the Providence of God* (London, 1710); R. Lambert, *A sermon preach'd to the Protestants of Ireland, now residing in London: at their anniversary meeting on October XXIII. 1708* (London, 1708); S. Palmer, *A sermon preach'd to the Protestants of Ireland now in London* (London, 1710); J. Ramsay, *A sermon preach'd to the Protestants of Ireland, now in London, at the parish church of St Mary le Bow, October 23 1713* (London, 1714); W. Stephens, *A sermon against Popery, preach'd to the Protestants of Ireland, now residing in London* (London, 1712).

186. Minutes of Corresponding Society, 1735–43, TCD, Ms. 5302, f. 35.

187. Ibid., ff. 22, 28, 35, 63, 127, 138, 140,

188. Ibid., f. 134.

189. A list of the preachers is in P. Fletcher, *A sermon preached before the Society corresponding with the Incorporated Society in Dublin . . . St Mary le Bow, 2 May 1759* (London, 1759), pp. 94–5.

190. Minutes of Corresponding Society, 1735–43, TCD, Ms. 5302, f. 162v.

191. R. T. Jenkins and H. Ramage, *The history of the Honourable Society of Cymmrodorion* (London, 1951); E. Jones (ed.), *The Welsh in London, 1500–2000* (Cardiff, 2001), pp. 54–87.

192.  M. D. George, 'Some caricatures of Wales and Welshmen', *National Library of Wales Journal*, v (1947–8), pp. 1–12; Hayton, 'From barbarian to burlesque', pp. 26–9; W. J. Hughes, *Wales and the Welsh in English literature* (London, 1924), ch. 3; P. Lord, *Words with pictures: Welsh images and images of Wales in the popular press, 1640–1860* (Aberystwyth, 1995), pp. 53–85.

193.  'Autobiography of Pole Cosby', p. 167; D. M. Beaumont, 'An Irish gentleman in England – the travels of Pole Cosby, c. 1730–1735', *Journal of the British Archaeological Association*, cxlix (1996), pp. 37–54.

194.  H. Ingoldsby to W. Smythe, 4 Feb. 1715[16], NLI, PC 445/4.

195.  H. Ingoldsby to W. Smythe, 3 April 1716, 20 March 1716[17], NLI, PC 445.

196.  H. Ingoldsby to W. Smythe, 30 July 1720, 9 Aug. 1720, NLI, PC 445.

197.  H. Ingoldsby to W. Smythe, 5 and 21 Sep. 1723, NLI, PC 445/7.

198.  H. Ingoldsby to W. Smythe, 14 and 21 Sep. 1723, 19 Oct. 1723, 2 June 1724, NLI, PC 445. For this development: E. McKellar, *The birth of modern London: the development and design of the city, 1660–1720* (Manchester, 1999), pp. 38–56; C. Spence, *London in the 1690s: a social atlas* (London, 2000).

199.  H. Ingoldsby to W. Smythe, 4 July 1724, 27 Aug. 1724, NLI, PC 445.

200.  H. Ingoldsby to W. Smythe, 12 Nov. 1723, 4 Dec. 1723, 18 and 22 Jan. 1723[4], 8 Feb. 1723[4], NLI, PC 445.

201.  H. Ingoldsby to W. Smythe, 27 Oct. 1724, NLI, PC 445.

202.  H. Ingoldsby to W. Smythe, 22 May 1725, 6 Sep. 1725, NLI, PC 445.

203.  T. Barnard, *The Abduction of a Limerick Heiress: social and political relationships in eighteenth-century Ireland* (Dublin, 1998), pp. 15–20.

204.  R. French, journal, 1751, NLI, Ms. 7375.

205.  J. Digby to W. Smythe, 21 April 1733, 25 Aug. 1733, NLI, PC 445.

206.  J. Digby to W. Smythe, 21 April 1733, 17 March 1736[7], NLI, PC 445; journal of Anne French, TCD, Ms. 5096; Barnard, 'French of Monivea', pp. 282–8.

207.  'Itinerarium Londinense', BL, Add. Ms. 27,951; *The Irish Register: or a list of the duchess dowagers, countesses, widow ladies and maiden ladies, widows and misses of large fortunes in England as registered by the Dublin Society* (Dublin, 1742); Hayton, 'From barbarian to burlesque', pp. 22–5.

208.  Barnard, 'What became of Waring?', pp. 185–212.

209.  J. Black, 'Occurrences', s.d. 5 May 1763, 14 Oct. 1763, 10 Nov. 1764, 29 July–2 Aug. 1766, PRONI, T 1073/16.

210.  G. Davis, 'Social decline and slum conditions: Irish migrants in Bath's history', *Bath History*, viii (2000), pp. 134–47.

211.  Petition of D. Flanagan, c. 1705, V & A, Ormonde Mss, 6/80.

212.  H. Howard to R. Howard, 19 March 1733[4], NLI, PC 227.

213.  A. Spurrett to R. Power, 14, 26 and 28 Sept. 1704, 3 Oct. 1704, Chatsworth, Spurrett letterbook, 1703–4; Barnard, *New anatomy*, p. 77.

214.  H. Green to R. King, 10 Jan. 1705[6], TCD, Mss 1995–2008/1189; W. Smythe to unknown, 18 Dec. 1711 and undated [?1711], NLI, PC 449.

215.  Abp. W. King to E. Southwell, 21 Jan. 1717[18]; Abp. W. King to W. Domville, 3 Feb. 1717[18], TCD, Ms. 2535, pp. 63–6, 75.

216.  Abp. W. King to Lord Fitzwilliam, 9 Aug. 1718, TCD, Ms. 2535, p. 350.

217.  Abp. W. King, account book, 1700–12, TCD, Ms. 751/2, ff. 119–132, 138–148v, 238–246v.

218.  Bp. J. Evans to Abp. W. Wake, 7 April 1716, Christ Church, Wake Ms. 12/32.

219.  A. Dobbs, *An essay on the trade and improvement of Ireland* (Dublin, 1729), p. 73; P. Delany, *A sermon preach'd before the Society corresponding with the Incorporated Society in Dublin . . . March 13th, 1743/4* (London, 1744), p. 16.

220.  Bp. J. Evans to Abp. W. Wake, 7 Nov. 1719, Christ Church, Wake Ms. 13/125: P. O'Regan, *Archbishop William King of Dublin (1650–1729) and the constitution of church and state* (Dublin, 2000).

221.  H. Colvill, account with E. Brice, 23 March 1731[2], PRONI, D 1556/16/7/10; H. Maxwell to E. Brice, 7 Jan. 1729[30], PRONI, D 1556/16/7/5; R. Maxwell to R. Maxwell, 26 June 1735, PRONI, D 4718/L/.

222. W. Longueville to T. Hales, 31 July 1686, Somerset CRO, DD/BR/ely, 3/11; H. Petty to Lady Petty, 14 Aug. 1687, BL, Add. Ms. 72,857/31; Abp. W. King, account book, 1700–12, TCD, Ms. 751/2, ff. 130v–132v; R. Waring to W. Leathes, 21 July 1721, 25 Sep. 1721, Suffolk CRO, Ipswich, de Mussenden–Leathes Mss, HA 403/1/2, 310, 314; *CARD*, iv, pp. 463–4; C. S. King, *A great archbishop of Dublin, William King, D.D., 1650–1729* (London, 1906), p. 19.

223. W. Waring to S. Waring, 30 June 1697, R. Waring to S. Waring, 12 May 1699; account of Mrs Waring's expenses at Bath, 1701; R. Smythe to W. Smythe, 31 May 1729, Smythe of Barbavilla Mss, private collection, Berkshire.

224. Bp. W. King's observations on the primatial visitation of Armagh, 1700, PRONI, DIO 4/29/1/2(6).

225. Abp. W. King to unknown, 7 March 1712[13], TCD, Ms. 750/4/1, 125; Abp. W. King to J. Swift, 14 April 1713, TCD, Ms. 750/4/1, 125; D. Ryder to Devonshire, 14 Oct. 1742, Chatsworth, Devonshire letters, box 1740–3, 297.0; R. Newcome to Hartington, 27 June 1753, Chatsworth, Devonshire letters, 1752–5.

226. Sir A. Cairnes to W. Conolly, 25 Sep. 1712, IAA, Castletown deposit, box 57; K. Conolly to Lady A. Conolly, 25 April 1745, IAA, Castletown deposit, box 76; O. Wynne to C. Kennedy, 11 Aug. 1711, NAS, GD 27/3/33.

227. Sir T. Vesey to D. Green, 8 Nov 1703, NLI, de Vesci Mss, J/5; A. Leech to Bp. T. Vesey, 24 Feb. 1717[18], NLI, de Vesci Mss, J/5; R. Mossom to Bp. T. Vesey, 1 May 1728; H. Bolton to Bp. T. Vesey, 7 Sep. 1728, NLI, de Vesci Mss, J/23; T. Harrison to J. Strype, 29 Aug. 1711, Cambridge UL, Add. Ms. 6, 434; O. Gallagher to O. St George, 2 Sep. 1729, PRO, C 110/46, 724.

228. Abp. W. King, account book, 1700–12, TCD, Ms. 751/2, ff. 136, 242; Abp. W. King to T. Foley, 18 March 1709[10], TCD, Ms. 2531, 161; Abp. W. King to H. Dodwell, 26 Jan. 1709[10], St Edmund Hall, Ms. 9, p. 147; Abp. W. King to S. Molyneux, 10 June 1713, TCD, Ms. 750/4, 164; Abp. W. King to F. Annesley, 11 June 1726, TCD, Ms. 750/8, 103; H. Boyle to J. Uniacke, 30 July 1720, PRONI, D 2707/A1/11/4A; R. Waring to W. Leathes, 6, 18, 22 Aug. 1722, Suffolk CRO, Ipswich, HA 403/1/3, 327–9; B. Badham to W. Cullen, 9 Dec. 1730, NLI, de Vesci Mss, J/6; R. Howard to Abp. W. King, 2 July 1726, TCD, Mss 1995–2008/2152.

229. J. Ware to H. Jodrell or H. Ware, 25 Nov. 1760, NLI, Ms. 116/46. Cf. D. Ó Murchadha, 'Memorial inscriptions of Irish interest from Bath Abbey', *Irish Genealogist*, viii (1993), pp. 530–45; *JRSAI*, xxxii, pp. 173–4.

230. Elinor O'Hara, account book, 1722–33, NLI, Ms. 36,387/7, pp. 57–65.

231. A. Philipps to unknown, 18 March 1733[4], NLI, Ms. 36,390/2.

232. R. Edgeworth, accounts, s.d. 17 Jan. 1743[4], 5 March 1743[4], 1753, 6 June 1754, 15 April 1756, NLI, Mss 1516, pp. 81, 88: 1520, p. 173, and at back, unpaginated; 1522, p. 125.

233. R. Edgeworth, accounts, s.d. 28 Sep. 1743, 2 March 1743[4], 8 May 1744, NLI, Ms. 1516, pp. 69, 83, 102.

234. Sir R. Bulkeley to M. Lister, 21 May [1690s], Bodleian, Lister Ms. 3, f. 45.

235. F. Bellew to Lord Raby, 28 Aug. 1717, BL, Add. Ms. 22,228, f. 42; H. Howard to R. Howard, 8 Sep. 1716, NLI, PC 227; E. Ormsby to O. Wynne, 20 Feb. 1769, PRONI, MIC/666/D/7/6.

236. P. Delany to M. Delany, 6 May 1747, Newport Public Library, Gwent, Delany Mss, 1/692; Delany, *Autobiography*, 1st series, iii, pp. 464–5; P. Delany, *Eighteen discourses and dissertations upon various very important and interesting subjects* (London, 1766), pp. 91–7; T. Pakenham to W. Smythe, 28 Sep. 1742, NLI, PC 449; W. Perceval to Lord Egmont, 3 Oct. 1748, 15 Nov. 1750; BL, Add. Ms. 47,000B, ff. 94, 115; cf. H. O'Neil to P. Maguire, 7 Feb. 1779, JRL, B 3/20/276; M. Busteed, 'Identity and economy on an Anglo-Irish estate: Castle Caldwell, Co. Fermanagh, *c.* 1750–1793', *Journal of Historical Geography*, xxvi (2000), pp. 184–5; 'Diary of Anne Cooke', p. 119; P. MacEvansoneya, 'An Irish artist goes to Bath: letters from John Warren to Andrew Caldwell, 1776–1784', *Irish Architectural and Decorative Studies*, ii (1999), pp. 149–50.

237. F. Kielmansegge, *Diary of a Journey to England in the Years 1761–1762* (London, 1902), pp. 126–7.

238. Davis, 'Irish migrants in Bath's history', pp. 134–47; R. S. Neale, *Bath: a social history 1680–1850* (London, 1981), pp. 71–2; J. A. Williams (ed.), *Post-reformation Catholicism in Bath*, Catholic Record Society Publications, 65 and 66 (1975–6), i, pp. 75–80; ii, pp. 28–33.

239. T. Vesey to D. Green, 8 Nov. 1703, NLI, de Vesci Mss, J/5; P. Stratford to Lady Eustace, 23 Nov. [1720], Tickell Mss, private collection, Devon.

240. N. Delacherois to D. Delacherois, 11 June 1770, 23 July 1770, 29 Sep. 1770, NAM, Ms. 7805–63; Green (ed.), 'Diary of journeys to London from the south of Ireland', p. 205.

241. T. Harrison to J. Strype, 5 June 1717, Cambridge UL, Add. Ms. 8/198; W. Andrews to Sir T. Vesey, 29 June 1728, NLI, de Vesci Mss, J/24; M. Coghill to E. Southwell, 21 June 1733, BL, Add. Ms. 21,123, f. 41; Bp. R. Howard to H. Howard, 22 May 1736, NLI, PC 227; P. T. Marcy, 'Eighteenth-century views of Bristol and Bristolians', in P. McGrath (ed.), *Bristol in the eighteenth century* (Newton Abbot, 1972), pp. 13–38; L. F. McNamara, 'The diary of an eighteenth-century Clare gentleman', *North Munster Antiquarian Journal*, xxii (1980), pp. 30–1; R. Sweet, 'Topographies of politeness', *TRHS*, 6th series, xii (2002), pp. 363–4.

242. 'Autobiography of Pole Cosby', p. 271.

243. K. Conolly to C. Eustace, 13 Aug. 1723, 10 Oct. 1723, Tickell Mss, private collection, Devon.

244. Marcy, 'Eighteenth-century views of Bristol', pp. 30–8; *A new present state of England*, 2 vols (London, 1750), i, p. 207; V. Waite, 'The Bristol Hotwell', in McGrath (ed.), *Bristol in the eighteenth century*, pp. 109–26.

245. T. C. Barnard, 'The cultures of eighteenth-century Irish towns', in P. Borsay and L. Proudfoot (eds), *Provincial towns in early modern England and Ireland; change, convergence and divergence*, Proceedings of the British Academy, cviii (2002), pp. 195–222.

246. R. Smythe to W. Smythe, 23 Feb. 1739[40], 14 Feb. 1740[1], Smythe of Barbavilla Mss, private collection, Berkshire; J. Mussenden to W. Leathes, 18 [ ] 1724, Suffolk CRO, Ipswich, de Mussenden–Leathes Mss, HA 403/1/6, 109.

247. P. Bellon, *The Irish spaw* (Dublin, 1684), pp. 50–1, 67, 74–6; P. Dun to W. King, 6 June 1684, TCD, Mss 1995–2008/24; 'Sir Thomas Molyneux, Bart., M.D., F.R.S.', *Dublin University Review*, xviii (Sep. 1841), p. 484.

248. W. Owen to J. Owen, 29 July 1690, UCNW, Penrhos Mss, v, 438.

249. Sir R. Bulkeley to ?M. Lister, 24 June 1686, Bodleian, Lister Ms. 35, f. 121v; Bp. N. Foy to Bp. W. King, 8 Sep. 1693, TCD, Mss 1995–2008/293; Bp. W. King to J. Bonnell, 4 Aug. 1696, TCD, Mss. 1995–2008/507; M. Ord to S. Waring, 15 Dec. 1705, private collection, Co. Down; J. Smythe to W. Smythe, 22 July 1713, NLI, PC 449; R. Smythe to W. Smythe, 13 Oct. 1713, Smythe of Barbavilla Mss, private collection, Berkshire.

250. Bp. W. King to J. Bonnell, 4 Aug. 1696, TCD, Mss 1995–2008/507.

251. J. Rutty, *An essay towards a natural, experimental and medicinal history of the mineral waters of Ireland* (Dublin, 1757), p. v.

252. Ibid., pp. xv, 137, 204, 287, 364.

253. Ibid., pp. 400–1.

254. Ibid., pp. 135, 159–60, 166.

255. W. Congreve to J. Kelly, 20 June 1704, NAS, RH 1/2/490; Barnard, *New anatomy*, p. 221.

256. Rutty, *Essay*, p. 77; H. French to R. Bourke, 2 Aug. 1754, NLI, Ms. 8475; A. Carpenter (ed.), *Verse in English from eighteenth-century Ireland* (Cork, 1998), pp. 307–8.

257. 'The Ballyspellan Spa', in Cambridge UL, Hib. 3.730.1 (52); A. Vesey to Sir T. Vesey, 27 April 1725, NLI, de Vesci Mss, J/14; A. Vesey to Sir T. Vesey, 11 April 1727, NLI, de Vesci Mss, J/11; E. Cooke to Mrs Sweet, 30 June 1729, Cooke Mss, Maidenhall, Co. Kilkenny; Lord Mountgarret to Lord Barrymore, 3 Aug. 1732, Bodleian, Carte Ms. 227, f. 72; cf. TCD, Ms. 1178, f. 23; J. Burgess, *An essay on the waters and air of Ballispellan* (Dublin, 1725); P. Henchy, 'A bibliography of Irish spas', *Publications of the Irish Bibliographical Society*, vi (1957), pp. 98–111; J. Loveday, *Diary of a tour in 1732 through parts of England, Wales, Ireland and Scotland* (Edinburgh, 1890), p. 46.

258. Rutty, *Essay*, pp. 170–7.

259. K. Myers, 'The Mallow Spa', *Mallow Field Club Journal*, ii (1984), pp. 11–12.

260. J. Wight, journal, s.d. 16 and 19 June 1753, Friends' Historical Library, Dublin; Oughton, autobiography, NAM, Ms. 8808–36–1, p. 62; J. Buckley, 'The journal of Thomas Wright, author of Louthiana (1711–1786)', *County Louth Archaeological Journal*, ii (1908–11), p. 185.

261. R. French, accounts, 15 June 1759–15 June 1760, NLI, Ms. 4918; A. Worthevale to J. Crone, 18 May 1767, 6 June 1767, Cork Archives Institute, Crone of Byblox Mss, PR 3, box 1.

262. E. Spencer to F. Price, 24 June 1746, NLW, Puleston Ms. 3580E; M. D. Jephson, *An Anglo-Irish miscellany: some records of the Jephsons of Mallow* (Dublin, 1964), pp. 356–7; Myers, 'The Mallow Spa', p. 12.

263. P. Delany to T. Tickell, 14 Aug. 1736, Tickell Mss, private collection, Devon.

264. J. Digby to W. Smythe, 19 June 1742, NLI, PC 445.

265. T. Taylor to Sir T. Taylor, 30 July 1749, n.s., NLI, Headfort Ms. F/3/24; see too: T. Barry to H. Hatch, 20 June 1759, NLI, Ms. 11,327/8; Rutty, *Essay*, pp. 363–401.

266. J. Bowes to Devonshire, 21 July 1758, Chatsworth, Devonshire letters, box Jan.–Oct. 1758.

267. R. Edgeworth, accounts, s. d. 7–14, 20 and 28 May 1767, 3 June 1767, NLI, Ms. 1533, pp. 169–72.

268. R. Edgeworth, accounts, s.d. 21 and 23 Aug. 1767, Sep. 1767, NLI, Ms. 1535, pp. 228, 232, 233–5.

269. R. Edgeworth, accounts, s.d. 20 May 1767, 5 June 1767, NLI, Ms. 1533, pp. 170, 173.

270. G. S. Cotter, *Poems consisting of odes, songs, pastorals, satyrs, &c.* 2 vols (Cork, 1788), i, pp. 197–9.

271. R. Porter (ed.), *The medical history of spas and waters* (London, 1990).

272. J. Leathes to W. Leathes, 1 Sep. 1714, Suffolk CRO, de Mussenden–Leathes Mss, HA 403/1/6, 14; O. Gallagher to O. St George, 24 Sep. 1726, PRO, C 110/46, 443; accounts of Blakes of Ballyglunin, *c.* 1753–63, NA, M 6933/16, s.d. 1752; 'Autobiography of Pole Cosby', p. 90.

273. Bp. E. Smythe to W. Smythe, 24 Sep. 1709, NLI, PC 445/1; T. Harrison to J. Strype, 5 and 28 Aug. 1718, Cambridge UL, Add. Ms. 9/261, 262; P. Delany to M. Delany, 6 May 1747, Newport Public Library, Gwent, Delany Mss, 1/692.

274. E. Echlin to C. Tickell, 7 Oct. 1754, Tickell Mss, private collection, Devon; Nancy Brabazon, account, 1759, Barber Mss, private collection, London, box I.

275. Annesley account book, 1761–6, s.d. 20 May 1761, PRONI, D 1854/8/17.

276. Mary, Lady Kildare to duchess of Leinster, 15 Oct. 1774, 2 Nov. 1774, NLI, Ms. 629/9, 11; 'Ant. Constitution', *A short and easy method of reducing the exorbitant pride and arrogance of the city of Dublin* (London, 1748), p. 31.

277. D. Keogh, 'The French Disease': the Catholic church and radicalism in Ireland, 1790–1800 (Dublin, 1993), p. 117; J. McVeagh (ed.), *Richard Pococke's Irish tours* (Dublin, 1995), p. 109.

278. Lucas, journal, s.d. 29 June 1741, 3 Sep. 1741, NLI, Ms. 14,101.

279. M. Symner, answers to interrogatories of S. Hartlib, *c.* 1658, Sheffield UL, Hartlib Mss, lxii/45.

280. Account of Fermanagh, pp. 6–7, Armagh Public Library, Physico-Historical Society; J. B. Cunningham, *A history of Castle Caldwell and its families* (Monaghan, *c.* 1980), pp. 36–7; J. Richardson, *The great folly, superstition, and idolatry, of pilgrimages in Ireland; especially of that to St Patrick's Purgatory* (Dublin, 1727).

281. H. Thomson, autobiography, Bodleian, Ms. Eng. Hist d. 155, p. 52.

282. ?Revd R. Hezlett to Bp. J. Garnett, 10 Feb. 1776, PRONI, D 668/E/38.

283. R. Barton, *Lectures in natural philosophy* (Dublin, 1751), pp. 168–75.

284. Revd W. Cope to Sir A. Acheson, 1 June 1752, PRONI, D 1606/1/8.

285. [R. Barton], *Some remarks, towards a full description of Upper and Lower Lough Lene, near Killarney, in the County of Kerry* (Dublin, 1751), sig. A2–A2v.

286. [Hickes], *The gentleman instructed*, p. 418.

*11  Society*

1.  J. Digby to A. French, 1 April 1737, NLI, Ms. 19,821; J. Digby to W. Smythe, 17 March 1736[7], 4 Dec. 1746, NLI, PC 445; Williams (ed.), *Correspondence of Swift*, iii, p. 319; iv, pp. 547–9, 556; v, p. 6.

2.  P. Delany, 'The great importance and wisdom of early industry, preached before the University in St Patrick's Cathedral, Dublin, 1720', in P. Delany, *Twenty sermons on social duties, and their opposite vices* (London, 1747), pp. 349–65.

3.  Bp. R. Howard to H. Howard, 28 Aug. 1730, NLI, PC 227.

4.  Lady A. Crosbie to W. Crosbie, 6 Jan. 1732[3], NLI, Talbot–Crosbie Mss, folder 5?5.

5.  A. Hill to S. Waring, 29 Jan. 1708[9], private collection, Co. Down.

6.  M. Mason to J. Mason, 14 Dec. 1737, Dromana, Co. Waterford, Villiers–Stuart Mss, T 3131, B/1/36.

7.  L. Clayton to Sir J. Perceval, 15 March 1685[6], BL, Add. Ms. 46,962, f. 240.

8.  A. Hill to G. Waring, 11 and 21 April 1705, 2 June 170[?5], private collection, Co. Down.

9.  A. Hill to G. Waring, 28 May 1705, private collection, Co. Down.

10. 'The autobiography of Pole Cosby, of Stradbally, Queen's County, 1703–1737(?)', *Journal of the County Kildare Archaeological Society*, v (196), pp. 96, 167.

11. M. Moore to J. Moore, 11 Dec. 1759; M. Moore to Margaret Moore, n.d., Barber Mss, private collection, London, box 1; confession of J. Meagher, *c.* 1691, RIA, Ms. 24 G 5/62; A. Reyler to M. Nugent, 12 April 1718, 8 March 1725[6], NA, M. 2372.

12. J. Smythe to W. Smythe, 23 Dec. 1729, NLI, PC 449.

13. J. Smythe to W. Smythe, 20 Oct. 1741, NLI, PC 449; above, pp. 112–13.

14. Barnard, *New anatomy*, pp. 288–94.

15. Monck Mason collections, ii, part iii, p. 544, Dublin Public Library, Gilbert Ms. 67; Minute Book of the Goldsmiths' Company, 1731–58, pp. 60, 125, 127, 171, 220–1, 323, Assay Office, Dublin Castle; Masters' Accounts, Weavers' Company, 1691–1714, s.d. 1701–2, 5 Aug. 1707, RSAI; Minute Book of Barber-Surgeons' Company, Dublin, 1703–57, TCD, Ms. 1447/8/1, ff. 58, 67v–68, 72v; extracts from records of the Tailors' Guild, Dublin, 1296–1753, Dublin Public Library, Gilbert Ms. 80, pp. 82, 86, 87; G. L. Barrow, 'Riding the franchises', *Dublin Historical Record*, xxxiii (1980), pp. 135–8; G. L. Barrow, 'The franchises of Dublin', *Dublin Historical Record*, xxxvi (1983), pp. 68–80.

16. Abp. W. King to Lady Carteret, 14 Aug. 1728, TCD, Ms. 750/9/93.

17. Petition on behalf of the 'poor societies belonging to the clothing trade', from W. Dames to Abp. W. King, 6 June 1728, Marsh's Library, Dublin, Ms. Z3.1.1, clxiv; case of the undertakers and journeymen broadcloth weavers to Abp. W. King, Marsh's Library, Dublin, Ms. Z3.1.1, clxv; E. B., *The defence of the whole society of wool-combers of the city and liberties of the city of Corke* (Cork, 1722); Barnard, *New anatomy*, pp. 284–6.

18. *Dublin Freeman's Journal*, no. 131, 26 July 1726.

19. H. N[elson], *A poem in honour of the antient and loyal society of journey-men-taylors, who are to dine at the King's Inns, on Monday the 25th inst., July; 1726* (Dublin, [1726]); H. Nelson, *A poem in praise of the loyal and charitable society of journeymen tailors* (Dublin, [1729]); H. Nelson, *Poem on the procession of journeymen tailors, July the 28th, MDCCXXIX* ([Dublin, 1729]); *CARD*, xi, pp. 496–8.

20. *Dublin Freeman's Journal*, no. 178, 29 Nov.–3 Dec. 1726.

21. W. S. Lewis (ed.), *Letters of Horace Walpole*, 48 vols (New Haven, 1937–1983), ix, p. 401.

22. *Schemes from Ireland for the benefit of the body natural, ecclesiastical and politick* (Dublin, 1732), p. 9.

23. Bp. R. Howard to H. Howard, 18 March 1730[1], NLI, PC 227; Mrs K. Conolly to Lady Anne Conolly, 21 Feb. 1746[7], IAA, Castletown deposit, box 76; E. K. Sheldon, *Thomas Sheridan of Smock Alley* (Princeton, 1967), pp. 76–107; H. Burke, *Riotous performances: the struggle for hegemony in the Irish theatre, 1712–1784* (Notre Dame, 2003), pp. 117–48.

24. Incorporated Society Board Book, 1761–75, s.d. 23 May 1766, TCD, Ms. 5225.

25. Masters' accounts, Weavers' Company, Dublin, 1691–1714, RSAI.
26. Account book, Guild of St Anne, Dublin, RIA, Ms. 12 P 1; Minute Book, Guild of St Anne, RIA, Ms. 12 D 1.
27. J. Perceval to Lord Perceval, 11 June 1731, BL, Add. Ms. 46,982, f. 98; W. H. G. Bagshawe, *The Bagshawes of Ford: a biographical pedigree* (London, 1886), p. 335; *A letter from Sir Richard Cox, Bart. to Thomas Prior, Esq.* (Dublin, 1749); *A letter from Sir Richard Cox, Bart. to the High Sheriff of the County of Cork relative to the present state of the linen-manufacture in that county* (Dublin, 1759).
28. Minute Book, Limerick Guild of Masons, 1747–57, s.d. 2 Feb. 1748[9], 12 Oct. 1753, Limerick Civic Museum.
29. Minute Book, Limerick Guild of Masons, 1747–57, s.d. 8 Oct. 1753, 24 May 1755, Limerick Civic Museum.
30. For May Day celebrations in England in the eighteenth century: N. Rogers, 'Crowds and political festivals in Georgian England', in T. Harris (ed.), *The politics of the excluded, c. 1500–1850* (Basingstoke, 2001), pp. 236–7.
31. J. Wight, journal, s.d. 22, 23 and 24 May 1752, 11 June 1752, 12, 14 and 18 May 1753, 11, 12 and 13 June 1753, Friends' Historical Library, Dublin, S. Bagshawe to C. Caldwell, 5 and 12 July 1751, JRL, B3/1/3 and 6; T. C. Barnard, *The abduction of a Limerick heiress: social and political relations in mid-eighteenth-century Ireland* (Dublin, 1999), pp. 11–12, 18–19; S. Derrick, *Letters written from Leverppole, Chester, Corke, the Lake of Killarney, Dublin . . .* , 2 vols (London, 1767), ii, p. 5; A. J. Guy, *Oeconomy and discipline: officership and administration in the British army, 1714–63* (Manchester, 1985), p. 41; 'Philopater', *A letter from a member of the corporation of Limerick to his friend* (?Dublin, 1726); *A true state of the present affairs of Limerick* (London, 1726).
32. 'Curate's address to the gown', in W. Young, notebook, TCD, Ms. 10,664, p. 20.
33. Vestry Book, St John's, Dublin, accounts, 1747–56, RCB, P. 328/5.2; N. Peacock, journal, s.d. 2 Sep. 1744, 29 Sep. 1745, NLI, Ms. 16,091.
34. J. Hewetson, *Memoirs of the house of Hewetson or Hewson of Ireland* (London, 1901), p. 115.
35. D. Muschamp to T. Fitzgerald, 11 Aug. 1695, NLI, de Vesci Mss, H/2.
36. W. Andrews to Sir T. Vesey, 7 Dec. 1727, NLI, de Vesci Mss, J/24.
37. Vestry Book, St John's, Dublin, s.d. 23 June 1763, RCB, P 328/5.2; Vestry Book, St Michan's, Dublin, 1723–61, RCB, P. 276/8.2.
38. R. Aylward to G. Legge, 5 April 1679, Staffordshire CRO, Dartmouth Mss, D 1778/iii/0/19, Staffordshire CRO, DW 1778/iii/O/18; J. Burward to Sir W. Abdy, 21 Nov. 1743, NLI, Ms. 7179.
39. Hume report, NLI, Ms. 6054, f. 11.
40. See above, pp. 96–7.
41. T. C. Barnard, 'Considering the inconsiderable: electors, patrons and Irish elections, 1659–1761', in D. W. Hayton (ed.), *The Irish Parliament in the eighteenth century: the long apprenticeship* (Edinburgh, 2001), pp. 107–27.
42. R. Edgeworth, accounts, s.d. 13 Jan. 1741[2], 26 Oct. 1742, NLI, Ms. 1515, pp. 92, 197; N. Peacock, journal, s.d. 25 July 1744, 10 Aug. 1745, 25 July 1746, 30 May 1748, 21 Nov. 1750, NLI, Ms. 16,091; 'The autobiography of Pole Cosby', pp. 168, 177–9, 'Diary of Anne Cooke', *Journal of the County Kildare Archaeological Society*, viii (1915–1917), p. 219.
43. Crosbie and Roche accounts, BL, Add. Ms. 20,715, ff. 45–45v; O. Wynne, account book, s.d. 29 Aug. 1747, NLI, Ms. 5781; R. Toler to H. Boyle, 23 June 1741, PRONI, D 2707/A1/11, 76; 'Memoir of the O'Mores of Balyna', p. 12, private collection, Co. Kildare; Revd J. Story, account book, s.d. 1 July 1760, June 1761, July 1765, June 1766, Aug. 1766, Bingfield, Co. Cavan, Story Mss; E. O'Leary, 'The O'More family of Balyna, circa 1774', *Journal of the County Kildare Archaeological Society*, ix (1918–21), p. 325; above, pp. 297, 332.
44. Payment of W. Flower to J. Wallis, 16 Aug. 1715, NLI, Ms. 11,468; W. French to Bp. R. Howard, n.d. [1730s], NLI, PC 225.

45. Paull, account book, s.d. 23 March 1725[6], NLI, Ms. 13,991, opening 30.

46. J. Methuen to unknown, 29 July 1697, PRO, SP 63/359/34; E. Southwell to Nottingham, 10 Jan. 1703 [4]; J. Methuen to unknown, 1704, PRO, SP 63/364/13; W. Butler to Sir D. O'Brien, 3 May 1711, NLI, Inchiquin Mss, no. 2621.

47. D. Hepburn to D. Graeme, 8 Feb. 1763, NAS, GD 190/3/319; J. Pratt, diary, s.d. 18 June 1746, Cloverhill, Co. Cavan, Purdon Mss.

48. J. Pratt, diary, s.d. 20 and 27 Oct. 1745, 3 Nov. 1745, 1, 14, 18 and 25 Dec. 1745, 16 and 23 March 1745[6], 27 April 1746, 2 June 1746, Cloverhill, Co. Cavan, Purdon Mss.

49. J. Pratt, diary, s.d. 10 Oct. 1745, 6 and 17 Jan. 1745[6], 3 and 4 March 1745[6].

50. J. Pratt, diary, s.d. 4 Nov. 1745.

51. J. Pratt, diary, s.d. 11 Jan. 1745[6], 18 April 1746, 1, 2 and 23 May 1746, 16 July 1746.

52. J. Pratt, diary, s.d. 25 Oct. 1745, 21 and 30 Nov. 1745, 6 Dec. 1745, 4 and 7 Jan. 1745[6], 25 April 1746, 5 May 1746.

53. J. Pratt, diary, s.d. 7 Oct. 1745, 12 Nov. 1745, 5 and 31 Dec. 1745, 6 and 11 Jan. 1745[6], 11 March 1745[6], 27 June 1746.

54. J. Pratt, diary, s.d. 3 and 8 June 1746, 3 Sep. 1746.

55. J. Pratt, diary, s.d. 2 June 1746.

56. J. Pratt, diary, s.d. 11, 23 and 30 Nov. 1745, 17 May 1746; account book of B. Pratt, from 1726, NLI, Ms. 5248.

57. J. Pratt, diary, s.d. 6, 9, 12 Sep. 1745, 4 Oct. 1745, 6 Nov. 1745, 2 and 28 Dec. 1745, 1 and 15 Jan. 1745[6], 7 and 15 May 1746, 18 Aug. 1746, 8 Nov. 1746, Cloverhill, Co. Cavan, Purdon Mss.

58. J. Pratt, diary, s.d. 4 Nov. 1745, 21 Dec. 1745, 14 and 29 July 1746, 1 Aug. 1746.

59. J. Pratt, diary, s.d. 4 Sep. 1746.

60. Genealogical notes on Robbins family, NLI, Ms. 13,314; genealogical notes in diary of J. Pratt, Cloverhill, Co. Cavan, Purdon Mss; J. Pratt, diary, s.d. 8, 12, 16 and 17 Sep. 1745, Cloverhill, Co. Cavan, Purdon Mss.

61. J. Pratt, diary, s.d. 17 March 1745[6], Cloverhill, Co. Cavan, Purdon Mss.

62. S. Winter, diary, 1762–3, s.d. 13 June 1762, 26 Sep. 1762, 21 Nov. 1762, 13 March 1763, 22 April 1763, 26 June 1763, NLI, Ms. 3855; N. Peacock, journal, s.d. 8 July 1751, NLI, Ms. 16,091; P. Fagan, 'The parish of Taghmon in the eighteenth century', *Ríocht na Midhe*, xii (2001), p. 115.

63. B. Burke, *The landed gentry of Ireland*, new edn (London, 1912), p. 774.

64. S. Winter, diary, s.d. 13 and 14 May 1762, 6 July 1762, 18 and 20 Aug. 1763, NLI, Ms. 3855.

65. S. Winter, diary, s.d. 15 July 1762, 14 April 1763, 11 Oct. 1763, 23 Oct. 1763, 17 Aug. 1764, NLI, Ms. 3855. On riding franchises, see too: J. Pratt, diary, s.d. 8 Aug. 1746, Cloverhill, Co. Cavan, Purdon Mss; Abp. W. King to Lady Carteret, 14 Aug. 1728, TCD, Ms. 750/9/93.

66. S. Winter, diary, s.d. 16 and 18 June 1762 , 24 June 1763, NLI, Ms. 3855.

67. S. Winter, diary, s.d. 28 June 1762.

68. J. Story, account book, s.d. Feb. 1757, Dec. 1757, Dec. 1758, Sep. 1760, Nov. 1761, Dec. 1761, May to Sep. 1762, Feb.–April 1763, July 1763, Oct. 1763, Dec. 1763, Jan. 1764, April 1764, May 1764, Dec. 1764, June 1766, Aug. 1766, Sep. 1766, Bingfield, Co. Cavan, Story Mss.

69. For a protest against the masons' exclusion of women, see Jane Moore's poems reprinted in A. Carpenter (ed.), *Verse in English from eighteenth-century Ireland* (Cork, 1998), pp. 530–4.

70. Minute Book, Weavers' Company of Dublin, 1734–60, s.d. 1 April 1755, RSAI; Barnard, *New anatomy*, pp. 73, 322; B. B. Butler, 'Lady Arbella Denny, 1707–1792', *Dublin Historical Record*, ix (1946–7), pp. 4–20; R. Raughter, 'A natural tenderness: the ideal and the reality of eighteenth-century female philanthropy', in M. G. Valiulis and M. O'Dowd (eds), *Women and Irish history: essays in honour of Margaret MacCurtain* (Dublin, 1997), pp. 71–87.

71. R. Black, travel journal, 1727, PRONI, T 1073/2.

72. Abp. W. King to Mrs H. Ormsby, 24 June 1710, 10 Feb. 1710[11], TCD, Ms. 2531, pp. 181, 196, 212; Abp. W. King to B. Foley, 2 Sep. 1710, 2 Jan. 1710[11], 8 May 1711, TCD Ms. 2531, pp. 196–7, 302, 334; P. Delany, *Twenty sermons on social duties, and their opposite vices* (London, 1747), pp. 47–73.

73. Recipe book of Dorothy Parsons *c.* 1668, Birr Castle, A/17; A. Rosse in C. A. Wilson (ed.), *Traditional country house cooking* (London, 1993), pp. 127, 135–55.

74. Recipe book of Diana Twigge, NA, M. 6231.

75. O. Elder, verses, NLI, Ms. 23,254, pp. 7–11, printed in Carpenter (ed.), *Verse in English from eighteenth-century Ireland*, pp. 343–6.

76. A. Cooke to S. Bagshawe, 20 Oct. 1758, JRL, B2/3/415.

77. Johnston-Liik, *HIP*, vi, p. 513.

78. 'Diary of Anne Cooke', pp. 105–110.

79. 'Diary of Anne Cooke', pp. 117–20.

80. 'Diary of Anne Cooke', pp. 123–4.

81. 'Diary of Anne Cooke', pp. 126–7, 215, 217–18.

82. 'Diary of Anne Cooke', pp. 217–19.

83. 'Diary of Anne Cooke', pp. 211–19, 447–55.

84. 'Diary of Anne Cooke', pp. 131, 209, 212.

85. C. Bagshawe to S. Bagshawe, 23 Sep. 1755, JRL, B3/1/25; Dowager Lady Caldwell to S. Bagshawe, 23 Jan. 1762, 11 March 1762, JRL, B2/3/309, 311.

86. N. Peacock, journal, s.d. 12 Oct. 1741, 14 Feb. 1742[3], 7 and 8 June 1744, 31 Dec. 1745, 6 Jan. 1745[6], 3 May 1746, 19 and 31 Dec. 1746, 3 May 1746, NLI, Ms. 16,091.

87. N. Peacock, journal, s.d. 1743, 27 Jan. 1742[3], 29 April 1745.

88. N. Peacock, journal, s.d. 25 Dec. 1745, 4 May 1747.

89. N. Peacock, journal, s.d., 27 Jan. 1747[8], 10 Feb. 1747[8], 19 March 1749[50], 1 Aug. 1750, 16 Nov. 1750.

90. N. Peacock, journal, s.d. 18 Aug. 1749.

91. S. Bagshawe to Mrs C. Bagshawe, 5 and 12 July 1751, JRL, B3/1/3, 6.

92. T. C. Barnard, 'The cultures of eighteenth-century Irish towns', in P. Borsay and L. Proudfoot (eds), *Provincial towns in early modern England and Ireland; change, convergence and divergence*, Proceedings of the British Academy, cviii (2002), pp. 206–7.

93. M. Mason to J. Mason, 31 Oct. 1737, 26 Nov. 1737, 10 Dec. 1737, Dromana, Villiers–Stuart Mss, B/1/19, 22, 27, 34; J. Alcock to H. Aland, 12 May 1739, Dromana, Villiers–Stuart Mss, B/5/2; H. Alcock to A. Mason, Dromana, Villiers–Stuart Mss, B/5/9.

94. M. Mason to J. Mason, 4 Jan. 1737[8], Dromana, Villiers–Stuart Mss, T 3131, B/1/47.

95. J. Alcock to H. Aland, 12 May 1739 , Dromana, Villiers–Stuart Mss, T 3131, B/5/2.

96. Memoir of H. Thomson, Bodleian, Ms. Eng. Hist. d. 155, ff. 40v–42v.

97. Revd J. Story, account book, s.d. Aug. 1762, Sep. 1762, Feb. 1763, April 1763, Oct. 1763, Dec. 1763, Jan. 1764, April 1764, May 1764, Dec. 1764, Bingfield, Co. Cavan, Story Mss.

98. W. G. Neely, *Kilkenny: an urban history, 1391–1843* (Belfast, 1989), p. 216.

99. J. Wight, journal, s.d. 20 June 1752, Friends' Historical Society, Dublin; S. Bagshawe to C. Caldwell, 5 July 1751, JRL, B 3/1/4; B. T. Balfour, accounts, s.d. 18 Feb. 1747[8], NLI, Ms. 10,277; Delany, *Autobiography*, 1st series, iii, p. 510; Derrick, *Letters written from Leverppole*, i, p. 61; *The Limerick directory* (Limerick, 1769), p. 38; J. McVeagh (ed.), *Richard Pococke's Irish tours* (Dublin, 1995), p. 92; *A tour through Ireland in several entertaining letters* (London, 1748), pp. 90, 173.

100. Captain Cobbe, description of Co. Antrim, 16 Dec. 1738, Armagh Public Library, Papers of the Physico-Historical Society.

101. A. Crone to J. Crone, 3 May 1773, Cork Archives Institute, Crone of Byblox Mss, PR 3, box 2; J. G. Evans, *Conflict, continuity and change in Wales, c. 1500–1603: essays and studies* (Aberystwyth, 1999), pp. 198–245; C. A. Hoover, 'Music and theatre in the lives of eighteenth-century Americans', in K. Carson, R. Hoffman and P. J. Albert (eds), *Of consuming interests* (Charlottesville and London, 1994), pp. 307–49; M. Humphreys, *The crisis of community: Montgomeryshire, 1680–1815* (Cardiff, 1996), pp. 167–8; P. Jenkins, *The making of a ruling class: the Glamorgan gentry 1640–1790* (Cambridge, 1983), pp.

253–4; D. Johnson, *Music and society in lowland Scotland in the eighteenth century* (London, 1972), pp. 4, 16–18, 25–8, 32–49; Legg (ed.), *Synge letters*, pp. 398, 406, 445, 446.

102.  A. Hamilton to Lady Panmure, 7 Sep. 1697, NAS, GD 45/14/238, 14. Cf. B. Boydell, *Music at Christ Church before 1800: documents and selected anthems* (Dublin, 1999); B. Boydell, 'The flourishing of music, 1660–1800', in K. Milne (ed.), *Christ Church cathedral Dublin: a history* (Dublin, 2000), pp. 298–314.

103.  M. Kelly, *Reminiscences*, ed. R. Fiske (London, 1975), pp. 2–10; J. C. Pilkington, *The real story of John Carteret Pilkington* (London, 1760), pp. 44–5.

104.  S. Bagshawe, fragmentary journal, JRL, B/15/3/1, s.d. 23 Dec. 1741; 27 Jan. 1741[2]; B. Boydell, *A Dublin musical calendar, 1700–1760* (Dublin, 1988), p. 75; B. Boydell, *Rotunda music in eighteenth-century Dublin* (Dublin, 1992); A. J. Guy (ed.), *Colonel Samuel Bagshawe and the army of George II, 1731–1762*, Army Records Society (London, 1990), p. 39.

105.  R. Edgeworth, accounts, s.d. 21 Dec. 1725, NLI, Ms. 1509, p. 37; R. Howard, account book, s.d. 10 Jan. 1749[50], NLI, Ms. 1725; 'A letter from Sir W[illia]m Fownes after enjoying the company of two young ladies at a concert of musick at my lodgings, Dublin, 1732', BL, Egerton Ms. 845A, f. 171.

106.  Delany, *Autobiography*, 1st series, ii, pp. 610, 626, 628, 629; iii, pp. 184, 587; Boydell, *Dublin musical calendar*, pp. 145, 284.

107.  Delany, *Autobiography*, 1st series, ii, pp. 336, 552, 580–1, 615; *A collection of the most celebrated Irish tunes* (?, 1747); D. O'Sullivan, *Carolan: the life, times and music of an Irish harper*, 2 vols (London, 1958), i, pp. 181–3; ii, p. 23.

108.  B. Smythe to W. Smythe, 17 Oct. 1730, NLI, PC 448.

109.  R. French, account book, NLI, Ms. 4919, ff. 64v, 65v, 67, 80; Boydell, *Dublin musical calendar*, pp. 101, 102, 268.

110.  R. French, account books, s.d. 15 June 1760–15 June 1761, NLI, Ms. 4615, p. 219; H. F. Berry, 'Notes from the diary of a Dublin lady in the reign of George II', *JRSAI*, 5th series, viii (1898), p. 143; W. Grattan Flood, 'The account book of a Dublin harpsichord maker, Ferdinand Weber, 1764–1783', *JRSAI*, xliv (1914), p. 338.

111.  R. Edgeworth, accounts, s.d. 12 April 1758, NLI, Ms. 1524, p. 82; Grattan Flood, 'Ferdinand Weber', p. 338.

112.  Barnard, 'French of Monivea', pp. 276, 281.

113.  Johnson, *Music and society in lowland Scotland*, pp. 12–13.

114.  St George Ashe to ?H. St George, 16/26 March 1689[90], TCD, St George Mss, photocopy, 175/2; K. T. Hoppen, *The common scientist in the seventeenth century: a study of the Dublin Philosophical Society, 1683–1708* (London, 1970), pp. 33, 127.

115.  Will of Revd C. Baldwin, 1747, NLI, Ainsworth report, no. 51; GEC, *Complete peerage*, ix, 235–6; Johnson, *Music and society in lowland Scotland*, pp. 68–84.

116.  R. Edgeworth, accounts, s.d. 18 Feb. 1726[7], 15 March 1737[8], 27 April 1761, NLI, Mss 1509, p. 116; 1512, p. 77; 1527, p. 99.

117.  R. Edgeworth, accounts, s.d. 1 Dec. 1757, 4 Jan. 1758, 7 Oct. 1758, 11 Nov. 1759, NLI, Mss 1523, p. 187; 1524, pp. 51, 161; 1525, p. 136. 'Mr Bird' the instructor was possibly the organist at St Anne's church; Boydell, *Dublin musical calendar*, p. 272.

118.  R. Edgeworth, accounts, s.d. 16 April 1734, 10 July 1734, 1 Jan. 1734[5], 12 March 1734[5], 3 April 1735, 24 July 1736, 17 July 1738, 30 Nov. 1738, 31 Dec. 1738, 24 Dec. 1740, 14 March 1740[1], 28 Dec. 1741, 13 and 15 Jan. 1741[2], 31 Aug. 1742, 1 Sep. 1742, 21 and 29 Dec. 1742, 12 and 16 March 1742[3], 17 Sep. 1746, 18 and 29 July 1749; 16 Feb. 1749[50]; 28 June 1756, 21 Dec. 1756, 22 Dec. 1757, 4 April 1758, 13 Aug. 1764, 12 Sep. 1764, 27 Oct. 1764, 29 Jan. 1765, 15 Aug. 1767, NLI, Mss 1512, p. 106; 1511, pp. 17, 26, 30, 119; 1512, pp. 125, 144, 150; 1514, pp. 84, 103; 1515, pp. 90, 92, 185, 186, 216, 232; 1517, p. 44; 1518, pp. 156, 157, 203; 1522, pp. 159, 213; 1523, p. 192; 1524, p. 70; 1528, pp. 87, 103, 128, 182; 1533, p. 217. Cf. Abp. W. King, account book, 1715–23, s.d. July 1720, TCD, Ms. 751/3, f. 125; Bp. F. Hutchinson, account book from 1729, s.d. 21 Dec. 1730, PRONI, DIO 1/22/2; Revd J. Story, accounts, s.d. April 1760, Bingfield, Co. Cavan, Story Mss.

119. Inventory of Burton, 11 Nov. 1680, BL, Add. Ms. 47,037, f. 22v; B. Taylor to Sir J. Perceval, 17 Dec. 1680, BL, Add. Ms. 47,037, f. 31.

120. A. J. Oughton, autobiography, NAM, Ms. 8808.36.1, p. 57; Thady Lawler, *An apology for pipes and pipers* (Dublin, *c.* 1730); O'Sullivan, *Carolan*, i, pp. 34–5.

121. Cork and Burlington, accounts, 1677–80, s.d. 14 June 1680; B. Gregory to W. Smythe, 30 Aug. 1733, NLI, PC 449; N. Peacock, journal, s.d. 15 May 1751, NLI, Ms. 16,091; Wynne, account book, from 1761, s. d. July 1761, NLI, Ms. 4199.

122. D. Ó Catháin, 'Revd Charles Bunworth of Buttevant: patron of harpers and poets', *JCHAS*, cii (1997), pp. 111–18; O'Sullivan, *Carolan*, i, pp. 72, 109, 112.

123. [Sydney Owenson], *Lady Morgan's Memoirs*, 2 vols (London, 1862), i, pp. 43–4; H. White, *The keeper's recital: music and cultural history in Ireland, 1770–1970* (Cork, 1998), pp. 15–17.

124. P. Perceval to Lord Perceval, 20 April 1716, BL, Add. Ms. 46,967, f. 55.

125. P. Perceval to Lord Perceval, 26 May 1716, BL, Add. Ms. 46,967, f. 69v.

126. Boydell, *Dublin musical calendar*, pp. 275, 288–9; J. Cousser, *A contest between Mars and Jupiter* (Dublin, 1721); D. Hunter, *Irish Musical Studies*, viii, forthcoming.

127. Balfour account book, 1697–1710, s.d. 11 June 1698, 29 Oct. 1698, 24 Dec. 1698; B. Boydell, 'The earl of Cork's musicians', *Records of Early English Drama*, 18 (1993), pp. 1–15; A. Fletcher, *Drama, performance and polity in pre-Reformation Ireland* (Cork, 2000).

128. *Ireland's lamentation* (London, 1689), p. 28.

129. N. Delacherois to D. Delacherois, 9 and 20 Aug. 1757, 20 March 1767, 10 May 1768, NAM, Ms. 7805.63.

130. Inventory of L. Delamain, 20 Jan. 1763, TCD, Ms. 2015/395; Barnard, *New anatomy*, pp. 79–80; R. Leppert, *Music and image: domesticity, ideology and socio-cultural formation in eighteenth-century England* (Cambridge, 1988), pp. 71–106.

131. A. Brodrick to St J. Brodrick, 13 and 31 May [*c.* 1684], Surrey CRO, Midleton Mss, 1248/1, ff. 195, 197.

132. J. Evelyn to J. Evelyn, 26 Oct. 1692, Evelyn Mss, formerly at Christ Church, Oxford, now in BL, Add. Ms.

133. Davis D. McElroy, *Scotland's age of improvement: a survey of eighteenth-century literary clubs and societies* (Washington, 1969), pp. 17–11, 27–30, 49–52.

134. J. Kelly, *'That damn'd thing called honour': duelling in Ireland, 1570–1860* (Cork, 1995), pp. 65–6; J. H. Lepper and P. Crosslé, *History of the Grand Lodge of Free and accepted Masons of Ireland*, 2 vols (Dublin, 1925).

135. Minutes of the Grand Lodge of Munster, 1726–31, Cork Archives Institute, U/177; W. J. Chetwode Crawley, *Caementaria Hibernica, being the public constitutions that have served to hold together the freemasons of Ireland, I, 1726–1730* (Dublin, 1895), pp. 7–11.

136. *A pocket companion for free-masons* (Dublin, 1735); F. D'Assigny, *A serious and impartial enquiry into the cause of the present decay of free-masonry in the kingdom of Ireland* (Dublin, 1744); W. G. Simpson, *The history and antiquities of freemasonry in Saintfield, Co. Down* (Downpatrick, 1924), p. 11.

137. P. Fagan, *Catholics in a Protestant country* (Dublin, 1998), pp. 126–58.

138. S. Leighton, *History of freemasonry in the province of Antrim, Northern Ireland* (Belfast, 1938), pp. 30–1.

139. *The fundamental laws, statutes and constitutions of the antient and most benevolent order of the friendly brothers of St Patrick* (Bath, 1770); Kelly, *'That damn'd thing called honour'*, pp. 95–6; R. Portlock, *The ancient and benevolent order of the friendly brothers of St Patrick. History of the London knots, 1775–1973* ([London, *c.* 1976]), pp. 1–3.

140. Oughton, autobiography, pp. 54–5, NAM, Ms. 8808–36–1.

141. S. H. Dorman, 'The Kinsale knot of the Friendly Brothers of St Patrick, A.D. 1754–1856', *JCHAS*, xix and xx (1913–14), pp. 178–83.

142. P. Guinness, 'The meeting book of the County of Kildare Knot of the Friendly Brothers of St Patrick 1758–1791', *Journal of the County Kildare Archaeological Society*, xix (2000–1), pp. 116–60.

143. Chetwode Crawley, *Caemenataria Hibernica, i, 1726–1730*, p. 14.

144. Henry Nelson, *The order of the procession of the journeymen builders, plaisterers, painters and free-masons* (n.p., n.d.). Cf. N[elson], *A poem in honour of the antient and loyal society of the journeymen-taylors*; Nelson, *A poem in praise of the loyal and charitable society of journeymen tailors*.

145. *CARD*, xi, p. 497.

146. Chetwode Crawley, *Caemenataria Hibernica, I, 1726–1730*, p. 11.

147. Ibid., p. 14; Lepper and Crosslé, *History of the Grand Lodge of Masons of Ireland*, i, pp. 98–9.

148. *The Limerick directory*, p. 42.

149. J. Fitzgerald, *The Cork remembrancer* (Cork, 1783), p. 165; L. Conlon, 'The influence of freemasonry in the eighteenth century', *Ríocht na Midhe*, ix (1997), pp. 137–55.

150. Minute Book, lodge 138, Coleraine, 1734–60, PRONI, D 668/O; Leighton, *Freemasonry in the province of Antrim*, pp. 129, 131; P. Mirala, 'The eighteenth-century masonic lodge as a social unit', *Ulster Folklife*, xliv (1998), pp. 60–8.

151. U. Im Hof, *The enlightenment* (Oxford, 1994), pp. 139–44.

152. C. Casey, 'Books and builders: a bibliographical approach to Irish eighteenth-century architecture', unpublished Ph.D. thesis, TCD, 2 vols (1991), i, pp. 144–63; C. Casey, '"De architectura": an Irish eighteenth-century gloss', *Architectural History*, xxxvii (1994), pp. 80–96.

153. M. Wills, account book, s.d. 19 April 1757, 17 Aug. 1774, IAA, 81/88.

154. Im Hof, *The enlightenment*, pp. 142–3; Chetwode Crawley, *Caemenataria Hibernica, I, 1726–30*, p. 14; ii, *1735–44* (Dublin, 1896), pp. 10–11; Lepper and Crosslé, *History of the Grand Lodge of Masons of Ireland*, i, pp. 138–41.

155. Fagan, *Catholics in a Protestant country*, pp. 126–58.

156. Minute Book, Youghal Hanover Society, PRONI, D 2707/C1/1; Barnard, 'Considering the inconsiderable', pp. 107–27; K. Wilson, *The sense of the people: politics, culture and imperialism in England, 1715–1785* (Cambridge, 1995), pp. 64–5.

157. Minute Book, Youghal Hanover Society, s.d. 28 Oct. 1762, 27 May 1779, 26 June 1786, 26 June 1787, PRONI, D 2707/C1/1.

158. Minute Book, Mallow Loyal Protestant Association, TCD, Ms. 7105, f. 2.

159. Ibid., ff. 15v, 18, 31v, 38, 51v.

160. 'Rules and resolutions of the Anna Liffy Club', *Journal of the County Kildare Archaeological Society*, xvii (1987–91), pp. 205, 212, 238.

161. Fitzgerald, *Cork remembrancer*, pp. 201, 203.

162. J. Kelly, 'The emergence of political parading, 1660–1800', in T. G. Fraser (ed.), *The Irish parading tradition: following the drum* (Basingstoke, 2000), pp. 18–19.

163. *A letter to . . . Sir Ralph Gore . . . concerning a lately published proposal for a voluntary subscription to erect a trophy in memory of the deliverance of this kingdom, by the glorious victory at the Boyne* (Dublin, 1732); HMC, *Stopford-Sackville Mss*, i, p. 168.

164. D. Clarke to W. Smythe, 16 April 1741, 5 Nov. 1743, NLI, PC 447; *Rules and orders to be observed and kept by the several and respective members of the Boyne Society* (Dublin, 1744); Kelly, 'The emergence of political parading', pp. 15–16.

165. E. Spencer to F. Price, 6 Dec. 1743, NLW, Puleston Mss, 3580E.

166. Minute Book, Dublin Florists' Society, s.d. 16 May 1760, 15 May 1761, 17 June 1763, RIA, Ms. 24 E 37; E. C. Nelson, 'The Dublin Florists' club in the mid-eighteenth century', *Garden History*, x (1982), pp. 142–8.

167. Minutes of the 'Medico-Politico-Physico-Classico-Puffical' society, pp. 84–5, RIA, Ms. 24 K 31.

168. E. Spencer to F. Price, 5 April 1746, NLW, Puleston Ms. 3580E; Bp. F. Hutchinson, account book, s.d. 16 Sep. 1729, PRONI, DIO 1/22/1; Revd J. Story, account book, 1756–66, s.d. June 1766, Bingfield, Co. Cavan, Story Mss; S. Conway, 'War and national identity in mid-eighteenth century British Isles', *EHR*, cxvi (2001), p. 881; Delany, *Autobiography*, 1st series, ii, p. 310.

169. J. Wight, journal, s.d. 22–23 May 1752, 11 June 1752, 9 Jan. 1755, 3 March 1756, Friends' Historical Society, Dublin; Fitzgerald, *Cork remembrancer*, p. 169.

170. O. St George to W. Conolly, 15 Oct. 1723, IAA, Castletown deposit, box 53; R. Wilson to O. St George, 4 Aug. 1724, PRO, C 110/46/334.

171. Muster of J. Lloyd's militia troop, NA, 999/612/40.

172. Lord Perceval to B. Taylor, 18 Aug. 1715, BL, Add. Ms. 46,966, f. 91v.

173. K. Conolly to Lady A. Conolly, 4 and 25 Feb. 1745[6], 13 May 1746, IAA, Castletown deposit, Conolly deposit, box 76; O. Wynne, account book, s.d. 19 April 1746, 4 June 1746, 30 Aug. 1746, NLI, Ms. 5781, pp. 362, 372, 385; T. Lloyd to W. Harris, 3 Jan. 1746[7], Armagh Public Library, Papers of the Physico-Historical Society; Bp. H. Maule to W. Harris, 1 Aug. 1748, Armagh Public Library, Papers of the Physico-Historical Society; *The Censor*, xxiv, 4–11 Nov. 1749.

174. C. Lucas, *Pharmacomastix* (Dublin, 1741), p. 33.

175. J. Pickard to Foley, 19 Feb. 1736[7], letterbook of J. Pickard, 1734–48, Dorset CRO, D/BLX, B.18.

176. R. Aylward to G. Legge, 5 April 1679, Staffordshire CRO, Dartmouth Mss, D 1778/iii/o/19.

177. Balfour account book, 1697–1710, s.d. 20 Aug. 1699, NLI, Ms. 9536; Abp. W. King, account book, 1700–15, s.d. Nov. 1710, TCD, Ms. 751/2, f. 259; A. Nickson, accounts with T. Wentworth, s.d. 28 May 1714, 4 Dec. 1714, 25 May 1716, 13 June 1716, 29 May 1719, 1 April 1720, Sheffield City Archives, WWM A 759, pp. 385, 388, 400, 401, 420, 427; C. Caldwell, letterbook, s.d. 22 Oct. 1744, PRO, CUST 112/10; R. Edgeworth, accounts, s.d. 18 Sep. 1721, 16 May 1722, 17 and 21 July 1722, 26 and 27 Oct. 1722, 30 Sep. 1725; 10 June 1749, 28 Sep. 1749, 10 Feb. 1758, 11 Sep. 1764, 30 Sep. 1767, 27 May 1769, NLI, Mss 1507, pp. 53, 85; 1508, pp. 9, 13, 16; 1509, p. 29; 1518, pp. 143, 169; 1524, p. 63; 1528, p. 102; 1533, p. 238; 1535, p. 179; Bp. F. Hutchinson, account book from 1729, s.d. 23 Aug. 1729, 6 Oct. 1729, 7 Aug. 1730, 5 Oct. 1730, PRONI, DIO 1/22/2.

178. Delany, *Autobiography*, 1st series, ii, p. 481.

179. Bp. F. Hutchinson, account book from 1729, s.d. 4 and 18 March 1733[4], PRONI, DIO 1/22/2.

180. N. Peacock, journal, s.d. 2 Jan. 1748[9], NLI, Ms. 16,091.

181. D. Mussenden to W. Leathes, 1 July 1719, Suffolk CRO, Ipswich, de Mussenden–Leathes Mss, HA 403/1/6, 28.

182. T. Kinsgbury to F. Price, 17 July 1736, NLW, Puleston Ms. 3584E, 28; J. Hawkshaw to F. Price, 7 Oct. 1736, 2 March 1737[8], NLW, Puleston, Ms. 3576E, 7 and 8.

183. Bp. F. Hutchinson, account book from 1729, s.d. 3 and 26 June 1729, 2 June 1731, 7 Jan. 1733[4], PRONI, DIO 1/22/2; recipe book, Carlow County Library, Vigors Mss; N. Peacock, journal, s.d. 9 June 1745, 11 and 14 July 1745, 24 Aug. 1745, 29 Sep. 1745, NLI, Ms. 16,091; R. Edgeworth, accounts, s.d. 2 May 1749, NLI, Ms. 1518, p. 133.

184. T. Kingsbury to F. Price, 12 March 1736[7], NLW, Puleston Ms 3584E/35; M. Ledwidge to W. Smythe, 30 Dec. 1748, NLI, PC 436.

185. P. Delany, *Sixteen discourses upon doctrines and duties* (London, 1754), pp. 335–8, 342–9; [E. S. Pery, Viscount Limerick], *Letter from an Armenian in Ireland, to his friends at Trebisond* (London, 1757), pp. 85–8.

186. *The beggars (of St Mary's parish) address, to their worthy representative, Hackball* (?Dublin, 1754).

187. K. A. Miller, A. Schrier, B. D. Boling and D. N. Doyle (eds), *Irish immigrants in the land of Canaan: letters and memoirs from colonial and revolutionary America, 1675–1815* (Oxford, 2003), p. 482. For Samuel Bryan as a grand juryman in Dublin, see Crown entry books, Co. Dublin, 1742, 1748, NA.

188. Derrick, *Letters written from Leverpoole*, i, pp. 49–50; *A tour through Ireland in several entertaining letters* (London, 1748), p. 118.

189. J. Wight, journal, s.d. 28 Aug. 1755, 29 July 1756, 1 Aug. 1756, Friends' Historical Library, Dublin.

190. R. Synge, Sermon preached, 25 Nov. 1683, Synge Mss, private collection, Greenwich; 'Curate's address to the gown', in W. Young, notebook, TCD, Ms. 10,664, pp. 1–50; Bp. R. Howard to H. Howard, 22 May

1736, NLI, PC 227; Delany, *Sixteen discourses upon doctrines and duties*, p. 235; Delany, *Twenty sermons on social duties*, p. 99.

191.    Abp. N. Marsh to Abp. T. Tenison, 10 April 1674, Lambeth Palace Library, Ms. 942/133; Jasper Brett, *The sin of with-holding tribute* (Dublin, 1721), p. 33.

192.    C. J. Berry, *The idea of luxury* (Cambridge, 1994); P. H. Kelly, ' "Industry and virtue versus luxury and corruption": Berkeley, Walpole and the South Sea Bubble crisis', *Eighteenth-Century Ireland*, vii (1992), pp. 57–74. T. C. Barnard, 'Integration or separation? Hospitality and display in Protestant Ireland, *c.* 1660–1800', in L. Brockliss and D. Eastwood (eds), *A union of multiple identities: the British Isles*, c. *1750–1850* (Manchester, 1997), pp. 127–46; T. C. Barnard, 'Public and private uses of wealth in Ireland, *c.* 1660–1760', in J. R. Hill and C. Lennon (eds), *Luxury and austerity: Historical Studies, XXI* (Dublin, 1999), pp. 66–83.

193.    Accounts of Blakes of Ballyglunin, *c.* 1753–63, NA, M. 6933/16; K. Harvey, *The Bellews of Mount Bellew: a Catholic gentry family in eighteenth-century Ireland* (Dublin, 1998), pp. 72–6.

194.    *The distress'd state of Ireland considered* (n.p., 1740), pp. 16, 49; *A letter to a member of parliament containing a proposal for bringing in a bill to revise, amend or repeal certain obsolete statutes, commonly called the Ten Commandments* (Dublin, 1738), pp. 15, 28–9, 47; D. Roche, *The people of Paris: an essay in popular culture in the eighteenth century* (Leamington Spa, 1987), pp. 127–93; *Schemes from Ireland for the benefit of the body natural, ecclesiastical and politick* (Dublin, 1732), pp. 17–18, 23.

# Index